THE LIFE OF THE PROPHET MUHAMMAD (SAW)

السيرة النبوية

As Seerah An Nabawiyya

VOLUME TWO

The Life of the Prophet Muhammad ﷺ

السيرة النبوية

As Seerah An Nabawiyya

VOLUME TWO

Imam Ibn Kathir

Translated by Professor Trevor Le Gassick

Reviewed by Dr Ahmed Fareed

Dar Ul Thaqafah
https://twitter.com/darulthaqafah
www.darulthaqafah.com

2019 CE – 1440 H

Translation of the Qur'ān

It should be perfectly clear that the Qur'ān is only authentic in its original language, Arabic. Since perfect translation of the Qur'ān is impossible, we have used the translation of the meaning of the Qur'ān throughout the book, as the result is only a crude meaning of the Arabic text.

Qur'ānic verses appear in speech marks proceeded by a reference to the Surah and verse number. Sayings (*Hadith*) of Prophet Muhammad ﷺ appear in inverted commas along with reference to the Hadith Book and its Reporter.

ﷺ - صلى الله عليه وسلم (Peace be upon him)

CONTENTS

FOREWORD

THE interrelationship and interaction of human cultures and civilisations has made the contributions of each the common heritage of men in all ages and all places. Early Muslim scholars were able to communicate with their Western counterparts through contacts made during the Crusades; at Muslim universities and centres of learning in Muslim Spain (al-Andalus, or Andalusia) and Sicily to which many European students went for education; and at the universities and centres of learning in Europe itself (such as Salerno, Padua, Montpellier, Paris, and Oxford), where Islamic works were taught in Latin translations. Among the Muslim scholars well-known in the centres of learning throughout the world were al-Rāzī (Rhazes), Ibn Sīnā (Avicenna), Ibn Rushd (Averroes), al Khwārizmī and Ibn Khaldūn. Muslim scholars such as these and others produced original works in many fields. Many of them possessed encyclopaedic knowledge and distinguished themselves in many disparate fields of knowledge.

In view of this, the Center for Muslim Contribution to Civilization was established in order to acquaint non-Muslims with the contributions Islam has given to human civilisation as a whole. The Great Books of Islamic Civilization Project attempts to cover the first 800 years of Islam, or what may be called Islam's Classical Period. This project aims at making available in English a wide selection of works representative of Islamic civilisation in all its diversity. It is made up of translations of original Arabic works that were produced in the formative centuries of Islam, and is meant to serve the needs of a potentially large readership. Not only the specialist and scholar, but the non-specialist with an interest in Islam and its cultural heritage will be able to benefit from the series. Together, the works should serve as a rich source for the study of the early periods of Islamic thought.

In selecting the books for the series, the Center took into account all major areas of Islamic intellectual pursuit that could be represented. Thus the series includes works not only on better-known subjects such as law, theology, jurisprudence, history and politics, but also on subjects such as literature, medicine, astronomy, optics and geography. The specific criteria, used to select individual books, were these: that a book should give a faithful and comprehensive account of its field; and that it should be an authoritative source. The reader thus has at his disposal virtually a whole library of informative and enlightening works.

Each book in the series has been translated by a qualified scholar and reviewed by another expert. While the style of one translation will naturally differ from another, the translators have endeavoured, to the extent it was possible, to make the works accessible to the common reader. As a rule, the use of footnotes has been kept to a minimum, though a more extensive use of them was necessitated in some cases.

This series is presented in the hope that it will contribute to a greater understanding in the West of the cultural and intellectual heritage of Islam and will therefore provide an important means towards greater understanding of today's world.

May God Help Us!

Muhammad bin Hamad Al-Thani
Chairman of the Board of Trustees

ABOUT THIS SERIES

THIS series of Arabic works, made available in English translation, represents an outstanding selection of important Islamic studies in a variety of fields of knowledge. The works selected for inclusion in this series meet specific criteria. They are recognized by Muslim scholars as being early and important in their fields, as works whose importance is broadly recognized by international scholars, and as having had a genuinely significant impact on the development of human culture.

Readers will therefore see that this series includes a variety of works in the purely Islamic sciences, such as Qur'ān, *hadīth*, theology, prophetic traditions (*sunna*), and jurisprudence (*fiqh*). Also represented will be books by Muslim scientists on medicine, astronomy, geography, physics, chemistry, horticulture, and other fields.

The work of translating these texts has been entrusted to a group of professors in the Islamic and Western worlds who are recognized authorities in their fields. It has been deemed appropriate, in order to ensure accuracy and fluency, that two persons, one with Arabic as his mother tongue and another with English as his mother tongue, should participate together in the translation and revision of each text.

This series is distinguished from other similar intercultural projects by its distinctive objectives and methodology. These works will fill a genuine gap in the library of human thought. They will prove extremely useful to all those with an interest in Islamic culture, its interaction with Western thought, and its impact on culture throughout the world. They will, it is hoped, fulfil an important rôle in enhancing world understanding at a time when there is such evident and urgent need for the development of peaceful coexistence.

This series is published by the Center for Muslim Contribution to Civilization, which serves as a research centre under the patronage of H.H. Sheikh Hamad bin Khalifa al-Thani, Amir of Qatar. It is directed by a Board of Trustees chaired by H.E. Sheikh Muhammad bin Hamad al-Thani, the former Minister of Education of Qatar. The Board is comprised of a group of prominent scholars. These include H.E. Dr Abul-Wafa al-Taftazani*, Deputy Rector of Cairo University, and Dr Yusuf al-Qaradhawi, Director of the Sira and Sunna Research Center. At its inception the Center was directed by the late Dr Muhammad Ibrahim Kazim, former Rector of Qatar University, who established its initial objectives.

The Center was until recently directed by Dr Kamal Nagi, the Foreign Cultural Relations Advisor of the Ministry of Education of Qatar. He was assisted by a

---

* Died 1994, may Allāh have mercy on him.

Board comprising a number of academicians of Qatar University, in addition to a consultative committee chaired by Dr Ezzeddin Ibrahim, former Rector of the University of the United Arab Emirates. A further committee acting on behalf of the Center has been the prominent university professors who act under the chairmanship of Dr Raji Rammuny, Professor of Arabic at the University of Michigan. This committee is charged with making known, in Europe and in America, the books selected for translation, and in selecting and enlisting properly qualified university professors, orientalists and students of Islamic studies to undertake the work of translation and revision, as well as overseeing the publication process.

CENTER FOR MUSLIM CONTRIBUTION TO CIVILIZATION

INTRODUCTION

THE work at hand in its original Arabic is, in a sense, the product of two minds:
the author himself, Abū al-Fidāʾ ʿImād al-Dīn Ismāʿīl b. ʿUmar b. Kathīr,[1] and,
to a lesser extent, its editor, Muṣṭafā ʿAbd al-Wāḥid. In his introduction to the
Arabic, ʿAbd al-Wāḥid points out that this work is in fact the culmination of a
search for a biography of the Prophet Muḥammad to which Ibn Kathīr makes
reference in his celebrated exegesis of the Qurʾān. There is, however, no extant
copy of any such independent biographical study traceable to Ibn Kathīr. That
such a study did exist is questionable, notwithstanding Ibn Kathīr's own allusion
thereto. Given the unavailability of this particular work, ʿAbd al-Wāḥid offers
the theory that the biography in question is none other than that which appears
in Ibn Kathīr's chief work, his opus on history, the *al-Bidāya wa al-Nihāya*.[2] He
argues that the *sīra* section of the latter work is so comprehensive in its analysis
of the life and times of the Prophet Muḥammad as to almost obviate the need for
any independent study of the same topic. The biography at hand, therefore, is the
same as found in the *al-Bidāya*. Nevertheless, ʿAbd al-Wāḥid must be commended
for the not inconsiderable task of editing and publishing this particular section as
an independent unit, and appropriately titling it *al-Sīra al-Nabawiyya li Ibn
Kathīr*.

Ibn Kathīr, whose ancestors are said to have been from Iraq, was himself
born around the year 1313 CE/700 AH in the Boesra district of eastern
Damascus. He died 74 years later, shortly after suffering a total loss of vision.
He counts as his tutors such illustrious personages as the eminent historian
Shams al-Dīn al-Dhahabī, the Mālikī jurist Abū Mūsā al-Qarāfī, and the cele-
brated Damascene polemicist and jurist Ibn Taymiyya al-Ḥarrānī.

Ibn Kathīr's was an era of the great political and social upheavals that posed
many challenges to the Muslim world at large, and in particular, to its scholars.
What with the scourge of the Tartars threatening the very existence of Islam as a
socio-political entity from the outside and the sectarian and ethnic strife created
by the Mamluk revolution doing much the same from within, Ibn Kathīr and his

---

1. According to R. Y. Curtis, *Authoritative Interpretation of Classical Islamic Tafsīr: Critical
Analysis of Ibn Kathīr's Tafsīr al-Qurʾan al-ʿAẓīm*. Unpublished dissertation. (Ann Arbor:
University of Michigan, 1989) (21), classical bibliographers have cited Ibn Kathīr's name in more
than one way. Al-Dhahabī for instance, in the supplement to his bibliography, *Dhayl Tadhkirat al-
Huffāẓ*, gives Ibn Kathīr's name as Ismāʿīl b. Umar b. Kathīr b. Ḍaw b. Kathīr b. Zarʿ. Other
versions have been given, however, such as appears in al-Ziriklī's *al-Aʿlam* (1: 320) and ʾUmar Riḍā
Kahhāla's *Muʿjam al-Muʾallifīn* (1: 28).

2. According to C. Brockelman in his *Geschichte der Arabischen Literatur* ii. 49, this historical
work of Ibn Kathīr is itself based on al-Birzālī's chronicle. For more information see also, Ibn
Ḥadjar al-Asqalānī, *al-Durar al-Kāmina* (Cod. Vienna, no. 1172).

colleagues, no doubt, had huge challenges with which to contend. In addition, the unrelenting pestilence and drought that had plagued the Levant and areas east thereof, made their burden all the more unwieldy. He died in 1387 CE/775 AH and lies buried in Damascus next to his master, Ibn Taymiyyah. He was mourned by his wife Zaynab, the daughter of his teacher, al-Mizzī, who, according to some reports, was an accomplished scholar in her own right. She bore him four sons, one of whom succeeded his father to the post of principal of the teaching academy al-Madrasa al-Ṣāliḥiyya.[3]

Ibn Kathīr, true to the pre-eminent tendencies of the academic milieu within which he functioned, brings to his study of the Prophet of Islam the method of the *muḥaddith*, the scholar of *ḥadīth* traditions, more assiduously than he does that of the traditional historian. In doing so, however, he has, I believe, substantially succeeded in combining two of the three sources available for the pursuit of the historical Muḥammad: the *ḥadīth* literature and the *sīra*; the Qurʾān, being the third such source, features less prominently, if not altogether rarely, in his study. Given the very extensive usage of *ḥadīth* material in this particular work, a word about the classical nature of such material and its contemporaneous validity would be appropriate at this point.

Early historical studies of Muslim society and culture, as A. A. Duri points out, "followed broadly two lines that were distinct from each other – that of *ḥadīth*, and that of the tribes (i.e. the *ayyām* anecdotes as narrated by the *akhbārīs* and the *ruwāt*), which is in a sense a continuation of pre-Islamic activities. "These two lines", he explains, "reflect the two major currents in early Islamic society – the Islamic and the tribal lines which influenced all aspects of life."[4] According to Muslim tradition, the learning and transmission of the sayings and actions of Muḥammad, his tacit approvals and disapprovals of the actions of others, and his general behaviour had religious significance second only to that of the Qurʾān. To that end Muslim scholars began the collection of such data as was related to the Prophet and his era even while he was still alive. At first, the system of oral retention was popular, but by the middle of the first century of the Muslim era, written compilations of *ḥadīth* traditions began to appear. By the end of the third quarter of that century, "a pattern was fixed for the learning and teaching of the *ḥadīth* which flourished in the second and third centuries."[5] A system of sorts for verifying the authenticity of such prophetic traditions was allegedly extant from the earliest of times – albeit in a

<hr>

3. Curtis, 23.

4. Professor Duri's article is in large measure an elucidation of what he calls "the tribal type of history." See in this regard "The Iraq School of History to the Ninth Century", in *Historians of the Middle East*, ed. B. Lewis and P. M. Holt (Oxford University Press, 1962).

5. M. M. Azami, *Studies in Early Hadith Literature* (Indianapolis: American Trust Publications, 1983), 186.

rather rudimentary manner. That system, however, was neither systematized nor rigorously applied until the advent of the civil wars (*fitna*), whereupon sources were no longer regarded, prima facie, as trustworthy, but were instead increasingly scrutinized to establish authenticity. Thus evolved the elaborate *isnād* system where every *hadīth* was scrutinized from two perspectives: the text (*matn*) containing the information transmitted as such, and the chain of transmitters (*sanad*) giving the names of all those responsible for transmitting such information from the Prophet himself.

As indicated earlier, Ibn Kathīr's method in this particular work is more that of the *hadīth* scholars than it is of the historian; al-Bukhārī, Muslim and more so, al-Bayhaqī, Ahmad b. Hanbal, and Abū Nuʿaym thus feature more prominently as sources for his biography than do historians such as Ibn Ishāq, Ibn Hishām or al-Tabarī. But, as ʿAbd al-Wāhid rightly points out, Ibn Kathīr, on occasion, is not averse to using some rather obscure historical works, some even that are no longer extant: the rare historical tractate of Mūsā b. ʿUqba, and the *al-Rawd al-Anf* of al-Suhaylī are examples thereof.

True to tradition, if not quite on the same scale as, for instance, Ibn Hishām, are Ibn Kathīr's copious citations of poetry, almost all of which seem to have been taken from Muhammad b. Ishāq's biography of the Prophet. The poems deal with a variety of themes and styles: there is, for instance, the unmistakable sarcasm of Kaʿab b. Zuhayr as reflected in his lampooning of the Prophet, followed by his subsequent retraction and apology as in the much celebrated poem, *Bānat Suʿād*; there is also the occasional celebration of pre-Islamic Arabian chivalry, as in the haunting ode of Abū al-Bakhtarī b. Hishām, when he speaks so movingly of his virtual self-immolation for the love of a friend. Then, of course, there are the evocative panegyrics of Hassān b. Thābit in defence of Islam, its Prophet, and his Companions.

Ibn Kathīr, oddly enough for someone who has plumbed the depths of *hadīth* methodology, frequently paraphrases, not just the many references to scholars such as Ibn Ishāq, but also, at times, the very *hadīth* material he so often quotes. He thus takes almost the same liberties with such material as he does with works on history, and the reader, particularly of the Arabic text, sometimes searches in vain for all but the gist of the traditions that he ascribes to, say, the *sahīh* of Bukhārī or that of Muslim. ʿAbd al-Wāhid offers two possible reasons for this anomaly; the one I believe to be somewhat more plausible than the other. It may well be, he suggests, that Ibn Kathīr was simply quoting from memory, seeing no need for any further textual verification, or it may also be that he is, in fact, using sources unavailable to us today. This latter hypothesis is, I believe, somewhat unconvincing for it requires, amongst other things, that Ibn Kathīr possessed not one, but an entire set of *hadīth* works unique to his library alone!

The text itself suffers from a singular lack of the literary cadence that makes the historical works of al-Ṭabarī, for instance, more of a pleasure to read. This seems to result from Ibn Kathīr's efforts to present an authentic description of the life and times of the Prophet of Islam, and to submit such data as is found in the popular biographical works to the scrutiny of *ḥadīth* literature. The flow of his text is, without question, a casualty of this exercise. But, as has been pointed out by a scholar of the Bible, "If we read biblical narrative (or in this case the *sīra* material) as a story, we abandon its historical truth. If we read it as literature, we will often find literary art in it, but this art takes us further from truth."[6] Not that the method of Ibn Kathīr is altogether without its redeeming features: it certainly provides useful information to scholars, particularly those of the traditional schools, who would prefer to have the classical sources for *sīra* studies close at hand.

The contents of works such as Ibn Kathīr's *sīra* are today regarded by many scholars of Islam as largely proto-historical, focusing, that is, on an era whose source documentation falls short of contemporary historiographical standards. It is, some say, the stuff of myth and legend, entwined in places with real historical data. For modern historians of Islam and the Middle East such as Maxime Rodinson, Patricia Crone et al., *sīra* material contains, in the first instance, virtually "nothing of which we can say for certain that it incontestably dates back to the time of the Prophet".[7] And so, "when doing research about the life and work of the Prophet Muḥammad", Rudi Paret warns, "we on principle distrust the traditional statement and explanation of facts given by later generations, in so far as they cannot be verified by internal evidence or in some other way."[8]

In addition, the work at hand may be seen by some to be no more than the product of one who had a variety of interests in the topic: one who was, at one and the same time, a historian, a scribe of "sacred biography", and also a devotee; the results of an endeavour such as Ibn Kathīr's, therefore, risk being perceived as less than the product of dispassionate scholarship.[9]

This critical approach to Islamic historiography emerged gradually in the 18th and 19th centuries. It was, understandably, only a matter of time before Albert Schweitzer's "quest of the historical Christ" would be appropriated by

6. See Robin L. Fox, *The Unauthorized Version: Truth and Fiction in the Bible* (New York: Alfred A. Knopf, 1992).

7. This particular statement appears in the introduction to Maxime Rodinson's own biography of the Prophet. See Maxime Rodinson, *Mohammed*. Trans. Anne Carter (London, 1971).

8. For the full text of this article see R. Paret, "Recent European Research on the Life and Work of Prophet Muhammad, *Journal of the Pakistan Historical Society*, Karachi, 1958.

9. See in this regard G. D. Newby, *The Making of the Last Prophet: A Reconstruction of the Earliest Biography of Muhammad* (Columbia: University of Southern California Press, 1989).

scholars of Islamic history in their search of the demythologized Muḥammad; after all, this kind of appropriation of the analytical tools indigenous to studies of Christianity for the unravelling of the Islamic historical experience has become almost a convention in Islamic and Middle Eastern studies. Yet the entire process is, I believe, fraught with questionable hypotheses, broad generalizations and a certain disregard for the spatio-temporal factors that shape ostensibly similar events. The application of New Testament heuristic tools such as Form and Redaction criticism to the corpus of information pertaining to the *sira* seems to betray a casual disregard for the *Sitz im Leben* of that very corpus. The life and work of Jesus is clearly different from that of Muḥammad; the former's mission – if it can be described as such – is, for example, singularly devoid of the political and socio-economic objectives that informed that of the latter. It is, therefore, hardly surprising, as F. E. Peters in his recent article "The Quest of the Historical Muhammad" points out, that "even though a great deal of effort has been invested in research into the life and times of Muḥammad, the results do not seem at all comparable to those achieved in research on Jesus, and the reasons are not at all clear."[10]

Ever since Gustav Weil presented his *Mohammad der Prophet, sein Leben und seine Lehre* in 1843, scholars have endeavoured to unravel the historical Muḥammad using a variety of tools and strategems. Initially the material offered by Muslim historians such as Ibn Isḥāq, Ibn Hishām and more, importantly, al-Ṭabarī was used almost unquestioningly by Christian scholars who, as Holt characterizes them, belonged mainly to "holy orders".[11] Their primary purpose, it would seem, was to provide a spirited defence of Christian theology and dogma against the claims of Islam and its adherents. The polemics that ensued were, in the main, reflective of the attitude that there was "not any rational inducement in all (that Muslims) believe or practice; insomuch that common sense must be discarded in order to embrace their system."[12] As for Muḥammad, he was for many in that era "so coarse and barbarous an imposter, that there is not a man, who does not or cannot perceive plainly his cheating and corruption."[13] Humphrey Prideaux, the 17th-century lecturer in Hebrew at Oxford, captured rather succinctly the disposition of scholars *vis-à-vis* the study of Muḥammad, in the rather long-winded title of his work, *The true nature of imposture fully display'd in the life of Mahomet. With a discourse annex'd*

10. F. E. Peters, "The Quest of the Historical Muhammad", in *International Journal of Middle East Studies* 23 (1991), 291 315.

11. See P. M. Holt, "The Treatment of Arab Historians by Prideaux, Ockley, and Sale," in *Historians of the Middle East*, ed. B. Lewis and P. M. Holt (Oxford University Press, 1962), 290–302.

12. Ibid., 300.

13. Ibid., 300.

for the vindication of Christianity from this charge. Offered to the consideration of the Deists of the present age.[14] Later Simon Ockley, the somewhat less acerbic and brusque vicar of Swavesey in Cambridgeshire, authored *The History of the Saracens*, a "much more solid contribution to historical knowledge" as Holt puts it, but one that nonetheless did "not fail to follow common form by stigmatizing Muḥammad in his first line, as 'the great Imposter' and then describing the Arab conquests as 'that grievous calamity'."[15] The liberalism that swept across Europe in the 18th century helped create a relatively less hostile attitude among European scholars towards Islam and its leader. We thus find during that era scholars such as Henri de Boulainvillier emerging. Boulainvillier, his theological affinities notwithstanding, assumed a decidedly more conciliatory tone in his biography of Muḥammad, *La vie de Mahomet*. For him, Christianity is undoubtedly superior to Islam but he is, none the less, quite charitable in his evaluation of his subject, and says: "With respect to the essential doctrines of religion, all that (Muḥammad) has laid down is true; but he has not laid down all that is true; and that is the whole difference between our religion and his."[16]

The quest itself began in earnest in the writings of the Belgian Jesuit, Henri Lammens. Whereas Theodor Noeldeke, prior to him, had largely failed in his attempts to unravel "the historical person of Muhammad", Lammens plodded on, and succeeded to some extent, in demonstrating "the possibility of the critical analysis of the *sīra*". Lammens' efforts, however, were directed, not at a biographical study of Muḥammad *per se*, but rather on the search for the secret of his personal appeal and the rapid expansion of his message. "Muhammad to him, was a historical problem as well as a symbol of Islam's obstinacy and insensitiveness to the missionary influence."[17]

Lammens also happened to be among the first to argue, with some conviction, that the *ḥadīth* traditions as well as the *sīra* material on the Prophet are, on the whole, fictitious. This inaugurated a new perspective on Islamic history: the emphasis shifted from a critique of the actors in that history to the questioning of the source material itself.

In the 19th century, the Hungarian scholar Ignaz Goldziher concluded that much of the *ḥadīth* material was but a "pious fraud . . . invoked by every group (in early Islam) for every idea it evolved; . . . through solid chains (*isnād*) of tradition, all such matters acquired an unbroken tie to the 'Companions' who had heard those pronouncements and statutes from the Prophet or had seen him act

14. Ibid., 291.
15. Ibid., 311.
16. P. M. Holt, *The Treatment of Arab History*, 300.
17. K. S. Salibi, "Islam and Syria in the Writings of Henri Lammens", in *Historians of the Middle East*, ed. B. Lewis and P. M. Holt (Oxford University Press, 1962), 330–342.

in pertinent ways."[18] Later Professor J. Schacht further explored the foregoing hypotheses by subjecting the *isnād* of a few legal traditions to an exhaustive scrutiny. He concluded that "hardly any of these traditions, as far as matters of religious law are concerned, can be considered authentic; they were put into circulation . . . from the first half of the second century onwards."[19] From this others were quick to extrapolate that even the biographical material is fraudulent. Crone thus states: "that the bulk of the *sira* . . . consists of second century *hadīths* has not been disputed by any historian, and this point may be taken as conceded."[20]

Not all Western scholars, however were as eager to jettison the classical material. W. M. Watt, writing in his *Muhammad at Mecca*, is clearly more reluctant than Crone, for example, to reject out of hand all such material, simply on the strength of Schacht's conclusion. He thus maintains that "In the legal sphere there may have been some sheer invention of traditions, it would seem. But in the historical sphere, in so far as the two may be separated, and apart from some exceptional cases, the nearest to such invention in the best early historians appears to be a 'tendential shaping' of the material . . ."[21]

It must be remembered, however, that traditional Muslim scholars display little awareness of the foregoing conundrum. The classical methodology of *hadīth* criticism as practised by early Muslim scholars, with its close scrutiny of the *isnād* and the *mutūn* of prophetic traditions, has, in the main, not been discredited, or even questioned, by Muslim scholars. If anything, that methodology has today been given a new lease of life by scholars such as Nāṣir al-Dīn al-Albānī, who, for example, regard the re-evaluation of the early sources as integral to what they call the Islamic renaissance (*al-Nahḍa al-Islamiyya*). Such a renaissance, Albānī argues, will fall far short of its goals, without a thoroughgoing purge of what remains of the spurious material that had crept into *hadīth* and *sira* works during the turbulent epoch of early Islamic history.[22] He thus set himself the task of appraising scholars and the Muslim laity alike to those traditions that were deemed spurious by the regimen of classical *hadīth* studies. His findings, which were first published under the title "al-Aḥādīth al-Ḍaʾīfah wa al-Mawdūʿah" in a weekly column in the magazine *al-Tamaddun al-Islamī*, now comprise a multi-volume work, appropriately titled *Silsilah al-Aḥādīth al-Ḍaʾīfah wa al-Mawdūʿah*.[23]

---

18. See Goldziher's chapter on the development of the law in Islam in *Introduction to Islamic Law and Theology*, (Princeton: Princeton University Press, 1981).

19. J. Schacht, *The Origins of Muhammadan Jurisprudence* (Oxford University Press, 1959).

20. Crone, *Slaves on Horses*, 14–15.

21. W. G. Watt, *Muhammad at Mecca* (Oxford Univesity Press, 1953), xiii.

22. M. N. Al-Albani, *Silsilah al-Aḥādīth al-Ḍaʾīfah wa al-Mawdūʿah*. Vol. i. Damascus?: Manshurāt al-Maktab al-Islami, 1376 h.

23. Ibid., 6.

Clearly not all contemporary scholars are as eager as Schacht et al. to ring the death knell on *hadīth* literature as a tool for unravelling early Islamic history. Azami for one, in his studies on early *hadīth* literature has attempted to show that *hadīth* literature is indeed the richest source for the investigation of that era, for it provides, among other things, material for the understanding of the legal, cultural and religious ideas of those early centuries. He maintains that the theories of Margoliouth, Goldziher and more recently, Schacht can no longer be incontestably accepted given the recent discoveries of manuscripts or research. According to him:

> "In the period referred to, works on the biography of the Prophet and on other historical topics were in a very advanced stage. We find that work on the biography of the Prophet was begun by the Companions. ʿAbd Allāh b. ʿAmr b. al-ʿĀṣ recorded many historical events. It is possible still to trace his work in the *ahādīth* narrated by ʿAmr b. Shuʿayb (d. 118 AH) as he utilized his great grandfather ʿAbd Allāh b. ʿAmr's books. ʿUrwah (d. 93 AH) in his biography of the Prophet names his authority and most probably he had obtained the information in writing. There are works mentioned here and there on a single topic of the Sirah, e.g. *Memorandum on the Servants of the Prophet*, a book on the ambassadors of the Prophet to different rulers and chieftains with their negotiations. There are references to the collections of the Prophet's letters in a very early period."[24]

But it is, in fact, these very sources that Azami cites that have, through the use of contemporary literary and hermeneutical tools, been relegated to no more than "the rubble of early Muslim history". For Patricia Crone therefore, the "inertia" of material such as appears heretofore "comes across very strongly in modern scholarship on the first two centuries of Islam."[25] "The bulk of it", she argues, "has an alarming tendency to degenerate into mere rearrangements of the same old canon – Muslim chronicles in modern languages and graced with modern titles."[26]

Others, such as Juynboll, have strived to arrive at the inevitable *solution inter-médiaire*, "a conceivable position that could be taken between the two points of view represented respectively by Muslim and Western scholarship."[27] For him therefore, the *hadīth* traditions "taken as a whole" do provide a fairly reliable rendition of early Islamic history, and "a judiciously and cautiously formulated overall view of what all those early reports . . . collectively point to, may in all likelihood be taken to be not very far from the truth of 'what really happened'."[28]

24. Azami, *Early Hadith*, 7–8.

25. See in this regard the introduction to her work, *Slaves on Horses: The Evolution of the Islamic Polity*. (Cambridge University Press, 1980).

26. Ibid., 13.

27. See G. H. A. Juynboll, *Muslim Tradition: Studies in chronology, provenance and authorship of early hadith*. (Cambridge University Press, 1983), 1.

28. Ibid., 7.

Finally, the true value of this particular work probably resides outside the context of the foregoing academic debate, for as Gadamer explains in *Truth and Method*,[29] "The meaning of a literary work is never exhausted by the intentions of its author; as the work passes from one cultural or historical context to another, new meanings may be culled from it which were perhaps never anticipated by its author or contemporary audience."[30]

Muneer Fareed
Reviewer of Volumes II–IV

29. H. G. Gadamer, *Truth and Method* (London, 1975).

30. This is in fact an interpretation of Gadamer's thoughts as espoused by T. Eagleton in his study, *Literary Theory: An Introduction* (Minneapolis: University of Minnesota Press, 1983), 71.

TRANSLATOR'S PREFACE

As has often been observed, translation is impossible, since the associations and emotive content of words in one language and culture differ from those of all others. Attempts at translation, therefore, inevitably represent strivings for compromise. While accuracy and precision are prime objectives, the ultimately necessary requirements for clarity and comprehension in the host language may require simplification or even omission from the original text. The dilemmas inherent in these conflicting objectives are at times irreconcilable, and this is particularly true when one is dealing, as here, with languages and cultures so far removed as ancient Arabic and modern English. This translation, composed in everyday, contemporary English, gives no impression of the ubiquitous rarities, oddities and archaisms of vocabulary and syntax that make the original extremely challenging to comprehend. It is hoped, of course, that the innumerable compromises that this translation represents will be accepted as good-faith attempts to convey the spirit and purpose of the original in a form that readers of English will not find impossibly daunting.

In some instances Ibn Kathīr repeats anecdotal *aḥādīth* with differing chains of authority that are almost identical in content; often, as will be seen, the accounts differ in only very few of their words and these are typically vocabulary rarities. While such variations between accounts may seem of scant interest to the Western reader, they have nevertheless been left complete and intact in this translation. Including them in full, as in the original work, gives a strong impression of the care with which these anecdotes have been handed down and the impression of their likely authenticity is therefore enhanced. This seems especially the case where the discrepancies involve vocabulary rarities that are synonymous. It seems that it would be just such words that would have been subjected to dispute, change or loss from memory.

Ibn Kathīr's objective was to appear authoritative and discriminating in his choices of inclusion and discussion of specific *aḥādīth*; to him the listing of all the names of his authorities and his comments on their reputations was an essential component of this lectures. The give-and-take of oral lecturing – of which this work is essentially a record – would have enabled immediate verbal clarification. Our English text, in contrast, has to stand by itself, and to present an inherent and visible logic and clarity; it must also give some impression of the reliability of the Arabic text that is indicated by its complexity, and by the care with which the names of quoted sources are given and at times evaluated.

A perpetual challenge in presenting this text has therefore been to leave the essential narratives clear and succinct while including yet simplifying the lines of authority on which their authenticity is based. The names of authorities quoted have been included in full, since their identities were of prime importance for the initial 'readership' of this work as well as to students and researchers today. However, the exact nature and relative value of the means of transmission from authority to authority and the suggestions implied of Ibn Kathīr's preference for certain sources over others, have not been conveyed with exactitude, since common English vocabulary is unable to convey some of the subtleties of the Arabic technical terms employed for this purpose. The essential completeness of the original text in this translation does, however, enable serious students of early Islamic materials to bring their own differentiation to bear by their knowledge of the reputations of the persons quoted.

Certain words common in this text – such as *Abū* and *sūrat* – change in their form in Arabic to accord with basic grammatical rules. Here, however, to avoid confusion for those readers who do not know Arabic, they have been left in the form in which they are most commonly met. Initial *hamza*, moreover, has been omitted. Since early Arabic manuscripts, like the Arabic printed version of this text, are devoid of quotation marks, the identity of the narrator is sometimes unclear. Similarly, it is occasionally difficult to discern whether comments at the end of an account are those of the transmitting authority or of Ibn Kathīr himself. Footnotes referring to these and similar textual difficulties have been kept to a minimum, while brief parenthetical explanatory comments have sometimes been inserted to aid the general reader.

Discriminating and knowledgeable readers and reviewers will no doubt find discrepancies and perhaps inaccuracies in this lengthy and demanding text, especially in the extensive poems quoted. For these the translator – and his reviewers, text editors and typesetters – apologize. But since this work offers intimate details not elsewhere available in English about Arabian history and the inspiration and leadership of Islam in its earliest formative period, it would seem unsatisfactory to leave it in a language and form accessible only to a small coterie of scholars. The evident religious historical and philosophical interest of this text suggests that all those associated with its production may properly take refuge and find consolation from criticism in the knowledge that 'to err is human'. To attempt the impossible, moreover, while perhaps foolhardy, is surely more laudable than to make no attempt at all.

Trevor Le Gassick
Ann Arbor, 1997

VOLUME II

Chapter: Concerning the migration of those Companions of the Prophet (ṢAAS) who escaped from persecution with their faith from Mecca to Abyssinia.

It has been recounted above how the polytheists abused those believers who lacked power or protection and treated them with severe violence and great humiliation.

God, Almighty and Glorious is He, had kept them away from His Messenger (ṢAAS), and had given him the protection of his uncle, Abū Ṭālib, as was mentioned above. And all praise and recognition is due to God.

Al-Wāqidī has related that their passage to Abyssinia occurred in the month of Rajab in the fifth year of the Mission, and that the first group to migrate consisted of eleven men and four women. He told how they made their way to the sea, either on foot or riding, and there they hired a boat to Abyssinia at a cost of one-half of one dinar.

These persons were: ʿUthmān b. ʿAffān and his wife Ruqayya, daughter of the Messenger of God (ṢAAS), Abū Ḥudhayfa b. ʿUtba and his wife Sahla, daughter of Suhayl, al-Zubayr b. al-ʿAwwām, Muṣʿab b. ʿUmayr, ʿAbd al-Raḥmān b. ʿAwf, Abū Salama b. ʿAbd al-Asad and his wife Umm Salama, daughter of Abū Umayya, ʿUthmān b. Maẓʿun, ʿĀmir b. Rabīʿa al-ʿAnzī, his wife Laylā, daughter of Abū Ḥathma, Abū Sabra b. Abū Ruhm, Ḥāṭib b. ʿAmr, Suhayl b. Bayḍāʾ and ʿAbd Allāh b. Masʿūd. God bless them all! Ibn Jarīr stated, "Others say, however, that the group consisted of 82 men, not counting their women and children. About ʿAmmār b. Yāsir we have doubts; if he was among them, they totalled 83 men."

Muḥammad b. Isḥāq stated, "When the Messenger of God (ṢAAS), witnessed the trials descending upon his Companions, he compared this with his own good state that derived from his own status with God and from his uncle Abū Ṭālib, and, recognizing that he was unable to prevent the evil befalling them, he told them, 'I wish you would go forth into the land of Abyssinia, for there is a king in whose realm no one is harmed, where truth prevails. Stay there until God gives you relief from your plight.'

"The Companions of the Messenger of God (ṢAAS), thereupon left for Abyssinia, fearing the unrest and fleeing with their faith unto God. This was the first emigration that occurred in Islam. The first Muslim to depart was ʿUthmān b. ʿAffān along with his wife Ruqayya, daughter of the Messenger of God (ṢAAS)."

Al-Bayhaqī related, similarly, from a *hadīth* of Yaʿqūb b. Sufyān, from ʿAbbās al-ʿAnbārī, from Bishr b. Mūsā, from al-Ḥasan b. Ziyād al-Burjumī, who said,

"Qatāda stated to us, 'The first man to emigrate to God Almighty along with his family was ʿUthmān b. ʿAffān, God be pleased with him.'

"I heard al-Naḍr b. Anas state, 'I heard Abū Ḥamza (by whom he meant Anas b. Mālik) say, "ʿUthmān b. ʿAffān, along with his wife Ruqayya, daughter of the Messenger of God (ṢAAS), left for Abyssinia. A long time elapsed without the Messenger of God (ṢAAS), having news of them, until a Quraysh woman came to him and said, 'O Muḥammad, I saw your son-in-law with his wife in his company.' 'In what state did you see them?' he asked.

"' "She replied, 'I saw him leading a decrepit old donkey on which his wife was mounted.'

"' "The Messenger of God (ṢAAS), exclaimed, 'May God be with them both! ʿUthmān is the first man since Lot, upon whom be peace, to take himself and his family into exile.'" '"

Ibn Isḥāq stated, "And (they also included) Abū Ḥudhayfa b. ʿUtba and his wife Sahla, daughter of Suhayl b. ʿAmr; and in Abyssinia she bore him a son, Muḥammad b. Abū Ḥudhayfa.

"And there were al-Zubayr b. al-ʿAwwām, Muṣʿab b. ʿUmayr, ʿAbd al-Raḥmān b. ʿAwf, Abū Salama b. ʿAbd al-Asad, along with his wife Umm Salama, daughter of Abū Umayya b. al-Mughīra, to whom Zaynab was born there. Also travelling were ʿUthmān b. Maẓʿūn, and ʿĀmir b. Rabīʿa, who was allied to the al-Khaṭṭāb family; he was from the tribe of ʿAnz b. Wāʾil. His wife was Laylā, daughter of Abū Ḥathma. Then there was Abū Sabra b. Abū Ruhm al-ʿĀmirī, with his wife Umm Kulthūm, daughter of Suhayl b. ʿAmr; the latter is also known as Abū Ḥāṭib b. ʿAmr b. ʿAbd Shams b. ʿAbd Wudd b. Naṣr b. Mālik b. Ḥisl b. ʿĀmir. He is also said to have been the first to arrive there.

"Also there was Suhayl b. Bayḍāʾ.

"These ten men, so I have been told, were the first Muslims to leave for Abyssinia."

Ibn Hishām stated, "ʿUthmān b. Maẓʿūn was in command of them, according to some scholars."

Ibn Isḥāq stated, "Then Jaʿfar b. Abū Ṭālib left, accompanied by his wife Asmāʾ, daughter of ʿUmays. ʿAbd Allāh b. Jaʿfar was born to him in Abyssinia."

The Muslims followed on after one another, eventually being reunited in Abyssinia.

Mūsā b. ʿUqba has claimed that the first migration to Abyssinia occurred when Abū Ṭālib and those who had allied with him in support of the Messenger of God (ṢAAS), went into the *shiʿb*.[1] There are differing views on this. But God knows best.

He also claimed that the departure of Jaʿfar b. Abū Ṭālib came only in the second migration to Abyssinia, after the return of some of those who had gone

---

1. The defile in Mecca where he was permitted by Quraysh to take up residence.

there initially. (They returned) when they heard that the polytheists had accepted Islam and were praying. When they arrived in Mecca, ҴUthmān b. Maẓ Ҵūn among them, they did not find it true that the polytheists had accepted Islam, as they had been told. Some of them then returned to Abyssinia, while others remained in Mecca. Other Muslims also went to Abyssinia at the time of the second migration. This will be explained hereafter.

Mūsā b. ҴUqba stated, "Ja Ҵfar b. Abū Ṭālib was among those who left the second time." But Ibn Isḥāq's referring to his having gone on the first migration is very plain, as will be shown. But God knows best.

However, he clearly was in a second group of the emigrants who went on the first migration; he acted as their spokesman and translator before the Negus and others. We will report this at length.

Then Ibn Isḥāq went on to list those who left in the company of Ja Ҵfar, God be pleased with them all.

They were: ҴAmr b. Sa ҵīd b. al-ҵĀṣ and his wife Fāṭima, daughter of Ṣafwān b. Umayya b. Muḥarrith b. Shiqq al-Kinānī.

And his brother Khālid, accompanied by his wife Umayna, daughter of Khalaf b. As ҵad al-Khuzā ҵī; she bore him Sa ҵīd and Amma, the latter ultimately marrying al-Zubayr by whom she gave birth to ҵAmr and Khālid.

Also there were ҵAbd Allāh b. Jaḥsh b. Ri³āb and his brother ҵUbayd Allāh, who was accompanied by his wife Umm Ḥabība, daughter of Abū Sufyān.

And Qays b. ҵAbd Allāh of the Banū Asad b. Khazīma along with his wife Baraka, daughter of Yasār, the freed-woman of Abū Sufyān.

And Mu ҵayqib b. Abū Fāṭima, a freed-man of Sa ҵīd b. al-ҵĀṣ. Ibn Hishām stated, "He was of (the tribe of) Daws."

And Abū Mūsā al-Ash ҵarī, that is ҵAbd Allāh b. Qays, an ally of the family of ҵUtba b. Rabī ҵa; we will discuss this later and also the authority.

And ҵUtba b. Ghazwān, Yazīd b. Zam ҵa b. al-Aswad, ҵAmr b. Umayya b. al-Ḥārith b. Asad, Ṭulayb b. ҵUmayr b. Wahb b. Abū Kathīr b. ҵAbd, Suwaybiṭ b. Sa ҵd b. Ḥuraymala and Jahm b. Qays al-ҵAbdawī, accompanied by his wife Umm Ḥarmala, daughter of ҵAbd al-Aswad b. Khuzayma, along with his two sons ҵAmr b. Jahm and Khuzayma b. Jahm. Also there was Abū al-Rūm b. ҵUmayr b. Hāshim b. ҵAbd Manāf b. ҵAbd al-Dār, Firās b. al-Naḍr b. al-Ḥārith b. Kalda, ҵĀmir b. Abū Waqqāṣ, brother of Sa ҵd, and al-Muṭṭalib b. Azhar b. ҵAbd ҵAwf al-Zuhrī, accompanied by his wife Ramla, daughter of Abū ҵAwf b. Ḍubayra, who bore in Abyssinia al-Muṭṭalib's son ҵAbd Allāh.

Also there were ҵAbd Allāh b. Mas ҵūd and his brother ҵUtba, al-Miqdād b. al-Aswad, al-Ḥārith b. Khālid b. Ṣakhr al-Taymī, accompanied by his wife Rayṭa, daughter of al-Ḥārith b. Jubayla; she bore him there Mūsā, ҵĀ³isha, Zaynab and Fāṭima.

Also there were ҵAmr b. ҵUthmān b. ҵAmr b. Ka ҵb b. Sa ҵd b. Taym b. Murra and Shammās b. ҵUthmān b. al-Sharīd al-Makhzūmī. He (Ibn Isḥāq) stated that he was named "Shammās" (i.e. perhaps "Sunny", tr.) because of his good looks; his original name was ʿUthmān b. ʿUthmān.

Then there were Habbār b. Sufyān b. ʿAbd al-Asad al-Makhzūmī and his brother ʿAbd Allāh, Hishām b. Abū Hudhayfa b. al-Mughīra b. ʿAbd Allāh b. ʿAmr b. Makhzūm, Salama b. Hishām b. al-Mughīra, ʿAyyāsh b. Abū Rabīʿa b. al-Mughīra, Muʿattib b. ʿAwf b. ʿĀmir, known as ʿAyhāma, he being an ally of the Banū Makhzūm.

Also included were Qudāma and ʿAbd Allāh, the two brothers of ʿUthmān b. Mazʿūn, al-Sāʾib b. ʿUthmān b. Mazʿūn, Hātb b. al-Hārith b. Maʿmar, accompanied by his wife Fātima, daughter of al-Mujallil and his two sons by her, Muhammad and al-Hārith. Also there were Hātib's brother Khattāb, accompanied by his wife Fukayha, daughter of Yasār, Sufyān b. Maʿmar b. Habīb and his wife Hasana, along with his two sons by her, Jābir and Junāda, as well as a son of hers by another husband. This son's name was Shurahbīl b. ʿAbd Allāh, a member of the family of al-Ghawth b. Muzāhim b. Tamīm; he was known as Shurahbīl b. Hasana.

And there were ʿUthmān b. Rabīʿa b. Ahbān b. Wahb b. Hudhāfa b. Jumah, Khunays b. Hudhāfa b. Qays b. ʿAdī, ʿAbd Allāh b. al-Hārith b. Qays b. ʿAdī b. Saʿīd b. Sahm, Hishām b. al-ʿĀs b. Wāʾil b. Saʿīd, Qays b. Hudhāfa b. Qays b. ʿAdī, accompanied by his brother ʿAbd Allāh.

Also there were Abū Qays b. al-Hārith b. Qays b. ʿAdī, along with his brothers al-Hārith, Maʿmar, al-Sāʾib, Bishr and Saʿīd, all sons of al-Hārith, along with the brother of Saʿīd b. Qays b. ʿAdī on his mother's side, his name being Saʿīd b. ʿAmr al-Tamīmī.

And ʿUmayr b. Riʾāb b. Hudhayfa b. Muhashshim b. Saʿīd b. Sahm, along with an ally of the Banū Sahm named Mahmiyya b. Jazʾ al-Zubaydī, Maʿmar b. ʿAbd Allāh al-ʿAdawī, ʿUrwa b. ʿAbd al-ʿUzzā, ʿAdī b. Nadla b. ʿAbd al-ʿUzzā, along with his son al-Nuʿmān, ʿAbd Allāh b. Makhrama al-ʿĀmirī, ʿAbd Allāh b. Suhayl b. ʿAmr, Salīt b. ʿAmr and his brother al-Sakrān, who was accompanied by his wife Sawda, daughter of Zamʿa, Mālik b. Rabīʿa and his wife ʿAmra, daughter of al-Saʿdī, and Abū Hātib b. ʿAmr al-ʿĀmirī, accompanied by their ally Saʿd b. Khawla from Yemen.

Also there were Abū ʿUbayda ʿĀmir b. ʿAbd Allāh b. al-Jarrāh al-Fihrī, Suhayl b. Baydāʾ, Baydāʾ being his mother, whose real name was Daʿd, daughter of Jahdam b. Umayya b. Zarib b. al-Hārith b. Fihr. He, Suhayl, was really Suhayl b. Wahb b. Rabīʿa b. Hilāl (b. Uhayb)[2] b. Dabba. And there were ʿAmr b. Abū Sarh b. Rabīʿa b. Hilāl b. Uhayb b. Mālik b. Dabba b. al-Hārith, ʿIyād b. Zuhayr b. Abū Shaddād b. Rabīʿa b. Hilāl b. Mālik b. Dabba. ʿAmr b. al-Hārith b. Zuhayr b. Abū Shaddād b. Rabīʿa and ʿUthmān b. ʿAbd Ghanm b. Zuhayr were two brothers. Saʿīd b. ʿAbd Qays b. Laqīt, along with his brother al-Hārith were of the Fihr tribe.

---

2. Ibn Hishām adds this link.

Ibn Isḥāq stated, "The number of those Muslims who migrated and went to Abyssinia, not counting the little children and those born there, totalled 83. This assumes that ῾Ammār b. Yāsir was among them, but there is some doubt about him."

I would comment that the inclusion by Ibn Isḥāq of Abū Mūsā al-Ash῾arī among those who migrated from Mecca to Abyssinia is very strange.

Imām Aḥmad stated, "Ḥasan b. Mūsā related to us that he heard Ḥudayj, brother of Zuhayr b. Mu῾āwiya say, on the authority of Abū Isḥāq, from ῾Abd Allāh b. ῾Utba, from Ibn Mas῾ūd, 'The Messenger of God (ṢAAS) sent us, a body of some 80 men, to the Negus. These included ῾Abd Allāh b. Mas῾ūd, Ja῾far, ῾Abd Allāh b. Arfaṭa, ῾Uthmān b. Maẓ῾ūn, and Abū Mūsā. These men went to the Negus.

"'Then Quraysh dispatched to him ῾Amr b. al-῾Āṣ and ῾Umāra b. al-Walīd with a gift.

"'When they went in to the Negus, they bowed down before him. Then they took up positions to the left and right before him and said, "A group of our people have taken up residence in your land, after having turned away from us and from our religion."

"'"Where are they?," he asked.

"'"In your land. Send for them," they suggested.

"'He did so and Ja῾far said, "I will be your spokesman today." And they followed him.

"'He made salutation, but did not bow down. They asked him, "What is wrong with you, not bowing down before the king?"

"'He replied, "We bow down only before God, the Almighty and Glorious."

"'"What is this all about?" he was asked.

"'He answered, "God has sent a messenger to us and told us to bow down to no one but God, the Almighty and Glorious. He also ordered us to pray, and to give alms."

"'῾Amr commented, "They differ with you about Jesus, son of Mary."

"'He (the Negus) asked, "What do you say about Jesus son of Mary and His mother?"

"'He (Ja῾far) replied, "We say as God did: He is His word and His spirit which He cast into the Virgin whom no man had touched and no child had been inside."

"'The king then picked up a stick from the ground and said, "O people of Abyssinia, and you, priests and monks; by God, they are not so much as the size of this stick away from what we say! Welcome to you and greetings to him from whom you come! I bear witness that he is the Messenger of God, and that it is him we find in the Bible. He is the Messenger of whom Jesus, son of Mary, made prophecy. You may reside wherever you wish; and, by God, were it not for my role as king, I would go to him so that I could be the one who carries his shoes for him!"

"'He then commanded that the present the two messengers had brought be returned to them.

"''Abd Allāh b. Masʿūd hurried forth thereafter, and lived to take part in the battle of Badr.

"'He claimed that the Prophet (ṢAAS) prayed for forgiveness for him (the king) when news of his death reached him.'"

The chain of authorities for this is excellent, and the narrative is good. It gives evidence that Abū Mūsā was among those who migrated from Mecca to Abyssinia, even though this *ḥadīth* is not recorded by some authorities. But God knows best.

This event is related on the authority of Abū Isḥāq al-Sabīʿī from another chain.

The *ḥāfiẓ* Abū Nuʿaym stated in *Dalāʾil* (*The Signs*), "Sulaymān b. Aḥmad related to us quoting from Muḥammad b. Zakariyyāʾ al-Ghulābī, from ʿAbd Allāh b. Rajāʾ from Isrāʾil. Also Sulaymān b. Aḥmad related to us from Muḥammad b. Zakariyyāʾ, from al-Ḥasan b. ʿAlluwiyya al-Qaṭṭān, from ʿIbād b. Mūsā al-Khutuli, from Ismāʿil b. Jaʿfar, from Isrāʾil.

"Also, Abū Aḥmad related to us, from ʿAbd Allāh b. Muḥammad b. Shīrawayh, from Isḥāq b. Ibrāhīm, he being Ibn Rāhawayh, from ʿUbayd Allāh b. Mūsā, from Isrāʾil, from Abū Isḥāq, from Abū Burda, from Abū Mūsā, who said, 'The Messenger of God (ṢAAS) ordered us to depart with Jaʿfar b. Abū Ṭālib, to the land of the Negus.'

"Quraysh heard of this and so they sent ʿAmr b. al-ʿĀṣ and ʿUmāra b. al-Walīd, having obtained a gift for the Negus.

"They went in to the Negus with the present, which he accepted, and they made obeisance before him.

"Then ʿAmr b. al-ʿĀṣ said, 'Certain people from our land have abandoned our religion. They are here in your country.'

"''In my country?' the Negus asked.

"''Yes,' they replied.

"So he sent for us and Jaʿfar told us, 'Let none of you speak. I will be your spokesman today.'

"And so we went to the Negus when he was seated on his throne, with ʿAmr b. al-ʿĀṣ on his right, ʿUmāra on his left, and the priests seated in two ranks. ʿAmr and ʿUmāra had told the king, 'They will not make obeisance to you.'

"When we arrived, some of his priests and monks there with him hurried to us and told us to bow down before the king. But Jaʿfar replied, 'We bow down only before God, the Almighty and Glorious.'

"When we reached the Negus, he asked, 'What prevents you from bowing down?'

"Jaʿfar replied, 'We bow down only before God.'

"The Negus then asked him, 'Well, what is this all about?'

"Ja᾽far explained, 'God sent a messenger among us; he is that same Messenger Jesus, son of Mary, God's prayers and peace be upon Him, said would come after himself, his name being "Aḥmad". He ordered us to worship God and to associate no god with Him, to perform the prayers, to pay alms, to be good, and to abstain from what is forbidden.'

"His speech astonished the Negus.

"When ᾽Amr b. al-᾽Āṣ saw this, he exclaimed, 'May God save the king! They disagree with you concerning Jesus, son of Mary.'

"The Negus then asked Ja᾽far, 'What does your master say about the son of Mary?'

"Ja᾽far replied, 'He says of Him what God stated – that he is God's spirit and His word, and that He brought him forth from the Virgin whom no man had approached and in whom there had been no child.'

"The Negus then picked up a stick from the ground and raised it up, saying, 'Ye priests and monks, these people do not add so much as the weight of this to what we say about the son of Mary.'

"'Welcome to you,' he continued, 'and greetings to him from whom you have come. I bear witness that he is the Messenger of God and that it is he of whom Jesus made prophecy. Were it not for the duties of my kingdom, I would go to him to kiss his shoes. Stay in my land as long as you wish.'

"He then ordered that food and fine garments be brought for us. And he said, 'Give back to those other two their gift.'

"'Amr b. al-᾽Āṣ was short, while ᾽Umāra was a handsome man. While at sea, they had been drinking. ᾽Amr had his wife with him and, after they had been imbibing, ᾽Umāra said to ᾽Amr, 'Tell your wife to kiss me!' ᾽Amr replied, 'You should be ashamed!' Then ᾽Umāra picked up ᾽Amr and flung him into the sea. ᾽Amr kept calling out to ᾽Umāra until he brought him back on to the boat.

"'Amr hated him for this, and told the Negus, 'If you were to leave, ᾽Umāra would take your place with your wife.' At that the Negus summoned ᾽Umāra and had air blown into his urethra so that he flew away with the wild birds."

The *ḥāfiz* al-Bayhaqī related it thus in *Dalā᾽il* (*The Signs*), through Abū ᾽Alī al-Ḥasan b. Sallām al-Sawwāq, from ᾽Ubayd Allāh b. Mūsā. He relates it similarly, with the same chain of authorities, up to the words, "He then ordered that food and fine garments be brought to us."

He then stated, "This chain of authorities is good; what it apparently shows is that Abū Mūsā was at Mecca, and that he did go with Ja᾽far, son of Abū Ṭālib, to Abyssinia.

What is true according to Yazīd b. ᾽Abd Allāh b. Abū Burda, on the authority of his grandfather Abū Burda, from Abū Mūsā, is that the departure of the Messenger of God (ṢAAS) became known to them while they were in Yemen. They therefore went out into exile along with some 50 persons in a boat that took them to the Negus in Abyssinia. They found that Ja᾽far b. Abū Ṭālib and his companions were already living there. Ja᾽far told them to stay, and they did stay with him until they joined the Messenger of God (ṢAAS), at the time of Khaybar.

He stated, "Abū Mūsā witnessed what took place between Jaʿfar and the Negus and reported this."

He also said, "And perhaps the narrator was using his imagination in saying, "The Messenger of God (ṢAAS), ordered us to depart." But God knows best.

This is how al-Bukhārī related this in his chapter on the migration to Abyssinia: "Muḥammad b. al-ʿAlāʾ related to us, quoting Abū Usāma, quoting Burayd b. ʿAbd Allāh from Abū Burda, from Abū Mūsā, who said, 'The departure of the Messenger of God (ṢAAS) became known to us while we were in Yemen. So we embarked on a boat which took us to the Negus, in Abyssinia. There we found Jaʿfar b. Abū Ṭālib, God bless him, and we stayed there with him until we left and joined the Prophet (ṢAAS), when Khaybar was conquered. And so the Prophet said, "For you people of the boat there are two migrations."'" Muslim related this in this way from Abū Kurayb and Abū ʿĀmir ʿAbd Allāh b. Barrād, both of whom used Abū Usāma as a source. They both related this at length in other places. But God knows best.

This narrative concerning Jaʿfar and the Negus was also related by the ḥāfiz Ibn ʿAsākir in his biography of Jaʿfar b. Abū Ṭālib. His account is on his own authority and that of ʿAmr b. al-ʿĀṣ, both of whom related the ḥadīth. It is also recounted by Ibn Masʿūd, as given above, and by Umm Salama, as will be shown later.

This following account given by Jaʿfar is extremely valuable. Ibn ʿAsākir related it from Abū al-Qāsim al-Samarqandī, from Abū al-Ḥusayn b. al-Naqūr, from Abū Ṭāhir al-Mukhalliṣ, from Abū al-Qāsim b. al-Baghawī, who said, "Abū ʿAbd al-Raḥmān al-Juʿfī related to us, from ʿAbd Allāh b. ʿUmar b. Abān, quoting Asad b. ʿAmr al-Bajalī, from Mujālid b. Saʿīd, from al-Shaʿbī, from ʿAbd Allāh b. Jaʿfar, from his father, who said, 'Quraysh sent ʿAmr b. al-ʿĀṣ and ʿUmāra b. al-Walīd with a gift from Abū Sufyān to the Negus. They told him – and we were there with him – 'Some low-class and silly people of ours have come to you. So hand them over to us!'

"He replied, 'No, not until I hear what they have to say.'"

Jaʿfar went on, "So he sent to us and asked, 'What's all this they say?'

"We replied, 'These are people who worship idols. God sent a messenger to us in whom we believed and trusted.'

"The Negus then asked them, 'Are these people slaves of yours?'

"'No,' they replied.

"'Do they have debts owing to you?' he then asked.

"'No,' they answered.

"'Then leave them alone,' he said.

"At this we left his presence, but ʿAmr b. al-ʿĀṣ told him, 'These people speak different things of Jesus from what you do.'

"He replied, 'If they do not say about Jesus as I do, I will not allow them to stay in my land a single hour of the day!'

"And so he sent for us, this second invitation being harder upon us than the first.

"The Negus asked, 'What does your master say about Jesus, son of Mary?'

"We replied, 'He says that He is the spirit of God and His word that He cast to a chaste virgin.'

"He then dispatched a messenger, saying, 'Summon to me such-and-such a priest, such-and-such a monk.'

"Some men of theirs came and he asked, 'What do you say concerning Jesus, son of Mary?'

"They replied, 'You are the most knowledgeable of us; what do you say?'

"The Negus replied, having picked something up from the ground, 'Jesus is no more different from what these people say than this much.'

"He then asked, 'Is anyone harming you people?'

"They replied, 'Yes.'

"So then a crier announced, 'Whoever harms any one of them is to be fined four dirhams.'

"Then he asked, 'Is this enough for you?'

"We replied, 'No.' So the king doubled the fine."

Ja῾far went on: "When the Messenger of God (ṢAAS) emigrated to Medina and proclaimed himself there, we told him (the Negus) 'The Messenger of God (ṢAAS) has proclaimed himself and gone to Medina; he has killed those we told you about. We wish to travel to him, so send us back.'

"'Yes, I will,' he replied. He gave us mounts and provisioned us, then said, 'Inform your master how I have treated you. This man, my friend, will go with you. I bear witness that there is no god but God and that he is the Messenger of God. Ask him to pray for forgiveness for me.'

Ja῾far went on: "So we left and went to Medina where the Messenger of God (ṢAAS) met us. He embraced me, then said, 'I don't know what pleases me more – the victory at Khaybar, or the arrival of Ja῾far!'"

This coincided with the victory at Khaybar. He then sat down.

The envoy of the Negus then said, "This man, Ja῾far, ask him how our master treated him."

So he, Ja῾far, said, "Yes, he acted in such-and-such a way, then gave us mounts and provisions and bore witness that there is no god but God and that you are the Messenger of God. He also told me, 'Ask him to pray for forgiveness for me.'"

The Messenger of God (ṢAAS) then arose, performed the prayer ablutions and prayed three times: "O God, forgive the Negus!" And the Muslims present said, "Amen".

Then Ja῾far said, "I then told the envoy of the Negus, 'Leave now, and tell your master what you saw of the Messenger of God (ṢAAS).'"

Ibn ʿAsākir commented after this *ḥadīth*: "It is *ḥasan gharīb* (good but unique)."

Regarding the narrative given by Umm Salama, Yūnus b. Bakayr stated, on the authority of Muḥammad b. Isḥāq, who said, "Al-Zuhrī related to me, from Abū Bakr b. ʿAbd al-Raḥmān b. Ḥārith b. Hishām, that Umm Salama, God bless her, said, 'When events turned threatening and even violent in Mecca for the supporters of the Messenger of God (ṢAAS), and actual harm was done to them because of their faith, while the Messenger of God (ṢAAS) was unable to defend them, being himself under the protection of his family and his uncle, so that he experienced none of their sufferings, he told them, "In Abyssinia there is a king who allows no one to be persecuted in his domain. So go to his country until such time as God provides for you some relief and solution to your troubles."

"'And so we did set out in groups and rejoined one another there. We found hospitality, friendship and security to engage in our religion in Abyssinia, and had no fear of harm.

"'When Quraysh saw that we had gained accommodation and security there, they were angered and agreed to make representations to the Negus to remove us from his country and send us back to them.

"'They therefore dispatched ʿAmr b. al-ʿĀṣ and ʿAbd Allāh b. Abū Rabīʿa. They gathered gifts for the king and for all his generals, without exception. They told their two envoys, "Give a present to each general before you speak among them, and then give the king his gifts. And if you are able to have him hand over the exiles to you without him speaking to them, then do so."

"'The envoys did go to the king, not having omitted giving the presents to each of his generals. They then addressed them, saying, "We have only come to see the king about some fools of ours who have abandoned their people and their religion, and who have not joined your faith. Their people have sent us to have the king return them to them. When we speak with him, then indicate that he should do so." They agreed to this.

"'The envoys then gave their gifts to the Negus. The most favoured of their gifts from Mecca to him were leather products.'"

Mūsā b. ʿUqba related that they presented to him a mare, a gown and a silk garment.

Umm Salama continued, "When they took their gifts in to him, they told him, 'O king, some of our foolish young have abandoned their people's religion and have not entered your faith. They have come here with a fabricated religion we do not know and have taken refuge in your land. Their tribes, their own fathers and uncles, have sent us to you so that you will return these people to them. They know them best. They will not adopt your faith, and you should prevent them from doing so.'

"The king was angered at this and replied, 'No! By God's life, I will not return them to them before summoning these people and talking to them to discover their views. They are a group who have taken refuge in my land and have chosen my company above that of all others. If they are indeed as your people say, I will return them to them. But if they are otherwise, I will protect them, give their people no access to them and no satisfaction.'"

Mūsā b. ꜥUqba related that his generals indicated to him that he should return them to their people, but the king refused, saying, "No! By God, I will not, not until I hear what they have to say and what their position is."

Umm Salama went on, "When the exiles came before him, they greeted him by saying, 'Peace be upon you', but they did not bow down before him. He addressed them, 'Will you not tell me why you do not greet me in the same manner as others of your people who have come to me? And tell me what it is you say about Jesus and what your religion is. Are you Christians?'

"'No,' they replied.

"'Are you Jews then?'

"'No.'

"'Do you worship in your people's religion?'

"'No.'

"'What is your religion?'

"'It is Islam.'

"'What is Islam?'

"'We worship God,' they replied, 'and we associate no other god with Him.'

"'Who was it brought you this faith?'

"'A man from among ourselves, whose face and genealogy we know. God sent him to us as He sent messengers to those who came before us. He ordered us to behave with kindness, honesty, trustworthiness and good faith. He forbad us to worship idols and ordered us to worship God alone who has no associate. We believed him and recognised God's words. We realized that what he presented came from God. But when we did all this our people behaved with enmity towards us and towards the truthful Prophet; they disbelieved in him and wanted to kill him. They wanted us to worship idols, and so we fled to you, bringing our faith and our blood to you away from our own people.'

"'By God,' he exclaimed, 'this is the very niche from which Moses' affair emerged!'

"'And regarding our greeting,' Jaꜥfar explained, 'the Messenger of God (ṢAAS) told us that the people of paradise greet one another with a wish for peace and he ordered us to do the same. We greeted you the same way we greet one another.

"'And regarding Jesus, son of Mary, he was the servant and messenger of God, His word that He cast to Mary and also His spirit. He was the son of the chaste Virgin.'

"The king then picked up a stick and said, 'By God, Mary's son did not add to this the weight of this stick more!'

"The Abyssinian leaders then said, 'By God, if the Abyssinians heard this they would depose you!'

"'By God,' he responded, 'I will never say anything about Jesus different from this; God did not acquiesce to the people about me when He restored my kingdom to me. Shall I then obey the people concerning God's religion? God forbid such a thing!'"

Yūnus stated, from Ibn Isḥāq, "And so the Negus sent for them and assembled them, nothing being more distasteful to ʿAmr b. al-ʿĀṣ and ʿAbd Allāh b. Abū Rabīʿa than that he should hear their words.

"When the Negus's messenger came to them, the exiles assembled and asked one another what to say.

"'What can we say?' they asked, and decided, 'By God, we will tell what we know and all about the religion we follow, what it was our Prophet (ṢAAS) brought to us, come what may!'

"When they went in to him their spokesman was Jaʿfar b. Abū Ṭālib, God be pleased with him. The Negus asked him, 'What is this religion you follow? Have you left the faith of your people without entering either Judaism or Christianity?'

"Jaʿfar replied, 'O king, we were a people of polytheism. We worshipped idols, ate the meat of animals that had died, offended rules of hospitality and permitted things forbidden, as in the shedding of one another's blood and so on. We completely ignored matters of right and wrong. And so God sent to us a prophet, from among ourselves, whose honesty and trustworthiness we knew well. He summoned us to pray to God alone and without associate, told us to respect rights of kinship, to honour rights of hospitality, to pray to God the Almighty and Glorious, to fast for Him and to worship none other than Him.'"

Ziyād stated, from Ibn Isḥāq, "And so he called us to God, to affirm His oneness, to worship Him, and to tear down all the other stones and idols we and our forefathers had worshipped apart from Him. He ordered us to be truthful in our speech, to keep to our trust, to respect kinship ties and hospitality rights and to abandon things forbidden and the shedding of blood. He forbad us to do anything immoral, to tell lies, to misuse the funds of orphans, or to make false accusations against women of virtue. He ordered us to worship God and to associate no other god with Him. He told us to pray, to give alms and to fast." He stated, "And he ennumerated for him all aspects of Islam.

"And so we believed in him and trusted him, following him in the instructions he brought from God. We worshipped God alone, without partner and associating no one with Him. We forbad what he had forbidden and considered permissible what he allowed us.

"But our people aggressed against us and harmed us, seeking to draw us out of our faith, to return us to the worship of idols instead of God, and to have us again consider permissible the abominations we had previously allowed.

"When they treated us with violence and persecution, besieged us and prevented us from performing our religion, we left for your country and chose you above all others. We desired your hospitality and hoped we would not be harmed in your domain, O king."

She (Umm Salama) went on to state, "The Negus replied, 'Did you bring anything with you from what he brought?'

"Jaᶜfar then recited to him a passage from KHYᶜṢ (*sūrat Maryam*: XIX) and, I swear, the Negus wept so hard his beard was soaked! And all his bishops cried so hard they wet their bibles!

"He then said, 'These words certainly come from the niche that Moses brought with him! Pass on, rightly guided! No, by God, I will not return them to you and I will not give you satisfaction.'

"So we did leave his presence. The more sensible of the two envoys, in our view, was ᶜAbd Allāh b. Rabīᶜa, for ᶜAmr b. al-ᶜĀṣ said, 'By God, I will go to him tomorrow and tell him something that will turn them all upside down: I will tell him that they claim that the god he worships, Jesus, son of Mary, is a servant (of God)!' But ᶜAbd Allāh b. Rabīᶜa told him, 'No, don't do that; even if they have opposed us, they are related to us and have a certain right.'

"But he insisted, 'By God, I will do it!'

"The next day he went in to the king and said, 'O king, they say terrible things about Jesus. Send for them and question them about him.'

"He did indeed do so, and nothing like this had happened to us before. We asked one another what we should say about Jesus if he were to ask about him. All agreed that we should definitely say about him what God had said and our Prophet had told us to say.

"The exiles then went in to the king who had his generals with him. He asked, 'What is it you say about Jesus, son of Mary?'

"Jaᶜfar replied, 'We say he is God's servant, His messenger, His spirit and His word that He cast into Mary, the chaste Virgin.'

"The Negus stretched his hand down to the ground and picked up a stick between two fingers, saying, 'Jesus, son of Mary is not more than the size of this little stick different from what you say.'

"His generals grumbled at this and he responded, 'Grumble away, by God! You people may leave now and you are *shuyūm* in my land! (The word *shuyūm* means in their language: those who are secure, i.e. those whose life is safe.) Whoever reviles you will be fined! (He repeated this phrase three times.) I'd rather not have *dabr* than that I harmed one man among you! (*Dabr* in their language means: gold.)' "

Ziyād stated, on the authority of Ibn Isḥāq, that what he said was, "I'd rather not have a *dabr* of gold." Ibn Hishām stated that others say the word *zabr* was used, meaning a mountain in their language.

The Negus then said, "I swear, God took no bribe from me when He returned my kingdom to me. And He did not acquiesce to the people about me; so am I to acquiesce to them about him? Return their presents to the two envoys. I don't need them. And, you two, get out of my country!"

The two men did depart in disgrace, with what they had brought having been returned to them.

Umm Salama continued, "And so we stayed on there in comfort and security.

"But soon a certain Abyssinian rose in revolt and challenged the rule of the Negus. And, I swear, nothing had ever caused us so much grief as this, since we feared that that rebel would defeat him and then there would be a king who might not recognise our rights as the Negus had done.

"And so we began saying prayers to God, supplicating Him to give victory to the Negus who went out to do battle.

"The Companions of the Messenger of God (ṢAAS) then asked one another which one of them should go and witness the engagement to see which side would be victorious.

"Al-Zubayr, one of the youngest of them, volunteered.

"They then blew air into a skin which they attached to his chest and he set off on it, swimming across the Nile. He came out on the other bank, went to the site where the two sides were meeting and witnessed the battle.

"God defeated and killed that rebel leader, giving the Negus victory over him.

"Al-Zubayr then returned to us, waving his shirt and yelling, 'Rejoice! God has given victory to the Negus!'"

Umm Salama concluded, "I swear by God we were never happier than at the Negus's victory. Thereafter we remained there with him, until some of us returned to Mecca while others stayed there."

Al-Zuhrī stated, "I related this *ḥadīth* on the authority of Umm Salama to ʿUrwa b. al-Zubayr and he asked, 'Do you know what was meant by the Negus's words? "I swear, God took no bribe from me when he returned my kingdom to me; so am I to accept a bribe about Him? And He did not acquiesce to the people about me; so am I to obey them about him?"'

"I replied, 'No; Abū Bakr b. ʿAbd al-Raḥmān b. al-Ḥārith b. Hishām, relating on the authority of Umm Salama, did not tell me that.'

"ʿUrwa explained, 'Well, ʿĀʾisha related to me that his father had been the king of his people and had a brother who had fathered twelve sons. Whereas his own father had only one son, the Negus himself. The Abyssinians discussed this among themselves and decided to kill the father of the Negus and to appoint his uncle over them in his place. For since the uncle had twelve sons of his own who would inherit the kingship, then Abyssinia would remain for a long time free from unrest. They therefore attacked and killed the father of the Negus and made his brother king.

"'The Negus then went to live with his uncle; eventually he had such influence over him that no one but he could direct his affairs. He was intelligent and judicious. When the Abyssinians saw his status with his uncle, they told one another, "We have seen how this young man ranks with his uncle, and we could never be safe if he ruled over us, because he knows we killed his father. If he became king, he would not fail to kill every nobleman among us. Let us therefore speak to the king about him so that he will kill or exile him from our land."

"'So they went to his uncle and told him, "We have seen how this young man ranks high with you, but you know that we killed his father and put you in his place. We could never be safe if he ruled over us, for he would kill us. You should either kill him or exile him from our land."

"'"What?" he responded, "You killed his father yesterday and today I am to kill him! No, but I will exile him."

"'So they took him out and stood him in the market where they sold him to a certain merchant for 600 or 700 dirhams who put him aboard a ship and sailed away with him.

"'When evening came, autumn storm clouds arose and his uncle went outside beneath them to pray for rain; he was struck by a thunderbolt which killed him.

"'They then went in fright to his sons but they turned out all to be idiots, with not a good one among them. The Abyssinians were most disturbed at this and some said to others, "You realize, by God, that the only king fit to solve your problems is the man you sold this morning. If you are concerned about Abyssinia, then go and get him before he leaves."

"'So they did set off to find him, located him and sat him on the throne and declared him king.

"'The merchant then said, "Return to me my money since you have taken my slave from me."

"'The Abyssinian replied that they would not and he said he would talk directly to the king.

"'He went to him and said, "O king, I bought a slave and those who sold it received the price for him. But then they acted unjustly with me regarding the slave by seizing him and not returning my money."

"'The first thing told about the stability and justice of his rule was that he replied, "Let his money be returned to him or let the hand of his slave be placed in his own so that he may take him wherever he wishes."

"'His people replied, "No, we will give him his money." And so they did.

"'That is why he said, "God did not take a bribe from me, so am I to take a bribe when He returns my kingdom to me? And He did not acquiesce to the people about me; so am I to obey the people about him?"'"

Mūsā b. ᶜUqba stated, "The father of the Negus had been the king of Abyssinia but died when the Negus was a small boy. The king had entrusted him to his own brother, saying, 'You rule your people until my son comes of age; thereafter, he shall be king.'

"But the king's brother wanted to rule and so he sold the Negus to a merchant. However, the uncle died that night and the Abyssinians restored the Negus, placing the crown on his head."

He then related it in brief. But Ibn Ishāq's account is better and fuller. But God knows best.

The account of Ibn Ishāq refers to ʿAmr b. al-ʿĀṣ and ʿAbd Allāh b. Abū Rabīʿa. Those of Mūsā b. ʿUqba, al-Umawī and others give the two envoys as ʿAmr b. al-ʿĀṣ and ʿUmāra b. al-Walīd b. al-Mughīra.

ʿUmāra was one of the seven persons against whom the Messenger of God (ṢAAS) spoke prayers when they ridiculed him on the occasion when they put the placenta of the sacrificial animal on his back when he was bent over in prayer at the *kaʿba*.

Similarly they were named in the previous accounts given by Ibn Masʿūd and Abū Mūsā al-Ashʿarī.

What is implied is that when they left Mecca, ʿAmr's wife was with him and also that ʿUmāra was a handsome young man. They were together in the boat and ʿUmāra was attracted to the wife of ʿAmr b. al-ʿĀṣ. So he threw ʿAmr into the sea to kill him, but he swam back to the boat. ʿUmāra then told him, "If I'd known you could swim so well, I wouldn't have thrown you in!" ʿAmr consequently hated him.

Having failed to achieve their objective with the Negus regarding the Emigrants, ʿUmāra ingratiated himself with some of the Negus's people. But ʿAmr warned the Negus of this and the latter had ʿUmāra bewitched so that he lost his mind and wandered off into the desert with the wild beasts.

Al-Umawī related his story at very great length, to the effect that he lived on into the time of the reign of ʿUmar b. al-Khaṭṭāb, when some of the Companions hunted him down and seized him. He then began saying, "Dispatch me! Dispatch me! Or I will die!" Since they did not dispatch him, he died right then and there. But God knows best.

It has been said that Quraysh sent twice to the Negus regarding the Emigrants. The first occasion involved ʿAmr b. al-ʿĀṣ and ʿUmāra, the second ʿAmr and ʿAbd Allāh b. Abū Rabīʿa. Abū Nuʿaym gives such a text in *Dalāʾil* (*The Signs*). But God knows best.

It is said that the second mission occurred after the battle of Badr. Al-Zuhrī stated this. Its purpose was to gain vengeance through the Emigrants there. But the Negus, God bless him, did not grant them any part of their request. But God knows best.

Ziyād related, from Ibn Ishāq, that when Abū Ṭālib saw Quraysh engaged in this he wrote to the Negus some verses urging him to act with justice and kindness towards those of his people who were living with him:

"Would that I knew how it is so far off for Ja'far and 'Amr, and it is relatives who can be the most bitter enemies.

And whether the actions of the Negus towards Ja'far and his companions are still kind, or whether some mischief-maker has hindered that.

You should know, may you avoid disaster, that you are noble, and that no alien would have complaint to you.

We know that God has given you much abundance, and that the means of all goodness is attached to you."

Yūnus stated, from Ibn Isḥāq, "Yazīd b. Rumān related to me that 'Urwa b. al-Zubayr said, 'It was really 'Uthmān b. 'Affān, God bless him, who spoke with the Negus and it is well-known that it was Ja'far, God bless him, who was the translator.'"

Ziyād al-Bakkā'ī stated, from Ibn Isḥāq, "Yazīd b. Rūmān related to me from 'Urwa, that 'Ā'isha, God bless her, said, 'After the Negus died, it was said that a light could still be seen at his grave.'"

Abū Dā'ūd related this from Muḥammad b. 'Amr al-Rāzī, from Salama b. al-Faḍl, from Muḥammad b. Isḥāq, as follows, "When the Negus, God bless him, died, we used to say that a light could still be seen at his grave."

Ziyād related, from Muḥammad b. Isḥāq, "Ja'far b. Muḥammad related to me that his father said, 'The Abyssinians gathered together and told the Negus, "You have abandoned our faith." Then they revolted against him.'

"He sent to Ja'far and his companions and prepared boats for them, telling them, 'Embark on these, and remain as you are. If I am defeated then leave for wherever you want. If I am victorious, then stay.'

"He then made his way to a document and wrote down the words, 'He testifies that there is no god but God and that Jesus is His slave, His messenger, His spirit and His word that he cast unto Mary.' He then placed the document inside his gown at his right shoulder.

"He then went outside to the Abyssinians who were lined up before him and said, 'O Abyssinians, am I not your rightful leader?' 'Yes,' they replied.

"'And how,' he asked, 'do you rate my conduct towards you?'

"'As fine conduct.'

"'So why are you discontented?'

"'You have abandoned our faith and claimed that Jesus is His slave and His messenger.'

"'And what is it you say of Jesus?' he asked them.

"'We say that he is the son of God.'

"Placing his hand across his chest over his gown, he then gave his testimony that, 'Jesus, son of Mary, was no more than this.' But he meant what he had written.

"His people were satisfied and left.

"This reached the Messenger of God (ṢAAS), and when the Negus died he prayed for him and sought God's forgiveness for him."

It is established in both *ṣaḥīḥ* collections, on the authority of Abū Hurayra, God be pleased with him, that the Messenger of God (ṢAAS) lamented the death of the Negus on the day he died and went with others to the place of prayer. There he lined up with them and four times recited the litany, *Allāhu Akbar*, God is most great. Al-Bukhārī stated: "*The Death of the Negus*. Abū al-Rabīʿ related to us, as did Ibn ʿUyayna, from Ibn Jurayj, from ʿAṭāʾ, from Jābir, who said, 'The Messenger of God (ṢAAS) stated on the day when the Negus died, "Today a good man died; arise and pray for your brother Aṣḥama."'"

This is also related from a *ḥadīth* of Anas b. Mālik, Ibn Masʿūd, and others.

In some accounts he is named Aṣḥama, though in one it is Maṣḥama. His name was Aṣḥama b. Baḥr. He was an honest, devout and intelligent man, just and honourable. May God be pleased with him.

Yūnus stated, from Ibn Isḥāq, "The name of the Negus was Maṣḥama." In one manuscript al-Bayhaqī has corrected this to Aṣḥam. 'The name means in Arabic *ʿaṭiyya*; gift. The word 'Negus' is the title for a king, equivalent to using the word 'Chosroe' or 'Heraclius'."

This, I observe, is how this text reads; no doubt he meant "Emperor", the title used for all kings who rule Syria along with the Roman peninsula. "Chosroe" is the title of those ruling Persia, "Pharoah" that for those ruling all Egypt, "al-Muqawqis" for he who rules Alexandria, "Tubbaʿ" for those ruling Yemen and al-Shaḥr, the "Negus" for those ruling Abyssinia, "Batlimus" for those ruling Greece, and, it is said, India, and "Khāqān" for those ruling the Turks.

Some scholars said that he only prayed for him because he kept his faith hidden from his people and there was no one there with him to pray for him the day he died.

These scholars thus maintain that for someone not present, if the funeral prayers were said for him in the place where he died, then such rites are not ordained for him in another country. This is why funeral prayers were said for the Prophet (ṢAAS) only in Medina and not by the people of Mecca or elsewhere. The same was true of Abū Bakr, ʿUmar, ʿUthmān and others of the Companions; it is not reported that funeral prayers were said for them in towns other than the ones in which they died. But God knows best.

I add the comment that the fact that Abū Hurayra, may God be pleased with him, witnessed the prayers for the Negus points to his having died after the conquest of Khaybar, the year when the remainder of the Emigrants to Abyssinia arrived along with Jaʿfar b. Abū Ṭālib, God bless him, namely on the day of the conquest of Khaybar.

It is therefore related that the Prophet (ṢAAS) said, "By God, I don't know which makes me happier – the conquest of Khaybar or the arrival of Jaʿfar b. Abū Ṭālib!"

They brought with them presents and treasures from the Negus, God be pleased with him; and accompanying them as passengers on their Yemeni boat were the followers of Abū Mūsā al-Ashͨarī and his people the Ashͨarīs, may God be pleased with them.

And with Jaͨfar and the presents of the Negus were the nephew of the Negus, Dhū Nakhtar, or Dhū Mikhmar, whom he had sent to serve the Prophet (ṢAAS) instead of his uncle.

Al-Suhaylī stated that the Negus died in Rajab in the year 9 of the *hijra*, *though there is dispute about that. But God knows best.*

Al-Bayhaqī stated, "The jurist Abū Isḥāq, Ibrāhīm b. Muḥammad b. Ibrāhīm al-Ṭūsī informed us, quoting Abū al-ͨAbbās Muḥammad b. Yaͨqūb, quoting Hilāl b. al-ͨAlā² al-Raqqī, quoting Abū al-ͨAlā² b. Mudrik, quoting Abū Hilāl b. al-ͨAlā², from his father, from Ghālib, from Abū Umāma, who said, 'The delegation from the Negus went in to see the Messenger of God (ṢAAS), and he arose to serve them. His Companions objected, saying, "Let us do that for you, O Messenger of God." He replied, "They honoured my Companions, and I wish to repay them."'"

He (al-Bayhaqī) then stated, "And Abū Muḥammad ͨAbd Allāh b. Yūsuf al-Aṣbahānī informed me, quoting Abū Saͨīd b. al-Aͨrābī that Hilāl b. al-ͨAlā² related, quoting my father, quoting Ṭalḥa b. Yazīd, from al-Awzāͨī, from Yaḥyā b. Abū Kathīr, from Abū Salama, from Abū Qatāda, who said, 'The delegation from the Negus went in to the Messenger of God (ṢAAS), and he arose to serve them. His Companions said, "We'll do that for you, O Messenger of God." He replied, "They honoured my Companions and I wish to repay them."'"

Ṭalḥa b. Yazīd narrated this, from al-Awzāͨī.

Al-Bayhaqī stated, "Abū al-Ḥusayn b. Bishrān related to us, quoting Abū ͨAmr b. al-Sammāk, quoting Ḥanbal b. Isḥāq, quoting al-Ḥumaydī, quoting Sufyān, quoting ͨAmr, as follows, 'When ͨAmr b. al-ͨĀṣ arrived from Abyssinia he sat at home. Since he would not go out to them, people wondered why this was. ͨAmr then said, "Ashama claims your man to be a prophet."'"

ͨUMAR B. AL-KHAṬṬĀB ACCEPTS ISLAM.

Ibn Isḥāq stated, "When ͨAmr b. al-ͨĀṣ and ͨAbd Allāh b. Abū Rabīͨa arrived back to Quraysh, having failed to achieve their aims with the supporters of the Messenger of God (ṢAAS) and having been rudely rejected by the Negus, ͨUmar b. al-Khaṭṭāb accepted Islam. He was a forceful man, capable of defending his supporters, and the Companions of the Messenger of God (ṢAAS) had protection through him and through Ḥamza, so that they could stand up to Quraysh.

"ͨAbd Allāh b. Masͨūd used to say, 'We were unable to pray at the *kaͨba* until ͨUmar accepted Islam; having done so, ͨUmar battled Quraysh until he was able to pray at the *kaͨba*, and we prayed with him.'"

I comment that it is well established in the *ṣaḥīḥ* collection of al-Bukhārī, that Ibn Masʿūd said, "We have been powerful ever since ʿUmar b. al-Khaṭṭāb accepted Islam."

Ziyād al-Bakkāʾī stated, "Misʿar b. Kidām related to me, from Saʿd b. Ibrāhīm, who said, 'Ibn Masʿūd stated, "The acceptance of Islam by ʿUmar was a victory, his migration was a help, and his reign was a mercy. We could not pray at the *kaʿba* until he accepted Islam; when he did so ʿUmar battled Quraysh until he was able to pray at the *kaʿba*, and we prayed with him."'"

Ibn Isḥāq stated, "The acceptance of Islam by ʿUmar occurred after the departure of some of the supporters of the Messenger of God (ṢAAS) to Abyssinia.

"'ʿAbd al-Raḥmān b. al-Ḥārith b. ʿAbd Allāh b. ʿAyyāsh b. Abū Rabīʿa related to me, from ʿAbd al-ʿAzīz b. ʿĀmir b. Rabīʿa, from his mother Umm ʿAbd Allāh, daughter of Abū Hathma, who said, 'We were preparing to depart for Abyssinia – ʿĀmir having gone off to get something we needed – when ʿUmar came along and stopped, he being a polytheist at the time. We had suffered violence and harm from him.

"'He said, "So you're leaving then, Umm ʿAbd Allāh?"

"'"Yes," I replied. "We're leaving for one of God's countries, since you have so maltreated and harmed us, so that God may provide us some way out."

"'He commented, "Well, God be with you!"

"'I saw in him a gentleness I never had before. He then left, our departure, so it seemed to me, having saddened him.

"'ʿĀmir then arrived with our things and I commented, "O father of ʿAbd Allāh, I wish you could have seen ʿUmar just now, his gentleness and concern for us."

"'He asked, "Do you look to his accepting Islam?"

"'"Yes, I do," I replied.

"'He commented, "That man you saw won't accept Islam before al-Khaṭṭāb's donkey does!"

"'He said this in despair at him, for all his harsh opposition to Islam that had been seen.'"

I comment that this refutes the claim of those who maintain that he brought the number of Muslims to 40. For the Emigrants to Abyssinia were more than 80 persons. Unless, that is, it be said that he was the 40th to convert after the departure of the Emigrants.

This is supported by Ibn Isḥāq's report here concerning the acceptance of Islam by ʿUmar, God bless him, individually, and the account of that.

Ibn Isḥāq stated, "The acceptance of Islam by ʿUmar, so I have been told, came about as a result of the conversion of his sister Fāṭima, daughter of al-Khaṭṭāb, who was married to Saʿīd b. Zayd b. ʿAmr b. Nufayl. Her husband had also converted, and they were concealing their conversion from ʿUmar.

"Nu°aym b. °Abd Allāh al-Naḥḥām, a member of the Banū °Adī tribe, had also converted but concealed this fact from his people.

"Khabbāb b. al-Aratt was attending the home of Fāṭima, daughter of al-Khaṭṭāb, to read the Qur'an to her. One day °Umar went out, his sword at his waist, looking for the Messenger of God (ṢAAS) who, along with a group of his followers, he had been told, were in a house at al-Ṣafā. The group with him, including men and women, totalled some 40 persons. Among these, along with the Messenger of God (ṢAAS), were his uncle Ḥamza, Abū Bakr b. Abū Quḥāfa, *al-Siddīq*, "the Trusting", and °Alī b. Abū Ṭālib, God be pleased with them, along with other Muslim men who had stayed behind in Mecca and not departed for Abyssinia.

"Nu°aym b. °Abd Allāh met him and enquired, 'Where are you heading, °Umar?'

"He replied, 'I'm looking for Muḥammad, that Ṣabian who has disunited Quraysh, ridiculed their dreams, criticized their religion and slandered their gods. I'm going to kill him!'

"Nu°aym told him, 'By God, you've lost your mind, °Umar! Do you think that °Abd Manāf would allow you to walk on the face of the earth once you killed Muḥammad? Why don't you go home and sort out your household!'

"'What about my household?'

"'Your brother-in-law and nephew Sa°īd b. Zayd and your sister Fāṭima. They have accepted Islam and become followers of Muḥammad (ṢAAS) in his religion. Look to them!'

"°Umar then returned to his sister Fāṭima where Khabbāb b. al-Aratt was; he had with him a manuscript of sūrat Ṭāhā that he was reading to her.

"When they heard °Umar's approach, Khabbāb hid inside a bedroom, or somewhere else in the house, and Fāṭima took the manuscript and hid it under her thigh. But °Umar had heard Khabbāb reciting it as he approached the door.

"As he came in, he demanded, 'What was that murmuring sound I heard?'

"'I heard nothing,' they both replied.

"'Well I did,' he insisted. 'And I've been told you are following Muḥammad in his religion.'

He then struck out at his brother-in-law Sa°īd b. Zayd, and when his sister Fāṭima rose to defend her husband he hit her and wounded her.

"When he did this, his sister and brother-in-law admitted, 'Yes, we have accepted Islam and do believe in God and in His Messenger. Do whatever you want!'

"When °Umar saw the blood on his sister he was sorry for what he had done and repentant and he told her, 'Give me that document you were just reading so that I can see what it is Muḥammad brings.' °Umar was literate.

"When he said that, she replied, 'We don't trust you with it.'

"'Don't be afraid,' he told her, and swore by his gods to return it to her when he had read it.

"When he said this she had hopes of his accepting Islam and so she said, 'But being a polytheist you are unclean, and only the purified may touch it.'

"So ʿUmar arose and washed himself, and she gave him the sheet on which *sūrat Ṭāhā* was written. When he had read a passage of it, he said, 'How fine, how wonderful these words are!'

"When Khabbāb b. al-Aratt heard this he came out and said, 'By God, ʿUmar, I do so hope that God has selected you because of the prayer of His Prophet (ṢAAS), for yesterday I heard him say, "O God, give help to Islam through Abū al-Ḥakam b. Hishām, or through ʿUmar b. al-Khaṭṭāb!" So come now to God, ʿUmar!'

"At that ʿUmar said, 'Khabbāb, lead me to Muḥammad so that I can accept Islam.'

"'He is in a house at al-Ṣafā with a group of his Companions,' Khabbāb replied.

"ʿUmar picked up his sword and put it on then left for the Messenger of God (ṢAAS) and his Companions. He knocked on the door and when they heard his voice, one of the Companions got up and looked outside through a chink in the door. He saw ʿUmar, wearing his sword, then went back in to the Messenger of God (ṢAAS) in a fright and exclaiming, 'O Messenger of God, it's ʿUmar b. al-Khaṭṭāb, armed with his sword!'

"Ḥamza said, 'Well, let him in. If he has come with good, we'll reciprocate, but if he's come in evil, we'll kill him with his sword.' The Messenger of God (ṢAAS) also said, 'Let him in!'

"So the Companion did so, and the Messenger of God (ṢAAS), got up and went across the room to meet him, taking him by his waist or by the place where his cloak joined, and giving him a strong pull, saying, 'What brings you, Ibn al-Khaṭṭāb? By God, I don't see you stopping until God sends down a thunderbolt upon you!'

"ʿUmar replied, 'O Messenger of God, I come to you to believe in God, in His messenger, and in what has come down from God!'

"At this the Messenger of God (ṢAAS) let out a great cry of *Allāhu Akbar*, and the people in the house all knew that ʿUmar had accepted Islam.

"The Companions of the Messenger of God left their places elated that now ʿUmar had accepted Islam along with Ḥamza, knowing that these two men would protect him and help them obtain justice from their enemies."

Ibn Isḥāq concluded, "This then, is the account given by the *hadīth* scholars of Medina concerning the acceptance of Islam by ʿUmar, God bless him."

Ibn Isḥāq stated, "ʿAbd Allāh b. Abū Najīḥ al-Makkī related to me, from his Companions ʿAṭā, Mujāhid and others, that regarding ʿUmar's acceptance of Islam, he himself would say, 'I used to be very remote from Islam. Before Islam I used to be a great man for wine; I loved drinking it. We used to have a place at al-Ḥazwara where we would meet.

"'One night I went out looking for my drinking partners, but found not one of them there. So I told myself I should go off to a wine dealer named so-and-so to get some for myself to drink.

"'But I could not find him. So I told myself I might as well go to the *ka῾ba* and circumambulate it seven or seventy times.

"'So I went to the mosque and there, standing praying, I saw the Messenger of God (ṢAAS). When he prayed he would face towards al-Shām, placing the *ka῾ba* between himself and it. The spot he prayed at was between the two corners, *al-aswad* (the one with the 'black stone') and *al-yamāni* (the one towards Yemen).

"'When I saw him, I told myself I might just as well spend the evening listening to Muḥammad. If I came too close to him to listen I might scare him, so I approached from the *ḥijr* side, passing beneath its covering and walking slowly while the Messenger of God (ṢAAS) continued standing there reciting the Qur᾿ān. Eventually I stood facing towards him with nothing there between us but the covering over the *ka῾ba*.

"'When I heard the Qur᾿ān my heart was touched by it, I wept and Islam entered within me.

"'I stayed where I was until the Messenger of God (ṢAAS) had finished his prayer and departed. When he left he would pass by the home of Ibn Abū Ḥusayn, whose dwelling happened to be at Dār al-Raqṭā῾, which was owned by Mu῾āwiya. I followed him until, as he went between the house of ῾Abbās and that of Ibn Azhar, I caught up with him. When he heard my voice he recognized me and thought I had followed him only to harm him. So he told me to keep away, then said, "What brings you here at this hour, Ibn al-Khaṭṭāb?"

"'I replied, "I have come to believe in God and in His messenger, and in what has come down from God."

"'The Messenger of God (ṢAAS) expressed thanks to God at this and then he said, "God has guided you, ῾Umar!" He then touched my chest and prayed for me to be constant.

"'After that I left and the Messenger of God (ṢAAS) went inside his house.'"

Ibn Isḥāq then commented, "God alone knows best which of these versions really happened."

I point out that I have investigated the manner in which ῾Umar, God bless him, accepted Islam and related all the statements and evidence thereto at length in the first part of the biography I devoted to him alone. All praise and credit be to God!

Ibn Isḥāq said, "Nāfi῾, the freed-man of Ibn ῾Umar, related to me that ῾Umar's son said, 'When ῾Umar accepted Islam, he asked, "Which man of Quraysh is best at making announcements?"

"'"Jamīl b. Ma῾mar al-Jumaḥī," he was told.

"'Next morning ῾Umar went to the man.' Ibn ῾Umar continued, 'So I followed him to see what he would do; I was a lad at the time, but understood all I saw.

"'When ʿUmar reached him, he asked, "Jamīl, do you know that I have accepted Islam and entered into the faith of Muḥammad (ṢAAS)?"'

"Ibn ʿUmar went on, 'Well, I swear, he had no sooner told him this than off he went, his gown trailing. ʿUmar followed him and I did so too until he stopped at the mosque gate, where he shouted at the top of his voice, "O Quraysh!" (They were there at that time in their chambers around the kaʿba.) "Ibn al-Khaṭṭāb has become a Ṣabian!"

"'ʿUmar, standing right behind him, yelled, "He lies! But I have become a Muslim. I do testify that there is no god but God and that Muḥammad is the Messenger of God!"

"'People were most enraged against him and soon he was battling hard against them, they against him. They kept up this fighting until the sun was high over their heads.

"'At last he was exhausted and sat down, while they stood all around him. He told them, "Do what you want! But I swear by God that if we were 300 men strong, either we'd have left the battlefield to you or you would have to us!"

"'While they were so engaged, a Quraysh sheikh finely dressed in a robe from Yemen and an embroidered shirt came up and stood there. He asked, "What's going on with you?"

"'"ʿUmar has become a Ṣabian," they replied.

"'"So what? If a man chooses to do something, what's it got to do with you? Do you think his tribe, the Banū ʿAdī, will give him over to you like this? Let the man go!"'

"Ibn ʿUmar went on, 'And I swear, they drew back like a garment being stripped from him.'

"'And when my father ʿUmar went off into exile to Medina, I asked him, "Father, who was that man who drove the people away from you at Mecca who was fighting you the day you accepted Islam?"

"'"That, my son." he replied, "was al-ʿĀṣ b. Wāʾil al-Sahmī."'"

This chain of authorities is extremely strong. It points to the tardiness of ʿUmar's acceptance of Islam. This is because Ibn ʿUmar fought at Uḥud for the first time, when he was 14. That battle, Uḥud, occurred in the year 3 AH. He was at the age of discrimination on the day his father accepted Islam, an event that must have occurred some 4 years before the emigration to Medina. And that is some 9 years after the beginning of the mission of the Prophet (ṢAAS). But God knows best.

Al-Bayhaqī said, "Al-Ḥākim related to us, al-Aṣamm informed us, quoting Aḥmad b. ʿAbd al-Jabbār, and Yūnus related to us, all from Ibn Isḥāq, who stated, 'Then 20 men came to the Messenger of God (ṢAAS) while he was in Mecca, or nearby; these were Christians, news having spread about him to them from Abyssinia. They found him at the meeting place and spoke with him and asked him questions, while the men of Quraysh were in their chambers there around the kaʿba.

"'When they had finished putting the questions they wanted to ask the Messenger of God, he invited them to come to God, the Almighty and Glorious, and he recited the Qur'ān to them. When they heard it, their eyes overflowed with tears. They then responded positively to him, believed in him and accepted and trusted him, recognising what had been described to them about him in their scripture.

"'When they arose to leave him, Abū Jahl and a group of Quraysh blocked their path and told them, "What a hopeless party you are! You were sent here by your co-religionaries back home to undertake an investigation for them and to return with information about this fellow, yet no sooner did you sit down in comfort with him than you abandoned your faith and believed all he told you. We've never known a group more foolish than you." Or words to that effect.

"'They replied, "We do not denigrate you; peace be upon you! We act as we see fit, as do you as you see fit. We spare no pains to attain what is good."'"

It is said that the group of Christians were from Najrān; but God alone knows whether that was so.

It is also said, though God alone knows, that the following verses were revealed about them, "And those to whom we gave the book before it do believe in it. When it is recited to them, they say, 'We do believe in it; it is the truth from our Lord. We were accepting (its message) even before it came.' Those shall receive their reward twice, for they have been steadfast and repay evil with good and expend from what We have given them. And when they hear idle gossip they turn away from it and say, 'We act as we see fit, as do you as you see fit. Peace be upon you; we do not desire the ignorant and foolish'" (sūrat al-Qaṣaṣ; XXVIII, v.52–5).

DIVISION

Al-Bayhaqī in his book *Dalā'il* (*The Signs*) entitles a chapter "On the contents of the document sent by the Prophet (ṢAAS) to the Negus."

He then relates, from al-Ḥākim, from al-Aṣamm, from Aḥmad b. 'Abd al-Jabbār, from Yūnus, from Ibn Isḥāq, as follows, "In the name of God, the most Merciful and Compassionate: this is a document from Muḥammad, the Messenger of God (ṢAAS), to the Negus, al-Aṣham, the great leader of Abyssinia: Peace be upon those who follow guidance, believe in God and His messenger, and testify that there is no god but God alone, Who has no partner, Who took no female partner for Himself, and Who has no child, and they testify that Muḥammad is His servant and His messenger. I call out to you in God's name, for I am His messenger. So submit (to Him) and be at peace! O People of the Book, come to an agreement that is equal between us both; that we will worship none but God and associate no other god with Him; that we will not take one another as masters to the exclusion of God. But if they do turn aside, then say, 'Bear witness that we are Muslims' (*sūrat Āl-ʿImrān*; III, v.63). But if you refuse, then upon you is the sin of those of your people who are Christians."

Al-Bayhaqī related it thus after the narrative of the migration to Abyssinia. There are various opinions concerning this account. It is clear that this document was to the Negus who, in addition to being a Muslim, (was also) the friend of Jaʿfar and his companions.

It relates to the time when he (Muḥammad) wrote to all the rulers on earth inviting them to God, the Almighty and Glorious, shortly before the conquest (of Mecca). He wrote to Heraclius, the head of the Romans and the Caesar of Syria, to Chosroe, the king of the Persians, to the ruler of Egypt as well as to the Negus.

Al-Zuhrī stated, "The letters to them from the Prophet (ṢAAS) were all the same, i.e. copies, and all quoted this same verse which comes from *sūrat Āl-ʿImran*, a chapter that is incontrovertibly from the Medina period. The verse comes from the early part of the *sūrat*."

Eighty-three verses of this *sūrat*, from its beginning, relate to the delegation from Najrān, as I asserted in my *Tafsīr* (*Exegesis*). And to God belong all praise and credit.

And so this document was to the second Negus, not to the first.

Regarding the words therein, "To the Negus al-Aṣham ..." perhaps the word "al-Aṣham" is an interpolation by the narrator, based on his understanding. But God knows best.

More relevant here than this is what al-Bayhaqī also narrated, from al-Ḥākim, from Abū al-Ḥasan b. ʿAbd Allāh al-Faqīh, of Merve, who stated, "Ḥammād b. Aḥmad related to us, quoting Muḥammad b. Isḥāq and Salama b. al-Faḍl, all from Muḥammad b. Isḥāq, who said, 'The Messenger of God (ṢAAS) sent ʿAmr b. Umayya al-Ḍamrī with a letter he wrote to the Negus concerning Jaʿfar b. Abū Ṭālib and his companions: "In the name of God the most Merciful and Compassionate: from Muḥammad, Messenger of God, to the Negus al-Aṣham, king of Abyssinia: Peace be upon you. I express to you my praises for God the King, the All-Holy, the Faithful, and the Protector; I testify that Jesus is the spirit of God and His word that He cast unto Mary, the good, chaste, unviolated Virgin. And so she bore Jesus, whom He created from His spirit and His breath, just as He created Adam by His hand and breath. I call upon you to believe the One God Who has no associate. To Him all obedience is due. (I call upon you, tr.) to follow me, to believe in me as well as in that which has come down to me. For I am the Messenger of God. And I have sent to you my nephew Jaʿfar along with a group of Muslims. When they come to you receive them hospitably. Do not be haughty, for I invite you and your forces to God the Almighty and Glorious. I have conveyed my message and given advice. So accept my advice. And peace be upon those who follow the true path."

"'The Negus wrote back to the Messenger of God (ṢAAS) as follows: "In the name of God, the most Merciful and Compassionate: To Muḥammad the Messenger of God from the Negus al-Aṣham b. Abjar: Peace be upon you, O Prophet of God, from God, along with the mercy and blessings of God. There is no god but Him who guided me to Islam. Your letter, O Messenger of God, in which you made reference to Jesus, has reached me. And, by the God of the heavens and the earth, Jesus is no more than what you stated. We recognize what you have been sent with to us. We have received your nephew and his friends with hospitality. And I do testify that you are the Messenger of God, that you speak the truth and are to be believed. I pledge my allegiance to you and to your nephew, accepting Islam at his hands for God, the Lord of the universe. I have sent to you, O Prophet of God, Arīḥa b. al-Aṣham b. Abjar, for I possess nothing but myself. If you wish for me to come to you, I will do so, O Messenger of God, for I testify that what you say is truth."'"

An Account of the disagreement of the Quraysh tribes of the Banū Hāshim and the Banū 'Abd al-Muṭṭalib in helping the Messenger of God (Ṣ.AAS). Also concerning their confinement of them in the quarter of Abū Ṭālib for a lengthy period and their writing an evil, brazen document to that effect. And the signs of the prophethood and proofs of the truth that became evident regarding all this.

Mūsā b. 'Uqba stated, from al-Zuhrī: "The polytheists thereafter became so violent in their actions against the Muslims that the plight of the latter became extreme. And Quraysh so united in their evil intent as to agree to kill the Messenger of God (ṢAAS) in full view.

"When Abū Ṭālib realized their purposes, he gathered the Banū 'Abd al-Muṭṭalib and told them to include the Messenger of God (ṢAAS) in their enclave and to protect him against those wishing to murder him.

"The Muslims and non believers of the tribe did agree to this, some out of a desire to uphold traditions of protection, others out of their faith and conviction.

"When Quraysh realized that these were in agreement to protect the Messenger of God (ṢAAS), the polytheists among them made a pact not to sit down with, nor to do business with them, nor to enter the homes of these people until they surrendered the Messenger of God (ṢAAS) to execution. They cunningly drew up agreements and pacts to the effect that they would never accept peace or reconciliation with the Banū Hāshim until they delivered him up for death.

"The Banū Hāshim therefore remained for three years confined to their enclave, suffering great deprivation. Their markets had been cut off; no food was allowed into Mecca for them, and all their business dealings were interrupted.

"Their purpose in all this was to spill the blood of the Messenger of God (ṢAAS).

"When it was bed time, Abū Ṭālib would tell the Messenger of God (ṢAAS) to sleep on the former's bed, and he would do the same, the intent being that anyone wishing to harm or assassinate him would be unaware of this. And while people slept, Abū Ṭālib made sure that one of his sons, brothers or nephews would lie on the bed of the Messenger of God (ṢAAS), and he would tell the latter to take their places instead."

"At the start of the third year certain men of the tribes of ʿAbd Manāf and Quṣayy, along with others whose mothers were from the Banū Hāshim, became critical of this and recognized that they were breaking the bonds of kinship and disregarding what was right. They therefore decided one night to revoke what they had previously agreed to, and to free themselves thereof.

"They discovered, however, that God had dispatched woodworm to attack their documents; they devoured everything making reference to their pact.

"It is said that these documents were hung from the ceiling of the temple. Every reference to God's name was devoured; all that remained was material relating to polytheism, injustice and destruction of ties of kindred.

"God, the Almighty and Glorious, made His messenger aware of what He had done to their documents, and the Messenger of God (ṢAAS) told this to Abū Ṭālib.

"But Abū Ṭālib responded, 'No! May the stars never mislead me!'

"He then hurried off with a band of the Banū ʿAbd al-Muṭṭalib and went to the mosque which was full of Quraysh. When the latter saw them heading for them they were surprised, believing them to be doing so because of the extent of their suffering and that they were coming to deliver the Messenger of God (ṢAAS) to them.

"Abū Ṭālib spoke to them as follows: 'Various things we don't need to tell you of have occurred between you. Bring now your deeds referring to the pacts you have made; perhaps now there can be peace between us all.'

"The reason he said this was because he was afraid they might look at the deeds before bringing them.

"They did now bring them down, proud of them and not doubting that the Messenger of God (ṢAAS) was to be delivered to them. They placed them down, saying, 'Well, the time has come for you to proceed to a reconciliation with your people. Only one man has caused this rupture between us. You have placed him in a position where he has brought the danger of destruction and corruption to your people.'

"Abū Ṭālib responded, 'I have only come to you now to offer you justice. My nephew has informed me – and he never lied to me – that God will have no part of that document there before you and that He has erased all of His names from it, leaving only references to your treachery, your breaking of the bonds of kin-ship and your unjust public demonstrations against us.

"'If what my nephew has said is so, then you should recognize that and, by God, we will never surrender him to you before the last of us is dead!

"'But if what he said is false, then we will deliver him to you for you to kill or to spare his life.'

"'We'll agree to that', they replied.

"They then opened up the deed and found that he (Muḥammad), the truthful and the trustworthy (ṢAAS) had proved correct. When Quraysh saw it to be as Abū Ṭālib had said, they said, 'By God, this has to be some magic done by your man!'

"They then reneged and reverted to even worse impiety and violence against the Messenger of God (ṢAAS) than before, doing their best to destroy him as they had formerly compacted.

"That group of men of the Banū ῾Abd al-Muṭṭalib responded by saying, 'It is others, not us, who are more blameworthy in telling lies and using magic. We very well know that the boycott of us you agreed on was closer to sorcery and magic than what we did. If you had not agreed to use magic the deeds before you would not have been spoiled and God's name would not have been erased while reference to your evil was retained. Is it we who rely on magic, or you?'"

"Thereafter some men of ῾Abd Manāf and Quṣayy, along with those of Quraysh born to women of the Banū Hāshim, including Abū al-Bakhturī, al-Muṭ῾im b. ῾Adī, Zuhayr b. Abū Umayya b. al-Mughīra, Zam῾a b. al-Aswad and Hishām b. ῾Amr, of the Banū ῾Āmir b. Lu᾽ayy (the last-mentioned having had charge of the deed), along with other prominent members of their community, stated that they disavowed the action.

"To this Abū Jahl, God damn him, responded, 'But this matter is not revocable!'

"Abū Ṭālib spoke verses regarding their deed and praised the men who had disavowed their former agreement, and he also commended the Negus."

Al-Bayhaqī stated, "Our sheikh, Abū ῾Abd Allāh, the *ḥāfiẓ*, also related it thus, that is through Ibn Lahī῾a, from Abū al-Aswad, from ῾Urwa b. al-Zubayr, meaning in the same context as that given by Mūsā b. ῾Uqba, God bless him."

We have previously told of Mūsā b. ῾Uqba that he stated, "The migration to Abyssinia only occurred following their entry into the enclave, and was the result of the Messenger of God (ṢAAS) having told them to do so." But God knows best.

I observe that it is most likely that Abū Ṭālib spoke his *lāmiyya*, his ode rhyming in 'l', as previously quoted, also only after they went into the enclave. And so making reference to it here is most appropriate. But God knows best.

Thereafter al-Bayhaqī related, through Yūnus, from Muḥammad b. Isḥāq, as having said, "When the Messenger of God (ṢAAS) set out to fulfil the mission entrusted to him, the Banū Hāshim and the Banū al-Muṭṭalib undertook to protect him and refused to deliver him. Even though they were opposed to him and were engaged in the same religion as their people at large, they were none the less reluctant to humiliate themselves and deliver him over, conscious of the loathing Quraysh had for him.

"The Banū Hāshim and the Banū al-Muṭṭalib having taken their stand and Quraysh having recognized that they had no access to Muḥammad, they met and agreed to write a document defining their relationship to the Banū Hāshim and the Banū ʿAbd al-Muṭṭalib. They agreed that they would not marry them nor allow their women to marry them, nor engage in buying or selling with them. They wrote a document to that effect which they hung up in the *kaʿba*.

"They then attacked the Muslims, restricting their movements and subjecting them to violence. Their plight and insecurity became extreme."

Thereafter Ibn Isḥāq related the story in full, telling of their entry into the enclave of Abū Ṭālib and of the severe trouble they suffered there, to such a degree that their children would be overheard inside writhing with the pangs of hunger.

Eventually most Quraysh regretted their plight and expressed their hatred for their accursed document. They then told how God, in His mercy, sent down woodworm against the document and these demolished every word relating to God, leaving therein only what referred to evil, to the boycott and to slanderous talk. Also related was how God Almighty informed the Messenger of God (ṢAAS) of this and how he told this to his uncle Abū Ṭālib.

He then went on to mention in full the remainder of the story as narrated by Mūsā b. ʿUqba.

Ibn Hishām stated, from Ziyād, quoting Muḥammad b. Isḥāq, "And when Quraysh saw that the supporters of the Messenger of God (ṢAAS) had gone to live in a land where they had attained security and where the Negus had offered his protection to those seeking refuge with him, that ʿUmar had accepted Islam and had now, along with Ḥamza, joined the Messenger of God (ṢAAS) and his Companions, and that Islam was spreading out into the tribes, they met and decided to write down a document. This would record their mutual agreement concerning the Banū Hāshim and the Banū ʿAbd al-Muṭṭalib. It specified that they would neither marry with them nor offer their womenfolk into marriage with them nor engage in any buying or selling with them. Having agreed to this, they wrote it down in a deed to which they gave their solemn pledge. They then suspended the document inside the *kaʿba* in affirmation of this.

"The man who wrote out the document was Manṣūr b. ʿIkrima b. ʿĀmir b. Hāshim b. ʿAbd Manāf b. ʿAbd al-Dār b. Quṣayy."

Ibn Hishām said, "He was also named as al-Naḍr b. al-Ḥārith. The Messenger of God (ṢAAS) said prayers against him and he lost the use of some of his fingers."

Al-Wāqidī stated, "The man who wrote down the agreement was Ṭalḥa b. Abū Ṭalḥa al-'Abdarī." My own view is that it is well established that the man was Manṣūr b. 'Ikrima, as Ibn Isḥāq related. It was he who lost the use of a hand; Quraysh used to say among themselves, "Look what happened to Manṣūr b. 'Ikrima!"

Al-Wāqidī said, "And the document was suspended in the middle of the ka'ba."

Ibn Isḥāq stated, "When Quraysh had done this the Banū Hāshim and the Banū al-Muṭṭalib allied with Abū Ṭālib and entered his enclave and joined forces with him.

"But Abū Lahab b. 'Abd al-'Uzzā b. 'Abd al-Muṭṭalib left the Banū Hāshim and gave his support to Quraysh.

"Ḥusayn b. 'Abd Allāh related to me that Abū Lahab met Hind, daughter of 'Utba b. Rabī'a when he parted with his own people and gave his support to Quraysh against them. He asked her, 'O daughter of 'Utba, have I not given my support to al-Lāt and al-'Uzzā and broken with those who have abandoned them and given their support against them?'

"'Yes, indeed,' she replied. 'And may God reward you well, O Abū 'Utba!'"

Ibn Isḥāq continued, "I was told that one of the things he would say was, 'Muḥammad promises me things I do not see that he claims to exist after death. What apart from that had he put in my hands?'

"He then blew into his hands and addressed them thus: 'May you both perish! I see nothing in you of what Muḥammad talks!'

"And so God Almighty sent down His words: 'May the hands of Abū Lahab perish, and may he perish too!'" (sūrat al-Lahab; CVI, v.1).

Ibn Isḥāq went on, "When Quraysh had agreed in this way and acted towards him as they did, Abū Ṭālib spoke the following verses:

'O do announce our disagreement to the Lu'ayy, to those Lu'ayy of the Banū Ka'b:

Do you not know that we have found Muḥammad to be a prophet like Moses of whom it is written in the very first books?

And that among men there is love for him and that none is better than those endowed by God with love,

And that the document you have put up is an evil thing, like the raging young camel?[3]

Wake up, wake up before the moist earth is dug (for your graves) and those without sin will be just like sinners.

Do not follow the orders of those who lie, and so cut your ties with us after friendship and kinship,

Drawing on an endless warfare; and the milk of war can turn very bitter to those who taste it.

3. Apparently a reference to the camel of Ṣāliḥ which was killed by his people, Thamūd, contrary to his express wish. See sūrat al Shu'arā; XXVI, v.155-8.

We will not, by the Lord of the temple, deliver up Aḥmad because of the tribulations of time or the agony,

And when our necks and hands and yours will otherwise be cut by glinting blades of Quṣāṣī steel.[4]

In a narrow battlefield where broken spears will be seen, over which vultures hover, like drinkers at a party,

And the space where the horsemen gallop and the heroes cry out will make it like a battle in a war.

Was our forefather Hāshim not courageous, and did he not advise his sons to thrust and to strike?

We do not tire of warfare before it tires of us, nor do we complain at whatever misfortunes may strike.

We are people who stay firm and prudent at times when the spirits of brave men fly off in terror.'"

Ibn Isḥāq stated, "And they remained under those conditions for two or three years in the utmost distress, with nothing getting into them unless secretly, from those members of Quraysh who wanted to keep ties with them.

"Abū Jahl b. Hishām, so they say, met Ḥakim b. Ḥizām b. Khuwaylid b. Asad with whom was a slave bearing wheat for Ḥizām's aunt Khadīja, daughter of Khuwaylid, who was in the enclave along with the Messenger of God (ṢAAS). Abū Jahl took hold of him and said, 'Are you taking food to the Banū Hāshim? I swear, you'll not go, you and your food, without me making a scandal about you in Mecca!'

"Abū al-Bakhtarī b. Hishām b. al-Ḥārith b. Asad then came up to him and asked, 'What's going on between you and him?'

"He replied, 'He's carrying food into the Banū Hāshim.'

"Abū al-Bakhtarī commented, 'This is food belonging to his aunt that she had sent him and he had at home. Would you prevent him from taking to her her own food? Get out of the man's way!'

"But Abū Jahl, God damn him, refused and they began to fight. Abū al-Bakhtarī picked up a camel's jawbone and struck him with it, giving him a head wound. He then stomped on him.

"Ḥamza b. ʿAbd al-Muṭṭalib was nearby and saw all this. But they did not like to tell the Messenger of God (ṢAAS) and his Companions of this incident lest they gloat over them."

THOSE WHO MOCKED.

The Messenger of God (ṢAAS) continued as before, calling upon his people by day and night, secretly and openly, calling out the commands of God Almighty, fearing no man.

---

4. Swords of Quṣas were reknowned for their high quality.

God having provided the Messenger of God (ṢAAS) with protection against Quraysh through the aid of his uncle and his relatives of the Banū Hāshim and the Banū ʿAbd al-Muṭṭalib, Quraysh were unable to treat him with the violence they wished. Consequently they set about mocking, ridiculing him and disputing with him.

The Qurʾān then began coming down concerning the evil deeds of Quraysh and those who had declared themselves to be his enemies.

Some of these were mentioned by name to us, while others were inferred among those polytheists to whom general reference was made.

Ibn Isḥāq mentions Abū Lahab and the revelation of a chapter concerning him; also, he referred to Umayya b. Khalaf and the revelation of the words of the Almighty, "Woe to every defaming slanderer!" (*sūrat al-Humaza*; CIV, v.1). The whole *sūrat* refers to the latter man.

Also there was reference to al-ʿĀṣ b. Wāʾil in the revelation, "And have you then seen him who disbelieved in our signs and who said, 'Certainly I will be awarded wealth and children'" (*sūrat Maryam*; XIX, v.77). Some part of this has been quoted previously.

And then there was Abū Jahl b. Hishām and his saying to the Prophet of God (ṢAAS), "You had better stop insulting our gods, or we will insult your God whom you worship." Regarding this, God's revelation came: "Do not insult those whom they worship besides God, for they, in enmity and without knowledge, will insult God" (*sūrat al-Anʿām*; VI, v.108).

Also, there was al-Naḍr b. al-Ḥārith b. Kalada b. ʿAlqama, or ʿAlqama b. Kalada according to al-Suhaylī and others, who used to sit down after the Prophet of God (ṢAAS) had finished one of his sessions in which he would recite the Qurʾān and pray to God. Al-Naḍr would then narrate tales of Rustum and Isfandiyār and the wars between them in ancient Persia. Then he would comment, "I swear by God, Muḥammad is no better a story-teller than me. His talk is only of ancient legends from which he borrows, just as I do."

And so God Almighty sent down: "And they say: 'These are only legends of the Ancients that he has borrowed; they are dictated to him morning and evening'" (*sūrat al-Furqān*; XXV, v.5). And also: "Woe to every sinful liar" (*sūrat al-Jāthiyya*; XLV, v.7).

Ibn Isḥāq stated, "One day, so we have been told, the Messenger of God (ṢAAS) sat down in the mosque with al-Walīd b. al-Mughīra. Al-Naḍr b. al-Ḥārith came over and sat with them; also present were several men of Quraysh.

"The Messenger of God (ṢAAS) spoke, but al-Naḍr argued with him. The Messenger of God (ṢAAS) then addressed al-Naḍr and ultimately silenced him. Having done so, he then recited to them all, 'You, along with that which you worship besides God, are the firewood for hell; you are on your way there. Were these gods they would not be ending up there; and all there will remain therein forever. Therein wailing is their lot, and therein they hear not' (*sūrat al-Anbiyāʾ*; XXI, v.98–100).

"The Messenger of God (ṢAAS) then arose just as ʿAbd Allāh b. al-Zibaʿrā al Sahmī approached and sat down.

"Al-Walīd b. al-Mughīra spoke to him, 'I swear, al-Naḍr b. al-Ḥārith's foregoing argument with Ibn ʿAbd al-Muṭṭalib (i.e. Muḥammad) was indeed short lived! Muḥammad (silenced him by) claiming that we and those gods of ours we worship are to be firewood for hell-fire!'

"ʿAbd Allāh b. al-Zibaʿrā replied, 'If I'd found him saying that, I'd have disputed with him. Ask Muḥammad: "Is everything besides God that is worshipped, along with those who worship them, to be firewood for hell? We worship angels, the Jews worship ʿUzayr, and the Christians worship Jesus."'

"Al-Walīd and those with him at the meeting were impressed by what Ibn al-Zibaʿrā had said, and thought he had made a cogent and winning argument.

"This was reported to the Messenger of God (ṢAAS) who replied, 'All those wanting to be worshipped aside from God will be there in hell with those who worship them. Those people merely worship devils, and those they (the devils) have ordered them to worship.'

"God Almighty then revealed, 'Those to whom good has already gone from us will be kept far away from it (hell). They will not hear its slightest sound, but will remain forever in what it is they have so desired'" (sūrat al-Anbiyāʾ; XXI; v.101–2).

This verse is referring to Jesus, ʿUzayr and those rabbis and monks who lived in obedience to God Almighty. And regarding their assertion that they were worshipping angels and that these were the daughters of God, He sent down: "And they say that God the Beneficent has taken a son for himself. All glory be to Him! No, (not that) but they are honoured servants" (sūrat al-Anbiyāʾ; XXI, v.26).

And then there were the verses following that.

Concerning the good impression made upon the polytheists by what al-Zibaʿrā said, God sent down: "And when the son of Mary is mentioned as an example, your people make a great outcry. They ask, 'Are our gods better, or is he?' They only raise this objection for argument's sake. They really are contentious people!" (sūrat al-Zukhruf; XLIII, v.57–8).

This argumentation they pursued was futile.

And they were aware of that, because they were an Arab people. It is part of their language that mā, i.e. "that which," in the above quotation implies in Arabic something that does not think. The statement: "You, along with that which you worship besides God are the firewood for hell; you are on your way there" (sūrat al-Anbiyāʾ; XXI, v.98) refers to the rocks fashioned as idols. It does not include the angels that they claimed to be worshipping inside these images. Nor does it include Jesus, ʿUzayr or any of the holy persons because that item of language, mā, cannot include them, directly or by implication.

They well knew that the comparison they were making to Jesus, son of Mary, was futile. As the Almighty stated, "They only raise this objection for argument's sake. They really are contentious people" (sūrat al-Zukhruf; XLIII, v.57–8).

God also stated, "He", (meaning Jesus) "was merely a servant whom We favoured" (that is, by prophethood) "and We made him an example for the people of Israel" (*sūrat al-Zukhruf*, XLIII, v.59). That is, as an indication of the totality of God's power to achieve His wishes, having created him from a female without a male. Similarly, God created Eve from a male without a female, and Adam without either, while He created all the rest of mankind from both male and female.

As God stated in another verse, "And certainly We are creating him as a sign for all mankind." That is, as a proof and an indication of His evident power, and as a "mercy from Him", by which He gives mercy to those He wishes.

Ibn Isḥāq also mentions al-Akhnas b. Sharīf and Almighty God's revelation regarding him: "And do not obey every base oath-maker" (*sūrat Nūn* or *al-Qalam*; LXVIII, v.10).

He referred also to al-Walīd b. al-Mughīra as having said, "Does God make revelation to Muḥammad and not me, even though I am chief and leader of Quraysh and also ignores Abū Mas῾ūd ῾Amr b. ῾Amr al-Thaqafi, lord of Thaqīf, even though we are the greatest men of the two towns?"[5] Regarding this statement, God sent down: "And they say, 'Why was this Qur᾽ān not revealed to some great men of the two towns?'" (*sūrat al-Zukhruf*, XLIII, v.31), along with other verses thereafter.

Ibn Isḥāq also referred to Ubayy b. Khalaf who said to ῾Uqba b. Abū Mu῾ayṭ, "Have I not heard that you sat down with Muḥammad and listened to him? I'll never set eyes on you again unless you spit in his face!" And ῾Uqba, that enemy of God, God damn him, did that! And so God sent down, "And a day (will come) when the evil-doer will bite his hands and say, 'Would that I had taken my path with the Messenger; woe is to me! How I wish I had not taken so-and-so as my friend!'" (*sūrat al-Furqān*; XXV, v.27, 28), along with following verses.

He also related, "And Ubayy b. Khalaf took an old, disintegrating bone to him and said, 'O Muḥammad, do you claim that God can restore this after it has disintegrated?' He then crumbled it in his hand and blew it into the air towards the Messenger of God (ṢAAS). He replied, 'Yes, I do say that. God will restore it and you too, even after you are like that. And then He will place you in the fire!' And God revealed, 'He coins a metaphor for us, forgetting his own creation, saying, "Who will give life to bones that are rotten?" Say, "He will give life to them who first created them! He has knowledge of all creation"'" (*sūrat Yāsīn*; XXXVI, v.78–9) to the end of that *sūrat*.

Ibn Isḥāq stated, "I have been told that once, when the Messenger of God (ṢAAS) was making a circumambulation of the *ka῾ba*, near its doorway, he was obstructed by al-Aswad b. al-Muṭṭalib, al-Walīd b. al-Mughīra, Umayya b. Khalaf and al-῾Āṣ b. Wā᾽il. They said to him, 'O Muḥammad, come on! We'll

5. Thaqīf were associated with al-Ṭā᾽if.

worship what you do if you'll worship what we do. Let's just co-operate, you and us, in the whole thing!'

"Regarding them God revealed, 'Say: "O you disbelievers! I will not worship what you worship"' (*sūrat al-Kāfirūn*; CIX; v.1–2).

"When Abū Jahl heard reference to the *al-zaqqūm* tree, he said, 'Do you know what this *al-zaqqūm* is? It is dates mashed in butter!' He added, 'Bring it along; we'll enjoy it!'

"And so God revealed, 'The *zaqqūm* tree is the food of sinners'" (*sūrat al-Dukhān*; XLIV, v.43–4).

Ibn Isḥāq also related, "Al-Walīd b. al-Mughīra was standing talking with the Messenger of God (ṢAAS) who was addressing him, wishing to convert him to Islam, when Ibn Umm Maktūm, that is, the son of ʿĀtika, daughter of ʿAbd Allāh b. ʿAnkatha, passed by. Ibn Umm Maktūm, who was blind, addressed the Messenger of God (ṢAAS) and began asking him to recite the Qurʾān. This so upset the Messenger of God (ṢAAS) as to anger him, and this was because he was interfering with his efforts to convert al-Walīd to Islam as he was hoping.

"When the blind man persisted, he turned away from him frowning and ignored him. And so God Almighty sent down, '... and he frowned and turned away when the blind man came to him ...' up to the words, '... exalted, purified'" (*sūrat ʿAbasa*; LXXX, v.1–14).

It is also said that the person who was talking to the Messenger of God (ṢAAS) when Ibn Umm Maktūm came along was Umayya b. Khalaf. But God knows best.

Ibn Isḥāq then related the names of those who returned to Mecca from the migration to Abyssinia. They did so when news reached them of the adoption of Islam by the Meccans. This information was incorrect, though there was a reason for it.

What is well established in the *ṣaḥīḥ* collections of traditions and elsewhere is that the Messenger of God (ṢAAS) sat down one day with the polytheists and God revealed to him, "By the star when it sets, your companion has not gone astray" (*sūrat al-Najm*; LIII, v.1–2). When he had recited this *sūrat* completely, he prostrated in prayer as did the Muslims, polytheists and spirits all.

But that (the prostrations of the polytheists along with the Muslims) had a reason which is mentioned by exegetes in their commentary on the words of Almighty God, "And we did not send before you any messenger or any prophet without him wishing something and the devil then influencing his wish; and so God annuls whatever the devil has inspired, and affirms His own signs. And God is knowledgeable, wise" (*sūrat al-Ḥajj*; XXII, v.52). They then refer to the story of the *gharānīq*.[6]

6. The word seems to have two possible connotations. It can mean either a high-flying crane or a particularly attractive young person, male or female. At issue here are two verses said, in the

We preferred to refrain from mentioning it openly here lest it come to the attention of those unable to place it in context. The origins of the story are, however, present in the *ṣaḥīḥ* collections.

Al-Bukhārī stated, "Abū Ma῾mar related to us, quoting ῾Abd al-Wārith, quoting Ayyūb, from ῾Ikrima, from Ibn ῾Abbās, who said, 'The Prophet (ṢAAS) prostrated himself in prayer having recited *sūrat al-Najam*, and all the Muslims, the polytheists and men and spirits alike prostrated too.'"

Al-Bukhārī is unique in giving this tradition; Muslim does not relate it.

Al-Bukhārī also stated, "Muḥammad b. Bashshār related to us, as did Ghundar and Shu῾ba, from Abū Isḥāq, who said, 'I heard al-Aswad say, quoting ῾Abd Allāh, "The Prophet (ṢAAS) recited *sūrat al-Najam* in Mecca and prostrated in prayer. And those there with him also prostrated except for one old man who picked up a handful of dust or dirt which he raised to his forehead, saying, 'This suffices for me.' And later I saw him killed as an unbeliever."'"

Muslim related this, as did Abū Dāūd and al-Nasā᾽ī, from a *ḥadīth* from Shu῾ba.

Imām Aḥmad (b. Ḥanbal) stated that Ibrahīm recounted to him, saying, "Rabbāḥ related to us, from Ma῾mar, from Ibn Ṭāwūs, from ῾Ikrima b. Khālid, from Ja῾far b. al-Muṭṭalib b. Abū Wadā῾a, who heard his father say, 'The Messenger of God (ṢAAS) recited *sūrat al-Najam* in Mecca and then prostrated, and all those there with him did the same. But I lifted up my head, declining to prostrate.' Al-Muṭṭalib had not then accepted Islam. After that he never heard anyone recite *sūrat al-Najam* without him prostrating along with the reciter."

Al-Nasā᾽ī related this from ῾Abd al-Malik b. ῾Abd al-Ḥamīd, from the account of Aḥmad b. Ḥanbal.

It may be gathered from this account and the preceding one that this man did prostrate, but then raised his head in pride. However, the old man whom Ibn Mas῾ūd considered an exception did not prostrate at all. But God knows best.

What is implied here is that when the narrator saw that the polytheists had prostrated themselves in imitation of the Messenger of God (ṢAAS) he believed that they had accepted Islam, made peace with him and that there was no longer any dispute between them.

The news of that quickly spread and reached the Emigrants in Abyssinia, and they believed it to be true. A group of them, hoping that was so, came back, while another group remained there. Each of them was well intentioned and correct in acting as they did.

Ibn Isḥāq gave the names of all of them that returned. These were: ῾Uthmān b. ῾Affān and his wife Ruqayya, daughter of the Messenger of God (ṢAAS), Abū Ḥudhayfa b. ῾Utba b. Rabī῾a and his wife Sahla, daughter of Suhayl, ῾Abd Allāh

works of tradition, to have immediately followed the reference to the goddesses of pre-Islam, al-Lāt, al-῾Uzzā and Manat, in *sūrat al-Najm*, v.19, 20. These extra verses, not in the Qur᾽ān but preserved in the tradition literature, suggest that these goddesses are *gharānīq* and that their intercession is to be hoped for on judgment day.

b. Jaḥsh b. Riʾāb, ʿUtba b. Ghazwān, al-Zubayr b. al-ʿAwwām, Muṣʿab b. ʿUmayr, Suwaybiṭ b. Saʿd, Ṭulayb b. ʿUmayr, ʿAbd al-Raḥmān b. ʿAwf, al-Miqdād b. ʿAmr, ʿAbd Allāh b. Masʿūd, Abū Salama b. ʿAbd al-Asad and his wife Umm Salama, daughter of Abū Umayya b. al-Mughīra, and Shammās b. ʿUthmān.

Also there were Salama b. Hishām and ʿAyyāsh b. Abū Rabīʿa who were imprisoned in Mecca until after the battles of Badr, Uḥud and *al-khandaq*.

There is some dispute over ʿAmmār b. Yāsir, as to whether or not he ever went to Abyssinia.

There also returned Muʿattib b. ʿAwf, ʿUthmān b. Maẓʿūn, his son al-Sāʾib, along with his two brothers Qudāma and ʿAbd Allāh, both sons of Maẓʿūn. Then there were Khunays b. Ḥudhāfa and Hishām b. al-ʿĀṣ b. Wāʾil, the latter being imprisoned in Mecca until after the battle of *al-khandaq*. ʿĀmir b. Rabīʿa and his wife Laylā, daughter of Abū Ḥathma, also returned, as did ʿAbd Allāh b. Makhrama.

ʿAbd Allāh b. Suhayl b. ʿAmr also returned, but he was imprisoned until the battle of Badr, when he joined the Muslims and fought on their side.

Also Abū Sabra b. Abū Ruhm returned, along with his wife Umm Kulthūm, daughter of Suhayl. As did al-Sakrān b. ʿAmr b. ʿAbd Shams and his wife Sawda, daughter of Zamʿa. He died in Mecca before the migration to Medina and the Messenger of God (ṢAAS), thereafter married his widow.

Saʿd b. Khawla, Abū ʿUbayda b. al-Jarrāḥ, ʿAmr b. al-Ḥārith b. Zuhayr, Suhayl b. Bayḍāʾ and ʿAmr b. Abū Sarḥ also returned.

They totalled 33 men; may God be pleased with them!

Al-Bukhārī stated, "ʿĀʾisha reported that the Messenger of God (ṢAAS) said, 'I was given a vision of your abode in exile, a place of date-palms between two tracts of black stones.'"

Some (of those who had returned from Abyssinia) then migrated to Medina, while the rest of those who had remained in Abyssinia did so as well.

And there is a report to this effect from Abū Mūsā and Asmāʾ, God be pleased with them both, from the Prophet (ṢAAS).

Already mentioned above is the account of Abū Mūsā, that being in both *ṣaḥīḥ* collections. The account of Asmāʾ, daughter of ʿUmays, will come later, if God wills it, and in Him is all trust. Her story relates to what happened after the battle of Khaybar, when the latecomers from among the emigrants to Abyssinia arrived.

Al-Bukhārī stated, "Yaḥyā b. Ḥammād related to us, quoting Abū ʿAwāna, from Sulaymān b. Ibrāhīm, from ʿAlqama, from ʿAbd Allāh, who said, 'We used to greet the Prophet (ṢAAS), while he prayed, and he would reply to us. But when we came back from the land of the Negus we would greet him the same way, but he would not reply. So we said to him, "O Messenger of God, when we used to greet you, you would reply to us. But since our return from the land of the Negus, you don't reply."'"

"He responded, 'Prayer keeps one engrossed.'"

Al-Bukhārī also related this, as did Muslim, Abū Dā°ūd and al-Nasā°ī, by different chains of authority, from Sulaymān b. Mahrān, from al-A°mash.

This substantiates the interpretation of those who explain the authentic account of Zayd b. Arqam that is in both *saḥīḥ* collections: "We used to talk during the prayer, until God's revealed verse was sent down, 'Stand up before God in humility' (*sūrat al-Baqara*; II, v.238). And so we were ordered to remain silent and were forbidden to talk."

However, those referred to here were the "Companions of the Prophet" generally, for Zayd himself was a "Companion", (but) from Medina, and the prohibition against speaking during the prayer was established in Mecca. And so the report is being applied to what had gone before.

Regarding his reference to this particular verse which is of the Medina period, it is indeed difficult to explain. Perhaps he believed that it was this verse that prohibited speaking during the prayers, when in fact there were other prohibitions of it along with it. But God knows best.

Ibn Isḥāq stated, "Among those emigrants who returned under an agreement of protection, or named to us as such, were °Uthmān b. Maẓ°ūn, protected by al-Walīd b. al-Mughīra, Abū Salama b. °Abd al-Asad, protected by his uncle Abū Ṭālib; his mother was Barra, daughter of °Abd al-Muṭṭalib.

"Regarding °Uthmān b. Maẓ°ūn, Ṣāliḥ b. Ibrāhīm b. °Abd al-Raḥmān b. Awf related to me from someone who was told the following about °Uthmān, 'When °Uthmān b. Maẓ°ūn saw the plight of the followers of the Messenger of God (ṢAAS), while he himself was able to come and go freely under the protection of al-Walīd b. al-Mughīra, he said, "By God, here I am moving about freely under the protection of a polytheist while my friends and followers in religion suffer harm and insult for God that do not afflict me, and this constitutes a great deficiency in me!"'

"So off he went to al-Walīd b. al-Mughīra and told him, 'O Abū °Abd al-Shams, you have fulfilled your pledge, but now I'm giving back to you your protection.'

"'Why is that, cousin?' he asked. 'Has any one of my people harmed you?'

"'No,' he replied, 'it's just that what I want is the protection of God, the Almighty and Glorious. I don't want the protection of anyone else.'

"'Well then,' al-Walīd said, 'you should go to the mosque and give me my protection back in public, just as I declared my protection over you.'

"And so they both did go to the mosque, where al-Walīd b. al-Mughīra announced, 'This is °Uthmān, and he has come to relieve me of my protection of him.'

"°Uthmān said, 'He speaks the truth. I have found him to be trustworthy and honourable in his protection, but I prefer to be protected only by God. I have given him back his pledge of protection.'

"ʿUthmān, God bless him, then left and joined an assembly of Quraysh who were being addressed by Labīd b. Rabīʿa b. Mālik b. Jaʿfar. ʿUthmān sat down with them. Labīd spoke a verse:

'Is not all but God vanity?'

"ʿUthmān commented, 'You speak the truth!'
"Labīd then said,

'And all pleasures must fade.'

"At this ʿUthmān protested, 'You lie! The pleasures of paradise will last forever!'

"Labīd commented, 'O men of Quraysh, those who sat with you used not to be so insulted; when did this come about so?'

"One man replied, 'This is just one of those fools allied with him; they have abandoned our faith. Don't take to heart what he says.'

"ʿUthmān spoke back to this man and they became angry with one another. The other man then got up and hit ʿUthmān in the eye, making it black. Al-Walīd, who was nearby and saw what had happened to ʿUthmān, commented, 'Well, nephew, your eye didn't need to suffer so; earlier you were fully protected!'

"ʿUthmān replied, 'Not so; I swear the only problem is that my good eye is in need of what the other one suffered for God's sake! Actually I am under the protection of One stronger and more capable than yourself, O Abū ʿAbd al-Shams!'

"To this al-Walīd replied, 'Come on now, nephew, just come back under my protection.'

"'No,' ʿUthmān told him."

Ibn Isḥāq stated, "Regarding Abū Salama b. ʿAbd al-Asad: my father, Isḥāq b. Yasār related to me that Salama b. ʿAbd Allāh b. Abū Salama told him that when Abū Salama sought the protection of Abū Ṭālib some men of the Banū Makhzūm went to the latter and asked him, 'O Abū Ṭālib, you've already given protection from us to your nephew Muḥammad; how is it you are now doing the same for one of our own men?'

"Abū Ṭālib replied, 'He sought out my protection, and he is my sister's son. And if I am not to protect my sister's son, how could I protect my brother's son?'

"Abū Lahab then arose and said, 'O men of Quraysh, you've treated this sheikh harshly, and you're constantly attacking him for giving protection to his own people. Either put an end to this, or let's all take his side in this so he attains his goal.'

"They replied, 'All right, Abū Lahab, we'll stop behaving contrary to your wishes.' He had been their ally and assistant against the Messenger of God (ṢAAS), and they wanted to maintain that.

"Abū Ṭālib had high hopes of him when he heard him speak thus and anticipated his aid regarding the Messenger of God (ṢAAS). And so he spoke the following verses urging Abū Lahab to support himself and the Messenger of God (ṢAAS):

'A man with Abū ͨUtayba as his uncle is secure from harm as in a pasture;

I tell him – though how could my advice benefit him – O Abū Muͨtib, hold your ground firmly,

And do not as long as you live accept a course you'll be blamed for, whenever you attend a gathering,

Leave the path of the weak to others than yourself, for you were not created to stay weak,

And fight, for fighting is just and you will never see a real warrior humbled until he surrenders.

And why is it, when they have done you no great harm, nor abandoned you when having victory or defeat?

May God punish ͨAbd Shams, Nawfal, Taym and Makhzūm for us with disaster and death,

For their deserting our alliance after friendship and affection in order to attain things forbidden.

You lie, by God's temple! Us dispossess Muḥammad? Not even at the enclave did you see (us) turn against (him).'"

Ibn Hishām stated, "We have omitted one verse from this poem."

An Account of the determination of Abū Bakr, "the Trusting", to emigrate to Abyssinia.

Ibn Isḥāq stated, "I was told by Muḥammad b. Muslim al-Zuhrī, from ͨUrwa, from ͨĀ³isha, that when Abū Bakr, 'the Trusting', God be pleased with him, experienced suffering in Mecca and witnessed the antagonism of Quraysh for the Messenger of God (ṢAAS) and his own supporters, he asked permission from the Messenger of God (ṢAAS) to move away and he granted him this request.

"And so Abū Bakr, God bless him, did leave and, having travelled a day or two away from Mecca, was met by Ibn al-Daghina, brother of the Banū al-Ḥārith b. Bakr b. ͨAbd Manāt b. Kināna, who was at that time the leader of the Aḥābīsh."

Al-Wāqidi gave this man's name as al-Ḥārith b. Yazīd, he being of the tribe of Bakr b. ͨAbd Manāt b. Kināna. Al-Suhaylī, however, gave his name as Mālik.

(ͨĀ³isha continued) "'What are you heading for, Abū Bakr?' the man asked. Abū Bakr replied, 'My people have offended me, treated me badly and forced me to leave.'

"'Why is that? By God, you're a credit to the tribe, aiding those in distress, and you are kindly towards the needy. Go back; you are under my protection!'

"He did return with him and, back in Mecca, Ibn al-Daghina stood up with him and stated, 'O Quraysh, I have placed the son of Abū Quḥāfa under my protection. Let no man do anything but good to him.'

"And they did leave him alone."

ʿĀʾisha went on, "Abū Bakr used to have a mosque at the gate of his home among the Banū Jumaḥ and there he would pray. He was a very sensitive man and would shed tears when reciting the Qurʾān. Young men, slaves and women would stand nearby astonished at his behaviour.

"Some Quraysh men went to Ibn Daghina and told him, 'O Ibn Daghina, surely you didn't protect this man to harm us? When he prays and recites what Muḥammad brought he is moved (to tears) and he then attracts attention; we fear that he may influence our young men, women and the weak. Go and tell him to go inside his house, where he can do as he wishes.'"

She went on, "So Ibn al-Daghina did go to Abū Bakr and told him, 'I didn't give you protection so that you could do your people harm. They take offence at the place you attend and feel that you are harming them. Go inside your house and do there whatever it is you want.'

"(Abū Bakr asked) 'So shall I give you back your protection and rely on God?'

"'Do return my protection.'"

"'Consider it returned.'"

"Ibn al-Daghina then stood and stated, 'O Quraysh, the son of Abū Quḥāfa has given me back my protection over him. Do with him whatever you wish.'"

The Imām al-Bukhārī alone gives an account of this *ḥadīth* and his account is nicely expanded. He stated, "Yaḥyā b. Bukayr related to me, quoting al-Layth, from ʿUqayl, Ibn Shihāb stated, and ʿUrwa b. al-Zubayr informed me, that ʿĀʾisha, the wife of the Prophet (ṢAAS) said, 'I have no consciousness of my parents not actively participating in the faith. Not a day would pass for us without the Messenger of God (ṢAAS) coming to us, either early in the day or late.

"'And when the Muslims were being persecuted Abū Bakr left, travelling in the direction of Abyssinia. When he reached Bark al-Ghimād, he was met by Ibn al-Daghina, who was chief of the Qāra. The latter asked him where he was heading. Abū Bakr replied, "My people expelled me, and so I want to travel in the land praying to my Lord."

"'Ibn al-Daghina commented, "But men like you, Abū Bakr, neither leave nor are expelled. You are charitable, maintain family ties, make sacrifices for others, are hospitable, and help out in times of disaster. I shall be your protector. So go back and worship your Lord in your own land."

"'So he went back and Ibn al-Daghina travelled with him. At evening Ibn al-Daghina made the rounds of the Quraysh chiefs and told them, "The like of Abū Bakr does not leave, nor is he expelled! Would you exile a man who is charitable, maintains family ties, makes sacrifices for others, is hospitable to guests, and helps out in times of disaster?"

"'Quraysh did not deny Ibn al-Daghina's right to give protection, but asked him, "Tell Abū Bakr to worship his Lord inside his house; there he can recite what he likes without harming us or advertising it. We're concerned that he might subvert our women and sons."

"'Ibn al-Daghina told that to Abū Bakr and the latter did therefore pray to his Lord in his house, without announcing what he was doing, and he recited only at home. But later Abū Bakr decided to build a mosque in the courtyard of his house and there he would pray and recite the Qurᵓān. The women of the polytheists and their sons would crowd around staring at him in wonder; Abū Bakr was a man prone to tears, and he could not restrain his eyes when he recited the Qurᵓān.

"'This upset the polytheist Quraysh leaders and they sent for Ibn al-Daghina. When he came, they told him, "We've acknowledged your protection of Abū Bakr on the understanding that he would worship his Lord in his house. But he has gone beyond that, built himself a mosque in his courtyard and openly prays and recites there. We're concerned that he will subvert our young men and our womenfolk. Make him stop. If he will restrict himself to worship at home, then well and good. But if he insists on so doing only in full view, then ask him to give back to you your protection. We don't want to break with you, but we cannot agree for Abū Bakr to advertise."'

"'Āᵓisha went on, 'Ibn al-Daghina then went to Abū Bakr and told him, "You know what it was I agreed to with you. Either you restrict yourself to that, or give me back my protection. I don't want the Arabs to hear it said that I've had my covenant broken because of a man to whom I had given my protection."

"'Abū Bakr replied, "Then I give you back your protection and will rely on that of God, Almighty and Glorious is He."'"

Al-Bukhārī then recounted the rest of the tradition concerning the emigration of Abū Bakr, God bless him, with the Messenger of God (ṢAAS), as will be described hereafter.

Ibn Isḥāq stated, "'Abd al-Raḥmān b. al-Qāsim related to me, from his father al-Qāsim b. Muḥammad, the son of b. Abū Bakr, 'the Trusting', as follows: 'He was confronted – that is Abū Bakr was confronted – after he had left the protection of Ibn al-Daghina, on his way to the ka῾ba by some fool from Quraysh who tossed dirt up over his head. Then al-Walīd b. al-Mughīra – or perhaps it was al-῾Āṣ b. Wāᵓil – passed by Abū Bakr, who spoke as follows: "Don't you see how this idiot is behaving?" He was told, "You brought this on yourself." Meanwhile Abū Bakr kept repeating, "O God, how forbearing You are!"'"

DIVISION

Ibn Isḥāq made mention of these incidents to show the contradiction between the pact made by Quraysh with the Banū Hāshim and the Banū al-Muṭṭalib, and their drafting of that damnable document against the latter and their confinement to the enclave, with all the resultant consequences. These are matters appropriate for consideration in this era. Al-Shāfi῾ī, God be pleased with him, therefore stated, "He who wishes to know about the *maghāzī*, the early military engagements, is reliant upon Ibn Isḥāq."

Ibn Isḥāq stated, "While the Banū Hāshim and the Banū al-Muṭṭalib were living in their house assigned to them by Quraysh in the document they had written, a certain group of Quraysh set about abrogating that document.

"No one took more pains to do this than Hishām b. ʿAmr b. al-Ḥārith b. Ḥabīb b. Naṣr b. Mālik b. Ḥisl b. ʿĀmir b. Luʾayy; this was because he was the nephew of Naḍla b. Hishām b. ʿAbd Manāf by his mother, and Hishām had close ties to the Banū Hāshim. He was, moreover, deemed highly by his people.

"When, at night, the Banū Hāshim and the Banū al-Muṭṭalib were restricted to their building in the enclave, he would, as I have been told, bring up a camel loaded down with food. When he reached the entrance to the enclave he would release the halter from the camel's head and strike its side to send it on down to them. Next time he would bring it loaded with wheat and do the same.

"He went to Zuhayr b. Abū Umayya b. al-Mughīra b. ʿAbd Allāh b. ʿAmr b. Makhzūm, whose mother was ʿĀtika, daughter of ʿAbd al-Muṭṭalib, and said, 'Zuhayr, does it please you to eat and dress well and to marry women while your uncles are where you know them to be, engaging in no buying nor selling, arranging no marriages, nor having any arranged with them? For my part, I swear that if they were the uncles of Abū al-Ḥakam b. Hishām and you were to ask him to treat them as you have been asked to do, he would never have agreed to your request.'

"'Shame on you, Hishām! What can I do? I'm just one man. If someone else would join me, I'd set about abrogating it.'

"Hishām replied, 'You have found one such man.' 'Who is that?' he asked. 'Myself,' came the answer. 'Well,' Zuhayr went on, 'find us a third then.'

"And so Hishām went to al-Muṭʿim b. ʿAdī and told him, 'Muṭʿim, are you pleased to have two clans of the Banū ʿAbd Manāf suffer while you look on, in agreement with Quraysh about that? By God, if you enable them to do this they will soon be treating you the same way.'

"'Damn it! What am I to do? I'm just one man,' Muṭʿim commented.

"Hishām replied, 'I have found you a second.' 'Who?' 'Myself.'

"'Then find a third,' Muṭʿim asked. 'I already have.'

"'Who is that?'

"'Zuhayr b. Abū Umayya.'

"'Then find us a fourth,' asked Muṭʿim.

"So Hishām went to Abū al-Bakhtarī b. Hishām and told him what he had said to Muṭʿim b. ʿAdī.

"Abū al-Bakhtarī asked, 'Can you find anyone else to help in this?'

"'Yes, I can,' Hishām replied.

"'Who?' he asked.

"'Zuhayr b. Abū ʿUmayya, Muṭʿim b. ʿAdī and myself are with you.'

"'Find us a fifth,' he asked.

"And so Hishām went to Zam°a b. al-Aswad b. al-Muṭṭalib b. Asad, spoke to him and reminded him of their kinship and their rights.

"'Is there anyone else helping in what you are inviting me to do?' asked Zam°a.

"'Indeed yes,' Hishām replied, naming the others.

"And so they agreed to meet at night on the promontory of Mt. al-Ḥajūn on the upper outskirts of Mecca. There they met and agreed to defy the document until they were able to revoke it. Zuhayr told them, 'I will begin and be the first to speak out.'

"Next morning they went off to their assembly meeting and Zuhayr attended wearing a ceremonial robe. He made seven circumambulations of the *ka°ba* then went before the gathering and said, 'O people of Mecca, shall we eat all kinds of food and dress at will while the Banū Hāshim are in distress, unable to engage in any trade? By God, I won't take my seat until this damnable boycott document is torn up!'

"Abū Jahl, who was over to one side of the mosque, retorted, 'By God, it will not be torn up!'

"Zam°a b. al-Asad then said, 'By God, you are the worst liar! We weren't pleased with the document when it was written.'

"'Zam°a speaks the truth,' Abū al-Bakhtarī joined in. 'We do not like or agree to what is written there.'

"Al-Mu°ṭim b. °Adī then spoke up, 'You are both right, and anyone denying that is a liar. We are innocent before God of the document and what is written on it.'

"Hishām b. °Amr then stated something similar.

"Abū Jahl observed, 'This is something decided at night, something discussed elsewhere.'

"Meanwhile, Abū Ṭālib was seated to one side of the mosque.

"Al-Mu°ṭim b. °Adī then arose to tear up the document but discovered that worms had already consumed it, all except for the words, 'In your name, O God!'

"It was Manṣūr b. °Ikrima who had written it and, so they say, his hand had become paralysed."

Ibn Hishām stated, "Some scholars relate that the Messenger of God (ṢAAS) told Abū Ṭālib, 'Uncle, God has sent worms to work upon the document of Quraysh and they have left alone only names relating to God and have removed the evil, boycott and lies from it.'

"Abū Ṭālib asked, 'Is it your Lord who told you this?'

"'Yes,' he replied.

"'Well, I swear by God,' Abū Ṭālib commented, 'no one has come in to you.'

"Abū Ṭālib then went out to Quraysh and asked, 'O Quraysh, my nephew has informed me of such-and-such things. Bring your document, and if it is as he says, then withdraw and remove the boycott. But if he is lying, I will hand my nephew over to you.'

"'We'll agree to that,' they said, and so compacted.

"They then looked and found it as the Messenger of God (SAAS) had said. But this only increased their malice.

"Thereupon the group of Quraysh men took their action to revoke the document."

Ibn Isḥāq stated that when it had been torn up and its contents revoked, Abū Ṭālib spoke the following verses in praise of those who had taken action to annul the document:

"Has our Lord's action reached our men at sea, despite their distance, for God is most kind to people,

And will tell them that the document has been torn up, and that all things that displease God come to nought.

Falsehood and deceit alternated and conjoined in it, but ultimately deceit is not bound to prevail.

Those uninvolved in it gathered together on a level plateau, while its fate remained undetermined.

It was an incident so worthy of being considered evil as to have arms and necks severed for it.

And for the people of all Mecca to leave in flight, their hearts quaking in fear of its evil,

The ploughman was left to ponder his options, whether because of it to head for low ground or for high,

So let him of Mecca's people whose prestige intoxicates him know that our glory in Mecca's heart is longer lived.

We grew up there when those there were few and we have always had our prestige and praise for us increase.

We fed our guests until they were forced to leave leftovers, and till the hands of those inundated with food began to give out.

God reward that group who united at al-Ḥajūn behind a chief who guides rightly and decisively,

Who sat on the heights at al-Ḥajūn as though they were kings, though even more noble and glorious than that.

Each hero helping in that, though walking with difficulty and impeded by his chainmail,

Courageously moving to great deeds, like a flame flaring in a torchbearer's hands

Men of the most noble of Luʾayy b. Ghālib whose faces burn in anger if they are insulted,

Men tall in stature, their swords reaching to the middle of their shanks, men for whom the clouds receive rain and bring joy.

Generous lords and sons of lords, urging their guests to eat, piling the food,

Constructing safety and paving the way for their tribesmen when we travel the country.

Every blame-free man strives to keep this peace; (every) leader of great renown for that reason.

They spent part of the night asleep then awoke quietly, while the rest still slept.

They sent back Sahl b. Bayḍā᾽ well pleased, and Abū Bakr and Muḥammad were delighted by it.

When was it that other clans helped out in our affairs, though of old, before that, we have been well liked?

In former times we never acquiesced in injustice, and achieved our aims without using violence.

O Tribe of Quṣayy, will you not consider, and do you want what tomorrow will bring?

The relationship between you and me is like the saying, 'O Mt. Aswad, you could explain it, if only you spoke.'"

Al-Suhaylī stated, "Aswad is the name of a mountain where a man was killed without anyone discovering his murderer. And so the relatives of the dead man recited the line, 'O Mt. Aswad, you could explain it, if only you spoke.' That is, 'O Mt. Aswad, if you spoke you could explain to us who it was killed him.'"

At this point Ibn Isḥāq quoted poetry of Ḥassān in praise of al-Muʿtim b. ʿAdī and Hishām b. ʿAmr for their having torn up that damnable, sinful and iniquitous document.

And here too al-Umawī quoted many lines of verse, whereas we have thought what Ibn Isḥāq transmitted to be sufficient.

Al-Wāqidī stated, "I asked Muḥammad b. Ṣāliḥ and ʿAbd al-Raḥmān b. ʿAbd al-ʿAzīz, 'When did the Banū Hāshim come out from the enclave?' They replied, 'In the tenth year, after the beginning of the mission that is, three years before the migration.'"

I add that in that year, following their release, Abū Ṭālib, uncle of the Messenger of God (ṢAAS) died, as also did his wife Khadīja, daughter of Khuwaylid, God bless her. An account of all this will come hereafter, if God, Almighty is He, so wishes.

DIVISION

Muḥammad b. Isḥāq related, following the account of the revocation of the document, many stories involving the enmity of Quraysh for the Messenger of God (ṢAAS), and how the Arab tribes and those making the lesser or the full pilgrimage to Mecca, or coming for some other reason, were driven away from (Muḥammad by the enemy). He also recounted how God made miracles happen through him to give proof of the veracity of the signs and guidance he brought, as well as to put to the lie the charges they were making against him of immorality, aggressiveness, deception and trickery, and accusations that he was mad, a magician, a soothsayer or a forger. But God was to give him victory.

Ibn Isḥāq then related the story of al-Ṭufayl b. ʿAmr al-Dawsī, but with an incomplete chain of authorities.

Al-Ṭufayl was an honoured and respected man of Daws. He came to Mecca where he was met by the Quraysh chieftains, who warned him about the Messenger of God (ṢAAS), and forbad him to meet with him or to listen to him talk.

Al-Ṭufayl related, "By God, they kept on at me until I agreed not to hear him nor to speak to him. I even stuffed my ears with cotton when I went to the mosque to prevent myself hearing anything he said; I didn't want to listen to him.

"I went to the mosque, and there was the Messenger of God (ṢAAS) standing in prayer at the *kaʿba*. I went over near to him, and God required me to hear some of what he said.

"And I heard wonderful speech. So I told myself, 'May my mother not be bereft! I swear, here am I, a man who is intelligent and a poet, and someone who can well distinguish good from bad! What prevents me from hearing what this man is saying? If what he says is good, I will accept it; if bad, I will reject it.'"

He went on, "So I stayed there until the Messenger of God (ṢAAS) went off home and I followed him till he went inside his house. Then I went in to him and said, 'O Muḥammad, your people have told me such-and-such.'

He continued, "And I swear, they so scared me that I stuffed my ears with cotton so as not to hear what you say. But then God insisted on making me hear your words. And I heard fine speech. So explain your situation to me.'

Al-Ṭufayl continued, "And so the Messenger of God (ṢAAS) explained Islam to me and recited the Qurʾān to me and, I swear, I never heard words more sweet than those, nor any matter more just.

"And so I accepted Islam and bore true witness, saying, 'O Prophet of God, I am a man who is obeyed by his people. I am now returning to them and will invite them to Islam. Pray to God to give me a sign that will help me with them when I do so.'

"And so he said, 'O God, give him a sign.'

"I then left for home and travelled till I came to a pass that enabled me to look down on to my village. But then there appeared between my eyes a light like that of a lamp. I said to myself, 'O God, not right in my face, for I fear that they will think it some exemplary punishment that has struck my face for my abandoning my faith.'

"Then the light moved and alighted on the head of my whip. And the villagers watched that light atop my whip that resembled a suspended candle, and they continued to do so as I was descending to them from the pass, right until I was there among them.

"When I dismounted, my father, an aged sheikh, came over to me, but I told him, 'Off with you, father; you and I must have nothing to do with one another.'

"'Why is that, my son?' he asked.

"'I have accepted Islam, and adopted the religion of Muḥammad (ṢAAS).'

"'Well, son, your religion shall be mine.'

"'Then go and wash yourself, clean your clothing and come to me so that I can instruct you in what I have been taught.'

"He did go and wash himself and cleaned his clothing. When he returned, I explained Islam to him and he accepted it.

"Then my wife came to me and I told her, 'Go away; you and I can have nothing to do with one another.'

"'Why is that, my father and my mother be your ransom?'

"'Islam has divided me from you; I have adopted the religion of Muḥammad (ṢAAS).'

"'Well, your religion is mine,' she said.

"I told her, 'Go to the *ḥimā*, the sacred shrine, of Dhū al-Sharā and purify yourself of it.' Dhū al-Sharā was an idol of Daws and the *ḥimā* was a shrine around it that they kept sacrosanct; it had a stream whose water descended from a mountain.

"She replied, 'May my father and mother ransom you, don't you fear something will happen to the children because of Dhū al-Sharā?'

"'Not at all; I guarantee that,' I replied.

"She did go and wash herself and, when she returned I explained Islam to her and she accepted it.

"I then called upon the Daws tribe to accept Islam, but they resisted. I went to see the Messenger of God (ṢAAS) in Mecca. I told him, 'O Messenger of God, fornication has defeated me with Daws; say a prayer to God for them.'

"He said, 'O God, lead Daws aright.' Then he said to me, 'Return to your people, preach to them and be kind to them.'

"And so I remained in Daws territory asking them to embrace Islam until the Messenger of God (ṢAAS), emigrated to Medina. Then the battles of Badr, Uḥud and the *khandaq*, the trench, took place. Thereafter I went to see the Messenger of God (ṢAAS), taking those of my people who had become Muslims, while he was at Khaybar. I set up camp, with some 70 or 80 tents of Daws families at Medina, and then we joined the Messenger of God (ṢAAS) at Khaybar; there he gave us an equal share of the spoils, along with the other Muslims.

"I remained with the Messenger of God (ṢAAS) until God conquered Mecca through him. Then I asked him, 'O Messenger of God, dispatch me to burn Dhū al-Kaffayn, the idol of ʿAmr b. Ḥumāma.'"

Ibn Isḥāq stated, "And he did leave to do so. As al-Ṭufayl set fire to the idol he spoke the verse,

> 'O Dhū al-Kaffayn, I am not one of your worshippers; our history is older than yours;
> I have stuffed your heart with fire.'

"He then returned to the Messenger of God (ṢAAS), and remained at Medina with him until the Messenger of God (ṢAAS) died.

"When the Arabs apostatized, al-Ṭufayl campaigned with the Muslims until they had subdued Ṭulayha and all of Nejd. Then he travelled with the Muslim forces to al-Yamāma, his son ʿAmr b. Ṭufayl accompanying him.

"On his way to Yamāma he had a vision and he asked his companions to interpret it to him. He recounted, 'I saw that my head had been shaved, a bird came forth from my mouth, and a woman met me and placed me in her vagina. Then I saw my son frantically searching for me, but he was withheld from me.'

"'Let's hope it's a good omen,' they told him.

"He said, 'I'm going to interpret it myself.'

"'What, then?' they asked.

"He explained, 'The shaving of my head means its being laid down. The bird exiting it is my soul. The woman who placed me in her vagina is the earth that will be dug out for me, and into which I will disappear. As for my son's searching for me, and then his being kept from me, I see him striving to have happen to him what has happened to me.'

"He was killed, God bless him, as a martyr in al-Yamāma, and his son was severely wounded but later recovered. Eventually he was martyred in the year of the battle of al-Yarmūk, during the caliphate of ʿUmar. God bless him."

That was how Muḥammad b. Isḥāq recounted the story of al-Ṭufayl b. ʿAmr, with an incomplete chain of authorities. There is testimonial to his account to be found in authenticated *ḥadīth* collections.

Imām Aḥmad stated, "Wakīʿ related to us, saying, 'Sufyān related to us, from Abū al-Zinād, from al-Aʿraj, from Abū Hurayra, as follows, "When al-Ṭufayl and his companions came to the Messenger of God (ṢAAS) and said, 'Daws are being difficult', he spoke the words, 'O God, give guidance to Daws and bring them.'"'"

Al-Bukhārī related this from Abū Nuʿaym, from Sufyān al-Thawrī.

Imām Aḥmad also stated, "Yazīd related to us, Muḥammad b. ʿAmr informed us, from Abū Salama, from Abū Hurayra, God be pleased with him, as follows, 'Al-Ṭufayl b. ʿAmr al-Dawsī arrived with his companions and they said, "O Messenger of God, Daws are being disobedient and difficult; say a prayer for them."'"

Abū Hurayra said, "And so the Messenger of God (ṢAAS) raised up his hands and I commented, 'Well, Daws are destroyed!' But he spoke, 'O God, give guidance to Daws and bring them (to Islam).'"

The chain of authorities for this is excellent, but the (other) scholars did not narrate it.

The Imām Aḥmad stated, "Sulaymān b. Ḥarb related to us, quoting Ḥammād b. Zayd, from Ḥajjāj al-Ṣawwāf, from Abū al-Zubayr, from Jābir, that al-Ṭufayl b. ʿAmr al-Dawsī came to the Prophet (ṢAAS) and said, 'O Messenger of God, don't you wish you had an impregnable, inaccessible fortress?' He replied, 'Daws had a fortress during the *jāhiliyya*.'"

The Messenger of God (ṢAAS) rejected that idea because of the rewards God had in store for the *anṣār*, "the Helpers".

"When the Prophet (ṢAAS) emigrated to al-Medina, al-Ṭufayl b. ʿAmr joined him, along with another of his people. They hated the town and (the second man, tr.) fell ill and, depressed, took an arrow head and used it to cut between his fingers. Blood streamed from his hands and did not stop until he was dead.

"Al-Ṭufayl saw the man in a dream in pleasant circumstances and observed that he had his hands covered. So he asked him, 'What did your Lord do?' He replied, 'He forgave me because I had gone to join His Prophet (ṢAAS).' Al-Ṭufayl asked, 'Why do I see you covering your hands?' He answered, 'I was told that what I had spoiled would never be restored!'"

The account continued, "And al-Ṭufayl recounted this to the Messenger of God (ṢAAS), who spoke the words, 'O God, do forgive him for his hands.'"

Muslim related this from Abū Bakr b. Abū Shayba and Isḥāq b. Ibrāhīm, both of them giving as their source an account of Ibn Ḥarb.

If it were asked, "What is the connection between this *ḥadīth* and what is established in both canonical collections from al-Ḥasan, from Jundub", he replied, "The Messenger of God (ṢAAS) replied, 'Among those who preceded you there was a man who became afflicted and depressed and so he took a knife and cut open his hand with it, the blood streaming out until he died. And God, Almighty and Glorious is He, said, "He foisted himself too hastily on Me, so I denied him paradise."'"

And so the answer could have several aspects. One is that the one man might have been a polytheist, the other a believer.

And God may have made of this one action an independent cause of his entering hell. And though his disbelief might have been self-sufficient (to confine him to hell), God none the less made reference to this act so that His people give heed. The second possibility is that the one could have been knowledgeable of what was forbidden, while the other was not, since he had so recently accepted Islam.

The third is that the one could have been doing what he did thinking it permissible, while the other did it knowing it to be impermissible, and, indeed, in error.

The fourth is that the one could have intended to kill himself by his afore-mentioned action, whereas the other, in contrast, might not have intended to kill himself but have had some other purpose.

The fifth is that the one might have been someone of few good deeds which did not measure up to the gravity of his aforementioned sin and so went to hell, while the other might have been a man of many good deeds which did equal his sin and therefore he did not go to hell but was forgiven because of his having joined the Prophet (ṢAAS).

The damage, however, did remain, though only in his hands. The rest of his form was good and he only covered the damaged part of it. And so when al-Ṭufayl b. ʿAmr saw him covering his hands and asked him what was the matter with him, he replied, "I was told that what I had spoiled would never be restored." When al-Ṭufayl told this story to the Messenger of God (ṢAAS) he prayed for him in the words, "O God, do forgive him for his hands." That is, "Do restore of them whatever was damaged."

What is certain is that God did respond to the Messenger of God (ṢAAS) concerning the companion of al-Ṭufayl b. ʿAmr.

The Story of Aʿshā b. Qays.

Ibn Hishām stated, "Khallād b. Qurra b. Khālid al-Sudūsī, and other sheikhs of Bakr b. Wāʾil told me, from certain scholars, that Aʿshā b. Qays b. Thaʿlaba b.ʿUkāba b. Ṣaʿb b. ʿAlī b. Bakr b. Wāʾil went to see the Messenger of God (ṢAAS) intending to accept Islam. He spoke the following verses in praise of the Messenger of God (ṢAAS),

'Did your eyes not close that night, O bleary-eyed one? You lay awake all night through restlessness.

And the sleeplessness was not for love of a woman, for before that you had forgotten your lover of Mahdad,

But I see that fate, that traitor, spoils what my hands restore.

I have thus lost age, youth and wealth, for by God this fate, how it changes!

I have constantly pursued wealth throughout my progression from childhood to youth to maturity to old age.

Daily I raced fast red-grey camels across the distance between al-Nujayr and Ṣarkhada.

O you enquiring where she has gone, she has an appointment with the people of Yathrib.

And if you enquire about me, then (know that) there are many kind-hearted ones who ask about Aʿshā, enquiring where he went.

My mount stretches her swift legs and draws them back, carefully turning out her hooves, not splaying them.

Sprightly she is, even in noonday heat, when you would imagine even the afternoon chameleon bending its neck.

I swore I'd not assuage her fatigue nor her sore feet until she reached Muḥammad.

When she should kneel at Ibn Hāshim's door, only then would it rest and receive, through his munificence, some generosity.

(He is) a prophet who sees what you do not, whose fame, I swear, has spread high and low in the land.

He has gifts and favours that do not end, and his giving today does not prevent him giving tomorrow.

Did you not, I repeat, hear the advice of Muḥammad, the Prophet of God, when he preached and testified?

If you did not travel with cargo of piety and after death met with others who have done so,

You will surely regret not being like them; so, therefore, prepare for a fate that is definitely arranged.

Beware of carrion; do not approach it, and do not take the share of that which some weapon has already allotted (to others)

And do not venerate raised monuments, nor worship idols, but pray to God alone.

Do not go near a free woman; her privacy is forbidden you; marry or be celibate.

Do not cut off ties with your relatives for some motive, nor take them as captives under restraint.

And glorify God at evening and at morning; do not praise the devil; praise only God. Do not ridicule those suffering poverty, and do not consider wealth man's way to eternity.'"

Ibn Hishām stated, "And when al-A^cshā was in Mecca or near thereto, some Quraysh polytheists stopped him and asked what business he had there. He told them that he had come seeking the Messenger of God (ṢAAS).

"One of the Quraysh commented, 'But Abū Baṣīr, he is forbidding sex!' Al-A^cshā responded, 'I swear, that's no desire of mine.'

"'But he's also forbidding wine,' the man objected.

"'Well, that's something I do hold dear; I'll go off and have my fill of it for a year, then I'll come back and accept Islam!'

"And leave he did. But he died that same year without returning to the Messenger of God (ṢAAS)."

Thus does Ibn Hishām tell this story here. He extracts a great deal from Muḥammad Ibn Isḥāq, God bless him, and this is one thing added to his account by Ibn Hishām, God bless him!

Wine was not in fact forbidden in Medina until after the fighting with the Banū al-Naḍīr, as will be explained hereafter.

It is apparent that the decision of al-A^cshā to accept Islam was taken only after the migration. There is evidence for this in his poetry. One verse reads,

"O you enquiring where she has gone, she has an appointment with the people of Yathrib."

It would have been more appropriate for Ibn Hishām to have recounted this anecdote within material relating to the post-migration period, rather than here. But God knows best.

Al-Suhaylī stated, "This is an error on the part of Ibn Hishām and those who follow him, for everyone agrees that use of wine was only prohibited in Medina after the battle of Uḥud."

He has also stated, "It is said that the person who spoke to al-A^cshā was Abū Jahl b. Hishām in the house of ^cUtba b. Rabī^ca."

Abū ^cUbayda, however, related that the one who spoke to him thus was ^cĀmir b. al-Ṭufayl in Qays territory while he was on his way to the Messenger of God (ṢAAS).

He stated, "And his saying '... then I will come to him and accept Islam' definitely does not bring him out of a state of disbelief. But God knows best."

Ibn Ishāq at this point recounted the story of the man from Irāsh and how he appealed to the Messenger of God (SAAS) against Abū Jahl over the price of a camel he had sold him, and how God abased Abū Jahl and forced him to make payment for it at the agreed time.

We recounted this in the material relating to the beginning of the revelation and the consequent harm done by the polytheists.

The Story of the contest with Rukāna and how the Prophet (SAAS) showed him a tree that he summoned and it came to him.

Ibn Ishāq quoted his father, Ishāq b. Yasār, as having related to him as follows: "Rukāna b. ʿAbd Yazīd b. Hāshim b. al-Muṭṭalib b. ʿAbd Manāf was the strongest man of Quraysh.

"Once he was alone in one of the defiles of Mecca with the Messenger of God (SAAS), who asked him, 'Rukāna, won't you fear God and accept my invitation to you?'

"He replied, 'If I knew that what you say is true, I would follow you.'

"The Messenger of God (SAAS) then asked him, 'If I were to wrestle you down would you know that what I say is true?'

"'Yes, I would,' Rukāna replied.

"'Come on then, let's wrestle,' the Messenger of God (SAAS) said.

"And so Rukāna did wrestle with him and when the Messenger of God (SAAS) went after him, he threw him down, powerless.

"Rukāna then said, 'Another round, Muhammad!'

"Once again he threw him. Rukāna then said, 'Muhammad, I swear, Muhammad, this is amazing! Can you really throw me?'

"He replied, 'I'll show you something even more amazing, if you like, if you will fear God and follow me.'

"'What is it?'

"'I'll call out to that tree you see and it will come to me.'

"'Call for it then.'

"He did so and it came and stood there right before the Messenger of God (SAAS). Then he told it, 'Go back to your place!' And it did so.

"And so Rukāna went to his people and told them, 'O Banū ʿAbd Manāf, you could have your man compete in magic with the whole world. I swear I've never seen a better magician than him.' He then recounted to them what he had seen and what he had done."

Ibn Ishāq related this story thus, with an incomplete line of transmission.

Abū Dāʾūd al-Tirmidhī related, from an account of Abū al-Hasan al-ʿAskalānī, from Abū Jaʿfar b. Muhammad b. Rukāna, from his father, Rukāna, who said he had wrestled the Prophet (SAAS) who had defeated him. Then al-Tirmidhī commented, "Strange! We know nothing of Abū al-Hasan, nor of Rukāna's son."

My comment is that Abū Bakr al-Shāfiʿī related, with an excellent chain of authorities, from Ibn ʿAbbās, God bless them both, that Yazīd b. Rukāna wrestled the Messenger of God (ṢAAS) who threw him three times, each time for a wager of 100 sheep. The third time Rukāna said, "Muḥammad, no one has ever put my back on the ground before you, and no one was more hateful in my sight before this than you! I testify that there is no god but God, and that you are the Messenger of God." At that the Messenger of God (ṢAAS) stood up from him and gave him back his sheep.

As for the story of his calling out to the tree and its going to him, many accounts of that, from several excellent sources, will appear in the chapter on "Proofs of Prophethood" after this biography, if God wills it, and in Him is our trust.

Earlier on, it was reported from Abū al-Ashdīn that he (Rukāna) wrestled the Prophet (ṢAAS) who threw him.

After this Ibn Isḥāq related the story of the arrival in Mecca of the Christians from Abyssinia, some 20 riders in number. They all embraced Islam. We gave this earlier, after the story of the Negus. And to God be all praise and credit.

Ibn Isḥāq stated, "The Messenger of God (ṢAAS) used to have some of his most vulnerable Companions sit close by him in the mosque, such Muslims as Khabbāb, ʿAmmār, Abū Fukayha Yāsar, the freed-man of Ṣafwān b. Umayya and Ṣuhayb. Quraysh would ridicule these people, telling one another, 'These are his companions, as you see, but has God really chosen them from among us to receive guidance and the true religion? If what Muḥammad brought were any good, they would not have joined him first; God would certainly not have put them before us.'"

And so God, Almighty and Glorious is He, revealed, "Do not drive away those who pray to their Lord morning and night seeking His face. You are not accountable for them in the least, nor are they for you. If you repulse them you will be acting unjustly. Thus have we put some to the test through others, so that they would say, 'Are they those of us whom God has favoured?' 'Does God not know best who gives thanks?' And when those who believe in our revelation come to you then say, 'Peace be upon you; your Lord has prescribed for Himself mercy so that if one of you does wrong in ignorance, then later repents and reforms – He is indeed merciful, forgiving'" (*sūrat al-Anʿām*; VI, v.52-4).

He went on: "The Messenger of God (ṢAAS) used often to sit at al-Marwa near the shop of a young Christian named Jabr, a slave of the Banū al-Hadramī. People would say, 'By God, it is merely Jabr who teaches Muḥammad most of what he says!'

"And so God Almighty revealed about their saying that, 'It is merely some mortal who teaches him. The language of him to whom they allude is foreign; yet this language is plain Arabic'" (*sūrat al-Naḥl*; XVI, v.105).

Then Ibn Isḥāq recounts how *sūrat al-Kawthar* (CVIII) was revealed concerning al-ʿĀṣ b. Wāʾil when he said of the Messenger of God (ṢAAS), "He is without a male child, that is, he has no male offspring. If he dies, memory of him will be gone." And so God Almighty stated, "He who hates you shall be childless." That is, he would not be remembered after his death, even if he were to have thousands of offspring. For remembrance, reputation and credibility do not depend on multiplicity of children and offspring. We discussed this *sūrat* in our *Tafsīr* (*Exegesis*). And to God be all praise.

It has been related from Abū Jaʿfar al-Bāqir that al-ʿĀṣ b. Wāʾil said the above following the death of al-Qāsim, the son of the Prophet (ṢAAS). He had reached an age when he could ride a mule and sit on a thoroughbred mount.

Ibn Isḥāq then related the revelation of the verse "… and they say, 'Now if only an angel had been sent down to him.' If We had sent down an angel, it would all have been finished!" (*sūrat al-Anʿām*; VI, v.8).

This referred to Ubayy b. Khalaf, Zamʿa b. al-Aswad, al-ʿĀṣ b. Wāʾil and al-Naḍr b. al-Ḥārith having said, "If only God had sent down for you an angel to tell the people about you."

Ibn Isḥāq stated, "The Messenger of God (ṢAAS), so we have been told, passed by al-Walīd b. al-Mughīra, Umayya b. Khalaf and Abū Jahl b. Hishām, and they insulted and mocked him. This angered him, and at that God Almighty revealed about them, 'Prophets before you were mocked, but it was their mocking that trapped them'" (*sūrat al-Anʿām*; VI, v.10).

I observe that God Almighty also stated, "Prophets before you were mocked. Yet they bore with fortitude the falsehoods and persecutions until Our help came to them. No one can change the words of God. And you have received information about the messengers sent" (*sūrat al-Anʿām*; VI, v.34). And the Almighty also said, "We will protect you against those who mock" (*sūrat al-Ḥajar*; XV, v.95).

Sufyān stated, quoting Jaʿfar b. Iyyās, from Saʿīd b. Jubayr, from Ibn ʿAbbās, that the "mockers" consisted of al-Walīd b. al-Mughīra, al-Aswad b. ʿAbd Yaghūth al-Zuhrī, al-Aswad b. al-Muṭṭalib Abū Zamʿa, al-Ḥārith b. ʿAyṭil, and al-ʿĀṣ b. Wāʾil al-Sahmī and that: "Gabriel came to him and the Messenger of God (ṢAAS) complained to him about them, pointing out al-Walīd. And so Gabriel gestured to his fingertips and said, 'So much for him!'

"He then pointed out to him al-Aswad b. al-Muṭṭalib and Gabriel gestured towards his neck, saying, 'So much for him!'

"He then pointed out al-Aswad b. ʿAbd Yaghūth and Gabriel gestured to his head, saying, 'So much for him!'

"He then pointed to al-Ḥārith b. Ayṭil and Gabriel gestured to his stomach, saying, 'So much for him!'

"Then al-ʿĀṣ b. Wāʾil passed by and Gabriel gestured towards the sole of his foot, saying, 'So much for him!'

"As for Al-Walīd, he later stopped by a man from Khuzāʿa who was mounting feathers on an arrow for him, but the arrow struck his fingertips and severed them.

"Al-Aswad b. ʿAbd Yaghūth had ulcers grow out of his head, and he died of them.

"Al-Aswad b. al-Muṭṭalib went blind. The cause of that was that he once dismounted under a gum tree and began calling out, 'O Son, help, can't you protect me! I'm dead!' His companions responded that they could see nothing, but he repeated, 'O Son, can't you protect me? I'm perishing! I'm being pricked with thorns in my eyes!' Again they said they saw nothing, but he kept saying the same until his eyes were blind.

"Al-Ḥārith b. ʿAyṭil was afflicted with yellow bile in his stomach until his excrement emerged from his mouth and he died of that.

"Al-ʿĀṣ b. Wāʾil one day had a thorn enter his head and caused it to be filled (with pus), and he died of this."

Others, however, narrate this account thus: "... and he rode to Ṭāʾif on a donkey that let him down on to a thorn and it pierced the sole of his foot and killed him."

Al-Bayhaqī related this tradition in much the same way.

Ibn Isḥāq stated, "The chief men who engaged in ridicule, as I was told by Yazīd b. Rawmān, from ʿUrwa b. al-Zubayr, were five in number. They were all men of maturity and highly regarded among their people. The Messenger of God (ṢAAS) spoke a curse against al-Aswad b. al-Muṭṭalib Abū Zamʿa: 'O God, blind his sight and make him bereft of his son!'

"The others were al-Aswad b. ʿAbd Yaghūth, al-Walīd b. al-Mughīra, al-ʿĀṣ b. Wāʾil, and al-Ḥārith b. al-Ṭalāṭil."

He also recounted that Almighty God revealed about them, "Announce what you have been ordered, and turn aside from the polytheists. We will take care of the mockers for you, those who establish another god alongside God. They shall learn!" (sūrat al-Ḥajar, XV, v.94–6).

He related, "Gabriel came to the Messenger of God (ṢAAS), while these men were circumambulating the kaʿba. Gabriel stood up, the Messenger of God (ṢAAS) at his side, while al-Aswad b. al-Muṭṭalib went by. Gabriel threw a green leaf into his face and he became blind.

"Al-Aswad b. ʿAbd Yaghūth next passed and Gabriel pointed at his stomach. It became swollen and so he died of dropsy.

"Al-Walīd b. al-Mughīra went by and Gabriel pointed at the scar of a wound at the base of his ankle that he had suffered years before when he had passed by a man of Khuzāʿa re-feathering an arrow, the head of which had caught on his robe and slightly cut him. After this, however, it burst open and so he died.

"Al-ʿĀṣ b. Wāʾil passed and Gabriel pointed to the underside of his foot. Al-ʿĀṣ later left on a donkey for Ṭāʾif. The donkey threw him on to a thorn which pierced his foot and killed him.

"Al-Ḥārith b. al-Ṭalāṭil went by and Gabriel pointed at his head. It filled with pus and so killed him."

Ibn Isḥāq then stated, "When al Walīd b. al-Mughīra felt the approach of death he made a request of his three sons Khālid, Hishām, and al-Walīd by name. He told them, 'Sons, I charge you with three tasks. My blood is on Khuzāʿa, and do not leave it unrevenged. I well know that they are innocent of it, but I fear that you may be maligned by it later. Thaqīf have debts owing me. Don't leave them alone until you get paid. And my dowry money is with Abū Uzayhir al-Dawsī; don't let him keep it from you.' Abū Uzayhir had married al-Walīd to a daughter of his but later had kept her from him and had not let him in to her up to the time he died. And he had taken the money al-Walīd had paid for her, which was her dowry.

"When he died the Banū Makhzūm hastened to Khuzāʿa seeking from them blood money for al-Walīd. They said, 'It was an arrow of one of your men that killed him!' Khuzāʿa refused and they spoke angry poetry against one another, and the situation deteriorated greatly between them. But then Khuzāʿa did pay some of the blood-money, and they made peace and reconciled."

Ibn Isḥāq stated, "Then Hishām b. al-Walīd attacked and killed Abū Uzayhir while he was at the Dhū al-Majāz market.

"He was a chief of his tribe and his daughter was Abū Sufyān's wife. This happened after the battle of Badr. Yazīd b. Abū Sufyān went out and gathered his men against the Banū Makhzūm since his father was then absent. When Abū Sufyān returned he was angered by what his son Yazīd had done and berated and struck him for it. He then paid the blood price for Abū Uzayhir and told his son, 'Did you plan to have Quraysh kill one another over one man from Daws?'

"Ḥassān b. Thābit wrote an ode goading Abū Sufyān over the spilling of Abū Uzayhir's blood. Regarding this poem, Abū Sufyān commented, 'It's a really bad idea of Ḥassān that we should kill one another, now, after our chiefs died at the battle of Badr.'

"When Khālid b. al-Walīd accepted Islam and was present at Ṭāʾif with the Messenger of God (ṢAAS), he asked the latter for payment of the interest due his father from the people of Ṭāʾif."

Ibn Isḥāq went on, "Some scholars informed me that the following verses were revealed about this, 'O you who believe, fear God and give up whatever interest payments are due, if you are indeed believers'" (sūrat al-Baqara; II; v.278).

Ibn Isḥāq stated, "And we know of no vengeance taken by Abū Uzayhir's people up to when Islam put an end to conflict between these men. Although Ḍirār b. al-Khaṭṭāb b. Mirdās al-Aslamī left with a group of Quraysh men into Daws territory. There they stayed with a woman named Umm Ghaylān, a freed-woman of Daws. She would comb the women's hair and prepare brides for marriage. The Daws wanted to kill the Quraysh for killing Abū Uzayhir, but Umm Ghaylān and some women who were with her stood in their way and protected the Quraysh men."

Al-Suhaylī said, "It is said that she hid him inside her clothing."

Ibn Hishām said, "In the days when 'Umar b. al-Khaṭṭāb ruled, Umm Ghaylān came to him, believing that Dirār was his brother. 'Umar told her, 'I am only his brother in Islam. I know of your favour to him. He gave her a gift as though she were a traveller.'"

He went on, "Dirār b. al-Khaṭṭāb met up with 'Umar b. al-Khaṭṭāb at the battle of Uḥud, and began striking him with the flat of his spear, saying, 'Save yourself, Ibn al-Khaṭṭāb, I shall not kill you!' 'Umar thus acknowledged this act of his after Islam. God bless them both.

DIVISION

Al-Bayhaqī related at this point the imprecation of the Prophet (ṢAAS) against Quraysh when they withheld from him, resulting in seven years similar to the seven in Joseph's case.

His account tallies with those in the *ṣaḥīḥ* collections narrated through al-A'mash, from Muslim b. Ṣubayḥ, from Masrūq, from Ibn Mus'ūd. He (the Prophet (ṢAAS)) said, "Five things have come to pass; *al-lizām*, the punishment, the Romans, the 'smoke,' the conflict, and the moon."

There is an account from Ibn Mus'ūd saying, "When Quraysh rejected the Messenger of God (ṢAAS), and refrained from accepting Islam, he (the Prophet (ṢAAS)) said, 'O God, bring down upon Quraysh for me the seven years like those for Joseph!'"

The account went on, "And they were afflicted for a year until everything was completely ruined. They were reduced to eating carrion, and some, out of hunger, hallucinated so that they would imagine seeing smoke all the way to the heavens. Then he prayed, and God gave them relief. 'Abd Allāh (b. Mus'ūd) thereafter recited the following verse, 'We are withdrawing from you the punishment for a while; but you will revert' (*sūrat al-Dukhān*; XLIV, v.15). They did revert and disbelieved, and so were put off till Judgement Day. Or he said, 'and they were put off till the battle of Badr.' 'Abd Allāh said, 'If the reference were really to Judgement Day, he would not have exposed them to the words, '... the day when we confront them with the great conflict. We will take revenge!' (*sūrat al-Dukhān*; XLIV, v.16). He said, 'At the battle of Badr.'

In (another) account from him, he said, "When the Messenger of God (ṢAAS) saw the people backing away, he said, 'O God, (inflict) seven years (of calamity) like those of Joseph.' And so they suffered a year so bad that they ate carrion, leather and bones. Abū Sufyān and other Meccans came to him and said, 'O Muḥammad, you claim to have been given your mission of mercy. Here your people are perishing. Pray to God for them.'

"And so the Messenger of God (ṢAAS) did say a prayer and profuse rain descended on them. It poured down on them for seven days and people complained about the volume of rain. And so he said the words, 'O God, around us, but not upon us!' The clouds were then withdrawn from above his head, and the people around them were watered."

He said, "The verse of *sūrat al-Dukhān* was mentioned earlier and it referred to the starvation that had afflicted them. This refers to God's statement, 'We are withdrawing from you the punishment for a while; but you will revert.' And the verses of *sūrat al-Rūm* (XXX), and those referring to the 'grievous hold' (of *sūrat al-Dukhān*; XLIV, v.16), and the 'splitting of the moon' (of *sūrat al-Qamar*; LIV, v.1), all came true at the battle of Badr."

Al-Bayhaqī stated, "What he means, though God alone knows best, is that the 'grievous hold', 'the smoke' and the verse relating to the *lizām*, God's punishment, all these (prophecies) came true at the battle of Badr."

He said, "Al-Bukhārī made reference to this account. He then mentioned it through 'Abd al-Razzāq from Ma'mar, from Ayyūb, from 'Ikrima, from Ibn 'Abbās, in the words, 'Abū Sufyān came to the Messenger of God (ṢAAS) seeking relief from the hunger because they had nothing to eat, even consuming spoiled meat. God Almighty then revealed the words, 'We brought punishment down on them, but they would not submit to their Lord, nor were they humble' (*sūrat al-Mu'minūna*; XXIII, v.76). And so the Messenger of God (ṢAAS) said a prayer for them, so that God gave them relief."

The *ḥāfiẓ* al-Bayhaqī stated, "There is given in the story relating to Abū Sufyān material suggesting that it applied to the period after the migration. Perhaps it happened twice. God knows best."

Division

Then al-Bayhaqī related the story of the Persians and the Byzantines and Almighty God's revelation of the verses: "Alif. Lam. Mīm. The Byzantines have been defeated in the neighbouring territory, yet after their defeat they will overcome, after a few years. God makes the decision, both before and after. And on a certain day the believers will rejoice at God's assistance. God assists whomever He wishes, for He is the Almighty, the Merciful" (*sūrat al-Rūm*; XXX, v.2).

He then related through Sufyān al-Thawrī, from Ḥabīb b. Abū 'Amr, from Sa'īd b. Jubayr, from Ibn 'Abbās, who said, "The Muslims would have liked the Byzantines to be victorious over the Persians because the former were the 'People of the Book'. The polytheists wanted the Persians to overcome the Byzantines because the former were idol worshippers. The Muslims mentioned this to Abū Bakr, who spoke about it with the Prophet (ṢAAS). The latter commented, 'They will prevail.' Abū Bakr related this to the polytheists who said, 'Set a term for us and if they do prevail, then you get so-and-so while if our side wins we get so-and-so.' Abū Bakr then related this to the Prophet (ṢAAS), who said, 'So now I've made it a wager!' He went on, 'In less than ten (days).' And thereafter the Byzantines were victorious."

We gave various lines of transmission for this *ḥadīth* in our *Tafsīr (Exegesis)* and recounted that the one who engaged in the wager with Abū Bakr was Umayya b. Khalaf, that the bet was for five young ostriches and that it had a time limit. To this "the Trusting", Abū Bakr, made an increased bet on the orders of the Messenger of God (ṢAAS). The victory did go to the Byzantines over the Persians and it occurred on the day the battle of Badr was fought. Or it may have been the day of the Ḥudaybiyya truce. God knows best.

It is also related through al-Walīd b. Muslim, who said, "Usayd al-Kilābī related to us that he heard al-ʿAlā> b. al-Zubayr al-Kilābī relate from his father, as follows, 'I saw the victory of the Persians over the Byzantines and then that of the Byzantines over the Persians. I then saw the victory of the Muslims over both Rome and Persia, and their conquering of Syria and Iraq. And all of that over a period of 15 years!'"

Section: Concerning the isrā>, *the night journey, of the Messenger of God (ṢAAS) from Mecca to Jerusalem, his ascent from there to heaven, and the signs he saw there.*

Ibn ʿAsākir related traditions about the night journey in materials telling of the early beginnings of the mission. Ibn Isḥāq, however, gave them in this location, some ten years after the mission.

Al-Bayhaqī related, through Mūsā b. ʿUqba, from al-Zuhrī whom he quoted as saying, "The Messenger of God (ṢAAS) was taken on the night journey one year prior to his departure to Medina."

He said, "And Ibn Lahīʿa related it thus, from Abū al-Aswad, from ʿUrwa."

Also, Al-Ḥākim related, from al-Aṣamm, from Aḥmad b. ʿAbd al-Jabbār, from Yūnus b. Bukayr, from Asbāṭ b. Naṣr, from Ismāʿīl al-Suddī, who said, "The five daily prayers were enjoined upon the Messenger of God (ṢAAS) at Jerusalem the night of his journey there, 16 months prior to his emigration."

According to al-Suddī's statement, then, the night journey occurred in the month of Dhū al-Qaʿda, whereas the reports of al-Zuhrī and ʿUrwa place it in Rabīʿ al-Awwal.

Abū Bakr b. Abū Shayba stated, "ʿUthmān related to us, from Saʿīd b. Mīnā>, that Jābir and Ibn ʿAbbās said, 'The Messenger of God (ṢAAS) was born in the year of the elephant, Monday the 12th of Rabīʿ al-Awwal, and on that same day and month he was appointed Prophet, was taken up to heaven, emigrated, and died.'"

The chain of transmission of the aforementioned *ḥadīth* is flawed. The *ḥāfiz* ʿAbd al-Ghanī b. Surūr al-Maqdisī, however, included it in his biography, and he also quoted a tradition whose chain of authorities is unsound. We made mention of it in the material relating to the virtues of the month of Rajab. This tradition states that the night journey took place on the night of the 27th of Rajab. But God knows best.

There are some who claim that the night journey took place on the first Friday night of Rajab, this having been the "night of the *al-raghā'ib*", the night of the great gifts, wherein the common system of prayer was first established. But there is no foundation for that. But God knows best. Some recite the following line concerning this:

> "It was a Friday night when the Prophet was made to ascend, the night of Friday, the first of Rajab."

This poetry is somewhat weak, but we have quoted it merely as testimonial for those who maintain this.

We gave reference to the traditions relating to this in detail regarding God's words, "Glory be to Him who carried His worshipper on a journey by night from the *masjid al-ḥarām*, the 'sacrosanct mosque', to the *masjid al-aqṣā*, the 'further mosque', whose precincts We had blessed that We may show him Our signs. He it is who hears all, sees all" (*sūrat al-Isrā'*; XVII, v.1).

Let us then record herewith the lines of authority and the sources and the support for or criticism of these. This will be convincing and sufficient in itself. And all praise and credit goes to God.

We will give here the gist of the words of Ibn Isḥāq, God bless him. Having recounted the earlier sections, he went on, "Then the Messenger of God (ṢAAS) was taken by night from the *masjid al-ḥarām* to the *masjid al-aqṣā*, the latter being the holy temple of Aelia. By then Islam had spread in Mecca into Quraysh and all the Arab tribes."

He continued, "Concerning the night journey of the Messenger of God (ṢAAS), I learned what follows from a *ḥadīth* that came down from Ibn Musʿūd, Abū Saʿīd, ʿĀʾisha, Muʿāwiya, Umm Hāniʾ, daughter of Abū Ṭālib, God bless them all, and al-Ḥasan b. Abū al-Ḥasan, Ibn Hishām al-Zuhrī, Qatāda and other scholars. Individually they gave information that combines in this account.

"The night journey of the Messenger of God (ṢAAS) was filled with trials and tribulations and (instances) of God's power and authority; it provides a lesson for men of intelligence, a guidance, a mercy and an affirmation for those with faith and belief. It was certainly an act of God.

"He carried him on this journey as and how He wished, to show him those of His signs He so desired. He thus surveyed some of the might of God, His will, power and authority by which He accomplishes His purposes.

"ʿAbd Allāh b. Masʿūd would say, as I have been informed, 'The Messenger of God (ṢAAS), was brought *al-Burāq*, that being the name of a mount on which previous prophets were carried; its stride was such that it could place its hooves as far as it could see. He was borne away on it.

"His companion (Gabriel) then took him off to see the signs between heaven and earth. Eventually he reached Jerusalem, where he found Abraham, Moses and Jesus, in a company of prophets assembled for him. He led them in prayer.

"Then he was brought three vessels, containing milk, wine and water. He said that he drank the vessel of milk and was told by Gabriel, 'You have been given guidance, and so has your nation.'"

Ibn Ishāq related through al-Ḥasan al-Baṣrī, but with an incomplete line of transmission, that Gabriel woke him up then conducted him to the door of the *masjid al-ḥarām*, where he set him upon *al-Burāq*, a white mount that was a cross between a mule and a donkey; on its flanks it had wings with which it set its feet in motion. It could place its hooves as far ahead as it could see. The account quotes the Messenger of God (ṢAAS) as saying, "He placed me upon it and then took me away, he not out-distancing me, nor I him."

I may add that in the *ḥadīth*, which came down from Qatāda, as related by Ibn Ishāq, it says that when the Messenger of God (ṢAAS) was about to mount *al-Burāq*, it became restive and so Gabriel placed his hand upon its neck where the mane grows and said, "Now Burāq, aren't you ashamed to do that? I swear, no servant of God more noble than Muḥammad has ever ridden you." He commented, "And it was so ashamed it burst out in sweat, then quietened down until I mounted it."

Al-Ḥasan stated, in his *ḥadīth*, "And so the Messenger of God (ṢAAS) departed, Gabriel accompanying him, until they reached Jerusalem. There he found Abraham, Moses and Jesus among a group of prophets. The Messenger of God (ṢAAS) acted as their Imām and led them in prayer."

He then explained his choice of the vessel of milk over that of the wine, and how Gabriel told him, "You have been given guidance, as has your nation, and you have been forbidden wine."

He went on, "And then the Messenger of God (ṢAAS) departed for Mecca and set about telling Quraysh of all that."

He recounted that most of the people disbelieved him and that one group reneged after having previously accepted Islam.

Abū Bakr, "the Trusting", responded by expressing his belief and said, "I give him credence in communication from heaven, early in the day or in the evening, so how should I not believe him regarding Jerusalem?"

(In his account al-Ḥasan) recounts that Abū Bakr asked him to describe Jerusalem, and that the Messenger of God (ṢAAS) did so.

And, he states, "From that day on Abū Bakr was known as *al-Ṣiddīq*, 'the Trusting'."

Al-Ḥasan said, "And on that subject God revealed, 'And we rendered the visions we showed you nothing but a way of testing people'" (*sūrat al-Isrā²*; XVII, v.60).

Ibn Ishāq related, quoting Umm Hāni² as his source, that she said, "It was from nowhere but my home that the Messenger of God (ṢAAS) made his night journey. He slept that night after having made the final evening prayer. When it was just before dawn he woke us up and when it was morning we prayed together and he said, 'O Umm Hāni', last evening I prayed with you in this valley, then I went to Jerusalem and prayed there. And now here I am having said the morning prayer with you, as you see.'

"He then arose to leave, but I took hold of the hem of his cloak and said, 'O Messenger of God, do not make that statement to people; they will surely disbelieve you and do you harm.'

"But he replied, 'By God, I will certainly tell it to them!' And he did tell them and they did disbelieve."

Ibn Isḥāq went on (and the Prophet (ṢAAS) told the sceptical, tr.) "And the proof of this is that I passed by the caravan of such-and-such a tribe in such-and-such a valley, and the sound of the animal (al-Burāq) startled them and so one of their camels ran away. I led them to it, being then on my way to al-Shām. Then I continued on until I reached Ḍajanān, where I passed a caravan of such-and-such a tribe. I found the people asleep. They had a vessel with water in it that they had covered over with something. I took off the cover and drank the water and replaced its cover. And the proof of this is that their caravan is now making its way down from the pass at al-Tanʿīm al-Bayḍā. Leading it is an ash-coloured camel on which are two sacks, one of which is black, the other black and white.

"On hearing this, people hurried to the pass. The first camel, which was as he had described to them, was insufficient proof for them, so they asked about the vessel and the camel, and those in the caravan did tell them just as the Prophet (ṢAAS) had recounted."

Yūnus b. Bukayr related, from Asbāṭ, from Ismāʿīl al-Suddī, that the sun had almost set before that caravan arrived and so he prayed to God, Almighty and Glorious is He, who slowed it down until they came, just as he had described it to them.

He stated, "And the sun was never slowed for anyone except on that day for him, and also for Yūshaʿ (Joshua) b. Nūn."

Al-Bayhaqī related this account.

Ibn Isḥāq stated, "A source I do not doubt quoted Abū Saʿīd as having said, 'I heard the Messenger of God (ṢAAS) say, "When I had finished in Jerusalem, the *miʿrāj*, the ladder, was brought to me. Never before did I see anything finer; it is that to which your dying turn their eyes at the point of death.

"'"My companion (Gabriel) led me up it until I reached one of the gates of heaven known as the *bāb al-ḥāfiẓa*, 'the guards' gate'. It is overseen by an attendant who is an angel, and his name is Ismāʿīl. He commands 12,000 angels, each of whom controls 12,000 more."'

"He (Abū Saʿīd) stated, 'The Messenger of God (ṢAAS) whenever he tells this *ḥadīth* recites, "And no one but He knows the armies of your Lord"'" (*sūrat al-Muddaththir*, LXXIV, v.34).

He then recounted the remainder of the *hadīth* and it is very lengthy. We gave it in full with all its lines of transmission in our *Tafsīr* (*Exegesis*), and discussed it there. It is one of the strangest of *hadīths*, and there is some weakness in its line of transmission.

The same is true of the text of the *hadīth* of Umm Hāni'. What is well established in the *sahīhayn* is the account of Shurayk b. Abū Nimr, from Anas, that the "night journey" took place from the mosque (the *ka'ba*), at the *hijr*, the sacred enclosure.

There are also several peculiarities in that text which we have discussed there. One such is his statement, "And this occurred before he received revelation." The fact is that their (the angels) coming on the first occasion was before he received revelation, but on that night nothing occurred. Then, on another night, the angels did come to him. So, he was not referring to the latter occasion when he said, "And that was before revelation came to him." In fact, he (Gabriel) came to him after he had received revelation.

The "night journey" certainly occurred after revelation (began), either shortly thereafter, as one group maintains, or much later, perhaps by as much as ten years, as others claim. And the latter is more likely.

The cleansing of his chest (by the angel) before the night journey was the second, or some say the third cleansing, and it was a prerequisite for the assembly on high and the Divine Presence.

He then rode upon *al-Burāq*, this being in veneration and honour of him. When he came to Jerusalem, he (Gabriel) inducted him into that circle by which the prophets were joined. He then entered Jerusalem and prayed at its prayer niche in salutation to that mosque.

Hudhayfa, God be pleased with him, denied his entry into Jerusalem, his tying up his mount, and his praying there. And this is strange. And a text that is affirmative is preferable to one that is negative.

There is also disagreement over his meeting the prophets and leading them in prayer, as to whether it was prior to his ascent to heaven, as the preceding account shows, or after his descent from there, as some accounts indicated. We will state that this latter view is to be preferred. But God knows best.

It is also said that his prayer with the prophets took place in heaven. Also there is disagreement over whether his making a choice between the vessels of milk, wine and water occurred in Jerusalem, as given above, or in heaven, as established in authentic traditions.

What is implied is that when the Messenger of God (ṢAAS) finished in Jerusalem the *mi'rāj*, the ladder, was set up for him; this was the ladder he used to ascend to heaven. The ascent was not upon *al-Burāq*, as some people imagine. *Al-Burāq* was tethered at the door of the mosque in Jerusalem to take him back to Mecca.

He rose one heaven to another on the ladder until he passed over the seventh heaven. Whenever he reached a heaven its favoured attendants and the most important angels and prophets therein would meet him.

He made reference to major persons from among the *mursalīn*, the messengers of God, like Adam in the nearest heaven, John and Jesus in the second, Idrīs in the fourth, Moses in the sixth, and Abraham in the seventh, leaning his back against the *bayt al-maʿmur*, the "eternal abode", that is entered each day by 70,000 angels who worship therein in prayer and circumambulation, and they do not return there again until Judgement Day.

He then ascended above their ranks and reached a level where the squeaking of pens could be heard.[7] There the *sidrat al-muntahā*, the "lote tree at the boundary",[8] stood high before the Messenger of God (ṢAAS); its leaves were like the ears of an elephant, its fruit like summits of Mt. Hidjr, and covered all about by great deeds and many splendid colours, with angels perching upon it as numerous as starlings on a tree. And there was a canopy of gold, bathed in the light of our Lord, All-Glorious is He.

There also he saw Gabriel, peace be upon him. He had upon him 600 wings with the space between each two wings as great as that between heaven and earth. It is Gabriel of whom God Almighty spoke thus: "And he certainly saw him in another revelation, at the *sidrat al-muntahā*, at which is the garden of eternity. When the tree was shrouded in its covering, sight did not turn aside, nor did it exceed its bound" (*sūrat al-Najm*; LIII, v.13–17). That is, it (i.e. sight, tr.) did not turn aside to the right or to the left, nor did it look up at that which was out of bounds.

This was both tremendous fortitude (on the part of Muḥammad) and a great show of respect (for God).

This second vision (that he had) of Gabriel, peace be upon him, in the natural form in which God created him, is in accord with the statements transmitted by Ibn Musʿūd, Abū Hurayra, Abū Dharr and ʿĀʾisha, God be pleased with them all.

The first vision (that Muḥammad had of Gabriel) was, in the words of the Almighty, when, "(an) all-powerful (angel) taught him, the one endowed with supreme power, who (appeared) in his natural form while in the highest point on the horizon. He then drew near and came close, until he was two bow lengths away, or closer. Then he made his revelation to His servant" (*sūrat al-Najm*; LIII, v.6–10).

That took place at al-Abṭaḥ.[9] Gabriel stretched out over the Messenger of God (ṢAAS), the enormity of his being dominating all between earth and sky, until there was only the space of a bow's length or two between them both.

---

7. A reference to the Islamic belief that angels, working as scribes in the service of God, record the fate and destiny of the universe as dictated to them by Him.

8. A tree believed to be positioned to the right side of God's throne.

9. The name of a place near Mecca.

This is what is authentic in the exegesis, as is affirmed by the words of the eminent Companions mentioned heretofore, God be pleased with them all. As for Shurayk's comment about Anas concerning the tradition relating to the night journey, "and then *al-Jabbār*, the Omnipotent, the Lord of Glory drew close and descended, becoming as close as a bow's length or two," this might be the understanding of the reciter, and so he inserted it into the *ḥadīth*. But God knows best.

Even if this interpretation is correctly preserved, it is no interpretation of the holy verse, but relates to something quite different from that at issue. But God knows best.

It was on that night that God Almighty and Glorious enjoined the daily prayers upon His servant Muḥammad (God's peace and blessings be upon him and upon his nation); these were to number fifty prayers each day and night. Thereafter he repeatedly went between Moses and his Lord, Almighty and Glorious is He, until finally the Lord, All Resplendent is He, and to Him is all credit due, decreed that they be five. He stated, "They are five and (yet) they are fifty, credit being ten times the number."

That evening speech came to him directly from the Lord, Almighty and Glorious is He. The Imāms of the orthodox faith are unanimous regarding this. They differ regarding his seeing Him. Some consider that he saw God twice, in his heart. Ibn 'Abbās and his adherents maintain this. Ibn 'Abbās generalized (in discussion) about the vision, but others have offered a more narrow interpretation.

Those who spoke in general terms about the vision include Abū Hurayra and Aḥmad b. Ḥanbal, God be pleased with them.

Some authorities, however, state their conviction that the vision was by means of his eyes.

Ibn Jarīr preferred this and insisted upon it, being followed in this by others of the more recent authorities.

Among those considering that the sight occurred through the naked eyes included Sheikh Abū al-Ḥasan al-Ash'arī, as reported by al-Suhaylī and it is the preferred view of Sheikh Abū Zakariyyā' al-Nawawī in his *fatāwa*,[10] his legal decisions.

One faction maintains that the vision never occurred, because of the *ḥadīth* in the *ṣaḥīḥ* collection of Muslim, from Abū Dharr. It states, "I said, 'O Messenger of God, did you see your Lord?' He replied, 'A light! How could I have seen it!' In another account the words are, 'I saw a light'."

These scholars say that the sight of the Everlasting could never be through eyes that are ephemeral.

Therefore God Almighty said to Moses, as is reported in certain holy texts, "O Moses, no mortal being can see me until he dies, nor any dry thing until it moves."

10. The plural of *fatwa*, a term used to denote the pronouncements of a *muftī*, one who delivers formal legal opinions.

The dispute over this question perplexed the early scholars just as it does those who succeeded them. God alone knows best.

Then the Messenger of God (ṢAAS) came back down to Jerusalem. And it seems clear that the prophets descended with him to express their respect for him on his return from the glorious Divine Presence, as is the custom for those who visit; visitors do not assemble with others before meeting that person to whom they have been summoned.

That is why when he passed by one of them Gabriel would say, as each approached to greet him, "This is so-and-so; greet him."

If he had met with them before his ascent he would not have needed introduction to them a second time.

Substantiation for this is given in his saying, "And when it was time for the prayer, I acted as their Imām." The only time for that, then, would have been the dawn prayer. He came forward as their Imām on the instruction of Gabriel, relaying what his Lord, Almighty and Glorious is He, told him.

Some scholars deduce from this that the most eminent Imām takes precedence over the master of the house, since Jerusalem was their (the other prophets) place of residence.

He then left there, riding on *al-Burāq*, and returned to Mecca. Next morning he was back, in a state of complete security, peace and dignity.

That night he saw such signs and things as to make anyone else who saw them, even in part, either utterly amazed or even insane.

He, however, became merely sombre, quiet that is, and was fearful that if he started to tell his people what he had seen they would have promptly disbelieved him.

And so at first he told them calmly that he had been to Jerusalem that night.

That was when Abū Jahl, God damn him, saw the Messenger of God (ṢAAS), in the sacred mosque sitting in sombre silence and spoke to him, asking, "Well, anything new?" He replied, "Yes." "What is it?" Abū Jahl asked. "I was taken this night to Jerusalem."

"To Jerusalem?"

"Yes."

Abū Jahl asked, "If I were to call your people over to you for you to tell them, would you say to them what you said to me?"

"Yes, I would," he replied.

Abū Jahl wanted to assemble Quraysh to hear that from him, and so too did the Messenger of God (ṢAAS) also want to gather them to tell them and so give them information.

Abū Jahl then said, "Come, O tribe of Quraysh!" They gathered there from their assemblies. He then said, "Well, tell your people what you told me."

The Messenger of God (ṢAAS) related to them what he had seen, that he had gone to Jerusalem that night and prayed there.

Amidst clapping and whistling of disbelief and derision at this report, the news spread quickly over Mecca.

People then went to Abū Bakr, God bless him, and told him that Muḥammad (ṢAAS) was saying such-and-such a thing.

He responded, "You are telling lies about him!"

They replied, "No, we swear it, he is saying that."

"Well," said Abū Bakr, "if he said that, he spoke the truth."

He then went to the Messenger of God (ṢAAS) who was surrounded by the pagans of Mecca, and asked him about that. He told him of it all and Abū Bakr asked him to describe Jerusalem, so that the polytheists would hear him and recognize the veracity of what he had told them. In the *ṣaḥīḥ* collection the account has it that it was the polytheists who asked the Messenger of God about that.

He said, "I then began telling them about His signs, and I became somewhat confused. And so God made Jerusalem clear to me until I could see it beyond ῾Uqayl's house, and I described it to them."

He (Ibn Isḥāq) went on, "In his description he was correct."

Ibn Isḥāq recounted the information we gave earlier about him telling them of his having passed by their caravan and of having drunk their water.

And so God provided proof for them and illuminated the straight path for them. Some did believe because of their conviction from God, while others disbelieved despite the proof they had.

As God Almighty said, "And we only made the visions we have shown you as a test for the people" (*sūrat al-Isrā᾽*; XVII, v.60). That is, they were a way of testing and trying them.

Ibn ῾Abbās said, "These were visions perceived by the eye that were shown to the Messenger of God (ṢAAS)."

This view, that of the majority of scholars both ancient and more recent, holds that the night journey was both a physical and a spiritual experience for the Messenger of God (ṢAAS). This is shown in the clear accounts of his making a journey and of his ascending on the ladder, and such-like. God therefore stated, "Glory be to Him who took his servant by night from the 'sacrosanct mosque' to the 'further mosque' whose precincts we have blessed, to show him our signs" (*sūrat al-Isrā᾽*; XVII, v.1). Such evocation of glory would only occur for truly great and extraordinary signs. And this proves that it was by both body and spirit, and the word "servant" gives expression to both of these together.

Also, if it had been a dream, the Quraysh polytheists would not have promptly expressed their disbelief and outrage. For that would not have been so important a matter. And so it shows that he did tell them that he had been taken on his night journey while awake, not asleep.

And then there is the statement of Shurayk, from Anas: "Then I awoke and found myself inside the *ḥijr*, the sacred enclosure." This is either to be considered an error of Shurayk, or it must be concluded that the movement from the one state to the other is to be noted as "wakefulness".

This will also be suggested in the *ḥadīth* from ʿĀʾisha, God bless her, when the Messenger of God (ṢAAS) went to Ṭāʾif but they disbelieved him. (In it) he said, "I returned in a state of depression, and I only came out of it at Qarn al-Thaʿālib."

Also there is the *ḥadīth* of Abū Usayd, when he brought his son to the Messenger of God (ṢAAS) for the *taḥnīk* ceremony.[11] He placed him in the lap of the Messenger of God (ṢAAS) who was engaged in conversation with the people. So Abū Usayd lifted his son up. Then the Messenger of God (ṢAAS), *istayqaẓa*, he "awoke or became aware", and did not find the boy there. He asked about him, and they said he had been lifted off; and so he named the boy *al-Mundhir*, the rooster or awakener.

This interpretation is preferable to considering it an error. But God knows best.

Ibn Isḥāq related as follows, "A member of Abū Bakr's family related to me that ʿĀʾisha, "mother of the believers", used to say, 'The body of the Messenger of God (ṢAAS), was never found to be missing, but God did journey away with his spirit.'"

He also said, "Yaʿqūb b. ʿUtba related to me as follows, 'When he was asked about the night journeys of the Messenger of God (ṢAAS), Muʿāwiya would say, "These were true visions from God."'"

Ibn Isḥāq stated, "That is not refuted by the statement of both these authorities, according to the words of al-Ḥasan, to the effect that, 'The following verse was revealed on that subject: "and We only made the signs We have shown you as a test for the people."'"

Similarly Abraham, peace be upon him, said, "O my son, I see in my sleep that I am sacrificing you" (*sūrat al-Ṣāffāt*; XXXVII, v.102). And in the *ḥadīth* literature there is the statement: "My eyes are asleep while my heart is awake."

Ibn Isḥāq stated, "God knows best which of that it was. He did go there and did see there what he saw of God Almighty, whether he was asleep or awake. All of that is, however, factual and true."

My own comment is that Ibn Isḥāq stopped at that point, having combined both possibilities in one whole. But one thing beyond doubt or disagreement is that he was certainly awake, for all the reasons given above.

It is not necessary to interpret the words of ʿĀʾisha, God bless her, that it was not his body, but his spirit that made the journey, as implying that he was asleep, as Ibn Isḥāq understood it. The journey might well have in fact occurred for his soul while he was awake and not asleep; he could have ridden *al-Burāq*, gone to Jerusalem, ascended into heaven and seen all he did while awake and not asleep.

11. This is an ancient Islamic custom of blessing a new-born by chewing dates and rubbing therewith the palate of the baby.

This may well be the purpose of ᶜĀ᾽isha, "mother of the believers", God bless her, as well as of those who agreed with her, and not what Ibn Isḥāq understood, which is that thereby they all implied that he was asleep. But God knows best.

I observe that we do not deny the occurrence of sleep visions before the experience of the night journey, as happened thereafter. For whenever he had visions they came (clearly) like the breaking of dawn. The *ḥadīth* dealing with the beginnings of revelation contained material to this effect. In such cases, what he saw when awake happen to him he had previously seen when asleep. That prior vision had been for the purpose of laying the foundation, making an introductory step, and giving him a sense of security and ease. But God knows best.

There is also disagreement among scholars over whether the night journey and the ascent took place on one night or whether each occurred on a different night. And some claim that the night journey came while he was awake and the ascent while he slept.

Al-Muhallab b. Abū Ṣufra has told, in his exegesis of al-Bukhārī's *ḥadīth* compendium, about some scholars maintaining that the night journey occurred twice, once with his spirit while he slept and once with both his body and his spirit when he was awake.

The *ḥāfiẓ* Abū al-Qāsim al-Suhaylī related this, from his teacher, the jurist Abū Bakr b. al-ᶜArabī.

Al-Suhaylī stated, "This view combines the accounts. In the *ḥadīth* of Shurayk, from Anas, are the words, 'And that related to what his heart saw while his eyes slept. His heart was not asleep.' At the end of his account the Messenger of God (ṢAAS) stated, 'Then I awoke and found myself in the *ḥijr*.'"

This was sleep. Something else would suggest wakefulness.

There are some who also claim that there were several journeys while he was awake. One scholar stated, "There were four night journeys." Some claim that some took place in Medina.

Sheikh Shihāb al-Dīn Abū Shāma, God bless him, tried to reconcile the differing interpretations of the night journey by grouping them variously. He concluded that there were three night journeys. One was from Mecca specifically to Jerusalem, mounted on *al-Burāq*. One again was from Mecca to heaven also upon *al-Burāq*, according to the *ḥadīth* of Ḥudhayfa, and one was from Mecca to Jerusalem and thereafter to heaven.

We comment that if it is merely the differences in the accounts that leads him to these three views, then the wording relating thereto differs even more than these three.

Anyone wishing to understand these matters should peruse the research materials we compiled in our book of exegesis relating to the words of the Almighty, "Glory be to Him who took his servant by night" (*sūrat al-Isrā᾽*; XVII, v.1).

Even if one concluded that such division was restricted to three possibilities relating to Jerusalem and to heaven, such mental computations have no impact on actual events. But God knows best.

It is strange that Imām Abū ʿAbd Allāh al-Bukhārī, God be pleased with him, gave the account of the night journey after recounting the death of Abū Ṭālib. He was thus in accord with Ibn Isḥāq in referring to the ascent to heaven in the later materials, but differed with him in reporting it after the death of Abū Ṭālib.

Ibn Isḥāq positioned his account of the death of Abū Bakr after the description of the night journey. But God alone knows how it really was.

This means that al-Bukhārī made a distinction between the night journey and the ascent. Each of these he therefore dealt with in a separate section.

His text reads, *Section on the night journey and the statement of God Almighty, 'Glory be to Him who took His servant by night.'*

"It was related to us by Yaḥyā b. Bukayr quoting al-Layth, from ʿUqayl, from Ibn Shihāb who said that Abū Salama b. ʿAbd al-Raḥmān related to him as follows, 'I heard Jābir b. ʿAbd Allāh say that he heard the Messenger of God (ṢAAS) say, "When Quraysh expressed their disbelief in me I was in the *ḥijr*. And God made clear Jerusalem to me and so I set about telling them its distinctive features while I viewed it."'"

Muslim, al-Tirmidhī and al-Nasāʾī related this from a *ḥadīth* of al-Zuhrī, from Abū Salama from Jābir.

Muslim, al-Nasāʾī and al-Tirmidhī also related it from a *ḥadīth* of ʿAbd Allāh b. al-Faḍl, from Abū Salama, from Abū Hurayra, from the Prophet (ṢAAS) in similar terms.

Al-Bukhārī's text goes on, *Section on the Ascent*:

"It was related to us by Hudba b. Khālid, from Hammām and Qatāda, from Anas b. Mālik, from Mālik b. Ṣaʿṣaʿa, that the Prophet (ṢAAS) related to them as follows about the night he was taken on a journey, 'While I was lying down there in the *ḥatīm*'[12] – or he may well have said the *ḥijr* – 'an apparition came to me and began cutting.' I (Mālik b. Ṣaʿṣaʿa, tr.) then heard him say, "And he split open from this to this." I asked al-Jārūd who was by my side, "What does he mean by that?" And he replied, "From the hollow of his neck down to his pubic hair." And I heard him say, from "his breastbone down to his pubic hair."'

"The Prophet (ṢAAS) went on, 'Then he withdrew my heart and a basin of gold filled with faith was brought to me. He then washed my heart and it was stuffed and replaced. After that I was brought a white mount that was smaller than a mule but larger than a donkey.'

"Al-Jārūd asked, 'Was that *al-Burāq*, Abū Ḥamza?' Anas responded, 'Yes'.

"The Prophet (ṢAAS) continued, 'It could span with its stride as far as it could see. I was mounted upon it and Gabriel led me away until he reached the lowest heaven. He asked for me to go in and a reply came, "Who is this?" "Gabriel," he replied. "And who is with you?" He replied, "Muhammad". "And

---

12. The semi-circular walled area next to the *kaʿba*.

has he been given a mission?" "Yes," Gabriel answered. "Then welcome to him! His arrival is a pleasure!"

"'And so he opened up. When I went in I found Adam therein. Gabriel said, "This is your father Adam; greet him!" I did so and he saluted me in return, saying, "Welcome to my pure son, to the pure Prophet!"

"'I was then taken up to the second heaven and when he asked to go inside, he was asked who it was. The same responses and questions as before followed and when I went in there were John and Jesus, who were cousins on the maternal side. Gabriel again introduced me and we exchanged the same greeting as with Adam.

"'Then I was taken up to the third heaven where Gabriel again asked entry and was met with the same questions and responses. When I went in, there was Joseph, whom I greeted, and I received welcome from him as before.

"'Taken to the fourth heaven, there were the same questions and responses and when I went in I found Idrīs there, exchanged greetings, and he welcomed me as before.

"'Brought up to the fifth heaven, the same questions and responses were made, and when I entered there was Aaron, with whom I exchanged greetings and from whom I received welcome.

"'Then at the sixth heaven the same questions and responses were made and when I entered, there was Moses, with whom I exchanged greetings and who made me welcome.

"'And when I went further on, he wept. When he was asked why, Moses replied, "I weep because a young man who has received his mission after me will have a greater number of his nation enter paradise than will of mine."

"'I was then taken to the seventh heaven where the same questions and responses were made. When I went in there was Abraham, with whom I exchanged greetings and who welcomed me.

"'Then I was raised up to the *sidrat al-muntahā*; there were four rivers, two open to see, two hidden. I asked Gabriel, "What is this, Gabriel?" He replied, "The two hidden rivers are those of paradise, while the two visible ones are the Nile and the Euphrates."

"'Then the *bayt al-ma°mur* was raised for me to see, wherein each day 70,000 angels enter. I was then brought a vessel of wine, another of milk, and a third of honey. I took the milk. Gabriel said, "That is *al-fiṭra*[13] that you and your nation follow."

"'Prayer was then enjoined on me, 50 prayers each day. Then I went back and when I passed by Moses, he asked, "What orders were you given?"

"'The Messenger of God (ṢAAS) replied, "I was ordered to pray 50 times each day."

"'Moses commented, "Your nation can't manage 50 prayers a day. I swear, I put people to the test before your time and I made some very severe requirements

13. The word has connotations of "God's way of creating", and therefore His plan or purpose. See the *Encyclopaedia of Islam*.

of the people of Israel. Return to your Lord and ask him for some relief for your nation."

"'And so I did return and ten prayers were lifted from me.

"'I went back to Moses, he said as he had before, I returned and ten more were removed.

"'Again back to Moses, I returned once more and ten more were removed.

"'Once more to Moses, he said as before, and I returned and was ordered to make ten prayers each day.

"'Moses then spoke as before, and again I returned and was ordered to make five prayers each day.

"'When I went back to Moses, he asked, "What were your orders?" I replied, "To make five prayers each day."

"'He commented, "Your people can't manage five prayers each day. I tried my people before your time and made severe requirements of the people of Israel. Return again and ask your Lord for some alleviation for your nation."

"'I replied, "I have already made such requests of my Lord as to make me ashamed; therefore I'd much rather accept and be satisfied." As I passed on, a voice called out to me, "I have completed my decree. I have alleviated the burden upon my servants."'"

Thus al-Bukhārī related this *hadīth* here. He also recounted it in other places of his compendium and so did Muslim, al-Tirmidhī and al-Nasāʾī through various chains from Qatāda, from Anas, from Mālik b. Ṣaʿṣaʿa.

We gave it by the account from Anas b. Malik from ʿUbay b. Kaʿb, as well as by the account of Anas from Abū Dharr. And we gave it by several paths from Anas, from the Prophet (ṢAAS).

We related all that in detail with its various chains of transmission and phraseology in our *Tafsīr* (*Exegesis*).

In this text there is no mention of Jerusalem. It is as though some of the sources omit some information because of the broad knowledge of it. Or they forgot it, or mention only what are in their views the most important matters. Sometimes they elaborate and give the entire account in detail, while at others they omit selectively to stress what they consider most useful. Those who make each account of the *isrāʾ* a separate experience, as we have indicated of some above, have strayed too far from the truth. This is so because each of these accounts includes reference to the greeting made to the prophets, and in each the Messenger of God (ṢAAS) is introduced to them. Also in each one prayer is made obligatory for him. How is it possible to claim that all these would have occurred several times? This is extremely unlikely and implausible. But God knows best.

Al-Bukhārī then stated, "Al-Ḥumaydī related to us, that Sufyān narrated to him from ʿAmr, from ʿIkrima, from Ibn ʿAbbās, who commented as follows about the words of God Almighty, 'And we only made the signs we have shown you as a test for the people.' He (Ibn 'Abbās,) said, 'These were visions seen by the eye, shown to the Messenger of God (ṢAAS) on the night he was taken to Jerusalem.' And of the *shajarat al mal'ūna*, the 'accursed tree', mentioned in the Qur'ān he said, 'It is the *al-zaqqūm* tree.'"[14]

DIVISION

On the morning following the night of his journey, Gabriel came to the Messenger of God (ṢAAS) at about noon. He then explained to him the manner of prayer and its times.

The Messenger of God (ṢAAS) told his followers to assemble and Gabriel led him in prayer all that day until the next, with the Prophet (ṢAAS) acting as the Imām of the Muslims, and following the example of Gabriel. This is told in the *hadīth* from Ibn 'Abbās and Jābir, "Gabriel led me in prayer twice at the house (of God)."[15]

He thus explained to him the two times, the beginning and the end, that is, of the five daily prayers. The expanse of time between them is called the *al-waqt al-muwassa'* the 'extended period', but he made no mention of such an extension of time for the prayer at sunset.

This is affirmed in the *hadīth* of Abū Mūsā, Burayda and 'Abd Allāh b. 'Amr, all of which are in the compendium of Muslim. Discussion of this occurs in our book *al-Aḥkām (The Regulations)*. And to God is all praise.

Also affirmed in the *hadīth* of the compendium of al-Bukhārī is the statement brought down from Ma'mar, from al-Zuhrī, from 'Urwa, from 'Ā'isha, who said, "When prayer was first prescribed it was just two *rak'āt*,[16] prostrations; this was subsequently established only for the prayer on travel, with more *rak'āt* being added for prayer when in residence."

Al-Awzā'ī related it thus, from al-Zuhrī, and al-Sha'bī gave it from Masrūq back to 'Ā'isha.

This is problematic in view of the fact that 'Ā'isha used to perform the prayer in its entirety while travelling, as also did 'Uthmān b. 'Affān. We discussed this matter with regard to God's words, "And if you journey in the world there is no blame on you if you shorten the prayer if you fear incitement from those who disbelieve" (*sūrat al-Nisā'*; IV, v.101).

Al-Bayhaqī stated, "Al-Ḥasan al-Baṣrī held the view that prayer while resident when first prescribed was made to be four *rak'āt*. He similarly referred to it, through a *hadīth* with an incomplete chain of authorities, regarding the prayer made by the Prophet (ṢAAS) on the morning after the night journey,

---

[14] A tree said to produce bitter, poisonous fruit.

[15] A reference to the *ka'ba* in Mecca.

[16] In Islam the daily prayers are made up of liturgies and physical movements that are divided into cycles each of which is called a *rak'a* (plural *rak'āt*).

namely to the effect that there should be four *rakʿāt* at midday, four in the late afternoon, three at sunset, with the prayers of the first two being recited aloud, four at night with just two being recited aloud, and two in the morning, both recited aloud."

My own view is that ʿĀʾisha may have meant that before the night journey the prayer consisted of two *rakʿāt*, recited twice, separately, and then, when the five were made compulsory they were kept the same while in residence, and that permission was given that two *rakʿāt* be prayed while travelling, as had been the case previously. Based on this explanation, there would be no controversy at all. But God knows best.

Section: Concerning the splitting of the moon in the time of the Prophet (ṢAAS).

God did provide the Messenger of God (ṢAAS) with a sign to prove the veracity of the guidance and religion of truth he brought, and that was at the time of his pointing (to the moon).

God Almighty spoke the following in His noble book, "The hour has drawn near and the moon has split asunder. And if they see a sign they turn away, saying, 'Just more trickery!' They call it deceit and follow their fancies, while all things are pre-determined" (*sūrat al-Qamar*; LIV, v.1 3).

Muslims are agreed that this did occur in the time of the Messenger of God (ṢAAS); traditions with complete lines of transmission, through numerous paths, provide decisive proof for those who examine it and comprehend it.

We will provide some of those easily available traditions, if God wills it and in Him is all faith and reliance. We detailed this in our *Tafsīr* (*Exegesis*), and there gave the various chains of authorities and differences in phraseology verbatim. Here we will refer to some aspects of these and will attribute them to well-known texts, with the power and strength from God.

That is related from Anas b. Mālik, Jubayr b. Muṭʿim, Ḥudhayfa, ʿAbd Allāh b. ʿAbbās, ʿAbd Allāh b. ʿUmar, and ʿAbd Allāh b. Masʿūd, God be pleased with them all.

Regarding the *ḥadīth* of Anas, Imām Aḥmad stated, "ʿAbd al-Razzāq related to us that Maʿmar related to him, from Qatāda, from Anas b. Mālik, who said, 'The people of Mecca asked the Prophet (ṢAAS) for a sign. And so the moon over Mecca was split twice. And he spoke the words, "The hour has drawn near and the moon has split asunder"'" (*sūrat al-Qamar*; LIV, v.1).

And Muslim related this, from Muḥammad b. Rāfiʿ from ʿAbd al-Razzāq.

This is one of the texts known as the *mursalāt al-ṣaḥāba*.[17] And it is plain that he received it from a large mass of the Companions, or from the Prophet (ṢAAS), or from everyone.

---

17. A statement of a Companion of the Prophet, and not of the Prophet himself.

Both al-Bukhārī and Muslim related this *hadīth* on a path through Shaybān. In his line of transmission al-Bukhārī added Sa'īd b. Abū 'Urūba. Muslim added Shu'ba to his. All three (sic) of them drew from Qatāda, from Anas. The tradition states that the people of Mecca asked the Messenger of God (ṢAAS) to show them a sign. He showed them the moon in two parts, so that they could see Mt. Ḥirā' between them both.

This is the phraseology of al-Bukhārī.

Regarding the traditions quoted by Jubayr b. Muṭ'im, the Imām Aḥmad stated, "Muḥammad b. Kathīr related to us, that Sulaymān b. Kathīr related to him, from Ḥusayn b. 'Abd al-Raḥmān, from Muḥammad b. Jubayr b. Muṭ'im, from his father, who said, 'The moon split in the time of the Messenger of God (ṢAAS), and became two parts; one was over this mountain, the other over that mountain. People said, "Muḥammad has performed a trick on us." Then they said, "He may have tricked us, but he can't trick everyone."'"

Aḥmad alone gives this *hadīth*.

Ibn Jarīr reported it similarly from a *hadīth* of Muḥammad b. Fuḍayl and others, from an account of Ḥusayn.

Al-Bayhaqī related it through Ibrāhīm b. Ṭahmān and Hushaym, both of them from Ḥusayn b. 'Abd al-Raḥmān, from Jubayr b. Muḥammad b. Jubayr b. Muṭ'im, from his father and grandfather. His account adds one further man to the chain of transmission.

As for Ḥudhayfa b. al-Yamān's tradition, Abū Nu'aym related in the *Dalā'il* (*The Signs*), on a line through 'Aṭā' b. al-Sā'ib from Abū 'Abd al-Raḥmān al-Sulamī, as follows: "Hudhayfa b. al-Yamān made an address to us at al-Madā'in. He gave thanks and praise to God and then said, 'The hour has drawn near and the moon has split asunder. Yes indeed, the time is near. And yes, the moon did split. The world really is close to partition. Today we have the race-track, and the race is tomorrow!'

"The next Friday I went with my father to the mosque. Again he praised God and repeated what he had said, adding, 'And yes, indeed, the winner is he who comes first on Fridays.'

"On our way back, I asked my father what he had meant when he said, 'the race is tomorrow!' He replied, 'For who first reaches paradise.'"

Regarding the tradition of Ibn 'Abbās, al-Bukhārī stated, "Yaḥyā b. Bukayr related to us that Bakr related to him, from Ja'far, from 'Irāk b. Mālik, from 'Ubayd Allāh b.'Abd Allāh b. 'Utba, from Ibn 'Abbās, who said, 'The moon did split during the time of the Prophet (ṢAAS).'"

Al-Bukhārī also, along with Muslim, related this from a *hadīth* of Bakr, who was Ibn Naṣr, from Ja'far. Regarding "... the time is near and the moon has split asunder. And if they see a sign they turn away, saying 'Just more trickery!'" He said, "That time is past. That was before the *hijra*. The moon did split, and people could see both parts of it."

Al-ʿAwfī related it thus, from Ibn ʿAbbās, God bless him, this being one of his *mursal*[18] traditions.

The *ḥāfiẓ* Abū Nuʿaym stated, "Sulaymān b. Aḥmad related to us, quoting Bakr b. Suhayl, quoting ʿAbd al-Ghanī b. Saʿīd, quoting Mūsā b. ʿAbd al-Raḥmān, from Ibn Jurayj, from ʿAṭāʾ, from Ibn ʿAbbās – also, it came from Muqātil, from al-Daḥḥāk, from Ibn ʿAbbās – with reference to God's words, 'The hour has drawn near and the moon has been split asunder' as follows, 'The polytheists gathered around the Messenger of God (ṢAAS); they included al-Walīd b. al-Mughīra, Abū Jahl b. Hishām, al-ʿĀṣ b. Wāʾil, al-ʿĀṣ b. Hishām, al-Aswad b. ʿAbd Yaghūth, al Aswad b. al-Muṭṭalib b. Asad b. ʿAbd al-ʿUzzā, Zamʿa b. al-Aswad and al-Naḍr b. al-Ḥārith, along with many other such men.

"'They said to the Prophet (ṢAAS), "If you are telling the truth, then split the moon for us into two parts, one half over Mt. Abū Qubays, the other over Mt. Quʿayquʿānʾ.' The Prophet (ṢAAS) asked them, "If I did so, would you believe?" "Yes, we would," they replied. It was a night of full moon, and so he asked God the Almighty and Glorious to grant him what they requested. That evening the moon did have one half removed and placed over Mt. Abū Qubays, the other being above Mt. Quʿayquʿān, while the Messenger of God (ṢAAS) called out, "O Abū Salama b. ʿAbd al-Asād, and al-Arqam b. al-Arqam, be a witness (to this event)."'"

Moreover, Abū Nuʿaym stated, "Sulaymān b. Aḥmad related to us, quoting al-Ḥasan b. al-ʿAbbās al-Rāzī, from al-Haytham b. al-ʿUmān, as did Ismāʿīl b. Ziyād, from Ibn Jurayj, from ʿAṭā, from Ibn ʿAbbās, who said, 'The people of Mecca went to the Messenger of God (ṢAAS) and said, "Is there some sign by which we can know that you are the Messenger of God?"'

"'Gabriel then came down and said, "O Muḥammad, tell the people of Mecca that they will rejoice this night when they will see a sign and benefit thereby."'

"'The Messenger of God (ṢAAS) informed them what Gabriel had said and they all went outside on the night of the splitting, that of the 14th, and the moon split into two halves, one above Mt. al-Ṣafā, the other over Mt. al-Marwa. They looked, turned away and wiped their eyes, then looked once more, saying, "O Muḥammad, this is nothing more than the trickery of a monk!"'

"'Then God revealed His words, "The hour has drawn near and the moon has split asunder"'" (*sūrat al Qamar*; LIV, v.1 3).

Al Daḥḥāk related from Ibn ʿAbbās as follows, "Rabbis came from the Jews to the Messenger of God (ṢAAS), and said, 'Show us a sign so we may believe in you.'

"He asked his Lord, and He showed them the moon split into two parts, one over Mt. al-Ṣafā, the other above Mt. al-Marwa. It remained so between early evening until night, with them looking on, and then it disappeared. They commented, 'This is just magic, a trick.'"

The *ḥāfiẓ* Abū al Qāsim al Ṭabrānī said, "Aḥmad b. ʿAmr al-Razzāz related to us, quoting Muḥammad b. Yaḥyā al-Qitaʿī, quoting Muḥammad b. Bakr quoting

---

18. A *mursal ḥadīth* is a statement of a Companion that he or she has not attributed to the Prophet himself.

Ibn Jurayj quoting ῾Amr b. Dīnār, from ῾Ikrima, from Ibn ῾Abbās, who said, 'In the time of the Messenger of God (ṢAAS), the moon was eclipsed and people said, "The moon is bewitched!" And so the words were revealed, "The hour has drawn near and the moon has split asunder. And if they see a sign they turn away saying, 'Just more trickery!'"'" (*sūrat al-Qamar*; LIV, v.1–3).

This has a fine chain of authorities; it states that the moon was eclipsed that night; perhaps its splitting occurred on the night of its eclipse and this is why what happened to it was hidden from most of the earth's inhabitants. However, this was in fact witnessed in many parts of the world. It is said that in some parts of India that became a point for dating, and that a building was constructed that night which was dated by the night when the moon split.

Regarding the tradition of Ibn ῾Umar, the *ḥāfiẓ* al-Bayhaqī stated, "We were informed by Abū ῾Abd Allāh, the *ḥāfiẓ*, and by Abū Bakr Aḥmad b. al-Ḥasan al-Qāḍī as follows: 'Abū al-῾Abbās al-Aṣamm related it to us, as did al-῾Abbās b. Muḥammad al-Dūrī, as did Wahb b. Jarīr, from Shu῾ba, from al-A῾mash, from Mujāhid.'"

Muslim said, "It is like the account of Mujāhid from Abū Ma῾mar, from Ibn Mas῾ūd."

Al-Tirmidhī stated, "This *ḥadīth* is *ḥasan* and *ṣaḥīḥ*."[19]

Regarding the tradition quoted by ῾Abd Allāh b. Mas῾ūd, the Imām Aḥmad said, "Sufyān related to us, from Ibn Abū Najīḥ, from Mujāhid, from Abū Ma῾mar, from Ibn Mas῾ūd, who said, 'The moon split into two parts during the time of the Messenger of God (ṢAAS) so that everyone looked at it. And so the Messenger of God (ṢAAS) said, "Bear witness!"'"

(Both of these authorities) drew this from an account of Sufyān, he being Ibn ῾Uyayna. And from a *ḥadīth* of al-A῾mash, from Ibrāhīm, from Abū Ma῾mar, from ῾Abd Allāh b. Samra, from Ibn Mas῾ūd, who said, "The moon split asunder while we were with the Messenger of God (ṢAAS) at Minā. The Prophet (ṢAAS) then said, 'Bear witness!' And one piece of the moon went off towards the mountain."

This phraseology is from al-Bukhārī.

Al-Bukhārī then said, "Abū al-Ḍaḥḥāk narrated it from Masrūq, from ῾Abd Allāh in Mecca, and Muḥammad b. Muslim followed him, from Ibn Abū Najīḥ, from Mujāhid, from Abū Ma῾mar, from ῾Abd Allāh, God bless him."

Abū Dā᾽ūd al-Ṭayālisī gave support to the *ḥadīth* of Abū al-Ḍuḥā, from Masrūq, from ῾Abd Allāh b. Mas῾ūd, who said, "The moon split in the time of the Messenger of God (ṢAAS), and Quraysh said, 'This is the trickery of Ibn Abū Kabsha.' They commented, 'See what travellers say to you! Muḥammad can't trick everyone.'

"He said, 'And travellers did arrive, and they said the same.'"

---

19. These are among the categories that *ḥadīth* scholars us to describe the *soundness of a chain* of transmission; the words mean "good" and "true".

Al-Bayhaqī stated, "Abū ʿAbd Allāh the *ḥāfiz* informed us, quoting Abū al-ʿAbbās, quoting al-ʿAbbās b. Muḥammad al-Dūrī, that Saʿīd b. Sulaymān related to us, that Hushaym related from Mughīra, from Abū al-Duḥā, from Masrūq, from ʿAbd Allāh, who said, 'The moon split asunder in Mecca, into two parts.'

"And the unbelievers of Quraysh told the people of Mecca, 'This is magic. The son of Abū Kabsha has tricked you by it. Look to travellers arriving. If they saw what you say, then he is correct, but if they did not see what you did, then it is magic he has tricked you with.'

"He went on, 'So travellers were questioned, and,' he said, 'they came from all directions. And they reported, "We did see it."'"

Abū Nuʿaym reported this the same way from a *ḥadīth* of Jābir, from al-Aʿmash, from Abū al-Duḥā, from Masrūq, from ʿAbd Allāh.

Imām Aḥmad stated, "Muʾammil related to us, that Isrāʾīl related, from Simāk, from Ibrāhīm, from al-Aswad, from ʿAbd Allāh, he being Ibn Masʿūd, who said, 'The moon split in the time of the Messenger of God (ṢAAS); I could see the mountain between the two splits in the moon.'"

Ibn Jarīr related it thus from a *ḥadīth* of Asbāṭ from Simāk.

The *ḥāfiz* Abū Nuʿaym stated, "Abū Bakr al-Ṭalḥī related to us, quoting Abū Ḥusayn Muḥammad b. al-Ḥusayn al-Wādiʿī, as did Yaḥyā al-Ḥimmānī, as did Yazīd, from ʿAṭāʾ, from Simāk, from Ibrāhīm, from ʿAlqama, from ʿAbd Allāh, who said, 'We were with the Prophet (ṢAAS), at Minā, when the moon split until it was in two parts, one of which was behind the mountain. The Prophet (ṢAAS) then said, "Bear testimony! Bear testimony!"'"

Abū Nuʿaym stated, "Sulaymān b. Aḥmad related to us, quoting Jaʿfar b. Muḥammad al-Qalānisī, as did Ādam b. Abū Iyās, as did al-Layth b. Saʿd, as did Hishām b. Saʿd, from ʿUtba, from ʿAbd Allāh b. ʿUtba, from Ibn Masʿūd, who said, 'The moon split while we were in Mecca. I saw one of its two pieces over the mountain at Minā while we were at Mecca.'

"ʿAḥmad b. Isḥāq related to us, as did Abū Bakr b. Abū ʿĀṣim, Muḥammad b. Ḥātim, and Muʿāwiya b. ʿAmr, from Zāʾida, from ʿĀṣim, from Zirr, from ʿAbd Allāh, who said, 'The moon split at Mecca and I saw it in two parts.'"

He then related from a *ḥadīth* of ʿAlī b. Saʿīd b. Masrūq, Mūsā b. ʿUmayr related to us, from Manṣūr b. al-Muʿtamir, from Zayd b. Wahb, from ʿAbd Allāh b. Masʿūd, who said, "I saw the moon, I swear by God, split in two parts, with Mt. Ḥirāʾ between them both."

Abū Nuʿaym related, through al-Suddī al-Saghīr, from al-Kalbī, from Abū Ṣāliḥ, from Ibn ʿAbbās, who said, "The moon split into two halves, one of which left while the other remained."

Ibn Masʿūd stated, "I saw Mt. Ḥirāʾ between the two halves of the moon. One half left and the people of Mecca were amazed at this, and said, 'This is just some faked-up trick; it will pass.'"

Layth b. Abū Sulaym reported Mujāhid as having said, "The moon split into two pieces in the time of the Messenger of God (ṢAAS) who said to Abū Bakr, 'Bear testimony, Abū Bakr!'

"And the polytheists said, 'He has bewitched the moon so that it split apart!'"

These various lines are strong in their links and provide decisive proof for those who consider them and the probity of these men. The version told by some storytellers, that the moon fell down to earth and entered one sleeve of the Prophet (ṢAAS), and came out of the other, has no foundation; it is a lie, an invention and untrue.

When the moon split it did not leave the sky. However, when the Prophet (ṢAAS) gestured towards it, it reacted by splitting and became two halves. One of these passed over until it was beyond Ḥirā³ and they saw the mountain between that one and the other. This is how Ibn Mas ͨūd related that he had witnessed it.

What we find in the account of Anas in the compendium of Aḥmad to the effect that, "The moon split 'twice' in Mecca" is controversial. Obviously he meant "into two parts". But God knows best.

Section: The death of Abū Ṭālib, uncle of the Messenger of God (ṢAAS), and thereafter that of Khadīja, daughter of Khuwaylid, and the wife, may God be pleased with her, of the Messenger of God (ṢAAS).

Some say that she preceded him in death, but the reverse is commonly known.

These were both sympathizers, he publicly, she privately. He remained a disbeliever while she was trusting and a believer; may God be pleased with her and please her.

Ibn Isḥāq stated, "Thereafter Khadīja and Abū Ṭālib both died, in one year.

"After the death of Khadīja troubles fell upon the Messenger of God (ṢAAS) in quick succession. She had been his trusted adviser in all his troubles and he would seek reassurance from her. The death of his uncle Abū Ṭālib meant he had lost a source of support and protection against his people.

"This occurred three years before his emigration to Medina.

"When Abū Ṭālib died, Quraysh harmed the Messenger of God (ṢAAS) to an extent they would never have dared during Abū Ṭālib's life; one fool of Quraysh even went so far as to throw dirt on his head.

"Hishām b. ͨUrwa related to me, from his father, as follows, 'The Messenger of God (ṢAAS) went into his house with the dirt still on his head. One of his daughters went to him, washing him off and weeping, while the Messenger of God (ṢAAS) told her, "Don't weep, child. God is your father's protector," while he also commented, "Quraysh never treated me so badly before Abū Ṭālib died."'"

Ibn Isḥāq previously reported that they might toss something harmful into his cooking pot when it was set up for him. When they did that, he stated, quoting ͨUmar b. ͨAbd Allāh from ͨUrwa, he would lift out on a stick whatever they had put there and take it to his door, saying, "O Banū ʿAbd Manāf, what kind of protection is this?" Then he would throw it out into the street.

Ibn Isḥāq stated, "When Abū Ṭālib became sick and Quraysh learned of his serious state, they noted how Ḥamza and ʿUmar had accepted Islam and how the prestige of Muḥammad had spread through the Quraysh tribes, so they decided to go to Abū Ṭālib to get him to reconcile his nephew to them. Otherwise, they concluded, he might subvert their authority completely.

"Al-ʿAbbās b. ʿAbd Allāh b. Maʿbad related to me, from a member of his family, from Ibn ʿAbbās, who said, 'When they went to Abū Ṭālib and spoke to him, the Quraysh leaders, including ʿUtba b. Rabīʿa, Shayba b. Rabīʿa, Abū Jahl b. Hishām, Umayya b. Khalaf and Abū Sufyān b. Ḥarb, along with others, said, "O Abū Ṭālib, you know what standing you have with us, and that your serious condition, of which you are aware, greatly concerns us. You also know of the dispute between us and your nephew. Would you now call him and reach a compromise by which he will do us no harm nor we him; let him tolerate our religion and we will his."

"'Abū Ṭālib sent for him and when he came, he told him, "O Nephew, these leaders of your people have gathered to reach a compromise with you and you with them."

"'The Messenger of God (ṢAAS) replied, "You all just need to say one word, uncle, and through it you can rule the Arabs and have the non-Arabs subject to you."

"'"Oh yes, I swear by your life," answered Abū Ṭālib, "along with ten words more!"

"'He told him, "Say, 'There is no god but God.' And repudiate whatever gods you worship besides Him!"

"'Those present clapped their hands and commented, "O Muḥammad, do you want to make all the gods into one? How strange."

"'Then they said to one another, "This man is not going to give us any part of what we want. We should leave and continue in the religion of our fathers until God decides between us and him." They then dispersed.

"'At that Abū Ṭālib said, "I swear, nephew, I don't think you asked anything excessive."

"'The Messenger of God (ṢAAS) had high hopes of him now and said to him, "O Uncle, if you were to say it I would intercede for you on Judgement Day."

"'Recognizing the eagerness of the Messenger of God (ṢAAS), Abū Ṭālib replied, "O Nephew, I swear that were it not for fear of the curses there would be on you and your relatives after me, and the fact that Quraysh would think that I had only said it out of fear of death, I would say it. I will not say it only to please you thereby."

"'When death approached Abū Ṭālib, al-ʿAbbās saw that he was moving his lips and so he put his ear close to hear. Then he said, "O Nephew, I swear my brother did say the word you asked of him!"

"'The Messenger of God (ṢAAS) replied, "I did not hear."

"'And God Almighty revealed about that group of men, "*Ṣād. By the Qur'ān of fine repute! Those who disbelieve act in pride and arrogance"'" (*sūrat Ṣād*; XXXVIII, v.1).

We have discussed this in the *Tafsīr* (*Exegesis*), and to God go all praise and credit.

Various scholars of the Shī'a and other extremists hold the view that Abū Ṭālib died a Muslim because of what al-'Abbās said in this *ḥadīth*, that is, "O Nephew, my brother did speak the word you told him to say: 'There is no god but God.'"

There are many ways to respond to this. One is that there is some question relating to the chain of authorities that includes one link defined as "a member of his family" about whom nothing is known. The doubt here rests on ignorance of both the person and his circumstances. Such a tradition is normally regarded as an *ḥadīth mawqūf*,[20] if it remains unsubstantiated.

Imām Aḥmad, al-Nasā'ī and Ibn Jarīr gave much the same chain, through Abū Usāma from al-A'mash (who said), "'Abbād related to us, from Sa'īd b. Jubayr …" He gave the account without, however, mentioning the words of al-'Abbās.

Al-Thawrī also related it, from al-A'mash, from Yaḥyā b. 'Ammāra al-Kūfī, from Sa'īd b. Jubayr, from Ibn 'Abbās. He gave it without the addition of the words of al-'Abbās.

Al-Tirmidhī related it and stated it to be a good tradition, as did al-Nasā'ī and Ibn Jarīr.

The wording of the tradition on the line given by al-Bayhaqī through al-Thawrī, from al-A'mash, from Yaḥyā b. 'Amāra, from Sa'īd b. Jubayr, quotes Ibn 'Abbās as saying, "Abū Ṭālib fell sick and men of Quraysh and the Prophet (ṢAAS) arrived at his home and there was a seat for one person at the head of Abū Ṭālib's bed. Abū Jahl arose to prevent him sitting there, all the while protesting to Abū Ṭālib about Muḥammad. He asked, 'Nephew, what is it you want from your people?'

"He replied, 'Uncle, all I want from them is a statement through which the Arabs will submit to them and which will bring them tribute from the non-Arabs. Just one statement.'

"'And what is that?'

"'There is no god but God,' he replied.

"They commented, 'What, make all the gods into one? That's ridiculous!'

"He went on, 'And God revealed about them, "*Ṣād. By the Qur'ān of fine repute! …*" and so on to the words, "… nothing but a forgery!"'" (*sūrat Ṣād*; XXXVIII, v.7).

Moreover Ibn Isḥāq's account is contradicted by one more authoritative, namely that of al-Bukhārī, who said, "Maḥmūd related to us, that 'Abd al-Razzāq

20. The term implies that the *ḥadīth* has an unknown person in its chain of transmission; it is therefore regarded as unsound.

related to them that Maʾmar informed them, from al-Zuhrī, from Ibn al-Musayyab, from his father, God bless him, that Abū Ṭālib was close to death when the Prophet (ṢAAS), along with Abū Jahl, went in to see him. He (the Prophet) said, 'Uncle, say, "There is no god but God!" One statement; (and) I will plead with God thereby on your behalf.'

"Abū Jahl and ʿAbd Allāh b. Abū Umayya then said, 'O Abū Ṭālib, are you leaving the faith of ʿAbd al-Muṭṭalib?' And they both continued talking to him until he spoke his last words to them, namely, '... in the faith of ʿAbd al-Muṭṭalib.'

"The Prophet (ṢAAS) said, 'I will seek forgiveness for you for as long as I am not restrained from doing so.'

"And so there was revealed, 'It is not appropriate for the Prophet and for those who believe to seek forgiveness for the polytheists, even though near relatives, after it has become plain to them that they would inhabit hell' (sūrat al-Tawba (or al-Barāʾa); IX, v.113). And there was also revealed, 'You cannot give guidance to those you love'" (sūrat al-Qaṣāṣ; XXVIII, v.56).

Muslim related this account from Isḥāq b. Ibrāhīm and ʿAbd Allāh, from ʿAbd al-Razāq.

They also drew it from a ḥadīth of al-Zuhrī, from Saʿīd b. al-Musayyab, from his father in similar words. In it he states, "The Messenger of God (ṢAAS) continued to suggest this to him while the other two repeated their words until he spoke his final words, '... in the faith of ʿAbd al-Muṭṭalib.' And he refused to utter the words 'There is no god but God.'

"The Prophet (ṢAAS) said, 'I will seek forgiveness for you.' And so God sent down, thereafter that is, the words, 'It is not up to the Prophet and those who believe to seek forgiveness for the polytheists, even though near relatives.'"

Concerning Abū Ṭālib, it was revealed, "You cannot give guidance to those you love."

Imām Aḥmad, Muslim, al-Tirmidhī and al-Nasāʾī related this from a ḥadīth of Yazīd b. Kaysān, from Abū Ḥāzim, from Abū Hurayra, who said, "When death was near for Abū Ṭālib, the Messenger of God (ṢAAS) came to him and said, 'Uncle, say "There is no god but God" and I will testify for you about it on Judgement Day.'

"He replied, 'If it were not for Quraysh insulting me and saying that it was only fear of death that made me say it, I would do so, and please you. I would not, however, say it only to please you.'[21]

"And so God, Almighty and Glorious is He, revealed, 'You cannot give guidance to those you love.'"

ʿAbd Allāh b. ʿAbbās, Ibn ʿUmar, Mujāhid, al-Shaʿbī, and Qatāda all stated that the above verse was revealed about Abū Ṭālib when the Messenger of God

---

21. The passage could also be translated, "Were it not for Quraysh insulting me by saying that it was only fear of death that induced me to say so, or that I did so in order to please you, I would have uttered this statement; but only to please you."

(ṢAAS) suggested to him that he say, "There is no god but God" and he refused to do so. Instead, he said that he subscribed to the faith of the elders. The last thing he said was that, "He is following the religion of ‘Abd al-Muṭṭalib."

All this is affirmed by al-Bukhārī's narration from Musaddad, who related from Yaḥyā, from Sufyān, from ‘Abd al-Malik b. ‘Umayr, from ‘Abd Allāh b. al-Ḥārith who said, "Al-‘Abbās b. ‘Abd al-Muṭṭalib related to us that he said, 'I asked the Messenger of God (ṢAAS), "What benefit were you to your uncle? He used to protect and defend you."

"'He replied, "He is in a shallow stream of hell-fire; if it were not for me, he would be in its lowest depths."'"

Muslim related this same account in his compendium by various paths, from ‘Abd al-Malik b. ‘Umayr.

Both these scholars narrated it in both their works from a *ḥadīth* of al-Layth, as follows, "Ibn al-Hādd related to me, from ‘Abd Allāh b. Khabbāb, from Abū Sa‘īd, that he heard the Prophet (ṢAAS) say when someone mentioned his uncle, 'Perhaps my intercession may help him on Judgement Day, and he will be placed in a shallow stream of hell-fire that will reach up to his ankles and cause his brain to boil.'"

This is the phraseology of al-Bukhārī. In one account the words used are, "… cause *umm dimāghihī*", the centre of his brain, instead of "*dimāghuhū*", his brain, to boil.

Muslim related, from Abū Bakr b. Abū Shayba, from ‘Affān, from Ḥammād b. Salama, from Thābit, from Abū ‘Uthmān, from Ibn ‘Abbās, that the Messenger of God (ṢAAS) said, "Abū Ṭālib receives more lenient punishment than any other inhabitant of hell; he wears two shoes of fire that cause his brain to boil."

In the *Maghāzī*, the history of the conquests, by Yūnus b. Bukayr, the statement given is "… and from them (his shoes) his brain will boil so that it streams down over his feet." Al-Suhaylī makes mention of this.

The *ḥāfiẓ* Abū Bakr al-Bazzār stated in his compendium, "'Amr — he being the son of Ismā‘īl b. Mujālid — related to us, saying that his father related to them, from Mujālid, from al-Sha‘bī, from Jābir, who said, 'The Messenger of God (ṢAAS) was asked, "Have you been of benefit to Abū Talib?"

"'He replied, "I drew him forth from hell-fire into a shallow stream of it."'"

Al-Bazzār alone gives this tradition.

Al-Suhaylī stated, "However, the Prophet (ṢAAS) did not accept the testimony of al-‘Abbās that his brother (Abū Ṭālib) had made the said statement and replied, 'I did not hear it because al-‘Abbās was at that time an unbeliever, from whom a testimony was unacceptable.'"

My comment is that this account thereof is in itself not to be considered authentic because of the weakness of its chain of transmission, as stated earlier.

Evidence for that is provided by the fact that he (al-‘Abbās) asked the Prophet (ṢAAS) thereafter about Abū Ṭālib and he told him what is stated above.

If, however, we accepted the argument for the authenticity of the afore-mentioned statement of Abū Ṭālib, we would, none the less, aver that he only said what he did upon seeing the angel after the death-rattle, when expression of faith cannot be of use to a soul.

But God knows best.

Abū Dāʾūd al-Ṭayālisī stated, "Shuʿba related to us, that Abū Isḥāq said, 'I heard Nājiyya b. Kaʿb say, "I heard ʿAlī say, 'When my father died, I went to the Messenger of God (ṢAAS), and told him, "Your uncle has died." He replied, "Go and bury him." I said, "He died a polytheist." So he replied, "Go and bury him and do not cause (a scene), then return to me."

"""'I did so, returned to him and he told me to wash.'"""

Al-Nasāʾī related this from Muḥammad b. al-Muthannā, from Ghundar, from Shuʿba.

Abū Dāʾūd and al-Nasāʾī related it from a *ḥadīth* of Sufyān, from Abū Isḥāq, from Nājiyya, from ʿAlī who said, "When Abū Ṭālib died, I said, 'O Messenger of God, that misguided old man your uncle has died. Who will bury him?'

"He replied, 'Go and bury your father. Do nothing to cause (a scene), then return to me.'

"When I returned to him he told me to wash, and I did so. He then said some prayers for me that gave me more pleasure than would have anything else on earth."

The *ḥāfiẓ* al-Bayhaqī said, "Abū Saʿd al-Mālīnī informed us, Abū Aḥmad b. ʿAdī related to us, quoting Muḥammad b. Hārūn b. Ḥumayd, quoting Muḥammad b. ʿAbd al-ʿAzīz b. Abū Razma, quoting al-Faḍl, from Ibrāhīm b. ʿAbd al-Raḥmān, from Ibn Jurayj, from ʿAṭāʾ, from Ibn ʿAbbās, who said, 'The Prophet (ṢAAS) returned after attending the funeral for Abū Ṭālib and said, "May your family ties be secure, and you be well rewarded, uncle."'"

He (al-Bayhaqī) went on to say that it was related from the Prophet (ṢAAS), though with an incomplete chain, with the addition "... and he did not stand at his grave."

He (al-Bayhaqī) also said, "This man, Ibrāhīm b. ʿAbd al-Raḥmān, who is mentioned in the context of the chain of authorities for this account, is that same al-Khawārizmī about whom there has been some controversy.

I note that several persons have related traditions from him, including al-Faḍl b. Mūsā al-Sinānī and Muḥammad b. Sallām al-Bīkandī. Nevertheless Ibn ʿAdī said, "He is not well known. And the traditions others have quoted from him are not sound."

We have already given accounts of the support and protection given by Abū Ṭālib to the Messenger of God (ṢAAS), how he defended him and his followers. We also quoted from the verses he spoke in their praise and of the love and sympathy for them these verses express, as well as the criticism and blame they contain for those who opposed and ridiculed them. These verses exemplify the eloquence, skill and fluency of the Hāshim and Muṭṭalibī clans, an ability to use the language that could not be matched, rivalled or excelled by any Arab.

In all of this he knew that the Messenger of God (ṢAAS) was truthful, innocent and right-guided, but his heart, nevertheless, did not believe.

There is a difference between the heart knowing and believing. We have affirmed this fact in our exegesis of the *Book of Faith* in the *ṣaḥīḥ* of al-Bukhārī.

Evidence for this is given in the words of the Almighty, "Those to whom we have brought the Book know it as they do their sons; (however) a group of them conceal the truth, while knowing it" (*sūrat al-Baqara*; II, v.146).

Regarding Pharoah's people, the Almighty said, "... and they denied them, though their souls were convinced ..." (*sūrat al-Naml*; XXVII, v.14). And Moses said to the Pharoah, "You know that it is only the Lord of the heavens and the earth who sent clear proofs, and I believe you, Pharoah, to be damned!" (*sūrat al-Isrā'*; XVII, v.102).

Some of the *salafī* or early authorities consider the Almighty's words "... they defend him yet reject him" (*sūrat al-Anʿām*; VI, v.26) to relate to Abū Ṭālib, since he used to defend the Messenger of God (ṢAAS) from harm even though he rejected the guidance and true religion he brought.

(This opinion) is related as from Ibn ʿAbbās, al-Qāsim b. Mukhaymira, Ḥabīb b. Abū Thābit, ʿAṭā' b. Dīnār, Muḥammad b. Kaʿb and others and it is open to question. But God alone knows best.

Preferable, though God knows best, is the other account from Ibn ʿAbbās to the effect that the verse refers to those who prevented people from believing in Muḥammad (ṢAAS). Mujāhid, Qatāda, al-Ḍaḥḥāk and others held this view. It is also the choice of Ibn Jarīr; though God knows best. Its implication is that this verse emphasizes the blame for the polytheists for preventing others from following him while themselves not benefitting from him either.

The Almighty therefore stated, "There are from among them those who listen to you over whose hearts we have placed covers that prevent them understanding, and holes in their ears; even if they see all signs they fail to believe in them. Even when they come to you to argue with you, those who disbelieve say, 'These are just legends of the ancients.' And they forbid others from (believing in it), and themselves keep away from it. It is only themselves they destroy, yet they do not sense this" (*sūrat al-Anʿām*; VI, v.25).

The phrase here: "... and they ..." indicates reference to a group. As for "they" as referred to in the subsequent comment, "... it is only themselves they destroy, yet they do not sense this", this gives evidence of the totality of the blame.

Such could not apply to Abū Ṭālib. On the contrary, he restrained people from harming the Messenger of God (ṢAAS), and his followers, using all action, speech, moral support and money available to him.

Nevertheless, God did not decree faith for him, in all His mighty wisdom, nor did He furnish him with the clear, irrefutable and decisive proofs whereby (one) is compelled to believe and submit.

And were it not for God's having forbidden us seeking forgiveness for disbelievers, we would certainly seek such forgiveness and mercy for him.

DIVISION

On the death of Khadīja, daughter of Khuwaylid and reference to some of her qualities and virtues, may God bless and please her and make the gardens of paradise her place of dwelling and repose. And He has indeed done that in a reference made by him who is truthful and believed, in which he announced her being in a home in paradise made of pearl shell where there is neither discord nor distress.

Yaʿqūb b. Sufyān said, "Abū Ṣāliḥ related to us, from al-Layth, who said that ʿUqayl related to him from Ibn Shihāb, as follows, "ʿUrwa b. al-Zubayr said, "Khadīja had died before the prayer was made obligatory.""

This was related also in another path from al-Zuhrī which had him say, "Khadīja died at Mecca before the departure of the Messenger of God (ṢAAS) for Medina, and before the prayer was made obligatory."

Muḥammad b. Isḥāq stated, "Khadīja and Abū Ṭālib died in the same year."

Al-Bayhaqī stated, "I was informed that Khadīja died three days after the death of Abū Ṭālib. It was ʿAbd Allāh b. Mandah who mentioned this in his book *al-Maʿrifa* (*Knowledge*), as did our sheikh Abū ʿAbd Allāh, the *ḥāfiẓ*.

Al-Bayhaqī stated, "Al-Wāqidī claimed that Khadīja and Abū Ṭālib both died in the same year they came out of the enclave, that is, three years before the emigration, and also that Khadīja died 35 days before the death of Abū Ṭālib."

My comment is that they mean before the five daily prayers were made obligatory, on the "night journey".

It would have been more appropriate for us to make reference to the deaths of Abū Ṭālib and Khadīja before the account of the "night journey", as al-Bayhaqī and others did. We have postponed it till after the "night journey" for a reason that you will see shortly. Discussion of this will effectively harmonize and order this section, as you will find, if God so wills it.

Al-Bukhārī stated, "Qutayba related to us, quoting Muḥammad b. Fuḍayl b. Ghazwān, from ʿUmāra, from Abū Zurʿa, from Abū Hurayra, who said, 'Gabriel came to the Messenger of God (ṢAAS), and said, "O Messenger of God, this is Khadīja who has brought a vessel of shortening — or food and drink. When she comes to you greet her from her Lord and from me and give her news of a house in paradise made of pearl shell and where there is neither discord nor distress.""

Muslim related this from a *ḥadīth* transmitted from Muḥammad b. Fuḍayl.

Al-Bukhārī stated, "Musaddad related to us, from Yaḥyā, from Ismāʿīl, who said, 'I asked ʿAbd Allāh b. Abū Awfā, "Did the Messenger of God (ṢAAS) give glad tidings to Khadīja?" He replied, "Yes, of a house of pearl shell devoid of discord or distress."""

Al-Bukhārī also related it, as did Muslim, in lines from Ismā<īl b. Abū Khālid.

Al-Suhaylī stated, "He only announced good news of her having a house made of *qaṣab*, pearl shell, in paradise, because she had won the *qaṣab*, the first prize, (in the race) to faith. There was to be 'no discord or distress' there because she never raised her voice to the Prophet (ṢAAS), never once caused him trouble or was discordant with him, and never harmed him."

Both scholars gave it in the *ṣaḥīḥ* collections, from a *ḥadīth* of Hishām b. <Urwa, from his father that <Ā>isha, God bless her, said, "The only one of the wives of the Prophet (ṢAAS) of whom I was jealous was Khadīja – who died before he married me – and this was because of how I would hear him mention her.

"And God ordered him to announce to her the tidings of a house of pearl shell for her in paradise; and if he slaughtered a sheep he would present to her friends as much of it as they wanted."

These are the words of al-Bukhārī.

In another version from <Ā>isha, she said, "I was never so jealous of any woman as I was of Khadīja; this was due to the frequency with which the Messenger of God (ṢAAS) would mention her. He married me three years after (her death). And his Lord, or Gabriel, ordered him to announce the tidings of her having a house of pearl shell in paradise."

In another of his variant wordings, she said, "I was never so jealous of any of the wives of the Prophet (ṢAAS) as I was of Khadīja. I did not see her, but he talked often of her. He sometimes slaughtered a sheep then would cut off its limbs for her and send them off to Khadīja's women friends. I would say, 'Why, it's as if Khadīja were the only woman in the world!' and he would reply, 'She was what she certainly was, and I had a son by her.'"

Then al-Bukhārī stated, "Ismā<īl b. Khalīl related to us, <Alī b. Mushir informed us, from Hishām b. <Urwa, from his father, that <Ā>isha said, 'Hāla, daughter of Khuwaylid, Khadīja's sister, asked to come in to see the Messenger of God (ṢAAS), and he thought of it as Khadīja's asking for entry; he was confused, then said, "O God, it's Hāla!"'"

<Ā>isha went on, "And so I was jealous and commented, 'Why think back on some red-mouthed old woman of Quraysh who died long ago and whom God has replaced for you with someone better!'"

Muslim related this thus, from Suwayd b. Sa<īd, from <Alī b. Mushīr.

This comment gives clear evidence that <Ā>isha was better than Khadīja, either in her personal or in her wifely qualities, for he did not contradict her or answer her back, as is obvious from the course of the account of al-Bukhārī, God bless him!

However, Imām Aḥmad said, "Mu>ammil Abū <Abd al-Raḥmān related to us, quoting Ḥammād b. Salama, from <Abd al-Malik – he being Ibn <Umayr – from Mūsā b. Ṭalḥa, from <Ā>isha, who said, 'One day the Messenger of God (ṢAAS) referred to Khadīja and began speaking excessive praise for her. I was overcome by that jealousy that affects women and I said, "O Messenger of God, God has awarded you with better than a red-mouthed old Quraysh woman!"'"

His account proceeds, "The face of the Messenger of God (ṢAAS) underwent such a change as I only ever saw when revelation happened or when he was imagining something and not knowing whether the outcome would be mercy or punishment."

He related it similarly on a path from Bahz b. Asad and ʿUthmān b. Muslim, both of these giving as authorities for it Ḥammād b. Salama, back to ʿAbd al-Malik b. ʿUmayr.

After the words, "red-mouthed" this last account added the phrase "who died ages ago". And then she said, "His face then flushed in such a way as I only ever saw when revelation came or he was imagining something that might mean either mercy or punishment."

Aḥmad alone gave this version. Its chain of authorities is excellent.

Imām Aḥmad also stated, and quoted Ibn Isḥāq as having said, "Mujālid related to us, from al-Shaʿbī, from Masrūq, that ʿĀʾisha said, 'When the Prophet (ṢAAS) mentioned Khadīja he would speak of her with the finest of praise. One day I got jealous and commented, "How often you refer to that old, red-mouthed woman; God has given you better than her in exchange!"

"'He replied, "God has not given me better than her in exchange. She believed in me when the people disbelieved, and trusted me when they distrusted. She shared her wealth with me when others denied me. And God endowed a son to me from her, yet He withheld from me having sons with other women."'"

Aḥmad is also alone in giving this tradition. Its chain of authorities is fair. Muslim frequently gave Mujālid as a source, and he is controversial. But God knows best.

Perhaps this statement, I refer to his saying "God endowed a son to me from her yet He withheld from me having sons with other women" was before the birth of Ibrāhīm, the son of the Prophet (ṢAAS) by Mary, and may have actually been before her arrival. This is clearly so, for all the sons of the Prophet (ṢAAS), as we have seen and will report hereafter, were born to Khadīja, except for Ibrāhīm who was born to Mary, God bless her, the Egyptian Coptic woman.

A number of scholars refer to this statement as evidence of the superiority of Khadīja over ʿĀʾisha, God be pleased with her and make her content.

Other scholars have questions about its chain of authorities.

Yet others interpret this matter as referring to ʿĀʾisha as having been better in intimacy. This is likely or even obvious. The reason for this is that ʿĀʾisha's closeness involved her youth, beauty and the pleasure of intimacy with her. She had not implied by her words, "God has given you better than her in exchange" that she considered herself more pure and virtuous than Khadīja. For this is a matter that is the prerogative of God, Almighty and Glorious is He. As He stated, "Do not attribute purity to yourselves; He knows best who is the most pious" (*sūrat al-Najm*; LIII, v.32). And God Almighty also stated, "Have you not seen those who attribute purity to themselves? It is God who attributes purity to whomever He wishes" (*sūrat al Nisā'*; IV, v.49).

This is an issue subject to much debate among scholars old and new. On one side of it there are those versions to which members of the Shī'a and others restrict themselves, considering no woman equal to Khadīja because of the greetings made to her by the Lord and because the only sons of the Prophet (ṢAAS), except for Ibrāhīm, were born to her. Also they refer to the fact that he married no other woman until she died, and out of his respect for her acceptance of Islam, and for her having been of those who trusted. She has the status of having believed at the beginning of the mission and of devoting herself and her wealth to the Messenger of God (ṢAAS).

There are also *sunni*, orthodox, scholars who take extreme positions and attribute to each of them special virtues, as is well-known. However, the strength of their orthodoxy leads them to prefer 'Ā'isha for having been the daughter of al-Ṣiddīq, Abū Bakr, "the Trusting", and to her having been more knowledge-able than Khadīja. For in no nation was there ever any woman the like of 'Ā'isha in her ability to memorize, in her knowledge, eloquence or intelligence. Moreover, the Messenger of God (ṢAAS) did not love any of his wives as much as he did her. And affirmation of her innocence came down from above the seven heavens. And she related after he had died a great deal of excellent and highly valued knowledge of him, to such an extent that many people make reference to the well-known *hadīth* "Take one half of your religion from al-Ḥumayrā'."[22]

The truth is that both of them have virtues so evident as to amaze and dazzle anyone who might have witnessed them. It is therefore best to defer this matter to God almighty.

One who possesses irrefutable proof, or is inclined to one view in this regard, ought to speak on the basis of such knowledge.

Anyone who is hesitant about any such matter will find that the best and the straightest path is for him to say, "God knows best".

Imām Aḥmad, al-Bukhārī, Muslim, al-Tirmidhī and al-Nasā'ī related, through Hishām b. 'Urwa, from his father, from 'Abd Allāh b. Ja'far, from 'Alī b. Abū Ṭālib, God bless him, who stated, "The Messenger of God (ṢAAS) said, 'The best of their women was Mary, daughter of 'Imrān, and the best of *their* women was Khadīja, daughter of Khuwaylid.'" By this he meant the best women of their eras.

Shu'ba related, from Mu'āwiya b. Qurra, that his father Qurra b. Iyyās, God be pleased with him, stated, "The Messenger of God (ṢAAS) said, 'There have been many perfect men, but only three perfect women. These were Mary, daughter of 'Imrān, Āsiyya, the wife of Pharoah, and Khadīja, daughter of

22. Apparently a nickname applied to 'Ā'isha. The word, a diminutive form, means high born, of great excellence, or fair-skinned.

Khuwaylid. The greater virtue of ʿÁʾisha over other women is like that of
al-tharīd[23] over other foods."

Ibn Mirdawayh related this in his *Tafsīr* (*Exegesis*), and this chain of authorities
is good back to Shuʿba and beyond.

Scholars agree that the quality shared by these three women, Āsiyya, Mary
and Khadīja is that each of them vouched for a prophet sent by God, gave them
the best of companionship, and believed when they were given their mission.

Mary gave the most complete and full support and credence to her son when
he received his mission.

Khadīja wished to have the Messenger of God (ṢAAS) marry her and gave her
wealth for that, as we have stated previously. She also had full faith in him when
revelation came down to him from God, Almighty and Glorious is He.

His statement "the greater virtue of ʿÁʾisha over other women is like that of
al-tharīd over other foods" is also firmly established in both ṣaḥīḥ compendia
through Shuʿba, from ʿUrwa b. Murra, from Murra al-Ṭayyib al-Hamdānī, from
Abū Mūsā al-Ashʿarī, who said, "The Messenger of God (ṢAAS) said, 'There
have been many perfect men, but of women there were only Āsiyya, Pharoah's
wife, and Mary, daughter of ʿImrān; and the greater virtue of ʿÁʾisha over other
women is like that of al-tharīd over other foods.'"

Al-tharīd is a dish made of bread and meat mixed together. It is the finest food
of the Arabs. As some poets have said:

"When bread is enriched with meat, that, by God's good grace, is *al-tharīd*."

His statement, "The greater virtue of ʿÁʾisha over other women" has the
implication of being comprehensive and encompasses all those women mentioned
as well as others; but it may apply equally to all women, excluding (the aforementioned three). The discussion about her (ʿÁʾisha's) status as compared to
those three women would then remain undecided, with the probability of there
being equality among them. Anyone wanting to express a preference for one of
these over the others would therefore need extrinsic proof. But God knows best.

*Section: On his marriage after the death of Khadīja, God bless her, to ʿÁʾisha,
daughter of Abū Bakr, and to Sawda, daughter of Zamʿa, God bless them both.*

What is true is that he contracted marriage first with ʿÁʾisha, as will be shown.

Al-Bukhārī stated in his chapter on his marriage to ʿÁʾisha as follows,
"Muʿalla b. Asad related to us, quoting Wuhayb, from Hishām b. ʿUrwa, from
his father, from ʿÁʾisha, that the Prophet (ṢAAS) told her, 'You have twice been
shown to me in my sleep dressed in a silk cloth. And he (Gabriel) says, "This is
your wife." And when I uncover her, it is you! And so I say that if this be God's
will, then may He bring it about!'"

---

23. The word refers to a culinary dish the base of which is bread to which may be added
marrow, eggs, meat and spices.

The text of al-Bukhārī reads, "*Chapter on Marriage to Virgins*. Ibn Abū Mulayka stated, 'Ibn ʿAbbās said to ʿĀʾisha, "The Prophet (ṢAAS) married no virgin other than yourself."'"

"Ismāʿīl b. ʿAbd Allāh related to us, as did his brother, from Sulaymān b. Bilāl, from Hishām b. ʿUrwa, from his father, from ʿĀʾisha, who stated, 'I said, "O Messenger of God, do you think that if you were to go down into a valley where there was one tree whose fruit had previously been eaten from, and another that had not been eaten from, at which of them would you graze your camel?" "At the one never eaten from." This implied that the Prophet (ṢAAS) married no other virgin but her.'"

Al-Bukhārī alone gives this tradition.

He then stated, "ʿUbayd b. Ismāʿīl related to us, that it was related to him by Abū Usāma, from Hishām b. ʿUrwa, from his father, that ʿĀʾisha said, 'The Messenger of God (ṢAAS) told me, "You were shown to me in my sleep being brought in a cloth of silk by an angel who said to me, 'This is your wife.' I withdrew the cloth from your face and it was you! So I said, 'If this be God's will, then may He bring it about!'"'"

In one account the wording is, "You were shown to me three nights in my sleep."

According to al-Tirmidhī Gabriel brought him her image in a piece of green silk and said, "This is your wife in this world and the next."

Al-Bukhārī's text reads, "*Chapter on Marriage between the Young and the Old*. ʿAbd Allāh b. Yūsuf related to us, as did al-Layth, from Yazīd, from ʿIrāk, from ʿUrwa, that the Messenger of God (ṢAAS) asked Abū Bakr for ʿĀʾisha's hand in marriage. Abū Bakr replied, 'But I'm your brother!' (the Prophet (ṢAAS)) responded, 'You are my brother in God's religion and His Book, and she is permitted to me.'"

The text of this tradition clearly suggests it to be *mursal*, incomplete,[24] even though al-Bukhārī and the authorities consider it uninterrupted. This is because it is a *ḥadīth* of ʿUrwa from ʿĀʾisha, God bless her. This is a tradition narrated by al-Bukhārī alone, God bless him.

Yūnus b. Bukayr stated, from Hishām b. ʿUrwa, from his father who said, "The Messenger of God (ṢAAS) married ʿĀʾisha three years after (the death of) Khadīja. At that time (of the contract) ʿĀʾisha had been a girl of six. When he married her she was nine. The Messenger of God (ṢAAS) died when ʿĀʾisha was a girl of eighteen."

This tradition is considered *gharīb* (unique in this line).

Al-Bukhārī had related, from ʿUbayd b. Ismāʿīl, from Abū Usāma, from Hishām b. ʿUrwa, from his father, who said, "Khadīja died three years before the emigration of the Prophet (ṢAAS). He allowed a couple of years or so to pass after that, and then he contracted marriage with ʿĀʾisha when she was six, thereafter consummating marriage with her when she was nine years old."

---

24. This is so because ʿUrwa, the narrator, is transmitting a conversation to which he was not a party, as is clear from the text. Also, he was too young to have witnessed this meeting.

What ʿUrwa stated here is *mursal*, incomplete, as we mentioned above, but in its content it must be judged as *muttaṣil*, uninterrupted.

His statement, "He contracted marriage with ʿĀʾisha when she was six, thereafter consummating marriage with her when she was nine" is not disputed by anyone, and is well established in the *ṣaḥīḥ* collections of traditions and elsewhere.

He consummated marriage with her during the second year following the emigration to Medina.

His contracting marriage with her took place some three years after Khadīja's death, though there is disagreement over this.

The *ḥāfiẓ* Yaʿqūb b. Sufyān stated, "Al-Ḥajjāj related to us, that Ḥammād related to him, from Hishām b. ʿUrwa, from his father, from ʿĀʾisha, who said, 'The Messenger of God (ṢAAS) contracted marriage with me (after) Khadīja's death and before his emigration from Mecca, when I was six or seven years old. After we arrived in Medina some women came to me while I was playing on a swing; my hair was like that of a boy. They dressed me up and put make-up on me, then took me to the Messenger of God (ṢAAS), and he consummated our marriage. I was a girl of nine.'"

The statement here "*muttawaffā Khadīja*", "Khadīja's death" has to mean that it was shortly thereafter. Unless, that is, the word *baʿda*, "after", originally preceded this phrase and had been omitted from the account. The statement made by Yūnus b. Bukayr and Abū Usāma from Hishām b. ʿUrwa, from his father, is, therefore, not refuted. But God knows best.

Al-Bukhārī stated, "Farwa b. Abū al-Maghrāʾ related to us, that ʿAlī b. Mushir related to him, from Hishām b. ʿUrwa, from his father, that ʿĀʾisha said, 'The Prophet (ṢAAS) contracted marriage with me when I was six. We went to Medina and took up residence with the Banū al-Ḥārith b. al-Khazraj. I fell ill and my hair was cut short so that all I had was a head of hair like a boy's. My mother, Umm Rūmān, came to me when I was on a swing in the company of my friends. She shouted to me and so I went to her not knowing what she wanted. She took me by the hand and sat me down at the door of the house; I was panting, but settled down somewhat. Then she took some water and, having wiped my face and head, led me into the house. There I found a number of the wives of the Companions of the Prophet (ṢAAS), and they addressed me with the words, "Blessings, good health and happy news!" Then she delivered me to them and they tidied me up. To my surprise it was the Messenger of God (ṢAAS) who came to me that morning. They gave me over to him; at the time I was nine.'"

Imām Aḥmad stated in the *musnad*,[25] of ʿĀʾisha, "the mother of the faithful", that "Muḥammad b. Bishr related to him, from Bishr and Muḥammad b. ʿAmr, who was told the following by Abū Salama and Yaḥyā: 'When Khadīja died, Khawla, daughter of Ḥakīm, the wife of ʿUthmān b. Maẓʿūn, came and said, "O

---

25. The word connotes a collection of *ḥadīth* arranged in accord with the names of the persons in their chains of transmission.

Messenger of God, wouldn't you like to get married?" He replied, "To whom?" "To either a virgin or to someone previously married, as you wish."

"""And who would the virgin be?" He asked. She replied, "That creation of God you enjoy above all others, ʿĀʾisha, daughter of Abū Bakr!"

"""And who would the previously married woman be?" he asked. "Sawda, daughter of Zamʿa," she answered. "She has expressed belief in you and has become your follower."

"""You may go," he told her, "and make mention of me to them."

"'She entered Abū Bakr's house and said to his wife, "Umm Rūmān, what goodness and blessings God brings you!" "How do you mean?" she enquired. "The Messenger of God (ṢAAS) has sent me to ask to become engaged to ʿĀʾisha!"

"""See Abū Bakr when he comes in," she replied.

"'Abū Bakr did come and Khawlā said, "O Abū Bakr, what goodness and blessings God brings you!"

"""How so?" he asked.

"""The Messenger of God (ṢAAS) has sent me to ask to become engaged to ʿĀʾisha!"

"""And would she be proper for him? After all, she is his brother's daughter," he responded.

"'So I returned to the Messenger of God (ṢAAS) and told him that and he replied, "Go back and tell him 'I am your brother, and you are mine, in Islam. Your daughter would be proper for me.'"

"'So I went back and told him this, and he replied, "Wait" and left. Umm Rūmān told me, "Muṭʿim b. ʿAdī has asked for her in marriage to his son; and, I swear, Abū Bakr never before broke an agreement he had made."'

"'Abū Bakr went in to see Muṭʿim b. ʿAdī who had his wife, Umm al-Ṣabī, with him. She commented, "Well, son of Abū Quḥāfa, are you perhaps having our friend change his religion and join yours if he gets married into your family?" Abū Bakr asked Muṭʿim b. ʿAdī, "Is this how you respond?" He replied, "It's she who said that."

"'And so Abū Bakr left, God having relieved him of the promise he had made to Muṭʿim. He returned home and told Khawlā, "Call for the Messenger of God (ṢAAS) to come to me." She did so and he agreed to her marriage to him, ʿĀʾisha at that time being six years old.

"'Khawlā then left and went in to see Sawda, daughter of Zamʿa, saying, "What goodness and blessings God brings you!" "How do you mean?" she asked. "The Messenger of God (ṢAAS) has sent me to ask you to marry him!" "I would like that," she replied. "Go in and tell Abū Bakr of that."

"'He was an elderly man, too old to have gone on the pilgrimage, so she went in to him and gave him the salutation used before the coming of Islam. "Who is that?" he asked. "The Messenger of God" (ṢAAS) she told him, "has sent me to arrange his marriage with Sawda." "A fine match! What does your lady say?" he responded. "She would like that," she replied. "Well, call her in to me," he told her. She did so and Abū Bakr said to Sawda, "My child, this woman claims that Muḥammad, son of ʿAbd Allāh b. ʿAbd al-Muṭṭalib, has sent asking to become engaged to you. It's a fine match. Would you have me marry you to him?" "Yes, I would," she replied. "Then call for him," he said.

"'And when the Messenger of God (ṢAAS) came, he did marry him to her.

"'Her brother ʿAbd b. Zamʿa then returned from the pilgrimage, his head covered with dirt. After greetings, he commented, "By your life, what a fool I am! The same day I cover my head with dirt[26] the Messenger of God (ṢAAS) marries Sawda, daughter of Zamʿa!"

"'Āʾisha stated, "We moved to Medina and took up residence among the Banū al-Ḥārith b. Khazraj in al-Sunḥ. The Messenger of God (ṢAAS) came into our house where he had a meeting with some of the men and women of the *anṣār*,[27] 'the Helpers'. My mother came to me while I was on a swing, going to and fro between two date-palms. She took me down from the swing; my hair was short like a boy's and she parted it, washed my face with some water and then led me over to the door. I was out of breath and (stopped) there until I became calmer. Then she took me in and there was the Messenger of God (ṢAAS) seated on a bed inside our house, in the company of a group of the *anṣār*, both men and women. She sat me down in his lap and said, 'These are your family; may God bless you by them and they by you.' The men and women then jumped up and left. The Messenger of God (ṢAAS) consummated our marriage there in our house; no camels or sheep were slaughtered for me. Eventually Saʿd b. ʿUbāda sent us a bowl of food such as he would provide whenever the Messenger of God (ṢAAS) was visiting his wives. At that time, I was nine."'"

This account, though seemingly incomplete is to be considered comprehensive.

This is an account of the same circumstances related by al-Bayhaqī through Aḥmad b. ʿAbd al-Jabbār, as follows, "ʿAbd Allāh b. Idrīs al-Azdī related to us, from Muḥammad b. ʿAmr, from Yaḥyā b. ʿAbd al-Raḥmān b. Ḥāṭib who reported, "Āʾisha said, "When Khadīja died Khawla, daughter of Ḥākim, came and said, 'O Messenger of God, would you like to be married?' 'To whom?' he enquired. 'It could, if you wish, be to a virgin or to a woman previously married,' she replied. 'Which virgin, and which previously married woman?' he asked. 'The virgin could be the daughter of that creation of God whom you love best; the previously married woman would be Sawda, daughter of Zamʿa. She has expressed belief in you and become your follower.' 'Make mention of me to them,' he told her."'"

The account hereafter relates the *ḥadīth* essentially as above.

---

26. Apparently placing dirt on the head was part of the pre-Islamic pilgrimage ritual in which he had engaged.

27. This refers to the people of Yathrib (later Medina) who accepted Islam and assisted the Muslim migrants from Mecca.

This tradition firmly establishes that his betrothal to 'Ā'isha preceded his marriage to Sawda, daughter of Zam'a.

However, he did consummate marriage with Sawda in Mecca, whereas that with 'Ā'isha was postponed until Medina, in the second year (after the hegira) as indicated above and hereafter.

Imām Aḥmad stated, "Aswad related to us, that it was related to him from Shurayk, from Hishām, from his father, from 'Ā'isha, who said, 'When Sawda grew old and she gave to me the day assigned to her, the Messenger of God (ṢAAS) shared the day given to me (by her) with his other wives. She was the first woman with whom he contracted marriage after myself.'"

Imām Aḥmad stated, "Abū al-Naḍr related to us, quoting 'Abd al-Ḥamīd, Shahr and 'Abd Allāh b. 'Abbās, that the Messenger of God (ṢAAS) became engaged to a woman from his people whose name was Sawda; she was a woman with many children, having some five or six from her husband who had died. The Messenger of God (ṢAAS) asked her, 'Is there something holding you back from me?' She replied, 'O Prophet of God, nothing prevents you from being the most beloved of mankind to me. But I would do you honour by preventing these boys from being at your head morning and night!'

"'Does anything else keep you from me?' he asked. 'No, I swear,' she replied. The Messenger of God (ṢAAS) then told her, 'God have mercy on you! The best of women ride on old camels; isn't that appropriate? The women of Quraysh are kind to a boy when young and they also take care of their husband however they can!'"

I observe that her husband before him was al-Sakrān b. 'Amr, brother of Suhayl b. 'Amr. He had accepted Islam and gone into exile to Abyssinia, as we reported before. He had then returned to Mecca and died there before the emigration, God be pleased with him!

All these accounts indicate that the marriage contract with 'Ā'isha was prior to that with Sawda, this being the statement of 'Abd Allāh b. Muḥammad b. 'Uqayl. Yūnus also related this from al-Zuhrī.

Ibn 'Abd al-Barr preferred the contract with Sawda to have preceded that with 'Ā'isha; he related this from Qatāda and Abū 'Ubayd.

He stated, "'Uqayl related it from al-Zuhrī."

DIVISION

Reference has previously been given to the death of Abū Ṭālib, the uncle of the Messenger of God (ṢAAS), and to his having been a supporter and defender of his, with all the moral, financial, verbal and practical help he could give.

When he died, foolish men of Quraysh were emboldened and engaged in such actions against him that they had not previously been able to undertake.

As al-Bayhaqī reported from al-Ḥākim, from al-Aṣamm: "Muḥammad b. Isḥāq al-San'ānī related to us, from Yūsuf b. Bahlūl, from 'Abd Allāh b. Idrīs, from Muhammad b. Ishāq, from someone else who told him, from ʿUrwa b. al-Zubayr, from ʿAbd Allāh b. Jaʿfar, who said, 'When Abū Ṭālib died, a foolish fellow of Quraysh stood in the way of the Messenger of God (SAAS), and threw dirt at him. He, the Messenger of God (SAAS), then returned home and one of his daughters came and wiped the dirt from his face, weeping. He told her, "Don't cry, daughter; God will protect your father."'"

He is supposed to have said during this conversation that Quraysh did not engage in any reprehensible actions against him until the death of Abū Ṭālib, at which point they began (to harass him).

Ziyād al-Bakāʿī related this from Muhammad b. Ishāq, from Hishām b. ʿUrwa, from his father, with an incomplete chain of authorities. But God knows best.

Al-Bayhaqī also related, from al-Ḥākim and others, from al-Aṣamm, from Ahmad b. ʿAbd al-Jabbār, from Yūnus b. Bukayr, from Hishām b. ʿUrwa, from his father, that the Messenger of God (SAAS) said, "Quraysh remained cowards until Abū Ṭālib died."

He then related this from al-Ḥākim, from al-Aṣamm, from ʿAbbās al-Dūrī, from Yahyā b. Maʿīn, who said, "We were related by ʿUqba al-Majdar, from Hishām b. ʿUrwa, from his father, from ʿĀʾisha, that the Prophet (SAAS) said, 'Quraysh remained cowards until Abū Ṭālib died.'"

The *hāfiz* Abū al-Faraj b. al-Jawzī related with a chain of authorities from Thaʿlaba b. Ṣuqayr and Ḥākīm b. Ḥizam who both said, "When Abū Ṭālib and Khadīja died, five days apart, he suffered two tragedies together. He kept to his house and rarely went out. Quraysh treated him worse than they would have ever intended before.

"News of this reached Abū Lahab, who came to him and said, 'O Muhammad, pass on freely as you want. Do whatever you did when Abū Ṭālib was alive. No, by al-Lāt, I swear no harm will befall you before I die.'

"Ibn al-Ghayṭala insulted the Messenger of God (SAAS), and so Abū Lahab went to him and punished him and he went off yelling, 'O tribe of Quraysh, Abū ʿUtba has become a Ṣabian!' Quraysh men then came and stood before Abū Lahab. He told them, 'I have not left the faith of ʿAbd al-Muṭṭalib. But I will prevent my nephew from being harmed and ensure his own freedom of action.'

"They commented, 'You have done well and right, and maintained your family ties.'

"The Messenger of God (SAAS) thereafter spent a period of some days coming and going without interference from Quraysh who respected Abū Lahab. But eventually ʿUqba b. Abū Muʿayṭ and Abū Jahl went to Abū Lahab and asked him, 'Has your nephew told you where your father has been sent?'

"Abū Lahab then asked him, 'Muhammad, where has ʿAbd al-Muṭṭalib been sent?'

"He replied, 'With his people.' So Abū Lahab went out to ʿUqba and Abū Jahl and told them, 'I did ask him. And he replied, "With his people."'"

"The two men commented, 'Well, he's claiming that he is in hell-fire then!'

"Abū Lahab then asked him, 'Muḥammad, is ʿAbd al-Muṭṭalib in the fire?'

"The Messenger of God (ṢAAS) replied, 'Whoever dies in the state ʿAbd al-Muṭṭalib was in does go into hell-fire.'

"Abū Lahab – God curse him – then announced, 'By God, I shall always be your enemy for your claiming that ʿAbd al-Muṭṭalib is in the fire!'

"At that Abū Lahab and the rest of Quraysh intensified their attacks upon him."

Ibn Isḥāq stated, "The group of men who used to harm the Messenger of God (ṢAAS) in his house were Abū Lahab, al-Ḥakam b. Abū al-ʿĀṣ b. Umayya, ʿUqba b. Abū Muʿayṭ, ʿAdī b. al-Ḥamrāʾ, and Ibn al Aṣdāʾ al-Hudhalī.

"These were neighbours of his; the only one of them to ever accept Islam was al-Ḥakam b. Abū al-ʿĀṣ.

"It is said that one of them would throw a sheep's uterus over him while he was praying, or toss it into his cooking pot if set up for him. Eventually the Messenger of God (ṢAAS) would take a position near a wall when praying and when they threw some such thing at him he would carry it outside on a stick, stand at his door and say, 'O Banū ʿAbd Manāf, what kind of neighbourliness is this?' Then he would toss it out into the street."

My own view is that most of the matter being related here occurred after the death of Abū Ṭālib. Though God knows best. It is certainly very appropriate to mention them here. These incidents included the throwing of a camel's placenta over his shoulders while he prayed, as Ibn Masʿūd related, and of Fāṭima's having come and removed it from him and having gone off and reviled them; when he had finished praying, he said prayers against seven of them. A similar incident was the account of ʿAbd Allāh b. ʿAmr b. al-ʿĀṣ of their having severely throttled him until Abū Bakr intervened, saying, "Would you murder a man merely for saying God is my Lord?" And there is the case of the intent of Abū Jahl, God damn him, to tread on his neck while he prayed, and of this being prevented.

Section: On his departure to the people of Ṭāʾif to call them to Almighty God, and to come to the aid of His faith; how they refused him this and he returned to Mecca.

Ibn Isḥāq stated, "When Abū Ṭālib died, Quraysh treated the Messenger of God (ṢAAS) worse than had ever been the case during the life of his uncle Abū Ṭālib.

"And so the Messenger of God (ṢAAS) left for Ṭāʾif seeking help from Thaqīf and their protection from his people. He hoped they would accept the message he brought them from God Almighty.

"He went to them alone.

"Yazīd b. Abū Ziyād related to me, from Muḥammad b. Kaʿb al-Kuraẓī, who said, 'When the Messenger of God (ṢAAS) arrived in Ṭāʾif, he made for a group of Thaqīf, their leaders and nobles, who were three brothers. They were ʿAbd

Yālīl, Masʿūd and Ḥabīb, all sons of ʿAmr b. ʿUmayr b. ʿAwf b. ʿUqda b. Ghiyara b. ʿAwf b. Thaqīf. One of these was married to a Quraysh woman of the Banū Jumaḥ.

"'He sat with them and invited them to God, asked them to help Islam and himself against those of his people who were opposing him. One of them replied, "He would tear off the covering of the *kaʿba* if it were God who had sent you!" Another said, "Did not God have anyone but you to send?" The third commented, "By God, I will never speak to you. If you were a messenger from God, as you claim, you are far too important for me to argue with, and if you are lying against God, then it would certainly not be appropriate that I talk to you."

"'And so the Messenger of God (ṢAAS) arose and left them, despairing of any good from Thaqīf. I have been told that he had asked them, "Since you have so behaved, at least keep it secret for me." The Messenger of God (ṢAAS) did not want his people to hear about this, since it would have encouraged them to oppose him.

"'However, they did not agree, and incited their fools and slaves to revile him and to shout out after him. A crowd gathered against him and forced him to seek refuge in a garden belonging to ʿUtba b. Rabīʿa and Shayba b. Rabīʿa, they both being there at the time. The Thaqīf fools who had been following him then withdrew.

"'He made for the shade of a grape vine, where he sat down, while the two sons of Rabīʿa watched him, having seen his ill-treatment by the Thaqīf fools.

"'As I have been told, the Messenger of God (ṢAAS) had met the woman from the Banū Jumaḥ and had told her, "Well, how is it we've been so treated by your husband's family?"

"'When he felt secure, as I have been told, he spoke the prayer, "O God, I complain to You about my weakness and inadequacy before the people. O You, most Merciful of all, You who are Lord of the oppressed, You who are my Lord, to whom would You entrust me, to those far away who greet me with displeasure, or to some enemy to whom You entrust me? As long as You are not angry with me, I will not care, but I would prefer your favour.

"'"I take refuge with the light of Your face that brightens the shadows, repairs the troubles of this world and the hereafter, ensuring that Your anger or discontent not alight upon me. May You be content and be pleased; all power and strength stem from You."

"'When Rabīʿa's two sons ʿUtba and Shayba saw what had happened to him, they felt compassion for him. They summoned a Christian servant they had called ʿAddās and told him, "Take a cluster of grapes, place it on a plate, then go over to that man and tell him to eat it."

"''ʿAddās did this; he placed it before the Messenger of God (ṢAAS), and told him to eat.

"'As the Messenger of God (ṢAAS) placed his hand upon it, he spoke the words, "In the name of God" then he ate. ʿAddās looked into his face and said,

"By God, people of this land do not say these words." The Messenger of God (ṢAAS) asked him, "Where are you from, 'Addās, and what is your religion?" He replied, "I am a Christian, and I come from Nineveh."

"'The Messenger of God (ṢAAS) then asked, "You mean from the village of that pious man Jonah, son of Amittai?"

"''Addās asked, "How do you know of Jonah, son of Amittai?"

"'The Messenger of God (ṢAAS) replied, "That man was my brother; he was a prophet and I am a prophet."

"''Addās bent low over the Messenger of God (ṢAAS), kissing his head, hands and feet.

"'The two sons of Rabī'a said to one another, "He's already corrupted our servant!"

"'When 'Addās came back to them, they commented, "What was wrong with you, 'Addās? Why did you kiss the head, hands and feet of that man?"

"'"On all earth there is none finer than this man; he has told me of something that no one but a prophet could know," he told them.

"'"Be careful", they warned him, "you don't let him turn you from your faith. Your religion is better than his."''"

Mūsā b. 'Uqba related this similarly but did not include the prayer and added the words, "The people of Ṭā'if positioned themselves in two lines along his path and as he passed by every time he raised and put down a foot they threw stones at it until his feet began to bleed. His feet streaming with blood, he withdrew and made his way beneath the shade of a palm tree, completely overcome. In that garden were 'Utba and Shayba, the two sons of Rabī'a. He disliked being at their place because of their enmity towards God and His Messenger."

Mūsā then related the story of 'Addās the Christian much as above.

Imām Aḥmad recounted from Abū Bakr b. Abū Shayba as follows, "Marwān b. Mu'āwiya al-Fazārī related to us, from 'Abd Allāh b. 'Abd al-Raḥmān al-Ṭā'ifī, from 'Abd al-Raḥmān b. Khālid b. Abū Jabal al-'Adwānī, from his father, that he saw the Messenger of God (ṢAAS) in the winter quarters of Thaqīf standing on a staff or a bow, having gone to them seeking their help. The source said, 'I heard him say, "By the heavens and he who comes by night" (*sūrat al-Ṭāriq*; LXXXVI, v.1) up to its end.'"

He went on, "So I became aware of it in the *jahiliyya*, before Islam, while I was a polytheist, then I recited it after accepting Islam.

"Thaqīf summoned me and asked, 'What did you hear from that man?' so I recited it to them. One of the Quraysh men there with Thaqīf said, 'We are very well acquainted with him; if we knew that what he says is true, we would follow him.'"

It is established in both *ṣaḥīḥ* collections, through 'Abd Allāh b. Wahb, who said, "I was told by Yūnus b. Yazīd from Ibn Shihāb, who told him, 'It was related to me by 'Urwa b. al-Zubayr that 'Ā'isha related to him that she said to the Messenger of God (SAAS), "Has any day been harder on you than that of the battle of Uhud?"

"'He replied, "The worst I suffered from your people was the day of al-ʿaqaba, when I presented myself to Ibn ʿAbdu Yālīl b. ʿAbd Kalāl, and he refused my request to him. I wandered off, dazed and depressed, and only came to myself at Qarn al-Thaʿālib. I raised my head and there above me was a cloud. Looking up, I saw Gabriel in it, and he called out to me, saying, 'God has heard what your people said to you, and how they rejected you. He has sent to you the angel of the mountain for you to order him to do with them whatever you like.'

"'"Then the angel of the mountain called out to me in greeting and said, 'O Muhammad, God has sent me. God has heard what your people said to you. I am the angel of the mountain; your Lord has sent me to you to order me to do whatever you wish. If you wish, you can bring down the two mountains the Akhshabayn upon them.' The Messenger of God (SAAS) replied, 'I hope that God will bring forth from their loins those who will worship God and associate no other god or person with Him.'"'"

DIVISION

Muhammad b. Isḥāq told how the jinn, the spirits, overheard the recitation made by the Messenger of God (SAAS) upon his return from Ṭāʾif when he spent the night at Nakhla and said the morning prayer with his Companions. The jinn who had been dispatched to him heard his reciting there.

Ibn Isḥāq stated, "They were seven in number. Concerning them God Almighty revealed His words, 'And when We dispatched towards you a group of jinn'" (sūrat al-Aḥqāf; XLVI, v.29).

My own comment is that we spoke about this in detail in the Tafsīr (Exegesis), and included some material relating to it above. But God knows best.

Then the Messenger of God (SAAS) entered Mecca on his return from Ṭāʾif and came under the protection of al-Muṭʿim b. ʿAdī. His people increased their anger and antagonism towards him and became ever bolder in their opposition. God is the one from whom to seek help, and reliance must be upon Him.

In his work on the maghāzī, the early military engagements, al-Umawī related that the Messenger of God (SAAS) sent Urayqiṭ to al-Akhnas b. Sharīf and asked him to give him protection in Mecca. But he replied, 'An ally of Quraysh cannot give protection for one of their own.'

"He then sent to Suhayl b. ʿAmr to give him protection, and he responded, 'The Banū ʿĀmir b. Luʾayy cannot give protection against those of the Banū Kaʿb b. Luʾayy.'

"He then sent him to al-Muṭʿim b. ʿAdī for his protection, who agreed, saying, 'Yes; tell him to come.'

"And so the Messenger of God (SAAS) did go to him and spent that night with him. When morning came, he and his six or seven sons, all wearing swords, went out with the Messenger of God (ṢAAS). They entered the mosque and told the Messenger of God (ṢAAS), 'Make your circumambulations.' And they sat, with their legs drawn up over their belted swords in the *maṭāf*, the space around the *kaʿba* for the circumambulations.

"Abū Sufyān came over to Muṭʿim and asked him, 'Are you giving protection or are you a follower?'

"He replied, 'No, I'm just protecting.'

"'Then you'll not be watched,' Abū Sufyān told him.

"He then sat with him until the Messenger of God (ṢAAS) had finished his circuits, and when he left al-Muṭʿim and his men went with him. Then Abū Sufyān went off to his seat."

The account went on, "This continued for a few days, then he was given permission to make the *hijra*, to leave for Medina.

"Shortly after the Messenger of God (ṢAAS) had left Mecca for Medina, al-Muṭʿim b. ʿAdī died. Ḥassān b. Thābit said, 'By God, I shall certainly eulogize him!' And part of what he spoke were the following verses:

> 'If honour could today render any one person
> everlasting, his honour would today select Muṭʿim.
> You protected the Messenger of God from them and they
> became your slaves for as long as pilgrims don the *iḥrām* and
> shout "*labbayka*".
> If all Maʿadd, Qaḥṭān or all the rest of Jurhum
> were asked about him,
> They would say, "He fulfils defence of his neighbour and
> protects if he takes on a difficult duty,"
> The shining sun above them does not look down on his like
> among them, one greater or more noble.
> Resolute if refusing, but kind by nature, sleeping well
> even if the night is dark and he protecting another.'

I observe that this is why the Prophet (ṢAAS) said, on the day the prisoners were taken at Badr, "If al-Muṭʿim b. ʿAdī were alive now and asked me about these stinking people, I would have given them over to him."

Section: On the call of the Messenger of God (ṢAAS) to the Arab tribes during the pilgrimage seasons to help and support him against those persecuting and denying him. None of them agreed, since God Almighty had reserved that great honour to the anṣar *(the "Helpers" or "Partisans") of Medina, may God be pleased with them.*

Ibn Isḥāq stated, "Then the Messenger of God (ṢAAS) returned to Mecca, where his people were even more antagonistic to him and his religion than before, except for a few persons of no power who did believe.

"The Messenger of God (ṢAAS) would present himself at the fairs when they were held, addressing the Arab tribes and inviting them to God, Almighty and Glorious is He. He would tell them that he was a prophet who had been given a mission, and would ask for their belief and their protection so that he could explain what God had entrusted to him."

Ibn Isḥāq continued, "One of our fellow scholars, a man in whom I trust, related the following to me, from Zayd b. Aslam, from Rabīʿa b. ʿIbād al-Duʾalī, and another person from whom Abū Zinād had narrated. I was also related this by Ḥusayn b. ʿAbd Allāh b. ʿUbayd Allāh b. ʿAbbās, who said, 'I heard Rabīʿa b. ʿIbād being addressed by my father who said, "I was once, when a young lad, with my father at Minā when the Messenger of God (ṢAAS) would stop at the camps of the Arab tribes and say to them, 'I am the Messenger of God to you. I tell you to worship God and to associate no other with Him and to abandon those others you revere; and you should have faith and belief in me and protect me so that I make evident that with which God sent me.'"

"'Behind him stood a squint-eyed, neatly dressed man, his hair in two braids and wearing a cloak from Aden. When the Messenger of God (ṢAAS) had finished his prayer and address, that man would say to the tribe, "This man is only trying to get you to strip al-Lāt and al-ʿUzzā off your necks, along with your allies the *jinn* of the Banū Mālik b. Uqaysh in favour of the wrongful innovation he himself brings. Do not obey him and do not listen to him."

"'I asked my father, "Who is that man who follows behind him and contradicts what he says?"

"'He replied, "That is his uncle, ʿAbd al-Uzzā b. ʿAbd al-Muṭṭalib, Abū Lahab.""'"

Imām Aḥmad recounted this *ḥadīth* from Ibrāhīm b. Abū al-ʿAbbās saying, "ʿAbd al-Raḥmān b. Abū Zinād related to us, from his father, who said, 'A man named Rabīʿa b. ʿIbād of the Banū al-Dīl informed me – he having been a polytheist before Islam who converted – as follows, "I saw the Messenger of God (ṢAAS) in the market of Dhū al-Majāz in the period before Islam was accepted; he was saying, 'O people, say, "There is no god but God" and you will prosper.' As people gathered around him there was one man with a handsome face, squint-eyed and wearing two plaits who would say, 'He's a Ṣabian, a liar.' And he would follow behind him wherever he went. I asked about him and was told he was his uncle Abū Lahab."'"

Al-Bayhaqī related this, through Muḥammad b. ʿAbd Allāh al-Anṣārī, from Muḥammad b. ʿAmr, from Muḥammad b. al-Munkadir, from Rabīʿa al-Dīlī, as follows, "I saw the Messenger of God (ṢAAS) at the market of Dhū al-Majāz following people into their homes and inviting them to God. Behind him came a squint-eyed man with flaming-red cheeks who was saying, 'Do not let this man lead you astray from your religion and that of your forefathers.' I asked who he was, and I was told that this was Abū Lahab."

Abū Nuʿaym related this similarly in the *Dalāʾil* (*The Signs*), through Ibn Abū Dhiʾb and Saʿīd b. Salama b. Abū al-Husām, both of them relating a similar account from Muḥammad b. al-Munkadir.

Al-Bayhaqī also related it through Shuʿba, from al-Ashʿath b. Salīm, from a man of Kināna, who said, "I saw the Messenger of God (ṢAAS) at the market of Dhū al-Majāz and he was saying, 'O people, say, "There is no god but God" and you will prosper.' And there was a man behind him tossing dirt at him. This was Abū Jahl and he was saying, 'O people, do not let this man lead you astray from your religion. He only wants you to give up worship of al-Lāt and al-ʿUzzā.'"

According to this account, these were words of Abū Jahl. This supposition might be illusory or it might sometimes have been Abū Jahl and sometimes the other, Abū Lahab. They might have taken turns in doing such harm to the Messenger of God (ṢAAS).

Ibn Isḥāq stated, "Ibn Shihāb al-Zuhrī related to me that the Messenger of God (ṢAAS) went to the tribe of Kinda, visiting them in their homes, including one of their leaders named Mulayḥ. He invited them to God, Almighty and Glorious is He, and offered himself to them, but they refused him."

Ibn Isḥāq said, "Muḥammad b. ʿAbd al-Raḥmān b. ʿAbd Allāh b. Ḥusayn related to me that the Messenger of God (ṢAAS) went to the Banū Kalb in their homes in a valley of theirs where they were called the Banū ʿAbd Allāh. He called them to the path of God and offered himself to them, saying, 'O Banū ʿAbd Allāh, God named well indeed your forefather ʿAbd Allāh' (i.e. 'the slave or servant of God'). But they could not accept from him what he proposed to them.

"Some of our friends related to me, from ʿAbd Allāh b. Kaʿb b. Mālik that the Messenger of God (ṢAAS) went to the Banū Ḥanīfa in their homes, called them to the path of God and offered himself to them. None of the Arabs gave him so rude a rejection as they did.

"Al-Zuhrī related to me that he went to the Banū ʿĀmir b. Ṣaʿṣaʿa and called them to the path of God, offering himself to them. One of their men, named Bayḥara b. Firās, replied to him, 'I swear, if I were to have this brave man of Quraysh, I could eat up the Arabs with him.' He then said to him, 'If we were to follow your orders and then God gave you victory against those opposing you, would we have power after you were gone?'

"He replied, 'God controls power and places it where He wishes.'

"Bayḥara commented in reply, 'Are we to present our throats to the Arabs in your defence and then, if God gave you victory, see power go elsewhere than to us? We'll have nothing to do with you!' And so they refused him.

"When the people there dispersed, the Banū ʿĀmir returned to a sheikh of theirs who, being elderly, was unable to attend the fairs with them. When they returned home they would tell him what had occurred at the fair. That year on their return he asked them who had been at the fair. They told him, 'A man of Quraysh, of the family of ʿAbd al-Muṭṭalib, came to us claiming to be a prophet and he asked us to defend him and aid him and take him back to our territory.'

"The old man put his hand to his head and said, 'Could your mistake be put right? Can its consequences be reversed? I swear no descendant of Ishmael ever made such a claim falsely. It has to be true. Where did your good judgement go?'"

Mūsā b. ʿUqba stated, quoting al-Zuhrī, "The Messenger of God (ṢAAS) would for the period of those years, present himself to the Arab tribes at each fair, speaking with each tribal leader but asking them only for their protection and support. He would say, 'I don't wish to force any one of you to do anything. Any of you who agree to what I ask may do so, but I would not compel anyone not so wishing. All I want is to guard myself against those wanting to kill me, so that I may fulfil my Lord's mission and carry out whatever decree He wishes regarding myself and those who support me.' But not one of them accepted him. Every one of those tribes reached the following conclusion: 'The man's own tribe knew him best; how could we accept as suitable for us someone who has subverted his tribe and whom they have expelled.'

"This rejection too was due to the honour God had in store for the *anṣār* (the 'Helpers') of Medina."

The *ḥāfiẓ* Abū Nuʿaym related through ʿAbd Allāh b. al-Ajlaḥ and Yaḥyā b. Saʿīd al-Umawī, who both took their information from Muḥammad b. al-Sāʾib al-Kalbī, from Abū Ṣāliḥ, from Ibn ʿAbbās, from ʿAbbās, who said, "The Messenger of God (ṢAAS) told me, 'I don't consider myself receiving protection from you or from your brother. Would you take me to the market tomorrow for us to stay in the homes of some of the tribespeople?' It was the time for the gathering of the Arab tribes.

"He (the Prophet (ṢAAS)) went on, 'These are Kinda and those who mix with them. They are the best of those from Yemen who make the pilgrimage. Those are the homes of Bakr b. Wāʾil; those belong to the Banū ʿĀmir b. Saʿṣaʿa. Choose for yourself.'"

ʿAbbas continued "He began with Kinda, asking them, 'From whom are you?' 'From Yemen,' they replied. 'From which tribe?' he asked. 'From Kinda.' 'From which sub-tribe?' he next enquired. 'From the Banū ʿAmr b. Muʿāwiya,' they told him.

"'Would you like to achieve good?'

"'How would that be?' they asked.

"'You would bear witness that there is no god but God, and would engage in prayer and believe in God's message.'"

ʿAbd Allāh b. al-Ajlaḥ quoted his father as having said, on the authority of the elders of his people, that Kinda replied to him (the Prophet (ṢAAS)), "If you are successful, will you grant us power after yourself?"

The Messenger of God (ṢAAS) replied, "Power rests with God; He places it where He wishes."

They responded, "We don't need what you bring."

Al-Kalbī went on to state, "And they (Kinda) said, 'have you come to us to keep us from our gods and have us go to war with the Arabs? Remain with your people. We have no need of you!'

"He then left them and went to Bakr b. Wā°il. He asked, 'Who are these people?' 'They are part of Bakr b. Wā°il.' 'From which sub-tribe?' he asked. He was told, 'From the Banū Qays b. Tha°laba.'

"'How many are they?' he asked.

"'Very numerous,' he was told.

"'How would their protection be?' he asked.

"They replied, 'We border on Persia; we have no protection from them or for them.'

"He told them, 'Grant God custody over yourselves and He will keep you safe until you descend upon their homes, marry their women and enslave their children. Then give praise to God three and thirty times, then give thanks to Him three and thirty times, and say He is most great four and thirty times.'

"'Who are you?' they asked.

"'I am the Messenger of God,' he replied. Then he left.

"When he had left," al-Kalbī said, "his uncle Abū Lahab had been following him and telling people, 'Do not accept what he says.' When he passed by them, they asked, 'Do you know this man?' He replied, 'Yes, he's from our élite. What about him makes you ask?' They told him what he had offered them, saying, 'He claims to be the Messenger of God.' Abū Lahab commented, 'Take no account of whatever he says. He's crazy, and talks off the top of his head.'

"'We saw that,' they commented, 'when he spoke as he did about Persia!'"

Al-Kalbī stated, "°Abd al-Raḥmān al-°Āmirī told me that elders of his tribe said, 'The Messenger of God (ṢAAS) came to us when we were at the °Ukāz fair. He asked, "From whom are these people?" We replied, "From the Banū °Āmir b. Ṣa°ṣa°a." "From which sub-tribe?" he asked.

"'We responded, "From the Banū Ka°b b. Rabī°a."

"'He asked, "How would protection be with you?"

"'We replied, "The best imaginable; we are invincible."

"'He stated to them, "I am the Messenger of God, and I am coming to you to protect me until I fulfil the mission of my Lord. I would not force any of you to anything."

"'They asked him, "From which part of Quraysh are you?"

"'"From the family of °Abd al-Muṭṭalib," he replied.

"'"What are your relations with the °Abd Manāf?" they asked.

"'"They were the first to deny and to drive me away," he told them.

"'"Well, we will neither drive you away nor believe in you; but we will protect you until you fulfil your Lord's mission."

"'So he took residence with them while they were attending the fair. And then Bayḥara b. Firāsh al-Qushayrī came to them and said, "Who is this man I now see with you; I don't know him?"

"""He is Muḥammad, son of ʿAbd Allāh, of Quraysh," they replied.

""""And what do you have to do with him?" he asked.

""""He claims to be the Messenger of God and he has asked us to protect him until he fulfils his Lord's mission," they replied.

""""And how did you respond?" he enquired.

""""We made him very welcome," they told him. "We said we would take him to our own territory and protect him as we do ourselves."

"'Bayḥara commented, "I know of no one at this fair going back home with anything worse than you are. You have begun a policy that will alienate people; the Arabs will attack you in unison. His people know him very well; if they had perceived good in him, they would have been most delighted with him. Will you support a man cast out and denied by his own people and give him shelter and aid? Your policy is dreadful."

"'He then approached the Messenger of God (ṢAAS), and told him, "Get up and join your people. I swear if you weren't here among my kin, I would strike you down!"

"'And so the Messenger of God (ṢAAS) got up and mounted his camel. That evil man Bayḥara then prodded the mount in its flank and it darted away with the Messenger of God (ṢAAS), and threw him.

"'With the Banū ʿĀmir on that day was Ḍabāʿa, daughter of ʿĀmir b. Qarṭ; she was one of the women who had accepted Islam with the Messenger of God (ṢAAS) in Mecca. She had come on a visit to the Banū ʿĀmir. She spoke out, "O people of ʿĀmir, you're not ʿāmir (i.e. civilized, cultured) to me! Could this really happen to the Messenger of God, right here among you without any one of you protecting him?"

"'Three of her relatives then attacked Bayḥara, while two assisted him. Each man fought with another, her supporters beating the others to the ground, sitting on their chests and slapping their faces.

"'The Messenger of God (ṢAAS) then spoke, "May God bless these men and damn the others!"

"'The three who had aided him later embraced Islam and died as martyrs in battle. These were Ghaṭīf and Ghaṭfān, two sons of Sahl and ʿUrwa – or ʿUdhra b. ʿAbd Allāh b. Salama. God be pleased with them.'"

The ḥāfiẓ Saʿīd b. Yaḥyā b. Saʿīd al-Umawī related this ḥadīth from his father in its entirety in his book of the maghāzī, the military campaigns.

The other men all perished. These were Bayḥara b. Firās, Ḥazn b. ʿAbd Allāh b. Salama b. Qushayr and Muʿāwiya b. ʿAbbāda, one of the Banū ʿUqayl, may God damn them utterly.

This is a curious tale; we give it here for its strangeness. But God knows best.

Abū Nuʿaym related a similar account, from a ḥadīth of Kaʿb b. Mālik, God bless him, relating to the story of ʿĀmir b. Ṣaʿṣaʿa and the rudeness of their reply to him.

Even stranger and lengthier than that was what Abū Nuʿaym, al-Ḥākim and al-Bayhaqī related; the text was given by Abū Nuʿaym, may God be pleased with them all. It comes from a *hadīth* of Abān b. ʿAbd Allāh al-Bajalī, from Abān b. Ṭaghlib, from ʿIkrima, from Ibn ʿAbbās, who quoted ʿAlī b. Abū Ṭālib as having said, "When God ordered His Messenger to present himself to the tribes of the Arabs, he left, along with myself and Abū Bakr, for Minā. There we were present at a *majlis*, a reception, given by the Arabs.

"Abū Bakr, God bless him, went forward and made his greetings. He was in the very vanguard of good, and an expert in genealogy. He asked, 'From whom do you people come?' 'From Rabīʿa,' came their reply.

"'From which Rabīʿa are you, from its mainstream or from a branch?'

"'From its greatest mainstream.'

"Abū Bakr asked them, 'Is ʿAwf of you, of whom it was said, "There is no *ḥarr*, no heat, in the ʿAwf valley?"'

"'No,' they told him.

"'Do Bisṭām b. Qays Abū al-Liwāʾ and Muntahā al-Aḥyāʾ belong to your tribe?'

"'No,' they replied.

"'Is al-Ḥawfazān b. Shurayk, the killer of kings and robber of their souls, a kinsman of yours?'

"'No,' they replied.

"'Is Jassās b. Murra b. Dhuhl, the protector of honour and defender of the neighbour, from you?'

"'No,' they said.

"'Is al-Muzdalif, he of the unique turban, from you?'

"'No,' they replied.

"'Are you related to the kings of Kinda?' he asked.

"'No,' they replied.

"'Are you related to the kings of Lakhm?' he asked.

"'No,' they replied.

"Abū Bakr, God bless him, then commented, 'So you're not from its mainstream, but from a branch.'

"At that a youth named Daghfal b. Ḥanẓala al-Dhuhlī, his beard beginning to sprout, jumped up and grabbed the bridle of Abū Bakr's camel, reciting, 'Those who ask of us will be asked of; as for the burden (of proof) we neither know it nor bear it (as a responsibility).'

"He also commented, 'Hey, you, you asked and we replied, hiding nothing from you. We want to ask you something; who are you?'

"He replied, 'A man of Quraysh.'

"The youth commented, 'Well said! You are a people of leadership and power, the vanguard and guide of the Arabs. What part of Quraysh?'

"He replied, 'I'm of the Banū Taym b. Murra.'

"The youth asked again, 'So you shot the bowman right through his mouth! Is Quṣayy b. Kilāb, he who killed at Mecca those trying to conquer it, a kinsman of yours? That man, Quṣayy, who drove the rest of them away and brought in his own people from all over and settled them in Mecca, took over the temple and set Quraysh in the dwellings? The man who was therefore known as "the unifier", and about whom a poet spoke the verse,

> "Was it not your father who was called 'the unifier',
> by whom God brought together the tribes of Fihr?"'

"Abū Bakr replied, 'No.'

"'Were not ʿAbd Manāf, the ultimate giver of advice, and Abū al-Ghaṭārif, the great leader, of your stock?'

"Abū Bakr replied, 'No.'

"'And ʿAmr b. ʿAbd Manāf Hāshim, who prepared bread and meat into the dish *al-tharīd* for his people and all of Mecca, was he not of you? The one of whom the poet said,

> "'ʿAmr al-ʿUlā prepared the *al-tharīd* for his people,
> while the men of Mecca were destitute and under famine,
> To him they attribute both the journeys, that of the
> winter and that of the summer,
> Quraysh were as an egg which when split open came to have
> its best part, its yoke, as the ʿAbd Manāf.
> (They are) the wealthy, as is no other known, and they
> are those who say 'come on in' to the guests.
> They are those who strike down pure-white sheep, those
> who protect the innocent with their swords.
> How fine for you, if you stay at their abode; they will
> protect you from all ills and accusations."'

"'No,' responded Abū Bakr.

"'Then,' the youth continued, 'you must be related to ʿAbd al-Muṭib, that venerable man of much praise, controller of the Mecca caravan, and feeder of the birds of the skies and the wild beasts, of the lions in the desert, he whose face shines forth like a moon on a dark night?'

"'No,' said Abū Bakr.

"'Then you must be of those who have the privilege of the *ifāḍa*?' (The signalling to the pilgrims to move from Arafāt to Minā.)

"'No,' said Abū Bakr.

"'Perhaps of those who have the privilege of the *ḥijāba*? (The guardianship of the holy places.)

"'No,' said Abū Bakr.

"'Then those with the privilege of the *nadwa*?' (Making an address to the pilgrims.)

"'No,' said Abū Bakr.

"'Then you must be of those who have the privilege of the *siqāya*? (The provision of drink for the pilgrims.)

"'No,' said Abū Bakr.

"'Are you then of those with the privilege of providing the *rifāda*?' (The provisioning of the pilgrims.)

"'No,' replied Abū Bakr.

"'Are you then of those who give bounteous aid?'

"'No,' said Abū Bakr and he pulled his bridle out of the hands of the youth, who then quoted the line,

> 'Sometimes it happens that distinction is moved on
> down, at other times up.'

"Then he commented, 'Well, I swear, O Brother of Quraysh, if you had continued to hold out I would have proven you to belong to the lowest class of Quraysh, not to its élite!'

"The Messenger of God (ṢAAS) now came over to us, smiling," ʿAlī went on, "and I commented to Abū Bakr, 'Well, this bedouin has turned out to be a disaster for you!' 'Yes indeed, Abū al-Ḥasan,' Abū Bakr replied, 'And, there's never a catastrophe without another that follows, and calamity is compounded by words.'"

ʿAlī continued his account, "We then went on to a meeting underway marked by calm and dignity. There were sheikhs of high rank and fine appearance there. Abū Bakr went forward and made greeting." "And," ʿAlī commented, "Abū Bakr was always in the vanguard of good.

"Abū Bakr asked them, 'From whom are you?' They replied, 'We are of the Banū Shaybān b. Thaʿlaba.'

"Abū Bakr turned to the Messenger of God (ṢAAS), and commented, 'I swear, no one has more ʿizz, power, in their people than these do.'"

In other accounts the words *ʿudhr*, responsibility, and *ghurar*, experience, are substituted for the word ʿizz, power, in the preceding sentence.

ʿAlī's account goes on, "Among this group were Mafrūq b. ʿAmr, Hāniʾ b. Qabīṣa, al-Muthannā b. Ḥāritha and al-Nuʿmān b. Shurayk.

"The man most comparable to Abū Bakr was Mafrūq b. ʿAmr; he was their most eloquent. He wore his hair in two braids that came down to his chest. He sat closest to Abū Bakr.

"Abū Bakr asked him, 'How many are you in number?'

"Mafrūq replied, 'We are more than 1,000 strong; and "a few men can't beat 1,000", as they say.'

"'And how would protection be with you?'

"'We go to the limit; and "every people has a forefather," (i.e. "we are proud and noble"),' Mafrūq responded.

"Abū Bakr asked, 'And how is it when you make war with your enemies?'

"Mafrūq answered, 'When we meet in battle, we are the angriest of men. We take greater pride in our steeds than our sons, care more for our swords than our sperm; victory rests with God. Sometimes He grants us victory, sometimes others victory over us. You seem to be a member of Quraysh?'

"Abū Bakr answered, 'If you have heard of him who is the Messenger of God, this is he here.'

"'We have heard,' Mafrūq answered, 'that he says he is.'

"He then turned to the Messenger of God (ṢAAS), and asked, 'What do you propound, O Brother from Quraysh?'

"The Messenger of God (ṢAAS) then came forward and sat down, while Abū Bakr arose and stood shading him with his cloak. The Messenger of God (ṢAAS) then spoke, 'I call upon you to bear witness that there is no god but God alone who has no associate, and that I am the Messenger of God. I ask you to shelter and protect me until I can carry out what God has ordered me to do. Quraysh have come out against God's commands and have denied His Messenger. They have sided with wrong against right. But God is All-Powerful, All-Praised.'

"'What else do you propound, O Quraysh brother?' he asked.

"The Messenger of God (ṢAAS) then recited to him, 'Say: Come! I shall recite for you what it was your Lord forbad you: that you must not associate another with Him, and that you must treat your parents with kindness' up to the words 'That He enjoined upon you that you might be pious' (sūrat al-Anʿām; VI, v.152–4).

"Mafrūq asked, 'And what else do you propound, O Quraysh brother? I swear these are not words of any earthly mortal; if they were, we would know them to be.'

"Then the Messenger of God (ṢAAS) recited to them, 'God enjoins justice, compassion and charity to your relatives. He forbids adultery, immorality and oppression. He exhorts you so that you will take heed' (sūrat al-Naḥl; XVI, v.90).

"Mafrūq commented, 'I swear, Quraysh brother, you are certainly advocating ethical conduct and good behaviour; and yet your people have denied, rejected and opposed you.'

"Apparently Mafrūq wanted to involve Hāniʾ b. Qubayṣa in the discussion and said, 'This is Hāniʾ b. Qubayṣa, our sheikh and religious leader.'

"Hāniʾ said, 'I heard what you said, O Quraysh brother, and believed what you said. I consider that our abandoning our religion and following you in yours because of one meeting we are having with you which had neither introduction nor follow-up, and without our giving it full consideration nor examining what the consequences would be of what you suggest – that would be a lapse in judge-ment, rashness and inadequate consideration for consequences. Lapse of judge-ment only comes with haste. We have behind us a people for whom we should be reluctant to make any pact. You should retire, as we should too; you should think it over, as we should.'

"Apparently Mafrūq wanted also to involve al-Muthannā b. Ḥāritha in the discussion, for he then said, 'This is al-Muthannā, our sheikh and military leader.'

"Al-Muthannā then spoke, 'I heard and liked what you said, O Quraysh brother. I was impressed by your words. But our answer should be that of Hāni' b. Qubaysa; for us to leave our religion and follow you after one sitting with us would be like us taking residence between two pools of stagnant water, one al-Yamāma and the other al-Samāwa.'

"The Messenger of God asked (ṢAAS), 'And what might those pools of stagnant water be then?'

"Al-Muthannā replied, 'One of these is where land extends to the Arab world, and the other is that of Persia and the rivers of Chosroe. We would be reneging on a pact that Chosroe has placed upon us to the effect that we would not cause an incident and not give sanctuary to a troublemaker. This policy you suggest for us is such a one that kings would dislike. As for those areas bordering Arab lands, the blame of those so acting would be forgiven and excuses for them be accepted, but for those areas next to Persia, those so acting would not be forgiven, and no such excuses would be accepted. If you want us to help and protect you from whatever relates to Arab territories alone, we should do so.'

"The Messenger of God (ṢAAS) replied, 'Your reply is in no way bad, for you have spoken eloquently and truthfully. (But) God's religion can only be engaged in by those who encompass it from all sides.'

"He then asked, 'Supposing it were only shortly after now that God were to award you their lands and properties and furnished you their young women, would you then praise God and revere Him?'

"Al-Nu'mān b. Shurayk replied, 'Would to God you could accomplish that, Quraysh brother!'

"The Messenger of God (ṢAAS) then recited to them, 'We have sent you as a witness, to bring good news and to warn, and to invite unto God, with His permission, and as a light-giving lantern.' (This quotation combines *sūrat al-Fath*; XLVIII, v.8 with *sūrat al-Aḥzāb*; XXXIII, v.46.)

"The Messenger of God (ṢAAS) then arose, holding on to the hand of Abū Bakr."

'Alī went on, "The Messenger of God (ṢAAS) then turned to us and said, "'Alī, what fine character the Arabs used to have, in the *jahiliyya*; how noble a time that was; they sought refuge in the life of this world.'"[28]

'Alī went on, "We proceeded on to a meeting being held by the Aws and the Khazraj. We remained with them until they pledged allegiance to the Prophet (ṢAAS)."

'Alī continued, "And they were true, steadfast friends. And the Messenger of God (ṢAAS) was delighted at the knowledge of Abū Bakr, God bless him, about their genealogies.

"Soon thereafter the Messenger of God (ṢAAS) went forth to address his Companions, telling them, 'Give much praise to God. For today the sons of

---

28. That is, from ignominy and boorishness.

Rabīʿa have triumphed over the people of Persia. They have killed their kings, and captured their troops and it was by me that they were given victory.'"

ʿAlī went on, "And the battle occurred at Qurāqir, by the side of Dhū Qār. And about this victory al-Aʿshā spoke the verses,

> 'My camel be a ransom for the Banū Dhuhl b. Shaybān and
> its rider at the clash, for it bore its burden well.
> They struck blows at the *ḥinw*, the bends of Qurāqir,
> against the vanguard of al-Hāmurz, until they fled.
> Glory be to the eyes that beheld those knights, like
> Dhuhl b. Shaybān, when they were in command.
> They rose up, and we did so too, with friendship
> between us, though we were overcome by the hardships of
> battle, clearly evident.'"

This *ḥadīth* is very strange. We have included it for its evidences of the proofs of the prophethood, its references to ethics and moral behaviour and its examples of the eloquence of the Arabs.

It also comes down through another line. It states, in that version, that when they battled against the Persians and met them at Qurāqir, a place near the Euphrates, they made their battle cry the name of Muḥammad (ṢAAS), and that it was thereby that they were made victorious over the Persians. Thereafter they converted to Islam.

Al-Wāqidī stated, "ʿAbd Allāh b. Wābiṣa al-ʿAbsī, told us, from his father, from his grandfather, who said, 'The Messenger of God (ṢAAS) came to us in our houses at Minā while we were staying there near the first *jamra*[29] which is next to the Khayf mosque. He was riding on his mount with Zayd b. Ḥāritha seated behind him. He called out an invitation to us, but we made no response to him; we were not given to make a good choice.

"'We had heard of him and of his preaching at the fairs; he stood and made a presentation and invitation to us, but we did not respond. We had with us Maysara b. Masrūq al-ʿAbsī and he said to us, "I swear by God, if we had believed this man and had taken him off to inside our territory, we would have triumphed. I swear by God, he will succeed and ultimately achieve all his objectives."

"'But our people replied, "Leave us alone. You'll not involve us in that over which we have no power."

"'The Messenger of God (ṢAAS) had high hopes of Maysara and spoke to him. Maysara replied, "How fine, how enlightening your words are! But my people oppose me. All a man has is his own people. And if they don't stand by him, then enmity is more extensive."

"'So the Messenger of God (ṢAAS) left and people went off to their families. Maysara told them, "Let's turn off to Fadak. There are Jews there whom we can ask about this man."

---

29. One of three pillars at Minā at which pilgrims cast stones.

"'So they did go off to the Jews. They brought out a book of scriptures they had, put it down and studied. It made mention of the Messenger of God (ṢAAS) as the *ummi*, unlettered, Arab prophet who would ride an ass, reward himself with a piece of bread, a man neither tall nor short, neither curly nor straight-haired, with a redness to his eyes, and light in complexion. "If," (the Jews concluded) "it is he who appealed to you, then respond to him and enter his religion. We envy him and will not follow him. We will suffer greatly from him. All Arabs will follow him or fight him, so be among those who follow him."

"'Maysara said, "O people, this matter is very clear."

"'His people replied, "We will return to the festival and meet him." They then went home to their lands, but their elders refused to allow their return, and so none of them did follow him.

"'When the Messenger of God (ṢAAS) migrated to Medina and performed the "farewell pilgrimage" Maysara met with him and he recognized him. Maysara asked, "O Messenger of God, I swear I've continued wanting to follow you ever since that day you dismounted with us. But, as you see, God saw fit to delay my accepting Islam. All those who were with me at that time have since died; where have they been taken, O Messenger of God?"

"'The Messenger of God (ṢAAS) replied, "All those who died in any other state than Islam are now in hell-fire."

"'Maysara commented, "Praise be to God who saved me!" He then accepted Islam fully and he was treated with respect by Abū Bakr.'"

Imām Muḥammad b. °Amr al-Wāqidī has examined closely and related individually details about those tribes to which the Messenger of God (ṢAAS) presented himself. These included the tribes of °Āmir, Ghassān, the Fazāra, the Murra, the Ḥanīfa, the Sulaym, the °Abs, the Naḍr b. Hawāzin, Tha°laba b. °Ukāba, Kinda, Ka°b, al-Ḥārith b. Ka°b, °Udhra, Qays b. al-Ḥaṭīm, and others.

The accounts of all these are very extensive; we have given here a goodly part of them, and to God belong all praise and credit.

Imām Aḥmad also stated, "Aswad b. °Āmir related to us, quoting Isrā°īl, from °Uthmān – meaning Ibn al-Mughīra – from Sālim b. Abū al-Ja°d, from Jābir b. °Abd Allāh, who said, 'The Prophet (ṢAAS) used to present himself to the tribes at the assembly at °Arafa, and say, "Will any man of you take me to his own people? For Quraysh have prevented me from delivering the words of my Lord. Almighty and Glorious is He!"

"'A man from Hamdān came to him thereafter and the Messenger of God (ṢAAS) asked him, "From whom are you?"

"'"From Hamdān," he replied.

"'"And do your people grant protection?"

"'"Yes."

"'Thereafter the man feared that his people might be watching him, so he came to the Messenger of God (ṢAAS), and said, "I will go to them and tell them, then I'll come to you next year."

"""All right," the Messenger of God (ṢAAS) agreed.

"'The man then left, and in the month of Rajab the delegation of the *anṣār*, (the Helpers), arrived.'"

This *ḥadīth* is reported, by various paths, by scholars of all four of *al-sunan al-arbaʿa*,[30] from Isrāʿīl. Al-Tirmidhī stated, "It is *ḥasan*, *ṣaḥīḥ*, good and authentic."

DIVISION

On the arrival of the delegation of the *anṣār*, the Helpers, year after year, and their pledging their loyalty to him time after time. And thereafter the Messenger of God (ṢAAS) moved away to them in Medina, residing there among them, as will be explained in detail, if God wills it and in Him is all trust.

An Account from Suwayd b. Ṣāmit, the Anṣārī.

His full name was Suwayd b. al-Ṣāmit b. ʿAṭiyya b. Ḥūṭ b. Ḥabīb b. ʿAmr b. ʿAwf b. Mālik b. al-Aws; his mother was Laylā, daughter of ʿAmr al-Najāriyya, the daughter of Salmā, daughter of ʿAmr, the mother of ʿAbd al-Muṭṭalib b. Hāshim. This Suwayd was the son of the maternal aunt of ʿAbd al-Muṭṭalib, the grandfather of the Messenger of God (ṢAAS).

Muḥammad b. Isḥāq b. Yasār stated, "The Messenger of God (ṢAAS) continued as he had for some time; whenever people met for the festival, he would go to them and invite the tribes to God and into Islam, presenting himself to them and the message of guidance and mercy he brought. Whenever he heard of any Arab of good repute coming to Mecca, he would meet him, invite him to God Almighty and present him his message."

Ibn Isḥāq continued, "'Āsim b. ʿAmr b. Qatāda informed me that the sheikhs of his tribe said that Suwayd b. al-Ṣāmit, a brother from the Banū ʿAmr b. ʿAwf came to Mecca, either for the *ḥajj*, the 'greater pilgrimage', or the *ʿumra*, the 'lesser pilgrimage'. Suwayd was known among his people as *al-Kāmil*, 'the perfect', for his strength, his poetry, his honour and his fine lineage. It was he who spoke the lines,

> 'Many men there are you call friends who would shock
> you to see the lies they tell of you in your absence.
> There before you his words may be sweet as honey, while
> in your absence they are an old sword at the base of your
> neck!
> What he shows you pleases you, while under his skin he's
> an amulet of deceit exploding behind your back.

---

30. A technical term used to identify the four compilers of the *ṣaḥīḥ* traditions, excluding al-Bukhārī and Muslim.

The eyes show you with suspicious glances what spite and
hatred he conceals.
    "Feather" me well; for long you have weakened me; the
best allies are those who "feather" without weakening.'

"Having heard of him, the Messenger of God (ṢAAS) went to see him and
invited him to God and to Islam. Suwayd replied, 'Perhaps what you have is like
what I have.'

"'What is it you have?' asked the Messenger of God (ṢAAS).

"'The *majalla* of Luqmān,' he replied. By this word he meant the 'wisdom' of
Luqmān.

"'Present it to me,' the Messenger of God (ṢAAS) asked, and when Suwayd
had done so, he commented, 'These words are fine. But what I have is better – a
Qur᾽ān that God has sent down to me to be a guide and a light.'

"The Messenger of God (ṢAAS) then recited the Qur᾽ān to him and invited
him into Islam. Suwayd did not draw away, but said, 'Those words were wonderful.'

"Suwayd then left and later came to Medina with his tribe. Shortly thereafter
he was killed by the Khazraj tribe, though some of his own people say that he was
a Muslim at the time of his death. His killing occurred before the battle at Bu῾ath."

Al-Bayhaqī related this, from al-Ḥākim, from al-Aṣamm from Aḥmad b. ῾Abd
al-Jabbār, from Yūnus b. Bukayr, from Ibn Isḥāq, in a shorter form.

THE ACCEPTANCE OF ISLAM BY IYĀS B. MU῾ĀDH.

Ibn Isḥāq stated that Al-Ḥusayn b. ῾Abd al-Raḥmān b. ῾Amr b. Sa῾d b. Mu῾ādh
related to him, from Maḥmūd b. Labīd, saying, "When Abū al-Ḥaysar, Anas b.
Rāfi῾ came to Mecca, accompanied by other men of the Banū ῾Abd al-Ashhal,
including Iyās b. Mu῾ādh, seeking a pact with Quraysh against the Khazraj tribe,
the Messenger of God (ṢAAS) heard of their coming and went to them. He sat
down among them and asked, 'Would you like something better than what it was
you came for?' 'What would that be?' they asked.

"He replied, 'I am the Messenger of God to all mankind. And I invite them to
worship God and to associate none other with Him. 'And,' he told them, 'the
book has been revealed to me.' He then told them of Islam and recited the
Qur᾽ān to them."

The account goes on, "Iyās b. Mu῾ādh, who was a young man, spoke up, saying, 'My people, I swear this is better than what you came for.'

"Abū al-Ḥaysar Anas b. Rāfi῾ then took up a handful of dirt from the river bed
and threw it into the face of Iyās b. Mu῾ādh, saying, 'Clear off! We came for
something different.'

"Iyās remained silent, and the Messenger of God (ṢAAS) left them, and they
returned into Medina. The battle of Bu῾ath was between the Aws and the
Khazraj tribes.

"And shortly thereafter Iyās b. Muʿādh died.

"Maḥmūd b. Labīd said, 'Some of his tribesmen who were present told me that they heard him constantly praising, glorifying and exalting God until he died. They did not doubt that he had died a Muslim. He had become conscious of Islam at that assembly when he had heard what the Messenger of God (ṢAAS) had to say.'"

My own comment is that this occurred on the day of the battle of Buʿāth, the name of a site at Medina. A major battle took place there which led to the death of a large number of the leaders of the Aws and the Khazraj; few of their prominent men survived it.

Al-Bukhārī related in his *ṣaḥīḥ* collection, from ʿUbayd b. Ismāʿīl, from Abū Umāma, from Hishām, from his father, from ʿĀʾisha, who said, "The battle of Buʿāth was one that God gave to His Messenger. The Messenger of God (ṢAAS) came to Medina when their leadership was divided, their elite having been killed."

Chapter: The commencement of the acceptance of Islam by the anṣār, *the "Helpers" of Medina, God bless them.*

Ibn Isḥāq stated, "When God wished to display His religion, exalt His Prophet and fulfil His promise to him, the Messenger of God (ṢAAS) set out in that season of the pilgrimage in which he met a number of the *anṣār*. He presented himself to the Arab tribes as he had been doing in previous seasons. While he was at al-ʿAqaba he met a group of the Khazraj tribe for whom God had good in store.

"ʿĀṣim b. ʿUmar b. Qatāda related to me that some of the leaders of his people said, 'When the Messenger of God (ṢAAS) met them he asked them, "Who are you?" "We are men of al-Khazraj," they replied. "Are you allies of the Jews?" he asked.

"'"Yes," they replied.

"'"Would you sit down so that I may talk with you?" he invited them, and they agreed.

"'So they did sit down and he called them to the path of God, explaining Islam to them. He also recited the Qurʾān to them.

"'One way in which God facilitated their (acceptance) of Islam was that the Jews were there with them in their country. These were followers of Scriptures and men of knowledge, though they themselves were polytheists and idol worshippers. They had previously attacked these Jews in their territories and whenever dispute had arisen, the latter had told them, "A prophet will now be sent. His day is coming. We will follow him and give you the same fate as that of the peoples of ʿĀd and Iram."

"'When the Messenger of God (ṢAAS) addressed these people, and invited them to God, they told one another, "This has to be the prophet the Jews foresaw; we should not let them get to him first!"

"'They therefore responded to his call for them to believe in him and accepted Islam, saying, "We have left our own people, for they have such discord and dissension between them not found in any other. Perhaps God may unite them through you. We will go forth among them and invite them to join you, presenting to them this religion we have accepted from you. If God should unite them around you, then no one will be dearer to us than you." They then left, returning to their territory, believing in him and the faith.'"

Ibn Isḥāq continued, "These men, so I have been told, were six in number. Of the Khazraj there was Abū Umāma As'ad b. Zurāra b. 'Uds b. 'Ubayd b. Tha'laba b. Ghanm b. Mālik b. al-Najjār. According to Abū Nu'aym, he was the first of the *anṣār* of the Khazraj to accept Islam.

"From al-'Aws there was Abū al-Haytham b. al-Tayyihān. It is said, however, that the first of them to accept Islam were Rāfi' b. Mālik and Mu'ādh b. 'Afrā'. But God knows best.

"Also there were 'Awf b. al-Ḥārith b. Rifā'a b. Sawād b. Mālik b. Ghanm b. Mālik b. al-Najjār, he being the son of 'Afrā', both these last being Najjāris; Rāfi' b. Mālik b. al-'Ajlān b. 'Amr b. Zurayq al-Zurqī; Quṭba b. 'Āmir b. Ḥadīda b. 'Amr b. Ghanm b. Sawwād b. Ghanm b. Ka'b b. Salama b. Sa'd b. 'Alī b. Asad b. Sārida b. Yazīd b. Jusham b. al-Khazraj al-Sulamī. From the Banū Sawwād; 'Uqba b. 'Āmir b. Nābī b. Zayd b. Ḥarām b. Ka'b b. Salama, also of al-Sulam, and then from the Banū Ḥarām; Jābir b. 'Abd Allāh b. Ri'āb b. al-Nu'mān b. Sinān b. 'Ubayd b. 'Adiyy b. Ghanm b. Ka'b b. Salama, also of al-Sulam, then from Banū 'Ubayd. God be pleased with all these men."

It is similarly related from al-Sha'bī, al-Zuhrī and others that those there that night were six men of the Khazraj.

Mūsā b. 'Uqba recounted, from al-Zuhrī and 'Urwa b. al-Zubayr, that at the first meeting between them and the Messenger of God (ṢAAS), they were eight in number and consisted of Mu'ādh b. 'Afrā', As'ad b. Zurāra, Rāfi' b. Mālik, Dhakwān, he being Ibn 'Abd Qays, 'Ubāda b. al-Ṣāmit, Abū 'Abd al-Raḥmān Yazīd b. Tha'laba, Abū Haytham b. al-Tīhān, and 'Uwaym b. Sā'ida. These all accepted Islam and made an appointment for the following year.

They then returned to their people and called on them to accept Islam. They also sent Mu'ādh b. 'Afrā' and Rāfi' b. Mālik to the Messenger of God (ṢAAS), asking him to send to them someone who could give them religious instruction. He responded by sending Muṣ'ab b. 'Umayr, who went and stayed with As'ad b. Zurāra.

This account goes on to conclude as Ibn Isḥāq's and more fully than that of Mūsā b. 'Uqba. But God knows best.

Ibn Isḥāq stated, "And when these men arrived in Medina to their people they told them of the Messenger of God (ṢAAS), and invited them to Islam. Eventually news of him spread among them to such a degree that not a single home of the *anṣār* was without knowledge of him.

"The following year 12 of the *anṣār* kept to their appointment to attend the festival (of the *ḥajj*); they were Abū Umāma Asʿad b. Zurāra and ʿAwf b. al-Ḥārith, mentioned above, along with his brother Muʿādh, both these being sons of ʿAfrāʾ, and Rāfiʿ b. Mālik, also mentioned above.

"Then there were Dhakwān b. ʿAbd Qays b. Khalada b. Mukhlid b. ʿĀmir, the son of Zurayq al-Zurqī. (Ibn Hishām said that he was a Helper who had also migrated from Mecca.)

"Also there were ʿUbāda b. al-Ṣāmit b. Qays b. Aṣram b. Fihr b. Thaʿlaba b. Ghanm b. ʿAwf b. ʿAmr b. ʿAwf b. al-Khazraj, along with their ally Abū ʿAbd al-Raḥmān Yazīd b. Thaʿlaba b. Khazma b. Aṣram al-Balawī, al-ʿAbbās b. ʿUbāda b. Naḍla b. Mālik b. al-ʿAjlān b. Yazīd b. Ghanm b. Sālim b. ʿAwf b. ʿAmr b. ʿAwf b. al-Khazraj al-ʿAjlānī, ʿUqba b. ʿĀmir b. Nābī, mentioned before, and Quṭba b. ʿĀmir b. Ḥadīda, mentioned before.

"These men were from Khazraj.

"From Aws there were two men, ʿUwaym b. Sāʿida and Abū al-Haytham, Mālik b. al-Tayhān." Ibn Hishām stated that al-Tayhān could also be spelled al-Tayyihān, as in the words *mayt*, dead, and *mayyit*.

Al-Suhaylī stated, "The full name of Abū al-Haytham b. al-Tayhān was Mālik b. Mālik b. ʿAtayk b. ʿAmr b. ʿAbd al-Aʿlam b. ʿĀmir b. Zaʿūr b. Jusham b. al-Ḥārith b. al-Khazraj b. ʿAmr b. Mālik b. al-Aws." And he also stated, "It is said that he was an Irāshī or a Balawī." But neither Ibn Isḥāq nor Ibn Hishām give him such a relationship. He also said, "The word *al-haytham* refers to an eaglet; it is also a type of plant."

By this he shows that these 12 men attended the festival that year with the intent of meeting with the Messenger of God (ṢAAS); they did so at al-ʿAqaba, where they pledged allegiance to him with a pledge known as the "women's pledge"; this occurred at the first (meeting) at ʿAqaba.

Abū Nuʿaym related that the Messenger of God (ṢAAS) recited to them God's words in *sūrat Ibrāhīm*, "And when Abraham said, 'O my Lord, render this country secure' (*sūrat Ibrāhīm*; XIV, v.35).

Ibn Isḥāq stated, "Yazīd b. Abū Ḥabīb related to me, from Marthad b. ʿAbd Allāh al-Yazanī, from ʿAbd al-Raḥmān b. ʿUsayla al-Ṣunābihī, from ʿUbāda, he being Ibn al-Ṣāmit, who said, 'I was among those who attended the first (meeting at) ʿAqaba. We were 12 men. We pledged allegiance to the Messenger of God (ṢAAS) by the so-called "women's pledge". That was before war was enjoined. It was to the effect that we would not associate any other with God, we would not steal, nor commit fornication, nor kill our children, nor make false accusations, nor disobey him in anything good. "If you keep to this," he told us, "you shall go to paradise. But if you commit any of these, then God will decide your fate; if He wishes He will either punish you or forgive you."'"

Al-Bukhārī and Muslim related this *ḥadīth* through al-Layth b. Saʿd, from Yazīd b. Abū Ḥabīb in much the same terms.

Ibn Isḥāq stated, "Ibn Shihāb al-Zuhrī recounted, from ʿĀʾidh Allāh Abū Idrīs al-Khawlānī that ʿUbāda b. al-Ṣāmit related to him, saying, 'We pledged to the Messenger of God (ṢAAS), on the night of the first (meeting at) 'Aqaba, that we would not associate any other with God, that we would not steal, commit fornication, kill our children, make false accusations, nor disobey him in anything good. (He told us) "If you keep to this, you shall have paradise. But if you give up any of this, and you are punished for it in this world, then that will provide atonement for you. But if it is overlooked until Judgement Day, it will be up to God to decide whether to punish or forgive you."'"

This *ḥadīth* is given in both *ṣaḥīḥ* collections and elsewhere with paths from al-Zuhrī in much the same version.

The words here, the "women's pledge", are a reference to the similarity between this and the revelation relating to the pledge later made by women in the year of the truce of al-Ḥudaybiyya. And on that occasion the revelation accorded with what had been revealed regarding the pledge he had required of his Companions on the night of al-'Aqaba. This is not strange, for a Qur'ānic revelation sometimes came in more than one location, as was affirmed by 'Umar b. al-Khaṭṭāb, as we have explained in both his biography and in the *Tafsīr* (*Exegesis*). And since this pledge resulted from revelation that was not recited,[31] it makes the aforementioned observation all the more plausible. But God knows best.

Ibn Isḥāq stated, "When the group left, the Messenger of God (ṢAAS) sent to them Muṣ'ab b. 'Umayr b. Hāshim b. 'Abd Manāf b. 'Abd al-Dār b. Quṣayy. He told him to recite the Qur'ān to them, to teach them Islam and to instruct them in the faith."

Al-Bayhaqī reported, on the authority of Ibn Isḥāq, who said, "'Āsim b. 'Umayr b. Qatāda related to me that the Messenger of God (ṢAAS) only sent Muṣ'ab when they wrote to him asking that he send him to them. It was he who was mentioned by Mūsā b. 'Uqba, as given above, even though in that case he applied to the first of the meetings what is here said of the second."

Al-Bayhaqī commented, "The account of Ibn Isḥāq is more complete."

Ibn Isḥāq stated, "'Abd Allāh b. Abū Bakr used to say, 'I don't know what this "first (meeting at) 'Aqaba" means.'" Ibn Isḥāq then commented, "Certainly, I swear it, there was an 'Aqaba meeting, and then another one."

All authorities agree that Muṣ'ab took up residence with As'ad b. Zurāra and that he was known in Medina as the *muqrī*, the reciter.

Ibn Isḥāq stated, "'Āsim b. 'Umar b. Qatāda related to me that he used to lead the prayer for them. This was because the Aws and the Khazraj disliked that they be led in prayer by one who belonged to the other tribe. God be pleased with them one and all."

Ibn Isḥāq stated, "Muḥammad b. Abū Umāma b. Sahl b. Ḥunayf related to me, from his father, from 'Abd al-Raḥmān b. Ka'b b. Mālik who said, 'When my

---

31. This refers to a genre of revelation different from that of the Qur'ān. It is therefore not *matlū*, recited, as liturgy in the Muslim daily prayers.

father had lost his sight, I used to lead him. When I would take him out to the Friday meeting, and he heard the call to prayer there he would say a prayer for Abū Umāma Asʿad b. Zurāra.'"

The account goes on, "'This went on for some time; he never heard the Friday call to prayer without praying for him and asking forgiveness for him. I told myself it was weakness on my part not to ask him why this was and said, "Why is it, father, that whenever you hear the Friday call to prayer, you pray for Abū Umāma?" He replied, "My son, he was the first to unite us in Medina at the *hazm al-nabīt*, in the quarter of the Banū Bayāḍa, in *al-baqīʿ*, the plain, known as the *baqīʿ al-Khaḍimāt*." "And how many were you there that day?" I asked. "We were 40 men," he replied.'"

Abū Dāʾūd and Ibn Māja told this *ḥadīth* through Muḥammad b. Isḥāq, God bless him.

Al-Dārquṭnī related, from Ibn ʿAbbās, that the Messenger of God (ṢAAS) wrote to Muṣʿab b. ʿUmayr telling him to establish the Friday prayer. But there is some peculiarity in the line of transmission he gives. God knows best.

Ibn Isḥāq stated, "ʿUbayd Allāh b. al-Mughīra b. Muʿayqib related to me, quoting ʿAbd Allāh b. Abū Bakr b. Muḥammad b. ʿAmr b. Ḥazm, that Asʿad b. Zurāra went off with Muṣʿab b. ʿUmayr to visit the homes of the Banū ʿAbd al-Ashhal and the Banū Ẓafr. Saʿd b. Muʿādh was the son of the maternal aunt of Asʿad b. Zurāra. He took him inside one of the gardens of the Banū Ẓafr at a well known as the 'Maraq well'. They sat there and received visits from some of the men who had accepted Islam.

"Saʿd b. Muʿādh and Usayd b. al-Ḥudayr were at that time leaders of their people of the Banū ʿAbd al-Ashhal; both were polytheists practising their nation's religion.

"When they heard of him, Saʿd said to Usayd, 'Go to those two men who have come to our homes to make fools of our weakest elements; rebuke them and forbid them from entering our quarters. If Asʿad b. Zurāra were not related to me, as you know, I'd save you the trouble. But he is my maternal aunt's son, and I can't approach him'

"And so Usayd b. Ḥudayr took his spear and went to them. When they saw him, Asʿad b. Zurāra said to Muṣʿab, 'This is his tribe's chief who has come to you; trust God through him.'

"Muṣʿab said, 'I will speak to him if he sits down.'

"Usayd stood glowering at them and asked them, 'Why did you both come here and make fools of our weak? Keep away from us if you value yourselves.'

"Mūsā b. ʿUqba said, 'At this point a youth commented, "It's you who have come to our homes with this strange threatening of yours to have our weak elements behave stupidly and advocate it to others."'"

Ibn Isḥāq stated, "Muṣʿab replied to him, 'Why not sit down and listen to us. If you like what you hear, you can accept it; if you dislike it you can ignore it.'

"He replied, 'You have spoken fairly.' He then put down his spear and sat with them. Muṣ῾ab then spoke to him about Islam and recited the Qur᾽ān to him.

"According to what is reported, they both said, 'By God, we recognized Islam in his face, from its radiant calm, even before he spoke.'

"Usayd then said, 'How beautiful, how wonderful that is! What does one do to enter this faith?'

"They told him, 'You wash, and clean yourself and your clothes. You then give testimony to the truth and say prayers.'

"Usayd then arose, washed, cleaned his clothes and made testimony to the truth. He then performed two prayer prostrations and told them, 'Behind me there is a man who if he follows you, will not leave behind any one of his people. I will send him to you now. He is Sa῾d b. Mu῾ādh.'

"He then took his spear and left for Sa῾d and his people who were sitting in their assembly. When Sa῾d b. Mu῾ādh saw him coming, he commented, 'I swear by God, Usayd is coming back to you with an expression quite different from when he left you.'

"When Usayd stopped at the assembly, Sa῾d asked him, 'Well, what did you do?' He replied, 'I spoke to both men and, I swear, I saw no harm in them. I warned them and they replied, "We will do whatever you wish." And I was informed that the Banū Ḥāritha had gone off to kill As῾ad b. Zurāra; that was because they knew that he is your aunt's son and wanted to harm you.'

"Sa῾d b. Mu῾ādh arose angrily at this, anxious because of what they had said about the Banū Ḥāritha. He took the spear in his hand and said, 'I can see, by God, that you have accomplished nothing!'

"Sa῾d then left to go to the two men and when he saw them to be untroubled, he realized that Usayd had merely wanted him to listen to them. He came to a stop, in a rage, and said to As῾ad b. Zurāra, 'By God, Abū Umāma, if we weren't relatives, you wouldn't behave this way to me. Will you behave in our very homes in ways that offend us?'

"As῾ad had told Muṣ῾ab, 'I swear, a leader has come to you who has such influence that if he follows you, no two others will hold back from you.'

"Muṣ῾ab therefore told him, 'Would you sit and listen; if you hear what you like, you can accept it; if you dislike it, we'll not bother you with it again.'

"Sa῾d replied, 'You speak fair.' He then put down his spear and sat. Islam was then explained to him, and the Qur᾽ān was recited to him."

Mūsā b. ῾Uqba recounted that it was the first part of *sūrat al-Zukhruf* (XLIII) that was recited to him.

"The account continued, 'And, I swear, we recognized Islam in his face even before he spoke, from its radiant calm.'

"Sa῾d then asked them, 'What does one do to accept Islam and enter this religion?'

"They told him, 'You wash, and clean yourself and your clothes. Then you give testimony to the truth and make two prayer prostrations.'

"Saʿd arose, performed the ablutions, washed both his garments, gave testimony to the truth and then performed two prayer prostrations.

"After that Saʿd took his spear and returned to his people's assembly, Usayd b. al-Ḥuḍayr accompanying him. When his people saw him coming, they said, 'My God, Saʿd is returning with quite a different expression from when he left.'

"When he stood there before them, he said, 'O Banū ʿAbd al-Ashhal, how do you view my position among you?'

"They replied, 'You are our leader, the wisest man among us, and the man with the happiest disposition.'

"Saʿd told them, 'It is forbidden for any man or woman among you to speak to me until you believe in God and His Messenger.'

"The account continues, 'And, I swear, by that evening every single man and woman there in the quarters of the Banū ʿAbd al-Ashhal had become Muslims.'

"Saʿd and Muṣʿab then returned to the home of Asʿad b. Zurāra and remained there calling upon people to join Islam until there was not a single one of the homes of the *anṣār* that did not have Muslims living there. Except, that is, for the homes of the Banū Umayya b. Zayd, Khaṭma, Wāʾil and Wāqif. These were of the Aws, that is, al-Aws b. Ḥāritha.

"This is because they had among them Abū Qays b. al-Aslat, known as Ṣayfī. Al-Zubayr b. Bakkār said, 'His name was al-Ḥārith, but also it was said to be ʿUbayd Allāh. His father's name was al-Aslat ʿĀmir b. Jusham b.Wāʾil b. Zayd b. Qays b. ʿĀmir b. Murra b. Mālik b. al-Aws. Al-Kalbī gave him the same genealogy. He was a poet and a leader of theirs; they would listen to him and obey. He kept them from Islam until after the battle of *al-khandaq*, "the battle of the trench".'"

I observe that this Abū Qays b. al-Aslat has poetry quoted by Ibn Isḥāq that is eloquent and good and reminiscent of the poetry of Umayya b. Abū al-Ṣalt al-Thaqafī.

Ibn Isḥāq commented concerning the above, "As news of the Messenger of God (ṢAAS) spread among the bedouins and the towns, this was reported in Medina. No Arab quarter was more knowledgeable about the affairs of the Messenger of God (ṢAAS), both before and after he became the subject of report, than this territory of the Aws and the Khazraj. This was because of what they had heard from the Jewish rabbis.

"When circumstances developed in Medina for him as they did and people discussed the dispute between him and Quraysh, Abū Qays b. al-Aslat, brother of the Banū Wāqif spoke some verses."

Al-Suhaylī gave his name as Abū Qays Ṣirma b. Abū Anas. The full name of Abū Anas was Qays b. Ṣirma b. Mālik b. ʿAdī b. ʿAmr b. Ghanm b. ʿAdī b. al-Najjār. And he said, "It was about him and ʿUmar that the following verse was revealed, 'It has been made lawful for you to visit with your wives on the night of the fast'" (*sūrat al-Baqara*; II, v.187).

Ibn Isḥāq commented, "He greatly liked Quraysh. He was a son-in-law of theirs, his wife being Arnab, daughter of Asad b. 'Abd al-'Uzzā b. Quṣayy. He had spent some years living among Quraysh with his wife.

"He spoke an ode in which he extolled sacrosanctity and advised Quraysh against war. In it he referred to their good qualities and their aspirations and reminded them of how God had tested them and how He had repelled from them those of the elephant and all their strategies. He also told them to leave the Messenger of God (ṢAAS) alone. In these verses, he said,

'O rider, if you do not object, then carry this message
from me to the tribe of Lu'ayy b. Ghālib.

The messenger of a man upset by your enmity, sad at the
distance between you, tired of it,

I had a place to stop at for my troubles, yet I did not
by it fulfil my needs and wishes.

Your abode, however, has two factions, each one clamouring
noisily, like the sound made by kindling and wood burning,

I bid you take refuge with God from your evil deeds, from
the evil of your desires and from the scorpion's sting,

From the display of bad morals, from evil plottings like
the prick of an awl, having great impact,

And remind them firstly of God and at the sanctioning of
things forbidden, like wombs of young maidens.

And tell them, "And God will make His judgement; abandon
warfare and let it depart from you."

When you incite it, you arouse something blameworthy; it
is an evil spirit for those related to you or not.

It severs family ties, can destroy a nation, use up the
fat from a camel's hump and withers.

For it fine, thin clothes are exchanged for coats of
chainmail and the rust-spotted garb of the warrior,

While musk and camphor are exchanged for clouds of dust,
the chain-links looking like locusts' eyes.

Beware lest war attach itself to you, for it is a pool
whose water is unhealthy and bitter to drink.

It seems attractive to nations, then they see its
consequences reveal it as an ugly old woman.

It burns up rather than cooks those who are weak, and
diverts your nobles to certain death.

Do you not know how it was in the war of Dāḥis; give
thought; and to the war of Ḥāṭib too.

How many great leaders were then struck down, fine,
up-standing men whose guests were never disappointed,

Great men, like fine charcoals, men to be revered, men of
pure character, of exemplary nobility,

Like water spread out in a waste-land as though poured
there by the winds of East or South,

Of which you are told by a truthful man who has knowledge
of its events, knowledge based on experience.

Buy weapons from a warrior, and remember well your
account, for God is the best accountant.

A man's patron is He, and chose a religion; and let there
be no guardian over you but the Lord of the stars.

Establish a *ḥanīf* religion for us, for You are a goal
for us, and one can be guided by great peaks.

And You are a light and protection for this people; You
are a refuge they go to, and dreams do not disappoint.

And if the people find a jewel, to You goes the credit
(lit. for You are the valley's centre, the rabbit's nose).

You ensure noble and ancient lineage, lines that are
refined and blemish-free.

Those in need see moving towards your abodes groups of
those destroyed, leading other groups.

Those most righteous have learned that your heights are
in all ways the best of all abodes.

It is the most wise and the best in conduct who, among
all the processions, are most given to the truth.

And so arise and pray to your Lord, and touch the pillars
of this temple amidst the mountains.

For among you from Him has come a favour and a proof on
the day of Abū Yaksūm, leader of the phallanges.

His forces will march over the plain, and his men will
traverse the clefts of the high mountains.

When the assistance of the Throne-possessor comes to you
armies of angels will repel them, raising dust and stones,

And they shall turn tail and flee, and only a few groups
will return from captivity to their people.

And if you perish, so let us die, along with festivals
long lived by; so will a man say who will not lie.'"

The war of Dāhis mentioned by Abū Qays in his poetry was famous and
occurred in the *jāhiliyya* period. According to Abū ʿUbayd Maʿmar b.
al-Muthannā and others, its cause was as follows: Qays b. Zuhayr b. Judhayma
b. Rawāḥa al-Ghaṭafānī owned a mare called Dāhis, and he ran her in a race with
a mare called al-Ghabrāʾ owned by Ḥudhayfa b. Badr b. ʿAmr b. Juʾayya, also of
Ghaṭafān. Dāhis came in first but Ḥudhayfa ordered it to be struck in the head.
Mālik b. Zuhayr jumped up and struck al-Ghabrāʾ in the head. At that Ḥamal b.
Badr struck Mālik. After, Abū Junaydab al-ʿAbsī met ʿAwf b. Ḥudhayfa and
killed him. Then a man of the Banū Fazāra met and killed Mālik. And so war
erupted between the Banū ʿAbs and Fazāra. Ḥudhayfa b. Badr, his brother
Ḥamal b. Badr and other groups were killed. A great deal of poetry, which it
would take much time to quote and explain, was written concerning this.

Ibn Hishām stated, "Qays started Dāḥis and al-Ghabrā' in the race, while Ḥudhayfa started al-Khaṭṭār and al-Ḥanfā'." The former account is more accurate.

As for the war of Ḥāṭib, the reference is to Ḥāṭib b. al-Ḥārith b. Qays b. Haysha b. al-Ḥārith b. Umayya b. Muʿāwiya b. Mālik b. ʿAwf b. ʿAmr b. ʿAwf b. Mālik b. al-Aws who had killed a Jew who was under the protection of the Khazraj. Zayd b. al-Ḥārith b. Qays b. Mālik b. Aḥmar b. Ḥāritha b. Thaʿlaba b. Kaʿb b. Mālik b. Kaʿb b. al-Khazraj b. al-Ḥārith b. al-Khazraj, he being known as Ibn Fusḥum, went out after this man Ḥāṭib, accompanied by a group of his men of the Banū al-Ḥārith b. Khazraj. They killed Ḥāṭib and this led to a war between the Aws and the Khazraj. The fighting was very fierce and ultimately the Khazraj were victorious. At that time al-Aswad b. al-Ṣāmit al-Awsī was killed by al-Mujadhdhar b. Dhiyād, an ally of the Banū ʿAwf b. al-Khazraj. This led to further wars between them that would be lengthy to relate.

The point is that Abū Qays b. al-Aslat gained nothing from all his knowledge and understanding when Muṣʿab b. ʿUmayr came to Medina and called upon its people to accept Islam, many of whom agreed.

So that, as has been said, not a house there was without a Muslim man or woman except that of the Banū Wāqif, Abū Qays's tribe, who held them back from Islam. It was also he who spoke the verses:

> "O Lord of mankind, some things have given pain,
> significant and trivial matters combined,
> O Lord of mankind, if we should have gone astray, then
> guide us to the proper path.
> Were it not for our Lord, we would be Jews, and the
> religion of the Jews lacks proper form.
> Were it not for our lord, we would be Christians, with
> the monks up in the mountains of Galilee.
> But when created, we were made *hanifs* from many
> generations back.
> We lead the camels to slaughter, passive and in shackles,
> their necks bare, but wearing saddles."

The gist of what he says is that he was undecided as to how to react to what he had heard about the mission of the Messenger of God (ṢAAS), so he prevaricated despite his learning.

The person who kept him back from Islam initially was ʿAbd Allāh b. Ubayy b. Salūl, after Abū Qays had informed him that the person who had announced his coming was a Jew; and so he dissuaded him from accepting Islam.

Ibn Isḥāq stated, "He did not accept Islam up to the time of the conquest of Mecca, he and his brother, and so he left."

Al-Zubayr b. Bakkār denied that Abū Qays accepted Islam. As did al-Wāqidī, who stated, 'He had intended to accept Islam when first the Messsenger of God

(SAAS) invited him to do so. ʿAbd Allāh b. Ubayy, however, criticized him for this and he pledged that he would not accept Islam until the next year. But he died in the month Dhū al-Qaʿda.'"

Others, as related by Ibn al-Athīr in his work *Usūd al-Ghāba* (*The Jungle Lions*) state that when death was close for him, the Prophet (SAAS) invited him to Islam and he was heard to say, "There is no god but God."

Imām Aḥmad stated, "Ḥasan b. Mūsā related to us, that Ḥammād b. Salama related to him, from Thābit, from Anas b. Mālik, that the Messenger of God (SAAS) visited an *anṣār* man and said, 'O *khāl*, "maternal uncle", say, "There is no god but God."' He replied, 'Do you say *khāl*, maternal uncle or ʿamm, paternal uncle?' 'No, I say *khāl*,' he replied. The man asked, 'So it is best for me to say, "There is no god but God?" The Messenger of God (SAAS) replied, 'Yes.'"

Aḥmad is alone in giving this *ḥadīth*.

ʿIkrima and others related that when he died, his son wanted to marry his father's widow, Kabīsha, daughter of Maʿan b. ʿĀṣim. She asked the Messenger of God (SAAS) about this and God revealed, "Do not marry those same women your fathers married" (*surat al-Nisāʾ*; IV, v.22).

Ibn Isḥāq stated, as did Saʿīd b. Yaḥyā al-Umawī in his work on the *maghāzī*, the military campaigns, "This man Abū Qays became a monk during the *jāhiliyya* period before Islam and adopted wearing a hair-cloth gown. He abandoned the idols, washed after being in a state of ritual impurity and kept away from menstruating women. He thought of adopting Christianity but then refrained. He took a house and made it into a mosque where he allowed no menstruating women entrance nor anyone in a state of ritual impurity. He said, 'I worship the God of Abraham when he had abandoned and expressed hatred for the idols.'

"This went on until the arrival of the Messenger of God (SAAS). He then accepted Islam and became a good Muslim.

"He was a respected elder and man of truth who glorified God in that *jāhiliyya* period, before Islam, in which he lived. He spoke fine verses on the subject. It was he who said,

> 'Abū Qays, about to leave, says, "Perform all you can of
> this my advice.
> I commend God to you, righteousness, piety and honour, but
> devotion to God comes first.
> If your people lead, do no envy them; if you attain
> leadership, then be just.
> If a disaster should befall your people, then place
> yourselves in front of your tribe.
> If a disastrous loss afflicts them, keep them company and
> bear up beneath whatever it is they place on you.
> If hardship afflicts you, remain pure, and if wealth
> should come to you, then be generous."'

"Abū Qays also said,

> 'Glorify God at dawn each day His sun rises, and at
> every crescent moon.
> He knows both what is plain and secret; nothing our Lord
> says is misguided.
> The birds are His that stray far away then return to
> their nests in the safety of the mountains.
> The wild beasts of the deserts are His; you see them in
> the sand tracts and the shades of the dunes.
> The Jews pray to Him and perform every ritual out of fear
> of disaster.
> The Christians bow down to Him and offer all feasts and
> celebrations to their Lord.
> The hermit monk is His; you see him live in poverty
> though formerly in ease.
> O my people, do not sever kinship's ties, but ever join
> the short to the long.
> Fear God when treating weak orphans; sometimes what is
> forbidden is considered fair.
> And know that orphans have an All-Knowing protector who
> guides without question.
> Do not consume the wealth of orphans; the wealth of
> orphans does have a protector.
> My people, do not ignore the bounds; there are limits to
> ignoring bounds.
> My people, do not feel secure in the future; beware of
> its deceit and of time's passage. Realize that time's
> passing destroys all things created, young and old alike.
> Resolve yourselves for goodness and piety; forsake
> indecency and do only right.' "

Ibn Isḥāq stated, "Abū Qays also composed another piece in which he records how God had honoured them by the gift of Islam and by having sent His Messenger (ṢAAS) down to them. The following line is part thereof:

> 'He resided among Quraysh a dozen years, preaching in
> case he should find there some helpful friend.' "

We will give the full text of this poem later, if God wills it, and in Him is all trust.

An Account of the second meeting at al-'Aqaba.

Ibn Isḥāq stated, "Muṣ'ab b. 'Umayr returned to Mecca and the *anṣār* Muslims came there along with those of their people who were making the pilgrimage and were still polytheists. (The *anṣār*) made a pact with the Messenger of God

(ṢAAS) at al-ʿAqaba, in the medial days of the *tashrīq*[32] when God granted them honour, ensured victory for the Prophet and glory for Islam and its people, and cast down idolatry and its supporters.

"Maʿbad b. Kaʿb b. Mālik related to me, that his brother ʿAbd Allāh b. Kaʿb, one of the most learned of the *anṣār*, told him that his father Kaʿb told him as follows, having been one of those who was present at al-ʿAqaba and pledged allegiance there to the Messenger of God (ṢAAS). He stated, 'We left in the company of those of our people who were polytheists; we had prayed and received religious instruction. With us was al-Barāʾ b. Maʿmūr, our elder and leader. When we had headed out on our journey from Medina, al-Barāʾ said, "I've had an idea, and I wonder whether or not you will agree with me on it." We asked what it was and he replied, "I think I will not leave this building – meaning the *kaʿba* – to my back. I shall pray towards it." We commented, "We've not heard that our Prophet (ṢAAS) never prays in any other direction than towards Syria[33] (i.e. Jerusalem). We don't want to contradict him."

"'He replied, "I am going to pray towards it."

"'"Well, we will not," we told him.

"'When time for prayer came we did face towards Syria, while he prayed in the direction of the *kaʿba* until we reached Mecca. We criticized him for persisting in doing this. Upon reaching Mecca, he told me, "Nephew, let's go off to the Messenger of God (ṢAAS), and ask him about what I've been doing on this journey. The disapproval I have seen in you has somewhat disturbed me."

"'So off we went, asking the whereabouts of the Messenger of God (ṢAAS). We had not seen him prior to that. We met a Meccan and asked after him, and he replied, "Do you know him?" "No," we replied. "Then do you know al-ʿAbbās b. al-Muṭṭalib, his uncle?" "Yes," we told him, for we did know al-ʿAbbās. He often came to us on business trips. The Meccan told us, "If you go to the mosque, he will be sitting next to al-ʿAbbās."

"'So we went in the mosque and there was al-ʿAbbās sitting with the Messenger of God (ṢAAS) by his side. We made greetings then sat down facing him. The Messenger of God (ṢAAS) asked al-ʿAbbās, "Do you know these two men, Abū al-Faḍl?" He replied, "Yes; this is al-Barāʾ b. Maʿmūr, his people's leader, and this is Kaʿb b. Mālik."'"

The account proceeds, "'I swear, I'll never forget what the Messenger of God (ṢAAS) then said: "You mean the poet?" "Yes," he replied.

"'Then al-Barāʾ b. Maʿmūr addressed him, "O prophet of God, I have come on this journey having been given guidance to Islam by God Almighty. I had the

32. During the pre-Islamic pilgrimage season, the *tashrīq* days, those between the 11th and the 13th of Dhu al-Ḥijja, were apparently given over to eating, drinking, and sensual pleasure. The *tashrīq* days were later incorporated into Islam, without, however, the aforementioned practices of the *jahiliyya*.

33. Lit. "Greater Syria". Jerusalem was often referred to as *al-Sham*, Syria, because it was a part of what was then Greater Syria.

idea of not facing my back to this building, so I prayed towards it. My friends opposed me in this, causing me concern. What do you think?"

"'"You already had a *qibla*, a direction for prayer, and should have kept to it," he replied.

"'And so al-Barāʾ reverted to the prayer direction adopted by the Messenger of God (ṢAAS), and so prayed along with us towards Syria.'"

The account concludes, "But his family claim that he continued his prayers towards the *kaʿba* until he died. But it was not as they said; we know better than they about it."

Kaʿb b. Mālik stated, "We then left on the pilgrimage, having made an agreement to meet the Messenger of God (ṢAAS) at al-ʿAqaba in the middle of the *tashriq* period. When we had finished the pilgrimage the night arrived for which we had an appointment with the Messenger of God (ṢAAS). We had kept our purpose unknown to those of our people who were polytheists, but there with us was ʿAbd Allāh b. ʿAmr b. Ḥarām Abū Jābir, one of our leaders. To him we spoke, telling him, 'Abū Jābir, you are one of our noble leaders, and we would like you to give up your practices; otherwise one day you will end up as fuel for hell-fire.' We then invited him into Islam, and told him of our rendezvous with the Messenger of God (ṢAAS) at al-ʿAqaba. He did accept Islam, was present at al-ʿAqaba and became a *naqib*, a leader."

Al-Bukhārī stated, "Ibrāhīm related to me, quoting Hishām, that Ibn Jurayj told them, from ʿAṭāʾ, that Jābir said, 'I, my father and my two maternal uncles were present at al-ʿAqaba.' ʿAbd Allāh b. Muḥammad stated, 'Ibn ʿUyayna said, "One of these two men was al-Barāʾ b. Maʿmūr."' ʿAlī al-Madīnī related to us, quoting Sufyān, "ʿAmr used to say, "I heard Jābir b. ʿAbd Allāh state, 'My two maternal uncles were present at al-ʿAqaba with me.'"'"

The Imām Aḥmad stated, "ʿAbd al-Razzāq related to us, quoting Maʿmar, from Ibn Khuthaym, from Abū al-Zubayr, that Jābir said, 'The Messenger of God (ṢAAS) remained for ten years in Mecca following people to their homes, going to ʿUkāẓ and Majanna during the festivals asking, "Who will give me refuge? Whoever will help me until I can fulfil the mission of my Lord will attain paradise." But he found no one to shelter or aid him. So much so that someone from Yemen or the Muḍar would appear and respond favourably to this plea, only to have his relatives and friends tell him, "Watch out that that man of Quraysh doesn't corrupt you!" And if the Messenger of God (ṢAAS) were to pass through their encampments, they would point their fingers at him.

"'This went on until God sent us from Yathrib (Medina) to him and we gave him refuge and believed in him. Our people would go off, believe in him, have the Qurʾān recited to them and then return to their own folk who would then accept Islam as they had. Eventually no *anṣār* home was devoid of Muslims displaying their faith in Islam.

"'At last we all consulted together and asked ourselves how long we were going to leave the Messenger of God (SAAS) doing his rounds and being harassed in the Meccan mountains in a state of fear.

"'So 70 of us men went to see him during the pilgrimage season. We made a rendezvous with him at the defile at al-ʿAqaba, going there in ones and twos until all were present. Then we asked him, "O Messenger of God what do you wish us to pledge to you?"

"'He replied, "You must pledge to hear and obey at times of both action and inaction, to give whether times are hard or easy, and to advocate goodness and prohibit evil. You must speak out for God and not fear any blame for supporting God. You must help and defend me if I come to you in the same ways you help and defend yourselves, your wives and your children. You will then attain paradise." And so we stood up before him and pledged allegiance. Asʿad b. Zurāra took him by the hand, he being one of the youngest there.'"

In the account of al-Bayhaqī, the text reads, "He was the youngest of the 70 except for myself. He (Asʿad) said, 'Slowly now, people of Yathrib! We only hurried here because we know that he is the Messenger of God. Bringing him out now, however, would be a provocation to all the Arabs that would cause you to lose your élite and would box you in with swords raised against you. If you are able to withstand that, then adopt him and it will be up to God to reward you. But if you are a people who have great fear for yourselves, then leave him and make that fact plain; that course would be more forgivable in God's sight.'

"'Keep away from us, Asʿad,' (they replied). 'We won't renege on this pledge. We will never deny it.'"

He continued, "So we all stood and pledged to him. He made us make promises and assured us paradise in return."

Imām Aḥmad related this also, as did al-Bayhaqī through Dāʾūd b. ʿAbd al-Raḥmān al-ʿAṭṭār.

Al-Bayhaqī's account adds to the chain of authorities al-Ḥākim back to Yaḥyā b. Sālim; both of them include ʿAbd Allāh b. ʿUthmān b. Khuthaym, from Abū Idrīs, with much the same content.

This chain of authorities is excellent and meets the criteria for *aḥādith* prescribed by Muslim; the scholars, however, did not cite it.

Al-Bazzār commented, "Several authorities quote it from Ibn Khuthaym, but we only know of Jābir being a link in this one account."

Imām Aḥmad stated, "Sulaymān b. Dāʾūd related to us, from ʿAbd al-Raḥmān b. Abū al-Zinād, from Mūsā b. ʿAbd Allāh, from Abū al-Zubayr, from Jābir, who said, "Al-ʿAbbās was holding the hand of the Messenger of God (SAAS), while the latter was verifying our pledges. When he had finished, the Messenger of God (SAAS) said, 'I have taken, and I have given.'""

Al-Bazzār stated, "Muḥammad b. Maʿmar related to us, quoting Qubayṣa, quoting Sufyān – he being al-Thawrī – from Jābir – meaning al-Juʿfī – from Dāʾūd – he being the son of Abū Hind – from al-Shaʿbī, from Jābir – meaning the son of 'Abd Allāh – who said, 'The Messenger of God (ṢAAS) said to the *anṣār* leaders, "Will you then give me refuge and protect me?" "Yes," they said, "and what will we receive?" "Paradise," he replied.'"

Al-Bazzār then added, "We know of this *ḥadīth* only from this one chain of authorities back to Jābir."

Ibn Isḥāq then related, from Ma'bad, from 'Abd Allāh, from his father Ka'b b. Mālik, who said, "That night we went to bed among our people in our caravan. But when one-third of the night had passed, we left the caravan to attend the rendezvous with the Messenger of God (ṢAAS). We slipped away, keeping ourselves hidden like sand-grouse and met in the defile at al-'Aqaba. We were 73 men in number and two of our women accompanied us, Nasība, daughter of Ka'b, mother of 'Umāra, a wife from the Banū Māzin b. al-Najjār, and Asmā', daughter of 'Amr b. 'Adī b. Nābī, one of the wives of the Banū Salama, she being the mother of Manī'."

Ibn Isḥāq quoted from an account of Yūnus b. Bukayr, giving their names and genealogies and the information that some sources give their number as 70; but the Arabs (i.e. the bedouin, tr.) often deal only in round numbers.

'Urwa b. al-Zubayr and Mūsā b. 'Uqba stated, "They were 70 in number, with one woman." He also said that 40 of them were adult, while 30 were youths, the youngest of them being Abū Mas'ūd and Jābir b. 'Abd Allāh.

Ka'b b. Mālik stated, "When we met at the defile we waited and the Messenger of God (ṢAAS) did come, accompanied by al-'Abbās b. 'Abd al-Muṭṭalib. At that time al-'Abbās was still following his people's religion, although he was keeping track of his nephew's affairs and watching over him.

"When they sat down, the first to speak was al-'Abbās b. 'Abd al-Muṭṭalib, who said, 'O Khazraj' – the Arabs used to know the *anṣār* as Khazraj, whether they were Khazraj or Aws – 'Muḥammad holds with us a position of which you are aware. We protect him from our people who think about him as we do. He is respected among his people and safe in his own town. But he is determined to join up with you. If you think you will keep trust with him in the invitation you have given him and will protect him from his opponents, then it's up to you to accept your responsibilities. But if you think you might deliver him over and abandon him after he has joined you, then leave him right now. He does have respect and protection among his own people and in his town.'

"We replied, 'We hear what you say. Speak to us, O Messenger of God, and take for yourself and for your Lord whatever you want.'

"The Messenger of God (ṢAAS) then spoke, recited the Qur'ān, invited people to God and acclaimed Islam. He said, 'I ask you to pledge that you will defend me as you do your women and children.'

"Al-Barā' b. Ma'mūr then took him by the hand and said, 'Yes indeed; we will, I swear by Him who sent you with the truth, protect you as we do our women from whatever threatens them. We pledge ourselves to you, O

Messenger of God, and we are, I swear it, warriors from father to son over many generations.'

"While al-Barāʾ was speaking to the Messenger of God (ṢAAS) he was interrupted by Abū al-Haytham b. al-Tayyihān, who said, 'O Messenger of God, we have certain ties to others' – meaning the Jews – 'and if we break these, we are concerned that if God gives you victory, you might return to your own people and abandon us.'

"The Messenger of God (ṢAAS) smiled at this and said, 'If your blood be sought, our blood shall be sought, and your destruction is mine as well. I am of you and you are of me. I will battle those you battle and make peace with those with whom you make peace.'"

Kaʿb b. Mālik went on, "The Messenger of God (ṢAAS) said, 'Bring forth twelve from among you to be leaders to take charge of their people's affairs.'

"They selected twelve men, nine from al-Khazraj, three from Aws."

These were, according to Ibn Isḥāq, Abū Umāma Asʿad b. Zurāra, mentioned above, Saʿd b. al-Rabīʿ b. ʿAmr b. Abū Zuhayr b. Mālik b. Imruʾ al-Qays b. Mālik b. Thaʿlaba b. Kaʿb b. al-Khazraj b. al-Ḥārith b. al-Khazraj, ʿAbd Allāh b. Rawāḥa b. Thaʿlaba b. Imruʾ al-Qays b. Mālik b. Thaʿlaba b. Kaʿb b. al-Khazraj b. al-Ḥārith b. al-Khazraj, Rāfiʿ b. Mālik b. al-ʿAjlān, mentioned above, al-Barāʾ b. Maʿmūr b. Ṣakhr b. Khansāʾ b. Sinān b. ʿUbayd b. ʿAdī b. Ghanm b. Kaʿb b. Salama b. Saʿd b. ʿAlī b. Asad b. Sārida b. Tazīd b. Jusham b. al-Khazraj, ʿAbd Allāh b. ʿAmr b. Ḥarām b. Thaʿlaba b. Ḥarām b. Kaʿb b. Ghanm b. Kaʿb b. Salama, ʿUbāda b. al-Ṣāmit, mentioned above, Saʿd b. ʿUbāda b. Dulaym b. Ḥāritha b. Abū Khuzayma b. Thaʿlaba b. Ṭarīf b. al-Khazraj b. Sāʿida b. Kaʿb b. al-Khazraj, and al-Mundhir b. ʿAmr b. Khunays b. Ḥāritha b. Lawdhān b. ʿAbd Wudd b. Zayd b. Thaʿlaba b. al-Khazraj b. Sāʿida b. Kaʿb b. al-Khazraj.

These were the nine men of the Khazraj.

From Aws there were three: Usayd b. Ḥuḍayr b. Simāk b. ʿAtīk b. Rāfiʿ b. Imruʾ al-Qays b. Zayd b. ʿAbd al-Ashhal b. Jusham b. al-Khazraj b. ʿAmr b. Mālik b. al-Aws, Saʿd b. Khaythama b. al-Ḥārith b. Mālik b. Kaʿb b. al-Naḥḥāṭ b. Kaʿb b. Ḥāritha b. Ghanm b. al-Salm b. Imruʾ al-Qays b. Mālik b. al-Aws, Rifāʿa b. ʿAbd al-Mundhir b. Zunayr b. Zayd b. Umayya b. Zayd b. Mālik b. ʿAwf b. ʿAmr b. ʿAwf b. Mālik b. al-Aws.

Ibn Hishām stated, "Some scholars include among these Abū al-Haytham b. al-Tayyihān instead of al-Rifāʿa, who is above mentioned." He is also included in the account of Yūnus quoting Ibn Isḥāq. And al-Suhaylī and Ibn al-Athīr in his *Usūd al-Ghāba* (*Jungle Lions*) included him.

Ibn Hishām gave testimony to this in a quotation he makes from Abū Zayd al-Anṣārī of poetry by Kaʿb b. Mālik giving reference to the twelve men selected that night of the second meeting at al-ʿAqaba:

"Tell Ubayy that his opinion is wrong; he died the
morning of the (meeting in) the defile, but death does come,
    May God deny what your soul craves; He watches over
man's affairs, seeing and hearing.
    And inform Abū Sufyān that, through Aḥmad, there has
appeared to us a shining light of God's guidance.
    Do not covet acquiring something you want; just take and
gather whatever it is you receive.
    Take care! Know that breaking vows with us was forbidden
you by the group when they gave allegiance.
    Both al-Barā' and Ibn 'Amr forbad it, and As'ad and Rāfi'
too forbid it.
    Sa'd al-Sā'idī forbad it, and Mundhir would cut off your
nose if you tried it.
    And Ibn Rabī', if you received his pledge, would not give him
up. Let no one expect that.
    Similarly Ibn Rawāḥa would not give him to you; to
protect him he would even take poison.
    Al-Qawqalī b. Ṣāmit too is far removed from what you try
to achieve, living up to the promise he made.
    Abū al-Haytham also is true to his pledge, secure in the
oath he had made.
    And you should have no hopes of Ibn Ḥuḍayr for what you
want; perhaps you should abandon your foolish error.
    And Sa'd, brother of 'Amr b. 'Awf, is far removed and
opposed to what it is you want.
    These are not stars that will arise in the dark of night
and repel bad luck from you."

Ibn Hishām stated, "Abū al-Haytham is mentioned here among these men,
whereas Rifā'a is not."

My own comment is that the poet also mentions Sa'd b. Mu'ādh who was
definitely not one of the leaders of the gathering that night.

Ya'qūb b. Sufyān recounted, from Yūnus b. 'Abd al-'A'la, from Ibn Wahb, from
Mālik who said, "The *anṣar* on the night of al-'Aqaba were 70 men; their leaders
were twelve in number, nine from Khazraj, three from Aws.

"An *anṣār* elder told me that Gabriel was indicating to the Messenger of God
(ṢAAS) which of these men he should appoint as leaders on that night of
al-'Aqaba, and Usayd b. Ḥuḍayr was one of those leaders."

Al-Bayhaqī related this.

Ibn Isḥāq stated, "'Abd Allāh b. Abū Bakr related to me that the Messenger
of God (ṢAAS) said to these leaders, 'You shall be those entrusted for your
people just as the apostles were for Jesus, son of Mary. I shall be entrusted with
my own people.' They replied, 'So be it.'

"ʿĀṣim b. ʿUmar b. Qatāda related to us that when this group met to pledge allegiance to the Messenger of God (ṢAAS), al-ʿAbbās b. ʿUbāda b. Naḍla al-Anṣārī, of the Banū Sālim b. ʿAwf, said, 'O Khazraj, do you know what it is you are pledging this man?' 'Yes,' they replied.

"He continued, 'You are pledging to go to war against all kinds of people. If you think that if you suffered great losses to your wealth and had your leaders killed, you would give him up, then do it now or suffer the punishment of this life and the next. If you think you will keep faith with him in what he has called upon you to do, despite loss of wealth and your leaders being killed, then do accept him. For he is, by God, the best in this world and the next.'

"They replied, 'We will take him regardless of loss of wealth or the death of our leaders. But what will we receive in return for this, O Messenger of God, if we keep faith with you?'

"'Paradise,' he replied.

"'Then hold out your hand,' they asked.

"He did so and they pledged allegiance to him.

"ʿĀṣim b. ʿUmar b. Qatāda commented, 'Al-ʿAbbās b. ʿUbāda only said this to emphasize the pact they were making.'

"ʿAbd Allāh b. Abū Bakr claimed that al-ʿAbbās had only said that to delay the pledge of allegiance that night in the hope that ʿAbd Allāh b. Ubayy b. Salūl, leader of the Khazraj would attend so that the action of the group would be even stronger. God knows best which of these is true."

Ibn Isḥāq stated, "The Banū al-Najjār claim that Abū Umāma Asʿad b. Zurāra was the first who touched his hand in allegiance. The Banū ʿAbd al-Ashhal, however, claim that it was Abū al-Haytham b. al-Tayyihān."

Ibn Isḥāq also said, "Maʿbad b. Kaʿb related to me from his brother ʿAbd Allāh, from his father Kaʿb b. Mālik, who said, 'The first man to touch the hand of the Messenger of God (ṢAAS) was al-Barāʾ b. Maʿrūr. Then all the rest pledged allegiance to him.'"

Ibn al-Athīr stated in his work al-Ghāba (The Jungle), "The Banū Salama claim that the first who pledged allegiance to him that night was Kaʿb b. Mālik."

It is established in the ṣaḥīḥ collection of al-Bukhārī and in that of Muslim, from a ḥadīth of al-Zuhrī, from ʿAbd al-Raḥmān b. ʿAbd Allāh b. Kaʿb, from his father, from Kaʿb b. Mālik in his ḥadīth when he absented himself from the battle of Tabūk. He stated, "I was present with the Messenger of God (ṢAAS) on the night of al-ʿAqaba when we pledged ourselves to Islam, and I would not rather have witnessed the battle of Badr than it, even though at Badr there were more men involved."

Al-Bayhaqī stated, "Abū al-Ḥusayn b. Bashrān informed us, quoting ʿAmr b. al-Sammāk, quoting Ḥanbal b. Isḥāq, quoting Abū Nuʿaym, and Zakariyyaʾ b. Abū Zāʾida, from ʿĀmir al-Shaʿbī, who said, "The Messenger of God (ṢAAS) went off with his uncle al-ʿAbbās to meet 70 of the anṣār at al-ʿAqaba, beneath a tree. He told them, 'Let your spokesman speak, but not talk too long. For there are polytheists watching you and if they have knowledge of you they will expose you.'

"Abū Umāma, their spokesman, said, 'Ask, Muḥammad, for your Lord whatever it is you want. Then after that ask for yourself what it is you want. Then tell us what reward we will have from God and from you if we do that.'

"He replied, 'For my Lord I ask you to worship Him and to associate no other god with Him. For myself, and my Companions, I ask you to give me refuge and to help me and protect me from what it is you protect yourselves.'

"They asked, 'What will we receive if we do that?'

"'You shall have paradise,' he replied.

"'Shall you have that?' they asked."

Ḥanbal also related this from Imām Aḥmad, from Yaḥyā b. Zakariyyāʾ, from Mujālid, from al-Shaʿbī, from Abū Masʿūd al-Anṣārī who, having recounted it, stated, "Abū Masʿūd was the youngest man there."

Aḥmad stated, from Yaḥyā, from Ismāʿīl b. Abū Khālid, from al-Shaʿbī, who said, "No one, old or young, ever heard such an address."

Al-Bayhaqī stated, "Abū Ṭāhir Muḥammad b. Muḥammad b. Muḥammad b. Muḥmish narrated to us from Muḥammad b. Ibrāhīm b. al-Faḍl al-Fahhām from Muḥammad b. Yaḥyā al-Dhuhlī from ʿAmr b. ʿUthmān al-Raqqī, as follows: 'Zuhayr related to us, from ʿAbd Allāh b. ʿUthmān b. Khuthaym, from Ismāʿīl b. ʿUbayd Allāh b. Rifāʿa, from his father, who said, "Skins of wine were brought out, but ʿUbāda b. al-Ṣāmit went up to them and pierced them open, saying, 'We have pledged to the Messenger of God (ṢAAS) that we will listen and obey, in action and at rest, expend our wealth in good times and bad, enjoin good and forbid evil, express our faith in God without fear of reproach, and assist the Messenger of God (ṢAAS) if he comes to Yathrib with the same protection we give ourselves and our children in body and soul. And we shall have paradise.'"

"'This was the pledge we made to the Messenger of God (ṢAAS).'"

This chain of authorities is strong and excellent but the scholars do not cite it.

Yūnus stated, from Ibn Isḥāq, "ʿUbāda b. al-Walīd b. ʿUbāda b. al-Ṣāmit related to me from his father, from his grandfather ʿUbāda b. al-Ṣāmit, who said, 'The Messenger of God (ṢAAS) had us pledge to him that we would fight, that we would listen and obey in good and bad times alike, regardless of the incentives or disincentives or pressure upon us, that we would not dispute among ourselves, that we would speak the truth wherever we were and hear no reproach in our worship of God.'"

Ibn Isḥāq stated in his account from Maʿbad b. Kaʿb, from his brother ʿAbd Allāh b. Kaʿb b. Mālik, who said, "When we pledged ourselves to the Messenger of God (ṢAAS) Satan called out from the top of the defile in the most piercing voice I have ever heard. He said, 'O people of the *jabājib*' – the word meaning 'houses' – are you going to support this reprehensible man and the fools with him who have tried to make war upon you?'

"The Messenger of God (ṢAAS) stated, 'That was Azabb of al-ʿAqaba. He's the son of Azyab.'"

Ibn Hishām suggested that the name given was "son of Uzayb".

"'Do you hear, O enemy of God,' he went on, 'I swear I will destroy you!'

"Then he told them, 'Return to your caravans.'"

The account continues, "Al-ʿAbbās b. ʿUbāda b. Naḍla said, 'O Messenger of God by Him who sent you with the truth, if you wish tomorrow we will fall on those at Minā with our swords!'

"The Messenger of God (ṢAAS) replied, 'We have not been ordered to do that; however, do go back to your caravans.'

"And so we returned to our beds and slept in them until morning.

"Next morning leaders of Quraysh came to us in our camps and said, 'O Khazraj, we have learned that you have come to this man of ours asking him to leave us and pledging to fight against us. We swear that there is no Arab group we would like less to do battle with than you.'

"Those of our people who were polytheists promptly swore that they had no knowledge of any such thing.

"And they spoke the truth; they knew nothing. We, meanwhile, were exchanging glances.

"Then Quraysh arose; they included al-Ḥārith b. Hishām b. al-Mughīra al-Makhzūmī who was wearing new sandals. I spoke to him as if I wanted to associate the entire group with what the polytheists had said. Then I said (changing the subject) "ʿAbū Jābir, seeing that you are one of our chiefs, can't you get sandals like those of that young Quraysh fellow?'

"Al-Ḥārith heard this, took off his sandals and hurled them at me, saying, 'By God, you can put them on!'

"Abū Jābir replied, 'Now easy there; you've annoyed the lad; give him back his sandals.'

"I replied, 'I swear, I'll not return them. They're a good omen; and if it proves true, I'll keep the sandals!'"

Ibn Isḥāq stated, "ʿAbd Allāh b. Abū Bakr related to me that they went to ʿAbd Allāh b. Ubayy b. Salūl and said much the same as Kaʿb had. He told them, 'This is a very grave matter; my people are not such as to divide over a matter like this. I have no knowledge of it.' The Quraysh leaders then left.

"The pilgrims then left Minā and some of them investigated the report further, finding it to have happened. They set about pursuing our people and caught up with Saʿd b. ʿUbāda at Adhākhir, along with al-Mundhir b. ʿAmr, a brother from the Banū Sāʿida b. Kaʿb b. al-Khazraj; both of these were 'leaders' (i.e. appointed at al-ʿAqaba, tr.).

"Al-Mundhir evaded them but they captured Saʿd b. ʿUbāda and tied his hands behind his neck with the cords holding his saddle and led him into Mecca, beating him and pulling him along by his hair which was very full.

"Saʿd reported, 'So there I was in their hands when up came a group of Quraysh among whom was one tall, handsome, fair-skinned man. I told myself, "If there is any good in any of their men, it has to be him."

"'But when he drew near he raised his hand and struck me hard. I told myself, "Well, I swear, after this there's no good in them at all!"

"'Well, there I was in their hands, being pulled along, when one of their men came up to me and said, "Too bad! Don't you have any pact or protection agreement with any Quraysh man?" I replied, "Yes, indeed I do. I used to give protection to Jubayr b. Mutʿim and his merchants on business trips and prevent those of my people who wanted to harm them. And also I protected al-Ḥārith b. Ḥarb b. Umayya b. ʿAbd Shams." He commented, "Cry out the names of the two men and tell of your connection to them."

"'So I did this and that man went off to look for those two merchants. He found them in the kaʿba and told them, "There's a man of Khazraj now out there in the valley being beaten and calling out for both of you." They asked, "Who is he?" "He is Saʿd b. ʿUbāda," he told them. "Well," they said, "he has spoken the truth. He did protect our merchants from some in his country who wanted to harm them."'"

The account continues, "The two men then went and released Saʿd from his attackers, and he fled. The man who struck Saʿd was Suhayl b. ʿAmr."

Ibn Hishām stated, "The man who gave him refuge was Abū al-Bakhtarī b. Hishām."

Al-Bayhaqī related with a chain of authorities from ʿĪsā b. Abū b. Jubayr, who said, "Quraysh heard someone speak out in the night on the mountain of Abū Qubays, 'If Saʿdān (i.e. "two Saʿds", tr.) be safe, then Muḥammad should not fear any opposition in Mecca.'

"Next morning, Abū Sufyān asked, 'Who is al-Saʿdān? Asʿad b. Bakr or Saʿd b. Hudhaym?'

"The second night they heard someone reciting,

'O Saʿd, Saʿd of al-Aws, may you be victorious; and
you, O Saʿd, Saʿd of Khazraj, a hero.
Answer to him who calls for guidance and beseech God for
paradise as those who know.
For God's reward to Him who seeks guidance is gardens of
paradise where birds fly.'

"Next morning Abū Sufyān said, 'I swear, it has to be Saʿd b. Muʿādh and Saʿd b. ʿUbāda!'"

DIVISION

Ibn Isḥāq stated, "When the *anṣār* who had pledged themselves to the Messenger of God (ṢAAS) on the night of the second meeting at al-ʿAqaba returned to Medina, they proclaimed their acceptance of Islam.

"Among their people there were still a few elders persisting in their polytheistic beliefs. One of these was ʿAmr b. al-Jamūḥ b. Zayd b. Ḥarām b. Kaʿb b. Ghanm b. Kaʿb b. Salama.

"His son Muʿādh b. ʿAmr was one of those who were present at al-ʿAqaba. ʿAmr b. al-Jamūḥ was a leader of the Banū Salama. He had a wooden idol, named Manāt, in his home; this was a practice common among those chieftains. They would treat these idols as gods and would venerate them and show them off. When the young men of the Banū Salama, Muʿādh, and Muʿādh b. Jabal accepted Islam, they would sneak in at night to that idol of ʿAmr, carry it out and toss it head first into pits used to contain the excrement of the Banū Salama. Next morning ʿAmr would ask, 'Who could have attacked our god tonight?' He would then look around for it and when he found it he washed it, purified it and scented it. Then he would say, 'I swear, if I knew who did that to you I would put him to shame!'

"When ʿAmr slept at night they would again seize it and do as before. ʿAmr again found it harmed as before and he would wash, purify and scent it. That night they returned and did the same, as he did. But this time he brought his sword and attached it to the idol saying, 'I swear I do not know who is doing this to you, but if there is any good in you, then defend yourself! You have this sword now.'

"That night while ʿAmr slept they returned to the idol, took the sword off its neck and then replaced it with a dead dog they attached to it. Then they threw it into one of the cesspools of the Banū Salama. Next day ʿAmr b. al-Jamūḥ did not see it in its place, so he went out to find it and did so in the cesspool, upside down and with the dead dog attached. When he saw it in this state he reflected upon his state and one of his people who had accepted Islam went and spoke to him, and, by God's mercy, he accepted Islam himself and remained a good Muslim. When he accepted Islam and knew what he now did of God, he reflected on his own state and what he had seen happen to the idol. He thanked God who had saved him from his former blindness and error and spoke the following verses,

> 'By God, if you had been a god, you would not have been
> hurled into a well tied to a dog!
> Yekh! for treating you as a god; now we have assessed
> you and (turned from) evil ways,
> Praise be to God the Almighty, the Benevolent, the
> Giver, the Provider, the establisher of the religions,
> He it was saved me before I was encased in the darkness
> of a grave.'"

Section: That gives the names of those who attended the second meeting at al-ʿAqaba, their number, according to Ibn Isḥāq, totalling seventy-three men and two women.

There were 11 men from Aws: Usayd b. Ḥuḍayr, one of the "leaders"; Abū al-Haytham b. al-Tayyihān, who was also at Badr; Salama b. Salāma b. Waqash, at Badr; Zuhayr b. Rāfiʿ; Abū Burda b. Niyār; Nuhayr b. al-Haytham b. Nābī b.

Majdaⁿa b. Ḥāritha; Saⁿd b. Khaythama, one of the "leaders" who was killed at Badr; Rifāⁿa b. ⁿAbd al-Mundhir b. Zunayr, a "leader", at Badr; ⁿAbd Allāh b. Jubayr b. al-Nuⁿmān b. Umayya b. al-Burak, at Badr, killed at Uḥud where he was a commander of the bowmen; Maⁿan b. ⁿAdī b. al-Jadd b. ⁿAjlān b. al-Ḥārith b. Ḍubayⁿa al-Balawī, an ally of the Aws, present at Badr and its aftermath and died a martyr in al-Yamāma; ⁿUwaym b. Sāⁿida, who attended Badr and thereafter.

From the Khazraj there were 62 men: Abū Ayyūb Khālid b. Zayd, who participated at Badr and thereafter, dying a martyr in Byzantine territory during the reign of Muⁿāwiya; Muⁿādh b. al-Ḥārith, along with his brothers ⁿAwf and Muⁿawwidh, sons of ⁿAfrāʾ, all at Badr; Umāra b. Ḥazm who witnessed Badr and thereafter, was killed in al-Yamāma; Asⁿad b. Zurāra Abū Umāma, one of the "leaders", who died before Badr; Sahl b. ⁿAtīk, at Badr; Aws b. Thābit b. al-Mundhir, at Badr; Abū Ṭalḥa Zayd b. Sahl, at Badr; Qays b. Abū Ṣaⁿṣaⁿa ⁿAmr b. Zayd b. ⁿAwf b. Mabdhūl b. ⁿAmr b. Ghanm b. Māzin, a commander of the rear-guard at Badr; ⁿAmr b. Ghaziyya; Saⁿd b. al-Rabīⁿ, one of the "leaders", who was at Badr and was killed at Uḥud.

Also there were ⁿAbd Allāh b. Rawāḥa, one of the "leaders"; he was present at Badr, Uḥud and the *khandaq*, "the trench". He was killed at the battle of Muʾta, acting as commander. Also there was Bashīr b. Saⁿd, at Badr, and ⁿAbd Allāh b. Zayd b. Thaⁿlaba b. ⁿAbd Rabbihī, who was shown how to call people to prayer. He was present at Badr.

Khallād b. Suwayd, who was present at Badr, Uḥud and *al-khandaq*. He died a martyr battling the Banū Qurayẓa; a millstone was hurled at him and it crushed him. It is said that the Messenger of God (ṢAAS) stated, "He will have the reward of two martyrs."

Also there was Abū Masⁿūd ⁿUqba b. ⁿAmr, at Badr. However, Ibn Isḥāq stated, "He was the youngest person to witness al-ⁿAqaba, and he was not present at Badr."

There was Ziyād b. Labīd, at Badr, Farwa b. ⁿAmr b. Wadhafa; Khālid b. Qays b. Mālik, at Badr; Rāfiⁿ b. Mālik, a "leader"; Dhakwān b. ⁿAbd Qays b. Khalda b. Mukhlid b. ⁿĀmir b. Zurayq. He it is who was called both *muhājirī* and *anṣārī*, "Emigrant" and "Helper", because he stayed with the Messenger of God (ṢAAS) in Mecca until his migration to Medina. He was present at Badr and was killed at Uḥud. Also there was ⁿAbbād b. Qays b. ⁿĀmir b. Khālid b. ⁿĀmir b. Zurayq, at Badr, and his brother al-Ḥārith b. Qays b. ⁿĀmir, also at Badr.

And al-Barāʾ b. Maⁿrūr, a "leader" and the first man to pledge allegiance (at ⁿAqaba) according to the claim of the Banū Salama. He died before the arrival of the Prophet (ṢAAS) in Medina and pledged to him a third of his wealth. The Messenger of God (ṢAAS) returned the money to his heirs. His son was Bishr b. al-Barāʾ; he was present at Badr, Uḥud and *al-khandaq*. He died a martyr at Khaybar as a result of eating, along with the Messenger of God (ṢAAS), from the poisoned sheep. God bless him!

Also there was Sinān b. Ṣayfī b. Ṣakhr, at Badr, al-Ṭufayl b. al-Nuⁿmān b. Khansāʾ, at Badr; he was killed at the battle of *al-khandaq*.

And there was Ma'qil b. al-Mundhir b. Sarḥ, at Badr, and his brother Yazīd b. Sinān al-Mundhir, at Badr; Mas'ūd b. Zayd b. Subay'; al-Daḥḥāk b. Ḥāritha b. Zayd b. Tha'laba, at Badr; Yazīd b. Khadhām b. Subay'; Jabbār b. Ṣakhr b. Umayya b. al-Khansā' b. Sinān b. 'Ubayd, at Badr; al-Ṭufayl b. Mālik b. al-Khansā', at Badr.

And Ka'b b. Mālik; Sulaym b. 'Āmir b. Ḥadīda, at Badr; Quṭba b. 'Āmir b. Ḥadīda, at Badr, and his brother Abū al-Mundhir Yazīd, at Badr also; and Abū al-Yusr Ka'b b. 'Amr, at Badr, and Ṣayfī b. Sawwād b. 'Abbād.

And Tha'laba b. Ghanama b. 'Adī b. Nābī, at Badr and martyred at *al-khandaq*. And his brother 'Amr b. Ghanama b. 'Adī; 'Abs b. 'Āmir b. 'Adī, at Badr; Khālid b. 'Amr b. 'Adī b. Nābī; and 'Abd Allāh b. Unays, an ally of theirs from Quḍā'a.

And 'Abd Allāh b. 'Amr b. Ḥarām, one of the "leaders", at Badr, martyred at Uḥud, and his son Jābir b. 'Abd Allāh; Mu'ādh b. 'Amr b. al-Jamūḥ, at Badr; Thābit b. al-Jadh', at Badr and martyred at al-Ṭā'if; 'Umayr b. al-Ḥārith b. Tha'laba, at Badr; Khadīj b. Salama, an ally of theirs from Baliy; Mu'ādh b. Jabal who witnessed Badr and thereafter; he died of the plague at 'Imwās in the Caliphate of 'Umar b. al-Khaṭṭāb.

And 'Ubāda b. al-Ṣāmit, a "leader", at Badr and thereafter; al-'Abbās b. 'Ubāda b. Naḍla, who stayed at Mecca until he emigrated from it. He also was known as a *muhājirī anṣārī*. He was martyred at Uḥud. And Abū 'Abd al-Raḥmān Yazīd b. Tha'laba b. Khazma b. Aṣram, an ally of theirs from the Banū Ghuṣayna from Baliy; 'Amr b. al-Ḥārith b. Labda; Rifā'a b. 'Amr b. Zayd, at Badr; 'Uqba b. Wahb b. Kalda, an ally of theirs, at Badr. He was one of those who left for Mecca and remained until he emigrated from there. He was one of those also called a *muhājirī anṣārī*. And Sa'd b. 'Ubāda b. Dulaym, a "leader"; al-Mundhir b. 'Amr, a "leader" and at both Badr and Uḥud. He was killed at Bi'r Ma'ūna, acting as a commander. It was he of whom it was said, "He was *manumitted only to die*."

The two women were Umm 'Umāra Nasība, daughter of Ka'b b. 'Amr b. 'Awf b. Mabdhūl b. 'Amr b. Ghanm b. Māzin b. al-Najjār, of Māzin and al-Najjār.

Ibn Isḥāq stated, "She, along with her sister and her husband Zayd b. 'Āṣim b. Ka'b and her sons Ḥabīb and 'Abd Allāh, was present with the Messenger of God (ṢAAS) during the war. This son of hers, Ḥabīb, was killed by Musaylima, "the liar", the latter asked him, 'Do you bear witness that Muḥammad is the Messenger of God?' 'Yes,' he replied. He asked, 'Do you bear witness that I am the Messenger of God?' He replied, 'I do not hear!' At that he began cutting off one member after the other from him until he died right there before him; he got nothing more from him. Umm 'Umāra was one of those who left for al-Yamāma with the Muslims when Musaylima was killed. When she came back she had 12 wounds caused by hits and cuts. God bless her.

The other woman was Umm Mani', Asmā', daughter of 'Amr b. 'Adī b. Nābī b. 'Amr b. Sawwād b. Ghanm b. Ka'b b. Salama. May God be pleased with them all.

Chapter: The beginning of emigration from Mecca to Medina.

Al-Zuhrī stated, from 'Urwa, that 'Ā'isha said, "The Messenger of God (ṢAAS), he being at Mecca at the time, addressed the Muslims as follows, 'I have been shown the place of your migration; I have been shown a salty, swampy plain with palm-groves between two tracts of rocks.'

"Some people migrated towards Medina when the Messenger of God (ṢAAS) said that, while other Muslims who had gone to Abyssinia returned and went there instead."

Al-Bukhārī related this.

Abū Mūsā stated that the Prophet (ṢAAS) said, "In my sleep I saw that I would be migrating from Mecca to a place where there were palm-groves. My imagination told me that it was to be in al-Yamāma or Hajar, but it turned out to be the town of Yathrib."

This *ḥadīth* is given at length by al-Bukhārī with a variety of chains of authority.

Muslim also related both of the above *aḥadīth* with lines of authority from Abū Kurayb. Muslim added 'Abd Allāh b. Murād and quoted both traditions on the authority of Abū Usāma, from Yazīd b. 'Abd Allāh b. Abū Burda, from his grandfather, Abū Burda, from Abū Mūsā 'Abd Allāh b. Qays al-Ash'arī, from the Prophet (ṢAAS), giving the whole *ḥadīth*.

The *ḥāfiz* Abū Bakr al-Bayhaqī stated, "The *ḥāfiz* Abū 'Abd Allāh informed us, quoting Abū al-'Abbās al-Qāsim b. al-Qāsim al-Sayārī of Merv, quoting Ibrāhīm b. Hilāl, quoting al-'Āmirī, from 'Alī b. al-Ḥasan b. Shaqīq, quoting 'Īsā b. 'Ubayd al-Kindī, from Ghaylān b. 'Abd Allāh al-'Āmirī, from Abū Zur'a b. 'Amr b. Jarīr, from Jarīr, that the Prophet (ṢAAS) said, 'God revealed to me, "Any one of these three places you go to will be the place of your migration: Medina, al-Baḥrayn or Qinnasrīn."'

"The scholars state that thereafter he decided for Medina, and told his Companions to migrate there."

This is a very strange *ḥadīth*. Al-Tirmidhī related it in a digression in his compendium, giving only one account, from Abū 'Ammār al-Ḥusayn b. Ḥurayth, from al-Faḍl b. Mūsā, from 'Īsā b. 'Ubayd, from Ghaylān b. 'Abd Allāh al-'Āmirī, from Abū Zur'a b. 'Umar b. Jarīr, from Jarīr, who said, "The Messenger of God (ṢAAS) said, 'God revealed to me, "Any one of these three places you go to will be the site of your migration: Medina, al-Baḥrayn or Qinnasrīn."'" He (al-Tirmidhī) then commented, "This tradition is *gharīb*, unique; we know of it only on the authority of al-Faḍl, and Abū 'Ammār alone narrated it."

I comment that this authority Ghaylān b. 'Abd Allāh al-'Āmirī is mentioned by Ibn Ḥibān in *al-Thiqāt* (*The Trustworthy Authorities*). However, he states, "He related, from Abū Zur'a, a spurious *ḥadīth* about the *hijra*, the emigration." But God knows best.

Ibn Isḥāq stated, "When God Almighty gave permission for warfare with His words, 'Permission (to fight) is being given to those against whom war is being wrongfully waged. God has power to give them victory, those who have been expelled unjustly from their homes merely for having said, "Our Lord is God"'' (*sūrat al-Ḥajj*; XXII, v.39–40).

"When God gave permission to do battle and that group of *anṣār* had followed him into accepting Islam and had agreed to give him and his Muslim followers aid and refuge, the Messenger of God (ṢAAS) ordered his supporters, both those who had previously emigrated and those who had stayed with him in Mecca, to leave in migration to Medina to join their Muslim brethren there. He told them, 'God has provided brothers and a home where you may be secure.'

"And so they left for Medina in groups.

"The Messenger of God (ṢAAS) stayed in Mecca waiting for his Lord to give him permission to emigrate from Mecca to Medina.

"The first of his supporters to emigrate to Medina of the Quraysh and of the Banū Makhzūm was Abū Salama ʿAbd Allāh b. ʿAbd al-Asad b. Hilāl b. ʿAbd Allāh b. ʿUmar b. Makhzūm. His migration took place one year before the pledge made at al-ʿAqaba. This was because, following his return from Abyssinia, he had been badly treated by Quraysh and had decided to return there, but, when he learned of fellow Muslims in Medina, he went there instead."

Ibn Isḥāq stated, "My father related to me, from Salama b. ʿAbd Allāh b. ʿUmar b. Abū Salama, from his grandmother Umm Salama, who said, 'When Abū Salama decided to depart for Medina, he saddled his camel for me, mounted me on it and put my son Salama in my lap. He then led us away.

"'When some men of the Banū al-Mughīra saw him they approached and said, "We can accept what you yourself do, but why should we allow this woman of ours to be taken off by you somewhere else?" She went on, "And they snatched the camel's bridle out of his hand and took me off it."

"'This angered the Banū ʿAbd al-Asad, Abū Salama's people, and they said, "By God, we'll not leave a son of ours with her now you've taken her away from our man." So they tugged at my son Salama and dislocated his arm. The Banū ʿAbd al-Asad then took him away, while the Banū al-Mughīra kept me among themselves. My husband, Abū Salama, then left for Medina. So I was separated from both my son and my husband.

"'Thereafter I would go out every morning and sit in the valley and weep till evening; I kept this up for about a year.

"'Then one day a man from my uncle's family, one of the Banū al-Mughīra, passed by, saw the state I was in and took pity on me. He told the Banū al-Mughīra, "Can't you let this poor woman go? You've separated her from both her son and her husband!"

"'They then told me I could join my husband if I liked.

"'So then the Banū ʿAbd al-Asad returned my son to me; I saddled a camel, took my son in my lap and headed out to my husband in Medina.

"'I was entirely alone. But eventually, at al-Tanʿim, I met ʿUthmān b. Ṭalḥa b. Abū Ṭalḥa, a relative of the Banū ʿAbd al-Dār, and he asked, "Where are you going, daughter of Abū Umayya?" I replied, "I'm heading for my husband in Medina." He said, "And there's no one with you?" "There is no one with me except God and this son of mine," I replied.

"'He commented, "You shouldn't be left like that."

"'He then took the camel's halter and began accompanying me. And, I swear, I was never in the company of any Arab more honourable than him. When we made a stop, he would make my camel kneel and then he would move away until I had dismounted. When I made a halt he would take my mount away, unload it, and tie it to a tree. He would then move off and make his bed beneath a tree. When it was time to leave, he would get my camel, lead it up, saddle it and then stand away from me. He would then say, "Do mount!" And when I mounted and was secure, he would come and take its halter and lead me away until we next stopped.

"'He continued behaving in this way until he brought me to Medina. When he saw the village of the Banū ʿAmr b. ʿAwf at Qubāʾ, he said, "Your husband is in this village. Abū Salama is living here. Go on in, with God's blessings." He then left, returning to Mecca.'

"She used to say, 'I know of no other family in all Islam who suffered like that of Abū Salama. And I swear I never had a more honourable companion than ʿUthmān b. Ṭalḥa.'"

This man, ʿUthmān b. Ṭalḥa b. Abū Ṭalḥa al-ʿAbdarī, accepted Islam after the Ḥudaybiyya truce. He emigrated along with Khālid b. al-Walīd. His father and brothers, al-Ḥārith, Kilāb and Musāfiʿ, were killed at Uḥud, along with his uncle ʿUthmān b. Abū Ṭalḥa. The Messenger of God (ṢAAS) handed over to him and to his cousin Shayba, head of the Banū Shayba, the keys of the *kaʿba* on the "conquest of Mecca"; he affirmed their being in their care in Islam as they had been in the *jahiliyya*. On that subject the Almighty revealed, "God orders you to give over matters of trust to those entitled to it" (*sūrat al-Nisāʾ*; IV, v.58).

Ibn Isḥāq stated, "The first of the emigrants to go there after Abū Salama was ʿĀmir b. Rabīʿa, an ally of the Banū ʿAdī. With him went his wife Laylā, daughter of Abū Hathma al-ʿAdawiyya. Then followed ʿAbd Allāh b. Jaḥsh b. Riʿāb b. Yaʿmur b. Ṣabra b. Murra b. Kabīr b. Ghanm b. Dūdān b. Asad b. Khuzayma, an ally of the Banū Umayya b. ʿAbd Shams, accompanied by his family and his brother ʿAbd, that is Abū Aḥmad."

Ibn Isḥāq gives his name as ʿAbd, though it is also said to have been Thamāma. Al-Suhaylī stated that the first of these names was correct.

"Abū Aḥmad was blind; however, he used to make his way all over the length and breadth of Mecca without any guide. He was a poet and had a wife named al-Fāriʿa, daughter of Abū Sufyān b. Ḥarb. His mother was Umayma, daughter of ʿAbd al-Muṭṭalib b. Hāshim.

"The home of Banū Jaḥsh was shut up when the migration occurred. ʿUtba b. Rabīʿa, al-ʿAbbās b. ʿAbd al-Muṭṭalib and Abū Jahl b. Hishām passed by it on their way up to the heights of Mecca. ʿUtba looked at its doors blowing open, unoccupied, and he sighed deeply and said,

'Every house, no matter how long safe, will one day be
beset by disaster and outrage.'"

Ibn Hishām, however, mentioned that this verse was a line from a poem by Abū Dāʾūd al-Iyyādī. Al-Suhaylī said that Abū Dāʾūd was Ḥanẓala b. Sharqī; also his name was given as Ḥāritha.

(Ibn Isḥāq continued) "ʿUtba then said, 'The home of Banū Jaḥsh has become devoid of its people.' Abū Jahl commented, 'No one at all will weep over that!' He then said, to al-ʿAbbās that is, 'All this is the work of your nephew! He has split us up and completely divided our community.'"

Ibn Isḥāq stated, "Abū Salama, ʿĀmir b. Rabīʿa and the Banū Jaḥsh took up residence at Qubāʾ with Mubashshir b. ʿAbd al-Mundhir; after this the Emigrants arrived in groups.

"Banū Ghanm b. Dūdān had accepted Islam and moved as Emigrants to Medina, men and women both. They consisted of ʿAbd Allāh b. Jaḥsh and his brother Abū Aḥmad, ʿUkāsha b. Miḥṣan, Shujāʿ and ʿUqba, both sons of Wahb, Arbad b. Jumayra, Munqidh b. Nubāta, Saʿīd b. Ruqaysh, Muḥriz b. Naḍla, Zayd b. Ruqaysh, Qays b. Jābir, ʿAmr b. Muḥsin, Mālik b. ʿAmr, Ṣafwān b. ʿAmr, Thaqf b. ʿAmr, Rabīʿa b. Aktham, al-Zubayr b. ʿUbayda, Tamām b. ʿUbayda, Sakhbara b. ʿUbayda and Muḥammad b. ʿAbd Allāh b. Jaḥsh. Their women included Zaynab, Ḥumna and Umm Ḥabība, daughters of Jaḥsh, Judāma, daughter of Jandal, Umm Qays, daughter of Muḥsin, Umm Ḥabīb, daughter of Thumāma, Āmina, daughter of Ruqaysh, and Sakhbara, daughter of Tamīm.

"Abū Aḥmad b. Jaḥsh spoke the following verses concerning their emigration to Medina:

'When Umm Aḥmad saw me leaving under the protection of
One supernatural whom I fear and revere,
She said, "If this is what you have to do, then take us
some place else, far from Yathrib."
I said to her, "Yathrib is not just a possible location;
man does whatever the All-Merciful wishes.
I head towards God and to the Messenger; and whoever
directs himself to God one day will not be disappointed.
What a lot of true, real friends we have left behind, and
a woman, too, who weeps tears and laments.
You think it is vengeance that distances us from our
land; we think that it is our aspiration that we seek.

I invited the Banū Ghanm to spare their bloodshed; for
there is a course open to people when the path to truth is
clear."

They responded, praise the Lord, when someone invited
them to the truth and to success, and they came united.

We, and our fellows who had left the true path and had
helped those using weapons against us, had become,

Like two battalions; one of these was successful in
achieving truth, rightly guided, while the other would be
punished.

Acting unjustly, they thought up lies; Satan made them
err away from the truth. They failed and caused to fail.

We delighted in the words of the Prophet Muḥammad and
those of us who supported truth acted well and were well
treated.

We are very closely related to them, though there is no
close relationship if there is no closeness.

What nephew would, after us, give you their trust; what
in-law after us could be respected?

One day you will learn which of us is closer to the
truth, when they have passed on and the people's dispute is
concluded."

(Ibn Isḥāq continued) "Then ʿUmar b. al-Khaṭṭāb left, along with ʿAyyāsh b.
Abū Rabīʿa, and went to Medina.

"Nāfiʿ related to me, from ʿAbd Allāh b. ʿUmar, from his father, saying,
'Having made up my mind to emigrate to Medina, I arranged a rendezvous with
ʿAyyāsh b. Abū Rabīʿa and Hishām b. al-ʿĀṣ at al-Tanāḍub of Iḍāt of the Banū
Ghifār, above Saraf. We agreed, "Any one of us who doesn't arrive there in the
morning must have been detained; in such a case the others must go ahead."

"'Next morning ʿAyyāsh and I were there at al-Tanādub. Hishām was
detained. He was enticed and apostatized.'

"'When we reached Medina we went to live among the Banū ʿAmr b. ʿAwf in
Qubāʾ. Abū Jahl b. Hishām and al-Ḥārith b. Hishām came over to see ʿAyyāsh
who was their cousin and their brother through their mother. They came to
Medina at a time when the Messenger of God (ṢAAS) was in Mecca. They
talked to ʿAyyāsh and told him, "Your mother has warned that she will not allow
a comb to touch her hair until she sees you, nor will she shelter from the sun."
ʿAyyāsh was worried about her, but I told him, "These people, I swear, only
want to entice you away from your faith; so beware of them. You can be sure that
if your mother gets lice she'll be sure to comb her hair, and if she finds Mecca's
heat severe, she'll surely seek shade!"

"'But ʿAyyāsh said, "I will remove my mother's oath; and I have money there
I can get." I told him, "You already know I'm one of the wealthiest men of
Mecca, and if you don't go, I'll give you half what I have!"

"'He refused my offer, insisting on leaving with them. When that was all he would do, I said, "Well, if you have to do it, then take this camel of mine. It is a splendid mount and docile. Keep on her back and if you get suspicious about them, then escape on her."'

"'He then rode off on her with them. Some way along Abū Jahl asked him, "Say, brother, I find my mount difficult to ride. Would you mind if I rode behind on yours?" "Sure," he responded. Then he made his camel kneel as the other two men dismounted to change mounts. But when they were all on the ground the others ran up at ʿAyyāsh and tied him up. Then they took him off to Mecca, subverted him and he apostatized.'

"'And,' the narrator ʿUmar said, 'we used to say, "God will not accept repentance from those who apostatize." And those who apostatized made similar statements about themselves.'

"He went on, 'This was so until the Messenger of God (ṢAAS) came to Medina and God revealed, "Say: 'O my servants who have harmed themselves, do not despair of God's mercy. God will forgive all sins. He is the All-Forgiving, the All-Merciful. Turn back to your Lord and submit to Him before punishment reaches you; then you shall not be helped. Follow the best that has been revealed to you from your Lord before punishment comes suddenly to you, and you are caught unawares.'"' (sūrat al-Zumar; XXXIX, v.53–5).

"ʿUmar went on, 'I wrote this down and sent it on to Hishām b. al-ʿĀṣ.

"'Hishām said, "When it reached me I began reading it at Dhū Ṭuwā, holding it this way and that, but I didn't understand it. Eventually I said, 'O God, make me understand this!' And God made me realize that it had been sent down specifically about us and what we used to tell ourselves and what was said about us."

"'So I went to my camel, mounted it and joined the Messenger of God (ṢAAS) in Medina.'"

Ibn Hishām recounted that it was al-Walīd b. al-Mughīra who brought Hishām b. al-ʿĀṣ and ʿAyyāsh b. Abū Rabīʿa to Medina. He stole them away from Mecca and brought them on his own mount while he walked beside them. He stumbled and bloodied his toe, and so spoke the line,

"Are you anything but a toe that bleeds; what happened to you was in God's cause!"

Al-Bukhārī stated, "Abū al-Walīd related to us, quoting Shuʿba, quoting Abū Isḥāq who heard al-Barāʾ say, 'The first to come to us were Muṣʿab b. ʿUmayr and Ibn Umm Maktūm, and they were followed by ʿAmmār and Bilāl.'

"Muḥammad b. Bashshār related to me, quoting Ghundar quoting Shuʿba, from Abū Isḥāq, who said, 'I heard al-Barāʾ b. ʿĀzib say, "The first to join us were Muṣʿab b. ʿUmayr and Ibn Umm Maktūm. They would read to the people. Then came Bilāl, Saʿd and ʿAmmār b. Yāsir, followed by ʿUmar b. al-Khaṭṭāb along with 20 of the supporters of the Prophet (ṢAAS)."

"'Then came the Prophet (ṢAAS); and I never saw the people of Medina so happy as they were to see him. So much so that the slave girls sang out, "The Messenger of God (ṢAAS) has come!" And he did not arrive until after I had read the verse in the Qur²ān: "Glorify the name of your Lord most high!" (*surat al-A²lā*; LXXXVII), along with other verses from *al-Mufaṣṣalāt.*'"[34]

Muslim related this in his *ṣaḥīḥ* collection from an *ḥadīth* of Isra²īl from Abū Isḥāq, from al-Bara² b. ²Āzib, in similar words.

In it there is the assertion that Sa²d b. Abū Waqqāṣ emigrated before the arrival of the Messenger of God (ṢAAS) in Medina. Mūsā b. ²Uqba, quoting al-Zuhrī, claimed that he emigrated only after the Messenger of God (ṢAAS); the information that precedes this however, is correct.

Ibn Isḥāq stated, "When ²Umar b. al-Khaṭṭāb and members of his family came to Medina, they included his brother Zayd b. al-Khaṭṭāb, ²Amr and ²Abd Allāh, the two sons of Surāqa b. al-Mu²tamir, Khumays b. Ḥudhāfa al-Sahmī, husband of his daughter Ḥafṣa, his cousin Sa²īd b. Zayd b. ²Amr b. Nufayl, Wāqid b. ²Abd Allāh al-Tamīmī, an ally of theirs, Khawlā b. Abū Khawlā and Mālik b. Abū Khawlā, two allies of theirs from the Banū Ijl, (and from) the Banū al-Bakayr, Ilyās, and Khālid, and ²Āqil and ²Āmir, and their allies from the Banū Sa²d b. Layth. They took up residence with Rifā²a ²Abd al-Mundhir b. Zunayr among the Banū ²Amr b. ²Awf at Qubā²."

Ibn Isḥāq stated, "Then the emigrants, God bless them, followed on after them. Ṭalḥa b. ²Ubayd Allāh and Ṣuhayb b. Sinān, took up residence with Khubayb b. Isāf, brother of the Banū al-Ḥārith b. al-Khazraj at al-Sunḥ. It is also said that Ṭalḥa stayed with As²ad b. Zurāra."

Ibn Hishām stated, "It was told to me that Abū ²Uthmān al-Nahdī said, 'I learned that when Ṣuhayb wished to emigrate the polytheists of Quraysh said to him, "When you came to us you were a poverty-stricken beggar. With us you grew wealthy and acquired status and now you want to take yourself and your money away! By God, that won't happen!"

"Ṣuhayb told them, 'If I were to make my money over to you, would you let me leave?'

"'Yes,' they agreed.

"That information reached the Messenger of God (ṢAAS), and he commented, 'Ṣuhayb made a profit! Ṣuhayb made a profit!'"

Al-Bayhaqī stated, "The *ḥāfiz* Abū ²Abd Allāh related to us, by dictation, that Abū al-²Abbās Ismā²īl b. ²Abd Allāh b. Muḥammad b. Mīkāl informed him, quoting ²Abdān al-Ahwāzī, quoting Zayd b. al-Juraysh, quoting Ya²qūb b. Muḥammad al-Zuhrī, quoting Ḥusayn b. Ḥudhayfa b. Ṣayfī b. Ṣuhayb, quoting his father and uncles, from Sa²īd b. al-Musayyab, from Ṣuhayb who said, 'The Messenger of God (ṢAAS) said, "I was shown the place of your emigration: a

---

34. That portion of the Qur²ān from *surat al-Ḥujurāt* to *surat al-Nās.*

salt-plain between two uplands and two lava-rock plains. That would either be Hajar or Yathrib.""

"He went on, 'The Messenger of God (SAAS) left for Medina accompanied by Abū Bakr. I had wanted to leave with him, but some young Quraysh men blocked my way. I remained up that night, not lying down, and they commented, "God has diverted him from you through his stomach!" But I made no complaint, and they went to sleep. So I left, but some of them caught up with me after I had gone some way and wanted to take me back. I told them, "If I were to give you some ounces of gold, would you let me go and be fair to me?" They did so and I followed them back to Mecca. I told them, "Dig beneath the threshold of the door; that's where the ounces of gold are. And if you go off to a certain woman, you can take two sets of vestments."

"'So I left and joined the Messenger of God (SAAS) at Qubā' before he moved out from there. When he saw me he said, "Well, Abū Yaḥyā, you made a good deal!" I replied, "O Messenger of God, no one got here to you before me, so it could only be Gabriel, peace be upon him, who informed you!"'"

Ibn Isḥāq stated, "Hamza b. ʿAbd al-Muṭṭalib, Zayd b. Ḥāritha, Abū Marthad Kannāz b. al-Ḥuṣayn and his son Marthad, both of the Ghanawī tribe, allies of Hamza; Anasa and Abū Kabsha, freed-men of the Messenger of God (SAAS); all these stayed with Kulthūm b. al-Hadm, brother of the Banū ʿAmr b. ʿAwf, at Qubā'. However, it is also said that they stayed with Saʿd b. Khaythama. It is stated, moreover, that Hamza stayed with Asʿad b. Zurāra. But God knows best."

He went on, "ʿUbayda b. al-Ḥārith and his two brothers al-Ṭufayl and Ḥuṣayn, Misṭaḥ b. Uthātha, Suwaybiṭ b. Saʿd b. Ḥuraymila, brother of the ʿAbd al-Dār, Ṭulayb b. ʿUmayr, brother of the Banū ʿAbd b. Quṣayy, Khabbāb, freedman of ʿUtba b. Ghazwān stayed with ʿAbd Allāh b. Salama, brother of Balʿajlān at Qubā'.

"ʿAbd al-Raḥmān b. ʿAwf and some other emigrants stayed with Saʿd b. al-Rabīʿ. Al-Zubayr b. ʿAwwām and Abū Sabra b. Abū Ruhm stayed with Mundhir b. Muḥammad b. ʿUqba b. Uḥayḥa b. al-Julāḥ at al-ʿUṣba, the home of the Banū Jaḥjabī. Muṣʿab b. ʿUmayr stayed with Saʿd b. Muʿādh. Abū Ḥudhayfa b. ʿUtba and Sālim, his freed-man, stayed with Salama."

Ibn Isḥāq stated, "Al-Umawī said that (some stayed) with Khubayb b. Isāf, brother of the Banū Ḥāritha. ʿUtba b. Ghazwān stayed with ʿAbbād b. Bishr b. Waqqāsh among the Banū ʿAbd al-Ashhal. ʿUthmān b. ʿAffān stayed with Aws b. Thābit b. al-Mundhir, brother of Ḥassān b. Thābit in the home of the Banū al-Najjār."

His account continues, "The unmarried emigrant men stayed with Saʿd b. Khaythama since he was unmarried. But God knows best about this."

Yaʿqūb b. Sufyān stated, "Aḥmad b. Abū Bakr b. al-Ḥārith b. Zurāra b. Muṣʿab b. ʿAbd al-Raḥmān b. ʿAwf related to us, quoting ʿAbd al-ʿAzīz b.

Muḥammad b. ʿUbayd Allāh, from Nāfiʿ, from Ibn ʿUmar, who said, 'We arrived from Mecca and took up residence at al-ʿUṣba, including ʿUmar b. al-Khaṭṭāb, Abū ʿUbayda b. al-Jarāḥ, and Sālim, freed-man of Abū Hudhayfa. It was Sālim who acted as their Imām because he had greater knowledge of the Qurʾān than the others.'"

Section: On the cause of the emigration of the Messenger of God (ṢAAS).

God Almighty revealed, "Say: O God, make my place of arrival good and make my place of departure good. And grant me an aid and authority from Yourself" (*sūrat Banī Isrāʾīl*; XVII, v.80).

And God did give him good guidance and inspired him to call out the above prayer to provide him prompt relief and a rapid departure. The Almighty gave him permission to migrate to the "Medina, the 'city', of the Prophet", where there were the *anṣār* and friends, a place where he could make his home in security and whose people would be his helpers.

Aḥmad b. Ḥanbal, and ʿUthmān b. Abū Shayba said, from Jarīr, from Qābūs b. Abū Zubyān, from his father, from Ibn ʿAbbās, that the Messenger of God (ṢAAS) was at Mecca when he was ordered to migrate and there was revealed to him the verse, "Say: O God, make my place of arrival good, and make my place of departure good. And grant me an aid and authority from Yourself."

Qatāda said, "The phrase 'place of arrival' referred to Medina, while the words 'place of departure' referred to his emigration from Mecca. The words 'grant me an aid and authority from Yourself' referred to God's book and His ordinances and restrictions."

Ibn Isḥāq stated, "The Messenger of God (ṢAAS) stayed on in Mecca after his supporters had emigrated, waiting for permission to be given to himself to leave.

"There remained there with him only those (Muslims) who had been detained or who had apostatized, except for ʿAlī, son of Abū Ṭālib, and Abū Bakr b. Abū Quḥāfa, God bless them both.

"Abū Bakr often asked the Messenger of God (ṢAAS) for permission to leave, but he would reply, 'Don't be in a hurry. God may well give you a companion.' And Abū Bakr hoped it would be him.

"When Quraysh saw that the Messenger of God (ṢAAS) had assembled a party and had supporters from others than their own people and from a town other than theirs, and saw his Companions moving out to join these others, they realized that the Muslims had found a new home with them and had acquired their protection.

"Quraysh were concerned that the Messenger of God (ṢAAS) would leave and join them, since they knew that he had decided to do battle with them.

"They therefore gathered in the *Dār al-Nadwa*, the house of assembly, the home of Quṣayy b. Kilāb, where all their decisions were made. They discussed there what they should do about the Messenger of God (ṢAAS), since they now feared him."

Ibn Isḥāq continued, "A colleague whose views I do not doubt, as did others I consider reliable, related to me, from ʿAbd Allāh b. Abū Najīḥ, from Mujāhid b. Jabr, that ʿAbd Allāh b. ʿAbbās said, 'The day arrived when they had agreed to meet to enter their assembly to discuss what to do about the Messenger of God (ṢAAS). That day is known as the *yawm al-zaḥma*, "the day of the gathering", and upon it Satan, God curse him, came before them in the form of a venerable sheikh dressed in a heavy cloak. He stood at the door of the house and, when they saw him they asked who he was. He replied, "I am come from Nejd, from the highlands; I have heard why you agreed to meet, and I've come to listen to what you say and perhaps offer some comment or advice." They invited him in.

"'He entered the meeting where the Quraysh nobles had assembled. They consisted of ʿUtba, Shayba, Abū Sufyān, Ṭaʿīma b. ʿAdī, Jubayr b. Muṭʿim b. ʿAdī, al-Ḥārith b. ʿĀmir b. Nawfal, al-Naḍr b. al-Ḥārith, Abū al-Bakhtarī b. Hishām, Zamʿa b. al-Aswad, Ḥakīm b. Ḥizām, Abū Jahl b. Hishām, Nabīh and Munabbih, sons of al-Ḥajjāj, and Umayya b. Khalaf, along with various others of their supporters from Quraysh.

"'They reminded one another what they had experienced from the behaviour of the Messenger of God (ṢAAS), and agreed that they felt insecure from the possibility that he and his supporters might make an attack upon them.

"'Having discussed the issue, one of them, said to have been Abū al-Bakhtarī b. Hishām, suggested, "Put him in irons and gaol him; then wait for him to have the same fate that befell poets like him before, such as Zuhayr and al-Nābigha. He would die as they had."

"'But the Najdī sheikh objected, saying "No; that's not a good plan. If you do shut him up, news of him will get right past the door you have locked on him and reach his supporters. They will promptly attack you and release him and then increase in numbers until they overcome you. That's not a good idea."

"'They consulted further and one suggested, "Let's exile him from our territory. Once he has gone, we shouldn't care where he ends up or what happens to him. So long as he is gone, we'll be rid of him and we'll be able to restore our affairs as they were before."

"'But the Najdī sheikh observed, "No, that's not a good idea for you. You know how sweet his talk is, and his reasoning, and how he convinces others of his message. If you do that you'd have no security against him going to live with some Arab tribe and using his speech and discourse to get them to follow him. Then he would lead them against you and perhaps defeat (or) dispossess you and do what they like with you. No, think of something else."

"'Abū Jahl b. Hishām then said, "I have an idea that hasn't occurred to you yet."

"' "What is it, Abū al-Ḥakam?" they asked him.

"'He replied, "I think we should select one young man from each tribe, and someone who is strong, of excellent lineage and reputation as a leader. We should give each one a sharp sword and they would go to him and use the swords to strike him in unison. They would kill him and we would then be rid of him. If they do this, his blood will be spread over all the tribes. And the Banū ˓Abd Manāf will not be able to do battle against them all. So they will accept blood money which we can pay them."

"'The Najdī sheikh commented, "What he says is right. This is the right idea, and no other."

"'Having agreed upon this, the assembly broke up.

"'Gabriel then came to the Messenger of God (ṢAAS) and told him, "Do not sleep tonight on the bed you usually use."

"'When it was fully dark that night the Quraysh men gathered outside his door, waiting for him to sleep so they could attack him. Having seen where they were, the Messenger of God (ṢAAS) said to ˓Alī b. Abu Ṭālib, "Sleep on my bed, wrapping yourself in this green cloak of mine from Haḍramaut; sleep in it. You'll not come to any harm from them." The Messenger of God (ṢAAS) was in the habit of sleeping in that cloak of his.'"

This story told by Ibn Isḥāq is also related by al-Wāqidī, with the chains of authority from ˓Ā³isha, Ibn ˓Abbās, ˓Alī, Surāqa b. Mālik b. Ju˓shum and others, the various accounts overlapping and saying much as above.

Ibn Isḥāq's account continues, "Yazīd b. Abū Yazīd related to me, from Muḥammad b. Ka˓b al-Quraẓī, who said, 'The men having met there at his door, Abū Jahl, who was among them, said, "Muḥammad claims that if you follow him you'll become kings of the Arabs and non-Arabs alike. Then you'll be given life after death and be provided with gardens like those of the Jordan. If you don't do that, then, he says, you will be slaughtered, given life after death but be put into hell-fire where you will be burned."'

"The Messenger of God (ṢAAS) then picked up a handful of dirt, saying, 'Yes, I do say that. And you are one of them!'

"Then God took away their sight from them and they could not see him. He began sprinkling the dirt on to their heads while he recited the following verses: 'Yā sīn. By the Qur³ān the wise. You are among those sent forth upon a straight path' up to the verse 'We have placed a barrier before them and a barrier behind them, and have covered them over so that they cannot see' (sūrat Yā Sīn; XXXVI, v.3–9). Every single man among them had dirt thrown on his head.

"He then left, and went where he wished.

"Someone who had not been there with these men then arrived and asked, 'What are you waiting for here?' They replied, 'For Muḥammad.' He commented, 'God damn you! Muḥammad just came out to you and he did not leave any single one of you without throwing dirt on your head. He then left and went elsewhere. Can't you see what has happened to you?'

"Each man then placed a hand on his head and found dirt there. Looking closely, they saw ˓Alī on the bed covered in the cloak of the Messenger of God (ṢAAS). They stayed there like that until morning; when ˓Alī arose from the bed, they said, 'By God, what he told us must have been true!'"

Ibn Isḥāq continued, "Concerning what they had agreed upon that day, God revealed, among others, the following verses, 'And when the disbelievers plotted to confine, kill or exile you they made plans; but God makes plans and He is the best planner of all' (*sūrat al-Anfāl*; VIII, v.30).

"And there was the verse, 'Or do they say he is a poet; we await for him incidents of fate.' Say: 'Do await! I with you am one who awaits!'" (*sūrat al-Ṭūr*, LII, v.30–1).

Ibn Isḥāq continued, "And so God gave His permission to His Prophet (ṢAAS) to emigrate."

Chapter: The emigration of the Messenger of God (ṢAAS) from Mecca to Medina accompanied by Abū Bakr "the Trusting", God be pleased with him.

That event marks the beginning of the Islamic era as was agreed upon by the *ṣaḥāba*, "the Companions", during the rule of ʿUmar, as we have shown in the biography of ʿUmar, God be pleased with him and with them all.

Al-Bukhārī stated, ʿMaṭar b. al-Faḍl related to us, quoting Rawḥ, quoting Hishām quoting ʿIkrima, from Ibn ʿAbbās, who said, "The Prophet (ṢAAS) received his mission when he was 40 years old. He continued in Mecca receiving revelation for 13 years and then was ordered to emigrate. He did so for 10 years, then died at the age of 63.

"His emigration took place in the month of Rabīʿ al-Awwal in the 13th year of his mission, on a Monday."

Similarly Imām Aḥmad recounted from Ibn ʿAbbās, who said, "Your Prophet was born on a Monday, left Mecca on a Monday, first received revelation on a Monday, entered Medina on a Monday and died on a Monday."

Muḥammad b. Isḥāq stated, "Whenever Abū Bakr asked permission from the Messenger of God (ṢAAS) to emigrate, he would be told, 'Don't be in a hurry. God may well give you a companion.' And Abū Bakr hoped it would be the Messenger of God (ṢAAS), and that he was really referring to himself.

"He therefore purchased two camels which he kept and fed at his home to be prepared."

According to al-Wāqidī, he paid 800 dirhams for them both.

Ibn Isḥāq continued, "A man in whom I have confidence related to me, from ʿUrwa b. al-Zubayr, from ʿĀʾisha, mother of the faithful, who said, 'The Messenger of God (ṢAAS) would go without fail to Abū Bakr's house either in the morning or the evening. Eventually that day arrived when God gave the Messenger of God (ṢAAS) permission to emigrate, to leave Mecca and his people there. He came to us that day at midday, a time unusual for him.

"'When Abū Bakr saw him, he said, "The Messenger of God (ṢAAS) can only have come at this hour because something has happened."

"'When he came in, Abū Bakr gave up his couch for him and the Messenger of God (ṢAAS) sat down. There was no one else in the house except myself and my sister Asmā³, daughter of Abū Bakr. The Messenger of God (ṢAAS) said, "Send away anyone else who is with you." Abū Bakr replied, "There are only my two daughters; what can be wrong, I pray you?"

"'"God has given me permission to leave, to emigrate," he replied.

"'"As companions then, O Messenger of God?" Abū Bakr asked.

"'"Yes, as companions," he answered.'

"'Ā³isha continued, 'And, I swear, before that day I never knew anyone who wept for joy until I saw Abū Bakr do so that day.

"'He then said, "O Prophet of God, these are two camels I have readied for this."'"

"They hired 'Abd Allāh b. Arqaṭ."

Ibn Hishām suggests an alternative name, 'Abd Allāh b. Urayqiṭ.

Ibn Isḥāq continued, "He was a polytheist, of the Banū al-Dīl b. Bakr, his mother of the Banū Sahm b. 'Amr. He was to act as their guide on the way and they gave him the two mounts to look after until needed.

"And, as I have been told, no one knew of the departure of the Messenger of God (ṢAAS) except 'Alī b. Abū Ṭālib and Abū Bakr, "the Trusting", and his family.

"'Alī was ordered to remain behind to return to people the items they had deposited with the Messenger of God (ṢAAS); anyone in Mecca who had concerns about things they owned would leave them in his care, such was his reputation for honesty and trustworthiness.

"Having decided to leave, the Messenger of God (ṢAAS) went to the house of Abū Bakr b. Abū Quḥāfa and they made their exit via a window at its rear."

Abū Nu'aym recounted, through Ibrāhīm b. Sa'd, from Muḥammad b. Isḥāq, who said, "I have been informed that as he was about to leave Mecca as an emigrant to Medina for God, he said, 'Praise be to God who created me when I had been nothing. O God, protect me from earthly terrors, misfortunes and mishaps in the nights and days to come. O God, accompany me on my journey and keep my family safe. Bless me in what You have granted me and humble me before Yourself. Raise me to the finest qualities in my character. Endear me to You, O Lord. And do not entrust (my fate) to people.

"'O Lord of the frail, you are my Lord. I take refuge in Your noble visage before which the heavens and the earth rejoice, the dark shadows dissipate and the troubles of those who are first and those who are last are made right. (I pray) that You spare me your anger and discontent. I appeal to You not to cease your favours and to spare me your sudden wrath, removal of your favour and all your anger. I will repay as best I can all your favours to me. And there is no power nor strength except in You.'"

Ibn Isḥāq continued, "They then made their way to a cave on Mt. Thawr, south of Mecca, which they entered. Abū Bakr ordered his son 'Abd Allāh to spend the day listening to what people were saying about them and then to bring them whatever news there might be. And he told ʿĀmir b. Fuhayra, his freed-man, to tend his flock during the day and then to bring them to the cave in the evening.

"ʿAbd Allāh b. Abū Bakr would spend the day among Quraysh listening to their planning and what they were saying regarding the Messenger of God (ṢAAS) and Abū Bakr. He would then visit them in the evening and report to them.

"ʿĀmir b. Fuhayra would tend his flock in the pasturage of the people of Mecca and in the evening he would bring them to Abū Bakr who would milk and slaughter them. When next morning ʿAbd Allāh, Abū Bakr's son would leave them to return to Mecca, ʿĀmir would follow him down with the flock in order to efface his footprints."

The following account from al-Bukhārī will give evidence of this.

Ibn Jarīr related from various sources that the Messenger of God (ṢAAS) preceded Abū Bakr in leaving for the cave on Mt. Thawr and that he told ʿAlī to guide his (Abū Bakr's) path to join him, and that he did so on the way. This account is strange and contradicts what is well known, that they travelled together.

Ibn Isḥāq continued, "Each evening Asmāʾ, daughter of Abū Bakr, may God be pleased with her, would bring them food to restore them.

"Asmāʾ said, 'When the Messenger of God (ṢAAS) and Abū Bakr had left, a group of Quraysh, including Abū Jahl b. Hishām, came and stood at Abū Bakr's door. I went out to them and they asked, "Where is your father, O Daughter of Abū Bakr?" I replied that I did not know, whereupon Abū Jahl, an evil and uncouth man, raised his hand and slapped me so hard on the cheek that my earring fell off. They then left.'

"Yaḥyā b. ʿAbbād b. ʿAbd Allāh b. al-Zubayr related to me that his father told him, that his grandmother Asmāʾ said, 'When the Messenger of God (ṢAAS) left, along with Abū Bakr, the latter took all his cash with him, some 5,000 or 6,000 dirhams. My grandfather, Abū Quḥāfa, whose sight was gone, came in thereafter and commented, "I swear, he's put you all into some difficulty by taking his money with him."

"'I replied, "No, father, he left us plenty." I then took some stones and placed them in a space in the house where my father used to put his money and placed a cloth over them. Then I took my grandfather's hand and told him, "Put your hand on this money." He did so and said, "Not bad at all. He did well by leaving you all this. This will be enough money for you."

"'But in fact he had left us nothing; I just wanted to reassure the old man.'"

Ibn Hishām stated, "A certain scholar told me that al-Ḥasan b. Abū al-Ḥasan al-Baṣrī said, 'The Messenger of God (ṢAAS) and Abū Bakr, went to the cave at night. Abū Bakr went in first and searched the cave to ensure there were no snakes or lions inside, thus using himself to protect the Messenger of God (ṢAAS).'"

The line of authorities here is incomplete at both ends.

Abū al-Qāsim al-Baghawī stated, "Dā’ūd b. ‘Amr al-Dabbī related to us, quoting Nāfi‘ b. ‘Umar al-Jumaḥī, from Ibn Abū Mulayka, that when the Messenger of God (ṢAAS) left with Abū Bakr for Mt. Thawr, Abū Bakr would first position himself ahead and then at the rear. The Prophet (ṢAAS) asked him why this was and he replied, 'When I'm behind you I'm afraid you'll be attacked from the front, and when I'm ahead of you I fear you'll be attacked from behind.'

"When they finally reached the cave on Mt. Thawr Abū Bakr said, 'Stay where you are until I put my hand inside and examine it; if there is some creature there it will attack me before you.'

"Nāfi‘ said, 'I have heard that there was a crevice inside the cave in which Abū Bakr placed his foot, fearing that some creature might emerge and harm the Messenger of God (ṢAAS).'"

This tradition is incomplete in its chain of authorities. But we have given several other testimonials for it in our biography of Abū Bakr, "the Trusting", God be pleased with him.

Al-Bayhaqī stated, "The *ḥāfiẓ* Abū ‘Abd Allāh informed us, quoting Abū Bakr Aḥmad b. Isḥāq, that Mūsā b. al-Ḥasan narrated that ‘Abbād related, quoting ‘Affān b. Muslim, quoting al-Sarī b. Yaḥyā, quoting Muḥammad b. Sīrīn, as follows, 'Some men were talking during the period of the rule of ‘Umar and apparently expressed their preference for ‘Umar over Abū Bakr. This reached ‘Umar and he commented, "By God, a single night or a single day of Abū Bakr would be better than the whole clan of ‘Umar! On the night when the Messenger of God (ṢAAS) went to the cave with Abū Bakr, the latter would walk in front for a while, then walk behind. Eventually the Messenger of God (ṢAAS) realized this and asked, 'Abū Bakr, why do you walk behind for a while, then go and walk ahead?' He replied, 'O Messenger of God, I think of pursuit and walk behind you, but then I think of ambush and so walk ahead of you.' The Messenger of God (ṢAAS) then asked, 'You mean if something happened you'd rather it be to you than to me?' 'Yes indeed, by Him who sent you with the truth,' he replied.

"'"When they reached the cave Abū Bakr said, 'Stay outside, O Messenger of God, until I make sure the cave is safe for you.' He went inside and made sure it was safe, but then remembered he had not checked out the crevice. So he said, 'Stay were you are, O Messenger of God, while I check again.' He then went back in, made sure the crevice was safe and said, 'Come on down, O Messenger of God.' And he did so."

"'‘Umar then commented, "By Him who holds my soul in His hand, that night was better than the whole clan of ‘Umar!"'"

Al-Bayhaqī related this comment from ‘Umar through a different chain. In that account the wording is "Abū Bakr sometimes walked ahead of the Messenger of God (ṢAAS) and at others behind him, sometimes to the left and at others to the right." That account also states that when the feet of the Messenger of God (ṢAAS) became sore, Abū Bakr would carry him on his back. Also, that when he went into the cave he blocked up all the crevices except one, and over that he placed his heel. Snakes then struck at him and his tears ran down. Seeing this, the Messenger of God (ṢAAS) told him, "Don't be sad; God is with us!"

There are some strange and unsatisfactory aspects to the course of this anecdote.

Al-Bayhaqī stated, "The *ḥāfiz* Abū ʿAbd Allāh and Abū Saʿīd b. Abū ʿAmr informed us as follows, ʿAbū al-ʿAbbās al-Aṣamm related to us, quoting ʿAbbās al-Dūrī, quoting Aswad b. ʿĀmir Shādhān quoting Isrāʾīl, from al-Aswad, from Jundub b. ʿAbd Allāh, who said, "Abū Bakr was with the Messenger of God (ṢAAS) in the cave when he hit his hand on a rock. He then spoke the following verse:

> 'You are nothing but a finger that bleeds; what
> happened to you was in God's cause!'""

Imām Aḥmad stated, "ʿAbd al-Razzāq related to us, quoting Maʿmar, quoting ʿUthmān al-Jazarī, that Miqsam, the freed-man of Ibn ʿAbbās, told him that Ibn ʿAbbās made the following comment about the verse in the Qurʾān. 'And when those who disbelieve were scheming to imprison you' (*sūrat al-Anfāl*; VIII, v.30). He said, 'Quraysh were engaged in discussion one night in Mecca and some of them suggested, "In the morning imprison him in shackles." They were referring to the Prophet (ṢAAS). Others of them said, "No; kill him!" Yet others said, "No, exile him!" God made his Prophet (ṢAAS), aware of that and so ʿAlī spent the night on his bed, while the Messenger of God (ṢAAS) went to the cave. The polytheists spent the night watching ʿAlī, thinking him to be the Prophet (ṢAAS). When morning came they attacked him and when they saw ʿAlī, God turned their trickery against them. They said, "Where is that master of yours?" He replied, "I don't know."

"'They followed his tracks, but these became too confused for them in the mountains. They climbed on up the mountain and passed by the cave but saw a spider's web over its opening. They said, "If anyone had gone inside here, the spider would not have put a web over its opening." And so he stayed there three nights.'"

The chain of authorities for this is good; it is one of the best accounts given relating to the spider's web over the mouth of the cave, which was God's protection for His Messenger (ṢAAS).

The *ḥāfiz* Abū Bakr Aḥmad b. ʿAlī b. Saʿīd al-Qāḍī stated in his collection of traditions relating to Abū Bakr as follows, "Bashshār al-Khaffāf related to us, quoting Jaʿfar, quoting Sulaymān, quoting Abū ʿImrān al-Jawnī, quoting al-Muʿallā b. Ziyād, that al-Ḥasan al-Baṣrī said, 'The Prophet (ṢAAS) hurried away with Abū Bakr to the cave. Quraysh came looking for him and when they saw the spider's web over the mouth of the cave, they said, "No one went in here."

"'The Prophet (ṢAAS) was at the time standing there praying while Abū Bakr watched. Abū Bakr then said to the Prophet (ṢAAS), "Those are your people searching for you. It's not for myself I am sad, but because I might see something terrible happen to you."

"'The Prophet (ṢAAS) replied, "Abū Bakr, don't be afraid. God is with us."'"

This tradition from Ḥasan is incomplete, but it is good as textual evidence. It includes, however, the praying of the Prophet (ṢAAS) in the cave; it was his custom to pray when something saddened him.

This same source, I mean Abū Bakr Aḥmad b. ʿAlī al-Qāḍī, related from ʿAmr al-Nāqid, from Khalaf b. Tamīm, from Mūsā b. Muṭīr, from his father, from Abū Hurayra, that Abū Bakr said to his son, "Son, if something should happen among the people, then go to the cave where I and the Messenger of God (ṢAAS) took refuge. Stay there and you will find sustenance come to you both morning and night."

A poet composed the following line:

"'David's web' is what protected the occupant of the
cave, and glory goes to the spider."

It is also said that two doves made their nest over its entrance. Al-Ṣarṣarī composed the following line on that:

"The spider roofed it over with his web, and the dove
having eggs remained at the entrance."

The *hadīth* dealing with this was related by the *ḥāfiẓ* Ibn ʿAsākir, through Yaḥyā b. Muḥammad b. Saʿīd, quoting ʿAmr b. ʿAlī, who said that ʿAwn b. ʿAmr Abū ʿAmr al-Qaysī, nicknamed ʿUwayn, related to us that Abū Muṣʿab al-Makkī said, "I am aware of Zayd b. Arqam, al-Mughīra b. Shuʿba and Anas b. Mālik as relating that on the night the Messenger of God (ṢAAS) went to the cave, God gave an order to a tree that emerged right in front of him and hid him. God also sent the spider that made a web between them, so hiding the face of the Messenger of God (ṢAAS). He then commanded two wild doves which came fluttering down and alighted between the spider and the tree. Now the young warriors of Quraysh approached, one from each of the tribes there, carrying sticks, bows and staves. When they got to within 200 yards of the Messenger of God (ṢAAS) the guide, who was Surāqa b. Mālik b. Juʿshum al-Mudlajī, said, 'That's the rock; but I don't know where he placed his foot.' The young warriors commented, 'You've not made a mistake since tonight began.' When morning came the guide told them to look in the cave. He went ahead of the rest until they were some 50 yards away from the Prophet (ṢAAS), and then there were the two doves. The guide came back and they asked him, 'What prevented you from looking in the cave?' 'I saw two wild doves at its entrance', he said, 'so I knew there was no one inside.'

"The Messenger of God (ṢAAS) heard him and knew that God had used the doves to save him and Abū Bakr. He then invoked a blessing upon them, and God brought them down to the holy shrine where, as you know, they proliferated."

This is a strange *ḥadīth* to come from this source. The *ḥāfiẓ* Abū Nuʿaym related it from an account from Muslim b. Ibrāhīm and others, from ʿAwn b. ʿAmr, he known as ʿUwayn, with chains of authority similar to these. That account states that all the doves of Mecca are descended from these two.

Also in this *ḥadīth* is the information that the tracker who guided the warriors was Surāqa b. Mālik al-Mudlajī.

Al-Wāqidī related from Mūsā b. Muḥammad b. Ibrāhīm, from his father, that the one who tracked for them was Kurz b. ʿAlqama.

My own comment is that it is likely that they both followed the trail. But God knows best.

God Almighty said, "Even if you do not aid him, God did so when those who disbelieved expelled him, he being the second of two, in the cave. (Therein) he said to his companion, 'Do not be sad; God is with us.' And so God sent down tranquillity upon him and aided him with troops you do not see, putting down very low the words of those who disbelieved; the words of God are the highest, for God is powerful, wise" (*sūrat al-Tawba* or *al-Barāʾa*; IX, v.40).

Reprimanding those who refrained from engaging in battle on the side of the Messenger of God (ṢAAS) the Almighty stated, "Even if you do not aid him." God will assist him, be his helper and ally. As He did help him, "when those who disbelieved expelled him" from his people in Mecca, in flight and accompanied by no one but his friend and Companion Abū Bakr.

Therefore He said, "being the second of two, when they were in the cave" where they stayed for three days until the search for them died down.

This was because when the polytheists lost track of the two men, as recounted above, they went off in all directions searching for them. They offered 100 camels to anyone who might turn in both or even one of them. They followed their tracks until they became confused. The tracker working for Quraysh was Surāqa b. Mālik b. Juʿshum, as mentioned above. They climbed the mountain where the two men were and went past the mouth of the cave. Their feet would move straight across the mouth of the cave without seeing the two men, God protecting them this way.

As Imām Aḥmad stated, quoting ʿAffān, quoting Hammām, quoting Thābit, from Anas b. Mālik, that Abū Bakr told him, "I said to the Prophet (ṢAAS), while we were inside the cave, 'If any one of them were to glance down at his feet he would see us below them!'

"He replied, 'Abū Bakr, how would you regard the safety of two people who had God as their third companion?'"

Al-Bukhārī and Muslim gave this *ḥadīth* in both their *ṣaḥīḥ* collections, from Hammām.

Some biographers state that when Abū Bakr said that the Prophet (ṢAAS) replied, "If they were to come to us from here, we would leave that way."

Abū Bakr then saw that the cave had opened up on its other side and it was now connected to the sea, and there was a boat tied up beside it.

This tradition is not objectionable in the sense of this being beyond the divine power. However, it does not have a chain of authorities that is strong; nor is it weak. We cannot assert anything purely by ourselves. We do, however, stand by tradition considered authentic and with chains of authority that are good. But God knows best.

The *ḥāfiẓ* Abū Bakr al-Bazzār stated, "Al-Faḍl b. Sahl related to us, quoting Khalaf b. Tamīm, quoting Mūsā b. Muṭayr al-Qurashī, from his father, from Abū Hurayra, that Abū Bakr said to his son, 'If some disturbance should break out among the people, go to the cave where you saw me hide with the Messenger of God (ṢAAS). Stay there and you will receive sustenance morning and evening.'"

Al-Bazzār then said, "We know of no one else but Khalaf b. Tamīm who related this *hadīth*."

My own comment is that Mūsā b. Muṭayr quoted here is a weak source of low regard; Yaḥyā b. Ma'īn gave the lie to him, and traditions from him are not accepted.

Yūnus b. Bukayr stated, from Muḥammad b. Isḥāq, that Abū Bakr, having entered the cave and behaved as related, and after the matter concerning Surāqa, which is still to be told, spoke some poetry, a part of which follows:

> "The Prophet said to reassure me, though I was not
> concerned, when we were in the dark of the shadows of the
> cave,
>   'Fear nothing, for God is our third, and he has
> guaranteed to me victory from Him.'"

Abū Nu'aym related this ode through Ziyād, from Muḥammad b. Isḥāq. He quoted it at great length along with another poem. But God knows best about these.

Ibn Lahī'a related, from Abū al-Aswad, from 'Urwa b. al-Zubayr, who said, "The Messenger of God (ṢAAS) remained in Mecca after the pilgrimage in which the *anṣār*, 'the Helpers', pledged themselves to him, for the remainder of Dhū al-Ḥijja, al-Muḥarram and Ṣafar.

"Then the polytheists of Quraysh joined together and plotted to kill the Messenger of God (ṢAAS) or to imprison or exile him. And so God gave him foresight of this and revealed the words, 'And when those who disbelieved were scheming to imprison you' (*sūrat al-Anfāl*; VIII, v.30). He then gave orders to 'Alī to sleep on his bed while he and Abū Bakr left. Next morning Quraysh went off searching for them everywhere."

Mūsā b. 'Uqba related it thus in his work on the military campaigns and stated that they went to the cave by night.

We also gave above a statement regarding this from Ḥasan al-Baṣrī, quoting Ibn Hishām.

Al-Bukhārī stated that Yaḥyā b. Bukayr related to him, quoting al-Layth quoting ʿUqayl, quoting Ibn Shihāb, who said that ʿĀʾisha stated, 'I have no awareness of my parents not practising the religion (Islam); and not a day passed for us without the Messenger of God (ṢAAS) visiting us at both ends of the day, in the morning and the evening. When the Muslims suffered harassment Abū Bakr left as an emigrant towards Abyssinia. He went as far as Bark al-Ghimād, where he met Ibn al-Daghina, the chieftain of the area.'"

She then recounted how he brought Abū Bakr back to Mecca and gave him protection. Her words are similar to our previous account of the migration to Abyssinia up to and including Abū Bakr's statement, "I therefore give back to you your protection and resign myself to the protection of God."

She (ʿĀʾisha) stated, "At that time the Prophet (ṢAAS) was at Mecca. He told the Muslims, 'I have been shown the place of your emigration; it has palm-groves between two rocky tracts.' These are the Ḥarratān.

"And so some people did leave for Medina, and some who had left for Abyssinia came back and went to Medina. Abū Bakr himself made preparations to leave for Medina. The Messenger of God (ṢAAS) told him, 'Take it slowly; I am hoping I will be permitted to leave.' Abū Bakr asked, 'You really do have hopes of that?' 'Yes,' he replied.

"Thereafter Abū Bakr restrained himself for the Messenger of God (ṢAAS), so that he could accompany him. He stabled two camels at his home, feeding them on mimosa leaves, crushed and mixed leaves, that is, for four months. Some, however, say he gave them fodder for six months."

Ibn Shihāb stated, "ʿUrwa reported that ʿĀʾisha said, 'One day, in the heat of noon, we were sitting in Abū Bakr's house when someone told him, "Here comes the Messenger of God (ṢAAS), heavily veiled, at a time he doesn't usually come!" Abū Bakr commented, "I swear, he can only have come at this time for one thing!"'

"'ʿĀʾisha went on, 'The Messenger of God (ṢAAS) arrived and asked to come in and was invited to do so. When he entered he said, "Ask everyone to leave." Abū Bakr responded, "But they are all like your own family, O Messenger of God."

"'He explained, "I have been given permission to leave." "As companions, then!" said Abū Bakr. "Yes," he replied.

"'Abū Bakr then said, "Do take one of these two mounts of mine." The Messenger of God (ṢAAS) replied, "I'll pay you for it."'

"'ʿĀʾisha went on, 'So we quickly prepared some equipment for them and put some provisions in a leather bag. Asmāʾ, Abū Bakr's daughter, cut off a piece of her girdle to tie up the mouth of the bag; she was thereafter known as "she of the two girdles".

"'Then the Messenger of God (ṢAAS) went with Abū Bakr to a cave on Mt. Thawr, where they stayed for three nights. Also with them during the night was

<Abd Allāh, Abū Bakr's son. He was a bright and intelligent lad and would leave them at dawn and be down among Quraysh by morning, as if he had spent the night there. He went back to them as soon as night fell with all the information he had gleaned of plans against them. <Āmir b. Fuhayra, Abū Bakr's freed-man, cared for a flock of sheep, which he would bring them after night fell; they would eat foods made with the milk they provided. Before dawn <Āmir b. Fuhayra would call the flock together and leave; he did this each one of those three nights.

"'The Messenger of God (ṢAAS) and Abū Bakr hired a man of the Banū al-Dīl, from the Banū <Abd b. <Adī, a skilled guide, a *khirrīt*. This man, though a follower of the faith of the Quraysh polytheists, had sworn an oath to the family of al-<Āṣ b. Wā>il al-Sahmī. They had thus placed their trust in him and handed over to him their two riding camels and made an arrangement with him to meet at the cave on Mt. Thawr three nights thereafter; he was to bring their mounts on the following morning. This guide and <Āmir b. Fuhayra did set off with the two men, conducting them along the coastal route.'"

Ibn Shihāb stated, "'Abd al-Raḥmān b. Mālik al-Mudlijī, he being the son of Surāqa's nephew, related that his father told him that he heard Surāqa b. Mālik b. Ju<sham say, 'Messengers from the Quraysh polytheists came to us putting a price on the head of either the Messenger of God (ṢAAS) or Abū Bakr for anyone who killed or captured either.

"'While I was sitting at a meeting being held by my people, the Banū Mudlij, one of their men arrived and stood there, while we sat, and said, "Surāqa, I've just seen some human forms in the distance towards the coast, and I think them to be Muḥammad and his companions."

"'Surāqa said, "I knew they would be them, but I told him, 'They are not them. You saw so-and-so and so-and-so whom we saw leave with our own eyes.'"

"'I remained for a while there in that meeting, then got up and went inside. I told my servant girl to bring over my mare which was behind a hillock and to keep it there for me. Then I took my spear and went out the rear of the house. I made marks with its head on the ground and kept its shaft down low until I reached my horse. I rode off on it and it took me ahead until I drew close to them. Suddenly my horse stumbled and I came off it. I got up and stretched my hand out to my quiver and took out my divining arrows. I sought guidance from them whether or not I should harm them. It came out as I did not want. But I got back on my horse, disobeying the arrows.

"'My horse drew me ever nearer to them until I could hear the Messenger of God (ṢAAS) reciting, without looking around, while Abū Bakr looked around constantly. Then two of my horse's legs sank deep into the ground, right up to the knees, and I was again thrown. I scolded her and she stood up, though scarcely able to pull her legs out. When standing upright there was dust coming up like smoke into the sky from the impression left by her legs. Again I sought advice from the divining arrows and it again came out against my wish.

"'I called out to them, reassuring them, and they stopped. I rode my horse up to them, it having dawned on me that my being kept from them was a sign that the Messenger of God (SAAS) was going to prevail. I told him, "Your people have put a price on your head!" and I related to them what people wanted to do with them. Then I offered them provisions, but they would not accept anything from me and told me to leave them alone. I asked him if he would write down a safe conduct for me, and he told ʿĀmir b. Fuhayra who did so on a piece of leather. The Messenger of God (SAAS) then left.'"

Muḥammad b. Isḥāq related this same story, from al-Zuhrī, from ʿAbd al-Raḥmān b. Mālik b. Juʿsham, from his father, from his uncle Surāqa. However, his account has him seeking advice from the divining arrows when he first left the house, with the arrow telling him what he did not like, that is, that he should not harm the Messenger of God (SAAS). It went on to mention his horse stumbling with him on four different occasions. All that related to his seeking advice from the divining arrows and being told what he did not like.– that he should not harm him. It has him reassuring them and asking for a document that would be a token from the Messenger of God (SAAS). The account states, "He wrote a document for me on a bone, or a scrap of leather, or a scrap of cloth." He also tells how he went to the Messenger of God (SAAS) when the latter was at al-Jiʿrāna on his way back from Ṭāʾif and that he said, "Today is one of keeping trust and of goodness; let him come near." The account ends, "So I approached him and accepted Islam."

Ibn Hishām stated, "The man relating this was ʿAbd al-Raḥmān b. al-Ḥārith b. Mālik b. Juʿsham.

"And what he said was correct.

"After Surāqa returned, whenever he met one of the pursuers, he would turn them back, saying, 'You've finished in this direction.'

"When it was known that the Messenger of God (SAAS) had arrived in Medina, Surāqa began telling people what he knew and had witnessed relating to him, and about what had happened to his horse. He gained some notoriety for this, and the leaders of Quraysh were afraid he would bring them discredit, and that that would be the cause of many people accepting Islam. Surāqa was the leader of the Banū Mudlij. Abū Jahl, God damn him, composed the following verses to them,

"O Banū Mudlij, I fear your fool Surāqa misleading
about Muḥammad's victory.
Take care that he not divide you so you become split,
after former glory and leadership."

Surāqa spoke the following in answer to Abū Jahl's poetry:

"O Abū al-Ḥakam, had you but been witness to what
happened to my horse when its legs sank,
You would have been amazed, and not doubted that

> Muḥammad is a prophet and a proof; so who can oppose him?
>   Take action, have your people leave him alone, for I
> think that some day his qualities will be clear to us.
>   In a matter you would wish to win, for all the people,
> altogether will make peace with him."

Al-Umawī gave this poetry in his work on the military campaigns with a chain of authorities from Abū Isḥāq. Abū Nu^caym related it with a chain through Ziyād, from Ibn Isḥāq. His account gives more poetry from Abū Jahl with verses that include overt disbelief.

Al-Bukhārī stated, with a chain of authorities back to Ibn Shihāb, who is quoted as saying, "^cUrwa b. al-Zubayr informed me that the Messenger of God (ṢAAS) met al-Zubayr in a caravan of Muslims who were merchants coming in from Syria, and that al-Zubayr clothed the Messenger of God (ṢAAS) and Abū Bakr in white garments.

"The Muslims in Medina heard of the departure of the Messenger of God (ṢAAS) from Mecca and would go each morning out to the rocky lava plain to wait for him, until the heat of noon would force them back.

"One day after they had returned to their homes, having waited a long time, one of the Jews went up on top of one of their forts for some reason, and he saw the Messenger of God (ṢAAS) and his Companions dressed in white emerging through the haze. The Jew felt compelled to shout out, 'O Arabs, here's your great man you've been awaiting!'

"The Muslims leapt for their weapons and met up with the Messenger of God (ṢAAS) beside the rocky lava plain. He turned off, along with them, to the right to where the Banū ^cAmr b. ^cAwf were; this was Monday in the month of Rabī^c al-Awwal.

"Abū Bakr stood up before the group, while the Messenger of God (ṢAAS) sat silently. The *anṣār* who had come and who had not before seen the Messenger of God (ṢAAS) began greeting Abū Bakr. But then the sun began striking the Messenger of God (ṢAAS), and Abū Bakr went over and shielded him from it with his cloak. And so everyone then knew which one was the Messenger of God (ṢAAS).

"The Messenger of God (ṢAAS) remained there with the Banū ^cAmr b. ^cAwf for some ten nights and founded the mosque 'whose foundations were based on piety'[35] and the Messenger of God (ṢAAS) prayed there.

"He then rode upon his camel, the people walking beside him, until it knelt down at the mosque[36] in Medina of the Messenger of God (ṢAAS) where that

---

35. A reference to the Qur>ān, *Sūrat al-Tawba*, IX, v.108, where the piety of its founders is mentioned.

36. A reference to the site of the Mosque of the Prophet in Medina which had not yet been constructed.

day some Muslim men were praying. It was a drying shed for dates and belonged to Suhayl and Sahl, two orphan youths in the care of Asʿad b. Zurāra. The Messenger of God (ṢAAS) said, when his camel knelt, 'This, if God wills it, will be the house.'

"He then asked to see the two youths and negotiated with them over the drying shed so that it could become a mosque. They replied, 'No, we will give it to you, Messenger of God!' But the Messenger of God (ṢAAS) refused to accept it from them as a gift and did buy it. He then built a mosque.

"The Messenger of God (ṢAAS) then set about bringing up the bricks for building it, along with the rest of the Muslims, saying as he did so the verse,

> 'This is not a load from Khaybar; this, O Lord, is
> more righteous more pure.'

"And also:

> 'No matter; the wages for this are those of the other
> world; be merciful, O God, on the Helpers and the
> Emigrants.'

"He quoted the verse of one of the Muslim men whose name is unknown to me. Ibn Shihāb said, 'We are not informed in the *ḥadīth* literature that the Messenger of God (ṢAAS) quoted any full line of poetry other than these.'"

This is the text as given by al-Bukhārī; only he, and not Muslim, gives it and he does so with testimony from other sources; his text, however, does not give the story of Umm Maʿbad, the Khuzāʿī woman.

We will report here from the beginning, as is appropriate.

Imām Aḥmad stated, "ʿAmr b. Muḥammad Abū Saʿīd al-ʿAnqazī related to us that Isrāʾīl related to him, from Abū Isḥāq, from al-Barāʾ b. ʿĀzib, who said, "Abū Bakr bought from ʿĀzib a horse's saddle, for 13 dirhams, telling him, "Tell al-Barāʾ to take it to my house." He replied, "No; not until you tell us what you did when the Messenger of God (ṢAAS) emigrated in your company.""

Abū Bakr stated, "We set off and travelled fast, by day and night until midday approached and was upon us. I strained my eyes to see some shade where we could shelter. I saw a rock and hurried down to it, and some shadow remained. I smoothed out a place for the Messenger of God (ṢAAS), and laid down a piece of leather for him, saying, 'Do lie down, O Messenger of God.' And he did so.

"I then left to see if I could locate any of the pursuers. I came upon a herdsman and asked him, 'Who employs you, lad?' He mentioned the name of a Quraysh man that I recognized. I asked him, 'Do you have any milk in your flock?' 'O yes,' he replied. 'Will you give me some?' I requested. He agreed and I told him to get some. He tethered a ewe and at my request he wiped the dirt off its udders and his hands. I had with me a container with a cloth over its mouth. He poured a little milk for me and I poured it out into a cup until it was all cool. I then went over to the Messenger of God (ṢAAS) and gave it to him;

he was awake. I asked him to drink, and he did so until I was content. I then asked, 'Should we continue with the travel?' And we left again, our pursuers still after us.

"But the only one of them to catch up with us was Surāqa b. Mālik b. Ju'sham, riding a horse. I asked, 'O Messenger of God, are our pursuers catching up?' 'Do not be worried, God is with us,' he replied.

"He caught up with us until there was only a spear's throw or two – or the words may have been two or three spear-throws – and I said, 'O Messenger of God, this pursuer is gaining on us!' And I wept. He asked, 'Why are you crying?' I replied, 'It's not for me I'm crying, but for you!'

"The Messenger of God (ṢAAS) said a prayer about him, saying, 'O Lord, protect us from him, as You wish.' The legs of his horse then sank down to its belly in firm ground and he fell off, saying, 'O Muḥammad, I know this is your work; say a prayer to God for me to save me from my plight! I swear I will mislead the pursuers behind me. This is my quiver; take an arrow from it, for you will pass by my camels and sheep at so-and-so, and you can take of them whatever you want.'

"The Messenger of God (ṢAAS) replied, 'I don't need them.' But he did say a prayer for him and he was released and returned to his people.

"The Messenger of God (ṢAAS) and I went further on and eventually reached Medina where people came out to meet him. They appeared on the roads and roofs and servants and young people thronged the streets, saying, 'God is Great! The Messenger of God (ṢAAS) has come! Muḥammad is here!'

"The people vied for the honour of having him stay with them. The Messenger of God (ṢAAS) therefore said, 'Tonight I will stay with the Banū al-Najjār who are related by blood to 'Abd al-Muṭṭalib, to honour them.' Next morning he was where he had been ordered to be.'

Al-Barā' said, "The first of the Emigrants to come to us was Muṣ'ab b. 'Umayr, a brother of the 'Abd al-Dār. Then came Ibn Umm Maktūm, the blind, one of the Banū Fihr, followed by 'Umar b. al-Khaṭṭāb, along with 20 riders. We asked them what had happened to the Messenger of God (ṢAAS), and they replied that he was coming later. And eventually he and Abū Bakr did arrive."

Al-Barā' went on, "The Messenger of God (ṢAAS) did not arrive until after I had recited chapters from *al-mufaṣṣal*."

The compilers of both *ṣaḥīḥ* collections include this account, from Isrā'īl, without the comment of al-Barā', that is, "The first of the Emigrants". Muslim is alone in giving this, and he related it through Isrā'īl.

Ibn Isḥāq stated, "The Messenger of God (ṢAAS) stayed for three nights in the cave along with Abū Bakr. Having lost knowledge of his whereabouts Quraysh offered a price of 100 camels to anyone who would return him. After the three nights, when the hue and cry had diminished, the man they had hired brought them their camels along with one for himself. Abū Bakr's daughter Asmā' also arrived with provisions in a leather table-cloth for them. But she forgot to tie it up and when they were about to depart she came out to tie it up but had no cord. So she untied her girdle to make a cord of it which she used to attach it. She used then to be called, 'she of the two girdles'."

Ibn Isḥāq stated, "Abū Bakr brought up the two mounts and offered the best of them to the Messenger of God (ṢAAS) and asked him to mount the camel. But the latter responded, 'I couldn't ride a camel that I don't own.' Abū Bakr told him, 'But please consider it yours'. 'No,' he replied, 'but what price did you pay for it?' He told him and the Messenger of God (ṢAAS) then said, 'Well, I'll take it for that.' 'It's yours,' Abū Bakr told him."

Al-Wāqidī related, with full chains of authorities, that the Messenger of God (ṢAAS) took the camel called *al-Qaṣwāʾ*. He also said, "Abū Bakr had bought both camels for 800 dirhams."

Ibn ʿAsākir related through Abū Usāma, from Hishām, from his father from ʿĀʾisha, who said, "(The camel he chose was) *al-Jadʿāʾ*." Al-Suhaylī related this similarly from Ibn Isḥāq, that it was *al-Jadʿāʾ*. But God knows best.

Ibn Isḥāq stated, "And so they rode off; Abū Bakr mounted ʿĀmir b. Fuhayra, his freed-man, behind himself to serve them both on the way.

"I was told that Asmāʾ said, 'When the Messenger of God (ṢAAS) departed with Abū Bakr, a number of Quraysh men came to us, including Abū Jahl'". Ibn Isḥāq then related how Abū Jahl struck her so hard on the cheek that he knocked off an earring, as told above.

"She went on, 'We remained for three nights without knowledge of the whereabouts of the Messenger of God (ṢAAS) until a man of the *jinn*, a spirit-man, arrived from the lower parts of Mecca, singing verses of Arabic songs. People followed him, listening to his voice without seeing him. Eventually he came out to the upper parts of Mecca, reciting,

> 'God, Lord of all men, awarded His very best reward to
> two Companions who stayed at the tents of Umm Maʿbad.
> They stayed there in good will, and then left; and
> lucky is he who becomes the Companion of Muhammad
> Their girl's position brings credit to the Banū Kaʿb,
> and her sitting there watching for the believers.'

"Asmāʾ said, 'When we heard what he said we knew where the Messenger of God (ṢAAS) was headed, towards Medina."

Ibn Isḥāq said, "They were four in number; the Messenger of God (ṢAAS), Abū Bakr, ʿĀmir b. Fuhayra, freed-man of Abū Bakr, and ʿAbd Allāh b. Arqaṭ." That is what Ibn Isḥāq states, but it is well known that the name of the fourth was ʿAbd Allāh b. Urayqiṭ al-Dīlī who at that time was still a polytheist.

Ibn Isḥāq stated, "When their guide, ʿAbd Allāh b. Arqaṭ, led them off, he took them down to the lower part of Mecca and from there along the coast, crossing over the route below ῾Usfān. He then took them along the lower parts of Amaj, then crossed the route after passing Qudayd, then from there across al-Kharrār and Thaniyyāt al-Marra to Liqf. He guided them past the Liqf well, then down to the Mijāj well and so to Marjaḥ Mijāj, then down again to Marjaḥ Dhū al-῾Aḍwayn and to the Dhū Kashr valley and so to al-Jadājid and al-Ajrad. Then he took them along Dhū Salam of the A῾dā᾽ valley, to the well at Ti῾hin, then past al-῾Ababid, across al-Qāḥa, down to al-῾Arj. One of their mounts was falling behind, so a man of Aslam called Aws b. Ḥajr mounted the Messenger of God (ṢAAS) on a camel called *Ibn al-Radā᾽* and led him into Medina; he sent with him a youth named Mas῾ūd b. Hunayda. Then their guide from al-῾Arj took them to Thaniyya al-῾Ā᾽ir on the right side of Rakūba; according to Ibn Hishām this place is known as Thaniyya al-Ghā᾽ir. Then he took them down the Ri᾽m valley and so to Qubā᾽, to the Banū ῾Amr b. ῾Awf. It was now Monday, the 12th of Rabī῾ al-Awwal and the heat was extreme, the sun almost having reached its zenith."

Abū Nu῾aym mentioned, through al-Wāqidī, approximately these same locations, though there is a discrepancy in some. God knows best.

Abū Nu῾aym stated that Abū Ḥāmid b. Jabala related to him that Muḥammad b. Isḥāq quoted from al-Sarrāj, who quoted from Muḥammad b. ῾Ubāda b. Mūsā al-Ijlī from his brother Mūsā b. ῾Ubāda, from ῾Abd Allāh b. Sayyār, from Iyās b. Mālik b. al-Aws al-Aslamī, who quoted his father as saying, "When the Messenger of God (ṢAAS) emigrated along with Abū Bakr, they passed by a camel of ours at al-Juḥfa. The Messenger of God (ṢAAS) asked, 'Who owns this camel?' 'A man from Aslam,' he was told. The Prophet (ṢAAS) turned to Abū Bakr, who commented, 'May you be safe, God willing!' The Prophet (ṢAAS) asked the man, 'What's your name?' 'Mas῾ūd,' he replied. The Prophet (ṢAAS) again turned to Abū Bakr, who commented, 'May you be happy. God willing!'"[37]

The account goes on, "My father then went to him and carried him on his way on a camel called *Ibn al-Radā᾽*."

I would comment that previously we learned from Ibn ῾Abbās that the Messenger of God (ṢAAS) left Mecca on a Monday and entered Medina on a Monday.

It is clear that there was a period of 15 days between his departure from Mecca and his arrival in Medina. This is because he spent three nights in the cave on Mt. Thawr, and then took the coastal road which is further than the main route.

On his way he passed by Umm Ma῾bad, daughter of Ka῾b of the Banū Ka῾b b. Khuzā῾a.

Ibn Hishām stated, "Yūnus quoted Ibn Isḥāq as saying that her name was ῾Ātika, daughter of Khalaf b. Ma῾bad b. Rabī῾a b. Aṣram.

"Al-Umawī, however, said that she was ῾Ātika, daughter of Tabī῾, an ally of Banū Munqidh b. Rabī῾a b. Aṣram b. Ṣanbīs b. Ḥarām b. Khaysa b. Ka῾b b. ῾Amr.

"This woman had sons named Ma῾bad, Nadra and Ḥunayda, all children of Abū Ma῾bad. His name was Aktham b. ῾Abd al-῾Uzzā b. Ma῾bad b. Rabī῾a b. Aṣram b. Ṣanbīs.

37. The passage has a pun on Aslam and 'safe', and on Mas῾ūd and 'happy'.

Her story is very well known and related from various paths all confirming one another.

The Story of Umm Ma'bad al-Khuzā'iyya.

Yūnus stated, from Ibn Isḥāq, "The Messenger of God (ṢAAS) stayed at the tent of Umm Ma'bad, whose name was 'Ātika, daughter of Khalaf b. Ma'bad b. Rabī'a b. Aṣram. The travellers wanted a meal served but she said, 'We have no food, no milch-camel and the only ewes we have are in heat.'

"The Messenger of God (ṢAAS) then asked to be brought one of her sheep. He wiped its teat with his hand, said a prayer and it gave milk into a tumbler, foaming. He said, 'Drink this, Umm Ma'bad!' She replied, 'No, you drink it; you have more right to it than me.' But he gave it back to her and she did drink it. He then called for another ewe in heat and did the same as before and this time he drank it. He then called for another ewe, did the same and gave it to his guide to drink. Again he did the same, giving it now to 'Āmir. And then they left.

"The Quraysh men, searching for the Messenger of God (ṢAAS), eventually came to Umm Ma'bad and asked her about him, saying, 'Have you seen Muḥammad who looks so-and-so?' And they described him to her.

"She replied, 'I don't know what you are saying, though a young man did come and get milk from ewes in heat.'

"'That's the one we want,' the Quraysh man told her."

The ḥāfiẓ Abū Bakr al-Bazzār stated that Muḥammad b. Ma'mar related to him from Ya'qūb b. Muḥammad, from 'Abd al-Raḥmān b. 'Uqba b. 'Abd al-Raḥmān b. Jābir b. 'Abd Allāh, who quoted his father as having related that Jābir stated, "When the Messenger of God (ṢAAS) and Abū Bakr left as Emigrants and entered the cave, there was a crevice that Abū Bakr blocked off with his heel until morning, for fear that something might come out at the Messenger of God (ṢAAS).

"They stayed in the cave for three nights, then left and stayed at the tents of Umm Ma'bad. She sent him the message, 'I see handsome faces; the tribal quarter is better equipped to honour you than I am.'

"That evening, while staying there in her camp, she sent over to them with a young son of hers, a ewe and a broad knife. The Messenger of God (ṢAAS) said, 'Take back the knife and bring us a *fariq*,' that is a *qadaḥ*, a bowl. She sent back a message that the ewe had no milk and had no lamb. He said, 'Do send us a bowl.' She brought one and he tapped the ewe on the back and it ruminated, and milk streamed forth. He filled the bowl and drank, gave it to Abū Bakr to drink, took more milk and sent it to Umm Ma'bad."

Then al-Bazzār stated, "We know of this anecdote being related only through this one chain. And regarding 'Abd al-Raḥmān b. 'Uqba, the only person we know who quoted from him was Ya'qūb b. Muḥammad, even though his ancestry was well known."

The *ḥāfiẓ* al-Bayhaqī recounted from a *ḥadīth* of Yaḥyā b. Zakariyyāʾ b. Abū Zāʾida from Muḥammad b. ʿAbd al-Raḥmān b. Abū Laylā who related it to him, quoting ʿAbd al-Raḥmān b. al-Aṣbahānī, who said, "I heard ʿAbd al-Raḥmān b. Abū Laylā quote Abū Bakr, 'the Trusting', as saying, 'I left Mecca with the Messenger of God (ṢAAS) and we reached a bedouin encampment. The Messenger of God (ṢAAS) noticed one tent off to one side and went towards it. When we dismounted we found that the only person there was a woman. She said, "O fellow slave of God, I'm just one woman, alone; you should go to our chief if you want hospitality." He made no response to her, it being evening by then, and a son of hers arrived herding some goats. She told him, "Take these goats over to those two men with this knife and tell them, 'My mother says that you should slaughter these and eat and feed us too.'"

"'When he arrived, the Messenger of God (ṢAAS) told him, "Take the knife away and bring a bowl." He replied, "But this ewe has not been with a male and has no milk." "Go and do it," he told him. When he had brought back a bowl the Messenger of God (ṢAAS) wiped the ewe's teat and it gave milk, filling the bowl. He then said, "Take this to your mother." She drank till she was satisfied and the lad returned. Now he told the boy, "Take this ewe away and bring me another." He did so and then brought a third ewe, did as before, and then the Messenger of God (ṢAAS) himself drank.

"'We stayed there that night, then left. She used to refer to him as *al-Mubārak*, "the blessed one". Her flock multiplied and eventually she brought them all in to Medina. Abū Bakr happened to pass by and he recognized her son and the son said to his mother, "Mother, that's the man who was with *al-Mubārak*, 'the blessed one'." She came over to him and asked, "O fellow slave of God, who was that man with you?" He asked, "You don't know who he is?" "No, I don't," she replied. "He is the Prophet of God," he told her. "Please, take me in to him," she asked.

"'He did so and the Messenger of God (ṢAAS) gave her food and gifts.'"

Ibn ʿAbdān added in his account of this, "She said, 'Lead me to him.' And so she came with me and gave to the Messenger of God (ṢAAS) some sour cheese and some bedouin goods. And he gave her clothing and gifts in return.'"

The account stated, "And I am certain he said, 'And she accepted Islam.'"

The chain of authorities for this is good.

Al-Bayhaqī stated, "This story is similar to that of Umm Maʿbad and it is evident that she is the one referred to here. But God knows best."

Al-Bayhaqī stated, "The *ḥāfiẓ* Abū ʿAbd Allāh informed us, as did Abū Bakr Aḥmad b. al-Ḥasan al-Qāḍī, both of whom said, ʿAbū al-ʿAbbās al-Aṣamm related to us, quoting al-Ḥasan b. Mukrim, Abū Aḥmad Bishr b. Muḥammad al-Sukkarī, quoting ʿAbd al-Malik b. Wahb al-Mudhḥijī, quoting Abjar b. al-Ṣabāḥ, from Abū Maʿbad al-Khuzāʿī, that the Messenger of God (ṢAAS), when he left by night, emigrating in the company of Abū Bakr, ʿĀmir b.

Fuhayra, freed-man of Abū Bakr, and their guide ʿAbd Allāh b. Urayqiṭ al-Laythī, passed by the two tents of Umm Maʿbad al-Khuzāʿiyya.

"Umm Maʿbad was a good, fearless, strong woman who would sit with her legs drawn up, wrapped in her garment, at the entrance to the tent and give out food and drink. They asked her whether she had any meat or milk they could buy from her. But they obtained none from her and she told them, 'If we had anything, you would not lack for hospitality, but our people are all out of provisions and we've been suffering drought.'

"The Messenger of God (ṢAAS) noticed a goat at the side of her tent and said, 'What about that goat, Umm Maʿbad?' She replied, 'She's a goat left over from the goats after the drought.' 'Does she give milk?' he asked. 'No, she's too dried up for that,' she replied. 'Would you permit me to milk her?' he asked. 'If she has any milk you can,' she replied.

"The Messenger of God (ṢAAS) called to the goat and stroked it, speaking God's name, wiped her teat and again invoked God's name. Then he called for a vessel large enough to satisfy them, and the goat opened its legs and milk poured out in a copious flow until it was full. He gave (the vessel to) her to drink, and then his Companions and thereafter they all had a second drink. When they were all quenched, he drank too, saying, 'The one who pours drinks last!' He put milk in it again, left it with her, and then they departed.

"He went on, 'Soon her husband, Abū Maʿbad, came home, leading emaciated goats, staggering they were so weak, and their brains scarcely functioning. When he saw the milk, he was amazed and said, 'Where did this milk come from, Umm Maʿbad? We don't have a milch-camel and the goat has not been with a male.' 'Well, a man who was blessed came past us and seemed from his speech to be such-and-such,' she replied. 'Describe him to me; I think he is that man the Quraysh are looking for,' he told her.

"She replied, 'I saw him to be a man of evident cleanliness, fine in character, his face handsome, slim in form, his head not too small, elegant and good looking, his eyes large and black, his eyebrows long, his voice deep, very intelligent, his eyelids brown, his brows high and arched, his hair in plaits, his neck long and his beard thick. He gave an impression of dignity when silent and of high intelligence when he talked. His logic was impressive, he was decisive, not trivial, not trite, his ideas like pearls moving on their string. He seemed the most splendid and fine-looking man from a distance and the very best of all from close-by, medium in height, the eye not finding him too tall nor too short. A tree-branch, as it were, between two others, but he was the finest-looking of the three, the best proportioned. He was the centre of his companions' attention. When he spoke, they listened well, and if he ordered, they hurried to obey, a man well helped, well served, never sullen, never refuted.'

"He – her husband – commented, 'That, I swear, has to be that man Quraysh are seeking. If I had chanced on him, I would have done my very best to follow him.'

"A voice was heard in Mecca, high up, somewhere between heaven and earth, that people could hear though no one see, reciting the verses,

'God, Lord of all men, awarded His very best reward to
two Companions who stayed at the two tents of Umm Ma'bad.
They stayed there in good will, and then left; and
lucky is he who becomes the Companion of Muḥammad.
O Quṣayy, God did not withhold from you actions that
will not be rewarded, nor leadership?
Ask your sister about her goat and bowl; if you were
to ask the goat, she would testify.
He asked her for a goat without young, and it gave milk
for him in plenty, its teat giving foam,
So he pledged (with the goat) (milk) for the milker,
such that it remained abundant at its commencement and at
its completion.'

"Next morning the people, those of Mecca that is, having missed their prophet went to the tents of Umm Ma'bad, trying to catch up with the Messenger of God (ṢAAS)."

Ḥassān b. Thābit responded with the verses,

"A people disappointed, having lost their prophet,
while those to whom he hurried were pleased,
He left a people and their spirits left them, and he
took up residence with a people with a light renewed.
Are those who mislead people out of blind stupidity
equal to those rightly guided by a guide?
A prophet, seeing about him what others do not see,
reciting the Book of God at every scene.
If one day he should speak the words of the unseen, it
is corroborated the same day or, at most, the morning of the
next.
Abū Bakr must be pleased by the pleasure his
grandfather enjoys at his accompanying him; whoever pleases
God will be happy.
Let the place of their woman please the Banū Ka'b, and
her sitting watching for the Muslims."

He stated – 'Abd al-Malik b. Wahb, that is – "I received information that Abū Ma'bad accepted Islam and emigrated to the Prophet (ṢAAS)."

The *ḥāfiẓ* Abū Nu'aym related this through 'Abd al-Malik b. Wahb al-Madhhijī, in the same terms. At the end of his account he added, "'Abd al-Malik said, 'I received information that Umm Ma'bad emigrated, accepted Islam, and joined the Messenger of God (ṢAAS).'"

Abū Nu'aym, moreover, related this through various routes, from Bakr b. Muḥriz al-Kalbī al-Khuzā'ī, from his father Muḥriz b. Mahdī, from Ḥarām b.

Hishām b. Hubaysh b. Khālid, from his father, from his grandfather Hubaysh b. Khālid, the Companion of the Messenger of God (ṢAAS), who stated that the Messenger of God (ṢAAS) when forced out of Mecca left there as an Emigrant, along with Abū Bakr, ʿĀmir b. Fuhayra and their guide ʿAbd Allāh b. ʿUrayqiṭ al-Laythī. They passed by the tent of Umm Maʿbad, a fearless, strong woman who would sit, legs drawn up and wrapped in her garment, at the entrance to the "leather tent." And he went on to relate the same (introductory material as in the prior account).

He went on, "And I think it was Muḥammad b. Aḥmad b. ʿAlī b. Makhlad who related to us, quoting Muḥammad b. Yūnus b. Mūsā, that is al-Kudaymī, quoting ʿAbd al-ʿAzīz b. Yaḥyā b. ʿAbd al-ʿAzīz, the freed-man of al-ʿAbbās b. ʿAbd al-Muṭṭalib, quoting Muḥammad b. Sulaymān b. Salīṭ al-Anṣārī, quoting his father, from his father Salīṭ al-Badrī, who said, 'When the Messenger of God (ṢAAS) left on the emigration accompanied by Abū Bakr, ʿĀmir b. Fuhayra with Ibn ʿUrayqiṭ guiding them on their path, they passed by Umm Maʿbad al-Khuzāʿiyya, she not knowing who he was. He asked her, "Umm Maʿbad, do you have any milk?" She replied, "No, I swear, our goats have not been with males." "What about that one?" he asked. "She is the last of the goats left after the drought."'" His account then relates the rest of the story much as given above.

Al-Bayhaqī then said, "It is likely that all these stories relate to one occasion."

He then related an anecdote similar to that about the goat of Umm Maʿbad al-Khuzāʿiyya, stating, "The *ḥāfiẓ* Abū ʿAbd Allāh related to us, by dictation, that Abū Bakr Aḥmad b. Isḥāq b. Ayyūb related to them, quoting Muḥammad b. Ghālib, quoting Abū al-Walīd, quoting ʿAbd Allāh b. Iyyād b. Laqīṭ, quoting Iyyād b. Laqīṭ, from Qays b. al-Nuʿmān, who said, 'When the Prophet and Abū Bakr left in secret they passed by a slave watching some goats. They asked him for milk. He replied, "I don't have one giving milk. I just have this one young female goat here who gave birth at the beginning of the winter, but her foetus was malformed and she has no milk left." "Call her over to me," he asked. He did so and the Messenger of God (ṢAAS) tethered her and stroked her teat and prayed until it began to flow. Abū Bakr then brought a vessel and he milked the goat, gave to Abū Bakr to drink, milked again, and gave to the shepherd, then milked again and drank.'

"The shepherd then asked, 'For heaven's sake, who are you? I never saw the like of you!'

"'Do you think you could keep it secret if I told you?' he asked. 'Oh yes,' he replied.

"'I am Muḥammad, the Messenger of God,' he told him.

"'You mean you're the one Quraysh say claims to be a Ṣabian?' he asked. 'Yes, they do say that,' he told him.

"'Well,' the shepherd said, 'I bear witness that you bring the truth, and that only a prophet could do as you have. I am your follower now.'

"'You can't be that right now,' he told him. 'Come and join us when you hear I have declared myself openly.'"

Abū Yaḥyā al-Mawṣulī related this, from JaꜤfar b. Ḥumayd al-Kufī, from ꜤAbd Allāh b. Iyyād b. Laqīṭ.

Abū NuꜤaym at this point related the story of ꜤAbd Allāh b. MasꜤūd stating, "ꜤAbd Allāh b. JaꜤfar related to us, quoting Yūnus b. Ḥabīb, Abū Dāᵓūd and Ḥammād b. Salama, from ꜤĀṣim, from Zirr, from ꜤAbd Allāh b. MasꜤūd who said, 'I was a teenage boy working as a shepherd for goats belonging to ꜤUqba b. Abū MuꜤayṭ at Mecca when the Messenger of God (ṢAAS) and Abū Bakr came by, having fled from the polytheists. They asked me whether I had any milk to give them to drink. I replied, "I'm held responsible; I'm not here to provide drink for you." They asked, "Do you have a young sheep that hasn't yet been with a ram?" "Yes, I do," I replied.

"'So I brought it to them and Abū Bakr tethered it, and the Messenger of God (ṢAAS) took hold of her teat and said a prayer. The teat flowed copiously and Abū Bakr brought a hollowed-out rock and milked into it. He and Abū Bakr drank and they served me. Then he told the teat to close, and it did so.

"'Later I went to the Messenger of God (ṢAAS) and asked him, "Teach me some of these fine words," meaning the Qurᵓān. The Messenger of God (ṢAAS) replied, "Consider yourself a well-taught lad!" I took from his mouth 70 *sūras* and no one can dispute me about them.'"

His words in this account, "Having fled from the polytheists" is not with reference to the time of the emigration but with regard to some circumstances prior thereto.

Ibn MasꜤūd was one who accepted Islam early and emigrated to Abyssinia and later returned to Mecca, as previously mentioned. This anecdote of his is firm and authentic, related in the *ṣaḥīḥ* collections and elsewhere. But God knows best.

Imām Aḥmad stated that ꜤAbd Allāh b. MuṣꜤab b. ꜤAbd Allāh, he being al-Zubayr, related to him, that his father had quoted Fāᵓid, the freed-man of ꜤAbādil, as having said, "I left town in the company of Ibrāhīm b. ꜤAbd al-Raḥmān b. SaꜤd; when we reached al-ꜤArj Ibn SaꜤd came. Now SaꜤd (his father) had been the man who had guided the Messenger of God (ṢAAS) on the road to Rakūba. Ibrāhīm asked him, 'What anecdotes did your father relate to you?' Ibn SaꜤd replied, 'My father told me that the Messenger of God (ṢAAS) came to them in the company of Abū Bakr. Abū Bakr had a daughter with us who was suckling at that time and the Messenger of God (ṢAAS) wanted to find a short route to Medina. SaꜤd told him, "This is the waste-land of Rakūba; out there are two thieves of Aslam who are known as the 'two disgraced men'. If you like we could get directions from them." The Messenger of God (ṢAAS) replied, "Yes, let's do that."

"'Saʿd went on, "So we went off and came into view of them, whereupon one of them said to the other, 'That is the man from Yemen.' The Messenger of God (ṢAAS) called over to them and explained Islam to them, and they accepted it. He then asked them their names and they replied, 'We're the "two disgraced men".' He commented, 'No, you're the "two honoured men"!' He then told them to lead him into Medina. So we left and reached the outskirts of Qubāʾ, and there he was met by the Banū ʿAmr b. ʿAwf. The Messenger of God (ṢAAS) asked, 'Where is Abū Umāma Asʿad b. Zurāra?' Saʿd b. Khaythama replied, 'So he scored (with you) before me, O Messenger of God; shouldn't I tell him that?'

"'"The Messenger of God (ṢAAS) then passed on until he could see the date-palms and the well there was full. He turned to Abū Bakr and said, 'O Abū Bakr, this is where I shall stay; I saw myself staying at a stream like that of the Banū Mudlij.'"'"

Aḥmad alone gives this account.

Section: On the entry of the Messenger of God (ṢAAS) into Medina, and where he established therein his dwelling, comprising matters related thereto.

It has been stated above by al-Bukhārī, on the authority of al-Zuhrī, from ʿUrwa, that the Prophet (ṢAAS) entered Medina at noon.

My own comment is that that could have been in the afternoon, because of what is established in both *ṣaḥīḥ* collections from the *ḥadīth* of Isrāʾīl, from Abū Isḥāq, from al-Barāʾ b. ʿĀzib, from Abū Bakr in his *ḥadīth* concerning the emigration. He stated, "We arrived at night and the people vied for the honour of having him stay with them. The Messenger of God (ṢAAS) therefore said, 'I will stay with the Banū al-Najjār who are related by blood to ʿAbd al-Muṭṭalib, to honour them.'"

This could have been, though God knows best, on the day of his arrival at Qubāʾ. He may have arrived at the outskirts of Medina in the heat of the afternoon and spent some time (resting) under the palm tree. He then proceeded on with the Muslims and stopped at Qubāʾ, that being at night. Furthermore, in stating that these events transpired after noon, he could have meant at night, for evening is indeed after noon.

Alternatively, that could refer to when he left Qubāʾ, travelling on and only reaching the Banū al-Najjār in the evening. This will be discussed later. But God knows best.

Al-Bukhārī recounted, from al-Zuhrī, from ʿUrwa, that he stayed with Banū ʿAmr b. ʿAwf at Qubāʾ, for a score or more nights and established the mosque at Qubāʾ during that period.

He then mounted up, the people accompanying him, and went on until his camel knelt with him at the site of his mosque. That place was a drying shed for dates owned by two orphaned youths named Sahl and Suhayl. He bought it from them and used it as a mosque. And that was among the Banū al-Najjār, may God be pleased with them.

Muḥammad b. Isḥāq stated, "Muḥammad b. Ja'far b. al-Zubayr related to me, from 'Urwa b. al-Zubayr, from 'Abd al-Raḥmān b. 'Uwaym b. Sā'ida, who said, 'Some of my tribesmen who were Companions of the Prophet (ṢAAS) said, "When we learned of the emigration of the Prophet (ṢAAS) from Mecca, we anticipated his arrival. We would go out, after saying the morning prayer, to the edge of the rock lava plain and await him. We would stay there until the sun would force us to seek shade, failing which, we would go indoors. It was the hot season at that time.

""Eventually the day arrived when the Messenger of God (ṢAAS) did come. We had sat as usual until there was no shade left and then we had entered our homes. But when we had done so, the Messenger of God (ṢAAS) arrived. The first to see him was a Jew, and he shouted at the top of his voice, 'Banū Qayla, your great man has come!'

""So we all went outside to the Messenger of God (ṢAAS), and found him in the shade of a date-palm, accompanied by Abū Bakr, a man of similar age. Most of us had not seen the Messenger of God (ṢAAS) before that, and people crowded around him, not knowing how to distinguish him from Abū Bakr. But when the shade moved away from the Messenger of God (ṢAAS) Abū Bakr stood up and shaded him with his cloak. And at that point we recognized him."""

The account given above from al-Bukhārī is similar to this one, as is that from Mūsā b. 'Uqba in his work on the *maghāzī*, the military campaigns.

Imām Aḥmad stated, "Hāshim related to us, quoting Sulaymān, from Thābit, from Anas b. Mālik, who said, 'I moved along through young men shouting, "Muḥammad has come!" And I'd move ahead but still see nothing.

"'But then the Messenger of God (ṢAAS) did come, accompanied by Abū Bakr. They hid in a ruin in Medina, then sent out a bedouin asking for the *anṣār*, the Helpers, to let them enter town. Thereupon some 500 of the *anṣār* went out to greet them, saying, "Do come on; you are safe and will be obeyed."

"'The Messenger of God (ṢAAS) and his Companion then came on in among them and the townspeople, even the old people as well came out to greet them, climbing on top of the houses and shouting, "Which one is he?" We never saw such a sight before.'"

"Anas said, 'I witnessed the day he entered among us and the day he died, and I never saw two such days as those.'"

Al-Bayhaqī related this from al-Ḥākim, from al-Aṣamm, from Muḥammad b. Isḥāq al-San'ānī, from Abū al-Naḍr Hāshim b. al-Qāsim, from Sulaymān b. al-Mughīra, from Thābit, from Anas, whose account was very similar.

In both *ṣaḥīḥ* collections, through Isrā'īl, from Abū Isḥāq, from al-Barā', we find that Abū Bakr says, in his account of the emigration, "When we arrived in Medina, the people came out filling the streets and the roof tops, with the young and the servants all shouting and repeating, 'God is most Great! The Messenger of God has arrived. God is most Great! Muḥammad has come! God is most Great! Muḥammad has come! God is most Great! The Messenger of God has come!' The next morning he moved on to where he had been ordered to go."

Al-Bayhaqī stated, "Abū ʿAmr al-Adīb told us, quoting Abū Bakr al-Ismāʿīlī, as follows, 'I heard Abū Khalīfa say, "I heard ʿāʾisha's son say, 'When the Messenger of God (ṢAAS) arrived in Medina the women and boys began chanting,

> "The full moon has risen over us, from the passes of
> al-Wadāʿ;
> We must give thanks, for what a supplicant has prayed
> to God."'"'"

Muḥammad b. Isḥāq stated, "The Messenger of God (ṢAAS), so they say, stayed at Qubāʾ with Kulthūm b. al-Hadam, a brother of the Banū ʿAmr b. ʿAwf, who was of the Banū ʿUbayd; it is also said, however, that he stayed with Saʿd b. Khaythama.

"Those who say he stayed with Kulthūm b. al-Hadam assert the following: that when the Messenger of God (ṢAAS) went outside the house of Kulthūm he would go and sit with people in the house of Saʿd b. Khaythama because this man was a bachelor, without family, and his house was therefore known as 'the bachelors' house. But God knows best.

"Abū Bakr, God bless him, stayed with Khubayb b. Isāf, of the Banū al-Ḥārith b. Khazraj at al-Sunh. It is also said he stayed with Khārija b. Zayd b. Abū Zuhayr, a brother of the Banū al-Ḥārith b. al-Khazraj."

Ibn Isḥāq also stated that ʿAlī b. Abū Ṭālib remained in Mecca for three days and nights until he had handed back the deposits made with the Messenger of God (ṢAAS).

"He then joined the Messenger of God (ṢAAS) and stayed with Kulthūm b. al-Hadm; apparently ʿAlī b. Abū Ṭālib stayed in Qubāʾ only a night or two.

"He would say, 'In Qubāʾ there was a Muslim woman who had no husband. I saw a man go to her in the depths of the night; he would knock on her door and she came out. He then gave her something he had with him which she took. I found her conduct very suspicious, so I asked her, "Who is it that knocks at your door every night; you go out to him and he gives you something I can't see properly. How can you do this, you being a Muslim woman without a husband?"

"'She replied, "The man is Sahl b. Ḥanīf. He knows I am a woman with no one and after dark he damages and destroys his people's idols then brings their remains to me. He tells me to use them as firewood."'

"ʿAlī, God be pleased with him, used to eulogize Sahl b. Ḥanīf in this way when he was killed in his company in Irāq."

Ibn Isḥāq went on, "The Messenger of God (ṢAAS) remained with Banū ʿAmr b. ʿAwf in Qubāʾ from the Monday through Thursday and founded a mosque there.

"Then God took him forth from among them on the Friday, though the Banū ʿAmr b. ʿAwf claim that he stayed there longer among them."

ʿAbd Allāh b. Idrīs quoted Muḥammad b. Isḥāq, as saying, "The Banū ʿAmr b. ʿAwf claim that he stayed there among them for 18 nights."

My own comment is, as was stated before from al-Bukhārī's account, through al-Zuhrī, from 'Urwa, that he stayed there for some 10 nights.

Mūsā b. 'Uqba quoted Mujma' b. Yazīd b. Ḥāritha as saying, "The Messenger of God (ṢAAS) stayed among us" – amongst the Banū 'Amr b. 'Awf at Qubā', that is – "for 22 nights."

Al-Wāqidī stated, "It is said he stayed among them for 14 nights."

Ibn Isḥāq stated, "When Friday came the Messenger of God (ṢAAS) was there among the Banū Sālim b.'Awf; he prayed that day in the mosque in the Rānūnā' valley, this being the first Friday he prayed in Medina.

"'Itbān b. Mālik and 'Abbās b.'Ubāda b. Naḍla came to him there along with some men of the Banū Sālim and told him, 'O Messenger of God, stay here among us enjoying our protection and our wealth.' He replied, referring to his camel, 'Give her free passage; for she is being guided.' And they cleared a path for her.

"She proceeded and got as far as the homes of the Banū Bayāḍa, where he was met by Ziyād b. Labīd and Farwa b. 'Amr, along with other men of the Banū Bayāḍa. They asked him, 'O Messenger of God, come and join us and share our protection and our wealth.'

"He replied, 'Make way before her, she has received a command.' And they cleared a path for her.

"She went on again and passed by the homes of the Banū Sā'ida where she was blocked by Sa'd b. 'Ubāda and al-Mundhir b. 'Amr along with some men of the Banū Sā'ida. They said, 'O Messenger of God, come to us and have our protection.' 'Make way before her,' he replied, 'she has received a command.' And they did so.

"On she went until she was opposite the home of Banū al-Ḥārith b. al-Khazraj. There her way was blocked by Sa'd b. al-Rabī', Khārija b. Zayd and 'Abd Allāh b. Rawāḥa, along with men of Banū al-Ḥārith b. al-Khazraj. They called out, 'Messenger of God, come to us; we have many to protect you.' But he replied as before.

"She proceeded further, as far as the homes of the Banū 'Adī b. al-Najjār, to whom he was related. The closest of these was the mother of 'Abd al-Muṭṭalib, Salmā, daughter of 'Amr, being one of their women. There were Salīṭ b. Qays and Abū Salīṭ, Usayra b. Abū Khārija and some men of the Banū 'Adī b. al-Najjār. They told him, 'O Messenger of God, join your own relatives and enjoy our wealth and protection.' 'Make way before her,' he replied, 'she has received a command.' And they did so.

"She went further, up to the homes of the Banū Mālik b. al-Najjār, where she knelt down before what is today his mosque. At that time it was a drying shed for dates owned by two orphan youths of the Banū Mālik b. al-Najjār, Sahl and Suhayl by name, sons of 'Amr. They were under the protection of Mu'ādh b. 'Afrā'."

My own comment, however, is that it has been related earlier, from the account of al-Bukhārī through al-Zuhrī, from ʿUrwa, that these youths were under the protection of Asʿad b. Zurāra. But God knows best.

Mūsā b. ʿUqba related that the Messenger of God (ṢAAS) passed by ʿAbd Allāh b. Ubayy b. Salūl while he was there in his house. The Messenger of God (ṢAAS) came to a stop, expecting to be invited into the house since he was at that time the chief of the Khazraj. But ʿAbd Allāh told him, "Look to those who invited you. Stay with them!"

The Messenger of God (ṢAAS) related this to a number of the *anṣār* and Saʿd b. ʿUbāda commented, apologizing for him, "Now God has granted you to us, O Messenger of God; whereas we had wanted to place a crown on his head and make him king over us."

Mūsā b. ʿUqba stated, "The *anṣār* had held a meeting before the Messenger of God (ṢAAS) left the Banū ʿAmr b. ʿAwf. They had gathered around his camel arguing over which of them should hold its reins, vying to honour and show their respect for the Messenger of God (ṢAAS).

"Whenever he passed by the home of one of the *anṣār* they would invite him inside, but he would say, 'Leave her alone; she has received a command. I will only stay where God decides.'

"When she arrived at the house of Abū Ayyūb she knelt before the door and he dismounted. He entered that house and stayed there until his mosque and its apartments were built."

Ibn Isḥāq stated, "When the camel of the Messenger of God (ṢAAS) first knelt he did not dismount and she got up and went a little further, while the Messenger of God left its rein free without his control. She then turned around and came back to where she had knelt and did so there again. She then shook herself, and sank to the ground stretching out fully. The Messenger of God (ṢAAS) then dismounted.

"Abū Ayyūb Khālid b. Zayd then picked up his bags and took them into the house. The Messenger of God (ṢAAS) stayed there with him.

"He asked who owned the drying shed and Muʿādh b. ʿAfrāʾ told him, 'It is owned by Sahl and Suhayl, two sons of ʿAmr. They are orphans under my care.' 'Then I will buy it from them and have it as a mosque,' said the Messenger of God (ṢAAS), and later he had it built."

The Messenger of God (ṢAAS) stayed in the home of Abū Ayyūb until he built his mosque and its living quarters; he and the Muslims, both Emigrants and Helpers, participated in its construction. An account of the building of the mosque will be given soon hereafter, if God wills it.

Al-Bayhaqī stated in *Dalāʾil* (*The Signs*), quoting from Abū ʿAbd Allāh, who stated that the *ḥāfiz* Abū al-Ḥasan ʿAlī b. ʿAmr informed him, quoting Abū ʿAbd Allāh Muḥammad b. Makhlid al-Dūrī, quoting Muḥammad b. Sulaymān

b. Ismāⓒīl b. Abū al-Ward, quoting Ibrāhīm b. Ṣirma, quoting Yaḥyā b. Saⓒīd, from Isḥāq b.ⓒAbd Allāh b. Abū Ṭalḥa, from Anas, who said, "The Messenger of God (ṢAAS) came to Medina, and when we entered the *anṣār* came along with other men and women and said, 'Come to us, O Messenger of God.' He replied, 'Leave my camel unimpeded; she has received a command.'

"She knelt at the door of Abū Ayyūb and servant girls of the Banū al-Najjār came out striking drums and chanting, 'We are girls of the Banū al-Najjār; how wonderful if Muḥammad were our neighbour.'

"The Messenger of God (ṢAAS) then came out to them and asked, 'Do you love me?' They replied, 'Oh yes, O Messenger of God!' 'And I,' he said, 'by God, love you all! By God, I love you all!'"

This is a strange tradition from this source. None of the authorities on tradition relate it, though al-Ḥākim gave it in his *Mustadrak* as will be related.

Al-Bayhaqī stated, "Abū ⓒAbd al-Raḥmān al-Sulamī related, quoting Abū al-Qāsim ⓒAbd al-Raḥmān b. Sulaymān al-Naḥḥās, the Qurʾān-reciter in Baghdad, that ⓒUmar b. al-Ḥasan al-Ḥalabī related to him, quoting Abū Khaythama al-Maṣīṣī, and ⓒĪsā b. Yūnus related, from ⓒAwf al-Aⓒrābī, from Thumāma, from Anas, who said, 'The Prophet (ṢAAS) passed by a quarter where the Banū al-Najjār lived. And there were servant girls striking drums and chanting,

> "We are girls of the Banū al-Najjār; how wonderful if
> Muḥammad were our neighbour."

"'The Messenger of God (ṢAAS) commented, "God knows that my heart loves you all!"'"

This was related by Ibn Māja, from Hishām b. ⓒAmmār, from ⓒĪsā b. Yūnus.

In the *ṣaḥīḥ* of al-Bukhārī it is stated from Maⓒmar, from ⓒAbd al-Wārith, from ⓒAbd al-ⓒAzīz, from Anas, who said, "The Prophet (ṢAAS) saw the women and boys coming – I believe he said that it was a wedding procession. So he stood up in full view and said, 'O God, these are the people I love most of all.' He repeated this three times."

Imām Aḥmad stated, "ⓒAbd al-Ṣamad b. ⓒAbd al-Wārith related to us, quoting his father, who quoted ⓒAbd al-ⓒAzīz b. Ṣuhayb, who quoted Anas b. Mālik, as follows: 'The Messenger of God (ṢAAS) set out for Medina with Abū Bakr riding behind him on the same mount. Abū Bakr was an elderly man who was well known, whereas the Messenger of God (ṢAAS), was youthful and not known.

"'If a person met Abū Bakr and said, "Abū Bakr, who is that man in front of you?" He would reply, "This man is showing me the path."

"'He would think he was referring to him showing him the road, but what he really meant was "the path of good".

"'Abū Bakr looked back and saw a horseman had caught up with them. So he said, "O Prophet of God, a rider has caught up with us!" The Messenger of God (ṢAAS) turned around and said, "O God, bring him down!" The man's horse then fell, tossed him and stood neighing. The man then said, "O Prophet of God, give me your orders!" He replied, "Stay where you are and don't let anyone catch up with me!"

"'So the man had started off the morning trying to catch the Messenger of God (SAAS) and by the end of it he was acting as his armed guard!

"'The Messenger of God (SAAS) alighted at the edge of the rock lava plain and sent a message off to the *anṣār*. When they came they greeted the two men and told them, "Mount up; you will be safe and you will be obeyed."

"'The Messenger of God (SAAS) and Abū Bakr then rode on, the *anṣār* all around them fully armed.

"'In Medina people were saying, "The Prophet of God, has come!" And they raised their glances to him, repeating that the Prophet had come.

"'He proceeded on and dismounted beside the house of Abū Ayyūb.

"'While he was talking to members of its household ʿAbd Allāh b. Salām heard of him while working in a palm-grove belonging to his family. He quickly stopped what he was doing, she[38] accompanying him, heard the Messenger of God (SAAS) then went back to his own people.

"'The Messenger of God (SAAS) asked, "Which of our people's houses is closest?" Abū Ayyūb replied, "Mine, O Messenger of God; this is my house, this my door." He asked, "Then go and prepare a place for us to rest." He went and did so, then returned and said, "O Messenger of God, I have prepared a place for your siesta. Do come, with God's blessings." They did so.

"'Now that the Messenger of God (SAAS) had arrived, ʿAbd Allāh b. Salām came to him and said, "I bear witness that you are really the Prophet of God, that you have brought the truth. The Jews know me to be their leader and the son of their former leader, their most learned man and son of their former most learned man. Call them and ask them."

"'When they came the Messenger of God (SAAS) addressed them, "O Jews, woe upon you! Fear God! By the God other than whom there is none, you well know that I am truly the Messenger of God, and that I bring you the truth. Accept Islam!"

"'But three times they replied, "We do not know this."'"

Al-Bukhārī alone relates this thus, on the authority of a Muḥammad not further identified and also from ʿAbd al-Ṣamad.

Ibn Isḥāq stated, "Yazīd b. Abū Ḥabīb related to me, from Marthad b. ʿAbd Allāh al-Yazanī, from Abū Ruhm al-Samāʿī, that Abū Ayyūb stated, 'When the Messenger of God (SAAS) took up residence in my house, he lived on the lower floor while I and Umm Ayyūb lived upstairs. I told him, "O Messenger of God, I really hate being above you, with you beneath me. Come along and live above, while we come down to the lower floor."

38. Ibn Isḥāq's account as elsewhere published refers to his aunt as working with him in the palm-grove; no doubt the reference is to her in this apparently abbreviated account. See p. 196.

“‘He replied, “Abū Ayyūb, it’s better for us and for our guests for me to live downstairs.”

“‘And so the Messenger of God (ṢAAS) remained down while we stayed above in the house. It happened that a large jug of water of ours broke and my wife and I had to mop it up as best we could with a velvet garment, since we had no other cloth. We used it to dry up the water, fearing to have any drop on the Messenger of God (ṢAAS) and so harm him.

“‘We used to prepare his evening meal for him and send it in to him. If when he returned it there were any morsels left we would try to see where his fingers had touched it and eat that part, hoping to be blessed by that. One night we sent him his supper, having included onions or garlic and he returned it without us detecting any marks of his hands on it. So I was shocked and went to him and asked, “O Messenger of God, you have sent back the food without me seeing any sign you have touched it.” He explained, “I sensed the smell of that plant in the food; I’m someone who whispers to others (and such an odour may be offensive to them), so why don’t you eat it.”

“‘We did so and never served him those vegetables again.’”

Al-Bayhaqī related this similarly, through al-Layth b. Saʿd, from Yazīd b. Abū Ḥabīb, from Abū al-Ḥasan, or Abū al-Khayr, Marthad b. ʿAbd Allāh al-Yazanī, from Abū Ruhm, from Abū Ayyūb, who told it.

Abū Bakr b. Abū Shayba related it from Yūnus b. Muḥammad al-Muʾaddib, from al-Layth.

Al-Bayhaqī stated, “The *ḥāfiẓ* Abū ʿAbd Allāh informed us, quoting Abū ʿAmr al-Ḥayrī, quoting ʿAbd Allāh b. Muḥammad, quoting Aḥmad b. Saʿīd al-Dāramī, quoting Abū al-Nuʿmān, quoting Thābit b. Yazīd quoting ʿĀṣim al-Aḥwal, from ʿAbd Allāh b. al-Ḥārith, from Aflaḥ, the freed-man of Abū Ayyūb, from Abū Ayyūb, who said that the Messenger of God (ṢAAS) resided with him, staying on the ground floor while he, Abū Ayyūb, lived upstairs. It occurred to Abū Ayyūb that he was walking on top of the Messenger of God (ṢAAS), and so he was careful to keep to the sides, where they also slept. He then spoke to the Messenger of God (ṢAAS) about that, commenting, ‘The lower floor is more appropriate for us; I can’t be above a ceiling when you are beneath it.’ And so the Messenger of God (ṢAAS) moved to the upper floor, while Abū Ayyūb moved to the lower.

“He used to prepare food for the Messenger of God (ṢAAS), and if it was returned he would ask about where he had placed his fingers and keep track of this. Once he made food for him that contained garlic and when the food came back he asked where the Messenger of God (ṢAAS) had placed his fingers. He was told, ‘He didn’t eat any.’ Abū Ayyūb was shocked and went up to him and asked, ‘Is it a forbidden food?’ The Prophet (ṢAAS) replied, ‘No, but I do dislike it.’ Abū Ayyūb commented, ‘I dislike whatever you dislike’; or he may have used the words, ‘whatever you have disliked.’ He also said, ‘The Prophet (ṢAAS) would be visited by angels.’”[39]

39. It is stated in another tradition that angels dislike the smell of garlic.

Muslim related this from Aḥmad b. Saʿīd.

It is established in both *ṣaḥīḥ* collections, that Anas b. Mālik said, "The Messenger of God (ṢAAS) was brought a large platter" – in one account it was a bowl – "containing green vegetables. He asked and was told what these were and when he looked at them, he did not want to eat them. He commented, 'You eat them; I have private conversations with people with whom you do not!'"

Al-Wāqidī recounted that when the Messenger of God (ṢAAS) stayed at the home of Abū Ayyūb, Asʿad b. Zurāra took hold of the nose-rein of the camel of the Messenger of God and it thus remained with him.

It is related from Zayd b. Thābit that he said, "The first gift made to the Messenger of God (ṢAAS), after he took up residence in the home of Abū Ayyāsh, was brought to him by myself. It was a big wooden bowl filled with bread, crumbled up with yoghurt and butter. I told him that my mother had sent the bowl. He commented, 'God bless her!' Then he called over his Companions and they ate. Then a wooden bowl came from Saʿd b. ʿUbāda, a mixture of bread and meat gravy.

"Not an evening went by without there being at the door of the Messenger of God (ṢAAS) three or four people who would come one after the other carrying food. He remained there in the home of Abū Ayyūb for seven months.

"While resident in the home of Abū Ayyūb, the Messenger of God (ṢAAS) sent his freed-man Zayd b. Ḥāritha and Abū Rāfiʿ, along with two camels and carrying 500 dirhams, to bring back Fāṭima and Umm Kulthūm, daughters of the Messenger of God (ṢAAS), his wife Sawda, daughter of Zamʿa and Usāma b. Zayd. Ruqayya had already emigrated with her husband ʿUthmān, while Zaynab remained with her husband, Abū al-ʿĀṣ b. al-Rabīʿ in Mecca. Umm Ayman, the wife of Zayd b. Ḥāritha, came with these, and so did ʿAbd Allāh b. Abū Bakr with the other children of Abū Bakr who included ʿĀʾisha, 'mother of the believers'. The Messenger of God (ṢAAS) had not yet consummated his marriage with her."

Al-Bayhaqī stated, "ʿAlī b. Aḥmad b. ʿAbdān informed us, quoting Aḥmad b. ʿUbayd al-Ṣaffār, quoting Khalaf b. ʿAmr al-ʿAkbarī, quoting Saʿīd b. Manṣūr, quoting ʿItāf b. Khālid, quoting Ṣādiq b. Mūsā, from ʿAbd Allāh b. al-Zubayr, that when the Messenger of God (ṢAAS) arrived in Medina his mount knelt down between the homes of Jaʿfar b. Muḥammad b. ʿAlī and al-Ḥasan b. Zayd. People came to him then saying, 'O Messenger of God, my house!' But his camel got up with him again and he said, 'Let her proceed; she is being divinely guided.'

"She then moved away with him and came to the place for the *minbar*, the pulpit, where it knelt down and shook itself. A shed was there where they were storing and drying dates. The Messenger of God (ṢAAS), alighted from his mount and went to the shade. Abū Ayyūb then approached him and said, 'O Messenger of God, my house is the one closest to you; shall I carry your baggage to my place?' 'Yes,' he said. So he took his baggage into the house. Another man then came to him and said, 'O Messenger of God, where are you staying?' He replied, 'A man stays wherever his baggage is.' The Messenger of God (SAAS) stayed there in the shed for 12 nights, until the mosque was built."

This was a great honour for Abū Ayyūb Khālid b. Zayd, God bless him, to have the Messenger of God (SAAS) stay with him.

It was related to us through Yazīd b. Abū Ḥabīb from Muḥammad b. 'Alī b. 'Abd Allāh b. 'Abbās, may God be pleased with him, that Abū Ayyūb came to Basra over which Ibn 'Abbās had been appointed governor by 'Alī b. Abū Ṭālib, may God be pleased with him. Ibn 'Abbās came out of his house and invited Abū Ayyūb to stay there, just as the latter had provided accommodation for the Messenger of God (SAAS) in his house. He also presented him with everything within the house; and when he came to leave, Ibn 'Abbās gave him 20,000 dirhams and 40 slaves.

Abū Ayyūb's house later passed into the hands of his freed-man Aflaḥ; al-Mughīra b. 'Abd al-Raḥmān b. al-Ḥārith b. Hishām bought it from him for 1,000 dinars, repaired it and donated it for the use of the poor of Medina who belonged to the household of the Prophet (SAAS).

Similarly his staying in the home of the Banū al-Najjār and God's choosing that for him, was also a great honour. In Medina there were many such complexes, nine in number. Each of these was separate and self-sufficient, with its own date-palms, gardens and families. Each one of their tribes were gathered in their own quarters, making them like adjoining villages. God chose for the Messenger of God (SAAS) the home of the Banū Mālik b. al-Najjār.

In both *ṣaḥīḥ* collections it is established from a *ḥadīth* of Shu'ba as follows, "I heard Qatāda quote Anas b. Mālik as stating, 'The Messenger of God (SAAS) said, "The best of the *anṣār* homes is that of the Banū al-Najjār, then comes that of the Banū al-Ashhal, then the Banū al-Ḥārith b. al-Khazraj, then the Banū Sā'ida; and in all the homes of the *anṣār* there is good."'"

"Sa'd b. 'Ubāda stated, 'I never saw the Messenger of God (SAAS), fail to express preference for others over us.' But he was told instead, 'He gave preference to you over many.'"

This quotation comes from al-Bukhārī.

Al-Bukhārī and Muslim also related this from a *ḥadīth* of Anas and Abū Salama, from Abū Usayd Mālik b. Rabī'a, and from a *ḥadīth* of 'Ubāda b. Sahl, from Abū Ḥumayd, from the Prophet (SAAS), in the same terms. In the *ḥadīth* of Abū Ḥumayd there is an addition: "Abū Usayd said to Sa'd b. 'Ubāda, 'Don't you think that the Prophet (SAAS) expressed favour for the *anṣār* and placed us last?' And so Sa'd went to the Prophet (SAAS) and asked, 'O Messenger of God, have you given preference to the homes of the *anṣār* and placed us last?' 'Well', he replied, 'does it not suffice you that you are among the very best?'"

Great honour and credit were firmly established for the people of Medina, the *anṣār*, both in this world and the next. God Almighty stated, "As for those who are first and foremost, of the *muhājirīn*, the Emigrants and the *anṣār*, 'the Helpers', and those who followed them in goodness, God is pleased with them, and they are with Him. He has prepared for them gardens beneath which rivers flow; they will live in them forever. That is the mighty success" (*sūrat al-Tawba* or *al-Barā'a*; IX, v.100). And God also stated, "And (give also) to those who lived in this area and had faith before them, loving those who emigrated to them, and they do not find in themselves any grudge because of what others were given, rather, preferring others over themselves, though they may themselves be in need. Those spared from the meanness of their selves shall be those who succeed" (*sūrat al-Ḥashra*; LIX, v.9).

The Messenger of God (ṢAAS) stated, "Had I not been compelled to perform the emigration personally, I would have been an *anṣārī*, a Helper; and if people had gone to any valley or defile, I would have gone to the valley or defile of the Helpers. The Helpers are as an undergarment, the people at large as an overgarment."

He also said, "The Helpers are my household and my own family."

And he said, "I am peace to those who make peace with them and war to those who make war upon them."

Al-Bukhārī stated that Ḥajjāj b. Minhāl related to him, quoting Shuʿba, quoting ʿAdī b. Thābit, as follows, "I heard al-Barāʾ b. ʿĀzib say, 'I heard the Messenger of God (ṢAAS) say' – or he said – 'the Messenger of God (ṢAAS), said, "The *anṣār* are loved only by those who believe and hated only by those who are hypocritical. Whoever loves them is loved by God, and whoever hates them is hated by God."'"

The other *hadīth* authorities also give this, except for Abū Dāʾūd, from an account of Shuʿba.

Al-Bukhārī also stated, "Muslim b. Ibrāhīm related to us, quoting Shuʿba, from ʿAbd al-Raḥmān b. ʿAbd Allāh b. Jubayr, from Anas b. Mālik, from the Prophet (ṢAAS) who said, 'A sign of faith is love for the Helpers; a sign of hypocrisy is hatred for the Helpers.'"

Al-Bukhārī also related it from Abū al-Walīd, al-Ṭayālisī and Muslim, from a *hadīth* of Khālid b. al-Ḥārith and ʿAbd al-Raḥmān b. Mahdī, all four of them quoting Shuʿba's account.

There are numerous verses of the Qurʾān and Prophetic Traditions that make reference to the virtues of the *anṣār*.

How fine are the verses spoken by Abū Qays Ṣirma b. Abū Anas, mentioned above, a poet from the Helpers, concerning the arrival of the Messenger of God (ṢAAS) among them, and of the help and comfort they gave to him and to his Companions, God bless them all.

Ibn Isḥāq stated, "Abū Qays Ṣirma b. Abū Anas also spoke the following, making reference to how God had honoured them by bringing them Islam and His Messenger (ṢAAS),

> 'A decade or so he stayed among Quraysh, preaching in
> hopes of finding agreeable friends,

Offering himself to those attending the fairs, but he
found no one to protect or invite him.

When he came to us his mind was put at ease and he
became pleased and contented,

He found friends and his mind became at ease, and he
received evident help from God.

He would tell us what Noah informed his people, and
what Moses said when he answered the call,

And so he came to fear no one, whether near or far away.

We gave of our best wealth and of ourselves amidst the
uproar and the shared sorrows,

Opposing all those people that he opposed, even those
who had been dear and close.

We know that there is nothing besides God, and that the
book of God has become our guide.

I would say, when praying at any temple, "Have pity, do
not show enmity towards us!"

I would say, when crossing any dangerous land, "Blessed
are You, the One relied upon."

Even if you step to one side the ways of death are
many, and it is not you who can preserve yourself.

And, by God, a man does not know how his course will
be, if he does not have God watch over him.

The thirsty date-palm will do its owner no good if it
becomes well-watered yet he becomes buried!'"

Ibn Isḥāq and others quoted this, as did 'Abd Allāh b. al-Zubayr al-Ḥumaydī
and others, from Sufyān b. 'Uyayna, from Yaḥyā b. Sa'īd al-Anṣārī, from an old
woman of the Helpers who said, "I saw 'Abd Allāh b. 'Abbās visiting Ṣirma b.
Qays as he spoke these lines."

Al-Bayhaqī related this.

DIVISION

Medina was also honoured by the emigration there of the Messenger of God
(ṢAAS), and it became a shelter to the good agents and worshippers of God, an
impregnable stronghold and fortress for the Muslims and a place where there
was guidance for all people.

There are innumerable traditions relating to its virtues, and these we will give
elsewhere, if God wills it.

It is established in both ṣaḥīḥ collections through Ḥabīb b. Yasāf, from Ja'far
b. 'Āṣim, from Abū Hurayra who said, "The Messenger of God (ṢAAS) stated,
'Faith fits into Medina like a snake into its hole.'"

Muslim also related this, from Muḥammad b. Rāfi', from Shabāba, from
'Āṣim b. Muḥammad b. Zayd b. 'Abd Allāh b. 'Umar, from his father, from Ibn
'Umar, from the Prophet (ṢAAS), in much the same words.

Also in the *ṣaḥīḥ* collections is the *ḥadīth* of Mālik, quoting Yaḥyā b. Saʿīd as saying that he heard Abū al-Ḥubāb Saʿīd b. Yasār report, "I heard Abū Hurayra say, 'The Messenger of God (ṢAAS) commented, "I was commanded to go to a town that eats up other towns; they call it 'Yathrib', but it is 'al-Madina'. It purifies men just as a bellows purifies the dross from iron."'"

Imām Mālik is unique among the four Imāms in giving Medina preference over Mecca.

Al-Bayhaqī stated, "The *ḥāfiz* Abū ʿAbd Allāh quoted Abū al-Walīd and Abū Bakr b. ʿAbd Allāh, both of whom said, 'Al-Ḥasan b. Sufyān related to us, quoting Abū Mūsā al-Anṣārī, quoting Saʿīd b. Saʿīd, quoting his brother, from Abū Hurayra, that the Messenger of God (ṢAAS) stated, "O God, you have brought me out of the town that is dearest to me; let me now dwell in the town dearest to You." And God sent him to dwell in Medina.'"

This *ḥadīth* is extremely strange.

It is very widely known and accepted that Mecca is better than Medina, except for that place that holds the body of the Messenger of God (ṢAAS).

Most authorities give many proofs of that, these being too many to refer to here; we have referenced their location in *al-Manāsik min al-Aḥkām* (*The Rites of the Ḥajj in the Sharīʿa*).

The most famous proof for them of this is in what Imām Aḥmad stated, namely, "Abū al-Yamān related to us, quoting Shuʿayb, quoting al-Zuhrī and Abū Salama b. ʿAbd al-Raḥmān that ʿAbd Allāh b.ʿAdī b. al-Ḥamrāʾ told him that he heard the Prophet (ṢAAS), while standing at al-Ḥazwara in the market of Mecca, say, 'By God, I swear that of all God's earth you are the best, and the dearest to me; and had I not been forced out of you I would never have left.'"

Aḥmad related the same, from Yaʿqūb b. Ibrāhīm, from his father, from Ṣāliḥ b. Kaysān, from al-Zuhrī.

Al-Tirmidhī related it thus, as did al-Nasāʾī and Ibn Māja, from a *ḥadīth* of al-Layth, from ʿUqayl, from al-Zuhrī. Al-Tirmidhī stated it to be "*ḥasan, ṣaḥīḥ*', "good and authentic".

Yūnus related this from al-Zuhrī. Muḥammad b. ʿAmr related it from Abū Salama b. ʿAbd al-Raḥmān, from Abū Hurayra. In my view the *ḥadīth* of al-Zuhrī is more reliable.

Imām Aḥmad stated, "ʿAbd al-Razzāq related to us, quoting Maʿmar, from al-Zuhrī, from Abū Salama b. ʿAbd al-Raḥmān, from Abū Hurayra, who said, 'The Messenger of God (ṢAAS) stood at al-Ḥazwara and said, "I know you to be of all God's earth the best, and the dearest to me; and if your people had not expelled me I would not have forsaken you."'"

Al-Nasāʾī related this thus from an account of Maʿmar.

The *ḥāfiz* al-Bayhaqī stated, "This is a mistake on Maʿmar's part."

Some authorities relate this from Muḥammad b. ʿAmr, from Abū Salama, from Abū Hurayra; it too is a misconception, the authentic version being that of the community of scholars.

Aḥmad also stated, "Ibrāhīm b. Khālid related to us, quoting Rabāḥ, from Ma'mar, from Muḥammad b. Muslim b. Shihāb al-Zuhrī, from Abū Salama, from some other scholars, that the Messenger of God (ṢAAS) said, while he was in the market place of al-Ḥazwara, 'By God, I swear that of all God's earth you are the best, and the dearest to me; and had I not been forced out of you, I would never have left.'"

Al-Ṭabrānī related it from Aḥmad b. Khulayd al-Ḥalabī, from al-Ḥumaydī, from Ibn Akh al-Zuhrī, from Muḥammad b. Jubayr b. Muṭ'im, from 'Abd Allāh b. 'Adī b. al-Ḥamrā'.

These are the various lines of transmission of this *ḥadīth* but the most reliable is the one given above. But God knows best.

The events of the first year of the hegira: An Account of the major events and happenings in the first year following the emigration of the Messenger of God (ṢAAS).

The *ṣaḥāba*, the "Companions", God be pleased with them, agreed in the year 16 AH – or some say 17 or 18 AH – during the Caliphate of 'Umar, on having the Islamic era begin with the year of the emigration.

This came about because a contractual document or agreement was referred to 'Umar by one man complaining against another. In it was stated that it came into effect in the month of Sha'bān. 'Umar asked, "Which Sha'bān? That of this, last or next year?"

He then assembled the Companions and discussed the need for a calendar whereby contracts concerning debts and other matters should come into effect. One speaker suggested, "Date as the Persians do." But this met no favour. For the Persians used to date by the reigns of their kings, one following the other.

Another man suggested, "Use the same dating system as the Byzantines." They used to date by the reign of Alexander, son of Phillip, the Macedonian. But this met no favour.

Another man suggested, "Date from the birth of the Messenger of God (ṢAAS)."

Another suggested, "No, date from his receiving the Mission."

Another suggested, "No, from his emigration."

Others suggested by the date of his death.

'Umar, God be pleased with him, preferred the date of his emigration, because it was so definite and well known, and the others agreed with him.

In his *ṣaḥīḥ* collection al-Bukhārī stated, under the heading: *The dating system and when it was established.* "'Abd Allāh b. Muslim related to us, quoting 'Abd al-'Azīz, from his father, from Sahl b. Sa'd, who said, 'They did not have the dating system start after the beginning of the mission of the Prophet (ṢAAS), nor after his death, but after his arrival in Medina.'"

Al-Wāqidī stated, "Ibn Abū al-Zinād related to us, from his father, who said, 'ʿUmar sought advice on a dating system and they agreed upon the emigration.'"

Abū Dāʾūd al-Ṭayālisī stated, from Qurra b. Khālid al-Sadūsī, from Muḥammad b. Sīrīn, who said, "A man went up to ʿUmar and said, 'Set a dating system!' He asked, 'What's that?' The man explained, 'It's something other peoples do; they record things in the form: in such-and-such a month of such-and-such a year.' 'Fine,' agreed ʿUmar, 'just set it up.'

"They then discussed the matter of the date from which it should begin. Some suggested from the beginning of the Mission of the Messenger of God (ṢAAS), others suggested from his death. Finally they agreed it should be from his emigration. Then they discussed at which month it should commence. Ramaḍān was suggested, and then al-Muḥarram, it being the time for the return of people from their pilgrimage and it was also a sacred month. They agreed on al-Muḥarram."

Ibn Jarīr stated, "Qutayba related to us, quoting Nūḥ b. Qays al-Ṭāʾī, from ʿUthmān b. Muḥsin, that Ibn ʿAbbās used to say in regard to the words of the Almighty, 'By the dawn and ten nights!' (surat al-Fajr, LXXXIX, v.1), that the reference was to al-Muḥarram, the dawn of the year."

It is related that ʿUbayd b. ʿUmayr stated, "Muḥarram is God's month; it is the beginning of the year and in it the *kaʿba* receives its new cover. It is the month from which people establish the date and in which coins are minted."

Aḥmad stated, "Rawḥ b. ʿUbāda related to us, quoting Zakariyyāʾ b. Isḥāq, from ʿAmr b. Dīnār, who said, 'The first man to put a date on a document was Yaʿlā b. Umayya in the Yemen. The Messenger of God (ṢAAS) came to Medina in Rabīʿ al-Awwal, and people marked that as the first of the year.'"

Muḥammad b. Isḥāq related from al-Zuhrī and Muḥammad b. Ṣāliḥ related from al-Shaʿbī, both saying, "The Banū Ismāʿīl dated from the fire of Abraham and then from the building by Abraham and Ismāʿīl of the temple, then from the death of Kaʿb b. Luʾayy, then from the [year of the] elephant. After that ʿUmar b. al-Khaṭṭāb began dating from the emigration. That was in the year 17 or 18 AH."

We made reference to this issue, giving the relevant chains of authority and lines of transmission in the biography of ʿUmar, and all praise be to God.

The conclusion is that they did make the beginning of Islamic history from the year of the emigration. They set its beginning from al-Muḥarram, this being well known. This is the consensus of the Imāms.

Al-Suhaylī and others quoted Imām Mālik as having said, "The Islamic year began in Rabīʿ al-Awwal, because that was the month when the Messenger of God (ṢAAS) emigrated."

He also made such an assertion elsewhere by referring to the Almighty's words, "certainly a mosque founded in piety from the first day" (surat al-Tawba or al-Barāʾa; IX, v.108). That is, from the first day of the arrival of the Prophet (ṢAAS) in Medina. This was the first day of the era, just as the Companions have agreed to its first year having been that of the emigration.

There is no doubt that this, as stated by Imām Mālik, God bless him, is appropriate. However, the actual practice is contrary to this. The first month of the Arabs is indeed al-Muḥarram. They thus made the first year of the calendar that of the emigration, and had it begin with al-Muḥarram (instead of Rabī' al-Awwal) so that there would be no confusion in the system. But God knows best.

Our comment is – and we rely on God's help – that the year of the blessed emigration begins while the Messenger of God (ṢAAS) was still resident in Mecca. He had received the pledge of the *anṣār*, "the Helpers", at the second 'Aqaba meeting, as we have explained, in the middle days of the *tashrīq* period, that is on the 12th of Dhū al-Ḥijja, preceding the year of the emigration.

The *anṣār* then went back and the Messenger of God (ṢAAS) permitted the Muslims to emigrate to Medina. One by one his Companions left for Medina to the point where no one was left in Mecca who could emigrate except for the Messenger of God (ṢAAS). Abū Bakr had kept himself back so as to be able to accompany the Messenger of God (ṢAAS) on the journey, as we have explained earlier. They then emigrated together, as is detailed above. 'Alī b. Abū Ṭālib was to leave later, at his command, to take care of the deposits entrusted to the Messenger of God (ṢAAS); he joined the other two men at Qubā'. The Messenger of God (ṢAAS) entered Medina on a Monday at approximately noon, when the heat was extreme.

Al-Wāqidī and others stated, "That occurred on the 2nd of the month of Rabī' al-Awwal." Ibn Isḥāq also related this, except that he did not stop there but preferred a date of the 12th of that month.

This is the popular view held by most scholars. The Messenger of God (ṢAAS) according to the best accounts, remained in Mecca following his receiving the Mission for 13 years.

This is what we learn in the account of Ḥammād b. Salama, from Abū Ḥamza al-Dabbī, from Ibn 'Abbās, who said, "The Messenger of God (ṢAAS) received the Mission at the age of 40 and remained living in Mecca for 13 years."

Ibn Jarīr related it similarly from Muḥammad b. Mu'ammar, from Rawḥ b. 'Ubāda, from Zakariyyā' b. Isḥāq, from 'Amr b. Dīnār that he (Ibn 'Abbās) used the words, "The Messenger of God (ṢAAS) stayed in Mecca 13."

It has been earlier stated that Ibn 'Abbās wrote down verses of Ṣirma b. Abū Anas b. Qays, including,

> "Some decades he stayed among Quraysh, preaching in
> hopes of finding agreeable friends"

Al-Wāqidī stated, from Ibrāhīm b. Ismā'īl, from Dā'ūd b. al-Ḥusayn, from 'Ikrima, from Ibn 'Abbās, that he cited that same verse as testimony (to the residence having been for 13 years).

Ibn Jarīr related the same, from al-Ḥārith, from Muḥammad b. Sa'd, from al-Wāqidī, but with reference to "15 pilgrimages", a very strange statement indeed.

Even stranger than that is what Ibn Jarīr stated, namely, "It was related to me from Rawḥ b. ʿUbāda, who said, 'Saʿīd related to us, from Qatāda, who said, "The Qurʾān was revealed to the Messenger of God (ṢAAS) over a period of 8 years in Mecca and 10 in Medina."'"

Al-Ḥasan used to say "over 10 years in Mecca and 10 in Medina."

This last statement to which al-Ḥasan al-Baṣrī subscribed, that he remained in Mecca 10 years, was one with which Anas b. Mālik, ʿĀʾisha, Saʿīd b. al-Musayyab and ʿAmr b. Dīnār all agreed, according to what Ibn Jarīr related of them.

And there is the account from Ibn ʿAbbās, related by Aḥmad b. Ḥanbal from Yaḥyā b. Saʿīd, from Hishām, from ʿIkrima. It has Ibn ʿAbbās as saying, "The Prophet (ṢAAS) received revelation at the age of 43 and he remained in Mecca for 10 years."

We recounted above that al-Shaʿbī stated, "Isrāfīl was linked with the Messenger of God (ṢAAS) for 3 years during which he communicated to him the Word and the Message. In one account, he would hear his voice but not see his person; and thereafter it was Gabriel."

Al-Wāqidī related that one of his sheikhs rejected that statement of al-Shaʿbī.

Ibn Jarīr tried to combine the statements of those who maintained that the Messenger of God (ṢAAS) stayed for 10 years in Mecca with those who considered it to have been 13 years by reference to what al-Shaʿbī had said. But God knows best.

Division

When the party of the Prophet (ṢAAS) came to Medina he first stayed, as stated above, at Qubāʾ in the home of the Banū ʿAmr b. ʿAwf. He remained there at the most for 22 nights, though some say it was 18, others 10 or so, and according to Mūsā b. ʿUqba, 3 nights.

What is widely accepted is what Ibn Isḥāq and others stated, namely that he was there at Qubāʾ from a Monday to a Friday.

He did establish during this period of disputed length, as we have indicated, the mosque at Qubāʾ.

Al-Suhaylī claimed that the Messenger of God (ṢAAS) founded it on the first day he arrived at Qubāʾ, citing to support this view the Almighty's words, "certainly, a mosque founded in piety from the first day" (*sūrat al-Tawba* or *al-Barāʾa*; IX, v.108). And he refuted those who would have the wording read "from the foundation of the first day".

It is a fine, much honoured mosque. God Almighty revealed about it, "certainly a mosque founded in piety from the first day is fully deserving of you standing (for prayer) inside it; therein are men who love that they be purified, and God loves those who purify themselves" (*sūrat al-Tawba* or *al-Barāʾa*; IX, v.108). We have discussed this in our *Tafsīr* (*Exegesis*). Therein we referred to the *ḥadīth* in the *ṣaḥīḥ* collection of Muslim to the effect of it being the mosque of Medina, and to the refutation of this.

We also made mention of the *hadīth* related by the Imām Aḥmad as follows: "Ḥasan b. Muḥammad related to us, quoting Abū Idrīs, quoting Shuraḥbil quoting 'Uwaym b. Sā'ida who said that it was related to him that the Messenger of God (ṢAAS) came to them in the mosque in Qubā' and said, 'God has given you much good praise for purifying yourselves, in the reference to your mosque; what is it you do to so purify yourselves?' They replied, 'We swear by God, O Messenger of God, that the only thing we know is that we had some Jewish neighbours who would wash their behinds after defecating, and so we washed like them.'"

Ibn Khuzayma included this *hadīth* in his *ṣaḥīḥ* collection and there are other testimonies to it.

It is also related from Khuzayma b. Thābit and Muḥammad b. 'Abd Allāh b. Salām and Ibn 'Abbās.

Abū Dā'ūd, al-Tirmidhī and Ibn Māja related from a *hadīth* of Yūnus b. al-Ḥārith, from Ibrāhīm b. Abū Maymūna from Abū Hurayra, from the Prophet (ṢAAS), who said, "The following verse was revealed about the people of Qubā': 'In it there are men who love to be purified, and God loves those who purify themselves.'" He then went on, "They would wash after excretion and this verse was revealed about them."

Al-Tirmidhī commented, "A unique tradition from this source."

My own comment is that this Yūnus b. al-Ḥārith is a weak authority. But God knows best.

One of those who stated that it referred to this mosque as the one "founded in piety" was 'Abd al-Razzāq who related, from Ma'mar, from al-Zuhrī, from 'Urwa b. al-Zubayr, and 'Alī b. Abū Ṭalḥa related it, from Ibn 'Abbās. It was related also from al-Sha'bī, al-Ḥasan al-Baṣrī, Qatāda, Sa'īd b. Jubayr, 'Aṭiyya al-'Awfī and 'Abd al-Raḥmān b. Zayd b. Aslam, along with others.

The Prophet (ṢAAS) used to visit it in later times and would pray there. He would go to Qubā' each Saturday, sometimes mounted and sometimes on foot. It is a *hadīth* from him that, "Prayer in the mosque at Qubā' is like an *'umra*."[40]

It is also stated in a *hadīth* that it was Gabriel, peace be upon him, who pointed out to the Prophet (ṢAAS) the place for the *qibla*, the prayer niche, for the mosque at Qubā'.

This mosque was the first built in Medina; indeed it is the first that was made for people in general in this community (of believers). In stating this about this mosque, we are excluding the mosque that Abū Bakr built at the entrance to his home in which to worship and pray; this is because it was for his personal household, not for the public at large. But God knows best.

The matters relating to the acceptance of Islam by Salmān have been referred to above in the chapter on the *bishārāt*, the early signs. They tell how when Salmān

---

40. This refers to the "lesser pilgrimage", a series of ceremonies and rituals performed either in conjunction with or independent of those of the complete pilgrimage. See the *Encyclopaedia of Islam* et alia.

the Persian heard of the arrival of the Messenger of God (ṢAAS) to Medina, he came and brought him something that he laid before him while he was at Qubāʾ, saying, "This is a donation." But the Messenger of God (ṢAAS) refrained from eating it and told his Companions to do so and they did eat it. Salmān then came a second time with something he presented saying, "This is a present." The Messenger of God (ṢAAS) then ate some of it himself and told his Companions to do the same, which they did. We gave the tradition earlier at length.

Section: On the acceptance of Islam by ʿAbd Allāh b. Salām, may God be pleased with him.

Imām Aḥmad stated, "Muḥammad b. Jaʿfar related to us, quoting ʿAwf, from Zurāra, from ʿAbd Allāh b. Salām, who said, 'When the Messenger of God (ṢAAS) arrived in Medina, the people ran away scared, as I did myself. But as I learned more about him I realized that he was no liar. The first thing I heard him say was, "Spread peace, feed others, pray at night while others sleep, and you will achieve paradise in peace."'"

Al-Tirmidhī related this, as did Ibn Māja, by various routes, from ʿAwf al-Aʿrābī, from Zurāra b. Abū ʿAwfa. Al-Tirmidhī stated that it was authentic.

This tradition requires that ʿAbd Allāh b. Salām had heard of the Prophet (ṢAAS) and saw him directly following his arrival at Qubāʾ, when he dismounted there among the Banū ʿAmr b. ʿAwf.

It is given above in the account of ʿAbd al-ʿAzīz b. Ṣuhayb, from Anas, that he met him when the Messenger of God (ṢAAS) dismounted at the home of Abū Ayyūb following his arrival from Qubāʾ to the quarters of the Banū al-Najjār as told above. It is possible that he did see him for the first time at Qubāʾ and then met with him after his arrival with the Banū al-Najjār. But God knows best.

In the account of al-Bukhārī, through ʿAbd al-ʿAzīz from Anas, the last-mentioned stated, "When the Prophet (ṢAAS) arrived, ʿAbd Allāh b. Salām came to him and said, 'I bear witness that you are the Messenger of God and that you bring the truth. The Jews recognize me as their leader and the son of their leader, their most learned man and the son of their most learned man. Summon them and ask them about me before they know that I have embraced Islam, because if they know I have done so they will say of me things that are untrue.'

"The Messenger of God (ṢAAS) then sent for the Jews and when they came he asked them, 'O Jews, woe upon you! Fear God! For, by God other than whom there is none, you certainly know that I am the Messenger of God, in truth, and that I bring you the truth. Therefore accept Islam!' They replied, 'We do not know it.' Three times this was repeated. Then the Messenger of God (ṢAAS) asked, 'Which of your men is ʿAbd Allāh b. Salām?'

"They replied, 'That is our leader, and the son of our leader, our most learned man and the son of our most learned man.' He then asked, 'What would you think if he accepted Islam?' They replied, 'God forbid! He would never accept Islam!'

"The Messenger of God (ṢAAS) then called out, 'Ibn Salām, come on out to them!'

"When he did so he addressed them as follows, 'O Jews, fear God! By God other than whom there is none, you do certainly know that he is the Messenger of God, and that he brings you the truth.' They replied, 'No, you are lying!' Thereupon the Messenger of God (ṢAAS) sent them away."

Those are the words used in the above account.

In one version the text states, "when he came out before them and gave testimony to the truth they said, 'You are the worst of us, and the son of the worst of us!' And they spoke ill of him. He then said, 'O Messenger of God, this is what I was fearing.'"

Al-Bayhaqī stated, "The *ḥāfiẓ* Abū ʿAbd Allāh told us, quoting al-Aṣamm, quoting Muḥammad b. Isḥāq al-Ṣanʿānī, quoting ʿAbd Allāh b. Abū Bakr, quoting Ḥumayd, from Anas, who said, "ʿAbd Allāh b. Salām heard of the arrival of the Prophet (ṢAAS) while he was out in some land he owned. He went to the Prophet (ṢAAS) and said, "I shall ask you three things for which only a prophet would know the answers. They are: What are the signs of the Day of Judgement? What is the finest food that the people of paradise would eat? And what causes a child to resemble his father or his mother?"

"'He replied, "Gabriel told me of these previously." "What, Gabriel?" he asked. "Yes," he replied. "But," commented ʿAbd Allāh b. Salām, "he is the angel who is the enemy of the Jews." The Messenger of God (ṢAAS) then recited, "Whoever is the enemy of Gabriel, who surely revealed it to your heart by God's permission" (*sūrat al-Baqara*; II, v.97).

"'He then said, "Regarding the signs of the Day of Judgement, the first will be a fire that comes at people from the East and leads them to the West. As for the prime food of paradise eaten by those that are there, that is a plentitude of whale's liver. And if the male's liquid precedes that of the female, he will resemble the child, while if the female's liquid precedes that of the male, she will resemble the child."

"'ʿAbd Allāh b. Salām exclaimed, "I testify that there is no god but God and that you are the Messenger of God; O Messenger of God, the Jews are a people of liars. If they learn of my accepting Islam before you ask them about me, they will lie to you."

"'The Jews arrived and the Messenger of God (ṢAAS) asked them, "What kind of man is the (one of you named) ʿAbd Allāh?" They replied, "He is the best of us and the son of the best of us; he is our leader and the son of our leader." "What," he then asked, "would you say if he were to accept Islam?" They replied, "May God spare him from that!"

"'ʿAbd Allāh then came forth and said, "I give testimony that there is no god but God, and that Muḥammad is the Messenger of God." They said, "You are the worst of us, and the son of the worst of us!" And they spoke ill of him.

"'He then commented, "This, O Messenger of God, is what I feared."'"

Al-Bukhārī related this from ʿAbd b. Ḥumayd from ʿAbd Allāh b. Abū Bakr. And he also related it from Ḥāmid b. ʿUmar, from Bishr b. al-Mufaḍḍal, from Ḥumayd.

Muḥammad b. Isḥāq stated, ʿAbd Allāh b. Abū Bakr related to me, from Yaḥyā b. ʿAbd Allāh, from a man of the family of ʿAbd Allāh b. Salām, who said, "Included in the statement reported as having been made by ʿAbd Allāh b. Salām, a learned rabbi, at his conversion to Islam, is the following, 'At Qubāʾ I heard of the Messenger of God (ṢAAS), and learned of his name, qualities and appearance, and that his coming was at a time when we were expecting him. I none the less remained secretive about this and silent until he came to Medina.

"'When he arrived in Qubāʾ, he stayed among the Banū ʿAmr b. ʿAwf. A man came and told me of his arrival; at that time I was at work at the top of a date-palm and my aunt Khālida, daughter of al-Ḥārith, was sitting below me.

"'When I heard the news of his arrival, I loudly praised God, and my aunt exclaimed, upon hearing that, "Why, you'd not have been more pleased at hearing of the coming of Moses, son of Aaron!"

"'I told her, "Yes indeed, Aunt. He is, I swear, the very brother of Moses, son of Aaron, and recognizing the same faith. He has been given the same mission assigned to Moses."

"'She responded, "O Nephew, is he the one whom we were told would be sent with news of Judgement Day?" "Yes," I told her, and she said, "Then so it is he."'

"ʿAbd Allāh continued, 'So I went to the Messenger of God (ṢAAS) and embraced Islam, returned to my household and ordered them to do the same. I kept my acceptance of Islam from my people, and told the Messenger of God (ṢAAS), "The Jews are a people of liars; I would like you to let me inside a house of yours, hide me from them, then ask them about me what status I have among them before you tell them of my conversion to Islam. If they knew that they would call me unreliable and would speak ill of me."' The account then continues approximately as above.

"ʿAbd Allāh continued, 'I then openly declared the acceptance of Islam by myself and by my household; my aunt Khālida, daughter of al-Ḥārith, also accepted the faith.'"

Yūnus b. Bukayr quoted Muḥammad b. Isḥāq as follows, "ʿAbd Allāh b. Abū Bakr related to me, quoting someone, from Ṣafiyya, daughter of Ḥuyay, who said, 'None of the children of my father or my uncle were more popular with them both than I was. Whatever child of theirs wanted their attention it was always me they put first. When the Messenger of God (ṢAAS) came to Qubāʾ, the village of the Banū ʿAmr b. ʿAwf, my father and my uncle, Abū Yāsir b. Akhṭab, went to him early in the morning and only returned at sunset, so tired out that they could scarcely walk, staggering from exhaustion. I raced over to greet them as was my custom, but, I swear, neither so much as looked at me. I heard my uncle Abū Yāsir ask my father, "Is that he then?" "Yes, I swear by God," he replied. "You recognize him from his character and description then?" "I certainly do, I swear it!" he responded. "So how will you relate to him?" he asked. "With enmity, I swear by God, for as long as I live!"'"

Mūsā b. 'Uqba recounted, from al-Zuhrī, that Abū Yāsir b. Akhṭab, following the arrival of the Messenger of God (ṢAAS) in Medina, went to him, heard him speak, spoke with him and then returned to his people. He told them, "People, obey me; God has sent you the one you have been awaiting. Follow him and do not oppose him.

"His brother Ḥuyayy b. Akhṭab, at that time the leader of the Jews, they both being of the Banū al-Naḍir, then went and sat and listened to the Messenger of God (ṢAAS), and returned to his people who were obedient to him. He told them, 'I come to you from being with a man whom, I swear it, I will for ever oppose.' His brother, Abū Yāsir, answered him, 'O cousin, obey me in this matter and disobey however you like thereafter without penalty.'

"Ḥuyayy insisted, 'No, by God, I will never obey you!' And so Satan took possession of him and his people followed him in his opinion."

As for Abū Yāsir, whose name was Ḥuyayy b. Akhṭab, his fate is unknown to me. Regarding Ḥuyayy b. Akhṭab, the father of Ṣafiyya, he expressed enmity for the Prophet (ṢAAS) and his Companions, and continued to do so, God damn him, until he was executed, bound, before the Messenger of God (ṢAAS) on the day the warriors of Banū Qurayẓa were killed. As we will relate, if God wills it.

DIVISION

When, on a Friday, the Messenger of God (ṢAAS) left Qubā' mounted on his camel *al-Qaṣwā'*, it was noon by the time he was in the quarter of the Banū Sālim b. 'Awf. He performed the Friday prayers there with the Muslims in a valley called Rānuwānā'.

This was the first Friday prayer which the Messenger of God (ṢAAS) performed with the Muslims in Medina, or perhaps the very first time of all. This is because – though God knows best – it had not been possible for him and his Companions in Mecca to have any Friday prayers with a sermon and joint open prayer. The strong opposition to him from the polytheists and the harm they were doing to him had precluded any such possibility.

An Account of the sermon of the Messenger of God (ṢAAS) that day.

Ibn Jarīr stated, "Yūnus b. 'Abd al-A'lā related to me, quoting Ibn Wahb, that Sa'īd b. 'Abd al-Raḥmān al-Jumaḥī reported that he was informed that the following was the content of the sermon of the Messenger of God (ṢAAS) on the first Friday he prayed in Medina, among the Banū Sālim b. ʿAmr b. ʿAwf, God bless them: 'Praise be to God; I give Him praise, and I ask His help. I ask for His forgiveness and for His guidance. I believe in Him, will not disbelieve in Him, and will do battle with those who do. I bear witness that there is no god but God, that He has no associate, that Muḥammad is His Servant and Messenger whom He has sent with guidance and the religion of truth and light, at a time without messengers, when there is little knowledge, the people are misguided, when the time is out of joint, and the day of retribution and fate is at hand.

"'Whoever obeys God and His Messenger is right-guided; whoever disobeys them is misled, and has erred and gone far astray.

"'I charge you to fear God; this is the best advice a Muslim can give a Muslim, to urge him on to the afterlife, to order him to fear God. Beware of what God has, of Himself, cautioned you. There is no better advice nor charge than this. It is an act of piety for those who accomplish this with apprehension and fear and a true means of assistance towards your aspirations from the afterlife.

"'Whoever cultivates, both openly and in secret, his relationship with God, seeking only God's favour thereby, shall receive recognition in the short term and reward after death, when a man will wish he had done differently than he had before, and would want to put great distance between himself and that behaviour. God bids you beware of Him, though He is merciful towards His worshippers.

"'Whoever believes His words and fulfils His promise will find nothing taken back therefrom, for God Almighty states, "Whatever I say shall not be changed, and I am not unjust towards my worshippers" (*sūrat Qāf*, L, v.29).

"'Fear God both in matters that are at hand and those that follow, in secret and openly, for "whoever fears God, God will remove his evil ways from him and give him great reward" (*sūrat al-Ṭalāq*, LXV, v.5). And "Whoever fears God and His Messenger will have won a mighty success."[41] Fearing God will forestall His disapproval, His punishment, His anger. Fearing God will bring satisfaction, please the Lord and elevate one's status.

"'Take advantage of your good fortune and do not be lax in matters pertaining to God. God has instructed you in His book, laid out for you His path, so that He may know those who speak the truth and those who lie. Do good, just as God does good to you. Oppose His enemies and strive energetically for God. It is He who chose you and named you "Muslims", so that those who perish do so for evident cause, while those who live do so for evident cause. There is no power but with God. Make frequent mention of God. Strive for what comes after death. For he who makes good his relationship with God will find his relationship with people satisfactory. That is because God passes judgement upon

---

41. Verse 71 of *sūrat al-Aḥzāb* (XXXIII) is somewhat different. It reads, "Whoever is obedient to God and His Messenger."

people, while they do not pass judgement upon Him. It is He who controls people, while they do not control Him. God is truly great! There is no power but with God, the Almighty and Glorious.'"

This is the text given by Ibn Jarīr; its chain of authorities is not complete.

Al-Bayhaqī's text reads, *"Chapter on the first address given by the Messenger of God (ṢAAS) after his arrival in Medina.* The *ḥāfiẓ* Abū 'Abd Allāh informed us, quoting Abū al-'Abbās al-Aṣamm quoting Aḥmad b. 'Abd al-Jabbār, quoting Yūnus b. Bukayr, from Ibn Isḥāq, who stated, 'Al-Mughīra b. 'Uthmān b. Muḥammad b. 'Uthmān related to me, along with al-Akhnas b. Sharīq, from Abū Salama b. 'Abd al-Raḥmān b. 'Awf, who said, "The first address given by the Messenger of God (ṢAAS) in Medina began with him standing before them and expressing appropriate praise and adoration for God, and then saying, 'O people, send forward for yourselves! You well know that any one of you may be struck down and so his flock be left with no shepherd. His Lord will then say to him – and there will be no interpreter or attendant to come between yourself and Him – "Did not My Messenger come to you and inform you? Did I not give you wealth and benefit? What is it you have sent forward for yourself?" And He will look to right and left but see nothing. Then the man will look in front of him and see only hell-fire. So, whoever is able to protect his face from the fire, even if only with a slice of dates, let him do so. If he finds nothing, then let him say one good word for thereby one good deed will be rewarded by 10 times its like, or even by 700 times. May peace be upon the Messenger of God, and the mercy and the blessings of God.'"'"

Then the Messenger of God (ṢAAS) proceeded with the second sermon by saying, "Praise be to God! I praise Him and I seek His help. We seek refuge with God from the evil of ourselves and of our deeds. Whoever is guided by God will not be misled while he who is misled shall have no guide. I bear witness that there is no god but God, Who is unique and without associate. The finest words are those of God's Book. Successful are those whose hearts have been embellished thereby by Him; those whom He has brought into Islam following disbelief and who chose these words above all human speech. Love those who love God and love Him with all your hearts. Do not tire of His words and of repeating them, nor harden your hearts towards them. From everything that God creates He makes His selection and choice. He has thus mentioned the best of these deeds and the best of persons who perform these deeds. He has also described healthy speech, along with those things He regards as lawful and those that are forbidden. So worship God and associate no other god or person with Him and fear Him as is His due. Be faithful to Him in those good things you utter with your mouths. Love one another, the spirit of God being between you. God is angry if vows to Him are broken. Peace be upon you, and God's mercy and blessings."

The chain of authorities for this tradition, though incomplete, does add strength to the previous address, even if the phraseology differs.

Section: On the building of the holy mosque during the period of the residence of the Messenger of God (ṢAAS) at the home of Abū Ayyūb, may God be pleased with him.

There are differences of opinion as to the length of his stay there. Al-Wāqidī stated seven months, while others refer to less than one month but God knows best.

Al-Bukhārī stated that Isḥāq b. Manṣūr related to him, from ʿAbd al-Ṣamad, who quotes a *hadīth* from his father, as follows, "Abū al-Ṭayyāḥ Yazīd b. Ḥumayd al-Ḍabbī related to us, quoting Anas b. Mālik, who said, 'When the Messenger of God (ṢAAS) came to Medina, he stayed in the upper part of the town in the quarter named for the Banū ʿAmr b. ʿAwf. He stayed among them for 14 nights, then sent a message to the chiefs of the Banū al-Najjār who came wearing their swords. It's as if I can still see the Messenger of God (ṢAAS) riding his camel with Abū Bakr mounted behind him and the chiefs of the Banū al-Najjār all around him until they reached the courtyard of Abū Ayyūb's house.

"'He used to pray wherever he happened to be when time for prayer came; he would even pray in sheep pens.

"'Then he ordered that the mosque be built. He summoned the chiefs of the Banū al-Najjār, and when they came he asked them, "O Banū al-Najjār, what price for this wall of yours?" They replied, "Oh no, by God, we'll seek its price from God, the Almighty and Glorious, alone!"'

"Anas Ibn Mālik then said 'This wall enclosed the following: the graves of polytheists, ruins and date-palms. The Messenger of God (ṢAAS) ordered that the graves be unearthed, the ruins levelled and the date-palms be cut down; this was done.

"'They (created a wall of) palm trees at the *qiblah* (the front of the mosque), and constructed its two door posts out of stones. They set about gathering stones, chanting in *rajaz* verse as they did so. The Messenger of God (ṢAAS) worked along with them, saying, "O God, there is no good but that of the after-life; please aid the Helpers and the Emigrants!"'"

Al-Bukhārī related this in other places, as did Muslim from a *hadīth* of Abū ʿAbd al-Ṣamad and ʿAbd al-Wārith b. Saʿīd.

A *hadīth* from the *ṣaḥīḥ* of al-Bukhārī quoted earlier, from al-Zuhrī, from ʿUrwa, stated that the mosque had been a *mirbad* — a shed for dates — belonging to two orphan youths, Sahl and Suhayl, who were under the care of Asʿad b. Zurāra. The Messenger of God (ṢAAS) made an offer of money to them but they replied, "No; we will give it to you, Messenger of God." But he refused, and bought it from them instead and then built a mosque on it.

The Messenger of God (ṢAAS) would chant as he moved the earth along with the others,

> "This load is not a load of Khaybar; this, O Lord, is
> cleaner and purer."

And he would say,

> "O God, real reward is that of the other world, so have
> mercy on the Helpers and the Emigrants."

Mūsā b. Uqba related that As ad b. Zurāra compensated the orphans for the land with some date-palms he had on land that was otherwise uncultivated but he also mentions the view that the Messenger of God (ṢAAS) bought it from them.

My own comment is that Muḥammad b. Isḥāq also related that the date shed was owned by two orphaned youths who were under the care of Mu ādh b. Afrā, and that they were Sahl and Suhayl, both sons of Amr. But God knows best.

Al-Bayhaqī related through Abū Bakr b. Abū al-Dunyā, quoting al-Ḥasan b. Ḥammād al-Ḍabbī, quoting Abd al-Raḥīm b. Sulaymān, from Ismā īl b. Muslim, from al-Ḥasan, who said, "When the Messenger of God (ṢAAS) built the mosque, his Companions helped him; he worked along with them, carrying the bricks so that his chest became brown. He told them, 'Build an *arish*, a trellis roof, like that of Moses.' I asked al-Ḥasan, 'What was the "trellis of Moses"?' He replied, 'When he raised his hands they would reach the *arish*, meaning the roof.'"

This *ḥadīth* is incomplete in its chain.

It is related from a *ḥadīth* of Ḥammād b. Salama, from Abū Sinān, from Ya lā b. Shaddād b. Aws, from Ubāda, that the Helpers collected money which they took to the Messenger of God (ṢAAS), saying, "O Messenger of God, build and embellish this mosque; how long do we have to pray beneath these palm fronds?" He replied, "I don't want to outdo my brother Moses; just a trellis roof like that of Moses."

This is a unique tradition from this source.

Abū Dā ūd stated, "Muḥammad b. Ḥātim related to us, quoting Abd Allāh b. Mūsā, from Sinān, from Firās, from Aṭiyya al- Awfī, from Ibn Umar, that the mosque of the Prophet (ṢAAS) initially had its walls made of palm trunks above which was a light roof made of palm fronds. It deteriorated in the Caliphate of Abū Bakr and he rebuilt it, again with palm trunks and fronds. It again fell apart in the Caliphate of Uthmān and he rebuilt it using bricks; it remains in a good state today."

This (tradition) is unique.

Abū Dā ūd also stated, "Mujāhid b. Mūsā related to us, quoting Ya qūb b. Ibrāhīm from his father, from Abū Ṣālih, from Nāfi from Ibn Umar, to the effect that the mosque had been built at the time of the Messenger of God (ṢAAS) from bricks and that it had a roof of palm fronds, with pillars made of palm trunks. Abū Bakr made no improvements to it, but Umar enlarged it, rebuilding it in the same manner as in the time of the Prophet (ṢAAS), that is, with bricks and palm fronds; he also restored its wooden pillars. Uthmān, God bless him, made changes and major additions. He had its walls built with cut stone and plaster, its pillars of stone and its roof of teak."

Al-Bukhārī related this similarly from ʿAlī b. al-Madīnī, from Yaʿqūb b. Ibrāhīm.

My own comment is that in adding to it, ʿUthmān b. ʿAffān, God bless him, was putting into effect the words of the Messenger of God (ṢAAS), "Whoever builds a mosque for God, even if only like the hollowed out nest of a sand-grouse, will have a house built for him by God in paradise."

The Companions living at that time agreed with him in this, and they made no changes after ʿUthmān. This gives support to the preponderant view of the scholars that the rules applicable to the original structure will also apply to the extensions made to that structure and thus, those who perform their prayer in that new section will also share in the virtues allotted to those who pray in the original section. Included in this is the waiver of the prohibition of undertaking a journey to any sacred place except the kaʿba and the Prophet's mosque.[42]

It was expanded in the time of al-Walīd b. ʿAbd al-Malik, the builder of the Damascus mosque. Its expansion was undertaken at his orders by ʿUmar b. ʿAbd al-ʿAzīz when he was governor of Medina. He added to it the ḥujrat al-nabawiyya, the burial chamber of the Prophet (ṢAAS). Substantial later additions were made to it. On the side of the prayer niche it was expanded, so much so that the original niche and the rawḍa, the promenade, became positioned after the front rows, as it is to be seen today.

Ibn Isḥāq stated, "The Messenger of God (ṢAAS) stayed with Abū Ayyūb until his mosque and apartments were built. The Messenger of God (ṢAAS) himself worked in it to inspire the Muslims with a desire to work there. Both Emigrants and Helpers co-operated busily in this. One Muslim worker spoke the verse,

"For us to sit while the Prophet worked would indeed be
misdirected action."

As they worked the Muslims chanted,

"There's no life but that of the hereafter; O God,
have mercy on both Helpers and Emigrants."

The Messenger of God (ṢAAS) himself spoke the words,

"There's no life but that of the hereafter; O God,
have mercy on both Emigrants and Helpers."[43]

42. This statement alludes to the teachings of the Prophet regarding the sanctity of the mosque. In one tradition he said that those who perform a single prayer in his mosque will have it increased a thousand fold.

43. The point of this quotation, in which the positions of the Arabic words for Emigrants and Helpers are transposed thus spoiling the meter, seems to be to provide evidence that the Prophet (ṢAAS) had no ear for verse, therefore further establishing the divine origin of the Qurʾān. See also Sir William Muir: *The Life of Muhammad* London, 1877, p. 184.

ʿAmmār b. Yāsir came in, overloaded with bricks, and said, "O Messenger of God, they're killing me by loading me with what they wouldn't carry!"

Umm Salama said, "I saw the Messenger of God (ṢAAS) wipe his hand through his long, thick hair – which was curly – and say, 'Alas, Ibn Sumayya, it's not them killing you but the evil gang who will!'"

This tradition is devoid of a link from this line; indeed it is problematic between Muḥammad b. Isḥāq and Umm Salama. Muslim, in his ṣaḥīḥ collection, joined it back to a ḥadīth of Shuʿba, from Khālid al-Hadhdhāʾ, from Saʿīd and al-Ḥasan, that is from the two sons of Abū al-Ḥasan of Baṣra, from their mother Khayra, the freed-woman of Umm Salama, from Umm Salama, who said, "The Messenger of God (ṢAAS) stated, 'The evil gang will kill ʿAmmār.'" He also related it from a ḥadīth of Ibn ʿAliyya, from Ibn ʿAwn, from al-Ḥasan, from his mother, from Umm Salama, which reports that the Messenger of God (ṢAAS) said to ʿAmmār as he was transporting rocks, "Alas for you, O Ibn Sumayya! The evil gang will kill you!"

ʿAbd al-Razzāq stated, "Maʿmar related to us, from al-Ḥasan, from his mother, from Umm Salama, who said, 'While the Messenger of God (ṢAAS) and his Companions were building the mosque, his men would carry the bricks one at a time, while ʿAmmār would carry two, one for himself and one for the Prophet (ṢAAS). So the latter patted him on the back and said, 'Ibn Sumayya, the others will get a reward, but you will receive two. And the last food for you will be a drink of milk and the evil gang will kill you!'"

This chain of authorities is in accordance with the criteria established in both ṣaḥīḥ collections.

Al-Bayhaqī and others tell us, through a group, from Khālid al-Hadhdhā, from ʿIkrima, from Abū Saʿīd al-Khudarī, who said, "While building the mosque we would be carrying bricks one by one, while ʿAmmār would bear them two at a time. The Prophet (ṢAAS) saw him and, while wiping the dust off him said, 'Alas, poor ʿAmmār! The evil gang will kill him. He will invite them to paradise, while they will invite him to the fire!' ʿAmmār commented, 'I seek refuge with God from strife!'"

Imām al-Bukhārī, however, related this ḥadīth from Musaddad, from ʿAbd al-ʿAzīz b. al-Mukhtār, from Khālid al-Hadhdhāʾ; and from Ibrāhīm b. Mūsā, from ʿAbd al-Wahhāb al-Thaqafī, from Khālid al-Hadhdhāʾ. However, that account does not mention his use of the words, "The evil gang will kill you!"

Al-Bayhaqī stated, "It is as if he left this out only due to what Muslim related from one route, from Abū Naḍra, from Abū Saʿīd, who said, 'Someone better than myself told me that the Messenger of God (ṢAAS) while setting about digging the khandaq, "the trench", wiped his head and said to ʿAmmār, "Alas for Ibn Sumayya! An evil gang will kill him!"'"

Muslim also related this, from a ḥadīth of Shuʿba, from Abū Muslim, from Abū Naḍra, from Abū Saʿīd who said, "One of my betters, Abū Qatāda, related to me that the Messenger of God (ṢAAS) said to ʿAmmār b. Yāsir, 'Alas for you, Ibn Sumayya! The evil gang will kill you!'"

Abū Dāʾūd Al-Ṭayālisī said, "Wuhayb informed us from Dāʾūd Ibn Abū Hind from Abū Naḍra, from Abū Saʿīd who said: "When the Prophet (ṢAAS) undertook the excavation of the trench, people generally carried one brick each. ʿAmmar however, who was recuperating from an ailment, carried two bricks at a time. Abū Saʿīd said: 'A Companion informed me that the Prophet (ṢAAS) would wipe the dust off his head and say: 'Alas for you, Ibn Sumayya! The evil gang will kill you!'"

Al-Bayhaqī stated, "He distinguished between what he had himself heard and what he heard from his Companions."

He said, "It seems that his reference to 'the trench' is imagined, or that he said this to him both while building the mosque and while digging the trench. But God knows best."

My own comment is that carrying bricks while digging a trench makes no sense. It seems obvious that there is confusion here. But God knows best.

This *ḥadīth* comes from the *Dalāʾil al-Nubuwwah* (*Signs of the Prophethood*) wherein the Messenger of God (ṢAAS) tells ʿAmmār that the evil gang will kill him.

In fact he was killed by the Syrians at the battle of Ṣiffīn, ʿAmmār having fought with ʿAlī and the Iraqis.

ʿAlī had greater right to rule than did Muʾāwiya. But their being called *bughāt*, unjust, does not imply that the supporters of Muʾāwiya have become unbelievers, as some ignorant persons do who belong to the Shīʿa, along with others as well. For even if they were essentially rebellious, they had in fact erred in their interpretation of the circumstances surrounding the conflict. And not everyone who undertakes interpretation is right; those who are right receive double reward, while those in error receive only one.

There are some who add after the words, "the evil gang will kill you" further words, "may my intercession not include them on Judgement Day". In making such an addition they are falsely attributing statements to the Messenger of God (ṢAAS); he did not say this, since it is not transmitted by any reputable source. But God knows best.

Regarding the words, "He invites them to paradise, while they invite him to the fire", they refer to ʿAmmār and his friends inviting the Syrians to friendship and to unity, while the Syrians wanted to give preference to some over those whose right was greater, which would result in the people being divided, each one having its own leader. This would have led to dissension and division within the nation and resulted inevitably from their philosophy and policies, even though this was not what they intended. But God knows best.

But the subject at hand here relates mainly to the building of the mosque of the Prophet, may the best of blessings and peace be upon its constructor.

The *ḥāfiz* al-Bayhaqī stated in *Dalāʾil* (*The Signs*) as follows, "The *ḥāfiz* Abū ʿAbd Allāh related to us by dictation, Abū Bakr b. Isḥāq related to us, ʿUbayd b.

Shurayk informed us, Nuʿaym b. Ḥammād related *to us, quoting* ʿAbd Allāh b. al-Mubārak, Ḥashraj b. Nubāta informed us, from Saʿīd b. Jumhān, from Safīna, freed-man of the Messenger of God (ṢAAS), who said, ʿAbū Bakr brought a stone and placed it down, then ʿUmar did the same, then ʿUthmān did the same. The Messenger of God (ṢAAS) commented, 'These will succeed to power after myself.'"

He (al-Bayhaqī) then related this from a *ḥadīth* of Yaḥyā b. ʿAbd al-Ḥamīd al-Ḥimmānī, from Ḥashraj, from Saʿīd, from Safīna, who said, "When the Messenger of God (ṢAAS) built a mosque he put down a stone, saying, 'Let Abū Bakr place a stone next to mine; let ʿUmar place his next to that of Abū Bakr, and let ʿUthmān place his next to that of ʿUmar.' The Messenger of God (ṢAAS) then said, "These shall be the Caliphs after me."

This *ḥadīth* through this line of transmission is *gharīb*, "unique".

What is well known is what Imām Aḥmad related, from Abū al-Naḍr, from Ḥashraj b. Nabāta al-ʿAbsī, and from Bahz and Zayd b. al-Ḥabbāb, and ʿAbd al-Ṣamad, and Ḥammād b. Salama, both authorities quoting Saʿīd b. Jamhān from Safīna, who said, "I heard the Messenger of God (ṢAAS) say, 'The Caliphate period will last for 30 years. Then thereafter will come the kingdom period.' Safīna then commented, 'Count! The Caliphate of Abū Bakr lasted 2 years, that of ʿUmar 10 years, that of ʿUthmān 12 years, and that of ʿAlī 6 years.'"

This wording is that of Aḥmad.

Abū Dāʾūd, al-Tirmidhī and al-Nasāʾī related it through various lines from Saʿīd b. Jamhān. Al-Tirmidhī stated, "This *ḥadīth* is *ḥasan*, 'good'. We know of it only in this form and with the alternate wording, 'The Caliphate after me will be for 30 years, and then will come a mordacious kingdom era.'" He then related the remainder of the tradition.

I would comment that when first built the mosque of the Prophet (ṢAAS) had no *minbar* from which to address the congregation. He would speak while leaning against a palm tree trunk in the wall next to the *qibla* near where he prayed. Eventually he began to use a *minbar*, as we will explain in its proper place. As he moved over towards it to make his address from it and passed by that tree trunk, it moaned like a love-lorne camel because it had always heard his speeches delivered near itself. And so the Prophet (ṢAAS) returned to it and hugged it until it settled down, just like a baby, and became quiet. Details of this will be given hereafter through various lines, from Sahl b. Saʿd al-Saʿīdī, Jābir, ʿAbd Allāh b. ʿUmar, ʿAbd Allāh b. ʿAbbās, Anas b. Mālik and Umm Salama, God be pleased with them.

What more appropriate than the comment made by al-Ḥasan al-Baṣrī after relating this story, from Anas b. Mālik, "O Muslims! A piece of wood so pining for the Messenger of God (ṢAAS)! Do not men hoping to meet him have even more right to yearn for him?"

INDICATIONS OF THE EXCELLENCE OF THIS NOBLE MOSQUE AND THIS EXALTED PLACE.

Imām Aḥmad stated, "Yaḥyā b. Anīs b. Abū Yaḥyā related to us, quoting his father, as follows, 'I heard Abū Saʿīd al-Khudarī say, "Two men, one from the Banū Khudra, the other from the Banū ʿAmr b. ʿAwf, disagreed over which mosque was referred to by the words in the Qurʾān, 'the mosque founded in piety' (*sūrat al-Tawba* or *al-Barāʾa*; IX, v.108). The Khudarī said, 'It is the mosque of the Messenger of God (ṢAAS).' The ʿAmrī insisted, 'No, it's the mosque at Qubāʾ.' So they went to the Messenger of God (ṢAAS) and asked him about it. He replied, 'It is this mosque,' referring to that of the Messenger of God (ṢAAS). 'In that one,' he went on, meaning the mosque at Qubāʾ, 'there is much good.'" '"

Al-Tirmidhī related this from Qutayba, from Ḥātim b. Ismāʿīl, from Anīs b. Abū Yaḥyā al-Aslamī. He characterized it as *ḥasan, ṣaḥīḥ*, "good", "authentic".

Imām Aḥmad, al-Tirmidhī and al-Nasāʾī related, from Isḥāq b. ʿĪsā, from al-Layth b. Saʿd, from Qutayba, from al-Layth from ʿImrān b. Abū Anas, from ʿAbd al-Raḥmān b. Abū Saʿīd, from his father, who said: "Two men argued over which was the mosque 'founded in piety'. Thereafter this account proceeded as above.

In the *ṣaḥīḥ* collection of Muslim, there is the *ḥadīth* of Ḥumayd al-Kharrāṭ, from Abū Salama b. ʿAbd al-Raḥmān, who is quoted as saying that he asked ʿAbd al-Raḥmān b. Abū Saʿīd, "What was it you heard your father say about the 'mosque founded in piety'?" He replied, "My father said, 'I went to the Messenger of God (ṢAAS) and asked him about the "mosque founded in piety". He picked up a handful of pebbles and dashed them to the ground, saying, "It is this, here, your mosque."'"

Imām Aḥmad stated, "Wakīʿ related to us, as did Rabīʿa b. ʿUthmān al-Tamīmī, from ʿImrān b. Abū Anas, from Sahl b. Saʿd, who said, 'Two men alive at the time of the Messenger of God (ṢAAS) differed over which mosque was "founded in piety". One of them said, "It is the mosque of the Messenger of God (ṢAAS)." The other said, "No, it's the mosque at Qubāʾ." So they went to the Messenger of God (ṢAAS) and asked him. He replied, "It is this mosque of mine."'"

Imām Aḥmad stated, "Abū Nuʿaym related to us, quoting ʿAbd Allāh b. ʿĀmir al-Aslamī, from ʿImrān b. Abū Anas, from Sahl b. Saʿd, from Ubayy b. Kaʿb, that the Prophet (ṢAAS) said, 'The mosque "founded in piety" was this mosque of mine.'"

These numerous sources come close to giving conclusive evidence that the mosque in question is that of the Messenger of God (ṢAAS).

ʿUmar, his son ʿAbd Allāh, Zayd b. Thābit, Saʿīd b. al-Musayyab and Ibn Jarīr all agreed with this.

Others say that there is simply no contradiction between the revelation of this verse being applied to the mosque at Qubāʾ and these traditions. This is so, they say, because this mosque (i.e. the Medina mosque) is simply more worthy of such than is the other since it is one of the three mosques referred to as those worth striving to attend. This is established in both *ṣaḥīḥ* collections from a *ḥadīth* of Abū Hurayra, who said, "The Messenger of God (ṢAAS) stated, 'Only three mosques should be the object of travel: this mosque of mine, the *ḥaram* mosque (in Mecca) and the *Bayt al-Maqdis* mosque (in Jerusalem).'"

In the *ṣaḥīḥ* collection of Muslim there is a tradition from Abū Saʿīd, from the Prophet (ṢAAS), who said, "Only three mosques should be the object of travel" and he named these. It is established in both *ṣaḥīḥ* collections that the Messenger of God (ṢAAS) said, "A prayer in this mosque of mine is better than a thousand prayers in any other, with the exception of the *ḥaram* mosque."

In the *ḥadīth* collection of Aḥmad, with a good chain of authorities, there is mention of an additional, bounty namely the words, "And that one is better."

In both collections, there is a *ḥadīth* of Yaḥyā al-Qaṭṭān, from Ḥabīb, from Ḥafṣ b. ʿĀsim, from Abū Hurayra, who said, "The Messenger of God (ṢAAS) stated, 'Between my house and my pulpit there is one of the gardens of paradise, and my pulpit stands by my pool.'"

There are numerous traditions referring to the virtues of this holy mosque. We will report these in the large work *al-Manāsik min Kitāb al-Aḥkām*, if God wills it. And in Him is all trust and reliance, and there is no power or strength except in God, the Powerful and Wise.

Imām Mālik and his associates support the view that the Medina mosque is superior to the *ḥaram* mosque because the latter was built by Abraham, and the former by Muḥammad (ṢAAS); it being obvious that Muḥammad (ṢAAS) was superior to Abraham, God bless him.

However, the majority opinion opposes this view and maintains that the *ḥaram* mosque is superior. This is because it is in a land made sacred by God at the time when He created the heavens and the earth. And it was made sacred by Abraham *al-Khalīl*, "the True Friend", peace be upon him, and Muḥammad, "the Seal of the Prophets". The (mosque in Mecca) is thus endowed with qualities not present in any other. Discussion of this issue however, belongs elsewhere; and one turns to God for help.

DIVISION

The Messenger of God (ṢAAS) built apartments around his mosque which would be dwellings for himself and his family. These were small dwellings with narrow courtyards.

Al-Ḥasan b. Abū al-Ḥasan al-Baṣrī stated, he having been a youth in the company of his mother Khayra, the freed-woman of Umm Salama, "I used to be able to reach up with my hand to the highest ceiling in the apartment of the Messenger of God (ṢAAS)."

I would observe, however, that al-Ḥasan al-Baṣrī was large in size and tall. God bless him.

Al-Suhaylī stated in *al-Rawḍ* (*The Gardens*), "The apartments of the Messenger of God (ṢAAS) were built of the stalks of palm leaves covered with mud and partly of stones stacked upon one another. The ceilings of all were made of palm fronds."

This account was related from al-Ḥasan al-Baṣrī.

His rooms were made of hair-cloth held together with juniper-tree wood.

In al-Bukhārī's work of history we learn that finger nails could knock on the door of the Messenger of God (ṢAAS); this shows that there were no cloth coverings over his doors.

He stated, "And after the deaths of the wives of the Messenger of God (ṢAAS) all these apartments were added to the mosque."

Al-Wāqidī, Ibn Jarīr and others said, "When ʿAbd Allāh b. Urayqiṭ al-Dīlī returned to Mecca, the Messenger of God (ṢAAS) and Abū Bakr dispatched Zayd b. Ḥāritha and Abū Rāfiʿ, both freed-men of the Messenger of God (ṢAAS) to bring back their families from Mecca. They sent with them two loads of goods and 500 dirhams with which to purchase a camel of Qudayd. They left and soon returned with the two daughters of the Messenger of God (ṢAAS), Fāṭima and Umm Kulthūm, his two wives, Sawda and ʿĀʾisha, and the latter's mother, Umm Rūmān, along with other members of his and Abū Bakr's family, including the latter's son, ʿAbd Allāh. On the road back, the mounts of ʿĀʾisha and her mother Umm Rūmān strayed apart and Umm Rūmān began calling out, 'Bride! My daughter!' ʿĀʾisha later said, 'I heard a voice say, "Let loose its bridle!' So I did this and it stopped, at God's will; we give praise to God the Almighty and Glorious.' They stayed at al-Sunḥ on the way. Eight months later, in Shawwāl, as we will relate, the Messenger of God (ṢAAS) consummated his marriage with ʿĀʾisha.

"Asmāʾ, daughter of Abū Bakr and wife of al-Zubayr b. al-ʿAwāmm arrived also; she was pregnant and near term with ʿAbd Allāh b. al-Zubayr, as we will relate in its proper place in material relating to the end of that year.

DIVISION

How the Emigrants suffered from the Medina fever, God be pleased with them all, though the Messenger of God (ṢAAS) was spared it through the strength and power of God; he prayed to his Lord who then drew it away from his city.

Al-Bukhārī stated, "ʿAbd Allāh b. Wahb b. Yūsuf related to us, quoting Mālik b. Hishām b. ʿUrwa, from his father, from ʿĀʾisha, who said, 'Abū Bakr and Bilāl fell sick around the time that the Messenger of God (ṢAAS) arrived in Medina. I went in to see them and asked, "How are you, father? Bilāl, how are you?"'

She said: "Whenever Abū Bakr developed a fever he would recite,

'Every man might arise among his family, yet his
death be closer than his sandal thongs.'

"When the fever was raised from Bilāl he would raise his voice and say,

'O how happy I would be to spend a night in a valley
covered with fresh grass and verdure,
Will I ever again descend to Majinna's waters, or see
Shāma and Ṭufayl?'"

῾Ā᾽isha went on, "So I went to the Messenger of God (ṢAAS) and told him and he said, 'O God, make Medina beloved by us as Mecca is, and more so; make it healthy and bless us in its foods. Turn aside its fever and send it off to al-Juḥfa!'"[44]

Muslim related this from Abū Bakr b. Abū Shayba from Hishām in abbreviated form.

In al-Bukhārī's account of it from Abū Usāma, from Hishām b. ῾Urwa, from his father, from ῾Ā᾽isha, there is an addition after the verses of Bilāl. In this he says, "O God, curse ῾Utba b. Rabī῾a, Shayba b. Rabī῾a and Umayya b. Khalaf alike for them having forced us out into the land of pestilence!"

"And so the Messenger of God (ṢAAS) said, 'O God, make Medina beloved by us, as Mecca is, and more so; make it healthy and bless us in its prosperity. Turn aside its fever and send it off to al-Juḥfa!'

"She said, 'When we arrived in Medina, we found it the most pestilential place on God's earth. It was just two basin-shaped valleys wet with *najl*, that is brackish water.'"

Ziyād quoted Muḥammad b. Isḥāq as follows, "Hishām b. ῾Urwa and ῾Umar b. ῾Abd Allāh b. ῾Urwa b. al-Zubayr related to me that ῾Ā᾽isha stated, 'When the Messenger of God (ṢAAS) arrived in Medina, it was the most pestilential place on God's earth. His Companions fell sick from fever and illness, but God kept that away from His Prophet. Abū Bakr, ῾Āmir b. Fuhayra and Bilāl, the two freed-men of Abū Bakr, were in one house, struck down by fever. I went in to them to visit them, that being before the *ḥijāb*, the veil, was prescribed for us. Only God knows how very sick they were. I approached Abū Bakr and said, "How are you, father?" He replied, in verse:

"Every man might arise among his family, yet his
death be closer than his sandal thongs!"

"'I exclaimed, "I swear, my father doesn't know what he is saying!" Then I went over to ῾Āmir b. Fuhayra and asked, "How are you, ῾Āmir?" He replied, in verse,

"I have found death before tasting it; a coward has
his demise right above him.
Every man fights hard with all his power, as a bull
protects its skin with its horns."

44. According to a footnote in the printed edition of Ibn Kathīr's text, the reference is to a town where largely Jews resided at the time, some 82 miles from Mecca.

"'I exclaimed, "By God, he doesn't know what he is saying!" Bilāl was in the habit of resting in the courtyard of the house whenever the fever struck him, then he would raise his voice and say,

"O how happy I would be to spend a night in Fakh, while
all around me was fresh grass and verdure.
Will I ever again descend to Majinna's waters, or see
Shāma and Ṭufayl?"'

"'Āʾisha went on, 'I told the Messenger of God (ṢAAS) what I had heard from them, saying, "They are raving, irrational from the intensity of the fever." He replied, "O God, make Medina beloved by us as Mecca is, and more so; make it healthy and bless us in its prosperity. Turn aside its fever to Mahyaʿa!" Mahyaʿa is a reference to al-Juḥfa.'"

Imām Aḥmad stated, "Yūnus related to us, quoting Layth, from Yazīd b. Abū Ḥabīb, from Abū Bakr b. Isḥāq b. Yasār, from ʿAbd Allāh b.ʿUrwa, from ʿUrwa, from ʿAʾisha, who said, 'When the Messenger of God (ṢAAS) arrived in Medina, Abū Bakr and ʿĀmir b. Fuhayra, Abū Bakr's freed-man, and Bilāl, fell sick.' ʿAʾisha asked permission from the Messenger of God (ṢAAS) to visit them, and he agreed. She then asked Abū Bakr, 'How are you?'

"He replied,

'Any man might arise among his family, yet his death be closer than his sandal thongs!'

"She then asked ʿĀmir and he replied,

'I have found death before tasting it; a coward has his demise right above him.'

"Then she asked Bilāl and he said,

'O how happy I would be to spend a night in Fakh, while all around me was fresh grass and verdure.'

"So she went to the Messenger of God (ṢAAS) and told him. He then looked up to heaven and said, 'O God, make Medina beloved by us as Mecca is, and more so; make it healthy and bless us in its foods. Turn aside its fever to Mahyaʿa.' This is a reference to al-Juḥfa, so they claim."

Al-Nasāʾī related this similarly from Qutayba, from al-Layth. The Imām Aḥmad related it through ʿAbd al-Raḥmān b. al-Ḥārith from her as above.

Al-Bayhaqī stated, "*The ḥāfiẓ* Abū ʿAbd Allāh related to us, quoting Abū Saʿīd b. Abū ʿAmr, both saying, 'Abū al-ʿAbbās al-Aṣamm related to us, quoting Aḥmad b. ʿAbd al-Jabbār and Yūnus b. Bukayr, from Hishām b. ʿUrwa, from his father, from ʿAʾisha, who said, "The Messenger of God (ṢAAS) came to Medina and it was the most pestilential place on God's earth. It was just two basin-shaped valleys wet with *najl*, brackish water."'"

Hishām stated, "Its pestilential nature was well known before Islam. When the valley was disease-ridden and a man were to arrive there, he would be told to neigh like a donkey; if he did this the valley's pestilence would not harm him. A poet once said, coming to Medina, "By my life, if I, fearing death, were to emit a donkey's neighing, I would be expressing my anxiety."

Al-Bukhārī related from a *ḥadīth* of Mūsā b.ʿUqba, from Sālim, from his father, that the Prophet (ṢAAS) said, "I saw what seemed like a black woman, her head in disarray, emerge from Medina and travel to Mahyaʿa, which is al-Juḥfa. I interpreted from this that Medina's pestilence had been transformed to Mahyaʿa, that is, to al-Juḥfa."

This wording is from al-Bukhārī. Muslim did not give this tradition. Al-Tirmidhī did relate it and pronounced it authentic, while al-Nasāʾī and Ibn Māja gave it from a *ḥadīth* of Mūsā b. ʿUqba.

Ḥammād b. Zayd related, from Hishām b. ʿUrwa, from ʿĀʾisha, who said, "When the Messenger of God (ṢAAS) arrived at Medina the pestilence was active." She related the tradition in full as above but gave the final words of the Messenger of God as "remove its fever to al-Juḥfa!"

Hishām stated, "A child born in al-Juḥfa never reached adolescence without being struck down by the fever."

Al-Bayhaqī related this in the *Dalāʾil al-Nubuwwah* (*Signs of the Prophethood*).

Yūnus stated, from Ibn Isḥāq, "When the Messenger of God (ṢAAS) arrived in Medina, the pestilence was active. All his Companions became seriously stricken with that. But God kept it away from his Prophet (ṢAAS)."

It is established in both *ṣaḥīḥ* collections, from Ibn ʿAbbās, who said, "The Messenger of God (ṢAAS) and his Companions arrived in Mecca flushed and feverish in the year they made the *ʿumrat al-qaḍāʾ*,[45] the 'fulfilment pilgrimage', and the polytheists said, 'There's a group of them arriving who are weakened by the Medina fever.' And so the Messenger of God (ṢAAS) ordered his Companions to jog around the *kaʿba* except between the two corners where they were permitted to walk. And it was only his concern for them that deterred him from making them jog throughout the performance of the ritual."

I observe that the *ʿumrat al-qaḍāʾ* took place in the year 7 AH, in the month of Dhū al-Qaʿda. Either his prayer to God to remove the pestilence elsewhere had been delayed to some time close to this, or that it had been removed but some few traces of it had remained. Or they were still suffering from some remaining effects of a previous affliction. But God knows best.

Ziyād stated, quoting Ibn Isḥāq, "Ibn Shihāb al-Zuhrī related from ʿAbd Allāh b. ʿAmr b. al-ʿĀṣ, that when the Messenger of God (ṢAAS) and his Companions arrived in Medina they became seriously ill from the Medina fever, to the extent that they had to say their prayers seated. However, God kept this affliction from affecting His Prophet (ṢAAS)."

The account states, "And so the Messenger of God (ṢAAS) went out before them while they were praying in this way and told them, 'You should know that

---

45. The name given to the *ʿumra* pilgrimage rites the Muslims performed then at Mecca which had been vacated by its inhabitants by prior agreement for this occasion. The circumstances of this will be detailed by Ibn Kathīr later in this text.

the prayer of someone seated is only half as valuable as that of someone standing.' At this the Muslims, despite their weakness and sickness, exerted themselves to stand, in order to gain grace."

Section: On the establishment of friendship between the Emigrants and the Helpers through the document he had drawn up between them. On the nature of that brotherly relationship he made between them, and on the friendly relations he established with the Jews who were in Medina.

In the city's Jewish quarters at that time there were the Qaynuqāʿ, Naḍīr and Qurayẓa tribes.

According to al-Ṭabarī they had settled in the Ḥijāz before the *anṣār*, the Helpers, in the days of Nebuchadnezar, when he had conquered Jerusalem.

When the Iram flood occurred and people had scattered in all directions, the Aws and the Khazraj tribes had settled in Medina with the Jews. They had established pacts of alliance with these Jews and imitated their ways because of the virtue they saw in them that they had acquired through the prophets.

However, God had bestowed guidance and Islam upon those who had been polytheists, while they, in their envy, pride and wrongheadedness, had failed to follow the truth.

Imām Aḥmad stated, "ʿAffān related to us, quoting Ḥammād b. Salama and ʿĀṣim al-Aḥwal, from Anas b. Mālik, as follows, 'The Messenger of God (ṢAAS) established a pact between the Emigrants and the Helpers in the house of Anas b. Mālik.'"

This was also related by Imām Aḥmad, al-Bukhārī, Muslim and Abū Dāʾūd, through various lines of transmission from ʿĀṣim b. Sulaymān al-Aḥwal, from Anas b. Mālik, who said, "The Messenger of God (ṢAAS) established a pact between Quraysh and the Helpers in my house."

Imām Aḥmad stated, "Naṣr b. Bāb related to us, from Ḥajjāj, he being Ibn Arṭat, who said, 'It was related to us by Surayj from ʿAbbād, from Ḥajjāj, from ʿAmr b. Shuʿayb, from his father and grandfather, to the effect that the Prophet (ṢAAS) wrote up a contract between the Emigrants saying that they would respect one another's strongholds, that they would treat with kindness those in distress and bring peace between the Muslims.'"

Aḥmad stated, "Surayj related to us, quoting ʿAbbād, from Ḥajjāj, from al-Ḥakam, from Qāsim, from Ibn ʿAbbās, much the same account."

Imām Aḥmad is alone in giving this.

The *ṣaḥīḥ* collection of Muslim quotes Jābir as saying, "The Messenger of God (ṢAAS) wrote an "*aqūla*', a blood-wit pact, for each sub-tribe."

Muḥammad b. Isḥāq stated, "The Messenger of God (ṢAAS) wrote a contract between the Emigrants and the Helpers in which he expressed conciliation towards the Jews and made a pact with them, confirming them in their religion and their properties. He stipulated their rights and obligations as follows, 'In the name of God, the Merciful, the Beneficent, this is a document from Muḥammad, the *ummi* (unlettered) Prophet, between the believers and Muslims of Quraysh and Yathrib and their followers, allies and supporters, establishing that they are one nation apart from all others. The Emigrants from Quraysh will maintain their current practice and will honour blood-money contracts between themselves and will treat their weaker members with kindness and justice. The Banū ‘Awf shall maintain their current practice, and honour their former blood-money contracts, each party treating their weaker members with kindness and justice, among all believers.’

"He then made reference to each clan of the Helpers and to the families of each home, mentioning the Banū Sā‘ida, the Banū Jusham, the Banū al-Najjār, the Banū ‘Amr b. ‘Awf and the Banū al-Nabīt.

"He went on to say, ‘The believers shall not leave anyone among them burdened by debts without giving to him in kindness and in paying for him any ransom money or blood-money he owes. A believer will not ally with any freed-man of a second believer against that man. Pious believers act against any of their own who practise evil or seek to bring harm, sin, aggression or corruption among believers. Believers will unite against anyone doing this, even if he be one of their own sons. No believer shall kill any believer for any non-believer. Nor shall he help any non-believer against a believer. God’s protection is all one; the least of them (believers) can offer protection to others. Believers are allies to one another, excluding others.

"‘Whatever Jews follow us shall receive help and equality. They shall not be maltreated nor will help be afforded others against them. Peace for all believers is one; no peace shall be accepted for any one believer to the exclusion of others when the battle is for God’s cause; among them equality and justice must prevail. In every expedition we engage in riders shall take turns on their mounts.

"‘Believers shall avenge one another for blood shed in God’s cause. Believers who are pious are well-guided on the straightest of paths. No polytheist shall be allowed to offer protection for the property or persons of Quraysh nor try to interfere with any believer. Anyone who has clearly aggressed against and caused the death of any believer shall be subject to retaliation for him unless the dead man’s executor can be satisfied. Believers as a whole shall take action against him and no excuse for their not doing so will be acceptable.

"‘It shall not be permissible for any believer who has accepted what is in this document and who believes in God and Judgement Day to give help or shelter to any wrong-doer. Any believer who does this shall be the object of God’s curses and anger on Judgement Day and neither compensation nor excuse will be acceptable from him. Any matter in which you disagree must be referred to God, Almighty and Glorious is He, and to Muhammad (SAAS).

"‘The Jews shall pay expenses along with the Muslims so long as they are allied in warfare. The Jews of the Banū ‘Awf are one nation with the believers; the Jews shall have their religion, the Muslims their own. This applies to their freed-men and to themselves, except for those who commit sins and are unjust. Such persons only harm themselves and their families.

"‘What applies to Banū ‘Awf shall also apply to the Jews of Banū al-Najjār, Banū al-Ḥārith, Banū Sā‘ida, Banū Jusham, Banū al-Aws, Banū Tha‘laba and

Jufna, and Banū al-Shuṭayba. The close associates of the Jews shall be viewed as themselves. None of them shall go to war without Muḥammad's permission. However, he is not (thereby) constrained from taking revenge for injury. Whoever attacks another may do so (to protect) himself and his family, but (act) not unjustly, for God condemns such acts. The Jews shall bear their own expenses, the Muslims theirs. Each must help one another against any who fight those who adopt this document. They must give one another advice and consultation; and do good and avoid evil. A man is not held blameworthy on behalf of his ally. Help must be given to those wronged. The centre of Yathrib shall be a sanctuary for those who agree to this document. One's neighbour shall be treated as oneself, without being harmed or sinned against. No property shall be encroached upon without the permission of its owner.

"'In the case of any dispute or incident occurring between those agreeing to this document, and involving consequences likely to be harmful, the matter must be referred to God and to Muḥammad, the Messenger of God. God acknowledges what is very good and very pious in this document. Quraysh and those who help them shall receive no protection. (Those accepting this document) must help one another against anyone attacking Yathrib. If they are called upon to make peace and do so and keep to it, they will be making peace; if they make a similar demand, then it is up to the Muslims to agree except if the warfare is over the Faith. Each participant shall receive whatever portion is due to him from his own side's winnings.

"'This document will not provide protection for anyone sinful or unjust. Whoever goes to war will be safe; whoever stays in the town will be safe – except for those who have sinned or been unjust. God provides protection for those who are good and pious.'"

Ibn Isḥāq gives it in approximately this form. Abū ʿUbayd al-Qāsim b. Salām, God bless him, criticized this *ḥadīth* at length in his *Kitab al-Gharīb* (*Book of the Strange*) and elsewhere.

Section: On the establishment by the Messenger of God (ṢAAS) of a pact of brotherhood between the Emigrants and the Helpers so that they would be friends.

As the Almighty stated, "And those who made their abode in the town and in the faith before them do love those who emigrated to them. They do not find in their hearts a need for what they are given, and prefer (them) even before themselves, despite their own poverty. Those who are saved from the meanness of themselves shall be successful" (*sūrat al-Ḥashr*; LIX, v.9). And He also said, "as for those with whom you made agreements, give them their due; God is witness to all things" (*sūrat al-Nisāʾ*; IV, v.33).

Al-Bukhārī stated, "Al-Ṣalt b. Muḥammad related to us, quoting Abū Usāma, from Idrīs, from Ṭalḥa b. Muṣarrif, from Saʿīd b. Jubayr, that Ibn ʿAbbās, commenting on the following verse, 'And to everyone we have appointed heirs' (*sūrat al-Nisāʾ*; IV, v.33), said 'The heirs of "those with whom you made agreements" were the Emigrants who settled in Medina. They inherited from the Helpers (and vice versa) instead of from their own family, based on the brotherhood pact established between them by the Prophet (ṢAAS). However, when the verse "and to everyone we have appointed agents" was revealed, this practice was abrogated. Then He stated that the following verse, "as for those with whom you have made agreements, give them their due", henceforth referred to help, hospitality and advice. Inheritance was thus stopped and instead, testamentary endowment was made for such persons.'"

Imām Aḥmad stated, "The following was quoted from Sufyān, 'I heard 'Āṣim say, on the authority of Anas, "The Prophet (ṢAAS) made a pact between the Emigrants and the Helpers in our home."' Sufyān commented, "He seems to be saying that he established brotherhood between them."

Muḥammad b. Isḥāq stated, "The Messenger of God (ṢAAS) established brotherhood between his fellow Emigrants and the Helpers, and said, from what I have heard – and God forbid our attributing to him what he did not say – he said, 'Become brothers in God's cause, each taking a brother for himself.'

"He then took the hand of 'Alī b. Abū Ṭālib and said, 'This is my brother.'

"The Messenger of God (ṢAAS), lord of the prophets, the leader of the pious, the Messenger of the Lord of the worlds, and the most important and peerless of men, and 'Alī b. Abū Ṭālib became brothers.

"Ḥamza b. 'Abd al-Muṭṭalib, lion of God and lion of His Messenger as well as his uncle, and Zayd b. Ḥāritha, the freed-man of the Messenger of God (ṢAAS), became brothers. It was Zayd that Ḥamza appointed his heir at the battle of Uḥud. Ja'far b. Abū Ṭālib Dhū al-Janāḥayn and Mu'ādh b. Jabal became brothers."

Ibn Hishām pointed out that at that time Ja'far was absent in Abyssinia.

Ibn Isḥāq went on: "Abū Bakr and Khārija b. Zayd al-Khazrajī, 'Umar b. al-Khaṭṭāb and 'Itbān b. Mālik, Abū 'Ubayda and Sa'd b. Mu'ādh, 'Abd al-Raḥmān b. 'Awf and Sa'd b. al-Rabī', al-Zubayr b. al-'Awwām and Salāma b. Salāma b. Waqsh, all became brothers. It is also said that al-Zubayr and 'Abd Allāh b. Mas'ūd, 'Uthmān b. 'Affān and Aws b. Thābit b. al-Mundhir al-Najjārī, Ṭalḥa b. 'Ubayd Allāh and Ka'b b. Mālik, Sa'īd b. Zayd and Ubayy b. Ka'b, Muṣ'ab b. 'Umayr and Abū Ayyūb, Abū Ḥudhayfa b. 'Utba and 'Abbād b. Bishr, 'Ammār and Ḥudhayfa b. al-Yamān al-'Absī, the ally of 'Abd al-Ashhal, all became brothers. It is also said, however, that 'Ammār and Thābit b. Qays b. Shammās became brothers."

I observe that this chain of authorities comes through two lines.

He went on, "Abū Dharr Barīr b. Junāda and al-Mundhir b. 'Amr, known as 'he who hurried on to death', Ḥāṭib b. Abū Balta'a and 'Uwaym b. Sā'ida, Salmān and Abū al-Dardā', Bilāl and Abū Ruwayḥa 'Abd Allāh b. 'Abd al-Raḥmān al-Khath'amī, one of the Faza' – all these became brothers."

He continued, "These are the men who were named to us from among his Companions between whom the Messenger of God (ṢAAS) established pacts of brotherhood. May God be pleased with them all."

I observe that there is controversy in some of what Ibn Isḥāq stated.

Regarding the brotherhood established between the Prophet and ʿAlī, some scholars deny this and maintain it to be untrue. Their argument is that this brotherhood was only established to bring about closer feelings and ties between these individuals. There was no sense, therefore, in declaring a brotherly state between the Prophet (ṢAAS) and one of (his) own, nor between two men both of whom were Emigrants, as was the case, according to him, between Ḥamza and Zayd b. Ḥāritha.

Unless the Prophet (ṢAAS) did not wish to place the interests of ʿAlī in the hands of anyone but himself. For he was someone for whom the Messenger of God (ṢAAS) had made contributions from his youth on, during the lifetime of Abū Ṭālib, as has been told above from Mujāhid and others.

That might also be the case with Ḥamza, who had looked after the interests of their freed-man Zayd b. Ḥāritha, and so established a brotherhood pact with him. But God knows best.

The same applies to Ibn Isḥāq's reference to the brotherhood between Jaʿfar and Muʿādh b. Jabal, which is subject to dispute, as ʿAbd al-Malik b. Hishām observed. For Jaʿfar b. Abū Ṭālib only arrived at the beginning of 7 AH at the time of the battle of Khaybar, as will be told hereafter. How, therefore, could there have been a tie of brotherhood made between him and Muʿādh b. Jabal immediately following the arrival of the Messenger of God (ṢAAS) in Medina? Unless, of course, the arrangement was that this would go into effect whenever he did arrive.

ʿIbn Isḥāq's statement, "Abū ʿUbayda and Saʿd b. Muʿādh became brothers," contradicts what Imām Aḥmad stated, namely, "It was related to us by ʿAbd al-Ṣamad, quoting Ḥammād, quoting Thābit, from Anas b. Mālik, that the Messenger of God (ṢAAS) established a brotherhood pact between Abū ʿUbayda b. al-Jarrāḥ and Abū Ṭalḥa."

Muslim related this also, being the only one to relate this from Ḥajjāj b. al-Shāʿir, from ʿAbd al-Ṣamad b. ʿAbd al-Wārith.

This seems more reliable than what Ibn Isḥāq recounted, of such a pact between Abū ʿUbayda and Saʿd b. Muʿādh. But God knows best.

Al-Bukhārī's text reads as follows, *"Chapter on how the Prophet (ṢAAS), established brotherhood between his Companions. ʿAbd al-Raḥmān b. ʿAwf stated, "The Prophet (ṢAAS), established a bond of brotherhood between myself and Saʿd b. al-Rabīʿ when we came to Medina."' Abū Juḥayfa stated, "The Prophet (ṢAAS) established brotherhood between Salmān the Persian and Abū al-Dardāʾ. God be pleased with him."*

Muḥammad b. Yūsuf related to us, quoting Sufyān, from Ḥumayd, from Anas, who said, "ʿAbd al-Raḥmān b. ʿAwf arrived and the Prophet (ṢAAS) established brotherhood between him and Saʿd b. al-Rabīʿ, the Helper. The latter suggested that he share his family and his property with him. ʿAbd al-Raḥmān replied, 'God bless you in both your family and your wealth. Show me the way to the market.'

There he made some profit from cottage cheese and fat. The Prophet (ṢAAS) saw him a few days later and he looked stained with yellow upon him. The Prophet (ṢAAS) asked him, 'What's the matter with you, ᶜAbd al-Raḥmān?' He replied, 'I married a woman from among the Helpers.' 'What did you give her as dowry?' he asked. 'The weight of 5 dirhams worth of gold,' he replied. The Prophet (ṢAAS) responded, 'Well, have a feast, if only with a sheep!'"

This is the sole account of this from this line. Al-Bukhārī related this also in other places as did Muslim from various lines, from Ḥumayd.

Imām Aḥmad stated, "ᶜAffān related to us, quoting Ḥammād, Thābit and Ḥamīd, from Anas, that ᶜAbd al-Raḥmān b. ᶜAwf came to Medina and the Messenger of God (ṢAAS) established a pact of brotherhood between him and Saᶜd b. al-Rabīᶜ, the Helper. Saᶜd said to him, 'Now brother, I'm the wealthiest man in Medina. Take a share that appeals to you. I have two wives. Look and see which of them you prefer and I'll divorce her!'

"ᶜAbd al-Raḥmān replied, 'May God bless you in your family and in your wealth. Show me the way to the market.' They did so and he engaged in buying and selling and made a profit. He ended up by bringing back some cottage cheese and cooking fat. Some time thereafter the Messenger of God (ṢAAS) (saw him) with traces of saffron upon him and asked him, 'What's the matter with you?' He replied, 'O Messenger of God, I married a woman.' 'What did you give her in dowry?' he asked. 'The weight of 5 dirhams worth of gold,' he replied. 'Well,' he commented, 'have a feast, if only with a sheep!'

"ᶜAbd al-Raḥmān observed, 'I was in such a state that if I had lifted a single rock I would have hoped to find gold and silver.'"

The additional comment given here by al-Bukhārī from ᶜAbd al-Raḥmān seems strange, for the only source given for it was Anas. Unless, of course, Anas was told this by ᶜAbd al-Raḥmān. God knows best.

Imām Aḥmad stated, "Yazīd related to us, that Ḥumayd informed him, from Anas, as follows, 'The Emigrants said, "O Messenger of God, we've never been to people who are better prepared to give help in hopes of so little or more willing to give from so much. They have spared us such difficulty and shared such comfort with us we're afraid they're the only ones getting rewards." He replied, "No, there's all the great praise you've given them, and you have also prayed to God for them."'"

The line of transmission of this *ḥadīth* is two-thirds in accord with the criteria for both *ṣaḥīḥ* collections. None of the authors of the six canonical books of traditions give this particular line. It is established in the *ṣaḥīḥ* collections along a different path.

Al-Bukhārī stated, "Al-Ḥakam b. Nāfiᶜ informed us, quoting Shuᶜayb, quoting Abū al-Zinād, from al-Aᶜraj, from Abū Hurayra, who said, 'The Helpers said, "Divide up the palm trees between us and our brothers." "No," he replied. They said, "You recompense us with your hard work, and we will have you share in the fruits." "We hear and obey," they responded.'"

He is alone in giving this *hadīth*.

ʿAbd al-Raḥmān b. Zayd b. Aslam said, "The Messenger of God (ṢAAS) told the Helpers, 'Your brothers have left behind their wealth and their children and have come forth to you.' They commented, 'Our property is to be divided up between us then.' The Messenger of God (ṢAAS) asked, 'Well, is there some alternative?' 'What could there be, O Messenger of God?' they asked. He replied, 'These are people who don't mind hard work; provide some for them and share the fruits.' 'We will,' they agreed."

We have previously mentioned the reports and references made concerning the virtues of the Helpers and their fine qualities confirmed by God's words, "And those who made their abode in the town and in the faith before them" (*sūrat al-Hashr*; LIX, v.9).

Chapter: On the death of Abū Umāma Asʿad b. Zurāra.

He was Ibn ʿAdas b. ʿUbayd b. Thaʿlaba b. Ghanm b. Mālik b. al-Najjār, one of the 12 leaders on the night of the pledge made by his people the Banū al-Najjār at al-ʿAqaba. He was present at all 3 meetings there, and was the first to make a verbal pledge of his allegiance to the Messenger of God (ṢAAS) at the second. He was a young man and was the first to bring the men together in Medina, at Naqīʿ al-Khaḍamāt in the plain of the Nabīt. This has been discussed above.

Ibn Isḥāq stated, "Abū Umāma Asʿad b. Zurāra died in these months, while the mosque was being built. He died from diptheria or from coughing."

Ibn Jarīr stated in his history, "Muḥammad b. ʿAbd al-Aʿlā informed us, Yazīd b. Zurayʿ related to us, from Maʿmar, from al-Zuhrī, from Anas, that the Messenger of God (ṢAAS) cauterized Asʿad b. Zurāra in the tongue."

The men in this chain of authorities are considered reliable.

Ibn Isḥāq stated, "ʿAbd Allāh b. Abū Bakr b. Muḥammad b. ʿAmr b. Ḥazm related to me, from Yaḥyā b. ʿAbd Allāh b. ʿAbd al-Raḥmān b. Asʿad b. Zurāra, who said, 'The Messenger of God (ṢAAS) stated, "The death of Abū Umāma is a great pity with respect to the Jews and the Arab hypocrites. They will say, 'If he were a prophet, his companion would not have died.' But I have no power from God over this for myself or for my friends."'"

This means that he has to have been the first man to die after the arrival in Medina of the Prophet (ṢAAS).

Abū al-Ḥasan b. al-Athīr has claimed in *al-Ghāba* (*The Jungle*) that he died in the month of Shawwāl, seven months following the arrival of the Messenger of God (ṢAAS) in Medina. But God knows best.

Muḥammad Ibn Isḥāq related, from ʿĀṣim b. ʿUmar b. Qatāda, that the Banū al-Najjār asked the Messenger of God (ṢAAS) to appoint a leader for them to succeed Abū Umāma Asʿad b. Zurāra. He replied, "You are my uncles and I am here among you; I will be your leader." He disliked the idea of singling out any one of them above the others. It was a credit to the Banū al-Najjār that they took pride among their peers in having the Messenger of God (ṢAAS) as their leader.

Ibn al-Athīr observed, "This fact refutes the statements of Abū Nu'aym and Ibn Mundah to the effect that As'ad b. Zurāra was leader of the Banū Sā'ida; in fact he led the Banū al-Najjār."

Ibn al-Athīr was correct in saying this.

Abū Ja'far b. Jarīr stated in his history work, "The first Muslim who died after the arrival of the Messenger of God (ṢAAS) in Medina was, so they say, the owner of his house, Kulthūm b. al-Hadm. He died soon after his arrival. The next to die was As'ad b. Zurāra, whose death was that same year of his arrival and before the construction of the mosque was completed. He died of either diptheria or from coughing."

I observe here that the full name of this man was Kulthūm b. al-Hadm b. Imru' al-Qays b. al-Ḥārith b. Zayd b. 'Ubayd b. Zayd b. Mālik b. 'Awf b. 'Amr b. 'Awf b. Mālik b. al-Aws, the Helper and member of the Aws tribe. Of the family of 'Amr b. 'Awf, he was a very elderly sheikh who had accepted Islam before the arrival of the Messenger of God (ṢAAS) in Medina. When the Messenger of God (ṢAAS) came there he stayed at night in Qubā' in Kulthūm's house, and then during the day would talk with his Companions in the home of Sa'd b. al-Rabī', God be pleased with them both, until he moved to the home of the Banū al-Najjār, as related above.

Ibn al-Athīr stated, "It has been said that he was the first Muslim to die following the arrival of the Messenger of God (ṢAAS), and that the death of As'ad b. Zurāra followed his. Al-Ṭabarī stated this."

Chapter: On the birth of 'Abd Allāh b. al-Zubayr in the month of Shawwāl in the year when the emigration occurred.

The first birth to the Emigrants in the Islamic era was 'Abd Allāh b. al-Zubayr. Similarly, al-Nu'mān b. Bashīr was the first child born to the Helpers after the emigration. God be pleased with them both.

Some claim that Ibn al-Zubayr was born 20 months after the emigration. Abū al-Aswad said this. Al-Wāqidī related this from Muḥammad b. Yaḥyā b. Sahl b. Abū Ḥathma, from his father, from his grandfather.

They claim that al-Nu'mān was born 6 months before al-Zubayr, some 14 months after the emigration.

The truth is as we have said above. Al-Bukhārī stated, "Zakariyyā' b. Yaḥyā related to us, quoting Abū Usāma, from Hishām b. 'Urwa, from his father, from Asmā', who said, regarding her pregnancy with 'Abd Allāh b. al-Zubayr, "When I emigrated, I was at term. When I came to Medina I stayed in Qubā' and gave birth to him there. Then I took him to the Messenger of God (ṢAAS) and placed him in his lap. He then called for a date, which he masticated then spat into his mouth. And so the first thing that entered the baby's stomach was the saliva of the Messenger of God (ṢAAS). He then gave him a date to chew on, prayed for him and blessed him. He was the first baby born in Islam." This account was followed by one of Khālid b. Makhlad, from ʿAlī b. Mushir, from Hishām, from his father, from Asmāʾ, to the effect that she was pregnant when she emigrated to the Prophet (ṢAAS).

Qutayba related to us, from Abū Usāma, from Hishām b. ʿUrwa, from his father, from ʿĀʾisha, who said, "The first child born in Islam was ʿAbd Allāh b. al-Zubayr. They brought him to the Prophet (ṢAAS) and he took a date which he chewed, then placed in the baby's mouth. And so the first food that entered his stomach was the saliva of the Prophet (ṢAAS)."

This refutes al-Wāqidī and others, because he reported that the Prophet (ṢAAS) sent Zayd b. Ḥāritha and Abū Rāfiʿ back to Mecca with ʿAbd Allāh b. ʿUrayqiṭ to bring his and Abū Bakr's children. They brought them back right after the emigration of the Prophet (ṢAAS). Asmāʾ was pregnant and near term, that is almost ready to deliver her child. When she did so the Muslims let out great shouts of "God is Most Great" in their joy at the birth because it had come to their attention that the Jews had used magic against them so that they would not have children following their emigration. And so God had refuted what the Jews were claiming.

DIVISION

The Messenger of God (ṢAAS) consummated his marriage with ʿĀʾisha in the month of Shawwāl that year.

Imām Aḥmad stated, "Wakīʿ related to me, quoting Sufyān, from Ismāʿīl b. Umayya, from ʿAbd Allāh b. ʿUrwa, from his father, from ʿĀʾisha, who said, 'The Messenger of God (ṢAAS) made a marriage contract with me in (the month of) Shawwāl and consummated the marriage in Shawwāl; and which of his wives did he favour more than myself?'"

ʿĀʾisha used to prefer to have her women marry in Shawwāl.

Muslim, al-Tirmidhī, al-Nasāʾī, and Ibn Māja related this on various paths from al-Thawrī. Al-Tirmidhī considered it *hasan ṣaḥīḥ*,[46] "good and authentic"; we know of it only from Sufyān al-Thawrī.

According to this the marriage of the Messenger of God (ṢAAS) to ʿĀʾisha took place in the seventh or eighth month after the emigration. Both statements were related by Ibn Jarīr, who commented earlier, in his treatment of his marriage with Sawda, on how he had married ʿĀʾisha after they had arrived in Medina, and that his marriage was at al-Sunḥ and during the daytime. This is in contrast to the normal practice of people today. In his marrying her in Shawwāl there is a refutation of those who express disfavour for marriage occurring between the two

---

46. The term designates a *hadith* that is deemed more clearly authentic than one designated as *hasan*, but less so than one considered *ṣaḥīḥ*.

feasts, out of fear of the couple's later separation. There is nothing to this, as is shown by what ʿĀʾisha said in reply to those people who imagined this for that time, that is, she said, "He made the marriage contract with me in Shawwāl and consummated the marriage in Shawwāl; and which of his wives did he favour more than myself?"

This shows that she understood from him that she was the wife he favoured most. And this belief of hers is shown to have been correct by various clear proofs, if only by that definite statement given in the *ṣaḥīḥ* collection of al-Bukhārī from ʿAmr b. al-ʿĀṣ which states, "I said, O Messenger of God, which person do you most favour?" He replied, "ʿĀʾisha." I then asked, "And which man?" "Her father," he replied.

DIVISION

Ibn Jarīr stated, "That same year, the first year of the hegira, the length of the *ṣalāt al-ḥaḍar*, the prayer while at home, was increased by two *rakʿāt*,[47] prayer cycles, or so it is said. Previously both the prayer at home and while travelling had been two *rakʿāt*. This came about after the arrival of the Messenger of God (ṢAAS) on the 12th of Rabīʿ al-Ākhir."

He said, "Al-Wāqidī maintained that there was no dispute among the people of Ḥijāz on this subject."

I observe that previously I have given the *hadīth* related by al-Bukhārī through Maʿmar, from al-Zuhrī, from ʿUrwa, from ʿĀʾisha, who said, "When first made obligatory, prayer was prescribed as needing two *rakʿāt*. This was affirmed for prayer while travelling, but it was increased for prayer while at home."

This was also related through al-Shaʿbī back to Masrūq.

Al-Bayhaqī related, from al-Ḥasan al-Baṣrī, that when the prayer at home was first made obligatory, it was established as four *rakʿāt*. But God knows best.

We discussed this in the exegesis of *sūrat al-Nisāʾ*, with regards to the words of the Almighty, "And when you travel over the earth, there is no blame on you if you shorten the prayer" (*sūrat al-Nisāʾ*; IV, v.101).

Chapter: On the call to prayer and its legitimacy upon the arrival of the Prophet (ṢAAS) in Medina.

Ibn Isḥāq stated, "When the Messenger of God (ṢAAS) was secure in Medina, his emigrant brothers gathered around him and the Helpers were united, Islam became firmly established. Prayer was instituted and the *zakāt*, the alms tax, and fasting were made obligatory. Punishments were prescribed, and those matters that were made permissible or forbidden were determined. Islam took firm hold there among them.

---

47. A *rakʿa* is an entire cycle of prayer, consisting of standing, bowing once and prostrating twice.

It was this community of Helpers to whom God made reference in the words, "And those who made their abode in the town and in the faith" (*sūrat al-Ḥashr*; LIX, v.9).

When the Messenger of God (ṢAAS) first came to Medina, the people would gather with him for prayer at the appointed times without any summons to them. The Messenger of God (ṢAAS) then wanted to have a horn blown like that the Jews use to call their people to prayer. But he grew to dislike this and ordered a hand bell be used. One was made to be struck to bring the Muslims to the prayer.

While this was the practice ʿAbd Allāh b. Zayd b. Thaʿlaba b. ʿAbd Rabbihī, the brother of Ibn al-Ḥārith b. al-Khazraj, saw a vision and came to the Messenger of God (ṢAAS) and said, "O Messenger of God, last night I had a vision. I saw a man pass me by who was wearing two green garments and he carried a bell in his hand. I asked him, 'Will you sell me that bell?' He responded, 'What will you do with it?' I replied, 'We'll use it to summon people to prayer.' He asked, 'Shall I tell you a better way?' 'What would that be?' I asked. He told me, 'You should call out, "Allāhu Akbar! Allāhu Akbar! Allāhu Akbar! (God is Most Great) I bear witness that there is no god but God. I bear witness that Muḥammad is the Messenger of God! I bear witness that Muḥammad is the Messenger of God! Come to prayer! Come to prayer! Come to salvation! Come to salvation! Allāhu Akbar! Allāhu Akbar! There is no god but God!"'

"Having been told this, the Messenger of God (ṢAAS) said, 'These are – if God wills it – visions of truth. Stand with Bilāl and deliver them to him so that he can use them to announce the call to prayer; he has a stronger voice than you.'

"When Bilāl made the call to prayer using these words ʿUmar b. al-Khaṭṭāb heard him while in his house and came out to the Messenger of God (ṢAAS) dragging his cloak behind him and saying, 'O Prophet of God, I swear by Him who sent you with the truth that I saw the same vision!'

"'All praise be to God!' exclaimed the Messenger of God (ṢAAS)."

Ibn Isḥāq went on, "Muḥammad b. Ibrāhīm b. al-Ḥārith related this *ḥadīth* to me, from Muḥammad b. ʿAbd Allāh Zayd b. Thaʿlaba b. ʿAbd Rabbihī, from his father."

Abū Dāʾūd, al-Tirmidhī, Ibn Māja and Ibn Khuzayma all related this *ḥadīth* through Muḥammad b. Isḥāq. Al-Tirmidhī, Ibn Khuzayma and others all deemed it authentic.

According to Abū Dāʾūd he (the vision) also taught him (ʿAbd Allāh b. Zayd) the *iqāma*,[48] saying, "Then, to begin the prayer, you say, 'God is Great! God is Great! I bear witness that there is no god but God! I bear witness that Muḥammad is the Messenger of God! Come to prayer! Come to salvation! The prayer has begun! The prayer has begun! God is Great! God is Great! There is no god but God!'"

Ibn Māja related this *ḥadīth* from Abū ʿUbayd Muḥammad b. ʿUbayd b. Maymūn from Muḥammad b. Salama al-Ḥarrānī from Ibn Isḥāq, as stated above.

---

48. The second call to prayer, indicating its commencement.

He then stated, "Abū ʿUbayd said, ʿAbū Bakr al-Ḥakamī informed me that ʿAbd Allāh b. Zayd, the Helper, spoke the following verse on this:

'Praise be to God, the Sublime, the Revered, great
praise for the call to prayer,
   For there having come to me the herald from God; honour
him as a herald to me!
   For three nights he dedicated thus, and each time he
came to me he brought me greater honour!'"

I observe that this poetry is strange for it implies that ʿAbd Allāh b. Zayd saw the vision for three nights before he informed the Messenger of God (ṢAAS).

The Imām Aḥmad related this from a *ḥadīth* of Muḥammad b. Isḥāq. And he stated, "Al-Zuhrī related from Saʿīd b. al-Musayyab, from ʿAbd Allāh b. Zayd, approximately the same account as given by Ibn Isḥāq from Muḥammad b. Ibrāhīm al-Taymī, but that account did not include the verses."

Ibn Māja stated, "Muḥammad b. Khālid b. ʿAbd Allāh al-Wāsiṭī related to us, quoting his father, from ʿAbd al-Raḥmān b. Isḥāq, from al-Zuhrī, from Sālim, from his father, to the effect that the Messenger of God (ṢAAS) asked the advice of the community on what to use to commence the prayer. They mentioned the horn, but he disliked this because of its use by the Jews. They then referred to the bell, but he disliked this because of its use by the Christians. That night a vision of the call to prayer came to a helper named ʿAbd Allāh b. Zayd and to ʿUmar b. al-Khaṭṭāb. The Helper made his way at night to the Messenger of God (ṢAAS) who gave orders to Bilāl, who made the call to prayer using it."

Al-Zuhrī stated, "Bilāl made an addition in the morning call to prayer, namely twice saying the words 'prayer is better than sleep'. The Messenger of God (ṢAAS) agreed to this. ʿUmar told him, 'O Messenger of God, I saw the same vision as he did but he preceded me.'"

Material relating to this section will be given in the chapter on the call to prayer in the large work *al-Aḥkām* (*The Statutes*). If God Almighty wills it, and in Him is our trust.

In a *ḥadīth* given by al-Suhaylī with the following line of authority through al-Bazzār, Muḥammad b. ʿUthmān b. Makhlid related, quoting his father, from Ziyād b. al-Mundhir, from Muḥammad b. ʿAlī b. al-Ḥusayn, from his father, from his grandfather, from ʿAlī b. Abū Ṭālib, who made reference to the *ḥadīth* respecting the *isrāʾ*, the ascent to heaven, as follows, "And an angel emerged from behind the screen and he made the call to prayer using this call. Each time he said a word, God Almighty verified it. Then the angel took the hand of Muḥammad (ṢAAS) and brought him forward. He then led the family of heaven, who included Adam and Noah, in the prayer." Al-Suhaylī then said, "You may view this *ḥadīth* as authentic for the support it gives and resemblance it has to the *ḥadīth* relating to the ascent to heaven."

But this *ḥadīth* is not, as al-Suhaylī maintained, authentic. In fact it is unacceptable. Ziyād b. al-Mundhir Abū al-Jārūd is he to whom is attributed the

"*Jārūdiyya* sect",[49] he being among those accused. Moreover, if this had been what the Messenger of God (ṢAAS) had heard on the night of his ascent to heaven, he would have ordered it to be used in the call to prayer immediately following the emigration. But God knows best.

Ibn Hishām stated that Ibn Jurayj quoted ʿAṭāʾ as having said, "I heard ʿUbayd b. ʿUmayr say, 'The Prophet (ṢAAS) had discussed with his Companions the use of a bell to summon people to prayer. While ʿUmar b. al-Khaṭṭāb was planning to buy two pieces of wood for the bell, he had a vision while he slept and was told, "Do not make a bell; instead call people to prayer."

"'ʿUmar went to the Prophet (ṢAAS) to tell him what he had seen. The Prophet had himself received revelation of that. ʿUmar was consequently very surprised to hear Bilāl make the call to prayer. The Messenger of God (ṢAAS) said to him, when he (ʿUmar) told him of his experience, "Revelation of this preceded you!"'"

This shows that the revelation had come in confirmation of what ʿAbd Allāh b. Zayd b. ʿAbd Rabbihī had seen in the vision or so some authorities state. But God Almighty knows best.

Ibn Isḥāq stated, "Muḥammad b. Jaʿfar b. al-Zubayr related to me, from ʿUrwa b. al-Zubayr, that a woman of the Banū al-Najjār told him, 'My house was one of the tallest around the mosque. Bilāl would make the call to prayer on top of it early each morning. He would come just before dawn and sit above the house waiting for daybreak. When he saw it he would stretch out and say, "O God, I praise You and seek Your help for Quraysh to adopt Your religion."' She concluded, 'And then he would make the call to prayer. I never knew him to miss one night.'"

That is, to miss saying those words.

Abū Dāʾūd was the only other to relate this.

Chapter: On the expedition of Ḥamza b. ʿAbd al-Muṭṭalib, may God be pleased with him.

Ibn Jarīr stated, "Al-Wāqidī claimed that in the month of Ramaḍān of that year the Messenger of God (ṢAAS) appointed Ḥamza b. ʿAbd al-Muṭṭalib over 30 of the Emigrants, having presented him with a white standard, to interfere with Quraysh caravans. Al-Wāqidī states that Ḥamza confronted Abū Jahl at the head of 300 Quraysh men, but that Majdī b. ʿAmr intervened between them, and so they did not engage in battle.

"He also said that it was Abū Marthad al-Ghanawī who carried the flag for Ḥamza."

Chapter: On the expedition of ʿUbayda b. al-Ḥārith b. ʿAbd al-Muṭṭalib.

Ibn Jarīr stated, "Al-Wāqidī also claimed that the Prophet (ṢAAS) in Shawwāl, at the beginning of the eighth month of that year, entrusted a white banner to ʿUbayda b. al-Ḥārith and ordered him to proceed into the Rābigh valley.

49. A denomination of the Zaydiyya Shīʿa founded by him and known by his name.

"His flag was carried by Misṭah b. Uthātha. He reached Thaniyyāt al-Murra, not far from al-Juḥfa, in the company of 60 Emigrants, there being no Helpers present. They met up with the polytheists at a well called Aḥyā'. They shot arrows at one another, but did not engage in sword play."

Al-Wāqidī stated, "The polytheists were 200 in number and were led by Abū Sufyān Ṣakhr b. Ḥarb. This is what we believed to be well established, though it is also said that they were led by Mikraz b. Ḥafṣ.

DIVISION

Al-Wāqidī stated, "In that same first year, in Dhū al-Qaʿda, the Messenger of God (ṢAAS) presented a white banner to Saʿd b. Abū Waqqāṣ and sent him to al-Kharrār; the flag was carried by al-Miqdād b. al-Aswad.

"Abū Bakr b. Ismāʿīl related to me, from his father, from ʿĀmir b. Saʿd, from his father, who said, 'I left with 20 men, by foot' – or he said 'with 21 men'. 'We would hide by day and travel by night. We got to al-Kharrār on the morning of the fifth. The Messenger of God (ṢAAS) had instructed me to go no further than al-Kharrār. The caravan had preceded me there by a day.'"

Al-Wāqidī stated, "The caravan consisted of 60; all those with Saʿd were Emigrants."

Abū Jaʿfar b. Jarīr stated, "It was the view of Ibn Isḥāq that these three expeditions mentioned by al-Wāqidī all occurred in the second year of the hegira."

I observe that the statements attributed to Ibn Isḥāq by Abū Jaʿfar are not seen as authentic by any who contemplates them, as we will show early in our work on the military expeditions in materials relating to the second year of the hegira. That work will follow the present one, if God wills it.

It is likely that what he means is that these expeditions occurred in the first year. We will give more details and comments on them when we get to them, if God Almighty wills it.

Al-Wāqidī gives full information and a well-organized historical account. He is one of the great Imams of this field of study. He is trustworthy and writes at length. We commented on what is both reliable and unreliable from him in our projected work *al-Takmīl fī Maʿrifat al-Thiqāt wa al-Duʿafāʾ wa al-Majāhīl* (*Full Information on those Authorities who are Trustworthy, Unreliable or Ignorant*). All praise and credit are due to God.

DIVISION

Those born in that blessed year, the first of the hegira, included ʿAbd Allāh b. al-Zubayr. He was the first to be born in Islam following the emigration, as al-Bukhārī related from his mother Asmāʾ and his aunt ʿĀʾisha, mother of the believers, both daughters of Abū Bakr, "the Trusting"; may God be pleased with both women.

There are those who say that al-Nu'mān b. Bashīr was born six months prior to him. According to that, Ibn al-Zubayr would have been the first child born to Emigrants following the emigration.

Some people suggest that they were both born in the second year of the hegira.

The former is obviously correct, as we have shown above. And all credit be to God. We will make reference to this second statement, if God Almighty wills it, in dealing with the end of that second year.

Ibn Jarīr stated, "It has been said that al-Mukhtār b. Abū 'Ubayd and Ziyād b. Sumayya were born in that first year. But God knows best."

Among the Companions who died that first year were Kulthūm b. al-Hadm al-Awsī, in whose home the Messenger of God (ṢAAS) stayed in Qubā' prior to his departure to the home of the Banū al-Najjār, as told above. Later that same year Abū Umāma As'ad b. Zurāra, the leader of the Banū al-Najjār, died, while the Messenger of God (ṢAAS) was still building the mosque. This has been related above. May God be pleased with both these deceased men.

Ibn Jarīr stated, "That year, the first of the hegira, Abū 'Uhayha died on his property in Ṭā'if. Also al-Walīd b. al-Mughīra died, as did al-'Āṣ b. Wā'il al-Sahmī in Mecca."

I observe that these men died while still polytheists. They did not accept God, the Almighty and Glorious.

An Account of what happened in the second year of the hegira.

In this year many military exeditions took place, the most important and glorious of these being the great battle of Badr, which occurred in Ramaḍān. It was the battle that God used to make a clear distinction between truth and falsehood, right guidance and error.

Now is the occasion to make mention of the military expeditions and the delegations sent. We therefore state (as follows), and we seek help from God in doing so.

THE BOOK OF MILITARY EXPEDITIONS.

Imām Muḥammad b. Isḥāq b. Yasār stated the following in his work of biography, after giving information about the Jewish rabbis and their declaration of enmity against Islam and the verses making mention of them. Of these men was Ḥuyayy b. Akhṭab and his two brothers, Abū Yāsir and Judayy. Also there were Sallām b. Mishkam, Kināna b. al-Rabī' b. Abū al-Ḥuqayq, Sallām b. Abū al-Ḥuqayq, otherwise known as Abū Rāfi' al-A'war. The latter was a trader of the Ḥijāz and one who was killed by the Companions at Khaybar, as will be shown later. Also, there were 'Amr b. Jaḥḥāsh, Ka'b b. al-Ashraf, he being of Ṭā'ī and of the Banū Nabhān; his mother was of the Banū al-Naḍīr. He was killed by the Companions before Abū Rāfiʿ, as will be shown, along with his two allies al-Ḥajjāj b. ʿUmar and Kardam b. Qays. God curse them all!

These men were from the Banū al-Naḍīr.

From the Banū Thaʿlaba b. al-Fityawn there was ʿAbd Allāh b. Ṣūriyā. There was no man in the Ḥijāz more learned in the Torah than he was.

I would observe here that he is said to have accepted Islam.

And there were Ibn Ṣalūbā and Mukhayrīq, the latter accepting Islam, as will be mentioned later, at the battle of Uḥud; he had been his people's rabbi.

From the Banū Qaynuqāʿ there was Zayd b. al-Laṣīt, Saʿd b. Ḥanīf, Maḥmūd b. Sayḥān, ʿUzayz b. Abū ʿUzayz, ʿAbd Allāh b. Ḍayf, Suwayd b. al-Ḥārith, Rifāʿa b. Qays, Finḥāṣ, Ashyaʿ, Nuʿmān b. Aḍā, Baḥrī b. ʿAmr, Shaʾs b. ʿAdī, Shaʾs b. Qays, Zayd b. al-Ḥārith, Nuʿmān b. ʿAmr, Sukayn b. Abū Sukayn, ʿAdī b. Zayd, Nuʿmān b. Abū Awfā, Abū Anas, Maḥmūd b. Daḥya, Mālik b. Ṣayf, Kaʿb b. Rāshid, ʿĀzir, Rāfiʿ b. Abū Rāfiʿ, Khālid, and Azār b. Abū Azār. The last-mentioned should be named Āzar b. Abū Āzar according to Ibn Hishām. Also there were Rāfiʿ b. Ḥāritha, Rāfiʿ b. Ḥuraymala, Rāfiʿ b. Khārija, Mālik b. ʿAwf, Rifāʿa b. Zayd b. al-Tābūt and ʿAbd Allāh b. Salām.

I observe that the last-mentioned had earlier accepted Islam, God be pleased with him. Ibn Isḥāq stated, "He was their rabbi and most learned man. His name had been al-Ḥusayn, and when he accepted Islam the Messenger of God (ṢAAS) named him ʿAbd Allāh."

Ibn Isḥāq stated, "From the Banū Qurayẓa there were al-Zubayr b. Bāṭā b. Wahb, ʿAzzāl b. Shamwīl, and Kaʿb b. Asad. The last-mentioned was the one who had signed for his tribe the agreement they broke in the year of the *aḥzāb*, the schisms. Also there were Shamwīl b. Zayd, Jabal b. ʿAmr b. Sukayna, al-Naḥḥām b. Zayd, Kardam b. Kaʿb, Wahb b. Zayd, Nāfiʿ b. Abū Nāfiʿ, ʿAdī b. Zayd, al-Ḥārith b. ʿAwf, Kardam b. Zayd, Usāma b. Ḥabīb, Rāfiʿ b. Rumayla, Jabal b. Abū Qushayr and Wahb b. Yahūdhā.

From the Banū Zurayq there was Labīd b. Aʿṣam, who had put a spell on the Messenger of God (ṢAAS).

From the Jews of the Banū Ḥāritha there was Kināna b. Ṣūriyā.

From the Jews of the Banū ʿAmr b. ʿAwf there was Qardam b. ʿAmr.

From the Jews of the Banū al-Najjār there was Silsila b. Barhām."

Ibn Isḥāq stated, "All these men were rabbis and men of evil intent and full of antagonism towards the Messenger of God (ṢAAS) and his Companions, God be pleased with them. They were those who asked the Messenger of God (ṢAAS) many questions in their desire to confuse and to express their obstinacy and disbelief. They were men who made difficulties for Islam and who tried to extinguish it. Exceptions to this were ʿAbd Allāh b. Salām and Mukhayrīq."

Ibn Isḥāq then related the acceptance of Islam by ʿAbd Allāh b. Salām, along with that of his aunt Khālida, as we mentioned above.

He also told of the conversion to Islam by Mukhayriq on the day of the battle of Uhud, details of which will come later. He told his people, it being a Sabbath, "O Jews, you well know that Muhammad has a right to expect your help." They replied, "But today is the Sabbath." He replied, "You shall have no Sabbath!" He then took his weapons and went off to battle. He made a charge upon his people who were staying behind, as follows, "If I should be killed today, then my properties are to go to Muhammad to dispose of as God shows him." He was a very wealthy man.

"He then joined the Messenger of God (SAAS) and fought until he was killed. God be pleased with him."

Ibn Ishaq stated, "The Messenger of God (SAAS) used to say, as I have been told, 'Mukhayriq was the best Jew.'"

DIVISION

Ibn Ishaq then listed the names of those hypocrites from Aws and Khazraj, who joined the Jews antagonistic to Islam.

From Aws there were: Zuwayy b. al-Harith, Julas b. Suwayd b. al-Samit, the Helper. It was about him that the verse was revealed, "They swear by God that they did not speak. But they did speak words of disbelief; they apostatized after accepting Islam" (sūrat al-Tawba or al-Barā'a; IX, v.74). This was because he said, after having withdrawn from the expedition against Tabūk, "If this man speaks the truth, then we are worse than donkeys!"

"The son of al-Julas's wife, a man named 'Umayr b. Sa'd reported this to the Messenger of God (SAAS) but al-Julas denied it, swearing that he had never said that. The verse was therefore revealed concerning him."

Ibn Ishaq went on, "It is claimed that he later truly repented and that he was known for his piety.

"Also there was his brother al-Harith b. Suwayd; it was he who killed al-Mujadhdhar b. Dhiyād al-Balawī and Qays b. Zayd, one of the Banū Dubay'a at the battle of Uhud. Al-Harith had gone to war on the Muslims' side, but he was a hypocrite and when the battle was joined he fought and killed both these men and joined the Quraysh forces."

Ibn Hishām stated, "Al-Mujadhdhar had killed his father Suwayd b. al-Samit in an engagement before the coming of Islam. Al-Harith was taking revenge upon him at the battle of Uhud."

This is what Ibn Hishām said, but according to Ibn Ishaq it was Mu'ādh b. 'Afrā' who killed him in a non-military engagement before the battle of Bu'āth, by shooting him with an arrow.

Ibn Hishām denied that it was al-Harith who killed Qays b. Thābit, on the grounds that Ibn Ishaq did not include the latter among those killed at Uhud.

Ibn Ishaq stated, "The Messenger of God (SAAS) had ordered 'Umar b. al-Khattāb to kill him if he could catch him. Al-Harith, however, sent a message to his brother al-Julās seeking forgiveness so that he could return to his people. And so it was, as I have been informed on the authority of Ibn 'Abbās, that God revealed, "How could God lead a people aright who have apostatized after having believed and given testimony that the Messenger is the truth, and after they had received proofs? God does not guide a people who are unjust" (*sūrat Āl-'Imrān*; III, v.86).

"Also there were Bijād b. 'Uthmān b. 'Āmir and Nabtal b. al-Ḥārith. It was about the latter that the Messenger of God (ṢAAS) said, 'Whoever would like to see Satan, let him look at this man!' He was a very tall, black man with a mass of hair, red eyes and flushed cheeks. He used to listen to what the Messenger of God (ṢAAS) said then report on it to the hypocrites. It was he who said, 'Muḥammad is just ears; he believes what anyone says to him!' God revealed concerning him, 'And among them are those who harm the Prophet by saying that he is ears' (*sūrat al-Tawba* or *al-Barā'a*; IX, v.61).

"And there was Abū Ḥabība b. al-Az'ar. He was one of those who built the mosque at al-Ḍirār. Also there were Tha'laba b. Ḥāṭib and Mu'attib b. Qushayr. It was these two who promised God that if He gave them of His bounty they would believe. They, however, broke their promise upon which the above was revealed . It was Mu'attib who said at the battle of Uḥud, 'If we had any say in it, we'd not be killed here!' A verse was then revealed about him. It was also he who said, at the battle of *al-Aḥzāb*, the 'schisms', 'Muḥammad used to promise us we would enjoy the treasures of Chosroe and Caesar, but we're not safe to go to the toilet!' The verse revealed about him was 'and when the hypocrites, and those in whose breasts is disease, say, "All that God and His Messenger have promised us is mere fancy"'" (*sūrat al-Aḥzāb*; XXXIII, v.12).

Ibn Isḥāq went on, "And there was al-Ḥārith b. Ḥāṭib."

Ibn Hishām commented, "Regarding Mu'attib b. Qushayr, and Tha'laba and al-Ḥārith, the two sons of Ḥāṭib, they were of the Banū Umayya b. Zayd and took part in the battle of Badr. These were not hypocrites, or so I have been told by a scholar whom I trust. Ibn Isḥāq in fact mentioned Tha'laba and al-Ḥārith as being of the Banū Umayya b. Zayd and gave their names as participants in the battle of Badr."

Ibn Isḥāq's account continues, "Also there were 'Abbād b. Ḥunayf, brother of Sahl b. Ḥunayf, and Baḥzaj, who participated in building the mosque, al-Ḍirār. And there were 'Amr b. Khidhām, 'Abd Allāh b. Nabtal, Jāriya b. 'Āmir b. al-'Aṭṭāf and his two sons Yazīd and Mujmi', also involved in the construction of the Ḍirār mosque. Mujmi' was a young man who had collected most parts of the Qur'ān and would pray with the others in prayer there. When the Ḍirār mosque was destroyed, after the Tabūk expedition, as will be explained hereafter, during the reign of 'Umar, the people of Qubā' asked the Caliph whether Mujmi' could lead them in prayer. He refused, saying, 'By God, was he not the Imām of the hypocrites in the Ḍirār mosque?'

"But Mujmiʿ swore by God that he knew nothing about them; and they say that ʿUmar let him go and that he did lead them in prayer.

"And there was Wadīʿa b. Thābit, also one of those who built the Ḍirār mosque. It was he who said, 'But we're only being sociable and having fun.' And a reference was made in the Qurʾān to that.

"And there was Khidām b. Khālid; it was he from whose house the Ḍirār mosque was made."

Ibn Hishām added to the names given by Ibn Isḥāq of the hypocrites of the Banū al-Nabīt b. al-Aws those of Bishr and Rāfiʿ, two sons of Zayd.

Ibn Isḥāq went on, "And there was Mirbaʿ b. Qayẓā; he was blind. It was he who said to the Messenger of God (ṢAAS), who was crossing through his garden on the way to the battle of Uḥud, 'I'll not allow you, even if you are a prophet, to pass through my garden!' And he picked up a handful of dirt and said, 'I swear, if I knew I would not strike anyone but yourself, I'd throw this at you!' The Muslims made for him to kill him, but the Messenger of God (ṢAAS) said, 'Leave him alone. This blind man is blind in his heart as well as in his sight.' Saʿd b. Zayd al-Ashhal, however, had already injured him with his bow.

"And there was Mirbaʿ's brother Aws b. Qayẓā, who made the comment, 'Our houses are exposed.' And so God said, 'They are not exposed; all they want is to take flight' (sūrat al-Aḥzāb; XXXIII, v.13).

"And there was Ḥāṭib b. Umayya b. Rāfiʿ. He was a powerful sheikh who was long set in the ways of pre-Islamic ignorance. He had a son who was among the best of Muslims. His name was Yazīd b. Ḥāṭib, and he was so injured at the battle of Uḥud that his wounds disabled him and he was borne to the home of the Banū Ẓafar.

"'Āṣim b. ʿUmar b. Qatāda related to me that the Muslims there, both men and women, gathered around him while he was dying and began telling him, 'Rejoice in the gardens of paradise, Ibn Ḥāṭib!' His father's hypocrisy then emerged and he began saying, 'Right! Gardens of rue! You have, by God, deluded this poor wretch about himself!"'

Ibn Isḥāq continued, "And there was Bashīr b. Ubayriq Abū Ṭuʿma, the man who stole the two breast-plates. It was of him that God spoke in the words, 'Do not argue for those who are treacherous to themselves' (sūrat al-Nisāʾ; IV, v.107).

"And there was Quzmān, the ally of the Banū Ẓufr, who killed seven men at Uḥud and then when in pain from his own wounds, killed himself, saying, 'I swear, I only fought in defence of my people!' He then died, God damn him!"[50]

---

50. In Ibn Isḥāq's text as translated by Guillaume, *op. cit.* p. 245, Quzmān is reported to kill seven polytheists and to have been well treated by the Muslims when he was wounded. It was, according to that text, when he was congratulated by the Muslims on his valour for the cause that he responded with the words attributed to him here, and that he then killed himself. Presumably he is being damned in this text both for denying that he had been fighting for Islam rather than for his people, and for committing suicide.

Ibn Isḥāq then stated, "There are no men or women of the Banū 'Abd al-Ashhal known as hypocrites; al-Ḍaḥḥāk b. Thābit, however, was charged with hypocrisy and love of the Jews."

All the above persons were from Aws.

Ibn Isḥāq stated, "And of Khazraj there were Rāfi' b. Wadī'a, Zayd b. 'Amr, 'Amr b. Qays, Qays b. 'Amr b. Sahl and al-Jadd b. Qays. It was the last-named who said, 'Give me leave; do not try me.'[51]

"And there was 'Abd Allāh b. Ubayy b. Salūl who was the chief hypocrite and leader of the Aws and Khazraj as well. They had previously agreed, before the coming of Islam, to appoint him their king, but when God led them to Islam before they did so, the accursed fellow was greatly offended and angered. It is he who said, 'If we get back to Medina the strong will definitely drive out of it the weak!'"

Very many verses were revealed about this man and also about Wadī'a, a man of the Banū 'Awf, as about Mālik b. Abū Qawqal, Suwayd and Dā'is who were all of his gang. About them the Almighty revealed, "If they are driven out, they will not go forth with them" (*sūrat al-Ḥashr*, LIX, v.12). This was when they allied secretly with the Banū al-Naḍīr.

DIVISION

Then Ibn Isḥāq made mention of those Jewish rabbis who had accepted Islam as if God-fearing men while in secret they were unbelievers; and they were followed by the worst of the hypocrites among whom were: Sa'd b. Ḥanīf and Zayd b. al-Laṣīt. It was the latter who commented, when the camel of the Messenger of God (ṢAAS) strayed, 'Muḥammad claims that information reaches him from heaven, yet he doesn't know the whereabouts of his camel!' The Messenger of God (ṢAAS) responded, 'I only know what God tells me; and He has guided me towards it. My camel is in this defile, her bridle caught in a tree.' Some of the Muslims then went and found it just so."

Ibn Isḥāq went on: "And there were Nu'mān b. Awfā, 'Uthmān b. Awfā and Rāfi' b. Ḥuraymala. The last-mentioned is the one of whom the Messenger of God (ṢAAS) said, so I have been told, when the man died, 'One of the great hypocrites has died today.'

"Also there was Rifā'a b. Zayd b. al-Tābūt. On the day of his death a great wind arose just as the Messenger of God (ṢAAS) was returning from Tabūk and he said, 'It is blowing due to the death of a great unbeliever.' And when they reached Medina they found that Rifā'a had died that day.

"Also there was Silsila b. Burhām, and Kināna b. Ṣūriyā.

"These, then, are the Jewish hypocrites who had accepted Islam."

Ibn Isḥāq went on, "These hypocrites would attend the mosque and listen to the Muslims' talk, ridiculing and making fun of their religion.

51. Presumably a reference to *sūrat al-Tawba* or *al-Barā'a*; IX, v.49.

"Some of them gathered in the mosque one day and the Messenger of God (ṢAAS) saw them talking among themselves, sitting together and speaking in low voices. The Messenger of God (ṢAAS) ordered that they be removed from the mosque and they were, forcibly.

"Abū Ayyūb went up to ʿAmr b. Qays, one of the Banū al-Najjār, who had been the guardian of their gods in the pre-Islamic era, took him by the foot and pulled him until he had got him outside, while the other man said, 'God damn! Would you evict me, Abū Ayyūb, from the date shed of the Banū Thaʿlaba?'

"Abū Ayyūb then went up to Rāfiʿ b. Wadīʿa al-Najjārī and grabbed him by the cloak, pulled at him hard, slapped his face and threw him out of the mosque, saying, 'Yekh! You dirty hypocrite!'

"ʿUmāra b. Ḥazm seized Zayd b. ʿAmr, who had a long beard, and pulled him along by it until he had evicted him from the mosque. ʿUmāra then clenched his fists and hit him with them hard in his chest, knocking him down. Zayd complained, 'ʿUmāra, you've grazed me!' At this ʿUmāra replied, 'Clear off with you, hypocrite! What God has in store for you is far worse! Don't ever come near the mosque of the Messenger of God (ṢAAS) again!'

"Abū Muḥammad Masʿūd b. Aws b. Zayd b. Aṣram b. Zayd b. Thaʿlaba b. Ghanm b. Mālik b. al-Najjār, who fought at Badr, went up to Qays b. ʿAmr b. Sahl, who was just a lad, the only youth among the hypocrites. Abū Muḥammad pushed Qays by the back of his neck till he had evicted him.

"One of the Banū Khudra approached a man called al-Ḥārith b. ʿAmr who wore his hair thick, seized him by it and pulled him violently across the ground until he had evicted him. At this the hypocrite yelled, 'You're being very rough, Abū al-Ḥārith!' 'You deserve it,' he was told, 'you enemy of God you, for what has been revealed about you. Don't you come near the mosque of the Messenger of God (ṢAAS) again; you're filth!'

"A man of the Banū ʿAmr b. ʿAwf went for the previous man's brother, Zuway b. al-Ḥārith and forcibly evicted him, expressing his disgust for him and saying, 'Satan and his work have charge of you!'"

Ibn Isḥāq then referred to the passages in *sūrat al-Baqara* (Qurʾān, II) and in *sūrat al-Tawba* (Qurʾān, IX) that refer to the hypocrites and offered full and effective explanations of these. God bless him!

An Account of the first military expedition, that of al-Abwāʾ, also called Waddān, and the first of the delegations sent.

This involved the dispatch of Ḥamza b. ʿAbd al-Muṭṭalib or ʿUbayda b. al-Ḥārith, as will be explained regarding the military expeditions.

Al-Bukhārī's text reads as follows: *Book of the Military Expeditions*. Ibn Isḥāq stated, "The first battle fought by the Messenger of God (ṢAAS) was that of al-Abwāʾ, followed by that of Buwāṭ, followed by that of al-ʿUshayra."

He then related how Zayd b. Arqam was asked how many military expeditions the Messenger of God (ṢAAS) had sent. He replied, "There were 19, in 17 of which he participated; the first of these was to al-ʿUsayra (or al-ʿUshayra)."

An account will follow in the sequel of the expedition to al-ʿUshayra, if God wills it, and in Him is all trust, along with the chains of authority and words used in reporting on it as well as comments about it.

Al-Bukhārī stated, in his *ṣaḥīḥ* collection from Burayda, "The Messenger of God (ṢAAS) set in motion 16 military expeditions."

Muslim quoted Burayda as saying that he accompanied the Messenger of God (ṢAAS) on 16 expeditions. He also quotes him as saying that the Messenger of God (ṢAAS) organized 19 expeditions and himself fought in 8 of them.

Al-Ḥusayn b. Wāqid stated, from Ibn Burayda, from his father, that the Messenger of God (ṢAAS) organized 17 expeditions and fought in 8, those at Badr, Uḥud, al-Aḥzāb, al-Muraysīʿ, Qudayd, Khaybar, Mecca and Ḥunayn, and that he sent out 24 raids.

Yaʿqūb b. Sufyān stated, "Muḥammad b. ʿUthmān al-Dimashqī al-Tanūkhī related to us, quoting al-Haytham b. Ḥumayd, quoting al-Nuʿmān from Makḥūl, that the Messenger of God (ṢAAS) organized 18 expeditions and himself fought in 8. The first of these was at Badr, followed by Uḥud, al-Aḥzāb, Qurayẓa, Biʾr Maʿūna, that against the Banū al-Muṣṭaliq of Khuzāʿa, Khaybar, Mecca, Ḥunayn and al-Ṭāʾif."

His placing that of Biʾr Maʿūna after that of Qurayẓa is open to dispute. The truth is that it followed Uḥud, as will be shown.

Yaʿqūb stated that Salama b. Shabīb related to him, from ʿAbd al-Razzāq, from Maʿmar, from al-Zuhrī, (who stated) "I heard Saʿīd b. al-Musayyab say, 'The Messenger of God (ṢAAS) organized 18 expeditions.' But on another occasion I heard him say 24. I don't know whether this was mere fancy or something he heard later."

Al-Ṭabrānī recounted from al-Dabarī, from ʿAbd al-Razzāq, from Maʿmar, from al-Zuhrī, who said, "The Messenger of God (ṢAAS) organized 24 expeditions."

ʿAbd al-Raḥmān b. Ḥumayd stated in his *ḥadīth* collection, "Saʿīd b. Sallām related to us, quoting Zakariyyāʾ b. Isḥāq and Abū al-Zubayr, from Jābir, who said, 'The Messenger of God (ṢAAS) organized 21 expeditions.'"

Al-Ḥākim recounted, through Hishām, from Qatāda, that the expeditions and night raids organized by the Messenger of God (ṢAAS) totalled 43. Al-Ḥākim then commented, "Perhaps he meant raids apart from the military expeditions, for in the work *al-Iklīl* (*Three Bright Stars*) more than 100 raids of the Messenger of God (ṢAAS) are arranged in order."

He went on, "A reliable scholar of Bukhārā told me he had read in the work of Abū ʿAbd Allāh Muḥammad b. Naṣr that the raids and delegations sent out totalled some 70, not counting the actual battles."

This information related by al-Ḥākim is very strange; and the statements he attributes in them to Qatāda are controversial.

Imām Aḥmad recounted, from Azhar b. al-Qāsim al-Rāsibī, from Hishām al-Dastuwāʾī, from Qatāda, that the military expeditions and raids of the Messenger of God (ṢAAS) totalled 43, consisting of 24 missions and 19 military expeditions. In 8 of these he himself participated, at Badr, Uḥud, al-Aḥzāb, al-Muraysīʿ, Khaybar, the conquest of Mecca, Ḥunayn, and al-Ṭāʾif.

Mūsā b. ʿUqba quoted al-Zuhrī as stating, "These were the military expeditions in which the Messenger of God (ṢAAS) fought: Badr in Ramaḍān of 2 AH; Uḥud in Shawwāl, 3 AH; and *al-khandaq*, which was also known as al-Aḥzāb and the 'Banū Qurayẓa battle', in Shawwāl, 4 AH. He then fought the Banū al-Muṣṭaliq and the Banū Liḥyān in Shaʿbān, 5 AH; at Khaybar in 6 AH; at the Yawm al-Fatḥ (Mecca) in Ramaḍān, 8 AH. Thereafter he fought at al-Ḥunayn and besieged the people of al-Ṭāʾif in Shawwāl, 8 AH. Then, in 9 AH Abū Bakr performed the pilgrimage, and in 10 AH the Messenger of God (ṢAAS) went on the so-called *ḥijjat al-wadāʿ*, the 'farewell pilgrimage'. He organized 12 expeditions that did not result in fighting. The first of his expeditions was that of al-Abwāʾ."

Ḥanbal b. Hilāl stated, from Isḥāq b. al-ʿAlāʾ, from ʿAbd Allāh b. Jaʿfar al-Raqqī, from Muṭrif b. Māzin al-Yamānī, from Maʿmar, from al-Zuhrī, who said, "The first verse revealed on making war was, 'Those who do battle are given permission (to do so), for they have been wronged' (*sūrat al-Ḥajj*; XX, v.39). This came after the arrival of the Messenger of God (ṢAAS) in Medina.

"The first battle witnessed by the Messenger of God (ṢAAS) was that at Badr, on Friday, 17th of Ramaḍān."

His account proceeds to his comments as follows, "He then went on the expedition against the Banū al-Naḍīr, then in Shawwāl, the battle of Uḥud took place, that is, in 3 AH. Thereafter he was at the battle of *al-khandaq* in 4 AH, fought the Banū Liḥyān in Shaʿbān of 5 AH, and fought at the battle of al-Fatḥ (i.e. the 'victory', at Mecca, tr.) in Shaʿbān 8 AH, followed by Ḥunayn in Ramaḍān 8 AH. The Messenger of God (ṢAAS) organized 11 expeditions in which he did not fight. The first on which he fought was al-Abwāʾ, then came al-ʿUshayra, Ghaṭafān, Banū Sulaym, al-Abwāʾ (sic), the first battle of Badr, Ṭāʾif, al-Ḥudaybiyya, al-Ṣafrāʾ, and Tabūk, the last expedition." He then went on to refer to the *buʿūth*, the delegations he sent.

This account that I have copied from the history of the *ḥāfiẓ* Ibn ʿAsākir is very strange. We will relate later, in its proper order, what truly occurred.

This is an area of expertise requiring care and proper training; as Muhammad b. ʿUmar al-Wāqidī related, from ʿAbd Allāh b. ʿUmar b. ʿAlī, from his father, who said, "I heard ʿAlī b. al-Ḥusayn say, 'We used to teach the military expeditions of the Prophet (ṢAAS) just as we would chapters from the Qurʾān.'"

Al-Wāqidī stated, "I heard Muḥammad b. ʿAbd Allāh say, 'I heard my uncle al-Zuhrī say, "In knowledge of the military expeditions there is knowledge of the hereafter as well as of this world."'"

Muḥammad b. Isḥāq gave further information concerning the military expeditions after having given that we have quoted above. In this he named the chief unbelievers from among the Jews and the hypocrites, God damn them all and gather them in the depths of hell.

He stated, "Then the Messenger of God (ṢAAS) prepared to do battle against them, to wage war and fight against his enemies and their allies as God had ordered him.

"The Messenger of God (ṢAAS) had arrived in Medina on a Monday when it was very hot, and the sun was near its zenith; it was the 12th of Rabī῾ al-Awwal. At that time he was 53 years old, and God had given him his mission 13 years before. He stayed there for the remainder of Rabī῾ al-Awwal and for Rabī῾ al-Ākhir, for both Jumādas, Rajab, Sha῾bān, Ramaḍān, Shawwāl, Dhū al-Qi῾da, Dhū al-Ḥijja, the polytheists being in charge of the pilgrimage that month, and al-Muḥarram. He then, in Ṣafar, at the start of the 12th month after his arrival there, went forth to do battle."

Ibn Hishām stated, "He left Sa῾d b. ῾Ubāda in charge of Medina."

Ibn Isḥāq went on, "He continued as far as Waddān; this was the expedition to al-Abwā᾽." Ibn Jarīr commented, "It is also known as the Waddān expedition."

Ibn Isḥāq continued, "He was heading for Quraysh and the Banū Ḍamra b. Bakr b. ῾Abd Manāt b. Kināna. The Banū Ḍamra made peace with him there; the one who actually did this was Makhshī b. ῾Amr al-Ḍamrī, who was their leader at that time.

"The Messenger of God (ṢAAS) then returned to Medina without having engaged in battle, remaining there for the rest of Ṣafar and the early part of Rabī῾ al-Awwal."

Ibn Hishām added, "This was the first expedition made by the Messenger of God (ṢAAS)."

Al-Wāqidī commented, "His banner was entrusted to his uncle Ḥamza; it was white."

Ibn Isḥāq went on, "While resident then at Medina, the Messenger of God (ṢAAS) dispatched ῾Ubayda b. al-Ḥārith b. al-Muṭṭalib b. ῾Abd Manāf b. Quṣayy along with 60 – or 80 – men, mounted and of the Emigrants; not one of them was a Helper. The party went as far as a well in Hijāz below Thaniyyat al-Murra, where he met a large contingent of Quraysh. There was no engagement with them, however, except that Sa῾d b. Abū Waqqāṣ did that day cast one arrow. That was the first arrow shot for God's cause after the coming of Islam.

"The two forces separated thereafter, the Muslims positioning a rear-guard. Miqdād b. ῾Amr al-Bahrānī, an ally of the Banū Zuhra, fled from the polytheists to the Muslims, along with ῾Utba b. Ghazwān b. Jābir al-Māzinī, an ally of the Banū Nawfal b. ῾Abd Manāf. These were really Muslims, but they had gone forth to have contact with the unbelievers."

Ibn Isḥāq continued, "῾Ikrima b. Abū Jahl was leader of the polytheists on that occasion."

Ibn Hishām related, from Ibn Abū ʿAmr b. al-ʿAlāʾ, that Abū ʿAmr al-Madanī said, "It was Mikraz b. Ḥafṣ who led them."

I observe that al-Wāqidī's account, heretofore, gives two statements, one that the leader was Mikraz, the second that it was Abū Sufyān Ṣakhr b. Ḥarb; but it seemed to him more likely that it was Abū Sufyān. God knows best.

Ibn Isḥāq then gave the ode attributed to Abū Bakr "the Trusting", written about this night raid. It begins,

> "Is it for your vision of Salmā in the flat desert
> plains you lay awake, and for something happening in the
> tribe?
> In Luʾayy you see a faction that no preaching, no
> messenger's mission could keep from unbelief.
> A truth-telling messenger came to them but they denied
> him and told him he could not stay among them.
> When we called them to the truth, they turned their
> backs and fled like panting dogs retreating to their
> lair."

He then gave the response of ʿAbd Allāh b. al-Zibaʿrā:

> "Is it because of the traces of a home now desolate
> amidst the sand dunes that you weep, your tears soon gone,
> And because of time's surprises, and destiny is all
> surprises, of things gone by and new.
> A great army that came to us, led by ʿUbayda who is
> called Ibn Ḥārith, in battle,
> So we would leave idols set up in Mecca, passed down by
> heir to noble heir."

Ibn Isḥāq goes on to give the complete ode. And nothing prevents us from doing the same except for the fact that Imām ʿAbd al-Malik b. Hishām, God bless him, who was an Imām in language, reported that many scholars, expert in poetry, deny the authenticity of both these poems.

Ibn Isḥāq further stated, "Saʿd b. Abū Waqqāṣ spoke the following verses concerning his having shot an arrow, or so they say,

> "Has the Messenger of God heard that I protected my
> companions with my arrow?
> Through it I well protected their front ranks over land
> both rough and easy.
> And no one shooting an arrow at an enemy will be
> counted before myself, O Messenger of God!
> And that was because your religion is that of truth; it
> was with truth and virtue that you brought it.
> By it the believers are saved, by it the unbelievers
> are punished at a place of boiling pitch.

> Take care, for you have erred, and do not decry me; woe
> upon you, Ibn Jahl, misleader of your tribe!"

Ibn Hishām commented, "Most authorities on poetry deny that this poem is to be attributed to Sa‘d."

Ibn Isḥāq stated further, "The banner given to ‘Ubayda, so I have been told, was the first awarded by the Messenger of God (ṢAAS) to any Muslim."

Al-Zuhrī, Mūsā b. ‘Uqba, and al-Wāqidī disputed Ibn Isḥāq in this and maintained that Ḥamza received a flag before ‘Ubayd b. al-Ḥārith. But God knows best.

It will be related hereafter, from a *hadīth* of Sa‘d b. Abū Waqqāṣ, that the first leader of these raids was ‘Abd Allāh b. Jahsh al-Asadī.

Ibn Isḥāq went on, "Some scholars maintain that the Messenger of God (ṢAAS) sent him out when he arrived from the mission to al-Abwā’ before he reached Medina. Mūsā b. ‘Uqba related it so from al-Zuhrī."

DIVISION

Ibn Isḥāq stated, "The Messenger of God (ṢAAS), while resident there, sent Ḥamza b. ‘Abd al-Muṭṭalib b. Hāshim to the sea coast near al-‘Īṣ along with 30 mounted men drawn from the Emigrants; there were no Helpers among them. Ḥamza confronted Abū Jahl b. Hishām and 300 mounted Meccans there on the shore. But Majdī b. ‘Amr al-Juhanī interposed himself between the opposing parties, for he was at peace with both. Both sides withdrew from one another and so no fighting occurred."

Ibn Isḥāq continued, "Some people say that Ḥamza's banner was the first awarded by the Messenger of God (ṢAAS) to any of the Muslims. This was because he had dispatched Ḥamza and ‘Ubayda at the same time; this confused people."

I comment that Mūsā b. ‘Uqba quoted al-Zuhrī as saying that he had dispatched Ḥamza before ‘Ubayda b. al-Ḥārith. He maintained that Ḥamza's mission came before the expedition to al-Abwā’. And that when the Messenger of God (ṢAAS) returned from al-Abwā’ he dispatched ‘Ubayda b. al-Ḥārith along with 60 Emigrants. He then related much as above.

It has been stated above that al-Wāqidī said, "The raid made by Ḥamza in Ramaḍān took place in 1 AH; ‘Ubayda's expedition came thereafter, in Shawwāl in the same year." But God knows best.

Ibn Isḥāq quoted from Ḥamza, God be pleased with him, poetry indicating that his banner was the first awarded in Islam. However Ibn Isḥāq stated, "If Ḥamza did speak this, then so it was. He only ever spoke the truth. But God knows best what happened. What we have heard from scholars was that ‘Ubayda was first. The poem is as follows:

> ‘O my people, contemplate wisdom and foolishness and
> failure in man's thought and intellect,
> About those who have wronged us while we have not
> violated their people or property.

As though we had been hostile to them, but we have no
hostility for them; all we told them is to be chaste and
just.
And we told them of Islam, but they do not accept it
and treat it as if it were a joke.
They kept this up till I was appointed to raid them
where they reside, seeking security in virtue.
At the order of the Messenger of God, being the first
to have his banner fly above me, it not having appeared
before.
A flag bringing victory, from a God of honour and power,
His deeds the best of all.
They left in the evening, gathered together, the
cooking pot of each of us boiling with the rage of his
Companions.
When we saw one another they made their mounts kneel
and tied up their mounts, and we tied ours an arrow's reach
away.
We told them, "Our connection to God is our aid. But
the only connection you have is to error."
Abū Jahl arose to fight there, acting in evil, but he
was disappointed, for God rejected Abū Jahl's tricks.
We had only thirty mounted men, while they numbered two
hundred, with one extra yet.
O Lu'ayy, do not obey your evil men; come over to
Islam, to the path that is plain.
For I fear that you will have pain wrought upon you and
you will cry out in regret and mourning.'"

Ibn Isḥāq went on, "And Abū Jahl b. Hishām, God damn him, spoke the following verses in response,

'I was amazed at the reasons for false worship and
ignorance and at those who seek to do harm through division
and idiocy,
At those who abandon the practices of our fathers and
forebears, those fine and noble leaders.'

He then quoted the rest of the poem.

Ibn Hishām stated, "Most poetry scholars deny that the first poem can be
attributed to Ḥamza, God be pleased with him, or the second to Abū Jahl, God
damn him!"

THE EXPEDITION TO BUWĀṬ, IN THE NEIGHBOURHOOD OF RAḌWĀ.

Ibn Isḥāq stated, "The Messenger of God (ṢAAS) sent an expedition against
Quraysh in the month of Rabīʿ al-Awwal, that is in 2 AH."

Ibn Hishām commented, "He left al-Sā>ib b. <Uthmān b. Maẓ<ūn in charge over Medina."

Al-Wāqidī stated, "He left Sa<d b. Mu<ādh in charge of it. The Messenger of God (ṢAAS) was accompanied by 200 mounted men. His banner was entrusted to Sa<d b. Abū Waqqāṣ. His purpose was to interfere with a Quraysh caravan which consisted of Umayya b. Khalaf with 100 men and 2,500 camels."

Ibn Isḥāq stated, "He proceeded until he reached Buwāṭ, near Raḍwā. He then returned to Medina without engaging in battle. He remained there for the remainder of Rabī< al-Ākhir and part of Jumādā al-Ūlā."

THE EXPEDITION TO AL-<USHAYRA.

He then made an expedition against Quraysh. This refers to the expedition known by the name "al-<Ushayra" or "al-<Usayra".

Ibn Hishām commented that he left Abū Salama b. <Abd al-Asad in charge of Medina.

Al-Wāqidī stated that his banner was carried by Ḥamza b. <Abd al-Muṭṭalib and stated, "The Messenger of God (ṢAAS) went forth to interrupt the Quraysh caravans going to Syria."

Ibn Isḥāq stated, "He made his way through the territory of the Banū Dīnār, then past Fayfā> al-Khayyār, and made camp beneath a tree in the Ibn Azhar valley at a place called Dhāt al-Sāq. He said his prayers there, where his mosque is now. Food was prepared for him there which he ate, and the others ate there with him. The remains of the supports used for his cooking pot are still known there. He used the water from a place called al-Mushayrib.

"He then moved on, leaving al-Khalā>iq to his left and traversed the <Abd Allāh defile. From there he kept left, coming down the Yalyal trail till it meets that of al-Ḍabū<a. He then crossed the Malal plain until he met the road at Ṣukhayrāt al-Yamām and then went on along it till he reached al-<Ushayra, in the Yanbu< valley.

"There he remained for Jumādā al-Ūlā and some nights of Jumādā al-Ākhira; there he made peace with the Banū Mudlij and their allies of the Banū Ḍamra, then returned to Medina, without having engaged in battle."

Al-Bukhārī stated, "<Abd Allāh related to us, quoting Wahb, quoting Shu<ba, from Abū Isḥāq, who said, 'I was standing next to Zayd b. Arqam when he was asked, "In how many military expeditions did the Messenger of God (ṢAAS) take part?" He replied, "Nineteen." "And on how many did you accompany him?" "Seventeen," he replied. "Which of them came first?" I enquired. "Al-<Ushayr – or al-<Usayr," he replied. I told this to Qatāda and he said it was "al-<Ushayr".'"

This *ḥadīth* is clear in stating that the first of the military expeditions was at al-<Ushayra, which can also be spelled "al-<Usayra", and that in both of these spellings the final feminine ending, the "a" may be dropped or a lengthened "a"

be substituted. However, what could be meant here is that al-ʿUshayra was the first expedition in which Zayd b. Arqam participated with the Messenger of God (ṢAAS), and there could have been earlier ones which he did not witness. This could reconcile between this *ḥadīth* and that of Ibn Isḥāq. But God knows best.

Muḥammad b. Isḥāq stated, "It was on that occasion that the Messenger of God (ṢAAS) made his comment to ʿAlī. Yazīd b. Muḥammad b. Khaytham related to me, from Muḥammad b. Kaʿb al-Quraẓī, quoting Abū Yazīd Muḥammad b. Khaytham, from ʿAmmār b. Yāsir, who said, "ʿAlī b. Abū Ṭālib and I were companions on the expedition to al-ʿUshayra in the Yanbuʿ valley. When the Messenger of God (ṢAAS) encamped there he remained for a month and made peace with the Banū Mudlij and their allies of the Banū Ḍamra. ʿAlī b. Abū Ṭālib said, "Abū al-Yaqẓān, how would you like for us to go and watch these men of the Banū Mudlij who are doing some work on a well of theirs?" So we went to them and watched for a while, then were overcome by sleep. We made our way over to a place where there were young date-palms growing and the ground was soft and there we slept. And, by God, we were eventually woken up by the Messenger of God (ṢAAS) moving us with his foot. We sat up, soiled with the earth there and it was then that he said to ʿAlī, 'What have you been up to, Abū Turāb?' (i.e. 'father of dirt') because of the soil that was upon him. We told him what had happened to us and he said, 'Shall I tell you who are the two most pitiable men?' We replied, 'Yes, do tell us.' He replied, 'They are Uḥaymir of the tribe of Thamūd who slaughtered the camel and the man who will strike you on this' – and he placed his hand on ʿAlī's head – 'so that this' – and he touched ʿAlī's beard – 'will become wet from it.'"

This *ḥadīth* is unique in this line given. From another line there is also testimony to reference being made to ʿAlī as 'Abū Turāb'. Similarly, in the *ṣaḥīḥ* of al-Bukhārī it states that ʿAlī left his house angry at Fāṭima and went and slept in the mosque. When the Messenger of God (ṢAAS) went to his house to ask after him, Fāṭima told him he had left angry. So the Messenger of God (ṢAAS) went to the mosque and woke him up and, wiping the dirt from him, told him, "Up you get, Abū Turāb! Up you get!"

THE FIRST EXPEDITION TO BADR.

Ibn Isḥāq stated, "Upon his return from al-ʿUshayra, the Messenger of God (ṢAAS) had been in Medina only a few days, less than ten, when Kurz b. Jābir al-Fihrī made a raid on the town. The Messenger of God (ṢAAS) went forth in search of him and travelled as far as a valley called Safwān, near Badr. This, then was the first expedition to Badr; Kurz evaded him and was not captured."

Al-Wāqidī stated, "His banner was entrusted to ʿAlī b. Abū Ṭālib."

Both Ibn Hishām and al-Wāqidī related that he had left Zayd b. Ḥāritha in command of Medina.

Ibn Isḥāq went on, "When the Messenger of God (ṢAAS) returned, he spent Jumādā, Rajab and Shaʿbān in Medina. He had previously sent out Saʿd with a party of eight Emigrants. He reached as far as al-Kharrār in the Ḥijāz."

Ibn Hishām stated, "Some scholars maintain that this mission of Saʿd's took place after that of Ḥamza. He returned without engaging in battle."

This is how Ibn Isḥāq briefly reported this. Al-Wāqidī's account of these three expeditions is given above; by this I mean those of Ḥamza in Ramaḍān, ʿUbayda in Shawwāl, and Saʿd in Dhū al-Qiʿda, all during 1 AH.

Imām Aḥmad stated that "ʿAbd al-Mutʿāl b. ʿAbd al-Wahhāb related to him, quoting Yaḥyā b. Saʿīd; and ʿAbd Allāh b. al-Imām Aḥmad stated that ʿSaʿīd b. Yaḥyā b. Saʿīd al-Umawī related to him, quoting his father, from Mujālid, from Ziyād b. ʿAlāqa, who quoted Saʿd b. Abū Waqqāṣ as having said, "When the Messenger of God (ṢAAS) came to Medina, he was visited by some of the Juhayna who told him, 'Now you have come to live among us, make a pact with us so we can join you.' He did so, and they accepted Islam. In Rajab the Messenger of God (ṢAAS) sent us out, a force of less than 100, with orders to make a raid on a quarter of the Banū Kināna, who were over next to the Juhayna. We did raid them, but there were many of them and we took refuge with the Juhayna who gave us protection. They asked us, 'Why are you fighting in the holy month?' We asked one another what to do and some of us thought we should go back to the Prophet of God (ṢAAS) and tell him. Others thought they should stay there. I, and some others decided we would do neither and would attack and cut off a Quraysh caravan. The arrangement over booty at that time was that you could keep anything you won.

"So we set off against the caravan, while some of our Companions went back to the Prophet (ṢAAS). When they told him the situation, he became very angry and red-faced and said, 'You left me as one group and you've returned divided! Those before you who became divided were only ever destroyed! I will appoint over you someone who is no higher than you in rank, but who will give you fortitude against hunger and thirst.'

"He then appointed over us ʿAbd Allāh b. Jaḥsh al-Asadī, who was the first commander in Islam."

Al-Bayhaqī related this in *Dalāʾil* (*The Signs*), from a *ḥadīth* of Yaḥyā b. Abū Zāʾida, from Mujālid, in much the same form. That account adds, after their words to their companions "Why are you fighting in the holy month?" that the others replied, "We are fighting in the holy month those who expelled us from the holy city!"

He then recounted it from a *ḥadīth* of Abū Usāma, from Mujālid, from Ziyād b. ʿAlāqa, from Quṭba b. Mālik, from Saʿd b. Abū Waqqāṣ. This account is similar, but it adds Quṭba b. Mālik in the chain of authorities between Saʿd and Ziyād. This is more appropriate. But God knows best.

This *ḥadīth* requires that the first of the raids was that of ʿAbd Allāh b. Jaḥsh al-Asadī and this is contrary to what Ibn Isḥāq recounted, namely that the first of these was entrusted to ʿUbayda b. al-Ḥārith b. al-Muṭṭalib. It also contradicts al-Wāqidī, who maintained that the first of the raids was entrusted to Ḥamza b. ʿAbd al-Muṭṭalib. But God knows best.

Chapter: On the expedition of ʿAbd Allāh b. Jaḥsh that was the cause for the great engagement at Badr.

This was the day of the *Furqān* (the line distinguishing good from evil) when the two forces met in battle. And God has power over all things.

Ibn Isḥāq stated, "In Rajab, following his return from the first expedition to Badr, the Messenger of God (ṢAAS) sent forth ʿAbd Allāh b. Jaḥsh b. Riʾāb al-Asadī along with eight Emigrants; their number included none of the Helpers. The names of these men were as follows: Abū Ḥudhayfa b. ʿUtba, ʿUkkāsha b. Miḥṣan b. Ḥurthān, an ally of the Banū Asad b. Khuzayma, ʿUtba b. Ghazwān, an ally of the Banū Nawfal, Saʿd b. Abū Waqqāṣ al-Zuhrī, ʿĀmir b. Rabīʿa al-Wāʾilī, an ally of the Banū ʿAdī, Wāqid b. ʿAbd Allāh b. ʿAbd Manāf b. ʿArīn b. Thaʿlaba b. Yarbūʿ al-Tamīmī, also an ally of the Banū ʿAdī, Khālid b. al-Bukayr, one of the Banū Saʿd b. Layth, also an ally of the Banū ʿAdī, and Sahl b. Bayḍā al-Fihrī. These seven men were led by their commander ʿAbd Allāh b. Jaḥsh, God be pleased with him."

Yūnus quoted Ibn Isḥāq as stating that there were eight men and their commander was their ninth. But God knows best.

Ibn Isḥāq stated, "He wrote a letter for ʿAbd Allāh b. Jaḥsh which he told him not to open until he had travelled for two days. After opening it he was to do as it ordered him, but not to force any of his companions to do so too.

"Having travelled for two days, he opened the letter. It stated, 'Having read this letter, proceed to Nakhla, between Mecca and Ṭāʾif. Stay there and observe Quraysh and report back to us news of them.' Having read the letter, he said, 'To hear is to obey!' And he told his men what was in the letter. He said, 'It forbids me from forcing any of you to comply with this. Those of you seeking martyrdom should go forward. Those reluctant to do this should return. As for myself, I shall proceed to fulfil the order of the Messenger of God (ṢAAS).'

"He then proceeded forward accompanied by his men, none of whom stayed behind. He travelled through Hijāz until he reached a mine above al-Furʿ known as Baḥrān. There Saʿd b. Abū Waqqāṣ and ʿUtba b. Ghazwān lost a camel they had that they had been riding, so they remained behind to look for it. ʿAbd Allāh b. Jaḥsh continued ahead with the rest of the party and made camp at Nakhla.

"There a Quraysh caravan in which was ʿAmr b. al-Ḥaḍramī – Ibn Hishām commented that his full name was ʿAbd Allāh b. ʿAbbād, one of the Ṣadif – along with ʿUthmān b. ʿAbd Allāh b. al-Mughīra al-Makhzūmī, and his brother Nawfal, along with al-Ḥakam b. Kaysān, the freed-man of Hishām b. al-Mughīra.

"When the caravan party saw them they were concerned because the Muslims had encamped near themselves. But ʿUkāsha b. Miḥṣan appeared before them, having cut his hair.[52] When they saw him, they felt secure. ᶜAmmār told them, 'You don't need to worry about them.'

"The Companions consulted about how to treat them. They realized that if they were to leave them unharmed, that night they would enter sacred territory and be safe, but if they were to kill them they would be doing so on the last day of the sacred month of Rajab. They were undecided and ill at ease about attacking them.

"But then they encouraged one another to do so, deciding eventually to kill those they could and to seize their goods. And so Wāqid b. ᶜAbd Allāh al-Tamīmī shot an arrow at ᶜAmr b. al-Ḥaḍramī and killed him, ᶜUthmān b. ᶜAbd Allāh and al-Ḥakam b. Kaysān were taken prisoner, and Nawfal b. ᶜAbd Allāh evaded them and escaped. ᶜAbd Allāh b. Jaḥsh and his men then returned to the Messenger of God (ṢAAS) with the caravan and the two prisoners.

"Some of ᶜAbd Allāh b. Jaḥsh's family maintain that ᶜAbd Allāh told his men, 'The Messenger of God (ṢAAS) is due one-fifth of what we have taken' and that he set this portion aside and divided up the rest between them. This was before the revelation came down concerning that fifth." When this revelation came down it was as ᶜAbd Allāh b. Jaḥsh had divided it, as Ibn Isḥāq observed.

"When they reached the Messenger of God (ṢAAS) he told them, 'I did not order you to kill anyone in the sacred month!' He suspended disposition of the caravan and the prisoners and refused to take any of it.

"When the Messenger of God (ṢAAS) said this, the raiders were very worried and thought they were ruined, and their fellow Muslims criticized them harshly for what they had done. Quraysh said, 'Muḥammad and his men have made it lawful to use violence in the sacred month; they have shed blood and taken booty and seized prisoners during it.' Those Muslims in Mecca opposing Quraysh, however, maintained that the action had occurred in Shaᶜbān. Some Jews said, 'You must consider this an omen against the Messenger of God (ṢAAS). The killing of ᶜAmr b. al-Ḥaḍramī by Wāqid b. ᶜAbd Allāh means as follows, "Amr" stands for "ᶜamarat al-ḥarb", (i.e. 'war has spread'). 'Al-Ḥaḍramī' stands for 'ḥaḍarat al-ḥarb', (i.e. 'war has come') 'Wāqid b. ᶜAbd Allāh' stands for 'wuqidat al-ḥarb', (i.e. 'war has been kindled'). God, however, turned this around against them.

"When people gossiped excessively about this, God Almighty sent down the following words to His Messenger (ṢAAS), "They will ask you about the sacred month, and about fighting in it. Say: 'fighting therein is a grave matter; but blocking off God's path and disbelief in Him and (hindering men from) the sacred mosque, and expelling its people from it, (all this) is extremely grave in God's view; and causing unrest is worse than killing. And they will not stop fighting you until they turn you from your religion, if they can!'" (sūrat al-Baqara; II, v.217).

---

52. That is, as if he had just fulfilled the rites of the pilgrimage.

This means "Even if you have fought in the sacred month, they have blocked you from God's path by disbelieving in Him, and also by keeping you from the holy mosque and expelling you from it when you were of its people. This is more grave in God's view than your fighting those of them you did. For causing unrest is worse than killing. That is, they used to seduce Muslims from their religion, trying to return them to disbelief from faith. This was worse in God's view than the fighting. Their conduct was far worse and they were completely unrepentant. This is why God Almighty stated, 'They will not stop fighting you until they turn you from your religion, if they can!'"

Ibn Isḥāq went on, "When the Qurʾān was revealed about this and God had alleviated the concerns of the Muslims, the Messenger of God (ṢAAS) took possession of the caravan and the two prisoners. Quraysh then sought to provide ransom for ʿUthmān and al-Ḥakam b. Kaysān, but the Messenger of God (ṢAAS) responded, 'We will not release them to you until our two men come forth.' He was referring to Saʿd b. Abū Waqqāṣ and ʿUtba b. Ghazwān. 'We are concerned', he told them, 'about your treatment of them. If you kill them, we will kill your men.'

"Saʿd and ʿUtba then came forth, and the Messenger of God (ṢAAS) ransomed them. Al-Ḥakam b. Kaysān accepted Islam and became a Muslim, remaining with the Messenger of God (ṢAAS) until he was killed, a martyr, at the battle of Biʾr Maʿūna. ʿUthmān b. ʿAbd Allāh stayed in Mecca where he died an unbeliever."

Ibn Isḥāq stated, "When ʿAbd Allāh b. Jaḥsh and his companions had been relieved of their anxiety when the revelation came in the Qurʾān, they sought reward. They asked, 'O Messenger of God, may we hope that this be considered an expedition for which we will be given reward as warriors for God's cause?' And so God revealed concerning them, 'Those who believe and those who have emigrated and those who have fought for God's cause, those persons may hope for the mercy of God, for God is merciful and forgiving' (*sūrat al-Baqara* II v.218). Through this God gave them very great hope."

Ibn Isḥāq continued, "The *ḥadīth* concerning this is from al-Zuhrī, and Yazīd b. Rūmān from ʿUrwa b. al-Zubayr."

Mūsā b. ʿUqba related, in his work on the military expeditions, from al-Zuhrī, a similar account, as did Shuʿayb from al-Zuhrī, from ʿUrwa. Their account stated, "Ibn al-Ḥaḍramī was the first man killed in fighting between Muslims and polytheists."

ʿAbd al-Malik b. Hishām stated, "He was the first person killed by the Muslims. And this was the first booty taken by the Muslims; ʿUthmān and al-Ḥakam b. Kaysān were the first prisoners taken by Muslims."

I comment that in his aforementioned report Imām Aḥmad quoted Saʿd b. Abū Waqqāṣ as having said, "ʿAbd Allāh b. Jaḥsh was the first *amīr*, commander, appointed in Islam."

We have given in our *Tafsīr (Exegesis)* various testimonies, with their chains of authorities, in support of what Ibn Isḥāq recounted.

One such is what was reported by *al-ḥāfiz* Abū Muḥammad b. Abū Hatim, namely, "My father related to us, quoting Muḥammad b. Abū Bakr al-Muqaddimī, quoting al-Mu'tamir b. Sulaymān, quoting his father, quoting al-Ḥaḍramī, quoting from Abū al-Siwār, from Jundab b. 'Abd Allāh, that the Messenger of God (ṢAAS) sent forth some men, having appointed Abū 'Ubayda b. al-Jarrāḥ – or 'Ubayda b. al-Ḥārith – as their commander. But when he came to leave, he wept in longing for the Messenger of God (ṢAAS) and sat down. And so he apppointed 'Abd Allāh b. Jaḥsh over them and wrote a letter to him, telling him not to read it until he reached a certain place. He told him, 'Do not force any of your men to proceed further with you.'

"When he read the letter, he spoke the words, 'We are God's and to Him do we return,' and said, 'To hear is to obey, both God and His Messenger.' He then told them what the letter contained. Two of their number then went back, while the rest stayed. They met up with Ibn al-Ḥaḍramī and killed him, not knowing whether that day was in the month of Rajab or Jumāda. The polytheists told the Muslims, 'You have killed a man in the sacred month!' God then revealed, 'They will ask you about the sacred month, and about fighting during it. Say: fighting then is a grave matter'" (*sūrat al-Baqara*; II, v.217).

Ismā'īl b. 'Abd al-Raḥmān al-Suddī al-Kabīr stated in his exegesis, from Abū Mālik, from Abū Ṣāliḥ, from Ibn 'Abbās, and from Murra, from Ibn Mas'ūd, from a group of the Companions regarding this verse, "They will ask you" that it referred to the Messenger of God (ṢAAS) having sent out a raiding party of seven men commanded by 'Abd Allāh b. Jaḥsh. Among them were 'Ammār b. Yāsir, Abū Ḥudhayfa b. 'Utba, Sa'd b. Abū Waqqāṣ, 'Utba b. Ghazwān, Sahl b. Bayḍā', 'Āmir b. Fuhayra and Wāqid b. 'Abd Allāh al-Yarbū'ī, an ally of 'Umar b. al-Khaṭṭāb.

(The narration states) "He wrote a letter for Ibn Jaḥsh and ordered him not to read it before he reached the Malal valley. When he arrived there he opened the letter. It told him to proceed on to the valley at Nakhla. He told his companions, 'Whoever desires death, let him proceed and appoint an executor; I have appointed one and am proceeding to carry out the orders of the Messenger of God (ṢAAS).'

"He proceeded further and Sa'd and 'Utba lost their mount and stayed behind to find it. Ibn Jaḥsh and his companions went on and encamped in the Nakhla valley. There they found al-Ḥakam b. Kaysān, al-Mughīra b. 'Uthmān and 'Abd Allāh b. al-Mughīra." His account then related how Wāqid killed 'Amr b. al-Ḥaḍramī and how they went back with the booty and the two prisoners. This was the first booty taken by the Muslims. The polytheists said, "Muḥammad claims that he obeys God. Yet it is he who makes killing lawful in the holy month, having killed our man in Rajab.' The Muslims responded that it was in Jumāda that they had killed him."

Al-Suddī stated, "Their killing of him occurred in the first night of Rajab, and the last night of Jumādā al-Ākhira."

I observe, that perhaps Jumādā was yet unfinished, and they believed the month would last through the 30th night. The new moon however, was seen that night. But God knows best.

Al-ʿAwfī related it thus, from Ibn ʿAbbās, that it occurred on the last night of Jumādā, which was also the first of Rajab, but they were not aware of this.

This is also given above in the *hadīth* of Jandab that was related by Ibn Abū Ḥātim.

In the account of Ibn Isḥāq previously given it is stated that that was the last night of Rajab, and that they feared that if they did not take the booty and seize the opportunity the polytheists would go on into the holy territory and they would then be unable to proceed; they therefore acted in full knowledge of it.

The account of al-Zuhrī, from ʿUrwa, is similar. Al-Bayhaqī related it too. But God alone knows which version is correct.

Al-Zuhrī quoted ʿUrwa as saying, "We have been informed that the Messenger of God (ṢAAS) paid the blood-money for Ibn al-Haḍramī and recognized the sacred nature of the holy month as he always had until God sent down his exemption." Al-Bayhaqī related this.

Ibn Isḥāq stated, "Abū Bakr 'the Trusting' spoke verses about the raid led by ʿAbd Allāh b. Jaḥsh in response to the polytheists and the charges they had made about making killing permissible in the holy month." Ibn Hishām, however, attributed these verses to ʿAbd Allāh b. Jaḥsh.

> "You consider killing in the holy month as a grave
> matter, but there are graver matters to those who view
> aright:
> (like) Your rejection of what Muḥammad says and your
> disbelief in him, and God sees and knows all.
> And your expelling its people from God's temple so that
> no one may be seen there prostrating before Him,
> Even though you blame us for killing him, more damaging
> to Islam is the evil-doer and the envier.
> We slaked our lances on Ibn al-Haḍramī at Nakhla when
> Wāqid set war alight in blood.
> While Ibn ʿAbd Allāh ʿUthmān is among us restrained by
> a strong leather strap."

Section: Concerning the change in the prayer direction in 2 AH before the battle of Badr.

Some authorities maintain that this occurred in Rajab of the second year of the hegira. Qatāda and Zayd b. Aslam stated this, in a tradition related from Muḥammad b. Isḥāq.

Aḥmad related, from Ibn ῾Abbās, evidence supporting this and that is what is clearly implied by the account of al-Barā᾽ b. ῾Āzib, as will be shown. But God knows best. It is also said to date from Sha῾bān in that year.

Ibn Isḥāq stated, after his account of the raid conducted by ῾Abd Allāh b. Jaḥsh, "It is said that the change in the direction of the prayer occurred in Sha῾bān, at the beginning of the 18th month following the arrival of the Messenger of God (ṢAAS) in Medina."

Ibn Jarīr related this through al-Suddī with a chain of authorities from Ibn ῾Abbās, Ibn Mas῾ūd and various Companions.

The great majority of scholars maintain that it was changed in fact in the middle of Sha῾bān, at the start of the 18th month following the hegira.

It was also related from Muḥammad b. Sa῾d, on the authority of al-Wāqidī to the effect that it was changed on a Tuesday in mid-Sha῾bān, though there is some dispute about this. God knows best.

We argued against this, with evidence, in the *Tafsīr* (*Exegesis*) regarding the words of the Almighty, "We see you turning your face about in the sky and we shall provide you with a *qibla* that will please you. Turn your face towards the Sacred Mosque; wherever you may be, turn your face towards it. Those to whom the Book has been brought know that it is the truth from their Lord. And God is not unaware of what they do" (*sūrat al-Baqara*; II, v.144).

(My commentary also examines) the objections made both before and after the change by foolish Jews, hypocrites and low-down ignorant people, and their criticisms were because this was the first abrogation that occurred in Islam.

Regarding this, God had previously stated in the course of the Qur᾽ān the permissibility of making abrogation. He had stated, "Whatsoever verse we may cancel or cause to be forgotten we replace with one better or similar. Do you not know that God is capable of all things?" (*sūrat al-Baqara*; II, v.106).

Al-Bukhārī had stated, "Abū Nu῾aym related to us, (that he had) heard Zuhayr (say) from Abū Isḥāq, from al-Barā᾽, who said that the Prophet (ṢAAS) prayed towards Jerusalem for 16 or 17 months, though it would have pleased him to have faced towards the *ka῾ba*. He also said that the first time he worshipped towards it was during the *al-῾aṣr* (late afternoon) prayer. Others were praying along with him at that time. Afterwards a man who had been with him there passed by some people in a mosque prostrated in prayer. He told them, 'I swear by God, I have prayed with the Prophet (ṢAAS) in the direction of Mecca.' They turned right then and there towards the *ka῾ba*. We didn't know what to say about people who had died or been killed before the direction for prayer was changed. And so God sent down, 'God is not one to consider your prayer as valueless; God is merciful and kind towards people'" (*sūrat al-Baqara*; II, v.143).

Muslim related this from another path.

Ibn Abū Ḥātim stated, "Abū Zur῾a related to us, quoting al-Ḥasan b. ῾Aṭiyya quoting Isrā᾽īl, from Abū Isḥāq, from al-Barā᾽, who said, 'The Messenger of

God (ṢAAS) had been praying towards Jerusalem for 16 or 17 months though he wanted to face towards the *kaʿba*. And so God sent down, "We see you turning your face about in the sky and we shall provide you with a *qibla* that will please you. Turn your face towards the Sacred Mosque" (*sūrat al-Baqara*; II, v.144). And so he did face towards the *kaʿba*.

"The foolish people – the Jews – asked 'What could it be that turned them from the prayer direction they had previously?' And so God sent down the verse, 'Say: To God belong both East and West; he guides whomever He wishes to the straight path'" (*sūrat al-Baqara*; II, v.142).

In short, the Messenger of God (ṢAAS) used to pray in Mecca towards Jerusalem, while the *kaʿba* was directly in front of him, so Imām Aḥmad related from Ibn ʿAbbās, God be pleased with him. And when he emigrated to Medina it was not possible for him to combine both and so he prayed towards Jerusalem immediately after his arrival there, keeping his back directed to the *kaʿba* for 16 or 17 months. This would require it to have been until Rajab of 2 AH. But God knows best.

The Messenger of God (ṢAAS) wanted to change his prayer direction towards the *kaʿba*, the *qibla* of Abraham, and often prayed and entreated God, Almighty and Glorious is He, to allow this. In doing so, he would raise his hands and sight to the sky in supplication. And so God, Almighty and Glorious is He, revealed the words, "We see you turning your face about in the sky and we shall provide you with a *qibla* that will please you. Turn your face towards the Sacred Mosque."

When the order came down to change the direction of prayer, the Messenger of God (ṢAAS) made an address to the Muslims and told them of this, as al-Nasāʾī related, from Abū Saʿīd b. al-Muʿalla, and this was at noon.

᛫ Some scholars say that the change was revealed between two prayers. Mujāhid and others stated this.

This is substantiated by what is given in both *ṣaḥīḥ* collections from al-Barāʾ. Namely, that the first prayer he made in Medina towards the *kaʿba* was that of *al-ʿaṣr*.

It is strange that the people of Qubāʾ did not hear of this until the early morning prayer of the next day, as is established in the *ṣaḥīḥ* collections, from Ibn ʿUmar. He stated, "While the people in Qubāʾ were at the morning prayer someone came to them and said, 'The Messenger of God (ṢAAS) has received tonight a Qurʾān revelation! He has been ordered to face the *kaʿba* in prayer, so you must too.' They had been facing towards Syria, but they now turned towards the *kaʿba*."

In the *ṣaḥīḥ* collection of Muslim, from Anas b. Mālik there is a similar account.

What is shown here is that when the change in the direction of the prayer to the *kaʿba* was decreed, and God Almighty abrogated the direction of prayer towards Jerusalem, various fools and ignorant people made criticisms, asking "What was it that turned them away from the direction of prayer they had before?"

They said this even though the unbelieving "People of the Book"[53] well knew that the order came from God, since they recognized the Messenger of God (ṢAAS) from the description of him given in their books, from the information there that Medina would be the place to which he would emigrate, and also that he would be ordered to face towards the *kaʿba* in his prayer. As God stated, "Those to whom the Book was brought know well that it is the truth from their Lord" (*sūrat al-Baqara*; II, v.144).

Despite all this, God Almighty responded to their question and mentioned them specificallly when He stated, "The fools will ask, 'What was it that turned them away from the direction of prayer they had before?' 'Say: To God belong both East and West; He guides whomever He wishes to the straight path'" (*sūrat al-Baqara*, II, v.142). That is, He is the Lord, the Judge and Ruler of the Universe, whose decree no one can revise, He who does as He wishes with His creation, He who decrees whatever He wishes in His law, He who leads whomever He wishes to the straight path, misleading whomever He wishes away from the right road; in all that, His is the wisdom to which all must agree and accept.

Then the Almighty stated, "And thus We have made you an intermediate nation" (*sūrat al-Baqara*; II, v.143). That is, the best "so that you may be witnesses to the people and have the Messenger be witness for you" (*sūrat al-Baqara*; II, v.143). That is, just as We have chosen for you the best of directions for your prayer, having led you to the *qibla* of your father Abraham, father of the prophets, to which thereafter Moses and those messengers before him also turned. Likewise We have made you the best of nations, the very essence of the world, the most noble of all groups, the most honourable of the ancient and the high-born, so that you may be witnesses on Judgement Day against those who have combined against you, and so that they may give testimony on that day to your great virtue.

This is so substantiated in a *marfūʿ*[54] account in the *ṣaḥīḥ* collection of al-Bukharī, from Abū Saʿīd, referring to Noah's testimony to this nation on Judgement Day. And if Noah should testify for them despite the fact of his own time having been so much before, then it is even more appropriate and proper a course for those after him.

God then mentioned His wisdom in sending his retribution to those who doubted and denied this reality, and His pleasure to those who believed and accepted this actuality. He said, "And We decreed the *qibla* you used to observe only to know who it is who follows the Messenger" (*sūrat al-Baqara*; II, v.143).

Ibn ʿAbbās commented, "That is, only to see those who follow the Messenger, and those who turn back upon their heels."

---

53. The term commonly applied to members of religions based upon Holy Books, most specifically to Jews and Christians.

54. A term denoting a tradition traceable in ascending order of traditionaries directly to the Prophet.

And "even though this was a grave matter" (*sūrat al-Baqara*; II, v.143). That is, even though this matter was difficult and of great impact and importance, except for those guided by God. For they had full faith and belief in it, and were without doubt or uncertainty, but rather were satisfied, had faith and took action, for they were obedient to the Great Ruler, the Mighty and All-Powerful, the Patient and All-Knowing, the Gracious and Omniscient.

And God's words, "God is not one to consider your prayer as valueless" (*sūrat al-Baqara*; II, v.143). That is, by His decision regarding facing towards Jerusalem and prayer towards it, (for) "God is merciful and kind towards people" (*sūrat al-Baqara*; II, v.143).

The accounts and proofs of this are very numerous and would take long to ennumerate; this issue is examined in the exegesis and we will include additional comments thereupon in our work *al-Aḥkām al-Kabīr* (*The Major Statutes*).

Imām Aḥmad recounted quoting ʿAlī b. ʿĀṣim, quoting Ḥuṣayn b. ʿAbd al-Raḥmān, from ʿAmr b. Qays, from Muḥammad b. al-Ashʿath, from ʿĀʾisha, who said, "The Messenger of God (ṢAAS) stated, in regards to the 'People of the Book', that is, 'They envy us for nothing so much as for our Friday to which God led us, but they erred from it, the *qibla* that God guided us to while they strayed, and our saying "Amen" after the Imām.'"

Section: On the institution of the fasting month of Ramaḍān in 2 AH, before the battle of Badr.

Ibn Jarīr stated, "It was in that year that fasting for the month of Ramaḍān was made obligatory. It is also said that it was declared obligatory in Shaʿbān of that year. It is related, moreover, that when the Messenger of God (ṢAAS) came to Medina, he found that the Jews were fasting for the day of ʿĀshūrāʾ. He asked them about it and they told him, 'This was the day when God rescued Moses.' He replied, 'But we have a greater claim to Moses than you do!' So he fasted it and told his people to do so too."

This *ḥadīth* is firmly substantiated in both *ṣaḥīḥ* collections from Ibn ʿAbbās.

God Almighty stated, "O believers, fasting has been prescribed for you as it was for those who preceded you, so that you may be properly pious. (It shall be) for a specific number of days. Those of you who are ill or travelling (shall fast) a different number of days. And those with the means to do so may redeem this by feeding a poor person. And whoever does more good than he is bound to do does good unto himself thereby; for you to fast is better for you, if only you knew it. It was the month of Ramaḍān in which the Qurʾān was revealed, as a guidance to man, and as clear proof of guidance and of the differentiation (between good and evil). Whoever of you are present that month, let them fast it; whoever is sick or travelling should fast a (like) number of other days" (*sūrat al-Baqara*; II, v.183–5).

We have written at sufficient length on this in the *Tafsīr* (*Exegesis*), giving those *aḥadīth* and related evidences relevant to it, along with the regulations arising therefrom. And all praise be to God.

Imām Aḥmad has stated, "Abū al-Naḍr related to us, quoting al-Mas'ūdī, quoting 'Amr b. Murra from 'Abd al-Raḥmān b. Abū Laylā, from Mu'ādh b. Jabal, who said, 'The prayer underwent three changes and fasting underwent three changes.' He referred to those respecting prayer, then went on, 'Regarding the changes in fasting, when the Messenger of God (ṢAAS) came to Medina, he began fasting three days each month, and he also fasted 'Āshūrā'.

"'Then God made fasting incumbent upon him and sent down the words, "O believers, fasting has been prescribed for you as it was for those who preceded you" (*sūrat al-Baqara*; II, v.183), and so on to the words, "And those with the means to do so may redeem this by feeding a poor person" (*sūrat al-Baqara*; II, v.184). As a result, those who wished to fast did so, while those who preferred to feed a poor person did so, and that was considered sufficient for them. Then God sent down another verse, "the month of Ramaḍān in which the Qur'ān was revealed" up to the words "whoever of you are present that month, let them fast it" (*sūrat al-Baqara*; II, v.185). This firmly prescribed fasting for those who were at home and healthy, and exempted those who were sick or travelling. It also established that the elderly unable to fast should be fed. These, then, were two changes.'"

(Mu'ādh b. Jabal) then said "Thereafter people would cat, drink and go to their women before retiring to bed; after retiring for sleep they would refrain from these. One Helper, however, a man named Ṣirma, once fasted while working until evening, went home to his family, performed the evening prayer and then retired without eating or drinking before the next morning, when he again began fasting. The Messenger of God (ṢAAS) saw him under great strain and so he asked him, 'How is it I see you under such great stress?' So he informed him.

He went on, "'Umar was in the habit of having sexual relations even after he had slept a while and he came to the Messenger of God and told him this. And so God sent down, 'It is lawful for you to visit your wives on the night of the fast; they are as apparel for you' and so on, to the words, 'and then complete the fast till the night' (*sūrat al-Baqara*; II, v.187)."

Abū Dā'ūd related this in his work, *Al-Sunan al-Mustadrak*, as did al-Ḥākim in his *Al-Mustadrak* quoting a *ḥadīth* of al-Mas'ūdī in similar terms.

In both *ṣaḥīḥ* collections there is a *ḥadīth* of al-Zuhrī from 'Urwa which quotes 'Ā'isha as saying, "'Āshūrā' was fasted until fasting in Ramaḍān was made obligatory. Thereafter, those who wished to continue with the fast (of 'Āshūrā') did so, while those who wished not to refrained." A similar account is given by al-Bukhārī from Ibn 'Umar and Ibn Mas'ūd."

This subject is examined in another section of the exegesis as well as in my work *al-Aḥkām al-Kabīr* (*The Major Statutes*). God is the source of all aid.

Ibn Jarīr stated, "In that year people were commanded to give the *zakāt al-fiṭr*.[55] It is said that the Messenger of God (ṢAAS) addressed the people ordering this a day or two before the *ʿīd al-fiṭr*".[56]

He also stated, "In that same year the Messenger of God (ṢAAS) said the *ṣalāt al-ʿīd* prayers for the first time and conducted the people to the *muṣallā*.[57] They set out in front of him carrying the *ḥarba*, a spearhead, that had belonged to Zubayr to whom it had been presented by the Negus. It would be carried forth before the Messenger of God (ṢAAS) on feast days."

I comment, and it was this year too, as several later authorities have reported, that the payment of *zakāt* alms was prescribed. Details of all this will be given following the account of the battle of Badr, if God wills it, and in Him is all confidence and reliance. And there is no power nor strength except in God, the All-High and Almighty.

THE GREAT BATTLE OF BADR; THE DAY OF THE FURQĀN, THE DIFFERENTIATION BETWEEN GOOD AND EVIL, THE DAY THE TWO HOSTS MET.

God Almighty stated, "God gave you assistance at Badr when you were weak; fear God then, and may you give Him thanks" (*sūrat al-ʿImrān*; III, v.123). He also said, "Even as your Lord sent you forth from your house with the truth, a faction of the believers were indeed reluctant. They disputed with you over the truth even after it had become clear, as if being led to death while they watched. And (remember) when God promised you that one of the two parties would be yours, and you wished that, for you, it would be the one that was unarmed, but God wished to fulfil the truth by His words and wipe the unbelievers out to the last. This was to fulfil the truth and to nullify falsehood, even if the evil-doers disliked this" (*sūrat al-Anfāl*; VIII, v.5–8).

We have discussed this in our exegesis of this *sūrat*. Here we will give reference appropriate to each passage.

Ibn Isḥāq, God bless him, stated, after giving his account of the expedition led by ʿAbd Allāh b. Jaḥsh: "The Messenger of God (ṢAAS) then heard that Abū Sufyān Ṣakhr b. Ḥarb was arriving from Syria with a great Quraysh caravan consisting of money and goods, as well as 30 or 40 men, who included Makhrama b. Nawfal and ʿAmr b. al-ʿĀṣ."

Mūsā b. ʿUqba stated, from al-Zuhrī, that this was two months after the killing of Ibn al-Ḥaḍramī. He also said that the caravan consisting of 1,000 camels carried property belonging to all of Quraysh except for Ḥuwayṭib b. ʿAbd al-ʿUzzā, and that this was why he was not present at Badr.

---

55. An obligatory donation given annually during the month of Ramaḍān.
56. The feast marking the end of the fasting of Ramaḍān.
57. A building or area set aside solely for prayer.

Ibn Isḥāq went on, "Muḥammad b. Muslim b. Shihāb, ᶜĀṣim b. ᶜUmar b. Qatāda, ᶜAbd Allāh b. Abū Bakr and Yazīd b. Rūmān related to me from ᶜUrwa b. al-Zubayr and others of our scholars, from Ibn ᶜAbbās, each of these having related to me a part of this *ḥadīth* which I have joined together in the following account about Badr. They said that when the Messenger of God (ṢAAS) heard that Abū Sufyān was arriving from Syria, he sent the Muslims out against them, saying, 'This caravan belongs to Quraysh, and will carry much wealth. Attack it; God may present it to you.'

"The men got ready, some pleased, others apprehensive because they had not thought the Messenger of God (ṢAAS) would make war. When Abū Sufyān approached Ḥijāz he sought information from each mounted man he encountered since he was concerned what might develop. Eventually he received news from some travellers that Muḥammad had readied a force of men against him and his caravan. This alarmed Abū Sufyān and he commissioned Ḍamḍam b. ᶜAmr al-Ghifārī, sending him on to Mecca with orders to go to Quraysh and get them to prepare for battle to save their property, by telling them that Muḥammad and his men were about to attack it. Ḍamḍam b. ᶜAmr raced into Mecca to do so."

Ibn Isḥāq stated, "An unimpeachable source related to me, from ᶜIkrima, from Ibn ᶜAbbās and Yazīd b. Rūmān related to me from ᶜUrwa b. al-Zubayr as follows: ᶜĀtika, daughter of ᶜAbd al-Muṭṭalib had, three nights prior to the arrival of Ḍamḍam, a dream that had terrified her. She sent for her brother al-ᶜAbbās b. ᶜAbd al-Muṭṭalib and told him, 'Last night, brother, I swear I had a vision that really scared me. I'm concerned that because of it some harm might come to you or your people, so please keep confidential for me what I'm about to tell you.'

"'What was it you saw?' he asked.

"She replied, 'I saw a man arrive mounted on a camel who came to a halt in the valley then shouted out at the top of his voice, "Come forth to your deaths in three days hence, you people of perfidy!" I saw people gather around him. He then entered the mosque, with the people following. While they were there around him, his camel took him to the top of the *kaᶜba*. Once there he called out as before: "Come forth to your deaths in three days, you people of perfidy!" His camel next took him up to the top of Mt. Abū Qubays where he shouted the same. Then he picked up a rock, flung it away and it came on down, bursting into fragments when it reached the bottom of the mountain. And no one house or building in Mecca escaped being pierced by one of its fragments.'

"Al-ᶜAbbās told her, 'That was some vision! Keep quiet about it. Don't tell anyone!'

"Al-ᶜAbbās then went off and met with al-Walīd b. ᶜUtba, who was a friend of his, told him of it and asked him to keep it confidential. Thereafter al-Walīd told it to his son ᶜUtba, and so soon the story was spread all about and all Quraysh were discussing it.

"Al-ᶜAbbās said, 'I arose early to circumambulate the *kaᶜba* and there was Abū Jahl b. Hishām sitting with a group of Quraysh leaders discussing ᶜĀtika's dream. When Abū Jahl saw me, he said, "Abū al-Faḍl, why don't you come and join us when you finish your circumambulation?" When I had finished I went over to him and sat down among them. Abū Jahl then asked me, "How long has your family of ʿAbd al-Muṭṭalib had this prophetess?" "How do you mean?" I asked. "I'm talking about the visions ʿĀtika saw," he replied. "What were they?" I enquired. He responded, "Aren't you ʿAbd al-Muṭṭalibs satisfied with having your men become prophets? Has it got to be your women too? ʿĀtika claims that in her vision a man said, 'Come forth in three days!' We're going to watch you closely for these three days and if what you say is true, so be it. But if three days pass with nothing happening, then we'll judge you the biggest liars of all the temple-worshippers among the Arabs!"'

"Al-ʿAbbās commented, 'I swear, I've never had any problem with him before. All I did was repudiate what he said and deny that she had seen anything.'

"He went on, 'We then parted company. That night every woman of the ʿAbd al-Muṭṭalib clan came to see me and said, "Have you agreed to let that dirty old reprobate attack first your men and then your womenfolk while you just listened? Didn't anything you heard him say offend you?" I replied, "I would have done something, but I never had a problem with him before. I swear I will confront him and if he repeats it, I'll take care of him for you!"'

"He went on, 'On the morning of the third day after ʿĀtika's vision, I was extremely angry, feeling I had let him get away with something I should have put a stop to. I went into the mosque and saw him. I swear I was making towards him to confront him to get him to retract what he had said – he was a slight man, with a face, voice and gaze that were all sharp – when he hurried off towards the door of the mosque. I asked myself what could be the matter with the fellow, and whether he was doing this because he feared I was about to confront him. But he had heard something I had not – the voice of Ḍamḍam b. ʿAmr al-Ghifārī who was out in the centre of the valley, standing by his camel. He had lopped its ears and turned its saddle back to front, rent his shirt and was yelling, "O Quraysh! The baggage camels! The baggage camels! Your goods being brought by Abū Sufyān have been waylaid by Muḥammad and his men! I don't think you can save them! Help! Help!"'

"Ibn ʿAbbās concluded, 'And so all this diverted us both from our personal conflict.

"'The Meccans then made quick preparations commenting, "Do Muḥammad and his men think it's going to turn out as it did with the raid on the caravan of Ibn al-Ḥaḍramī? No way! By God, they'll find out differently!"'"

Mūsā b. ʿUqba related the vision of ʿĀtika in much the same terms as did Ibn Isḥāq. He stated, "And when Ḍamḍam b. ʿAmr spoke in this fashion the Meccans were very worried about ʿĀtika's vision and went forth to battle feeling insecure and fearing the worst."

Ibn Isḥāq stated, "The Meccans used to respond in two ways. They either went forth themselves or sent another in their place. Not one of their leaders stayed behind now, except for Abū Lahab b. ʿAbd al-Muṭṭalib; he sent al-ʿĀṣī b. al-Mughīra in his place. He hired him for a debt of 4,000 dirhams al-ʿĀṣī owed him that he could not pay.”

Ibn Isḥāq stated, “Ibn Abū Najīḥ related to me that Umayya b. Khalaf had made up his mind to stay behind; he was a dignified old sheikh, tall and portly. ʿUqba b. Abū Muʿayṭ came up to him, while he was sitting there in the mosque with some of his family, carrying a censer with lit scented embers which he placed before him, saying, ‘Here, Abū ʿAlī, enjoy the perfume! You’re just a woman!’

“Umayya responded, ‘God damn you, and what you bring!’ He then got himself ready and left with the others.”

This, then, is the anecdote as given by Ibn Isḥāq. Al-Bukhārī told it quite differently. He stated, “Aḥmad b. ʿUthmān related to me, quoting Shurayḥ b. Maslama, quoting Ibrāhīm b. Yūsuf, from his father, from Abū Isḥāq quoting ʿAmr b. Maymūn, that he heard ʿAbd Allāh b. Masʿūd relate the following from Saʿd b. Muʿādh. Saʿd recounted that he was a friend of Umayya b. Khalaf and that when Umayya visited Medina he would stay with him, just as Saʿd would stay with Umayya when he came to Mecca.

“After the Messenger of God (ṢAAS) had moved to Medina, Saʿd went to stay with Umayya in Mecca while performing the ʿumra, the ‘lesser pilgrimage’. Saʿd asked Umayya, ‘Would you look out for me some time when it’s empty there and I can circumambulate the kaʿba?’ Umayya accompanied him forth at close to midday, but they were met by Abū Jahl, who said, ‘(Abū) Ṣafwān, who is this with you?’ He replied, ‘This is Saʿd.’ Abū Jahl said (to Saʿd) ‘What’s this? Do I really see you going in safety around Mecca when you’ve given shelter to the Sabians and proclaimed your help and protection for them? I swear, if you weren’t in the company of Abū Ṣafwān you’d not return home safely!’

“Saʿd replied, raising his voice, ‘If you were to block my way here I’d do worse to you by blocking yours to Medina!’

“Umayya asked him, ‘Saʿd, don’t raise your voice to Abū al-Ḥakam; he is the leader of our valley.’

“Saʿd responded, ‘Let’s talk no more of it; and, I swear, I’ve heard the Messenger of God (ṢAAS) say that they are going to kill you!’ Umayya asked, ‘In Mecca?’ Saʿd replied, ‘I don’t know.’

“Umayya was very much afraid at this.

“When he returned home he asked his wife, ‘Umm Ṣafwān, do you know what Saʿd told me?’ ‘What did he say?’ she asked. ‘He claims that Muḥammad told them they would kill me! I asked him whether in Mecca, and he said he didn’t know. So, I swear, I’m not leaving Mecca,’ Umayya told her.

“When the day of the battle of Badr arrived, Abū Jahl assembled the Meccan force by asking them to save their caravan. Umayya did not want to go to battle, but Abū Jahl came to him and said, ‘Abū Ṣafwān, when people see that you are staying behind, you, one of the valley leaders, they will remain with you.’

"Abū Jahl kept on at him until Umayya responded, 'You win! I'll purchase the finest camel in Mecca!'

"He then told his wife, 'Umm Ṣafwān, get my equipment ready!' 'But have you forgotten what your Yathrib friend told you?' 'No,' he replied, 'I only want to go a little way with them.'

"After leaving, Umayya tied up his camel at every stop they made, right on up to Badr, where God took his life."

Al-Bukhārī also told this elsewhere, on the authority of Muḥammad b. Isḥāq, from ʿUbayd Allāh b. Mūsā, from Isrāʾīl, from Abū Isḥāq, that account being similar.

Al-Bukhārī alone gives this.

Imām Aḥmad related it from Khalaf b. al-Walīd, from Abū Saʿīd, both of them quoting Isrāʾīl. In Isrāʾīl's account Umayya's wife commented, "I swear, Muḥammad never lies."

Ibn Isḥāq stated, "When they had gathered their equipment and were assembled to depart, Quraysh remembered the dispute they had with the Banū Bakr b. ʿAbd Manāt b. Kināna. They expressed fear that they might attack their rear. This quarrel related to a son of Ḥafṣ b. al-Akhyaf of the Banū ʿĀmir b. Luʾayy who had been killed by a man of the Banū Bakr, on the orders of ʿĀmir b. Yazīd b. ʿĀmir b. al-Mulawwaḥ. His brother Mikraz b. Ḥafṣ took revenge for him, killing ʿĀmir by plunging his sword into his stomach.

"He then brought the sword by night and hung it up in the curtains of the kaʿba. Quraysh therefore feared the Banū Bakr for what had occurred between them."

Ibn Isḥāq went on, "Yazīd b. Rūmān related to me, from ʿUrwa b. al-Zubayr, who said, 'When Quraysh were ready to leave they remembered their problem with the Banū Bakr and that almost diverted them. But Iblīs, Satan, appeared to them in the form of Surāqa b. Mālik b. Juʿsham al-Mudlijī, one of the nobles of the Banu Kināna. He told them, "I will give you protection against Kināna attacking you from your rear." They therefore hurried away to battle.'"

I observe that this illustrates the words of the Almighty, "Do not be like those who left their homes exulting and showing off before men, blocking people from the way of God, for God was aware of what they were doing. And when the devil made their works look good to them, he said, 'No one will overcome you today; I will be your protector.' But when the two factions met he turned on his heels, saying, 'I am quit of you; I see what you do not see. I fear God! God is fierce in punishing.'" (sūrat al-Anfāl; VIII, v.47–8).

He, God curse him, deceived them, so that they left, with him following behind them, stage by stage, bringing his troops and his banners with him, as several of them reported. And so he delivered them to their deaths. When he saw the strife, and the angels coming down to help and sighted Gabriel, he turned on his heels and said, "I am quit of you; I see what you do not see. I fear God!"

This is similar to the words of God Almighty, "like the devil, when he says to man, 'Disbelieve!' and when man disbelieves, he says, 'I am quit of you; I fear God, the Lord of the worlds'" (*sūrat al-Ḥashr*, LIX, v.16).

And God Almighty said, "And say: 'The truth has come; and falsehood has vanished; falsehood is ever bound to vanish'" (*sūrat Banū Isrāʾīl* or *al-Isrāʾ*; XVII, v.81).

And so when Satan, God damn him, on that day saw the angels descend to give victory, he fled. He was the first to flee, though he had been the chief encourager and helper of Quraysh, deceiving them and making them false promises. Satan's promises were only to mislead.

Yūnus stated, quoting Ibn Isḥāq, "Quraysh went forth with a sense of anxiety and weakness. They consisted of 950 warriors led by 200 cavalry. They had slave girls with them striking tambourines and chanting invective against the Muslims."

He lists day by day those providing food for the Quraysh force.

Al-Umawī stated, "The first person to slaughter for them following their departure from Mecca was Abū Jahl. He slaughtered ten camels. At ʿAsfān Umayya b. Khalaf slaughtered nine, and Suhayl b. ʿAmr ten more at Qadīd. At Qadīd they turned off to the wells in the direction of the sea coast and remained a day there. Shayba b. Rabīʿa slaughtered nine more for them. Next morning they reached al-Juḥfa, where ʿUtba b. Rabīʿa slaughtered ten and the next morning, at al-Abwāʾ, Nubīh and Munbih, two sons of al-Ḥajjāj slaughtered ten. Next, al-ʿAbbās b. ʿAbd al-Muṭṭalib slaughtered ten, and Abū al-Bakhtarī ten more at the well at Badr. They then ate from their provisions."

Al-Umawī stated, "My father related to us, quoting Abū Bakr al-Hudhalī, as follows, 'The polytheists had with them 60 horses and 600 coats of mail, while the Messenger of God (ṢAAS) had with him 2 horses and 60 coats of mail.

This, then, was how they left Mecca and moved towards Badr.

Regarding the activities of the Messenger of God (ṢAAS), Ibn Isḥāq stated, "The Messenger of God (ṢAAS) moved out with his men several days after the start of Ramaḍān. He appointed Ibn Umm Maktūm to lead the people in prayer and he sent back Abū Lubāba from al-Rawḥāʾ to administer Medina.

"He entrusted the banner, which was white, to Muṣʿab b. ʿUmayr, while he was preceded by two black flags one, called *al-ʿUqāb*, the standard, carried by ʿAlī b. Abū Ṭālib, the other borne by one of the Helpers."

Ibn Hishām stated that the Helpers' flag was carried by Saʿd b. Muʿādh. Al-Umawī said it was with al-Khabbāb b. al-Mundhir.

Ibn Isḥāq went on, "The Messenger of God (ṢAAS) appointed Qays b. Abū Saʿṣaʿa, a brother of the Banū Māzin b. al-Najjār, over the rear guard."

Al-Umawī said that they had two horses, on one of which rode Muṣʿab b. ʿUmayr, and on the other al-Zubayr b. al-ʿAwwām. Saʿd b. Khaythama had charge of the right flank, al-Miqdād b. al-Aswad that of the left.

Imām Aḥmad recounted, from a *ḥadīth* of Abū Isḥāq, from Ḥāritha b. Maḍrab, who quoted ʿAlī as saying, "The only horseman we had at Badr was al-Miqdād."

Al-Bayhaqī related, through Ibn Wahb, from Abū Sakhb, from Abū Muʿāwiya al-Balkhī, from Saʿīd b. Jubayr, from Ibn ʿAbbās, that ʿAlī told him, "We only had two horses with us – that of al-Zubayr and that of al-Miqdād b. al-Aswad." He was referring to the battle of Badr.

Al-Umawī stated, "My father related to us, quoting Ismāʿīl b. Abū Khālid, from al-Taymī, who said, 'At the battle of Badr the Messenger of God (ṢAAS) had with him two horsemen, al-Zubayr b. al-ʿAwwām on the right flank, al-Miqdād b. al-Aswad on the left."

Ibn Isḥāq stated, "They had with them 70 camels they would ride in turn. The Messenger of God (ṢAAS) shared one with ʿAlī and Marthad b. Abū Marthad, while Ḥamza and Zayd b. Ḥāritha, along with Abū Kabsha and Anisa, two freedmen of the Messenger of God (ṢAAS), took turns with another."

This is what Ibn Isḥāq stated, may God Almighty have mercy on him.

Imām Aḥmad stated, "ʿAffān related to us, from Ḥammād b. Salama, ʿĀṣim b. Bahdala related to us, from Zirr b. Ḥubaysh, from ʿAbd Allāh b. Masʿūd, who said, 'At Badr we were three to a camel. Abū Lubāba and ʿAlī were the Companions of the Messenger of God (ṢAAS).' He also said, 'They were the ones taking turns riding with him, and they told him, "Let us walk." He replied, "You are no stronger than me; nor can I dispense with the reward more than you can."'"

Al-Nasāʾī recounted this, from al-Fallās, from Ibn Mahdī, from Ḥammād b. Salama.

I would comment that this might have been before Abū Lubāba was sent back from al-Rawḥāʾ, and that it was thereafter that he shared with ʿAlī and Marthad instead of Abū Lubāba. But God knows best.

The Imām Aḥmad stated, "Muḥammad b. Jaʿfar related to us, quoting Saʿīd, from Qatāda, from Zurāra b. Abū Awfā, from Saʿd b. Hishām, from ʿĀʾisha, who said that the Messenger of God (ṢAAS) ordered that the bells be cut off the necks of the camels at the battle of Badr."

This line of transmission accords with the criteria of both *ṣaḥīḥ* collections. However, al-Nasāʾī recounted it from Abū al-Ashʿath, from Khālid b. al-Ḥārith, from Saʿīd b. Abū ʿUrūba, from Qatāda.

Our teacher, the *ḥāfiz* Sheikh al-Mizzī, stated in *al-Aṭraf* (*The Extremes*): "It was Saʿīd b. Bishr who quoted directly from Qatāda. And also Hishām gave it from Qatāda, from Zurāra, from Abū Hurayra." But God knows best.

Al-Bukhārī stated that Yaḥyā b. Bukayr related to him, quoting al-Layth, from ʿUqayl, from Ibn Shihāb, from ʿAbd al-Raḥmān b. ʿAbd Allāh b. Kaʿb b. Mālik, who quoted ʿAbd Allāh b. Kaʿb as reporting, "I heard Kaʿb b. Mālik say, 'The only expedition in which the Messenger of God (ṢAAS) participated, that I did not attend, except for the raid on Tabūk, was the battle of Badr. And God did not reproach anyone who stayed behind from it. Because when the Messenger of God (ṢAAS) went forth on it he was heading for the Quraysh caravan; God, however, brought the Muslims into contact with their enemies unexpectedly.'"

Al-Bukhārī is alone in giving this.

Ibn Ishāq stated, "The Messenger of God (ṢAAS) made his way out towards Mecca via the upper part of Medina. His path then led by al-'Aqīq, Dhū al-Ḥulayfa and Ūlāt al-Jaysh. From there he passed by Turbān, Malal, Ghamīs al-Ḥamām, Ṣukhayrāt al-Yamāma, al-Sayyāla, Fajj al-Rawḥā' and Shunūka, this being the direct route.

"Arriving at 'Irq al-Ẓabiyya he met a bedouin. They asked him about other people, but received no news from him. The Muslims told him, 'Pay your respects to the Messenger of God! (ṢAAS).' The man asked, 'Do you have the Messenger of God (ṢAAS) among you?' 'Yes,' they replied. The man then did greet him, but asked, 'If you're the Messenger of God, then tell me what is inside the belly of this female camel of mine.' Salama b. Salāma b. Waqsh responded, 'Don't you put questions to the Messenger of God! (ṢAAS). Come on over to me, and I'll tell you that. You mounted her and so she has a little goat inside her belly from you!' The Messenger of God (ṢAAS) commented, 'You've used obscene language to the man!' He then turned away from Salama.

"The Messenger of God (ṢAAS) made a halt at Sajsaj, where there is the well of al-Rawḥā', and proceeded on to al-Munṣaraf, where he left the Mecca road which goes to the left and took that to the right, towards al-Nāziyya, heading for Badr. He continued on this path for some way, crossing a valley called Ruḥqān, between al-Nāziyya and the al-Ṣafrā' pass. He crossed through the pass, then emerged from it and continued to near al-Ṣafrā'. From there he sent Basbas b. 'Amr al-Juhanī, an ally of the Banū Sā'ida, and 'Adī b. Abū al-Zaghbā', an ally of the Banū al-Najjār, on to Badr to seek any news of Abū Sufyān Ṣakhr b. Ḥarb and his caravan."

Mūsā b. 'Uqba stated that he had dispatched them both before he left Medina and that when they returned and reported on the status of the caravan, he sent people ahead to it.

If what both Mūsā b. 'Uqba and Ibn Ishāq stated is correct, then he sent them forward twice. But God knows best.

Ibn Ishāq, God bless him, went on, "The Messenger of God (ṢAAS) proceeded ahead and approached al-Ṣafrā', a village set between two mountains. He asked what were the names of the two mountains and was told that one was called Musliḥ and the other Mukhri'. He then asked about the people living on them and they were named as the Banū al-Nār and the Banū Ḥurāq, two sub-tribes of Ghifār. The Messenger of God (ṢAAS) did not like these names, thinking them an ill-omen,[58] and so he left them and al-Ṣafrā' to his left, making his way along a valley called Dhafirān. Having gone through it, he made camp."

____

58. The words *musliḥ* and *mukhri'* can both be interpreted as "he who defecates"; *al-nār* means fire, and *ḥurāq* means conflagration.

Ibn Isḥāq continued, "There he received the news that Quraysh had set out to protect their caravan.

"He told his men about this, and asked their opinion.

"Abū Bakr arose and spoke, giving good advice.

"ʿUmar b. al-Khaṭṭāb arose and spoke, giving good advice.

"Al-Miqdād b. ʿAmr then got up and said, 'Carry on as ever God tells you, O Messenger of God. We are with you. We will certainly not say to you what the people of Israel said to Moses – that is, "You and your Lord go and fight together; we are staying here!" Rather, (we say) you and your Lord go and fight together, and we will fight along with you! By Him who sent you with the truth, if you were to take us even to Bark al-Ghimād,[59] we would fight with you all over the place until you reached it!'

"The Messenger of God (ṢAAS) expressed his appreciation and blessed him. He then said, 'Now you advise me, men!' He was really addressing the Helpers, because they were the majority and because, when they had given him allegiance at al-ʿAqaba they had told him, 'We are free of responsibility for you until you reach our territory. When you join us, you will be under our protection, and we will then protect you as we do our own sons and women.' The Messenger of God (ṢAAS) was therefore apprehensive that they would feel obliged to help him only against those enemies attacking him in Medina, and that they had no duty to proceed against an enemy beyond their lands.

"When he said this, Saʿd b. Muʿādh responded, 'Is it us you are asking, O Messenger of God?' When he said that it was, Saʿd affirmed, 'We do believe in you and bear witness that you bring the truth. We have given you our oaths and agreement to listen to and to obey all your commands. Proceed as ever you decide, for we are with you. I swear, if you were to plunge into the sea, we would do so with you, not one of us would remain behind. We would have no reluctance to accompany you in confronting our enemy tomorrow. We are stoic in battle, trustworthy in the fray. Let us hope that God will give you pleasure in us. Go forward with God's blessings!'

"The Messenger of God (ṢAAS) was delighted with Saʿd's words and they spurred him on. He then said, 'Go forward in good spirits! God has promised me I shall take one of the two parties. I swear by God I feel I can already see their destruction!'"

This was how Ibn Isḥāq, God have mercy on him, related it. And there are various testimonies to it.

One such is what al-Bukhārī related in his *ṣaḥīḥ* collection. He stated that, "Abū Nuʿaym related to him, quoting Isrāʾīl, from Mukhāriq, from Ṭāriq b. Shihāb, who quoted Ibn Masʿūd as having said, 'I witnessed a scene involving al-Miqdād b. al-Aswad such as to make me more his friend than I would have

---

59. Apparently the reference is to a place some five days' journey away from Mecca towards Yemen; presumably the name is used to imply a distant and inaccessible place.

been from what was reported of him. He went to the Prophet (ṢAAS) while he was praying against the polytheists. Al-Miqdād said, "We will not say as Mūsā's people did to him, 'You go off with your Lord and fight along with Him; we're staying here!' Instead, we will fight on your right and your left, and in front of you and behind you!"'

"(Ibn Mas‘ūd went on) 'At that I saw the face of the Prophet (ṢAAS) light up in delight.'"

Al-Bukhārī alone gave this; Muslim did not. The former related it several places in the ṣaḥīḥ collection, from a ḥadīth of Mukhāriq. Al-Nasā’ī also recounted it from his ḥadīth; his version states, "At the battle of Badr, Miqdād rode a horse." He then related it.

Imām Aḥmad stated, "‘Ubayda related it to us, he being the son of Ḥumayd, from Ḥumayd al-Ṭawīl, from Anas, who said, 'The Messenger of God (ṢAAS) sought advice concerning going to battle at Badr. First Abū Bakr gave him advice and again he sought it from all. Then ‘Umar gave him advice and again he sought it. One of the Helpers observed, 'The Messenger of God (ṢAAS) wants your advice, O Helpers.'

"One of them said, 'Well, O Messenger of God, we'll not speak as the people of Israel did to Moses, that is, "Go off with your Lord and fight; we're staying here!" If you were to race all the way to Bark al-Ghimād, we'd follow you!'"

Two-thirds of this chain of authorities meets the conditions for being considered ṣaḥīḥ, "authentic".

Aḥmad also stated, "‘Affān related to us, quoting Ḥammād, from Thābit, from Anas b. Mālik, that the Messenger of God (ṢAAS) sought advice when he learned of the approach of Abū Sufyān. Abū Bakr spoke, and he turned away from him. Then ‘Umar spoke, and he turned away from him. Sa‘d b. ‘Ubāda then said, 'It's to us the Messenger of God (ṢAAS) is wanting to respond. By Him in whose hand is my soul, if you were to order us to plunge into the sea we would do so. And if you told us to race all the way to Bark al-Ghimād we would do so.'

"And so the Messenger of God (ṢAAS) urged his men forward.

"They set off and reached Badr. People came to them with reports of Quraysh, and one of these was a black youth of the Banū al-Ḥajjāj whom they captured. The Companions of the Messenger of God (ṢAAS) asked him about Abū Sufyān and those men with him. He would respond, 'I have no knowledge of Abū Sufyān. But it was Abū Jahl b. Hisham, ‘Utba b. Rabī‘a and Umayya b, Khalaf.' When he said this they beat him. When they did so, he would then say, 'Yes, I will tell you! It was Abū Sufyān.' When they let him go and asked him, he said, 'I have no knowledge of Abū Sufyān. But it was Abū Jahl, ‘Utba, Shayba and Umayya.' When he said this too, they would beat him.

"Meanwhile the Messenger of God (ṢAAS) was standing there praying. When he saw this scene, he left, saying, 'By Him who holds my soul in His hands, you beat him when he speaks the truth, and you leave him alone if he lies!"

"He went on, 'The Messenger of God (ṢAAS) said, "This is the place where so and so shall fall. He then placed his hands on the ground here and here." And no one effaced the place where the Messenger of God (ṢAAS) had placed his hand.'"

Muslim related this from Abū Bakr, from ʿAffān in a similar form.

Ibn Abū Ḥātim related in his *Tafsīr* (*Exegesis*), as did Ibn Mardawayh, and the wording is his, through ʿAbd Allāh b. Lahīʿa, from Yazīd b. Abū Ḥabīb, from Aslam, from Abū ʿImrān, who said he had heard Abū Ayyūb al-Anṣārī say, "The Messenger of God (ṢAAS) said, while we were in Medina, 'I have received information that Abū Sufyān's caravan is approaching. Do you want us to go out against it in the hope that God will grant it to us as booty?' We replied, 'Yes.'

"'And so he went forth as did we too. When we had travelled for a day or two, he asked us, "What should we do about their force? They have been informed of our advance." We replied, "No; we just don't have the strength to do battle with them. We came seeking the caravan."

"'Again he asked what we thought of engaging them in battle and we replied as before."

"'Then al-Miqdād b. ʿAmr arose and said, "In such case we would not say to you what Moses' people told him – that is, 'You and your Lord can go off and fight; we're staying here.'"

"'We wished that our people, the "Helpers", had spoken as al-Miqdād had done, preferring that to great wealth. And then God the Almighty and Glorious made revelation to His Messenger, with the words, "just as your Lord brought you forth from your house with the truth. A group of the believers are reluctant"'" (*sūrat al-Anfāl*; VIII, v.5).

He then related the rest of the *ḥadīth* as above.

Ibn Mardawayh also related, through Muḥammad b. ʿAmr b. ʿAlqama b. Waqqāṣ al-Laythī, from his father, from his grandfather, who said, "The Messenger of God (ṢAAS) went forth to Badr and, having gone as far as al-Rawḥāʾ, there he addressed his force. 'What do you think?' he asked them. Abū Bakr replied, 'O Messenger of God, we have heard that they are so-on and so-forth.' Again he asked them what they thought, and ʿUmar responded as Abū Bakr had done. But he asked a third time what they thought.

"Saʿd b. Muʿādh then asked him, 'O Messenger of God, is it us you ask? By Him who honoured you and sent down the Book to you, I've never travelled this road before and so have no knowledge of it. But if you were to travel on to Bark al-Ghimād, in Yemen, we'd accompany you. We'll not be like those who told Moses, "Go off with your Lord and fight; we're staying here." Instead, you go off with your Lord and fight, and we will follow you. And if you proceeded for one purpose and God gave you another, then recognize what God has charged you with and proceed. Make or break with whomever you wish, make war or peace with whomever you wish, and take from our wealth whatever you wish.'"

There was a revelation in the Qur>ān concerning Sa<d's words, "Just as your Lord brought you forth from your home with the truth. A group of the believers are reluctant" (*sūrat al-Anfāl*; VIII. v.5).

Al-Umawī related this in his work on the military expeditions and he added, after his words, "and take from our wealth whatever you wish" the phrase "and give us what you wish. And what you take from us will be dearer to us than what you have left. Whatever orders you give us we will follow completely. And, I swear, if you were to go on until you reached al-Bark of Ghamdān, we would go with you."

Ibn Isḥāq stated, "The Messenger of God (ṢAAS) travelled on from Dhafrān and traversed the passes called al-Aṣāfir. From there he went down to a town called al-Dābba, leaving al-Ḥannān on his right. This is a huge sandhill, like a mountain, and from there he went on down to near Badr. He and another man then rode on further."

Ibn Hishām stated that this man was Abū Bakr.

Ibn Isḥāq went on, "This was related to me by Muḥammad b. Yaḥyā b. Ḥabbān. They went on and finally stopped near an old bedouin sheikh. He asked him about Quraysh and about Muḥammad and his Companions and what news he had of them. The old man replied, 'I'll not tell you until you tell me to whom you belong.'

"The Messenger of God (ṢAAS) replied, 'You tell us and we'll tell you.' The sheikh asked, 'This for that?' 'Yes,' he agreed.

"The old man then said, 'I have been told that Muḥammad and his Companions left on such and such a day. And if the person who told me this spoke the truth, then today they should be at such and such a place.' This was the name of the very place where the Messenger of God (ṢAAS) actually was. 'And,' he went on, 'I was told that Quraysh left on day so-and-so. And if the person who told me this spoke the truth, then today they should be at such-and-such.' This was the place where Quraysh then were.

"When he had finished his report, he asked, 'And who are you?' The Messenger of God (ṢAAS) replied, 'We are from *mā>*, "water".' He then left. As he did so the old man was asking, 'What's that about *mā>*? You mean you're from the *mā>*, the water, of Iraq?'"

Ibn Hishām said that this man's name was Sufyān al-Ḍamrī.

Ibn Isḥāq stated, "The Messenger of God (ṢAAS) then returned to his Companions. That evening he dispatched <Alī b. Abū Ṭālib, al-Zubayr b. al-<Awwām and Sa<d b. Abū Waqqāṣ, along with a number of his men, to the well at Badr to seek news; it was Yazīd b. Rūmān who told me this, from <Urwa b. al-Zubayr.

"They came across a watering-party of Quraysh among whom were Aslam, a youth of the Banū al-Ḥajjāj, along with <Arīḍ Abū Yasār, a youth of the Banū al-<Āṣ b. Sa<d. They brought them back and questioned them, while the

Messenger of God (ṢAAS) was standing praying. The youths told them they were water carriers sent to bring them water.

"The Muslim force disliked what they said and, believing they were under the command of Abū Sufyān, beat them. After they had been severely beaten, the youths said that they were from Abū Sufyān. The Muslims then released them.

"The Messenger of God (ṢAAS) bowed and prostrated in prayer twice and said, 'When they spoke the truth you beat them and when they lied you released them! They did speak the truth, by God. They are of Quraysh. Now, you two, tell me about Quraysh!' They responded, 'They are beyond that sandhill you can see over on the far side of the valley.' That sandhill was called al-ʿAqanqal.

"The Messenger of God (ṢAAS) asked them, 'How many men do they have?' 'Very many,' they replied. 'How many in number?' he asked. 'We don't know,' they answered. 'How many camels do they slaughter each day?' he next asked. 'Some days nine, others ten,' they told him. The Messenger of God (ṢAAS) concluded, 'So their force must be between 900 and 1000 men.'

"He then asked them, 'What Quraysh nobles do they have among them?'

"They replied, 'ʿUtba b. Rabīʿa, Shayba b. Rabīʿa, Abū al-Bukhtarī b. Hishām, Ḥākim b. Ḥizām, Nawfal b. Khuwaylid, al-Ḥārith b. ʿĀmir b. Nawfal, Ṭuʿayma b. ʿAdī b. Nawfal, al-Naḍr b. al-Ḥārith, Zamʿa b. al-Aswad, Abū Jahl b. Hishām, Umayya b. Khalaf, Nabīh and Munabbih, two sons of al-Ḥajjāj, Suhayl b. ʿAmr and ʿAmr b. ʿAbd Wudd.'

"The Messenger of God (ṢAAS) went out to his men and told them, 'This Mecca has thrown at you slices of its very liver!'"

Ibn Isḥāq stated, "Basbas b. ʿAmr and ʿAdī b. Abū al-Zaghbāʾ had gone on ahead to Badr and halted at a hill near the well. They then took a water-skin they had and went to fetch water. Majdī b. ʿAmr al-Juhanī was there at the well and ʿAdī and Basbas heard two girls from the village laying claims on the water. The one under obligation was saying to her companion, 'The caravan will arrive tomorrow or the day after. I will work for them, then pay you what I owe you.' Majdī answered, 'You are right.' He then made a settlement between them.

"ʿAdī and Basbas overheard that, mounted their camels and left, riding back to the Messenger of God (ṢAAS) and telling him what they heard.

"Abū Sufyān led the caravan cautiously ahead to the well and asked Majdī b. ʿAmr, 'Did you see anyone?' He replied, 'I saw no one suspicious, except for two riders who dismounted over at that hill, took water in a skin they had, then left.'

"Abū Sufyān made his way to where they had dismounted and picked up some of the droppings of their camels, broke it up and found it contained date-stones. He then said, 'I swear this is from feed of Yathrib.'

"He then hurried back to his men, struck his camel to direct it away from the road and headed it towards the sea coast, leaving Badr to his left and moving off at top speed.

"Quraysh advanced and at al-Juḥfa Juhaym b. al-Ṣalt b. Makhrama b. al-Muṭṭalib b. ʿAbd Manāf had a vision. He said, 'I had a vision in my sleep, while half-way between waking and sleeping, of a man riding a horse and leading a camel, who came to a halt. He then said, "ʿUtba b. Rabīʿa, Shayba b. Rabīʿa, Abū al-Ḥakam b. Hishām, Umayya b. Khalaf and so on, are all killed!' He went on to enumerate other chiefs of Quraysh as well who were killed at Badr.

"Juhaym went on, 'I then saw him strike the upper chest of his camel and send it on into the camp. And every single tent there was splattered with its blood.'

"When Juhaym's vision was reported to Abū Jahl, God damn him, he said, 'So he too is a prophet from the ʿAbd al-Muṭṭalib family! He'll know tomorrow who will be killed, if we meet in battle!'"

Ibn Isḥāq continued, "Thinking he had saved his caravan, Abū Sufyān sent word to Quraysh, 'You came out to do battle in order to protect your caravan, people and wealth; God has now saved these, so go back!'

"But Abū Jahl b. Hishām said, 'By God, we'll not turn around until we reach Badr!'"

Badr was a place where the Arabs would hold a fair and market each year.

(Abū Jahl went on) "'We'll stay there three days, slaughter some camels, eat well, drink wine and the entertainers will play music for us. The bedouin will get to hear of our journey and of our gathering there, and they will always respect us for it. Let's proceed ahead.'

"Al-Akhnas b. Sharīq b. ʿAmr b. Wahb al-Thaqafī, an ally of the Banū Zuhra, who lived in al-Juḥfa, said, 'O Banū Zuhra, God has saved your wealth for you and has now rendered your companion Makhrama b. Nawfal safe; since you only came out to protect him and the wealth he bears, put the blame for cowardice on me and go back. There is no need for you to go to battle when you have suffered no loss. Don't do as he says.'

"And they did go back; not one member of the Zuhra tribe took part in the battle of Badr. They obeyed him because they recognized his authority.

"Every sub-tribe of Quraysh except the Banū ʿAdī did participate. Not a single one of them took part.

"And so the Banū Zuhra went back with al-Akhnas; not a man from these two tribes engaged in the battle."

Ibn Isḥāq went on, "And so the force proceeded. There was some debate between Ṭālib b. Abū Ṭālib, who was present there, and some of the Quraysh. They told him, 'We well know, you men of the Banū Hāshim, that even though you have come out with us, that your sympathy lies with Muḥammad.' And so Ṭālib went back to Mecca with some other men. On that subject he spoke the following verses,

'O God, if Ṭālib goes to battle with a force allied to
fight in great troops like there,

> Then let him be the one despoiled, not the despoiler,
> the one defeated, not the one defeating.'"

Ibn Ishāq went on, "Quraysh proceeded and made camp on the far side of the valley, behind the sandhill called al-ʿAqanqal. The floor of the valley, called Yalyal, was between Badr and the huge sandhill, al-ʿAqanqal, behind which were Quraysh. The well at Badr was on the other side of the valley, nearest to Medina."

I would comment that on this subject the Almighty said, "You were on the nearer side, they on the further, and the caravan was below you" (that is, over towards the coast) "and had you made appointment for this you would have failed to keep it; however, (the battle did take place) in order for God to bring about something already ordained" (*sūrat al-Anfāl*; VIII, v.42).

Ibn Ishāq went on, "And God dispatched the heavens (with rain). The valley was soft ground and the water from the sky merely dampened the earth for the Messenger of God (ṢAAS) and his force but did not impede their progress. But Quraysh had such rain fall upon them that they could not move ahead."

I comment that on this God spoke, "And He sent down upon you water from the sky to purify you thereby, to remove from you the devil's filth, to strengthen your hearts and to steady your feet" (*sūrat al-Anfāl*; VIII, v.11).

Here God refers to cleansing them both inside and out, to steadying their feet and giving them courage, to thwarting the devil and his inspiring them with fear and doubts. This action was to give strength both within and without. He sent down His help for them from above, as exemplified in His words, "when your Lord revealed to the angels that I am with you. And so make those who believe; for I shall cast terror into the hearts of the unbelievers. Therefore strike above their necks" (upon their heads, that is) "and strike off all their finger-tips" (so that they cannot grip their weapons). "This is because they were hostile to God and to His Messenger. And God is violent in His punishment of those who are hostile to God and His Messenger. Taste that then! And (know) that the punishment of hell is for disbelievers" (*sūrat al-Anfāl*; VIII, v.12–14).

Ibn Jarīr stated, "Hārun b. Ishāq related to me, quoting Musʿab b. al-Miqdām, quoting Isrāʾīl quoting Abū Ishāq, from Hāritha, from ʿAlī b. Abū Tālib, who said, 'That night – the one preceding the morning when the battle of Badr occurred – it drizzled and we took shelter from it beneath the tree and under leather shields. The Messenger of God (ṢAAS) remained up praying and he exhorted us for the battle ahead.'"

The Imām Ahmad stated, "ʿAbd al-Rahmān b. Mahdī related to us, from Shuʿba, from Abū Ishāq, from Hāritha b. Midrab, from ʿAlī, who said, 'The only horseman we had at the battle of Badr was al-Miqdād. From what I saw, all slept except for the Messenger of God (ṢAAS) who remained beneath a tree praying and weeping until morning came.'"

This *hadīth* will be given hereafter at greater length.

Al-Nasāᵓī related this from Bundār, from Ghundar, from Shu‘ba. Mujāhid stated, "He sent down upon them rain which settled the dust and compressed the soil for them. It pleased them to have their feet tread upon it."

I comment that the night before Badr was the eve of Friday, the 17th of Ramaḍān, 2 AH. The Messenger of God (ṢAAS) spent that night near the stump of a tree there, praying. He kept prostrating himself and repeating, "O Everlasting One! O Self-Reliant One!" (sūrat al-Baqara; II, v.255).

Ibn Isḥāq stated, "The Messenger of God (ṢAAS) went out to urge his men on to the well, and when he reached the nearest source at Badr, he stopped there.

"It was related to me by some men of the Banū Salama, that they had been told that al-Ḥubāb b. Mundhir b. al-Jamūḥ said, 'O Messenger of God, is this the place about which God revealed to you that we should not advance beyond nor stop before? Or is this a question of opinion, warfare and tactics?'

"He replied, 'It's one of opinion, warfare and tactics.'

"Al-Ḥubāb then said, 'Well, O Messenger of God, this isn't a place to stop. We should go ahead till we get to the well nearest to their force and stop there. We should then stop up the wells behind it and build a cistern and fill it with water. Then we can fight them and have water to drink, while they'll have none.'

"The Messenger of God (ṢAAS) commented, 'You've had a good idea!'"

Al-Umawī stated, "My father related to us as follows: 'Al-Kalbī claimed, quoting Abū Ṣāliḥ, from Ibn ‘Abbās, who said, "As the Messenger of God (ṢAAS) was gathering the men into groups with Gabriel on his right, an angel came to him and said, 'O Muḥammad, God greets you with peace.' The Messenger of God (ṢAAS) replied, 'He is peace; from Him comes peace, and to Him peace goes.' The angel then said, 'You are to do as al-Ḥubab b. Mundhir told you.'"

"'The Messenger of God (ṢAAS) then asked, "O Gabriel, do you know this man?" He replied, "I don't know all the people of heaven, but he is truthful. He is no devil."

"'The Messenger of God (ṢAAS) and those with him arose and proceeded on to the well nearest to the Quraysh force, where they halted. He then ordered that the other wells be blocked and built a cistern at the well where he had stopped and filled it with water. They then threw the water jugs into it.'"

Some say that when al-Ḥubāb b. al-Mundhir made his suggestion to the Messenger of God (ṢAAS) an angel descended from the sky while Gabriel was there with him. The angel said, "O Muḥammad, your Lord greets you with peace and says to you that you are to do what al-Ḥubāb advised you." The Messenger of God (ṢAAS) looked up at Gabriel who said, "I don't know all the angels, but he is an angel, not a devil."

Al-Umawī stated that they halted at the well that was nearest to the polytheists at midnight and made camp there. They completely filled the cistern, and so the polytheists had no water.

Ibn Isḥāq stated, "ʿAbd Allāh b. Abū Bakr related to me that he was informed that Saʿd b. Muʿādh stated, 'O Prophet of God, should we not build you a cover where you could stay and near which we could tether your mounts, and then we can meet our enemy. If God gives us victory over our enemy, that will be fine by us; but if the opposite happens, you can mount up and join those of our people behind us; those who stayed do not love you any less than we do. If they had thought you would be going into battle, they would not have stayed. God will protect you through them and they will give you sincere counsel and will fight hard with you.'

"The Messenger of God (ṢAAS) thanked him and prayed for him. Then a shelter was constructed for the Messenger of God (ṢAAS) where he stayed."

Ibn Isḥāq stated, "When morning came, the Quraysh force advanced.

"When the Messenger of God (ṢAAS) saw them coming forward into the valley from their position behind the sandhill at al-ʿAqanqal, he said, 'O God, these men advancing are Quraysh in all their vanity and pride; they are antagonistic to You and are calling Your Prophet a liar. O God, give us Your victory You promised us! O God, destroy them this morning.'

"The Messenger of God (ṢAAS) then said, having seen ʿUtba b. Rabīʿa in the Quraysh force mounted on a red camel, 'Whatever good may be in them resides in the man mounted on the red camel. If they were to obey him, they would be well guided.'

"Khufāf b. Aymāʾ b. Raḥaḍa, or his father Aymāʾ b. Raḥaḍa al-Ghifārī, had sent to Quraysh a son of his with some slaughtered camels which he was donating to them, telling them, 'If you wish us to provide you with weapons and men we will do so.' Quraysh sent back with his son the following response, 'You have maintained family ties and fulfilled your duty. If we are only fighting men, we will not lack the power. But if we are fighting God, as Muḥammad claims, no one could stand up to Him.'

"When the Quraysh force made camp, some of their men came forward to the water cistern of the Messenger of God (ṢAAS); they included Ḥakīm b. Ḥizām. The Messenger of God (ṢAAS) said, 'Let them come.' And every man who drank that day was killed, except for Ḥakīm b. Ḥizām, who survived. He later accepted Islam and became a good Muslim; whenever he later made a serious oath, he would say, 'By Him who saved me at the battle of Badr.'"

I would comment that the troops of the Messenger of God (ṢAAS) consisted of 313 men, as will be shown in a chapter we will give following the account of the battle in which we will list their names in alphabetical order, if God wills it.

In the *ṣaḥīḥ* collection of al-Bukhārī, from al-Barāʾ, there is the *ḥadīth*: "We used to relate that those Muslims present at Badr totalled 300 men and some tens more, the same number as the companions of Ṭālūt, who crossed the river along with him; and all those who did so were believers."

Al-Bukhārī also quotes from the same source as follows, "I and Ibn ῾Umar were deemed too young to participate in the battle of Badr. The Emigrants there numbered some 60 men, while the Helpers totalled some 240."

Imām Aḥmad related from Naṣr b. Ri᾿āb, from Ḥajjāj, from al-Ḥakam, from Muqsim, from Ibn ῾Abbās, who said, "Those participating at Badr totalled 313, while the Emigrants numbered 76. The defeat occurred on Friday, 17th Ramaḍān."

God Almighty stated, "And recall when God showed them to you in your sleep as few; and if He had showed them to you as many, you would have lost courage, and would have disputed about the matter. However, God granted salvation" (sūrat al-Anfāl; VIII, v.43).

That related to a dream he had that night. It is said that he slept in the shelter and that he told his men that they should not fight until they received permission. When the Quraysh force approached, Abū Bakr began to wake him up, saying, "O Messenger of God, they are getting close! Wake up!" God had showed them to him in his sleep as being few in number.

Al-Umawī related this, and it is very strange.

The Almighty stated, "And when He showed them to you, when you met, as few in number in your sight, as He diminished you in theirs, in order to bring about a matter already decreed" (sūrat al-Anfāl; VIII, v.44).

When the two sides were to engage in battle, God made each of them fewer in the view of the other so that they would have courage to face each other, there being very great wisdom in this.

This is not contrary to the statement of God Almighty: "There was a sign for you in the two sides battling together, one fighting for God, the other unbelieving and seeing them by their own sight as twice their own like. And God aids with His victory those He wishes" (sūrat Āl-῾Imrān; III, v.12).

The meaning according to the most authentic statements is that the unbelievers did indeed view the believers as twice their number. This was when the battle and swordsmanship had begun, God cast weakness and terror into the hearts of the unbelievers. He first led them on by showing them as few in the initial engagement and then aided the believers by making them seem twice as many as they were so that the enemy was weakened and overcome. For this reason God stated, "God aids with his help those He wishes. And there is a lesson in that for those who have vision" (sūrat Āl-῾Imrān; III, v.12).

Isrā᾿il stated, from Abū Isḥāq, Abū ῾Ubayd and ῾Abd Allāh, "They were made fewer in number in our sight on the day of the battle of Badr, to the point where I said to a man by my side, 'Do you think they are 70 strong?' He replied, 'I see them as 100!'"

Ibn Isḥāq stated that Abū Isḥāq b. Yasār and other scholars related to him that sheikhs of the Helpers had said, "When the Quraysh force felt secure they sent out ῾Umayr b. Wahb al-Jumaḥī with orders to estimate the size of the force of the Messenger of God (ṢAAS).

"He circled the camp on his horse and returned, saying, 'They are approximately 300 men in number; but be patient while I check out whether they have any others hidden or in reserve.'"

"He rode far off into the valley but saw nothing. So he came back and told them, 'I saw nothing more; but what I did see, O Quraysh, was camels bearing death. The Yathrib mounts bear imminent death. They are people whose only aid and refuge is their swords. I swear I don't foresee any of them being killed before he kills one of you. And if they do kill of you a like number as their own, what good will it be to live after that? Consider carefully.'

"When Ḥakīm b. Ḥizām heard that he walked through the force to ʿUtba b. Rabīʿa and said, 'Al-Walīd, you are a leader and a commander of Quraysh; do you wish to be remembered with pride by your people until the end of time?'

"'How do you mean, Ḥakīm?' he asked. 'Take your force back and deal with the issue of your ally ʿAmr b. al-Ḥaḍramī.' 'Consider it done,' he agreed, 'you have my guarantee of it. He was under my protection and so it is my duty to pay his bloodwit and provide compensation for what was taken from him. Go and talk to Ibn al-Ḥanẓaliyya – meaning Abū Jahl – he is the only one I fear might make trouble.'

"ʿUtba then arose to speak, saying, 'O Quraysh, by fighting Muḥammad and his Companions you will accomplish nothing. If you do attack him, each of you will always be looking at others who will dislike looking back at you; you will be known to have killed their cousin or a member of their tribe. Go home and leave Muḥammad up to the other Arabs. If they kill him that will be accomplishing your aims and if otherwise, he will find you not to have been exposed to (the risk of) what you now plan.'

"Ḥakīm went on, 'So I went on to Abū Jahl whom I found to have put on a coat of mail and was getting it ready. I told him, "Abū al-Ḥakam, ʿUtba has sent me to you." And I told him what he had said. He replied, "I swear, his lungs filled with terror when he saw Muḥammad and his men. By God, we will not return until God decides the issue between us and Muḥammad. ʿUtba is not sincere in what he says. He sees Muḥammad and his men as fodder for camels awaiting slaughter, and his own son is there among them. He's scaring you for his own sake."'

"Abū Jahl then sent for ʿĀmir b. al-Ḥaḍramī and told him, 'This ally of yours wants our force to return home. Yet you see before you your vengeance; stand up and demand your rights for the slaying of your brother.'

"ʿĀmir b. al-Ḥaḍramī arose, uncovered his head and proclaimed, 'Woe for ʿAmr! Woe for ʿAmr!'

"And so the mood for warfare became heated and the attitude of the Quraysh force hardened and they became set in their evil course, while ʿUtba's advice was ignored.

"When Abū Jahl's words 'his lungs filled with terror' reached ʿUtba, he exclaimed, 'That fellow with the filthy yellow backside will find out whether it's me or him whose lungs filled in terror!'

"'Utba then looked for a steel helmet to put on his head. But he could not find one with the army that was big enough for his skull. Realizing this, he wrapped his head in a cloth he had."

Ibn Jarīr related through al-Musawwar b. 'Abd al-Malik al-Yarbū'ī, from his father, from Sa'īd b. al-Musayyab, who said, "While we were at the home of Marwān b al-Ḥakam, his doorkeeper came in and said, 'Ḥakīm b. Ḥizām asks if he can come in.' Marwān said that he could, and when Ḥakīm came in, he said to him, 'Welcome to you, Abū Khālid, do sit close by.' He then moved away from the central cushion, taking a seat with the cushion next to him. He then greeted him and said, 'Tell us about the battle of Badr.'

"Ḥakīm then said, 'We went out as far as al-Juḥfa, at which point one entire Quraysh tribe went back, none of their polytheists consequently being at Badr. We then went on to al-'Udwa where we stopped as the Almighty had said. I then went to 'Utba b. Rabī'a and asked, "Abū al-Walīd, how would you like to enjoy honour for this day for as long as you live?" "What should I do?" he asked. I replied, "Ask of Muḥammad only compensation for the death of your ally, al-Ḥaḍramī; be satisfied with his blood-money and the force will go home."

"'"You have convinced me," he said, "go on to Ibn al-Hanẓaliyya (meaning Abū Jahl) and tell him his cousin asks him if he is willing to now return home with his men."

"'So I went to him (Abū Jahl) and found him with a group of his men all around him. There too, standing in front of him, was Ibn al-Ḥaḍramī who was saying, "I have cancelled my contract with 'Abd Shams; now it stands with the Banū Makhzūm."

"'I said to him (to Abū Jahl), "'Utba b. Rabī'a asks you whether you will now return with your men?" He replied, "Are you the only messenger he could find?" I answered, "No; and I'd be the messenger for no one but him."'

"Ḥakīm went on, 'I hurried off to 'Utba to be sure I would miss nothing that happened. He was leaning over Aymā' b. Raḥaḍa al-Ghifārī, who had donated to the polytheists ten camels for slaughter.

"''Abū Jahl then appeared, looking extremely mean, and said to 'Utba, "Have your lungs filled with terror then?" 'Utba replied, "You'll find out!" At that Abū Jahl drew his sword and slapped the flank of his horse with it. Aymā' b. Raḥaḍa commented, "This is a bad omen." And at that point warfare began.

"''The Messenger of God (ṢAAS) had established very effective battle lines for his force.'"

Al-Tirmidhī related, from 'Abd al-Raḥmān b. 'Awf, that Ḥakīm used the words, "It was during the night that the Messenger of God (ṢAAS) established us in battle lines at Badr."

Imām Aḥmad related, from an account of Ibn Lahī'a, as follows, "Yazīd b. Abū Ḥabīb related to me that Aslam Abū 'Imrān related to him that he heard Abū Ayyūb say, 'The Messenger of God (ṢAAS) established our battle lines at

Badr, and our heralds went out in front of our lines. The Prophet (ṢAAS) looked over at them and said, "With me! With me!"'"

Aḥmad alone gives this account. The line of transmission is good.

Ibn Isḥāq stated, "Ḥabbān b. Wāsiʿ b. Ḥabbān related to me, from sheikhs of his tribe, that when the Messenger of God (ṢAAS) lined up his forces at the battle of Badr, he held an arrow which he used to indicate how they should adjust their position. He passed by Sawwād b. Ghaziyya, an ally of the Banū ʿAdī b. al-Najjār, and a little ahead of the line. He poked him in the belly with the arrow, saying, 'Straighten up, Sawwād!'

"He replied, 'O Messenger of God, I swear by Him who sent you with the truth and justice that you hurt me! So let me retaliate!'

"The Messenger of God (ṢAAS) promptly uncovered his stomach and said, 'Retaliate then!' Sawwād hugged him and then kissed his stomach. The Messenger of God (ṢAAS), asked, 'Why did you do that, Sawwād?' He replied, 'O Messenger of God, you can see what is about to happen; I wanted my last contact with you to be my skin touching yours.'

"The Messenger of God (ṢAAS) then spoke a prayer for him."

Ibn Isḥāq stated, "ʿĀṣim b. ʿUmar b. Qatāda related to me that ʿAwf b. al-Ḥārith, he being ʿAfrāʾ's son, said, 'O Messenger of God, what is it about His worshippers that pleases God?' 'For them to charge into the enemy unprotected by helmet or chain-mail,' he replied.

"At this ʿAwf removed the suit of chain-mail he wore, threw it aside, then drew his sword and fought until he was killed; may God be pleased with him!"

Ibn Isḥāq went on, "Having arranged the position of his forces, the Messenger of God (ṢAAS) returned to his shelter and went in, accompanied by Abū Bakr, no one else being there with him."

Ibn Isḥāq and others also said, "Saʿd b. Muʿadh, God be pleased with him, was standing at the door of the shelter wearing his sword. With him were some of the Helpers standing guard over the Messenger of God (ṢAAS) fearing he might be attacked by the polytheist enemies, while choice horses stood there at the ready for the Messenger of God (ṢAAS) to ride back to Medina if necessary, as Saʿd b. Muʿadh had suggested."

Al-Bazzār related in his *Musnad* (collection of *aḥādīth*), from an account of Muḥammad b. ʿUqayl, that ʿAlī (once) addressed the forces, saying, 'Who is the bravest of all the people?' 'It is you, O Commander of the Faithful!' they responded.

"'Well,' he commented, 'I have never refused anyone's challenge, but it was in fact Abū Bakr. We made a shelter for the Messenger of God (ṢAAS) to prevent his being attacked by one of the polytheists. And, I swear, it was Abū Bakr alone who came over to us, holding his drawn sword above the head of the Messenger of God (ṢAAS). And when anyone came towards him, Abū Bakr would raise his sword before him. This man was the bravest of all.'

"ʿAlī went on, 'Once I saw the Messenger of God (ṢAAS) in the hands of some Quraysh men, some blocking his way, others jostling him, and saying, "You made the gods into just one!" And, I swear, the only one of us who intervened was Abū Bakr, striking and pushing and jostling them, saying, "Shame on you! Would you kill a man for saying that God is his Lord?"'

"ʿAlī then raised up the mantle he wore and wept, his beard wet with tears. He said, 'Were the believers among Pharoah's people better than him?' The crowd was silent, and ʿAlī went on, 'By God, an hour of Abū Bakr is better than an earth full of the believers from among Pharoah's people. Those were people who concealed their belief, while he was a man who made his faith public.'"

Al-Bazzār then stated, "We know of this anecdote only from this account."

This reflects the special distinction of Abū Bakr; it was he who was with the Messenger of God in the shelter, just as he had been with him in the cave. May God be pleased with him and please him!

"The Messenger of God (ṢAAS) was meanwhile making invocations, pleas and prayers saying, among other things, 'O God, if this force perishes, You will never again be worshipped on earth!' He cried out to God the Almighty and Glorious, 'O Lord, fulfil what You promised me; O God, give me aid!'

"In saying this he would raise his hands so high that his cloak would slip down over his shoulders, and Abū Bakr, God bless him, would stand close behind him repositioning it for him and saying, in sympathy at the effusiveness of his supplication, 'O Messenger of God, lessen your appeals to your Lord; He will fulfil His promise to you.'"

This, then, is how it is related by al-Suhaylī, from Qāsim b. Thābit. Abū Bakr only used the words meaning "lessen your appeals to your Lord" out of his concern for what he saw as his being so engrossed in his prayer and supplications that his mantle had slipped down over his shoulders. By saying these words he was in effect asking, "Why are you so exhausting yourself; God has made you a promise of His help." Abū Bakr, God bless him, was a tender-hearted man with great empathy and compassion for the Messenger of God (ṢAAS).

Al-Suhaylī related that his teacher, Sheikh Abū Bakr b. al-ʿArabī, said, "The Messenger of God (ṢAAS) was in a situation of *khawf*, fearing, while Abū Bakr was in one of *rajāʾ*,[60] hoping. And this was really a time of fearing." By this he meant that *khawf* (in this instance) was more appropriate, "because it was up to God to do as He wished; and he feared that God would not be worshipped thereafter. His fear was therefore worship."

I would comment that the view of some Sufi ascetics that this situation was analogous to that of the day in the cave is to be rejected. For this person did not make mention of the weakness of his viewpoint, nor the consequences thereof.

---

60. These are terms used especially by Muslim mystics to describe the attitudes one can adopt in one's relationship to the Divine being.

In any case, the contending forces did confront one another in battle, the outcome resting in the hands of the All-Merciful. The greatest of the prophets called upon his Lord's help, his Companions too raising their voices loud in invocation of the Lord of heaven and earth, Who hears all prayers and discovers all heroic action.

The first of the polytheists to be killed was al-Aswad b. ʿAbd al-Asad al-Makhzūmī.

Ibn Isḥāq stated, "This was a mean and disreputable fellow who had said, 'I swear to God I will drink from their cistern or destroy it, or die before I get there!' And when he came forth to do battle, Ḥamza b. ʿAbd al-Muṭṭalib went out to confront him. When they met, Ḥamza struck him and off came his foot and half his leg, before he had reached the cistern. He fell down on his back, his leg spurting blood back towards his companions. He then crawled on in the direction of the cistern, plunging into it intending, so they say, to fulfil his oath. Ḥamza pursued him and struck him again and again until he had killed him, there in the cistern."

Al-Umawī stated, "At that ʿUtba b. Rabīʿa became excited and determined to demonstrate his bravery. He came forth with his brother Shayba on one side of him and his son al-Walīd on the other and, standing out in the centre between the two lines, they issued a challenge for single combat. Three young men from the Helpers went out to confront them; they were ʿAwf and Muʿādh, the two sons of al-Ḥārith, their mother being ʿAfrāʾ, along with ʿAbd Allāh b. Rawāḥa, so they say. 'And who are you?' they were asked, and they replied, 'We are from among the *anṣār*, "the Helpers".' 'We have no quarrel with you,' they were told."

In one account it is said that the Quraysh warriors then said, "These are our honourable peers, but send forth some of our own people." Their herald then called out, "O Muḥammad, send forth our peers from our own people."

"The Prophet (ṢAAS) replied, 'You go, ʿUbayda b. al-Ḥārith, and you Ḥamza, and you, ʿAlī.'"

According to al-Umawī, the Messenger of God (ṢAAS) was displeased when the three Helpers stepped forth. This was because this was the first battle pitting his men against his enemies, and he would have preferred his warriors to have been from his own tribe. He therefore ordered the first three men to withdraw and ordered out the three men named above.

Ibn Isḥāq stated, "When the three combatants approached the three Quraysh warriors, the latter asked their names." (This is an indication that they were wearing armour and they could not be recognized by their weapons.) "ʿUbayda, Ḥamza and ʿAlī each gave their names in turn. The Quraysh champions then commented, 'Worthy peers.'

"ʿUbayda then stepped forward, he being the oldest of them, and faced ʿUtba, while Ḥamza addressed Shayba and ʿAlī stood before al-Walīd b. ʿUtba.

"Ḥamza soon killed Shayba, as ʿAlī did al-Walīd. ʿUbayda and ʿUtba exchanged blows and each brought the other down. Ḥamza and ʿAlī then turned their swords against ʿUtba and finished him off. They then picked up their fallen comrade and carried him back to their side. May God be pleased with him."

It is established in both *ṣaḥīḥ* collections from a *ḥadīth* of Abū Mijlaz, from Qays b. ʿUbād, that Abū Dharr used to swear on oath that this verse, "These two are adversaries who dispute about their Lord" (*sūrat al-Ḥajj*; XXII, v.19) was revealed about Ḥamza and his opponent and about ʿUtba and his, referring to their coming forth at Badr.

This is the wording al-Bukhārī gives in explaining this verse.

Al-Bukhārī stated, "Ḥajjāj b. Minhāl related to us, quoting al-Muʿtamir b. Sulaymān, who said, 'I heard my father say that Abū Mijlaz related to him, from Qays b. ʿUbād, who quoted ʿAlī b. Abū Ṭālib as having said, "I will be the first person who kneels before the All-Merciful one, Almighty and Glorious is He, among the adversaries on Judgement Day."'

"Qays stated, 'And it was about them that the verse was revealed, "These two are adversaries who dispute about their Lord."' He went on, 'This referred to those who stood forth to do battle at Badr – ʿAlī and Ḥamza, ʿUbayda and Shayba b. Rabīʿa, and ʿUtba b. Rabīʿa and al-Walīd b. ʿUtba.'"

Al-Bukhārī alone gives this.

We have discussed this at sufficient length in our *Tafsīr* (*Exegesis*); and to God be all praise and credit.

Al-Umawī stated, "Muʿāwiya b. ʿAmr related to us, from Abū Isḥāq, from Ibn al-Mubārak, from Ismāʿīl b. Abū Khālid, from ʿAbd Allāh al-Bahiyy, who said, "ʿUtba, Shayba and al-Walīd, stood forth to do battle and Ḥamza, ʿUbayda and ʿAlī went out to face them. The Quraysh champions said, "Speak, so we may know you." Ḥamza replied, "I am *Asad Allāh*, 'God's lion', and the lion of the Messenger of God; I am Ḥamza, son of ʿAbd al-Muṭṭalib." They responded, "A worthy peer." ʿAlī then said, "I am *ʿAbd Allāh*, 'God's slave', and the brother of the Messenger of God." ʿUbayda said, "I am he who is among the allies." Each then engaged in man-to-man conflict, and God killed them.'"

Hind spoke the following on that subject,

> "Eyes of mine, make copious tears flow down for the
> best of heroes who did not turn aside.
> His people called out to him on the morning when the
> Banū Hāshim and the Banū al-Muṭṭalib did battle,
> Making him taste the sharpness of their swords, raising
> him aloft even after he had been destroyed."

This was why Hind swore she would eat Ḥamza's liver.

The ʿUbayda referred to here was the son of al-Ḥārith b. al-Muṭṭalib b. ʿAbd Manāf. They carried him to the Messenger of God (ṢAAS), and placed him on a bed next to where he stood. The Messenger of God (ṢAAS) then honoured him by allowing his cheek to rest on his foot.

"ʿUbayda then said, 'O Messenger of God, if Abū Ṭālib could only see me, he would know that it was to me his words applied, "We will serve him until we are laid out before him, uncaring even of our sons and our wives."'

"He then, God be pleased with him, died, and the Messenger of God (ṢAAS) said, 'I bear witness that you are a martyr!'"

Al-Shāfiʿī, God bless him, related this.

The first Muslim killed in the battle was Mihjaʿ, the freed-man of ʿUmar b. al-Khaṭṭāb; he was shot with an arrow.

Ibn Isḥāq stated, "He was the first man killed. Then Ḥāritha b. Surāqa, one of the Banū ʿAdī b. al-Najjār, was shot at as he drank from the cistern. An arrow hit him in the throat, and so he died."

It is established in the ṣaḥīḥ collections, from Anas, that Ḥāritha b. Surāqa was killed at Badr. He was in the vanguard and was struck by a stray arrow which killed him. His mother later came to the Messenger of God (ṢAAS) and said, "O Messenger of God, tell me about Ḥāritha. If he is in heaven, I will be content. Otherwise, let God show me what to do." That is, to engage in mourning for him, a practice not yet forbidden. The Messenger of God (ṢAAS) replied, "Have you gone crazy? There are eight gardens there, and your son has earned the very highest of paradise!"

Ibn Isḥāq stated, "The forces moved slowly towards one another. The Messenger of God (ṢAAS) had told his men not to attack until he gave them the order. He said, 'If the enemy should surround you, then force them back with arrows.'"

In his ṣaḥīḥ collection, al-Bukhārī quotes Abū Usayd as saying, "The Messenger of God (ṢAAS), told us at the battle of Badr, 'If they close in on you' – meaning the polytheists – 'then shoot at them and gather up your arrows.'"

Al-Bayhaqī stated, "Al-Ḥākim informed us, quoting al-Aṣamm, that Aḥmad b. ʿAbd al-Jabbār related to us, from Yūnus b. Bukayr, from Abū Isḥāq, quoting ʿAbd Allāh b. al-Zubayr, as follows, 'The Messenger of God (ṢAAS) made the battle-cry of the Emigrants at Badr, "O Banū ʿAbd al-Raḥmān!" (that is, "O tribe of the worshipper of the All-Merciful") and that of al-Khazraj, "O Banū of ʿAbd Allāh" (that is "O tribe of the worshipper of God"), that of al-Aws, "O Banū ʿUbayd Allāh" (that is, "O tribe of the slaves of God"). He named his cavalry "God's horsemen."'"

Ibn Hishām stated that the war cry used at Badr by the ṣaḥāba, the Companions, was "One! One!"

Ibn Isḥāq stated, "While the Messenger of God (ṢAAS) was in the shelter with Abū Bakr, God bless him, he called out to God the Almighty and Glorious for help. As the Almighty stated, 'When you sought aid from your Lord, and he answered you, saying, "I will help you with 1,000 angels, following after one another. And God made of it nothing but glad tidings, to ease your hearts by it. And victory comes only from God. God is powerful, wise"'" (sūrat al-Anfāl; VIII, v.9, 10).

Imām Aḥmad stated that Abū Nūḥ Qurād related to him, quoting 'Ikrima b. 'Ammār, quoting Simāk al-Ḥanafī, father of Zumayl, quoting Ibn 'Abbās, quoting 'Umar b. al-Khaṭṭāb, as follows, "At the battle of Badr, the Messenger of God (ṢAAS) looked over at his force numbering some 300 and viewed the polytheists, totalling more than 1,000. He then turned in the direction of the *qibla*, wearing his shawl and pants and spoke the words, 'O God, fulfil what you promised me; O God, if this force perishes You will never again be worshipped on earth.'

"He kept up his appeals and prayers to his Lord until his mantle fell down. Abū Bakr then came and replaced it, remaining close behind him. He then said, 'Let your appeals to your Lord be enough now. He will fulfil what He has promised you.' And so God revealed, 'When you sought aid from your Lord, and He answered you, saying, "I will help you with 1,000 angels, following after one another"'" (*sūrat al-Anfāl*; VIII, v.9).

He then related the conclusion of the *ḥadīth* as will come hereafter.

Muslim, Abū Dā'ūd, al-Tirmidhī, Ibn Jarīr and others all related this, from a *ḥadīth* of 'Ikrima b. 'Ammār al-Yamānī. 'Alī b. al-Madīnī and al-Tirmidhī declared it authentic.

Others also stated, from Ibn 'Abbās, al-Suddī, Ibn Jarīr and others, that this verse was revealed concerning the prayers said by the Prophet at Badr.

Al-Umawī and others stated that the Muslims shouted out loudly to God, Almighty and Glorious is He, seeking His aid.

As for the words of the Lord "with 1,000 angels, following after one another", it implies that "they are following on towards you and giving aid to your party".

Al-'Awfī related this *ḥadīth* from Ibn 'Abbās along with Mujāhid, Ibn Kathīr, 'Abd al-Raḥmān b. Zayd and others. Abū Kudayna stated, from Qābūs, from Ibn 'Abbās, that the word *murdifīn*, i.e. "following after one another", meant that each angel was followed by another one. In another account from him, with the same chain of authorites *murdifīn* is taken to imply that each came immediately after the other. Abū Ẓabyān, al-Ḍaḥḥāk and Qatāda said this.

'Alī b. Abū Ṭalḥa al-Wālibī related from Ibn 'Abbās, who said, "God provided His Prophet and the believers with 1,000 angels. Gabriel was there with one wing of 500, while Michael had another wing of 500. This is very well known."

However, Ibn Jarīr stated, "Al-Muthannā related to me, quoting Isḥāq, quoting Ya'qūb b. Muḥammad al-Zuhrī, quoting 'Abd al-'Azīz b. 'Imrān, from al-Raba'ī, from Abū al-Ḥuwayrith, from Muḥammad b. Jubayr, from 'Alī, who said, "Gabriel came down along with 1,000 angels on the right flank of the Prophet (ṢAAS) where Abū Bakr was, while Michael came down with 1,000 angels on the left flank of the Prophet (ṢAAS) where I was.'"

Al-Bayhaqī related this in his work *Dalā'il* (*The Signs*), from a *ḥadīth* of Muḥammad b. Jubayr, from 'Alī. He added the words, "And Isrāfīl came down with 1,000 angels."

He related in that account that he was stabbed that day by a lance, with the result that his armpit was reddened with blood, and that 3,000 angels came down.

This is strange, and there is some weakness in its chain of authorities. If true, the account would strengthen even further the prior statements. This is substantiated by the alternative reading of some authorities who read the word *murdafina*,[61] with an "a" following the "d". But God knows best.

Al-Bayhaqī stated, "Al-Ḥākim informed us, quoting al-Aṣamm, while Muḥammad b. Sinān al-Qazzāz related to us, quoting ʿUbayd Allāh b. ʿAbd al-Majīd Abū ʿAlī al-Ḥanafī, quoting ʿUbayd Allāh b. ʿAbd al-Raḥmān b. Mawhab, quoting Ismāʿīl b. ʿAwf b. ʿAbd Allāh b. Abū Rāfiʿ, from ʿAbd Allāh b. Muḥammad b. ʿUmar b. ʿAlī b. Abū Ṭālib, from his father, from his grandfather, who said, 'At the battle of Badr, I fought for a while, then hurried to see what the Messenger of God (ṢAAS) was doing. When I got there, I found him prostrate in worship, saying, "*Yā Ḥayy! Yā Qayyūm!*" "O Living One! O Eternal One!"; he was saying nothing else. I returned to the fighting, then came back to find him still prostrate and still repeating the same. Again I went off to battle, and once more returned to find the same. He kept saying this till God gave him victory.'"

Al-Nasāʾī related it in *al-Yawm wa al-Layla* (*Day and Night*) from Bundār, from ʿUbayd Allāh b. ʿAbd al-Majīd Abū ʿAlī al-Ḥanafī.

Al-Aʿmash stated, from Abū Isḥāq, from Abū ʿUbayda, from ʿAbd Allāh b. Masʿūd, who said, "I never heard any worshipper imploring God more strongly than did Muḥammad (ṢAAS) at the battle of Badr. He was saying, 'O God, I beseech you in the name of Your promise and Your pact! O God, if this force perishes, You will not be worshipped!' He then turned, and it was as if the moon had cleft its face! He said, 'I seem to be seeing the enemy's destruction in the late evening!'"

Al-Nasāʾī related this from a *ḥadīth* of al-Aʿmash.

He also said, "When we met in battle at Badr, the Messenger of God (ṢAAS) arose, and I never saw anyone implore God more strongly for his rights than did the Messenger of God (ṢAAS)." And he related as above.

It has been definitively stated in the *ṣaḥīḥ* collection of Muslim, on the authority of Anas b. Mālik, as stated, above, how the Prophet (ṢAAS) gave details of the circumstances of the deaths at Badr of the polytheists leaders. This information will also be reported later from the *ṣaḥīḥ* collection of Muslim on the authority of ʿUmar b. al-Khaṭṭāb.

The conclusion to be drawn from the *ḥadīth* of Ibn Masʿūd is that he gave notice of this on the actual day of the engagement. This is appropriate. The other two accounts, from Anas and from ʿUmar, suggest that he gave this information one day prior thereto.

There is no objection to combining between these. He could have given this information a day or more before, and (again) an hour before, on the actual day of the battle. But God knows best.

---

61. Changing the vowel i to a has the effect of changing the word from an active to a passive participle.

Al-Bukhārī related through several different lines of transmission, from Khālid al-Hadhā', from 'Ikrima, from Ibn 'Abbās, that the Prophet (ṢAAS), while in a pavilion he had at Badr, spoke the words, "O God, I appeal to Your pact and to Your oath! If You wish it, You will not be worshipped ever again after this day!" Abū Bakr took him by the hand and said, "That is enough, O Messenger of God! You are pestering your Lord." The Messenger of God (ṢAAS) then went outside, walking vigorously in his armour, speaking the verse, "The force will be defeated! They will retreat! The hour will come, and it will be most bitter!" (sūrat al-Qamar; LIV, v.45).

This verse was revealed in Mecca. Its truth was substantiated at the battle of Badr, as Ibn Abū Ḥākim related, as follows, "My father related to us, quoting Abū al-Rabī' al-Zahrānī, quoting Ḥammād, from Ayyūb, from 'Ikrima, who said, 'When the verse was revealed, "The force will be defeated! They will retreat!" 'Umar asked, "Which force will be defeated, and which will be supreme?" And 'Umar (later) said, "On the day of the battle of Badr, I saw the Messenger of God (ṢAAS) walking vigorously in his chain-mail and reciting, 'The force will be defeated! They will retreat! Their hour will come, and it will be most bitter!' I then realized how it was to be interpreted."'"

Al-Bukhārī related, through Ibn Jurayj, from Yūsuf b. Māhān, who heard 'Ā'isha say, "While I was a girl playing in Mecca, there was revealed to Muḥammad the words, 'Their hour will come, and it will be most bitter.'"

Ibn Isḥāq stated, "The Messenger of God (ṢAAS) began appealing to his Lord for the aid He had promised him, saying, 'O God, if this force perishes, You will not be worshipped.' Abū Bakr was saying meanwhile, 'O Prophet of God, diminish your appeals to your Lord. God will fulfil for you what He has promised you.'

"The Prophet (ṢAAS) had a brief nap while he was in the shelter. When he awoke, he said, 'Be joyful, Abū Bakr, God's help will come to you; I saw Gabriel taking his horse by the reins and leading it. And on its front teeth there was al-naq'!' By this word he meant 'dust'."

Ibn Isḥāq continued, "The Messenger of God (ṢAAS) then went outside to the men and urged them on, saying, 'Every man who fights them bravely and advances without retreating will have God give him entry into heaven.'

"'Umayr b. al-Ḥumām, a brother of the Banū Salama had some dates in his hand that he was eating. He shouted, 'Great! Great! Is all that stands between me and paradise to have them kill me?' He then tossed away the dates, took his sword and fought the enemy until he was killed. God bless him!"

Imām Aḥmad said, "Hāshim b. Sulaymān related to us, from Thābit, from Anas, who said, 'The Prophet (ṢAAS) sent Basbas off as a scout to see what had become of Abū Sufyān's caravan. He then returned to the house where only I and the Prophet (ṢAAS) were present, as far as I know, except for some of his wives. He (Basbas) then made his report to him.'

"Anas went on, 'Thereupon the Messenger of God (SAAS) went out and made an address, saying, "We have a request to make: whoever presently has a camel may ride with us." Some men there sought permission to fetch their camels from the upper parts of the town but he replied, "No; only those who have their camels present."

"'The Messenger of God (SAAS) and his men then set off and arrived at Badr before the polytheists. When the latter did arrive, the Messenger of God (SAAS) said, "None of you may advance for any purpose unless I am right behind."

"'When the polytheists advanced, the Messenger of God (SAAS) said, "Go forth towards a garden the size of the heavens and the earth combined."'

"Anas continued, 'At this ʿUmayr b. al-Hammām al-Anṣārī asked, "O Messenger of God, could a garden really be the size of the heavens and earth combined?" "Yes," he replied. ʿUmayr then said, "Fine! Fine!" The Messenger of God (SAAS) asked him, "What makes you say 'fine'?" ʿUmayr replied, "O Messenger of God, by God, it is only because of my hope of being one of its people." "You certainly will be," responded the Messenger of God (SAAS).

"'ʿUmayr then took some dates out of his quiver and began eating them. He then said, "If I were to live long enough to eat these dates, it would be a long life!" He then threw away all the dates he had and engaged them in battle until he was killed, God bless him.'"

Muslim related this anecdote from Abū Bakr b. Abū Shayba and a group of authorities, from Abū al-Naḍr Hāshim b. al-Qāsim, from Sulaymān b. al-Mughīra.

Ibn Jarīr recounted that while ʿUmayr fought he spoke the verses,

> "Racing on to God, my only provision is my piety and
> action for the life to come,
> And my persistence in fighting for God; for all other
> provisions soon become exhausted,
> Except for piety, goodness and right-guidedness."

Imām Aḥmad stated, "Ḥajjāj related to us, quoting Isrāʾīl, from Abū Isḥāq, from Ḥāritha b. Miḍrab, from ʿAlī, who said, 'When we got to Medina we fell sick from its fruits and the marshes there. The Messenger of God (SAAS) was preparing for Badr. When we received news that the polytheists were advancing, the Messenger of God (SAAS) moved out to Badr, it being the site of a well. We arrived there ahead of the polytheists but we did discover two men there. One was of Quraysh, the other a freed-man of ʿUqba b. Abū Muʿīṭ. The man of Quraysh escaped, but we took the freed-man and asked him how large was their force. He replied, "I swear, their numbers are great and their morale is very high." When he said this, the Muslims would beat him.

"'Eventually they took him to the Messenger of God (SAAS) who asked him how many they were, and the freed-man replied as before. The Prophet (SAAS) tried hard to get him to tell their numbers, but he refused. The Prophet (ṢAAS) then asked how many camels they were slaughtering for food. He replied that it was ten each day. The Prophet (ṢAAS) then said, "Their force numbers 1,000; each slaughtered camel would feed 100 men and their attendants."

"'That night rain drizzled down on us and we moved beneath a tree and took shelter from the rain beneath leather shields. The Messenger of God (ṢAAS) set about praying to his Lord, saying, "O God, if this force is destroyed, You will not be worshipped."

"'When dawn came, he called out, "Come to prayer, O worshippers of God!" The men emerged from beneath the tree and the leather shields, and the Messenger of God (ṢAAS) prayed with us and urged the men on to battle. He then said, "The Quraysh force is over behind those red slopes of the mountain."

"'When the enemy force drew near and we lined up to face them, there was one man among them mounted on a red camel. The Messenger of God (ṢAAS) called out, "ʿAlī, summon Ḥamza!" This Quraysh man was the closest to us. The Messenger of God (ṢAAS) asked, "Who is it on the red camel?" When Ḥamza came, he said the man was ʿUtba b. Rabīʿa. He was advising them against going to war, telling them, "Tie it up to my head; tell people, 'ʿUtba b. Rabīʿa turned cowardly.' Though you well know I'm no more cowardly than any one of you."

"'Abū Jahl heard of this and said, "You say this? I swear, were it anyone else who spoke thus, I would set my sword upon him! Your lungs have filled your belly with fear!"

"'He (ʿUtba) then said, "You dare to revile me, you yellow-bottomed one! You will discover today which one of us is cowardly."

"'ʿUtba, his brother Shayba and his son al-Walīd went forth challengingly and called out, "Who will come and oppose us?" Some young warriors from among the Helpers stepped forward, but ʿUtba called out, "We don't want them. We will do battle against our own relatives of the Banū ʿAbd al-Muṭṭalib."

"'At this the Messenger of God (ṢAAS) said, "Off you go, Ḥamza, and you ʿAlī and you too, ʿUbayd Allāh b. al-Ḥārith b. al-Muṭṭalib."

"'God then killed ʿUtba and Shayba, sons of Rabīʿa, and al-Walīd, ʿUtba's son. ʿUbayda was wounded; of their men we killed 70 and took 70 prisoner.

"'One of the Helpers brought in al-ʿAbbās b. al-Muṭṭalib as a prisoner, and al-ʿAbbās said, "O Messenger of God, this is not the man who captured me. A bald, fine-looking man on a piebald horse whom I had not seen with your men was he who took me prisoner." The Helper insisted, "No; it was I who captured him, O Messenger of God!"

"'But he replied, "Keep quiet! God gave you the help of a noble angel."'

"ʿAlī went on, 'Of the Banū ʿAbd al-Muṭṭalib we captured al-ʿAbbās, ʿUqayl and Nawfal b. al-Ḥārith.'"

This account is good. It corroborates what is given above and will come hereafter. Imām Aḥmad alone gives it in full. Abū Dāʾūd gave part of it, quoting a *ḥadīth* of Isrāʾīl.

When the Messenger of God (ṢAAS) had come out of the shelter and urged the men on to fight, they remained in their battle lines, firm and frequently invoking God's name, as the Almighty had ordered them to do in the words, "O believers, when you meet a force in battle, remain firm and invoke frequently the name of God" (sūrat al-Anfāl; VIII, v.45).

Al-Umawī stated, "Muʿāwiya b. ʿAmr related to us, from Abū Isḥāq, who quoted al-Awzāʿī as having stated, 'It used to be said that rarely did an armed force remain firmly in place. Those who can stay in place at such times, cast their eyes down and make frequent mention of God are likely to remain safe from the charge of hypocrisy.'"

ʿUtba b. Rabīʿa said to his men at the battle of Badr, "Do you not see them" – referring to the force of the Prophet (ṢAAS) – "how they crouch down on their mounts, keeping firmly in place, licking their lips like al-ḥayyāt, 'serpents'? Or he may have used the word al-afāʿī, 'snakes'."

Al-Umawī stated in his work on the military expeditions, "When the Prophet (ṢAAS) urged the Muslims on to battle, he promised that each man would keep any spoils they took and said, 'By Him in whose hands is my soul, any man who fights them hard and valiantly, advancing and not retreating, who is killed, will be allowed entry to heaven by God.'"

Al-Umawī's account then repeats the anecdote relating to ʿUmayr b. al-Hamām given above.

The Messenger of God (ṢAAS) himself fought with heart and soul, as did Abū Bakr, just as they had exerted themselves in the shelter in prayer and entreating. Thereafter, they went forth, and urged on the men to fight, themselves participating physically, thus combining their two noble functions.

The Imām Aḥmad stated, "Wakīʿ related to us, quoting Isrāʾīl, from Abū Isḥāq, from Ḥāritha b. Miḍrab, from ʿAlī, who said, 'I saw at Badr how near we kept to the Messenger of God (ṢAAS), while he was the one of us most close to the enemy. He was one of the bravest men there that day.'"

Al-Nasāʾī related this from a ḥadīth of Abū Isḥāq, from Ḥāritha, quoting ʿAlī as having said, "When the forces engaged and the battle grew fierce we sought protection with the Messenger of God (ṢAAS)."

Imām Aḥmad stated, "Abū Nuʿaym related to us, quoting Misʿar, from Abū ʿAwn, from Abū Ṣālih al-Ḥanafī, from ʿAlī who said that he and Abū Bakr were told at Badr, 'With one of you is Gabriel and with the other is Michael. Isrāfīl, a great angel, will witness the battle but not fight.' Or the words used were 'will witness the ranks.'"

This account is similar to the information preceding, namely, that Abū Bakr was on the right flank, and that at Badr when the angels descended Gabriel was there with 500 of them on one flank, the right along with Abū Bakr, while Michael was on the other, the left, with 500 more angels, along with ʿAlī.

In a ḥadīth related by Abū Yaʿlā, through Muḥammad b. Jubayr b. Muṭʿim, ʿAlī is quoted as saying, "At Badr, I was swimming in the water-hole when a great wind arose, then another, then another. Finally Michael came down along with 1,000 angels. He took up position on the right of the Messenger of God (ṢAAS) where Abū Bakr was positioned. Isrāfīl came to the left flank where I was, with another 1,000 angels. Gabriel was present, also with another 1,000." ῾Alī then said, "That day the water reached up to my armpits."

The author of *al-῾Iqd*[62] and others maintain that the finest verse ever spoken by the Arabs is that of Ḥassān b. Thābit,

> "And a well at Badr when Gabriel and Muḥammad held back
> their mounts, beneath our banner."

Al-Bukhārī stated, "Isḥāq b. Ibrāhīm related to us, quoting Jarīr, from Yaḥyā b. Sa῾īd, from Mu῾ādh b. Rifā῾a b. Rāfi῾ al-Zurqī, who quoted his father, who had been one of those present at Badr, as saying, 'Gabriel came to the Messenger of God (ṢAAS) and asked, "How do you consider those of you who were at Badr?" He replied, "As the best of Muslims," or some such phrase. Gabriel commented, "Likewise those of the angels who were present at Badr."'"

Al-Bukhārī alone gives this *ḥadīth*.

God Almighty had said, "When your Lord reveals to the angels that I am with you. And so strengthen those who believe; for I shall cast terror into the hearts of the unbelievers! Therefore strike above their necks" (meaning their heads) "and strike off all their finger-tips" (*sūrat al-Anfāl*; VIII, v.12).

In the *ṣaḥīḥ* collection of Muslim, through ῾Ikrima b. ῾Ammār, from Abū Zumayl, (it states) that Ibn ῾Abbās said, "While one of the Muslim warriors was vigorously pursuing one of the unbelievers ahead of him he heard above him the noise of a whip striking and a rider's voice saying, 'Giddy up, Ḥayzūm!' When the Muslim warrior looked at the polytheist in front of him, he found him prostrate on the ground. Examining him more closely he found that the man's nose had been smashed and his face split apart by a blow from a whip, all having turned dark in colour. The warrior, a Helper, went and told this to the Messenger of God (ṢAAS) who said, 'You speak true. That was help from the third heaven.' That day they killed 70 and captured 70 more."

Ibn Isḥāq stated, "῾Abd Allāh b. Abū Bakr b. Ḥazam related to me, from someone who related it to him, from Ibn ῾Abbās, from a man of the Banū Ghifār, who said, "I and a cousin of mine were present at Badr, though we were still polytheists then. We were up on a mountain waiting for the battle to take place and to see who would win, when a cloud approached. When it drew near the mountain we heard the sound of horses galloping and a voice saying, 'Giddy up, Ḥayzūm!' My companion suffered a heart attack and died on the spot, while I almost expired, but later recovered.'"

Ibn Isḥāq went on, "῾Abd Allāh b. Abū Bakr related to me, from a man of the Banū Sā῾ida, from Abū Usayd Mālik b. Rabī῾a, who was present at Badr, who

---

62. Presumably the reference is to *al-῾Iqd al Farīd* by Ibn ῾Abd Rabbihi, d. 940 AH.

said, his sight by then having gone, 'If I were there today at Badr and had my sight back, I would show you the defile from which the angels emerged. I would have no doubt whatsoever about it.

"'When the angels came down and Satan saw them, God revealed to them the verse, "I am with you. And so make firm those who believe" (*surat al-Anfāl*; VIII, v.12). "Making them firm" referred to the fact that the angels would come to someone in the form of a person they would know and would say, "Be glad! For they are as nothing, and God is with you. Attack them!"'"

Al-Wāqidī stated that Ibn Abū Ḥabība related to him, from Dāʾūd b. al-Ḥusayn, from ʿIkrima, from Ibn ʿAbbās, who said, "The angel would appear in the form of someone they knew and would say, 'I went close to them and heard them say, "If they attack us, we'll not hold firm. They are as nothing." And so on.'" This relates to the words, "When your Lord reveals to the angels that I am with you. And so make firm those who believe."

When Satan saw the angels he turned on his heels and said, "I'm quit of you. I see what you do not see." He was then in the guise of Surāqa.

Abū Jahl came forward haranguing his men and saying, "Don't be scared by the nonsense Surāqa is telling you. He has a rendezvous with Muḥammad and his men." He then said, "By al-Lāt and al-ʿUzzā, we'll not return until we scatter Muḥammad and his men into the mountains. Don't kill them; take them prisoner."

Al-Bayhaqī related, through Salāma, from ʿUqayl, from Ibn Shihāb, from Abū Ḥāzim, from Sahl b. Saʿd, who said, "Abū Usayd stated, he being by then blind, 'Cousin, I swear by God, that if you and I were at Badr and God were to restore my sight, I'd show you the defile through which the angels came out to us; I'd do so without any doubt or difficulty at all.'"

Al-Bukhārī related, from Ibrāhīm b. Mūsā, from ʿAbd al-Wahhāb, from Khālid, from ʿIkrima, from Ibn ʿAbbās, that the Messenger of God (ṢAAS) said on the day of the battle at Badr, "This is Gabriel over here, holding the head of his horse and fully accoutred for battle."

Al-Wāqidī stated, "Ibn Abū Ḥabība related to us, from Dāʾūd b. al-Ḥusayn, from ʿIkrima, from Ibn ʿAbbās, and Mūsā b. Muḥammad b. Ibrāhīm al-Taymī informed us, from his father, and ʿĀbid b. Yaḥyā related to me, from Abū al-Ḥuwayrith, from ʿUmāra b. Ukayma al-Laythī, from ʿIkrima, from Ḥakīm b. Ḥizām, who all said, 'When the time for battle arrived, the Messenger of God (ṢAAS) stood with his arms raised imploring God's aid and fulfilment of His promise, saying, "O God, if they prevail over this force, then polytheism too will prevail and You will have no religion left." Meanwhile Abū Bakr was saying, "I swear that God will give you aid and will make you content." And then God sent down 1,000 angels descending *en masse* and surrounding the enemy.'"

"The Messenger of God (ṢAAS) said, 'Rejoice, Abū Bakr! I saw Gabriel wearing a yellow turban, holding the reins of his horse, up there between heaven and earth! When he came down to earth, I lost sight of him for a while, but then he appeared again; he was dusty all over and he was saying, "God's aid did come to you when you prayed to Him!"'"

Al-Bayhaqī related from Abū Umāma b. Sahl who quoted his father as saying, "My son, I saw for myself at Badr that all any of us had to do was to point to the head of a polytheist and it would fall from his body before a sword even touched it!"

Ibn Isḥāq stated, "My father related to me, quoting some men of the Banū Māzin, quoting Abū Wāqid al-Laythī, as saying, 'I was pursuing one of the polytheists, wishing to strike him, when his head came off – before my sword reached him! I realized that someone other than myself had killed him.'"

Yūnus b. Bukayr stated, from ‘Īsā b. ‘Abd Allāh al-Taymī, from al-Rabī‘ b. Anas, who said, "Our men could differentiate the ones the angels had killed from those they had struck by the blow having occurred above their necks, and by their finger-tips looking as if they had been burned by a branding iron."

Ibn Isḥāq stated, "A reliable source related to me, from Muqsim, from Ibn ‘Abbās, who said, 'The distinguishing dress of the angels at Badr was the white turbans they wore that hung down over their backs. Except for Gabriel, that is; he had on a yellow turban.'"

Ibn ‘Abbās stated, "The only battle in which the angels participated was at Badr. At the other battles they constituted auxiliaries and reinforcements that did not actually fight."

Al-Wāqidī stated, "‘Abd Allāh b. Mūsā b. Abū Umayya related to me, from Muṣ‘ab b. ‘Abd Allāh, from a freed-man of Suhayl b. ‘Amr, who quoted Suhayl b. ‘Amr as saying, 'At the battle of Badr, I saw white men on piebald horses riding between heaven and earth, bearing banners, killing and taking prisoners.'

"And Abū ‘Ubayd used to say, he being by then blind, 'If I were there at Badr with you now and had my sight back, I could show you the defile from which the angels came without any doubt or confusion.'"

Al-Wāqidī went on, "Khārija b. Ibrāhīm related to me, quoting his father as saying, 'The Messenger of God (ṢAAS) said to Gabriel, "Which one of the angels was it who said at Badr, 'Giddy up, Ḥayzūm?'" Gabriel answered him, "O Muḥammad, I am not familiar with every denizen of the heavens!"'"

I comment that this is a *ḥadīth mursal*;[63] it refutes those, like al-Suhaylī and others, who maintain that Ḥayzūm is the name of Gabriel's horse. But God knows best.

Al-Wāqidī stated, "Isḥāq b. Yaḥyā related to me, from Ḥamza b. Ṣuhayb, from his father, who said, 'I can't tell you how many were the severed arms and deep wounds I saw at the battle of Badr that did not bleed!'"

Muḥammad b. Yaḥyā related to me, from Abū ‘Uqayl, from Abū Burda b. Niyār, who said, "I gathered up three heads at Badr and placed them before the

---

63. One in which the Prophet is quoted without mention of the Companion who narrated the statement.

Messenger of God (SAAS) telling him, 'Two of these I myself killed. Regarding the third, I saw a tall man kill him and I then took his head.'

"The Messenger of God (SAAS) responded, 'O, that was so-and-so, one of the angels.'"

Mūsā b. Muḥammad b. Ibrāhīm related to me, quoting his father, as saying, "Al-Sāʾib b. Abū Ḥubaysh used to relate, during the period of ʿUmar's rule, 'I swear, it was no man who took me prisoner.' 'Who was it then?' he would be asked, and he would respond, 'When Quraysh were defeated, so was I with them. A tall, long-haired man on a white horse took me and tied me up. Then along came ʿAbd al-Raḥmān b. ʿAwf and found me there bound. He called out to the men, "Who was it captured this man?" Eventually he took me to the Messenger of God (SAAS) who asked, "Who was it took you prisoner?" I told him I did not know, but I was reluctant to tell him what I had seen. The Messenger of God (SAAS) then said, "It was an angel who took you prisoner. Take your captive away, Ibn ʿAwf."'"

Al-Wāqidī stated, "ʿĀbid b. Yaḥyā related to me, as did Abū al-Ḥuwayrith, from ʿImāra b. Ukayma, from Ḥakīm b. Ḥizām, who said, 'At the battle of Badr, I witnessed striped cloth come down from the sky and it blocked off the horizon. And then the valley streamed with water. It occurred to me that this was something from heaven with which Muḥammad was to be helped. And it was not long before there was the defeat and the advance of the angels to the forefront.'"

Isḥāq b. Rāhawayh stated, "Wahb b. Jarīr b. Ḥāzim related to us, saying, 'My father told me, from Muḥammad b. Isḥāq, who said, "My father quoted to me Jubayr b. Muṭʿim as saying, 'Before the enemy force was defeated, and while the men were still fighting, I saw something like a black striped cloth descend from the sky, like black ants; I had no doubt it was the angels, and soon the enemy force was defeated.'"'"

The angels descended to give their help and the Messenger of God (SAAS) saw them when he took a nap and, upon waking up, he told Abū Bakr the good news, saying, "Rejoice at this, Abū Bakr; for Gabriel was there, leading his horse and with dust all over him." By this he meant from the battle.

The Messenger of God (SAAS) then left the shelter, dressed in chain-mail, and began urging on the men to battle. He told them of heaven and gave them encouragement in news of the coming of the angels. The men were meanwhile still in their battle ranks, not yet having advanced against their enemy. The result was that they felt tranquility and confidence.

They felt that calmness that is the sign of confidence, security and faith, just as God stated, "When He caused calm to overcome you, as a security from Him" (sūrat al-Anfāl; VIII, v.11). This similarly happened to them thereafter, at the battle of Uḥud, as in the reference in the Qurʾān.

This is why Ibn Masʿūd remarked, "Calm in the battle ranks is a sign of faith; calm during the prayer is a sign of hypocrisy."

God Almighty stated, "If you sought judgement, it has come to you. If you desist, it will be better for you. If you go back, so will we. Your forces will serve you nothing, no matter how numerous they are. God is with the believers" (*sūrat al-Anfāl*; VIII, v.19).

Imām Aḥmad stated, quoting Yazīd b. Hārūn and Muḥammad b. Isḥāq al-Zuhrī from 'Abd Allāh b. Tha'laba that Abū Jahl said, when the two sides met in battle, 'O God, he (Muḥammed) was willing to destroy the ties of kinship, and the one to introduce us to that which was foreign to us, so destroy him this morning.' It was Abū Jahl who 'sought judgement'."

Ibn Isḥāq related it thus in his biography. Al-Nasā°ī related it through Ṣāliḥ b. Kaysān, from al-Zuhrī. And al-Ḥākim related it also from a *ḥadīth* of al-Zuhrī. He then said, "It is authentic and in accordance with the criteria of both scholars (al-Bukhārī and Muslim); though neither one of them mentioned it."

Al-Umawī stated, "Asbāṭ b. Muḥammad al-Qurashī related to us, from 'Aṭiyya, from Muṭrif, concerning God's words, 'If you sought judgement, it has come to you' that Abū Jahl said, 'O God, assist the better of the parties, the more noble of the tribes, and the more numerous of the forces.'" And the words came down, "If you sought judgement, it has come to you."

'Alī b. Abū Ṭalḥa quoted Ibn 'Abbās as saying, regarding the words, "And when God promises you that one of the two parties is yours" (*sūrat al-Anfāl*; VIII, v.7). "The caravan belonging to the people of Mecca approached on its way to Syria. Those in Medina got news of this and they went forth, accompanied by the Messenger of God (ṢAAS) to attack the caravan.

"News of this reached the Meccans and they hurried out to the caravan to prevent the Prophet (ṢAAS) and his force from seizing it. The caravan outstripped the Messenger of God (ṢAAS); God had promised them one of the two parties, and they had wanted to meet up with the caravan.

"The Messenger of God (ṢAAS) did set forth with the Muslims heading for the enemy force, but they were reluctant to leave, being aware of the strength of their opponents. The Prophet (ṢAAS) made a halt with his Muslims at a place where there was a large sandhill between them and the wells. The Muslims were extremely tired, and Satan made them discontented by whispering to them, 'You claim to be partisans of God and to have His Messenger among you, yet it was the polytheists who reached the wells before you did, leaving you like this.'

"Then God sent down upon them a heavy rain. The Muslims drank and cleaned themselves and God withdrew Satan's evil from them. The sand became packed down and so both men and their animals could walk easily upon it. They then went out to fight the enemy force, and God aided his Messenger and the believers with 1,000 angels. Gabriel was there with 500 angels on one flank, and Michael was on the other with another 500 angels.

"Satan also brought a force of devils, including some of his own progeny, these being in the guise of men of the Banū Mudlij. Satan himself was in the form of Surāqa b. Mālik b. Jaʿsham; he addressed the polytheists, saying, 'No one will defeat you today. I shall protect you!'

"When the battle lines were drawn, Abū Jahl spoke the words, 'The one more worthy of the truth, provide him with assistance.'

"The Messenger of God (ṢAAS) raised up his hands and prayed, 'O God, if this force is destroyed, You will never be worshipped on earth.'

"Gabriel told him to pick up a handful of soil. He did so and threw it into the faces of the polytheists. Every one of those whose eyes, nostrils or mouth any of this soil touched turned and retreated.

"Gabriel went towards Satan and at the time when the former saw him his hand was holding that of a polytheist. Satan withdrew his hand and retreated, along with his party of devils. The polytheist asked him, 'I thought you claimed to be our protector?' He replied, 'I see what you do not. I fear God, for God is mighty in His punishment.' He said this when he saw the angels."

Al-Bayhaqī related this in *Dalāʾil (The Signs)*.

Al-Ṭabrānī stated, "Masʿada b. Saʿd al-ʿAṭṭār related to us, quoting Ibrāhīm b. al-Mundhir al-Ḥizāmī, quoting ʿAbd al-ʿAzīz b. ʿImrān and Hishām b. Saʿd, from ʿAbd Rabbihī b. Saʿīd b. Qays al-Anṣārī, from Rifāʿa b. Rāfiʿ, who said, 'When Satan saw how the angels dealt with the polytheists at Badr, he was afraid that the same would happen to him. Al-Ḥārith b. Hishām was staying very close to him, believing him to be Surāqa b. Mālik; Satan struck al-Ḥārith hard in the chest, then hurried away and threw himself into the sea, raising his hands into the air and pleading, "O God, I ask you to look kindly down upon me!" He was afraid that he was going to be killed. Abū Jahl came up and called out, "O people, do not be disturbed by the rambling of Surāqa b. Mālik; he was about to attend a meeting with Muḥammad! And don't be scared by the killing of Shayba, ʿUtba and al-Walīd; their time had come. I swear by al-Lāt and al-ʿUzzā, we'll not go back home before we have scattered them into the mountains. I don't expect any of you to kill any of them. Just capture them roughly and make them aware of their bad behaviour in parting company with you and in abandoning al-Lāt and al-ʿUzzā."'"

"Abū Jahl then quoted the line:

> 'Fierce warfare will not take revenge on me, spry like
> a two-year old camel; I am young in years.
> It was for such as this that my mother bore me.'"

Al-Wāqidī related, from Mūsā b. Yaʿqūb al-Zamʿī, from Abū Bakr b. Abū Sulaymān, from Abū Ḥatma, (who said), "I heard Marwān b. al-Ḥakam ask Ḥakīm b. Ḥizām about the battle of Badr. The sheikh was reluctant, but when Marwān insisted Ḥakīm said, 'We met and engaged in battle, and I heard a sound of something falling from the sky to the ground, making a noise like pebbles dropping into a brass basin. Then the Prophet (ṢAAS) picked up a handful of dirt and threw it. And we were defeated.'"

Al-Wāqidī stated, "Isḥāq b. Muḥammad b. ʿAbd al-Raḥmān b. Muḥammad b. ʿAbd Allāh related to us, from ʿAbd Allāh b. Thaʿlaba b. Ṣuqayr (who said), "I heard Nawfal b. Muʿāwiya al-Dīlī say, 'We were defeated at Badr as we heard a noise like that of pebbles dropping into a bowl, right inside us and behind us! That had a terrifying impact on us.'"

Al-Umawī stated, "My father related to us, quoting Ibn Abū Isḥāq, quoting al-Zuhrī from ʿAbd Allāh b. Thaʿlaba b. Ṣuqayr, that Abū Jahl said, when the forces met, 'O God, in the morning destroy the one who introduced us to that which was foreign to us and who ruined the family ties.' This was the 'judgement sought'.

"While they were in this state, God had encouraged the Muslims in meeting their enemy and had so diminished their enemy in their eyes that they were eager to fight them. The Messenger of God (ṢAAS) took a nap in the shelter, then woke up and said, 'Rejoice, Abū Bakr; Gabriel is here, wearing a turban and holding the reins of his horse he is leading, with dust upon him. God and His forces have come to you.'

"The Messenger of God (ṢAAS) issued orders picked up a handful of pebbles, went outside and faced the enemy and said, 'You are disgraced!' He then cast the pebbles out over them and said to his men, 'Attack!'"

The defeat soon came. God killed some of their leaders and took some prisoner. Ziyād stated, quoting Ibn Isḥāq, "The Messenger of God (ṢAAS) then picked up a handful of pebbles, approached Quraysh carrying them and said, 'You are disgraced!' He cast the pebbles out over them and ordered his men, 'Attack them!' The defeat then occurred and God killed some of their chieftains and captured others."

Al-Suddī al-Kabīr stated, "The Messenger of God (ṢAAS) said to ʿAlī at the battle of Badr, 'Give me some pebbles from the ground!' He handed him some pebbles with dirt on them which he threw into the faces of the enemy. None of the polytheists escaped having a little of that dirt enter their eyes. The Muslims forced them back, killing and capturing them. God revealed on that subject, 'You did not kill them; it is God who killed them. It was not you who threw when you threw, but God who threw'" (sūrat al-Anfāl; VIII, v.17).

ʿUrwa, ʿIkrima, Mujāhid, Muḥammad b. Kaʿb, Muḥammad b. Qays, Qatāda, Ibn Zayd, and others all spoke similarly, agreeing that this verse came down about the battle of Badr.

The Messenger of God (ṢAAS) did the same during the expedition of Ḥunayn, as we will explain in the proper place, if God wills it, and in Him we trust.

Ibn Isḥāq reported that when the Messenger of God (ṢAAS) urged his men on to battle, cast the dirt at the polytheists and God Almighty defeated them, he went back up into the shelter accompanied by Abū Bakr. Saʿd b. Muʿādh, along with some of the Helpers stood guard at its door, bearing swords, concerned that some of the polytheists might attack the Prophet (ṢAAS).

Ibn Isḥāq stated, "When his men busied themselves in taking prisoners, the Messenger of God (ṢAAS) noticed, so I have been told, some discontent in the face of Saʿd b. Muʿādh at what they were doing. He therefore asked him, 'Do I see you dislike what our men are doing, Saʿd?' He replied, 'Yes, by God, O Messenger of God; this is the first battle God has waged against the polytheists and I would have preferred the men to be massacred rather than kept alive!'"

Ibn Isḥāq went on, "Al-ʿAbbās b. ʿAbd Allāh b. Maʿbad related to me, from some of his family, from ʿAbd Allāh b. ʿAbbās, that the Prophet (ṢAAS) said to his Companions that day, 'I have learned that some men of the Banū Hāshim, and others, have been forced to come out and did not want to do battle against us. If any of you should meet up with any men of the Banū Hāshim, do not kill them. If one of you should meet Abū al-Bakhtarī b. Hishām b. al-Ḥārith b. Asad, he should not kill him. Anyone meeting al-ʿAbbās b. ʿAbd al-Muṭṭalib (the uncle of the Messenger of God (ṢAAS)) should also not kill him; he only came forth reluctantly.'

"Abū Ḥudhayfa b. ʿUtba b. Rabīʿa then asked, 'Should we then kill our own sons and brothers yet leave al-ʿAbbās alone? I swear by God, if I meet up with him, I'll attack him with my sword!'

"This comment reached the Messenger of God (ṢAAS) and he said to ʿUmar, 'O father of Ḥafṣ' – ʿUmar swore this was the first time he had ever used this name when addressing him – 'shall the face of the uncle of the Messenger of God be struck with a sword?'

"'O Messenger of God,' ʿUmar replied, 'let me strike Abū Ḥudhayfa's neck with my sword; he's turned hypocrite!'

"Abū Ḥudhayfa stated, 'I never felt safe, having made that comment that day. I always feared that the only thing that would mitigate it would be my martyrdom.'

"And he was killed as a martyr at the battle of al-Yamāma. God be pleased with him."

THE DEATH OF ABŪ AL-BAKHTARĪ B. HISHĀM.

Ibn Isḥāq stated, "The Messenger of God (ṢAAS) only forbad the killing of Abū al-Bakhtarī because in Mecca he had been the most protective of the Messenger of God. He never harmed him, nor allowed anyone to mistreat him. He had also been one of those who had annulled the document boycotting the Messenger of God (ṢAAS). Al-Mujadhdhir b. Dhiyād al-Balawī, an ally of the Helpers met up with him and told him, 'The Messenger of God (ṢAAS) has forbidden us from killing you.' Abū al-Bakhtarī had with him a friend who had come forth from Mecca in his company, a man named Junāda b. Malīḥa, of the Banū Layth. Abū al-Bakhtarī asked, 'And what about my friend?'

"Al-Mujadhdhir replied, 'No, by God, we'll not excuse your friend; it was about you alone the Messenger of God (ṢAAS) gave orders.' Abū al-Bakhtarī said, 'Well then, I and he will die together. I'll not have the womenfolk of Mecca say of me that I abandoned my friend because of my own will to live!'

"Abū al-Bakhtarī spoke the following verse as he began to battle al-Mujadhdhir,

'No free man abandons his comrade until he dies or sees
his way.'

"They fought, and al-Mujadhdhir b. Dhiyād killed him. On this subject he spoke the verses,

'Should you have not known or forgotten my lineage, be
sure that I descend from Balī,
Men who fight using Yazanī spears, striking down the
high and mighty,
Either tell Abū al-Bakhtarī's son that he's an orphan
now, or tell my son the same of me.
I am he whose lineage is known to be from Balī; I
thrust home my spear so hard it almost folds over.
I slaughter my foe with a sharp Mashrafī blade, racing
to death like a milch-camel to milking,
You will never see Mujadhdhir inventing a lie.'

"Al-Mujadhdhir then went to the Messenger of God (ṢAAS) and told him, 'I swear by Him who sent you with the truth, I did try to take him prisoner to bring him to you, but he insisted on fighting me. So I fought back and killed him.'"

Chapter: On the death of Umayya b. Khalaf.

Ibn Ishāq stated, "Yaḥyā b. 'Abbād b. 'Abd Allāh b. al-Zubayr related to me, from his father, and 'Abd Allāh b. Abū Bakr and others related to me, from 'Abd al-Raḥmān b. 'Awf, who said, 'Umayya b. Khalaf had been a friend of mine at Mecca. My name at that time was 'Abd 'Amr, and when I became a Muslim I renamed myself 'Abd al-Raḥmān. When we met in Mecca, he addressed me by saying, "Hey, 'Abd 'Amr, don't you like the name your father gave you?" "That's right," I replied. He then said, "Well, I don't know this 'al-Raḥmān' name; let's give you some name just for you and me that I can call you. You don't respond to your first name and I can't call you by what I don't recognize." When he addressed me by 'Abd 'Amr, I did not respond. So I told him, "Abū 'Alī, name me whatever you want." "Then you can be 'Abd al-Ilāh", he said, and I agreed to this.

"'Thereafter, when I passed him, he would address me as 'Abd al-Ilāh, and I would respond and talk with him.

"'At the battle of Badr, I passed by him as he was standing with his son 'Alī, holding his hand. I was carrying some coats of chain-mail I had got as spoils and when he saw me he called out, "'Abd 'Amr!" I made no reply, so he then called out, "ʿAbd al-Ilāh!" "Yes?" I then responded. He asked, "Don't you think I'm worth more to you than those coats of chain-mail you're carrying?" "Yes, you are," I replied.

"'So I put down the chain-mail and took him and his son by the hands. As I did so he commented that he had never seen the like of that day and asked, "Don't you have need of milk?"[64] I then walked off with them both.'"

Ibn Isḥāq went on, "ʿAbd al-Wāḥid b. Abū ʿAwn related to me, from Saʿd b. Ibrāhīm, from his father, from ʿAbd al-Raḥmān b. ʿAwf, who said, 'Umayya b. Khalaf said to me as I walked between him and his son, holding hands with them both, "ʿAbd al-Ilāh, who is that man distinguished by an ostrich feather across his chest?" I replied, "That is Ḥamza." He commented, "He's the one who ruined us."

"'As I was leading them on, Bilāl saw him with me, Umayya having been the one who had so persecuted him for his adoption of Islam. Bilāl shouted out, "Hey, there's that polytheist-in-chief Umayya b. Khalaf! I'll not live on if he does!" I responded, "Now Bilāl, he's my prisoner." "I'll not live on if he does," he insisted. He then began shouting at the top of his voice, "O partisans of God, here's Umayya b. Khalaf, the worst polytheist of all! I'll not live on if he does!" Men soon surrounded us till they had us in a sort of enclosure, with me protecting him all the while. Then one man took his sword and struck the leg of Umayya's son, making him fall down. Umayya then let out a cry such as I never heard before. I told him to try to escape, though there was no chance of this, and I could do nothing for him. After that our men fell on them with their swords and killed them.'"

The account concludes, "ʿAbd al-Raḥmān used to say, 'May God have mercy on Bilāl; he deprived me of both my chain-mail and my two prisoners!'"

Al-Bukhārī related this in similar terms in his ṣaḥīḥ collection. In the chapter dealing with the power of attorney, he stated, "ʿAbd al-ʿAzīz related to me, he being the son of ʿAbd Allāh, quoting Yūsuf, he being the son of al-Mājishūn, from Ṣāliḥ b. Ibrāhīm b. ʿAbd al-Raḥmān b. ʿAwf, who quoted his father as saying that his father, ʿAbd al-Raḥmān b. ʿAwf said, 'I corresponded with Umayya b. Khalaf asking him to take care of my personal affairs in Mecca while I looked after his in Medina. When I used the word "al-Raḥmān" in my name, he responded, "I don't know any 'al-Raḥmān'; write to me in the name you had before." So I wrote to him as "ʿAbd ʿAmr." At Badr I went out to the mountain to protect him when the men were asleep, but Bilāl caught sight of him and came out and stood where there was a group of the Helpers and yelled, "Umayya b. Khalaf! I'll not live on if Umayya b. Khalaf does!"

"'So he and a group of the Helpers took off after us. Fearing they would catch up with us, I left behind for them his son to deter them. But they killed him and pursued us; he was a heavy man. When they caught up to us, I told him to kneel down and when he did so I shielded him with myself. But they reached him with

---

64. According to Ibn Hishām, he was suggesting that he would be able to offer milch-camels as ransom for himself and his son.

their swords while he was beneath me, and one of them cut my leg with his sword.' And ᶜAbd al-Raḥmān b. ᶜAwf used to show us the mark on the back of his leg."

Yūsuf heard Ṣāliḥ relate this, his father being Ibrāhīm.

Al-Bukhārī, alone of all the authorites, gave this account. In the collection of *ḥadīth* attributed to Rifāᶜa b. Rāfiᶜ, it was he who killed Umayya b. Khalaf.

THE DEATH OF ABŪ JAHL, GOD DAMN HIM!

Ibn Hishām stated, "As Abū Jahl advanced that day he spoke the following verse as he fought,

> 'Violent warfare will not take revenge on me, spry like
> a two-year old camel; I am young in years.
> It was for such as this that my mother bore me.'"

Ibn Isḥāq stated, "When the Messenger of God (ṢAAS) had finished with his enemy, he ordered that the body of Abū Jahl be sought among those killed.

"Regarding who was the first to find Abū Jahl, I was told by Thawr b. Zayd, from ᶜIkrima, from Ibn ᶜAbbās, and also by ᶜAbd Allāh b. Abū Bakr, as follows, 'Muᶜādh b. ᶜAmr b. al-Jamūḥ, a brother of the Banū Salama, said, "I heard our men say that Abū Jahl was amid some bushes, and that he could not be reached."

"'When I heard this, I made him my business and went off for him. When I could do so, I attacked him and gave him such a blow as to sever his foot and half his leg. I swear, the only thing I can compare it with as it flew off was like the kernel of a nut emerging after having been struck by a nutcracker. His son ᶜIkrima struck me on my shoulder and off came my arm, which remained attached only by the skin of my side. The battle drew me away from him, and I spent the whole day fighting while dragging my arm behind me. When it began hurting, I kept my foot on it as I walked ahead until I had removed it.'"

Ibn Isḥāq went on, "Muᶜādh lived on after that into the reign of ᶜUthmān.

"Then Muᶜawwidh b. ᶜAfrā᾽ passed by Abū Jahl, who was already badly wounded, and struck him till he disabled him completely. Muᶜawwidh left him on the point of death and fought on until he was killed.

"ᶜAbd Allāh b. Masᶜūd next passed by Abū Jahl, the Messenger of God (ṢAAS) having issued the order that he be sought from among those killed. The Messenger of God (ṢAAS) had told them, so I have been informed, 'If when you search he is hidden among the dead, look for someone with a scar on his knee. He and I, when we were youths, were once sitting crowded together at a feast given by ᶜAbd Allāh b. Judᶜān. I was a little slimmer than him, and I gave him a push making him fall down on his knees, one of which received a wound that left a permanent scar.'"

"Ibn Masᶜūd stated, 'When I found him he was on the point of death. When I recognized him I put my foot on his neck; he had once held me captive in

Mecca and hurt me and kicked me. I asked him, "So God has put you to shame then, you enemy of God!" He replied, "And how has He shamed me?" he asked. "Aren't I the most noble man you have killed? Tell me which side won the day?" "It went to God and to His Messenger," I told him.'"

Ibn Isḥāq went on, "Men of the Banū Makhzūm claim that Ibn Masʿūd used to say, ʿAbū Jahl said to me, 'You've climbed very high, for having been just a herdsman!' I then severed his head and took it to the Messenger of God (ṢAAS) and told him, 'This, O Messenger of God, is the head of God's enemy.' 'Is it really, by God other than Whom there is none?' (This was the oath the Messenger of God used to speak.) I responded, 'Yes, by God other than whom there is none.' I then threw Abū Jahl's head down in front of him and he praised God."

This is an account given by Ibn Isḥāq, God be pleased with him.

It is established in both *ṣaḥīḥ* collections, through Yūsuf b. Yaʿqūb b. al-Mājishūn, from Ṣāliḥ b. Ibrāhīm b. ʿAbd al-Raḥmān b. ʿAwf, from his father who quoted ʿAbd al-Raḥmān b. ʿAwf, as saying, "At Badr I was standing in the battle line and when I looked to my right and my left I found myself to be between two Helpers, both of whom were young men. I had hoped to be positioned between two men who would be weaker than these. One of them asked me, winking, 'Uncle, would you know Abū Jahl?' 'Yes,' I replied, 'what need have you of him?' He replied, 'I've heard that he curses the Messenger of God (ṢAAS). I swear by Him who holds my soul in His hand, if I were to see him, I'd not leave him before the death of whichever of us had his time come first.'

"I was amazed to hear this. Then the young man on my other side winked at me and asked me the same. I looked right over at Abū Jahl, moving around his men and commented, 'Can't you see? That's the man over there you're asking about.' Thereupon the two men charged at him with their swords drawn and struck him until they had killed him. They then went off to the Messenger of God (ṢAAS) and informed him and he asked which of them had killed him. Each one said he had. The Messenger of God (ṢAAS) then asked, 'Have you both wiped your swords clean?' They replied, 'No.' He then examined the swords and concluded that they had indeed both killed him. He decided that Abū Jahl's spoils should go to Muʿadh b. ʿAmr b. al-Jamūḥ, the other man being Muʿadh b. ʿAfrāʾ."

Al-Bukhārī stated, "Yaʿqūb b. Ibrāhīm related to us, quoting Ibrāhīm b. Saʿd, from his father, from his grandfather, who quoted ʿAbd al-Raḥmān as having said, 'I was there in the line at Badr and happened to look to my left and right and found those next to me to be young men. I wasn't feeling very comfortable at their position, when one of them asked me, keeping his question secret from his companion, "Uncle, point out Abū Jahl to me." "What will you do to him?" I asked. He replied, "I swore to God that if I saw him I would kill him or die in front of him." The other man asked me in confidence the same question. Nothing pleased me more than to be in that position between them both. I pointed Abū Jahl out to them and they flew at him like falcons and struck him down. These men were two sons of ʿAfrāʾ.'"

In both *ṣaḥīḥ* collections, moreover, there is an account from Abū Sulaymān al-Taymī quoting Anas b. Mālik as saying, "The Messenger of God (ṢAAS) asked, 'Who will find out what became of Abū Jahl?' Ibn Masʿūd offered to do so and went off and located him; he had been struck down by ʿAfrā²'s two sons and was on the point of death. Ibn Masʿūd then took him by the beard and asked, "Are you Abū Jahl?" He replied, "Is any man superior whom you have killed?" Or he said, "It is his people who killed him!"'"

According to al-Bukhārī, from Abū Usāma, Ismāʿīl b. Qays quoted Ibn Masʿūd as having said that he went to Abū Jahl and asked him, "Has God disgraced you then?" He replied, "Aren't I the most noble man you have killed?"

Al-Aʿmash stated, from Abū Isḥāq, from Abū ʿUbayda, from ʿAbd Allāh, who said, "When I reached Abū Jahl he was stretched out, wearing a helmet and holding a fine sword. My own sword was a poor one. I was about to sever his head with my sword, remembering how my own head had been struck with swords in Mecca till the hands of my attackers tired. Then I picked up his sword, whereupon he raised his head and asked, 'Which side won the day? Us or them? And aren't you our young herdsman from Mecca?'

"ʿAbd Allāh went on, 'So I killed him. Then I went to the Prophet (ṢAAS) and told him I had killed Abū Jahl. He exclaimed, "Did you really, by God other than Whom there is none!" He made me swear it three times. He then arose and went outside, with me accompanying him, and cursed them (those polytheists killed in battle).'"

Imām Aḥmad stated, "Wakīʿ related to us, quoting Isrāʾīl, from Abū Isḥāq, from Abū ʿUbayda, who said, "ʿAbd Allāh stated, "When I reached Abū Jahl at the battle of Badr, I found that his leg had been severed, but he was still using his sword to defend himself. I said, 'Praise be to God for disgracing you, you enemy of God!' He responded, 'Is he any but a man killed by his own people!'

"""I set about fighting him with a blunt sword I had and struck him on the hand. His sword fell, and I picked it up and hit him with it till I had killed him."'

"ʿAbd Allāh went on, 'I then went to the Prophet (ṢAAS) as though walking on air, and told him. He responded, "Is it really so, by God other than Whom there is none!" He repeated this three times. I then replied, "It really is, by God other than whom there is none!"'

"ʿAbd Allāh continued, 'The Messenger of God (ṢAAS) then went out, accompanied by myself, stood over him and said, "Praise be to God! God has disgraced you, you enemy of God! This man was the Pharoah of his people!"'"

In another account, Ibn Masʿūd stated, "And he gave me his sword as booty."

Abū Isḥāq al-Fazārī stated, from al-Thawrī, from Abū Isḥāq, from Abū ʿUbayda, from Ibn Masʿūd, who said, "I went to the Messenger of God (ṢAAS) at the battle of Badr and told him I had killed Abū Jahl. He replied, 'Is it really so, by God other than whom there is none?' I replied, 'It really is, by God other than whom there is none!' I said this twice or thrice.'

"The Prophet (ṢAAS) responded, 'God is Great! Praise be to God who fulfilled His promise, and aided His servant and defeated the parties by Himself.' He then added, 'Go and show him to me.' I went and did so and he said, 'This is the Pharoah of this nation.'"

Abū Dāʾūd and al-Nasāʾī related it from a *hadith* told by Abū Isḥāq al-Sabīʿī.

Al-Wāqidī stated, "The Messenger of God (ṢAAS) stood where the two sons of ʿAfrāʾ had died and said, 'God bless the two sons of ʿAfrāʾ; they were partners in the killing of the Pharoah of this nation, the leader-in-chief of the polytheists.' Someone asked, 'O Messenger of God, who was it who killed him along with them?' He replied, 'The angels; and also Ibn Masʿūd participated in killing him.'"

Al-Bayhaqī related this.

Al-Bayhaqī stated, "Al-Ḥākim related to us, quoting al-Aṣamm, quoting Aḥmad b. ʿAbd al-Jabbār, quoting Yūnus b. Bukayr, from ʿAnbasa b. al-Azhar from Abū Isḥāq, who said, 'When the Messenger of God (ṢAAS) received at Badr the good news of the death of Abū Jahl, he asked (the informant) to swear thrice that he had indeed seen him dead. He did so whereupon the Messenger of God (ṢAAS) prostrated in prayer.'"

Al-Bayhaqī then related through Abū Nuʿaym, from Salama b. Rajāʾ, from al-Shaʿthāʾ, a woman of the Banū Asad, from ʿAbd Allāh b. Abū ʿAwfā, that the Messenger of God (ṢAAS), prayed two *rakʿāt* (four prostrations) when he was given the good news of the victory, and when he was brought Abū Jahl's head.

Ibn Māja stated, "Abū Bishr Bakr b. Khalaf related to us, quoting Salama b. Rajāʾ, who said, 'Shaʿthāʾ related to me, from ʿAbd Allāh b. Abū Awfā, that the Messenger of God (ṢAAS) made two prostrations in prayer on the day he was brought the head of Abū Jahl.'"

Ibn Abī Dunyā stated, "My father related to me, quoting Hishām, quoting Mujālid from al-Shaʿbī, that a man said to the Messenger of God (ṢAAS), 'As I passed by Badr, I saw a man coming out of the battle-field being struck by a man with an iron staff he had until he disappeared into the ground. When he next appeared, the man would hit him again, and this happened several times.'"

The Messenger of God (ṢAAS) then said, "That was Abū Jahl b. Hishām being tortured until Judgement Day."

Al-Umawī stated in his work on the military expeditions, "I heard my father say that al-Mujālid b. Saʿīd related to him, from ʿĀmir, who said, 'A man came to the Messenger of God (ṢAAS) and said, "I saw at Badr a man seated while another man struck him on the head with an iron rod until he disappeared into the ground." The Messenger of God (ṢAAS) commented, "That was Abū Jahl; an angel had been appointed to do that to him whenever he came up. He is going to go on sinking down into the ground until Judgement Day."'"

Al-Bukhārī stated, "ʿUbayd b. Ismāʿīl related to us, quoting Abū Usāma, from Hishām, from his father, who said, 'Al-Zubayr stated, "At Badr I met up with ʿUbayda b. Saʿīd b. al-ʿĀṣ who was fully accoutred, so that nothing of him could be seen except his eyes. He was known by the nickname 'Abū al-Kirsh', i.e. 'pot-belly'. He told me he was Abū al-Kirsh and I charged at him with a javelin, struck him in the eye and he died."'

"Hishām stated, 'I was informed that al-Zubayr said, "I put my foot on him and trod down, only managing to extract it with difficulty for its two blades had bent over."'"

'Urwa stated, "The Messenger of God (ṢAAS) asked for it and he gave it over. When the Messenger of God (ṢAAS) died, it being still in his possession, Abū Bakr requested and received it. When Abū Bakr died, 'Umar b. al-Khaṭṭāb requested and received it. When 'Umar died, he (al-Zubayr, tr.) took it, but 'Uthmān requested it and he gave it to him. When 'Uthmān was killed, it went to 'Alī's family. Then 'Abd Allāh, al-Zubayr's son, asked for it and had possession of it until he was killed."

Ibn Hishām stated, "Abū 'Ubayda related to me, quoting other scholars learned in the early military engagements, that 'Umar b. al-Khaṭṭāb said to Sa'īd b. al-'Āṣ as he passed by, 'You seem to me annoyed about something; do you think I killed your father? If I had, I would not apologize to you for doing so. However, it was my uncle al-'Āṣ b. Hishām b. al-Mughīra whom I killed. I did pass by your father, but he was acting like a bull scraping the earth with his horn. So I avoided him and it was his nephew 'Alī who sought him out and killed him.'"

Ibn Isḥāq stated, "'Ukkāsha b. Miḥṣan b. Ḥirthān al-Asadī, an ally of the Banū 'Abd Shams, used his sword to fight with at Badr until it broke off in his hand. He went to the Messenger of God (ṢAAS) who then gave him a wooden club and told him, 'fight with this, 'Ukkāsha!'

"When 'Ukkāsha took it from the Messenger of God (ṢAAS) and brandished it, it turned into a fine, long, white steel sword. He fought using it until God gave victory to the Muslims. That sword was named al-'awn, 'the helper'; he had it at all the battles he witnessed with the Messenger of God (ṢAAS), until ultimately he was killed by Ṭulayḥa al-Asadī, during the wars of apostasy. Ṭulayḥa spoke an ode about this, part of which was,

> "The evening I left Ibn 'Aqram lying prostrate, and
> 'Ukkāsha al-Ghanamī on a battle-field."

Ṭulayḥa later accepted Islam, as will be related hereafter.

Ibn Isḥāq stated, "'Ukkāsha was he who said, when the Messenger of God (ṢAAS), gave his nation the good news that 70,000 of them would enter heaven without either testing or punishment, 'Pray to God to make me one of them.' The Prophet (ṢAAS) then spoke the words, 'O God, make him one of them!'"

This ḥadīth is given in all the ṣaḥīḥ, "authentic", and ḥisān, "good", collections of traditions, as well as elsewhere.

Ibn Isḥāq stated, "The Messenger of God (ṢAAS) said – so I have been told – 'We have the finest horseman of all the Arabs.' 'And who is he then?' he was asked, and he replied, 'ʿUkkāsha b. Miḥṣan.' Ḍirār b. al-Azwar commented, 'He's one of our men, Messenger of God.' He replied, 'He's not one of yours. He's one of ours by alliance.'"

Al-Bayhaqī related, from al-Ḥākim, through Muḥammad b. ʿUmar al-Wāqidī, "ʿUmar b. ʿUthmān al-Khashnī related to me, from his father, from his maternal aunt, who said, 'ʿUkkāsha b. Miḥṣan stated, "My sword broke at Badr, so the Messenger of God (ṢAAS) gave me a stick and suddenly it became a long, white sword. I fought with it until God defeated the polytheists." He kept it with him until he died.'"

Al-Wāqidī stated, "Usāma b. Zayd related to me, from Dāʾūd b. al-Ḥusayn, from some men of the Banū al-Ashhal, several of whom said, 'The sword of Salama b. Ḥuraysh broke during the battle of Badr. Without a sword, he was unable to fight, so the Messenger of God (ṢAAS) gave him a staff he carried made of a green palm tree frond. He told him, "fight with this!" And it turned into a fine sword. He kept it with him until he was killed at the battle of Jisr Abū ʿUbayda.'"

HOW THE PROPHET (ṢAAS) REPLACED QATĀDA'S EYE.

Al-Bayhaqī stated, in the *Dalāʾil* (*The Signs*), "Abū Saʿd al-Mālīnī informed us, quoting Abū Aḥmad b. ʿAdī, quoting Abū Yaʿlā, quoting Yaḥyā al-Himmānī, quoting ʿAbd al-ʿAzīz b. Sulaymān b. al-Ghasīl, from ʿĀṣim b. ʿUmar b. Qatāda, from his father, from his grandfather Qatāda b. al-Nuʿmān, that his eye was wounded at Badr and that its pupil came down on to his cheekbone. They were about to slice it off, but asked the Messenger of God (ṢAAS) who said that they should not do this. He then said a prayer for him, covering his cheek with his palm. And later you could not tell which of his eyes had been struck!"

According to one account, this became his better eye.

An account came down to us from the Commander of the Believers, ʿUmar b. ʿAbd al-ʿAzīz that when he was told this account by ʿĀṣim b. ʿUmar b. Qatāda, he also recited,

> "I am the son of him on whose cheek his eye descended,
> which was replaced so well by the hand of the Chosen-One."

Upon hearing this, ʿUmar b. ʿAbd al-ʿAzīz, God bless him, quoted very appropriately the verse of Umayya b. Abū al-Ṣalt about the sword of Ibn Dhū Yazin,

> "These fine qualities are not like two bowls with milk
> merely whitening the water that soon becomes urine."

ANOTHER SIMILAR ACCOUNT.

Al-Bayhaqī stated, "The *ḥāfiẓ* Abū ʿAbd Allāh informed us, quoting Muḥammad b. Ṣāliḥ, quoting al-Faḍl b. Muḥammad al-Shaʿrānī, quoting

Ibrāhīm b. al-Mundhir, quoting ʿAbd al-ʿAzīz b. ʿImrān, quoting Rifāʿa b. Yaḥyā, quoting Muʿādh b. Rifāʿa b. Rāfiʿ, from his father Rāfiʿ b. Mālik, who said, 'At the battle of Badr, the enemy was gathered around Ubayy b. Khalaf and when I drew near him, I saw that his chain-mail had been damaged beneath his arm pit. So I stabbed him there with my sword. At Badr I was also hit by an arrow and my eye was gouged out. The Messenger of God (ṢAAS) spat on it and said a prayer for me. And no harm had been done to me.'"

This account is unique from this line; its chain of transmission is excellent, but the (major) scholars did not quote it. Al-Ṭibrani, however, related it from a *hadīth* of Ibrāhīm b. al-Mundhir.

Ibn Hishām stated, "And Abū Bakr called for his son ʿAbd al-Raḥmān who was at that time on the side of the polytheists, not yet having accepted Islam. Abū Bakr asked him, 'Well, where's my property now, evil one?' ʿAbd al-Raḥmān replied, in verse,

"All that remains are weapons and the horse Yaʿbūb, and
a sword with which to kill silly old men."

By this he meant that all that was left was equipment for warfare and a horse, named Yaʿbūb, on which misguided old men could be fought. This is what he said in his state of disbelief.

We have been informed in al-Umawī's work on the military campaigns that the Messenger of God (ṢAAS) and Abū Bakr went out and walked among the dead, the former commenting, "We're splitting the chieftains apart," the latter reciting the verse,

"Of powerful men who were against us; they were very
haughty and evil!"

An Account of how the heads of the unbelievers were thrown into the well at the battle of Badr.

Ibn Isḥāq stated, "Yazīd b. Rūmān related to me, from ʿUrwa, from ʿĀʾisha, who said, 'When the Messenger of God (ṢAAS) ordered that those killed should be thrown into the burial pit, it was done. Umayya b. Khalaf, however, was not thrown in because he had swollen up in his armour and quite filled it. When they went to take him out of it, his body fell apart so they left him in it and threw on him the earth and the stones they had removed.

"'Having thrown them into the pit, he stood over them and said, "O denizens of the pit, have you found what your Lord promised you to be true, for I have found what my Lord promised me?"'

"She went on, 'His Companions asked him, "O Messenger of God, are you talking to people who are dead?"

"'He replied, "They have learned that what their Lord promised them was true'" (sūrat al-Rūm; XXX, v.52).

"'Ā'isha stated, 'People say that he spoke the words, "They heard what I said to them." However, what he said was, "they have learned"'"

Ibn Isḥāq stated that Ḥumayd al-Ṭawīl related to him, from Anas b. Mālik who said, "The Companions of the Prophet (ṢAAS) heard him saying in the middle of the night, 'O denizens of the pit, O 'Utba b. Rabī'a, O Shayba b. Rabī'a, O Umayya b. Khalaf, O Abū Jahl b. Hishām,' and he went on to enumerate those in the pit. 'Have you found what your Lord promised you to be true, for I have found what my Lord promised me to be true.'

"The Muslims said, 'O Messenger of God, are you calling out to decaying bodies?'

"He replied, 'You do not hear any better than they what it is I say; but they cannot answer me.'"

Imām Aḥmad related this from Ibn Abū 'Adī, from Ḥamīd, from Anas. His account was similar. This tradition conforms to the criteria of both the sheikhs (al-Bukhārī and Muslim).

Ibn Isḥāq stated, "A scholar related to me that the Messenger of God (ṢAAS) said, 'O denizens of the pit, you were very bad relatives of the prophet who was your Prophet. You called me a liar, while the people believed in me. You expelled me, while they gave me shelter. You fought me, while they aided me. Have you found what your Lord promised you to be true? I have found what my Lord promised me to be true.'"

I would comment that this is one of those aḥādīth that 'Ā'isha, God bless her, used to interpret (differently), believing them to contradict the verses in the Qur'ān. These have been documented in a single volume.

In this case the passage contradicted, in her view, is the verse, "And you do not make those in the graves listen" (sūrat al-Fāṭir; XXXV, v.22). This verse however does not contradict the previous statement. The view of the majority of the Companions is correct in the light of the aḥādīth that contradict her views, God bless her and be pleased with her.

Al-Bukhārī stated that 'Ubayd b. Ismā'īl related to him, from Abū Usāma, from Hishām b. 'Urwa, from his father, who said, "Someone mentioned in 'Ā'isha's presence that Ibn 'Umar quoted the Prophet (ṢAAS) as having said, that the dead would be persecuted in their graves because of the weeping of their families. She commented, 'God have mercy on him, no! What the Messenger of God (ṢAAS) said was, "They will be tortured for their faults and their sins, and their families are weeping for them now."'

"She went on, 'That is like the account saying, "The Messenger of God (ṢAAS) stood at the trench in which were the polytheists who had been killed at Badr and he spoke to them, and commented, 'They do listen to what I say.'" However, what he said was, "They now know that what I was telling them was true." She then recited, "you do not make the dead to hear" (sūrat al-Rūm;

XXX, v.52) and "you do not make those inside the graves hear" (*sūrat al-Fāṭir*; XXXV, v.22). She commented, "When they had taken their places in hell-fire, that is." Muslim related it from Abū Kurayb, from Abū Usāma.

The assertion concerning hearing the dead after their burial comes in more than one *ḥadīth*, as we will establish, if God wills it, in our book on funerals in *al-Aḥkām al-Kabīr* (*The Major Statutes*).

Al-Bukhārī then stated, "'Uthmān related to me, quoting 'Abda, from Hishām, from his father, from Ibn 'Umar, who said, 'The Messenger of God (ṢAAS) stood at the burial pit at Badr and said, "Have you found what your Lord promised you to be true?" He then said, "They now listen to what I tell them!"'"

"This was related to 'Ā'isha and she commented, 'The Prophet (ṢAAS) really said, "Now they know that what I used to tell them was the truth."' She then recited, 'you do not make the dead to hear' to the end of that verse."

Muslim related this from Abū Kurayb, from Abū Usāma, and from Abū Bakr b. Abū Shayba, from Wakī', both of them quoting Hishām b. 'Urwa.

Al-Bukhārī stated, "'Abd Allāh b. Muḥammad related to us, (that) he heard Rawḥ b. 'Ubāda (say), 'Sa'īd b. Abū 'Arūba related to us, from Qatāda, who said, "Anas b. Mālik reported to us, from Abū Ṭalḥa, that the Messenger of God (ṢAAS) ordered on the day of the battle at Badr that 24 of the chiefs of Quraysh be thrown into a dirty, refuse-laden old well. Whenever he went forth against an enemy he would stay for three nights out in an open area. On the third day at Badr he ordered his mount to be readied and it was saddled. He then set off, followed by his Companions who told one another that he had to have some important reason to be leaving. He came to a stop at the lip of the well and began calling out their names, referring also to their fathers' names by saying, 'You so-and-so, son of so-and-so' etc. 'Would you now be pleased to have obeyed God and His Messenger? We have found that what our Lord promised us was true. Have you found what your Lord promised you to be true?'"'

"'Umar then said, 'Messenger of God, why do you talk to bodies that have no spirits in them?'

"The Prophet (ṢAAS) replied, 'By Him who holds the soul of Muḥammad in His hand, you do not hear what I say any better than do they!'"

Qatāda stated, "God gave them life until He had made them hear his words, to reprimand, denigrate, and punish them, to make them feel sorry and regretful."

The rest of the scholars gave this tradition, except for Ibn Māja, from various lines, back to Sa'īd b. Abū 'Urūba.

Imām Aḥmad related it from Yūnus b. Muḥammad al-Mu'adib, from Shaybān b. 'Abd al-Raḥmān, from Qatāda, who said that Anas b. Mālik gave this *ḥadīth*, in similar form, but without making reference to Abū Ṭalḥa. This chain of authorities is good, but the prior one is more reliable and more clear. But God knows best.

Imām Aḥmad stated, "ʿAffān related to us, quoting Ḥammād, from Thābit, from Anas, that the Messenger of God (ṢAAS) left the dead at Badr unburied for three days, till they became putrid. He then went out, stood near them and said, 'O Umayya b. Khalaf, O Abū Jahl b. Hishām, O ʿUtba b. Rabīʿa, O Shayba b. Rabīʿa, have you found what your Lord promised you to be true? I have found what my Lord promised me to be true.'"

He continued, "ʿUmar heard his voice and asked, 'O Messenger of God, do you call out to them after three days, and do they hear? God Almighty said, "You do not make the dead to hear."' He replied, 'By Him in whose hand is my soul, you do not hear any better what I say than they do. But they cannot reply.'"

Muslim related this from Hudba b. Khālid, from Ḥammād b. Salama.

Ibn Isḥāq stated, "Ḥassān b. Thābit spoke the following verses,

'I recognized Zaynab's home on the dunes, traced like a
line of revelation on a clean sheet,
The winds blow over them and all the dark clouds
pouring down heavy rain,
Its traces are worn and have become defaced that once
were the abode she enjoyed.
Give up remembering her every day and cast off the
agony of your sad heart,
And relate shamelessly, honestly and without inventing
lies.
Tell what the All-Powerful did in the morning at Badr,
giving us success over the polytheists,
That morning when their force seemed as great as Mt.
Ḥirāʾ, its dimensions plain at sunset.
When we engaged them our force was like forest lions,
young and mature alike,
Ahead of Muhammad whom they defended against his
enemies in the fires of warfare,
Sharp, thin swords in their hands, all well-tried
and bone cutting,
The Banū al-Aws in the vanguard, helped by the Banū
al-Najjār, men in the firm faith.
We left Abū Jahl prostrate, and ʿUtba on the ground,
And Shayba we left there, along with other men of noble
lines.
When we threw them upside down into the pit, the
Messenger of God called to them,
"Do you not now find my words were true? And God's
command does take by the heart."
They did not speak but if they had they would have
said, "You spoke true; your views were correct."'"

Ibn Isḥāq stated, "When the Messenger of God (ṢAAS) ordered they be thrown into the pit, 'Utba b. Rabī'a was dragged there. The Messenger of God (ṢAAS) looked, so I have been told, into the face of Abū Ḥudhayfa, son of 'Utba, and he looked sad and distressed. He asked some such question as, 'Abū Ḥudhayfa, are you very upset at your father's fate?'

"He replied, 'No, I swear, O Messenger of God. I've no problems with my father's fate; but I once knew him as a man of reason, judgement and goodness, and hoped those qualities would lead him to Islam. When I saw what his fate was and how he had died in disbelief despite my hopes for him, I was saddened.' Hearing this, the Messenger of God (ṢAAS) treated him with kindness and said a prayer for him."

Al-Bukhārī stated, "Al-Ḥumaydī related to us, quoting Sufyān, quoting 'Amr, from 'Aṭā', from Ibn 'Abbās, who said, quoting the verse of the Qur'ān, 'those who exchanged disbelief for God's favour' (surat Ibrāhīm; XIV, v.28), 'These, I swear, were the disbelievers of Quraysh.' 'Amr commented, 'They were Quraysh; and Muḥammad was God's favour.' And regarding the verse, 'And their people came to dwell in a waste-land abode' he commented, 'This referred to the hell-fire, after the battle of Badr.'"

Ibn Isḥāq stated, "Ḥassān b. Thābit spoke the following verses,

> 'My people are those who gave refuge to their Prophet
> and who believed him, while the earth's inhabitants were
> unbelievers,
> Except for certain special peoples who preceded the
> virtuous Helpers, aiding them,
> Rejoicing in their words at God's decree, for there
> having come to them one noble in line, chosen.
> "Welcome indeed! Welcome in ease and security!" How
> fine the Prophet, fine the decree, and the protection!
> They had him stay in a place where nothing was to fear
> from those neighbours who lived close by;
> The Helpers shared their wealth with them when they
> arrived as Emigrants, while the fate of the deniers was the
> fire.
> We went and they did too, to their fate; had they but
> known for sure they would not have gone.
> He set them in conceit, then delivered them up; the
> vile are careless of those who empower them.
> He told them, "I am your neighbour." Then he brought
> evil upon them, including punishment and disgrace.
> We then met up against them and they turned away from
> their leaders who were aiding them, and one faction of them
> fell far down.'"

Imām Aḥmad stated, "Yaḥyā b. Abū Bakr and 'Abd al-Razzāq related to us, as follows, 'Isrā'īl related to us, from 'Ikrima, from Ibn 'Abbās, who said, "When the Messenger of God (ṢAAS) had finished with the slain, he was told, 'Pursue the caravan; there's nothing protecting it now.' Al-ʿAbbās, in shackles, called out to him, 'It behoves you not!' 'Why not?' he asked. He replied, 'Because God promised you one of the two parties and He has fulfilled His promise to you.'"'"

The total number of polytheist leaders killed at Badr were 70, this taking place in the presence of 1,000 angels.

It was no doubt God's decree that a majority of those who survived would accept Islam. If He had wished He could have sent down just one angel against them and destroyed them to the last man. But the (angels) killed only those totally devoid of good.

For among those angels was Gabriel, whom God Almighty had once ordered to destroy the cities of the people of Lot. There were seven of these cities and they consisted of a variety of nations, animals, lands and farms, and God only knows what. He lifted these cities up until he had raised them to the very heavens on the edge of his wing. He then turned them upside down and lowered them, pursuing them with stones that struck them. This was as we described it in our account of the people of Lot.

God had planned for the warfare of the believers against the unbelievers. The Almighty had laid out his judgements about that in saying, "And when you meet in battle those who disbelieve, then strike their necks until you have defeated them. Then take them prisoner. Later set them free either as a favour or for ransom until the war is concluded. That will be how it is; if God had wished he would have inflicted full retribution upon them. But He acted to try some of you through others" (*sūrat Muḥammad*; XLVII, v.4).

The Almighty also stated, "Fight them! God will punish them through your hands and will disgrace them. He will give you victory over them and He will assist you against them, relieving the hearts of a people who are believers. He will remove the anger from their hearts and He will grant forgiveness to those He wishes" (*sūrat al-Tawba*; IX, v.14, 15).

The death of Abū Jahl came about at the hands of a youth from the Helpers. Thereafter ʿAbd Allāh b. Masʿūd was placed over him; he grasped Abū Jahl by the beard and stood upon his chest, until he said, "You have reached remarkable heights, for a herdsman!" ʿAbd Allāh then cut off his head and took it and placed it before the Messenger of God (ṢAAS).

By this God comforted the believers. And this was more effective than if He had made a bolt of lightning strike Abū Jahl down, or made the roof of his house fall upon him, or if he had died a natural death. But God knows best!

Among those polytheists killed at Badr, Ibn Isḥāq mentions some Muslims who had come to battle along with them only out of fear. These Muslims had been persecuted and enticed away from Islam. Among these were al-Ḥārith b. Zamʿa

b. al-Aswad, Abū Qays b. al-Fākih, Abū Qays b. al-Walīd b. al-Mughīra, ῾Alī b. Umayya b. Khalaf, and al-῾Āṣ b. Munabbih b. al-Ḥajjāj.

Ibn Isḥāq stated, "It was regarding them that the Almighty revealed, 'Those whom the angels made to die were unjust to themselves. They say, "What were your circumstances?" They will reply, "We were powerless on earth." They shall ask them, "Was God's earth not spacious enough for you to move away elsewhere?" Those persons shall have hell as their abode, and bad will be their fate'" (sūrat al-Nisā᾽; IV, v.97).

The prisoners taken at Badr that day totalled 70 and discussion relating to them will follow, if God wills it. These included some members of the family of the Messenger of God (ṢAAS), that is, his uncle al-῾Abbās b. ῾Abd al-Muṭṭalib, his cousin ῾Aqil b. Abū Ṭālib, and Nawfal b. al-Ḥārith b. ῾Abd al-Muṭṭalib.

Al-Shāfi῾ī, al-Bukhārī and others have used this as evidence in support of the view that not everyone who possesses a relative is obliged to set him free. They use this to refute the ḥadīth of al-Ḥasan, from Ibn Samra regarding this. But God knows best.

Abū al-῾Āṣ b. al-Rabī῾ b. ῾Abd Shams b. Umayya, the husband of Zaynab, daughter of the Prophet (ṢAAS) was one of those prisoners.

DIVISION

The Companions differed over what to do with the prisoners taken at Badr. There were two views – that they should be killed, or that they should be freed in return for ransom.

As Imām Aḥmad stated, "῾Alī b. ῾Āṣim related to us, from Ḥumayd, from Anas, and from another man mentioned, from al-Ḥasan, who said, 'The Messenger of God (ṢAAS) sought the advice of his men concerning what to do with the prisoners taken at Badr. He told them, 'God has placed them in your power.'"

He went on, "῾Umar arose and said, 'O Messenger of God, strike their necks!' The Messenger of God (ṢAAS) turned away from him.

"He then again asked them the same question. Abū Bakr arose and said, 'O Messenger of God, we consider you should pardon them and accept ransom for them.'

"At this the unhappiness on the face of the Messenger of God (ṢAAS) disappeared; he did pardon them and accepted ransom for them.

"And God Almighty revealed the words, 'Were it not decreed by God beforehand you would have suffered mightily'" (sūrat al-Anfāl; VIII, v.68). Aḥmad alone quoted this tradition.

He also related – and the following wording is his – as did Muslim, Abū Dā᾽ūd and al-Tirmidhī, stating it to be authentic, as did ῾Alī b. al-Madīnī, who also affirmed its authenticity, from a ḥadīth of ῾Ikrima b. ῾Ammār, as follows, "Simāk al-Ḥanafī Abū Zumayl related to us, quoting Ibn ῾Abbās, quoting ῾Umar b. al-Khaṭṭāb, who said, 'At the battle of Badr, the Messenger of God (ṢAAS) looked out and saw his force to be some 300 strong, while that of the polytheists was more than 1,000.'"

He then related the *hadīth* as above as far as the words, "and 70 of them were killed, while 70 were taken prisoner."

And the Messenger of God (ṢAAS) asked the advice of Abū Bakr, ʿAlī and ʿUmar about them. Abū Bakr responded, "O Messenger of God, these are your close relatives, your tribal brothers; I think you should accept ransom from them. What we receive from them will give us power against the unbelievers; and God might well give them guidance so that they become allied to us."

The Messenger of God (ṢAAS) then asked, "Well, what do you think, O ʿUmar b. al-Khaṭṭāb?" ʿUmar went on, "I replied, 'By God, I don't agree with Abū Bakr. I think you should hand over to me so-and-so,' referring to someone closely related to ʿUmar, 'and I'll strike his neck. And if you hand ʿAqīl over to ʿAlī, he can strike his neck. And if you hand over to Ḥamza so-and-so, his brother, he can strike his neck. That way God will know that we feel no leniency towards the polytheists. These men are their chieftains, their very leaders.'

"The Messenger of God (ṢAAS) liked what Abū Bakr had said and did not like my view. And so he did accept ransom from them."

The following day, ʿUmar said, "I went to the Prophet (ṢAAS) early in the morning; he was with Abū Bakr and they were weeping. I asked, 'O Messenger of God, tell me why you and your Companion are weeping. If I find reason to weep, I'll do so. If not I would pretend to weep at your weeping!'

"The Messenger of God (ṢAAS) replied, 'I'm weeping at how you Companions proposed to me that I accept ransom. Your punishment for doing so was proposed to me and it was closer than this tree,' referring to a tree nearby.

"And God Almighty sent down, 'It is not proper for a prophet to take captives before he has caused slaughter in the land. You desire the things of this world, while God wishes for the after-life. And God is All-Powerful, All-Wise! Were it not decreed by God beforehand you would have suffered mightily for what you took'" (*sūrat al-Anfāl*; VIII, v.67, 68).

This refers to the ransom. God then did make permissible the acceptance of spoils. He then went on to complete the *hadīth*.

Imām Aḥmad stated that Abū Muʿāwiya related to him, quoting al-Aʿmash, from ʿAmr b. Murra, from ʿUbayda, from ʿAbd Allāh, who said, "At the battle of Badr, the Messenger of God (ṢAAS) asked, 'What do you say concerning these prisoners?' Abū Bakr replied, 'O Messenger of God, they are your people, your relatives. Let them live; be lenient to them. Perhaps God will forgive them.'"

ʿAbd Allāh went on, "ʿUmar said, 'O Messenger of God, they exiled you and called you a liar. Bring them close and strike their necks!'

"ʿAbd Allāh b. Rawāḥa suggested, 'O Messenger of God, find a valley with many trees, make them enter it, then set it on fire around them!'"

ʿAbd Allāh went on, "The Messenger of God (ṢAAS) went back inside without giving him any response. Some people said he was going to do as Abū Bakr had suggested, others that he would take ʿUmar's advice, still others that he would take that given by ʿAbd Allāh b. Rawāḥa. Then he came out to them and said, 'God softens the hearts of men concerning Him, so that they become softer than soft. And God hardens the hearts of men so that they become harder than stone. You, Abū Bakr, are like Abraham who said, "Whoever follows me is of me, and whoever disobeys me, then You are Forgiving, Merciful" (*sūrat Ibrāhīm*; XIV, v.36). You, Abū Bakr, are like Jesus, who said, "If You punish them, they are Your servants; if You forgive them, then You are the All-Powerful, the Wise" (*sūrat al-Māʾida*; V, v.118). You, ʿUmar, are like Noah, who said, "O Lord, do not leave on the earth any place for the unbelievers" (*sūrat Nūḥ*; LXXI, v.26). And ʿUmar, you are like Moses, who said, "O God, destroy their wealth and make their hearts hard, for they will not believe until they see the painful punishment" (*sūrat Yūnus*; X, v.88). You are a support. Let none be exempt from either ransom or having their head smitten.'"

ʿAbd Allāh continued, "I asked, 'Except for Suhayl b. Bayḍā? For I have heard him talk of Islam.'" He went on, "But he remained silent."

ʿAbd Allāh then said, "And I was never more afraid that there should fall upon me some stone from heaven than I was that day, until he said the words 'Except for Suhayl b. Bayḍā'."

He went on, "And so God revealed, 'It is not proper for a prophet to take captives before he has caused slaughter in the land. You desire the things of this world, while God wishes for the after-life; and God is All-Powerful, All-Wise. And were it not for a decree'" (*sūrat al-Anfāl*; VIII, v.67–8).

Al-Tirmidhī related it thus, as did al-Ḥākim, from a *ḥadīth* of Abū Muʿāwiya. Al-Ḥākim stated, "The chain of authorities is authentic, though they (al-Bukārī and Muslim) did not narrate it." Also, Ibn Mardawayh related it through ʿAbd Allāh b. ʿUmar and Abū Hurayra in similar words. And it is similarly related from Abū Ayyūb al-Anṣārī.

Ibn Mardawayh related, and so did al-Ḥākim in the *al-Mustadrak*, (*The Compendium*), from a *ḥadīth* of ʿUbayd Allāh b. Mūsā, (as follows), "Isrāʾīl related to us, from Ibrāhīm b. Muhājir, from Mujāhid, from Ibn ʿUmar, who said, 'When the prisoners were taken at the battle of Badr, al-ʿAbbās was among them; he was captured by a Helper.' He went on, 'The Helpers had warned him they would kill him. That information reached the Messenger of God (ṢAAS) who said, "I did not sleep tonight because of my uncle al-ʿAbbās. The Helpers are saying they are going to kill him."' ʿUmar asked, 'Should I go to them?' 'Yes,' he replied.

"ʿUmar went to the Helpers and asked them to release al-ʿAbbās to him. They replied, 'No; by God we'll not release him!' ʿUmar then asked them, 'What if that is the pleasure of the Messenger of God?' They replied, 'If that is his pleasure, then take him.' So ʿUmar did take him and when he had control over him, ʿUmar asked him, "ʿAbbās, accept Islam! I swear, for you to accept Islam would please me more than if al-Khaṭṭāb, my father, were to do so. And that would be only for the pleasure I would see your acceptance of Islam giving to the Messenger of God.'

"He went on, 'The Messenger of God (ṢAAS) asked the advice of Abū Bakr, who replied, "They are of your family, release them." He asked the advice of ʿUmar, who said, "Kill them!" The Messenger of God (ṢAAS) then asked ransom for them and so God revealed, "It is not proper for a prophet to take captives before he has caused slaughter in the land"'" (sūrat al-Anfāl; VIII, v.67).

Al-Ḥakim then stated in his ṣaḥīḥ collection, "This ḥadīth has an authentic chain of transmission, but the two authorities (al-Bukhārī and Muslim) did not narrate it."

Al-Tirmidhī related, as did al-Nasāʾī and Ibn Māja, from a ḥadīth of Sufyān al-Thawrī, from Hishām b. Ḥassān, from Muḥammad b. Sīrīn, from ʿUbayda, from ʿAlī, who said, "Gabriel came to the Prophet (ṢAAS) and said, 'Ask your Companions to make a choice about the prisoners; if they want there to be ransom, so be it. If they want to kill them, so be it, provided that in a future year a similar number be killed of them.'

"They commented, 'So it's to be ransom or some of us will be killed!'"

This is a very strange ḥadīth. Some authorities relate it with an incomplete line of authorities, from ʿUbayda. But God knows best.

Ibn Isḥāq stated, from Ibn Abū Najīḥ, from ʿAṭāʾ, from Ibn ʿAbbās, who said, concerning the verse "were it not for a decree from God that came before, you would have suffered mightily for what you took" (sūrat al-Anfāl; VIII, v.68). "He is saying, 'Were it not for the fact that I do not punish those who disobey me until I have approached them, I would have made you suffer mightily for what you took.'"

It is similarly related from Ibn Abū Najīḥ, also from Mujāhid. Ibn Isḥāq and others chose it.

Al-Aʿmash stated, "He had previously made plain that he would not punish anyone who had taken part in the battle of Badr." It is similarly related from Saʿd b. Abū Waqqāṣ, Saʿīd b. Jubayr and ʿAṭāʾ b. Abū Rabāḥ.

Mujāhid and al-Thawrī stated, "'were it not for a decree from God that had come previously.' That is, in forgiving them."

Al-Wālibī stated, from Ibn ʿAbbās, "It had previously been stated in the Qurʾān that the 'spoils and ransom for prisoners are permitted to you'. And this is why God later stated, 'and so enjoy whatever you have taken as booty, well and legally'" (sūrat al-Anfāl; VIII, v.69).

It was related similarly from Abū Hurayra, Ibn Masʿūd, Saʿīd b. Jubayr, ʿAṭāʾ, al-Ḥasan, Qatāda and al-Aʿmash, and Ibn Jarīr selected it.

This last statement is considered preferable because of what is substantiated in the ṣaḥīḥ collections, from Jābir b. ʿAbd Allah, who stated, "The Messenger of God (ṢAAS), stated, 'I was given five things not given to any prophet before myself: I was given victory through fear (within Quraysh) for a month; the earth was made for me into a mosque, and a pure place; booty was made permissible for me while it had not been made so for anyone before myself; I was given intercession; and prophets were previously sent to their people, while I was sent to all mankind.'"

Al-A'mash related, from Abū Ṣāliḥ, from Abū Hurayra, who quoted the Prophet (ṢAAS) as saying, "Booty was not made permissible to leaders other than ourselves."

The Almighty therefore stated, "so enjoy whatever you have taken as booty, well and legally".

And so God Almighty made it permissible to take booty and ransom for prisoners.

Abū Dā'ūd stated, "'Abd al-Raḥmān b. al-Mubārak al-'Absī related to us, quoting Sufyān b. Ḥabīb, quoting Shu'ba, from Abū al-'Anbas, from Abū al-Sha'thā', from Ibn 'Abbās, that the Messenger of God (ṢAAS) placed a price of 400 dirhams as ransom for the non-Muslims at Badr. This sum was in fact the least taken for any one of them as ransom, while the largest amount taken for any one of them was 4,000 dirhams."

God promised those who believe that there will be returned to them what was taken from them, in this world and the next. The Almighty stated, "O Prophet, tell the prisoners now in your hands, 'If God knows there is good in your hearts, He will give you better than what has been taken from you, and He will forgive you'" (sūrat al-Anfāl; VIII, v.70).

Al-Wālibī stated, from Ibn 'Abbās: "Revelation came down about al-'Abbās, and he ransomed himself for 40 awqiyya of gold. And he commented, 'And so God did give me 40 slaves,' referring to those who worked for him in his business. He went on, 'And I hope for that forgiveness that God – most highly is He to be praised – has promised.'"

Ibn Isḥāq stated, "Al-'Abbās b. 'Abd Allāh b. Ma'bad related to me, from some of his family, from Ibn 'Abbās, who said, 'The night following the Battle of Badr, after the prisoners had been bound, the Messenger of God (ṢAAS) at first could not get to sleep. His Companions asked him why he could not sleep and he replied, "I have been hearing my uncle al-'Abbās groaning in his fetters." So they untied him, he became silent and the Messenger of God (ṢAAS) went to sleep.'"

Ibn Isḥāq concluded, "And he was a wealthy man, who ransomed himself with 100 awqiyya of gold."

My own comment is that this money was on behalf of himself, and for his nephews 'Aqīl and Nawfal, as well as for his ally, 'Utba b. 'Amr, one of the Banū al-Ḥārith b. Fihr, as the Messenger of God (ṢAAS) had told him to do when he claimed to have accepted Islam. The Messenger of God (ṢAAS) commented, "What was evident was that you were against us. God knows best about your accepting Islam, and He will reward you."

Al-'Abbās claimed that he had no money and so he was asked, "Where is the money that you and Umm al-Faḍl buried when you told her, 'If I should be killed on my expedition, then this is for my sons al-Faḍl, ʿAbd Allāh and Qathm?'

"Al-ʿAbbās responded, 'By God, I certainly know you're the Messenger of God; no one except myself and Umm al-Faḍl knew that.'"

Ibn Isḥāq related this from Ibn Abū Najīḥ, from ʿAṭāʾ, from Ibn ʿAbbās.

It is established in the ṣaḥīḥ of al-Bukhārī, through Mūsā b. ʿUqba that Al-Zuhrī stated, "Anas b. Mālik related to me as follows, 'Some Helpers requested to see the Messenger of God (ṢAAS). They asked him, "Give us permission and we will leave the ransom money for our sister's son al-ʿAbbās." He replied, "No, by God, you won't leave a single dirham for him!"'"

Al-Bukhārī stated, "Ibrāhīm b. Ṭahmān said, from ʿAbd al-ʿAzīz b. Ṣuhayb, from Anas, that the Prophet (ṢAAS) was brought money from al-Baḥrayn and ordered that it be distributed in the mosque. It was the largest sum of money that was ever brought to him. Al-ʿAbbās came to him and said, 'O Messenger of God, give me some; I paid ransom for myself and for ʿUqayl.' 'Take some,' he told him. Al-ʿAbbās stuffed money into his gown, then moved away, dragging it, but was unable to do so. He asked, 'Tell someone to lift it up for me!' 'No, I won't,' he replied. 'Then you lift it upon me,' he asked. 'No, I won't,' he repeated. Al-ʿAbbās then scattered some of the money and made to go, again dragging it, but he could not. Again he asked, 'Tell someone to lift it up on me!' 'No, I won't,' he said. Al-ʿAbbās scattered some more of the money then lifted it up on his shoulders and left. The Messenger of God (ṢAAS) gazed after him until he was lost to our sight, amazed at his cupidity. And the Messenger of God (ṢAAS) did not rise to collect a single dirham of the money."

Al-Bayhaqī stated, "Al-Ḥākim told us, quoting al-Aṣamm, from Aḥmad b. ʿAbd al-Jabbār, from Yūnus, from Asbāṭ b. Naṣr, from Ismāʿīl b. ʿAbd al-Raḥmān al-Suddī, who said, 'The ransom for al-ʿAbbās and his two cousins ʿAqīl b. Abū Ṭālib and Nawfal b. al-Ḥārith b. ʿAbd al-Muṭṭalib amounted to 400 dinars for each man. Then the Almighty threatened the rest, saying, "If they want to betray you, they have previously betrayed God. And so He took control of them. And God is knowledgeable, wise"'" (sūrat al-Anfāl; VIII, v.71).

DIVISION

It is well known that the prisoners at Badr numbered 70, while the number of polytheists killed was also 70, as was related in more than one aḥadīth that have been given above and will be given hereafter, if God wills it. This is also stated in a ḥadīth of al-Barāʾ b. ʿĀzib, in the ṣaḥīḥ collection of al-Bukhārī, namely that at Badr they killed 70 and captured 70.

Mūsā b. ʿUqba stated, "At the battle of Badr 6 Muslims of Quraysh were killed and 8 of the Helpers, while 49 of the polytheists were killed and 39 were taken prisoner."

Al-Bayhaqī related it thus from him and went on to state that Ibn Lahīʿa reported it similarly, from Abū al-Aswad, from ʿUrwa, concerning the number of the Muslims who died as martyrs, and the number of polytheists who were killed. ·

Al-Bayhaqi continued, "Al-Ḥākim related to us, quoting al-Aṣamm, quoting Aḥmad b. ʿAbd al-Jabbār, from Yūnus b. Bukayr, from Muḥammad b. Isḥāq, who said, 'At Badr 11 of the Muslims died as martyrs, 4 from Quraysh and 7 from among the Helpers, while more than a score of the polytheists were killed.'"

In another passage, al-Bayhaqi stated, "With the Messenger of God (ṢAAS) there were 40 prisoners, while their dead were of a similar number."

Al-Bayhaqī then related, through Abū Ṣāliḥ, al-Layth's secretary, from al-Layth, from ʿUqayl, from al-Zuhrī, who said, "The first of the Muslims killed was Mihjaʿ, the freed-man of ʿUmar, and a Helper. More than 70 of the polytheists were killed that day, a similar number of them being taken prisoner."

Al-Bayhaqi went on, "Ibn Wahb related it from Yūnus b. Yazīd, from al-Zuhrī, from ʿUrwa b. al-Zubayr. He commented, "It is this that we have related that is the most authentic account of the number of polytheists killed and taken prisoner."

He then gave evidence of this, referring to what both he and al-Bukhārī had derived through Abū Isḥāq, from al-Barāʾ b. ʿĀzib, stating, "At the battle of Uḥud, the Messenger of God (ṢAAS) placed ʿAbd Allāh b. Jubayr in command of the archers, and they hit 70 of us. The Prophet (ṢAAS) and his men had struck down 140 of the polytheists at Badr, 70 being killed and 70 being taken captive."

I would comment that the fact is that the total number of polytheists at Badr was between 900 and 1,000.

Qatāda asserted that they were 950 men, as if he were deriving his information from what we have stated. But God knows best.

In the *ḥadīth* of ʿUmar given above, it is stated that they were more than 1,000; however, the first account is what is authentic, since the Prophet (ṢAAS) stated, "The enemy force was between 900 and 1,000."

The Muslim forces that day totalled some tens above 300 men, as evidence shows that will be given hereafter, if God wills it, along with their names.

It has been previously stated in the *ḥadīth* of al-Ḥakam, from Miqsam, from Ibn ʿAbbās, that the battle of Badr took place on Friday, the 17th of Ramaḍān; ʿUrwa b. al-Zubayr also stated this, as did Qatāda, Ismāʿīl, al-Suddi al-Kabīr and Abū Jaʿfar al-Bāqir.

Al-Bayhaqī related, through Qutayba, from Jarīr, from al-Aʿmash, from Ibrāhīm, from al-Aswad, from ʿAbd Allāh b. Masʿūd, who said with reference to the *laylat al-qadr*.[65] "Search for it with 11 nights remaining of the month, for Badr took place on the morning of that date."

____

65. The term refers to that night in the month of Ramaḍān when revelation of the Qurʾān first occurred.

Al-Bayhaqī stated, "It is related of Zayd b. Arqam that he was questioned about the *laylat al-qadr* and he replied, 'The night of the 19th, without doubt.' He went on, 'And the day known as *al-furqān*[66] when the two forces met in battle.'"

Al-Bayhaqī stated, "It is well known from the works of the scholars of the early military campaigns that that occurred on the 17th of Ramadān."

Al-Bayhaqī then stated, "Abū al-Ḥusayn b. Bishrān informed us, quoting Abū ʿAmr b. al-Sammāk, quoting Ḥanbal b. Isḥāq, quoting Abū Nuʿaym, quoting ʿAmr b. ʿUthmān, who quoted Mūsā b. Ṭalḥa, as saying, ʿAbū Ayyūb al-Anṣārī was asked about the battle of Badr, and he replied, 'It was either on the 17th or the 13th, or when either 11 or 17 days remained of the month.'"

This is very strange.

The *ḥāfiẓ* Ibn ʿAsākir recounted in the biography of Qubāth b. Ashyam al-Laythī, through al-Wāqidī and others, with lines of authority going back to him, that Qubāth was present at Badr on the side of the polytheists and that he recounted their defeat despite the small size of the force of the Messenger of God (ṢAAS). He stated, "I kept saying to myself, 'I only ever saw women take flight from such as this.' I swear, if the Quraysh women had gone forth to battle bearing only easily-drawn bows, they would have turned back Muḥammad and his men! And following the battle of *al-Khandaq*, 'the trench', I wished I had gone to Medina and had looked into what Muḥammad was saying. Islam had now entered my spirit." He went on, "I then went there and asked after him and was told he was over in the shade of the mosque with a group of his Companions. So I went there, but I was unable to distinguish him from the others. I made my greetings and he asked me, 'So, Qubāth b. Ashyam, you're the man who said of Badr, "I only ever saw women take flight from such as this?" I replied, 'I bear witness that you are the Messenger of God! This is something I never uttered, not even muttering it. It's only what I said to myself. And were you not a prophet, you'd not know of it! Let me now pledge to you my allegiance to Islam!' And I accepted Islam."

DIVISION

The Companions, God be pleased with them, disagreed among themselves over who should receive the spoils gained from the polytheists at Badr.

When the polytheists retreated, the Muslims performed three functions. One group remained on watch guarding the Messenger of God (ṢAAS) aware that any one of the polytheists might come back and attack him.

Another group pursued the polytheists, killing and capturing them.

A third group gathered the spoils of the battle from various places.

Each of these groups maintained that their activities were important and entitled them to a greater share than the rest.

66. The term refers to that "clear differentiation" that occurred between the forces of good and evil at the battle of Badr.

Ibn Isḥāq stated, "ʿAbd al-Raḥmān b. al-Ḥārith and others related to me from Sulaymān b. Mūsā, from Makḥūl, from Abū Umāma al-Bāhilī, who said, 'I asked ʿUbāda b. al-Ṣāmit about the *sūrat al-Anfāl*, (*The Spoils*). He replied, "It was revealed about those of us who took part in the battle at Badr after we had begun quarreling about the spoils and were behaving badly. God therefore took them away from us and gave them over to the Messenger of God (ṢAAS) who divided them *ʿan bawāʾ*, equally, that is, among the Muslims."'"

Aḥmad related this similarly from Muḥammad b. Salama, from Muḥammad b. Isḥāq.

By the word given above for "equally" it is meant that the spoils were split between those who had gathered them, those who had chased the enemy, and those who had remained near the banners. No one group was given the preferential treatment they claimed.

This does not contradict the concept of spoils being divided into five parts, each fifth being allotted to a specific recipient, as some scholars might maintain, including Abū ʿUbayda and others. But God knows best. In fact, the Messenger of God (ṢAAS) received his sword *Dhū al-Fiqār* from the booty taken at Badr.

Ibn Jarīr stated, "He similarly chose a camel that had belonged to Abū Jahl that had a silver ring through its nose. This was also before the issuance of the edict about the fifth."

Imām Aḥmad stated, "Muʿāwiya b. ʿAmr related to us, quoting Ibn Isḥāq, from ʿAbd al-Raḥmān b. al-Ḥārith b ʿAbd Allāh b. ʿAbbās b. Abū Rabīʿa, from Sulaymān b. Mūsā, from Abū Sallām, from Abū Umāma, from ʿUbāda b. al-Ṣāmit, who said, 'We went forth with the Prophet (ṢAAS) and I witnessed Badr with him. When the forces met and God defeated the enemy, one group went off after them, putting them to flight and killing them, another group sought and gathered up the booty, while a third group kept watch over the Messenger of God (ṢAAS), so that the enemy would not do him harm. When night came and the forces gathered back together, those who had assembled the booty said, "We gathered it and no one else has any right to it." Those who had pursued the enemy said, "You have no greater right to it than us; we drove the enemy away from the booty and we defeated them." Those who had guarded the Messenger of God (ṢAAS) said, "We feared some harm might come to him from the enemy, and so we devoted ourselves to him." And so it was that God sent down, "They ask you about the spoils. Say, 'The spoils belong to God and to His Messenger. So fear God, reconcile and obey God and His Messenger, if you are indeed believers'"' (*sūrat al-Anfāl*; VIII, v.1).

"And so the Messenger of God (ṢAAS) divided the booty among the Muslims. Whenever he raided enemy territory he would divide the spoils into fourths. But if he pursued a retreating (army) he would divide it into thirds. He had a dislike for booty."

Al-Tirmidhī and Ibn Māja related the latter part of this, from a *ḥadīth* of al-Thawrī, from ʿAbd al-Raḥmān b. al-Ḥārith. Al-Tirmidhī stated, "This is a *ḥadīth ḥasan*,[67] a 'good *ḥadīth*'." Ibn Ḥibbān related it in his *ṣaḥīḥ* collection, as did al-Ḥākim in his *al-Mustadrak* (*The Compendium*) from a *ḥadīth* of ʿAbd al-Raḥmān. Al-Ḥākim stated, "This is authentic according to the criteria of Muslim, but he did not narrate this tradition."

Abū Dāʾūd, al-Nasāʾī, Ibn Ḥibbān and al-Ḥākim related, on various lines from Dāʾūd b. Abū Hind, from ʿIkrima, from Ibn ʿAbbās, the following: "At the battle of Badr, the Messenger of God (ṢAAS) stated, 'Those who have done so-and-so shall receive such-and-such.' The younger men made haste to carry this out, while the older men stayed near the banners. When the booty had been collected the men gathered to claim their share. The older men asked that they not be given less credit than the rest, saying they had acted as a safeguard against the sudden attack by any enemy force. There was much dispute and so God Almighty revealed, 'They ask you about the spoils. Say, "The spoils belong to God and to His Messenger. So fear God, reconcile and obey God and His Messenger, if you are indeed believers"'" (*sūrat al-Anfāl*; VIII, v.1).

We have made extensive comments elsewhere, too lengthy to explore here, on the reason for the revelation of this verse.

The meaning of the words is that decisions over the spoils devolve upon God and His Messenger to judge in accord with the best interests of the worshippers regarding this life and the after-life. The Almighty therefore stated, "The spoils belong to God and to His Messenger. So fear God, reconcile and obey God and His Messenger, if you are indeed believers."

He then went on to recount the events and outcome of the battle of Badr, concluding, "And know that whatever thing you have taken as spoils of war, then one-fifth of it is for God and for His Messenger and for the kinfolk, orphans, the poor and wayfarers" (*sūrat al-Anfāl*; VIII, v.41). It is evident that this verse explains God's commands regarding the spoils of war which He has made subject to Himself and to His Prophet (ṢAAS). The Almighty has clarified and determined this in accord with His wish. This is the view of Abū Zayd.

Abū ʿUbayd al-Qāsim b. Salām, God bless him, claimed that the Messenger of God (ṢAAS) divided up the booty taken at Badr equally between the men and that he did not divide it into fifths. The edict relating to the division into fifths was revealed after this, cancelling the previous practice.

Al-Wālibī related this similarly, from Ibn ʿAbbās, and Mujāhid, ʿIkrima and al-Suddī attested to it. However, there is controversy over this. And God knows best. The controversy relates to whether the above verses came prior to or following the verse referring to the division into fifths, since all relate to the battle of Badr. It seems necessary to consider them to have been revealed all together

____

67. Al-Tirmidhī used this term to define a *ḥadīth* whose narrators were known to have defective memories.

at one time and not separately, with some having come later, as would be necessary if some had cancelled others.

Then there is the *hadīth* in both *sahīh* collections relating to 'Alī, God be pleased with him. This tells how, regarding Hamza's having cut off the two humps of his two old mare camels, and of his stating that one of these was part of the fifth part set aside at Badr. His statement directly contradicts Abū 'Ubayd's contention that the spoils at Badr were not divided into five parts. God knows best; but they were divided into five according to the accounts of al-Bukhārī, Ibn Jarīr and others; this is the correct and preferable view. But God knows best.

DIVISION

The return of the Messenger of God (ṢAAS) from Badr to Medina and the events on that journey by which his Lord gave him help and assistance.

It has previously been stated that the engagement took place on Friday, the 17th of Ramadān, 2 AH.

It is established in both *sahīh* collections that following an engagement against an enemy, the Messenger of God (ṢAAS) would thereafter spend three days in an open area. His normal period of three days so spent at Badr, however, ended, as related above, after two days when he mounted his camel and stood above the pit at Badr, berating those dead polytheists who had been dragged there.

Thereafter he departed, taking with him the prisoners and the great quantity of booty. He had sent on ahead two heralds to Medina to announce the victory over those who had associated others with God and denied and disbelieved in Him. One of these heralds was 'Abd Allāh b. Rawāha, whom he sent to the upper parts of Medina. The other, Zayd b. Hāritha, he sent to the city's lower parts.

Usāma b. Zayd stated, "The news reached us when we had finished levelling the earth over Ruqayya, daughter of the Messenger of God (ṢAAS). Her husband, 'Uthmān b. 'Affān, God bless him, had remained behind to nurse her at the orders of the Messenger of God (ṢAAS) who had assigned to him a share in the spoils of Badr."

Usāma stated further, "When my father, Zayd b. Hāritha, arrived, I went to him and found him standing at the prayer shrine, swamped by people. He was saying, ''Utba b. Rabī'a has been killed, as also had been Abū Jahl b. Hishām, Zam'a b. al-Aswad, Abū al-Bakhtarī al-'Ās b. Hishām, Umayya b. Khalaf and Nubayh and Munabbih, the two sons of al-Hajjāj.' I asked him 'Father, is this true?' He replied, 'Son, I swear it is so.'"

Al-Bayhaqī stated, citing a line of authorities through Hammād b. Salama, from Hishām b. 'Urwa, from his father, from Usāma b. Zayd, that the Prophet (ṢAAS) had left 'Uthmān and Usāma b. Zayd to look after his daughter. Then Zayd b. Hāritha arrived, mounted on *al-'Adbā'*, the camel of the Messenger of God (ṢAAS), with the good news. Usāma said, "I heard the tumult and so went outside. There I found Zayd who had brought the good news. But, I swear, I didn't really believe it until I saw the prisoners. The Messenger of God (ṢAAS) had assigned to ʿUthmān a share in the spoils."

Al-Wāqidī stated, "The Messenger of God (ṢAAS) following his return from Badr, performed the evening prayer at al-Athīl.[68] When he had finished one *rakʿa* he smiled. Someone later asked why he was smiling and he replied that he could see Michael with dust on his wing, who had smiled at him and said, 'I was looking for the rest.' And Gabriel had come to him when he had finished fighting the enemy at Badr, riding a mare, its forelock knotted and the furrows of its head covered with dust. He had said, 'O Muḥammad, my Lord has sent me to you and told me not to leave you until you are content. Are you content?' 'I am,' he had replied."

Al-Wāqidī stated, "They related that the Messenger of God (ṢAAS) sent Zayd b. Ḥarītha and ʿAbd Allāh b. Rawāḥa ahead from al-Athīl and they arrived on Sunday in the heat of late morning. ʿAbd Allāh b. Rawāḥa parted from Zayd b. Ḥarītha at al-ʿAqīq and began calling out, still on his mount, 'O Helpers, rejoice at the safety of the Messenger of God (ṢAAS), and at the killing and capture of the polytheists! The two sons of Rabīʿa have been killed, along with the two sons of al-Ḥajjāj, Abū Jahl, Zumʿa b. al-Aswad and Umayya b. Khalaf, while Suhayl b. ʿAmr has been taken prisoner!'

"ʿĀṣim b. ʿAdī stated, 'I went up to him and accompanied him, saying, "Is that the truth, Ibn Rawāḥa?" He replied, "It certainly is! And tomorrow the Messenger of God (ṢAAS) will arrive with the prisoners in chains." He then went to the homes of the Helpers, one after the other, in the upper part of the town, telling them the good news. The children chanted along with him, "The evil Abū Jahl is dead!" He continued on until he reached the home of the Banū Umayya, when Zayd b. Ḥarītha arrived on the camel called *al-Qaswāʾ* belonging to the Messenger of God (ṢAAS) announcing the good news. When he reached the prayer shrine he shouted, still mounted, 'ʿUtba and Shayba, the two sons of Rabīʿa have been killed! And the two sons of al-Ḥajjāj! Umayya b. Khalaf is dead, as are Abū Jahl, Abū al-Bakhtarī, and Zamʿa b. al-Aswad. Suhayl b. ʿAmr Dhū al-Anyāb has been taken captive, along with many others!'

"Some people refused to believe Zayd and began saying, 'Zayd b. Ḥarītha has only come because he's been defeated!' This confused and scared the Muslims.

"Zayd arrived when we had finished levelling the earth over Ruqayya, the daughter of the Messenger of God (ṢAAS), at al-Baqīʿ, and one of the hypocrites commented to Usāma, 'Your master has been killed, and all those with him!' Another said to Abū Lubāba, 'Your friends have scattered, and they'll never unite around him again. His Companions have died for him, and Muḥammad has been killed. This we know to be his own camel. And Zayd is so confused he doesn't know what he is saying. He's come in defeat.' Abū Lubāba said, 'God will refute what you are saying.' The Jews commented, 'Zayd has only come in defeat.'

68. A place near Medina, between Badr and Wādī al-Ṣafrāʾ.

"Usāma said, 'So I went off alone with my father and asked, "Is it really true, what you are saying?" He replied, "Yes indeed, son; I swear by God what I say is true."

"'This encouraged me and I returned to that hypocrite telling him, "You are spreading lies about the Messenger of God (ṢAAS) and about the Muslims! We're going to have you up before the Messenger of God, and he'll execute you!" He replied. "It's only what I hear people saying."'

"He went on, 'The prisoners were brought in, in the custody of Shaqrān, the freed-man of the Messenger of God (ṢAAS). He had participated at Badr with the rest. They were 49 men in number.'"

Al-Wāqidī stated, "According to the sources, they totalled 70; and there is no doubt about this."

He went on, "The Messenger of God (ṢAAS) met with the city leaders who congratulated him on the victory God had given him. Usayd b. al-Ḥuḍayr told him, 'O Messenger of God, praise be to God who has given you victory and made you content. By God, O Messenger of God, nothing would have kept me from joining you at Badr if I had thought you would be meeting an enemy in battle; but I thought you were going after a caravan. If I had known it was an enemy, I'd not have stayed behind.'

"The Messenger of God (ṢAAS) replied, 'You speak the truth!'"

Ibn Isḥāq stated, "Then the Messenger of God (ṢAAS) began his journey back to Medina, taking the prisoners with him. Amongst them were ʿUqba b. Abū Muʿayṭ and al-Naḍr b. al-Ḥārith. In charge of the booty he had appointed ʿAbd Allāh b. Kaʿb b. ʿAmr b. ʿAwf b. Mabdhūl b. ʿAmr b. Ghanm b. Māzin b. al-Najjār.

"One of the Muslims who composed doggerel verse, who according to Ibn Hishām was said to be ʿAdī b. Abū al-Zaghbāʾ, spoke the lines,

'Water your camels, Basbas, for there's no place for
them to halt at Dhū al-Ṭalḥ.
Nor in the deserts of ʿUmayr is there any corral;
though the people's mounts can't be kept penned in.
It's smarter to get them on the road; God has given
victory, and al-Akhnas has fled.'"

Ibn Isḥāq continued, "The Messenger of God (ṢAAS) then went forward and, having come through the pass at al-Ṣafrāʾ, he halted at a hill between the pass and al-Nāziyya called Sayar, near a willow tree. There he divided up equally the spoils that God had bestowed upon the Muslims from the polytheists. Then he moved on to al-Rawḥāʾ, where he was met by Muslims congratulating him on the victory that God had given him and his Muslim force. Salama b. Salama b. Waqsh – as I have been told by ʿĀṣim b. ʿUmar and Yazīd b. Rūmān – asked them, 'What are you congratulating us about? All we faced were bald old women, like camels bound for sacrifice, and we slaughtered them!'

"The Messenger of God (ṢAAS) smiled at this and said, 'Hey, cousin, those were the *al-malaʾ*, chiefs!'"

Ibn Hishām observed, "He was referring to the nobles and the leaders."

THE DEATHS OF AL-NAḌR B. AL-ḤĀRITH AND ʿUQBA B. ABŪ MUʿAYṬ, GOD DAMN THEM!

Ibn Isḥāq stated, "While the Messenger of God (ṢAAS) was at al-Ṣafrāʾ, al-Naḍr b. al-Ḥārith was killed by ʿAlī b. Abū Ṭālib, or so I was told by a scholar from Mecca. After they had moved on to ʿIrq al-Zabiyya, ʿUqba b. Abū Muʿayṭ was executed.

"When the Messenger of God (ṢAAS) ordered his death, ʿUqba asked him, 'Who will look after my children, Muḥammad?' 'The fire!' he responded. The man who killed him was ʿĀṣim b. Thābit b. Abū al-Aqlaḥ, a brother of the Banū ʿAmr b. ʿAwf, as I was told by Abū ʿUbayda b. Muḥammad b. ʿAmmār b. Yāsir."

Mūsā b. ʿUqba also stated this in his work on the military expeditions. He claimed that the Messenger of God (ṢAAS) killed no other person taken captive.

He stated, "And when ʿĀṣim b. Thābit came up (to kill him) ʿUqba asked, 'O tribe ȯf Quraysh, why am I to be killed out of all those here?'

"He replied, 'For your enmity towards God and His Messenger.'

"Ḥammād b. Salama stated, from ʿAṭā b. al-Sāʾib, from al-Shaʿbī, who said, 'When the Prophet (ṢAAS) ordered the execution of ʿUqba, he asked, "Will you kill only me from among Quraysh?"

"'The Messenger of God (ṢAAS) replied, "Yes. Do you know how this man treated me? He came up while I was prostrate in prayer behind the *maqām*,[69] placed his foot on my neck and pressed down on it. I thought my eyes were going to come out, before he lifted up his foot. On another occasion he brought a sheep's entrails which he threw over my head while I was prostrate in prayer. Fāṭima came and washed it off my head."'"

Ibn Hishām stated, "It is also said that it was ʿAlī b. Abū Ṭālib who killed ʿUqba, according to al-Zuhrī and other scholars."

I would comment that these two men were among the most evil of God's servants, the most stubborn, wicked, envious and disbelieving of men and they had been very active in satirizing Islam and its supporters. God damn them! And He did, indeed!

Ibn Hishām stated, "Qutayla, daughter of al-Ḥārith, sister of al-Naḍr b. al-Ḥārith, spoke the following verses about the death of her brother,

> 'O rider, al-Athīl is a landmark since the morning of
> the fifth night, and you are fortunate.
> Inform there a dead man of a greeting that the finest
> of all are still waving,
> From me to you, and of tears that are shed in

---

69. The "shrine of Abraham", near the *kaʿba*.

profusion, flooding out, while others are repressed.
     Will al-Naḍr hear if I call to him; or can a dead man
hear who cannot speak?
     Muḥammad, you, the finest son of a woman noble among
her people, and her husband a fine stallion,
     It would not have harmed you to forgive him, for a
valorous man often forgives, despite his anger or rage.
     Or you could have accepted ransom, and the largest sum
ever paid would have been provided,
     And al-Naḍr was the closest in ties to you of all your
captives, and the worthiest, if any were to be freed.
     The swords of his father's sons would then have charged
for God, with wombs being split asunder on His behalf,
     Stoically he was led to death, worn out and bound, but
servile.'"

Ibn Hishām stated, "And it is said, though God alone knows best, that the
Messenger of God (ṢAAS) said, when those verses were recited to him, 'If only
this had reached me before his death, I would have spared him!'"

Ibn Isḥāq stated, "At that place the Messenger of God (ṢAAS) was met by Abū
Hind, the freed-man of Farwa b. ʿAmr al-Bayāḍī, his cupper. He had with him
a wine-skin filled with *hays*, that being dates in a butter sauce, a gift for the
Messenger of God (ṢAAS). He accepted it and recommended Abū Hind to the
Helpers.
     "The Messenger of God (ṢAAS) then went on into Medina, arriving there
one day before the prisoners."

Ibn Isḥāq stated, "Nabīh b. Wahb, brother of the Banū ʿAbd al-Dār, related to
me that the Messenger of God (ṢAAS) divided up the prisoners among his
Companions following their arrival and said, 'Behave well towards them.'
     "Abū ʿAzīz b. ʿUmayr b. Hāshim, a brother of Muṣʿab b. ʿUmayr by the same
father and mother, was among the captives. Abū ʿAzīz stated, 'My brother Muṣʿab
b. ʿUmayr passed me by while one of the Helpers was tying me up. Muṣʿab said,
"Bind his hands fast. His mother is wealthy, and she'll ransom him from you."'
     "Abū ʿAzīz went on, 'I was with a group of Helpers bringing me from Badr.
When they had their midday and evening meals, they gave me the bread and ate
the dates themselves, in accordance with the instruction given them by the
Messenger of God (ṢAAS) regarding us. Every piece of bread that came into
their hands they passed on to me. I was embarrassed and would return the bread,
but they would pass it back untouched.'"
     Ibn Hishām stated, "This Abū ʿAzīz was the standard-bearer of the poly-
theists at Badr, following al-Naḍr b. Ḥārith.
     "And after his brother had made his comment to Abū al-Yusr, the man who
had me captive, Abū ʿAzīz commented, 'Brother, is this how you treat them?'
Muṣʿab replied, 'He's more my brother than you are!'

"His mother asked what was the highest price paid to ransom a Quraysh man. She was told, 'Four thousand dirhams.' She therefore ransomed him with four thousand dirhams she sent."

I comment that the given name of this Abū ʿAzīz was Zurāra, according to what Ibn al-Athīr stated in his work *Ghābat al-Ṣaḥāba* (*Compendium of Companions*). Khalīfa b. Khayāṭ included him in his list of names of the Companions. He was Muṣʿab b. ʿUmayr's brother on his father's side. They had another paternal brother who was Abū al-Rūm b. ʿUmayr. Those who would have him as killed at Badr as an unbeliever are in error. That person was really Abū ʿAzza, as will be told hereafter. But God knows best.

Ibn Isḥāq stated, "ʿAbd Allāh b. Abū Bakr related to me, that Yaḥyā b. ʿAbd Allāh b. ʿAbd al-Raḥmān b. Saʿd b. Zurāra said, 'When the prisoners were brought in, Sawda, daughter of Zamʿa, wife of the Prophet (ṢAAS) was with the family of ʿAfrāʾ, who were engaged in mourning for ʿAfrāʾ's two sons, ʿAwf and Muʿawwidh. This was before the veil was made required for the wives of (the Prophet). Sawda said, "I swear by God, there I was when someone came in and said, 'They've brought in the prisoners!' So I went off to my house, where the Messenger of God was, and there I found Abū Yazīd Suhayl b. ʿAmr in a corner of the room with his hands tied with a rope behind his neck. I couldn't restrain myself from saying, at the sight of Abū Yazīd, 'O Abū Yazīd! You gave yourself up then! Couldn't you have died a noble death!'

"'"I swear, I was then quite startled to hear the Messenger of God (ṢAAS) call out from inside the house, 'Sawda, are you stirring up trouble for God and for His messenger!' I replied, 'O Messenger of God, by Him who sent you with the truth, I couldn't restrain myself from saying as I did when I saw Abū Yazīd with his hands tied up at his neck!'"'"

Information will follow hereafter in detail recounting the arrival of the prisoners in Medina, and how and at what cost they were ransomed. If God wills it so, that is.

An Account of the joy of the Negus, God bless him, at the outcome of the battle of Badr.

The *ḥāfiẓ* al-Bayhaqī stated, "Abū al-Qāsim ʿAbd al-Raḥmān b. ʿUbayd Allāh al-Ḥurfī of Baghdad informed us, quoting Aḥmad b. Salmān al-Najjād, quoting ʿAbd Allāh b. Abū al-Dunyā, quoting Ḥamza b. al-ʿAbbās quoting, ʿAbdān b. ʿUthmān, quoting ʿAbd Allāh b. al-Mubārak, quoting ʿAbd al-Raḥmān b. Yazīd, quoting Jābir, from ʿAbd al-Raḥmān, a man from Ṣanʿā, who said, 'One day the Negus sent for Jaʿfar b. Abū Ṭālib and his Companions and when they went in to him they found him in his house sitting on the ground dressed in rags. Jaʿfar said, "We felt very sorry for him when we saw him, in this state, and when he observed this in our faces, he explained, 'I have good news for you that will make you rejoice. A spy has come to me from your land and has told me that God has given victory to his Prophet, defeated his enemy, taken captive so-and-so and so-and-so, and killed so-and-so and so-and-so. The forces met in a valley called Badr where many thorny trees grow. It's as if I can see it now, for I used to look after camels there for my master, a man of the Banū Damra.'"

"'Ja‘far then asked the Negus, "Why are you sitting on the ground, without even a carpet, dressed in those old clothes?" He replied, "We agree with what God sent down to Jesus – that it is the duty of God's worshippers to behave in humility when God performs some favour for them. Since God has favoured me with the victory of his Prophet (ṢAAS), I am acting in humility in this way for him."'"

Chapter: On the arrival of the news of those stricken at Badr to their families in Mecca.

Ibn Isḥāq stated, "The first to arrive in Mecca with news of the Quraysh casualties at Badr was al-Ḥaysumān b. ‘Abd Allāh al-Khuzā‘ī. When he was asked for news, he reported the deaths of ‘Utba b. Rabī‘a, Shayba b. Rabī‘a, Abū al-Ḥakam b. Hishām, Umayya b. Khalaf, Zam‘a b. al-Aswad, Nubayh and Munabbah, and Abū al-Bakhtarī b. Hishām.

"As he ennumerated the Quraysh nobles, Ṣafwān b. Umayya commented, 'That makes no sense; ask him about me!' So they asked him what had happened to Ṣafwān b. Umayya, and he responded, 'He's over there, sitting in the *ḥijr*; I saw the deaths of his father and his brother when they were killed.'"

Mūsā b. ‘Uqba stated, "When the news reached Mecca and was verified, the women cut off their hair; and many horses and riding camels were slaughtered."

Al-Suhaylī recounted, from the book *Dalā’il* (*The Signs*) of Qāsim b. Thābit, whose author said that at the time of the battle of Badr the people of Mecca heard a spirit calling out,

> "The *ḥanīfs* brought a battle to bear at Badr because of
> which the power of Chosroe and Caesar will collapse,
> It sent men of Lu’ayy to their death, and brought forth
> unmarried women to strike the ground in despair.
> Woe to him who becomes Muḥammad's enemy, deliberately
> straying from the right path and getting lost!"

Ibn Isḥāq stated, "Ḥusayn b. ‘Abd Allāh b. ‘Ubayd Allāh b. ‘Abbās related to me, from ‘Ikrima, the freed-man of Ibn ‘Abbās, who said, 'Abū Rāfi‘, the freed-man of the Messenger of God (ṢAAS) said, "I was a slave of al-‘Abbās b. ‘Abd al-Muṭṭalib at the time when Islam had entered us, the people of the house. Al-‘Abbās accepted Islam, as did Umm al-Faḍl and myself as well. Al-‘Abbās was concerned about his people and disliked opposing them and so he concealed his acceptance of Islam. He was a man of great wealth that was scattered amongst his people. Abū Lahab had stayed behind from Badr and had sent al-‘Āṣ b. Hishām

b. al-Mughīra in his place. This was the practice; any man who could not go to battle sent another in his place.

"""When he received news of those of Quraysh who were struck down at Badr, God humiliated and disgraced Abū Lahab, while we experienced a sense of power and pride. I was a weak man and I used to make arrows, sharpening them in the pavilion near *zamzam*, the sacred well. I was seated there active in this, with Umm al-Faḍl sitting there with me, happy at the news we had received, when in came Abū Lahab, dragging his feet in annoyance. He sat down at one side of the pavilion, his back facing mine. As he sat there people announced, 'Here's Abū Sufyān, al-Mughīra b. al-Ḥārith b. ʿAbd al-Muṭṭalib, who has arrived.' Abū Lahab called out, 'Come on in to me; you must have some news.'

"""Abū Sufyān came and sat down, people standing all around. Abū Lahab then spoke, 'Cousin, tell me what happened to everyone.'

""""Well,' he reported, 'I swear that no sooner had we joined battle with them, than we turned our back to them and they killed and captured us just as they liked. But, I swear, I don't blame them; we faced men dressed in white mounted on piebald horses between heaven and earth. I swear, they spared nothing, and nothing could withstand them.'""

"Abū Rāfiʿ went on, 'I then raised the tent rope with my hand and commented, "By God, those were the angels!"

"'At that Abū Lahab raised his fist and hit me a very hard blow in the face. I charged at him, but he fought back and knocked me to the ground. He then knelt down on me, beating me. I was a weak man. Then Umm al-Faḍl took hold of one of the tent supports and began hitting him with it, making a nasty wound in his head and shouting, "So you think he's powerless now that his master is away!'

"'He got up and left, humiliated. And by God, he only lived seven more days before God afflicted him with the pustules that killed him.'"

Yūnus, quoting Ibn Isḥāq, added, "His two sons left him unburied for three days after his death and he began to decompose. Quraysh greatly feared those pustules, just as they did the plague. Eventually one of the Quraysh said to his sons, 'Aren't you ashamed that your father is decomposing in his house, without you burying him?' They replied, 'We're scared of those terrible pustules.' The man insisted, 'If you do it, I'll help you.' And they did not wash him and merely threw water over him from a distance, not going close to him at all. They then carried him to the heights of Mecca, placed him against a wall and covered him over with stones."

Yūnus said, quoting Ibn Isḥāq, "Yaḥyā b. ʿAbbād b. ʿAbd Allāh b. al-Zubayr related to me, from his father, from ʿĀʾisha, mother of the believers, who said she always veiled herself with her gown until she had passed beyond the place where Abū Lahab was buried."

Ibn Isḥāq stated, "Yaḥyā b. ʿAbbād related to me as follows, 'Quraysh mourned their dead. Then they told one another not to do this because when Muhammad and his supporters heard of it they would revile them. They also agreed not to seek reassurance by making enquiry about the captives to discourage the Messenger of God (ṢAAS) from making heavy demands for their ransom.'"

I observe that God's forcing them to forego mourning for their dead was part of the totality of His punishment of those of them that remained alive at that time. For weeping for the dead contributes to the recovery of the grieving heart.

Ibn Isḥāq stated, "Al-Aswad b. al-Muṭṭalib was afflicted with the loss of three of his sons, Zamʿa, ʿAqīl and al-Ḥārith, and he wished to mourn properly for them. He heard a woman in the night bewailing her loss and, because he was himself blind, he asked his son, 'Go and see if mourning has become permissible. Are Quraysh now bewailing their dead? Perhaps I will now be able to lament the loss of Abū Ḥakīma' – he was referring to his son Zamʿa – 'for I am in great pain.'

"When the boy returned, he reported that it was merely a woman lamenting the loss of a camel that had gone astray. It was then that al-Aswad spoke the verses,

> 'Is she weeping because a donkey of hers has gone
> astray and so insomnia keeps her from sleeping?
> Do not weep over a young camel, but over Badr that
> ruined all hopes,
> Over Badr and the elite of the Banū Ḥuṣayṣ and Makhzūm
> and the tribe of Abū al-Walīd.
> And weep, if you weep at all, for Abū ʿAqīl and for
> Ḥārith, the lion of lions.
> Weep for them all, and do not hold back, for there is
> none the like of Abū Ḥakīma.
> After them it is other men who rule, and had it not
> been for Badr, they would not have come to lead.'"

DIVISION

The payment of ransom money by Quraysh to the Messenger of God (ṢAAS) for their men who were captive.

Ibn Isḥāq stated, "Abū Wadāʿa b. Ḍubayra al-Sahmī was among the prisoners. The Messenger of God (ṢAAS) commented, 'He has a son in Mecca who is a wealthy, shrewd merchant; no doubt he will come and seek to ransom his father.' When Quraysh advised that there would be no hurry in ransoming the prisoners so that Muḥammad and his Companions would not seek larger sums, al-Muṭṭalib b. Abū Wadāʿa, the man to whom the Messenger of God (ṢAAS) had referred, agreed and also advised against haste. But he left secretly at night and went to Medina, where he ransomed and removed his father, having paid 4,000 dirhams."

I comment that this was the first prisoner ransomed. Then Quraysh sent to ransom their prisoners and Mikraz b. Ḥafṣ b. al-Akhyaf went to ransom Suhayl b. ʿAmr, who had been taken captive by Mālik b. al-Dukhshum, brother of the Banū Sālim b. ʿAwf. Mālik spoke the following verses on this,

"I captured Suhayl and I would not want for him any
prisoner from any other nation.

Khindif knows that, if injustice be done, Suhayl is the
man to charge.

I struck with a sharp sword until it bent, forcing
myself on against that hare-lipped man."

Ibn Isḥāq stated, "Suhayl was a man who had a split lower lip."

He went on, "Muḥammad b. ʿAmr b. ʿAṭāʾ, a brother of the Banū ʿAmr b.
Luʾayy related to me, that ʿUmar b. al-Khaṭṭāb said to the Messenger of God
(ṢAAS), 'Let me extract the two front teeth of Suhayl b. ʿAmr; his tongue will
protrude and he will never speak ill of you again. The Messenger of God
(ṢAAS), said, 'I will not mutilate him, for if I did, God would mutilate me, even
though I am a prophet.'"

I observe that this *ḥadīth* is incomplete in its line of authorities; indeed, it may
be defined as *muʿdal*, "problematic".

Ibn Isḥāq stated, "I have been informed that the Messenger of God (ṢAAS)
said to ʿUmar about this, 'Maybe he will take a stand for which you will not
criticize him.'"

I observe that this refers to the stand adopted in Mecca by Suhayl when, following the death of the Messenger of God (ṢAAS) some of the Arabs rebelled.
Hypocrisy arose in Medina and elsewhere, and Suhayl stood up and gave a public address in Mecca in which he urged the people to remain firm in the true
ḥanīf religion. This will be related in its proper place.

Ibn Isḥāq stated, "When Mikraz negotiated with them about Suhayl and ultimately satisfied them, they said, 'Give us what is ours.' He replied, 'Take me
hostage in his place and let him go until he sends you his ransom money.' They
released Suhayl and kept Mikraz with them."

Ibn Isḥāq quoted some poetry of Mikraz that Ibn Hishām suggested might not
be authentic. But God knows best.

Ibn Isḥāq stated, "ʿAbd Allāh b. Abū Bakr related to me, saying, "ʿAmr b. Abū
Sufyān Ṣakhr b. Ḥarb was among the prisoners.'"

Ibn Isḥāq stated, "His mother was the daughter of ʿUqba b. Abū Muʿīṭ."

Ibn Hishām, however, said that his mother was ʿUqba's sister; and he added
that it was ʿAlī b. Abū Ṭālib who had captured him.

Ibn Isḥāq stated, "ʿAbd Allāh b. Abū Bakr related to me, as follows, 'Abū
Sufyān was advised to ransom his son, ʿAmr. He replied, "Shall blood and
money combine against me? They killed Ḥanẓala, and shall I now ransom ʿAmr?
Let him remain with them; they can keep him as long as they want!"'

"While he was thus imprisoned in Medina, Saʿd b. al-Nuʿmān b. Akkāl, a
brother of the Banū ʿAmr b. ʿAwf and also related to the Banū Muʿāwiya, went
forth on pilgrimage, accompanied by his young wife. He was elderly and a
Muslim and had sheep at al-Baqīʿ. He left for there on pilgrimage with no idea
he would be imprisoned at Mecca, since he was a pilgrim; Quraysh only ever

treated well those who came as pilgrims. But Abū Sufyān b. Ḥarb attacked him in Mecca, imprisoning him in retaliation for this son 'Amr. Abū Sufyān spoke the following verses on this,

> 'O tribe of Ibn Akkāl, answer his request; you had a
> pact together, so do not surrender the chief in his
> maturity.
> The Banū 'Amr is lowly, contemptible, if they do not
> release their prisoner's fetters.'"

Ḥassān b. Thābit spoke the following verses in response,

> "If Sa'd had been free to act that day in Mecca, he would
> have killed many of you before he was captured.
> Using a sharp sword or a bow of *nab'a* wood, its string
> twanging when its arrows shoot."

He went on, "The Banū 'Amr b. 'Awf went to the Messenger of God (ṢAAS) and told him what had happened and asked him to give them 'Amr b. Abū Sufyān so they could release him and receive their own man in exchange. The Prophet (ṢAAS) agreed and they sent 'Amr to Abū Sufyān, who released Sa'd."

Ibn Isḥāq went on, "Abū al-'Āṣ b. al-Rabī' b.'Abd al-'Uzzā b. 'Abd Shams b. Umayya was among the captives, the son-in-law of the Messenger of God (ṢAAS), husband of his daughter Zaynab."

Ibn Hishām added, "It was Khirāsh b. al-Ṣimma, of the Banū Ḥarām, who had captured him."

Ibn Isḥāq continued, "Abū al-'Āṣ was a respected Meccan credited with much wealth and goods. His mother was Hāla, daughter of Khuwaylid, sister of Khadīja, daughter of Khuwaylid. It was Khadīja who had asked the Messenger of God (ṢAAS) to marry her daughter Zaynab to him, and he never disagreed with her; this occurred before the beginnings of revelation.

"The Messenger of God (ṢAAS) had married his daughter Ruqayya, or Umm Kulthūm, to 'Utba b. Abū Lahab. And when revelation began, Abū Lahab said, 'Let Muḥammad look after his own!' He ordered his son 'Utba to divorce Ruqayya with the promise to give him any woman he wanted. He did so before having consummated the marriage. She was then married by 'Uthmān b. 'Affān, God bless him. They approached Abū al-'Āṣ and said, 'Leave your wife and we will marry you to any Quraysh woman you desire.' He replied, 'No, by God! I will not leave her, and I do not want any other woman from Quraysh for my wife.' The Messenger of God (ṢAAS), so I have been told, used to commend his son-in-law for this."

I comment that the evidence of his praise for his son-in-law is well established in the *ṣaḥīḥ* collection, as will be shown.

Ibn Isḥāq stated, "The Messenger of God (ṢAAS) had no authority in Mecca to allow or to forbid, since he was powerless. Islam had divided Zaynab, daughter of the Messenger of God (ṢAAS), from Abū al-ʿĀṣ, but he was not able to bring about their separation."

I comment that it was only in the year of the truce of al-Ḥudaybiyya, in the year 6 AH that God made it unlawful for Muslim women to marry polytheists, as will be shown hereafter, if God wills it.

Ibn Isḥāq stated that Yaḥyā b. ʿAbbād b. ʿAbd Allāh b. al-Zubayr related to him, from his father who quoted ʿĀʾisha as having said, "When the Meccans sent ransom money for their men who were prisoners, Zaynab, daughter of the Messenger of God (ṢAAS), sent money on behalf of Abū al-ʿĀṣ. She sent the necklace for him that Khadīja had given her upon her marriage to Abū al-ʿĀṣ. She said, 'When the Messenger of God (ṢAAS) saw it, he was greatly touched for her and said, "If you should think fit to deliver her prisoner to her and to return to her what is hers, then do so." They replied, "Yes, Messenger of God." And they did release him and returned her property to her.'"

Ibn Isḥāq stated, "Those named to us as having been freed by the Messenger of God (ṢAAS) without ransom having been paid for them include: of the Banū Umayya, Abū al-ʿĀṣ b. al-Rabīʿ, and of the Banū Makhzūm, al-Muṭṭalib b. Ḥanṭab b. al-Ḥārith b. ʿUbayd b. ʿUmar b. Makhzūm. He was taken prisoner by one of the Banū al-Ḥārith b. al-Khazraj. He had been left in their custody until he was released, whereupon he rejoined his own people."

Ibn Isḥāq went on, "The Messenger of God (ṢAAS) had required of him (Abū al-ʿĀṣ) that he allow free movement to Zaynab, which meant that she could emigrate to Medina. And Abū al-ʿĀṣ did keep to his agreement, as will be told."

It is at this point that Ibn Isḥāq related this; however, we have deferred telling of it, since that is more appropriate. But God knows best.

We have previously related how al-ʿAbbās b. ʿAbd al-Muṭṭalib, uncle of the Prophet (ṢAAS), ransomed himself and ʿUqayl and Nawfal, sons of his two brothers, for 100 *awqīya* of gold.

Ibn Hisham stated, "It was Abū Ayyūb Khālid b. Zayd who captured Abū al-ʿĀṣ."

Ibn Isḥāq stated, "Ṣayfī b. Abū Rifāʿa b. ʿĀʾidh b. ʿAbd Allāh b. ʿUmar b. Makhzūm was left in the custody of his captives. They agreed with him that he would send them his ransom and so let him free; but he did not keep his word. On that subject Ḥassān b. Thābit spoke the lines,

> 'Sayfī's word was not one to be trusted, like the trail
> of some fox that rested at a watering hole.'"

Ibn Isḥāq continued, "Abū ʿAzza ʿAmr b. ʿAbd Allāh b. ʿUthmān b. Uhayb b. Ḥudhāfa b. Jumaḥ was a poor man with daughters to support. He said, 'O Messenger of God, you know my state of finances. I am poor and have a family, so be gracious to me.' The Messenger of God agreed to be gracious to him on condition that he did not support anyone else against him. Abū ʿAzza spoke the following lines in praise of the Messenger of God (ṢAAS) for this action,

'Who is it will tell the Messenger, Muḥammad, from
me, "You are truth; and the All-Powerful is to be praised.
    You are a man who calls to the truth and to right
guidance, with witness for you from God the Almighty.
    You are a man given a position of power among us,
there being steps both easy and high up to where you are.
    You are someone whose opponents are unhappy being
fought, while those with whom you make peace are content.
    But when I think of Badr and those who fought it, I am
overcome again by sorrow and depression.'"

I comment that thereafter this Abū ʿAzza broke the pact he had made with the
Messenger of God (ṢAAS), and he fell under the influence of the polytheists and
rejoined them. At the battle of Uḥud he was again taken captive, and he again
asked the Messenger of God (ṢAAS) to set him free. But the latter replied, "I'll
not let you stroke your beard and say that you deceived Muḥammad twice!" And
so his head was cut off at Uḥud, as will be related in the account of that engagement.

It is said that it was of him that the Messenger of God (ṢAAS) spoke as follows, "A believer will not be bitten twice from the same lair." This is one of those
proverbs uttered only by the Messenger of God (ṢAAS).

Ibn Isḥāq stated, "Muḥammad b. Jaʿfar b. al-Zubayr related to me, from ʿUrwa
b. al-Zubayr, as follows, "ʿUmayr b. Wahb al-Jumaḥī was sitting with Ṣafwān b.
Umayya in the *hijr* shortly after the losses that were suffered at Badr. He,
ʿUmayr, was one of the devilish Quraysh provocateurs, a man who had grievously
harmed the Messenger of God (ṢAAS) and his Companions at Mecca. His son
Wahb b. ʿUmayr was one of those taken captive at Badr.'"

Ibn Hishām stated, "The person who captured him was Rifāʿa b. Rāfiʿ, one of
the Banū Zurayq."

Ibn Isḥāq went on, "Muḥammad b. Jaʿfar related to me, from ʿUrwa, that
ʿUmayr made mention of the fate of those caste into the pit at Badr, at which
Ṣafwān said, 'I swear, there's nothing good in life now they are gone.' ʿUmayr
agreed, 'You are right. Were it not for a debt I can't pay and children whose survival after me concerns me, I would ride off to Muḥammad to kill him; I have
cause against them, since my son is a prisoner in their hands.'

"Ṣafwān b. Umayya seized the opportunity to say, 'Consider your debt my
responsibility; I will redeem it and consider your children as my own, caring for
them as long as they live. Everything I have will be theirs.'

"ʿUmayr suggested, 'Keep this matter a secret between us both.' Ṣafwān
agreed.

"ʿUmayr then called for his sword, sharpened it, put poison on it and left for
Medina. While ʿUmar b. al-Khaṭṭāb was there talking with a group of Muslims
about Badr and recalling how God had honoured them and how He had treated

their enemy, ʿUmar saw ʿUmayr b. Wahb having just dismounted at the door to the mosque, wearing his sword. ʿUmar commented, 'There's that dog ʿUmayr b. Wahb, that enemy of God; he's come here only to do some mischief. It is he who sowed discord among us and estimated our numbers for the enemy at Badr!'

"ʿUmar then went in to the Messenger of God (ṢAAS) and told him, 'O Prophet of God, that enemy of God ʿUmayr b. Wahb is here wearing his sword.' He told him to let him enter, so ʿUmar went and seized the sheath of ʿUmayr's sword and wrapped it tightly around his neck, telling the Muslim Companions there to go and sit with the Messenger of God (ṢAAS), and to guard him against that evil fellow who could not be trusted.

"He then took him in to the Messenger of God (ṢAAS), and when the latter saw him with ʿUmar holding his sword sheath around his neck, he said, 'Release him, ʿUmar; come near, ʿUmayr.' ʿUmayr went over to him and said, 'May your morning be good!' This was the mode by which people greeted one another before Islam. The Messenger of God (ṢAAS) responded, 'God has honoured us with a greeting better than that, ʿUmayr. That is *salām*, peace, the greeting used by the people of paradise.'

"'Well,' ʿUmayr replied, 'it's a greeting you've not been using for long.'

"'So what brings you, ʿUmar?' the Messenger of God (ṢAAS) asked.

"'I have come about that captive you have; treat him well,' ʿUmayr replied.

"'Why are you wearing a sword around your neck?'

"'God curse the swords! Have they done us any good?'

"'Seriously, why did you come?'

"'That's the only reason,' ʿUmayr insisted.

"'On the contrary, you sat in the *hijr* with Ṣafwān b. Umayya; you discussed the fate of the dead in the pit, then you said, "Were it not for a debt I can't pay and children whose survival after me concerns me, I would ride off to Muḥammad to kill him." And so Ṣafwān b. Umayya took responsibility for your debt and your family if you would kill me. But God prevented you from doing that.'

"ʿUmayr declared, 'I testify that you are the Messenger of God! We used to call you a liar when you brought us news from heaven and the revelations that came to you, but only Ṣafwān and I were present on that occasion, and I well know that only God could have told you of it. Praise be to God who led me to Islam and to where I am now!' He then gave testimony to the truth of Islam.

"The Messenger of God (ṢAAS) ordered, 'Give your brother instruction in the religion! Teach him the Qurʾān and release his prisoner to him!' They did so.

"ʿUmayr then said, 'O Messenger of God, I vigorously tried to extinguish the light of Islam and was very harsh towards those who followed God's religion. I would like you to give me permission to go to Mecca where I will call others to God, to His Messenger and to Islam. Perhaps God will guide them. Otherwise I will persecute them in their religion just as I used to maltreat your Companions in theirs.'

"The Messenger of God (ṢAAS) gave permission· to him and he did go to Mecca.

"Ṣafwān had been saying, following ʿUmayr b. Wahb's departure, 'Rejoice at an event soon to happen that will make you forget Badr!'

"He would ask riders about ʿUmayr, and eventually one came who told him of ʿUmayr's acceptance of Islam. He swore that he would never say another word to him and never do him any favour."

Ibn Isḥāq continued, "When ʿUmayr arrived back in Mecca he set about preaching for Islam and persecuting those who opposed it. Many people accepted Islam due to him.

"And it was ʿUmayr b. Wahb, or al-Ḥārith b. Hishām, who saw the enemy of God, Satan, when he turned on his heels and fled, saying, 'I'll have nothing to do with you, I see what you do not.' Satan was then in the form of Surāqa b. Mālik b. Juʿshum, the leader of Mudlij."

DIVISION

Hereafter Imām Ibn Isḥāq, God bless him, wrote on the revelations in the Qurʾān that relate to the battle of Badr. This is the passage from the first to the last of *sūrat al-Anfāl* (*The Spoils*; VIII). He wrote well and at length. We have examined this in detail in our work of exegesis and those wishing to read this should look at it there. And all praise and credit are due to God.

DIVISION

He then begins giving the names of those Muslims who participated at Badr. He listed these names in the order of the Emigrants and then the Helpers, beginning with those of Aws and going on to those of Khazraj. He concludes with the statement, "The total number of Muslims, whether Emigrants or Helpers, who either witnessed Badr or who were credited with a share of the spoils from it, totalled 314 men.

"The Emigrants totalled 83 men.

"From Aws there were 61 men.

"From Khazraj there were 170 men."

Al-Bukhari listed them in his *ṣaḥīḥ* compendium in alphabetical order following the names of the Messenger of God (ṢAAS), Abū Bakr, ʿUthmān and ʿAlī, may God be pleased with them all.

What follows is a list of the names of the Muslims who were present at Badr arranged alphabeticaly. This is derived from the book *al-Aḥkām al-Kabīr* (*The Major Statutes*) by the *ḥāfiz* Ḍiyāʾ al-Dīn Muḥammad b. ʿAbd al-Wāḥid al-Maqdisī and others. This alphabetical listing is preceded by the name of their chief and their pride, the leader of all the progeny of Adam, Muḥammad, Messenger of God (ṢAAS).

THE NAMES OF THOSE AT BADR ARRANGED ALPHABETICALLY.

THE LETTER ALIF.

Ubayy b. Ka'b al-Najjārī, leader of al-Qurrā'; al-Arqam b. Abū al-Arqam; Abū al-Arqam 'Abd Manāf b. Asad b. 'Abd Allāh b. 'Umar b. Makhzūm al-Makhzūmī; As'ad b. Yazīd b. al-Fākih b. Yazīd b. Khalda b. 'Āmir b. al-'Ajlān.

Aswad b. Zayd b. Tha'laba b. 'Ubayd b. Ghanm – Mūsā b. 'Uqba gave the same. Al-Umawī said, "There is doubt over Sawwād b. Rizām b. Tha'laba b. 'Ubayd b. 'Adī." Salama b. al-Faḍl stated, quoting Ibn Isḥāq, that the name was Sawwād b. Zurayq b. Tha'laba. Ibn 'Ā'idh gave it as Sawwād b. Zayd.

Usayr b. 'Amr al-Anṣārī Abū Salīṭ, also known as Usayr b. 'Amr b. Umayya b. Lawdhān b. Sālim b. Thābit al-Khazrajī; Mūsā b. 'Uqba did not mention him.

Anas b. Qatāda b. Rabī'a b. Khālid b. al-Ḥārith al-Awsī, also so named by Mūsā b. 'Uqba, though al-Umawī named him Anīs in his biography (of the Prophet (ṢAAS)).

I comment that Anas b. Mālik was the servant of the Messenger of God (ṢAAS) according to the account of 'Umar b. Shabba al-Numayrī. Muḥammad b. 'Abd Allāh al-Anṣārī related to us, from his father, from Thumāma b. Anas, who said, "Anas b. Mālik was asked whether he had been present at Badr, and that he replied, 'Where would I have been, to be absent from Badr, may you be motherless!'"

Muḥammad b. Sa'd stated, "Muḥammad b. 'Abd Allāh al-Anṣārī informed us, my father related to us, from a freed-man of Anas b. Mālik, that the latter asked Anas whether he had been present at Badr. He replied, 'May you be motherless, where would I have been, to be absent from Badr?'"

Muḥammad b. 'Abd Allāh al-Anṣārī stated, "Anas b. Mālik went forth to Badr with the Messenger of God (ṢAAS) as a servant in service to him."

Our teacher, the sheikh and *ḥāfiẓ* Abū al-Ḥajjāj al-Mizzī stated in his *tahdhīb*, his educational text, "Thus al-Anṣārī stated, but none of the authors of the works on the military expeditions said this."

Anas b. Mu'ādh b. Anas b. Qays b. 'Ubayd b. Zayd b. Mu'āwiya b. 'Amr b. Mālik b. al-Najjār; Anasa al-Ḥabashī, freed-man of the Messenger of God (ṢAAS); Aws b. Nābit b. al-Mundhir al-Najārī.

Aws b. Khawlī b. 'Abd Allāh b. al-Ḥārith b. 'Ubayd b. Mālik b. Sālim b. Ghanm b. 'Awf b. al-Khazraj al-Khazrajī. Mūsā b. 'Uqba gave his name as Aws b. 'Abd Allāh b. al-Ḥārith b. Khawlī. Aws b. al-Ṣāmit al-Khazrajī, brother of 'Ubāda b. al-Ṣāmit; Iyyās b. al-Bukayr b. 'Abd Yālīl b. Nāshib b. Ghayra b. Sa'd b. Layth b. Bakr, ally of the Banū 'Adī b. Ka'b.

THE LETTER BĀ᾽.

Bujayr b. Abū Bujayr, ally of the Banū al-Najjār, Baḥḥāth b. Tha῾laba b. Khazama b. Aṣram b. ῾Amr b. ῾Imāra al-Balawī, an ally of the Helpers; Basbas b. ῾Amr b. Tha῾laba b. Kharsha b. Zayd b. ῾Amr b. Sa῾īd b. Dhubyān b. Rashdān b. Qays b. Juhayna al-Juhanī, an ally of the Banū Sā῾ida, he being one of the scouts, along with ῾Adī b. Abū al-Zaghbā᾽, referred to above; Bishr b. al-Barā᾽ b. Ma῾rūr al-Khazrajī, who died at Khaybar from the poisoned mutton; Bashīr b. Sa῾d b. Tha῾laba al-Khazrajī, father of al-Nu῾mān b. Bashīr, said to have been the first man to pledge his allegiance to Abū Bakr; Bashīr b. ῾Abd al-Mundhir Abū Lubāba al-Awsī, who was sent back by the Messenger of God (ṢAAS) from al-Rawḥā᾽ to take charge of Medina; he was assigned a full share in the spoils of Badr.

THE LETTER TĀ᾽.

Tamīm b. Ya῾ār b. Qays b. ῾Adī b. Umayya b. Jadāra b. ῾Awf b. al-Ḥārith b. al-Khazraj; Tamīm, the freed-man of Khirāsh b. al-Ṣimma; Tamīm, the freed-man of the Banū Ghanam b. al-Sallam. Ibn Hishām stated, "He was the freed-man of Sa῾d b. Khaythama."

THE LETTER THĀ᾽.

Thābit b. Aqram b. Tha῾laba b. ῾Adī b. al-῾Ajlān; Thābit b. Tha῾laba. This Tha῾laba was known as al-Jadha῾ b. Zayd b. al-Ḥārith b. Ḥarām b. Ghanm b. Ka῾b b. Salama.

Thābit b. Khālid b. al-Nu῾mān b. Khansā᾽ b. ῾Usayra b. ῾Abd b. ῾Awf b. Ghanm b. Mālik b. al-Najjār al-Najjārī; Thābit b. Khansā᾽ b. ῾Amr b. Mālik b. ῾Adī b. ῾Āmir b. Ghanm b. ῾Adī b. al-Najjār al-Najjārī.

Thābit b. ῾Amr b. Zayd b. ῾Adī b. Sawwād b. Mālik b. Ghanm b. ῾Adī b. al-Najjār al-Najjārī; Thābit b. Hazzāl al-Khazrajī; Tha῾laba b. Ḥāṭib b. ῾Amr b. ῾Ubayd b. Umayya b. Zayd b. Mālik b. al-Aws; Tha῾laba b. ῾Amr b. ῾Ubayd b. Mālik al-Najjārī; Tha῾laba b. ῾Amr b. Miḥṣan al-Khazrajī; Tha῾laba b. ῾Anma b. ῾Adī b. Nābī al-Sulamī; Thaqf b. ῾Amr, of the Banū Ḥijr, of the clan of the Banū Salīm, he being an ally of the Banū Kathīr b. Ghanm b. Dūdān b. Asad.

THE LETTER JĪM.

Jābir b. Khālid b. Mas῾ūd b. ῾Abd al-Ashhal b. Ḥāritha b. Dīnār b. al-Najjār al-Najjārī; Jābir b. ῾Abd Allāh b. Ri᾽āb b. al-Nu῾mān b. Sinān b. ῾Ubayd b. ῾Adī b. Ghanm b. Ka῾b b. Salama al-Sulamī, one of those who were present at al-῾Aqaba.

I comment that Jābir b. ʿAbd Allāh b. ʿAmr b. Ḥarām, al-Sulamī also, is mentioned by al-Bukhārī among those at Badr. He gives a line of authorities from Saʿīd b. Manṣūr, from Abū Muʿāwiya, from al-Aʿmash, from Abū Sufyān quoting Jābir as saying, "I drew water from the well for my companions at the battle of Badr."

This line of authorities is according to Muslim. However, Muḥammad b. Saʿd stated, "I mentioned this *hadīth* to Muḥammad b. ʿUmar – meaning al-Wāqidī – and he commented, 'This is ficticious and comes from the Iraqi scholars.' He refuted Jābir's having been present at the battle of Badr."

Imām Aḥmad b. Ḥanbal stated, "Rawḥ b. ʿIbāda related to us, quoting Zakariyyāʾ b. Isḥāq, quoting Abū al-Zubayr, that he heard Jābir b. ʿAbd Allāh say, 'I went on 19 military expeditions with the Messenger of God (ṢAAS), but I was not present at either Badr or Uḥud. My father prevented me. After my father was killed at Uḥud, I never missed any one of the military engagements of the Messenger of God (ṢAAS).'"

Muslim related this from Abū Khaythama, from Rawḥ.

Jabbār b. Ṣakhr al-Sulamī; Jabr b. ʿAtīk al-Anṣārī; Jubayr b. Iyyās al-Khazrajī.

THE LETTER ḤĀʾ.

Al-Ḥārith b. Anas b. Rāfiʿ al-Khazrajī; al-Ḥārith b. Aws b. Muʿādh b. Akhū Saʿd b. Muʿādh al-Awsī; al-Ḥārith b. Ḥāṭib b. ʿAmr b. ʿUbayd b. Umayya b. Zayd b. Mālik b. al-Aws, who was sent back by the Messenger of God (ṢAAS) on the road to Badr, and he awarded him a share of the spoils; al-Ḥārith b. Khazma b. ʿAdī b. Abū Ghanm b. Sālim b. ʿAwf b. ʿAmr b. ʿAwf b. al-Khazraj, an ally of the Banū Zaʿūrā b. ʿAbd al-Ashhal; al-Ḥārith b. al-Ṣimma al-Khazrajī, who was sent back by the Messenger of God (ṢAAS) because his leg was broken en route; he gave him a full share in the spoils.

Al-Ḥārith b. ʿUrfuja al-Awsī; al-Ḥārith b. Qays b. Khalda Abū Khālid al-Khazrajī; al-Ḥārith b. al-Nuʿmān b. Umayya al-Anṣārī; Ḥāritha b. Surāqa al-Najjārī, who was struck by a stray arrow while he was with the observers and was elevated to paradise; Ḥāritha b. al-Nuʿmān b. Rāfiʿ al-Anṣārī; Ḥāṭib b. Abū Baltaʿa al-Lakhmī, an ally of the Banū Asad b. ʿAbd al-ʿUzzā b. Quṣayy.

Ḥāṭib b. ʿAmr b. ʿUbayd b. Umayya al-Ashjaʿī, of the Banū Dahmān. This name is given thus by Ibn Hishām from a source other than Ibn Isḥāq. Al-Wāqidī gave it as Ḥāṭib b. ʿAmr b. ʿAbd Shams b. ʿAbd Wudd; Ibn ʿĀʾidh gave it thus in his work on the military expeditions. Ibn Abū Ḥātim stated, "Ḥāṭib b. ʿAmr b. ʿAbd Shams was a name I heard from my father who said that this man's identity was unknown."

Al-Ḥubāb b. al-Mundhir al-Khazrajī; it is said that the banner of Khazraj was in his care on that day.

Ḥabīb b. Aswad, freed-man of the Banū Ḥarām, of the Banū Salama. Mūsā b. ʿUqba stated, "The name was Ḥabīb b. Saʿd, instead of Aswad." Ibn Abū Ḥātim stated, "Ḥabīb b. Aslam was the freed-man of the tribe of Jusham b. al-Khazraj, and a Helper and a man who participated in the battle of Badr."

Ḥurayth b. Zayd b. Thaʿlaba b. ʿAbd Rabbihi al-Anṣārī, a brother of ʿAbd Allāh b. Zayd, *who was shown al-nidāʾ,[70] the call to prayer.*

Al-Ḥusayn b. al-Ḥārith b. al-Muṭṭalib b. ʿAbd Manāf; Ḥamza b. ʿAbd al-Muṭṭalib b. Hāshim, an uncle of the Messenger of God (ṢAAS).

THE LETTER KHĀʾ.

Khālid b. al-Bukayr, brother of Iyās referred to above; Khālid b. Zayd Abū Ayyūb al-Najjārī; Khālid b. Qays b. Mālik b. al-ʿAjlān al-Anṣārī; Khārija b. al-Ḥumayr, an ally of the Banū Khansāʾ, of the Khazraj, a man also named as Ḥāritha b. al-Ḥumayr whom Ibn ʿĀʾidh called "Khārija"; but God knows best. Khārija b. Zayd al-Khazrajī, son-in-law of Abū Bakr; Khabbāb b. al-Aratt, an ally of the Banū Zahra, one of the original Emigrants, a man whose origins were in the Banū Tamīm, though some say in Khuzāʿa; Khabbāb, freed-man of ʿUtba b. Ghazwān, one of the original Emigrants; Khirāsh b. al-Ṣimma al-Sulamī; Khubayb b. Isāf b. ʿInaba al-Khazrajī; Khuraym b. Fātik who was included among these by al-Bukhārī; Khalīfa b. ʿAdī al-Khazrajī; Khulayd b. Qays b. al-Nuʿmān b. Sinān b. ʿUbayd al-Anṣārī al-Sulamī; Khunays b. Ḥudhāyfa b. Qays b. ʿAdī b. Saʿd b. Sahm b. ʿAmr b. Ḥuṣayṣ b. Kaʿb b. Luʾayy al-Sahmī, who was killed at Badr, thus making Ḥafṣa, daughter of ʿUmar b. al-Khaṭṭāb, a widow; Khawwāt b. Jubayr al-Anṣārī, who was accorded a share of the spoils, though he was not himself present at Badr; Khawlā b. Abū Khawlā al-ʿIjlī, an ally of the Banū ʿAdī, one of the original Emigrants; Khallād b. Rāfiʿ; Khallād b. Suwayd and Khallād b. ʿAmr b. al-Jumūḥ, men of Khazraj.

THE LETTER DHĀL.

Dhakwān b. ʿAbd Qays al-Khazrajī; Dhū al-Shimālayn b. ʿAbd b. ʿAmr b. Naḍla of Ghabshān b. Salīm b. Malkān b. Afṣā b. Ḥāritha b. ʿAmr b. ʿĀmir of the Banū Khuzāʿa, an ally of the Banū Zuhra who was martyred that day. Ibn Hishām stated that his name was ʿUmayr and that he was only called Dhū al-Shimālayn, i.e. "he with the two left hands" because he was left-handed.

THE LETTER RĀʾ.

Rāfiʿ b. al-Ḥārith al-Awsī; Rāfiʿ b. ʿUnjada: Ibn Hishām *stated that ʿUnjada was his mother;* Rāfiʿ b. al-Muʿallī b. Lūdhān al-Khazrajī who was killed that day; Rabīʿ b. Rāfiʿ b. al-Ḥārith b. Zayd b. Ḥāritha b. al-Jidd b. ʿAjlān b. Ḍubayʿa.

---

70. This was a vision that he was shown while asleep of how the call to prayer was to be made to the Muslim community. See p. 222 above.

Mūsā b. ʿUqba gave his name as Rabʿī b. Abū Rāfiʿ. Rābiʿ b. Iyyās al-Khazrajī; Rabīʿa b. Aktham b. Sakhbara b. ʿAmr b. Lakīz b. ʿĀmir b. Ghanm Dūdān b. Asad b. Khuzayma, an ally of the Banū ʿAbd Shams of the Banū ʿAbd Manāf, he having been one of the original Emigrants; Rakhīla b. Thaʿlaba b. Khālid b. Thaʿlaba b. ʿĀmir b. Bayāḍa al-Khazrajī; Rifāʿa b. Rāfiʿ al-Zurqī, a brother of Khallād b. Rāfiʿ; Rifāʿa b. ʿAbd al-Mundhir b. Zunayr al-Awsī, a brother of Abū Lubāba; Rifāʿa b. ʿAmr b. Zayd al-Khazrajī.

THE LETTER ZĀʾY.

Al-Zubayr b. al-ʿAwwām b. Khuwaylid b. Asad b. ʿAbd al-ʿUzzā b. Quṣayy, the son of the aunt of the Messenger of God (ṢAAS), and his disciple.

Ziyād b. ʿAmr. Mūsā b. ʿUqba gave his name as Ziyād b. al-Akhras b. ʿAmr al-Juhanī. Al-Wāqidī gave it as Ziyād b. Kaʿb b. ʿAmr b. ʿAdī b. Rifāʿa b. Kulayb b. Bardhaʿa b. ʿAdī b. ʿAmr b. al-Zibaʿrā b. Rushdān b. Qays b. Juhayna. Ziyād b. Labīd al-Zurqī; Ziyād b. al-Mazīn b. Qays al-Khazrajī; Zayd b. Aslam b. Thaʿlaba b. ʿAdī b. ʿAjlān b. Ḍubayʿa; Zayd b. Hāritha b. Shuraḥbīl, freed-man of the Messenger of God (ṢAAS); Zayd b. al-Khaṭṭāb b. Nufayl, brother of ʿUmar b. al-Khaṭṭāb, God bless them both; Zayd b. Sahl b. al-Aswad b. Harām al-Najjārī Abū Ṭalḥa, God be pleased with him.

THE LETTER SĪN.

Sālim b. ʿUmayr al-Awsī; Sālim b. Ghanm b. ʿAwf al-Khazrajī; Sālim b. Maʿqil, freed-man of Abū Ḥudhayfa; al-Sāʾib b. ʿUthmān b. Maẓʿūn al-Jumaḥī, who was present with his father; Sabīʿ b. Qays b. ʿAysha al-Khazrajī; Sabra b. Fātik, who is mentioned by al-Bukhārī; Surāqa b. ʿAmr al-Najjārī; Surāqa b. Kaʿb, also al-Najjārī; Saʿd b. Khawlā, freed-man of the Banū ʿĀmir b. Luʾayy, one of the original Emigrants; Saʿd b. Khaythama al-Awsī, martyred that day; Saʿd b. al-Rabīʿ al-Khazrajī who was martyred at the Battle of Uḥud; Saʿd b. Zayd b. Mālik al-Awsī: al-Wāqidī gave his name as Saʿd b. Zayd b. al-Fākih al-Khazrajī; Saʿd b. Suhayl b. ʿAbd al-Ashhal al-Najjārī; Saʿd b. ʿUbayd al-Anṣārī; Saʿd b. ʿUthmān b. Khalda al-Khazrajī Abū ʿUbāda. Ibn ʿĀʾidh gave his name as Abū ʿUbayda.

Saʿd b. Muʿādh al-Awsī, and it was he who was entrusted with the Aws banner.

Saʿd b. ʿUbāda b. Dulaym al-Khazrajī: several authorities, including ʿUrwa, al-Bukhārī, Ibn Abū Ḥātim and al-Ṭibrānī include him among those who were present at Badr. In the ṣaḥīḥ of Muslim, there is material substantiating that when the Prophet (ṢAAS) was preparing to meet the Quraysh force, Saʿd b. ʿUbāda said, "O Messenger of God, perhaps you would like us to make ..." But the truth is that it was Saʿd b. Muʿādh who said this.

It is well known that Asʿad b. ʿUbāda was sent back from the road; it is said this was so that he should take charge of Medina. It is also said to have been because he was bitten by a snake and was not able to proceed to Badr. Al-Suhaylī related this from Ibn Qutayba. But God knows best.

Sa°d b. Abū Waqqāṣ, who was Mālik b. Uhayb al-Zuhrī, one of the so-called "ten";[71] Sa°d b. Mālik Abū Sahl: al-Wāqidī stated that he had made preparations to go forth but fell sick and died before he had left.

Sa°īd b. Zayd b. °Amr b. Nufayl al-°Adawī, nephew of °Umar b. al-Khaṭṭāb. It is said that he arrived from Syria after they returned from Badr; the Messenger of God (ṢAAS) gave him a share of the spoils.

Sufyān b. Bishr b. °Amr al-Khazrajī; Salama b. Aslam b. Ḥuraysh al-Awsī; Salama b. Thābit b. Waqsh b. Zaghba; Salama b. Salāma b. Waqsh b. Zaghba; Salīm b. al-Ḥārith al-Najjārī; Salīm b. °Amr al-Sulamī; Salīm b. Qays b. Fahad al-Khazrajī; Salīm b. Milḥān, brother of Ḥarām b. Milḥān al-Najjārī; Simāk b. Aws b. Kharasha Abū Dujāna, also known as Simāk b. Kharasha; Simāk b. Sa°d b. Tha°laba al-Khazrajī, who was the brother of Bashīr b. Sa°d referred to above; Sahl b. Ḥunayf al-Awsī; Sahl b. °Atīk al-Najjārī; Sahl b. Qays al-Sulamī; Suhayl b. Rāfi° al-Najjārī, who had owned the site of the mosque built by the Prophet (ṢAAS) as was related above; Suhayl b. Wahb al-Fihrī who was the son of Bayḍā°, his mother; Sinān b. Abū Sinān b. Miḥsan b. Ḥirthān, a *muhājirī*, an Emigrant, an ally of Banū °Abd Shams b. °Abd Manāf; Sinān b. Ṣayfī al-Sulamī; Sawwād b. Zurayq b. Zayd al-Anṣārī: al-Umawī gave his name as Sawwād b. Rizām; Sawwād b. Ghaziyya b. Uhayb al-Balawī; Suwaybiṭ b. Sa°d b. Ḥarmala al-°Abdarī; Suwayd b. Makhshī Abū Makhshī al-Ṭā°ī, ally of the Banū °Abd Shams: his name is said to have been Azyad b. Ḥimyar.

THE LETTER SHĪN.

Shujā° b. Wahb b. Rabī°a al-Asadī; Asad b. Khuzayma, ally of the Banū °Abd Shams, one of the original Emigrants. Shammās b. °Uthmān al-Makhzūmī: Ibn Hishām said that his name was °Uthmān b. °Uthmān, but he was named Shammās for his good looks and his resemblance to a Shammās of the pre-Islamic era; Shaqrān, freed-man of the Messenger of God (ṢAAS): al-Wāqidī stated, "He was not awarded any share in the spoils. He was in charge of the captives. He was given money by everyone who had control over the prisoners and so he received more than a share of the spoils would otherwise have been."

THE LETTER ṢĀD.

Ṣuhayb b. Sinān al-Rūmī, one of the original Emigrants; Ṣafwān b. Wahb b. Rabī°a al-Fihrī, brother of Suhayl b. Bayḍā°: he was martyred that day; Ṣakhr b. Umayya b. Khansā° al-Sulamī.

-----

71. Ten early converts to Islam reported to be assured places in paradise. See footnote Vol. I, p. 113.

THE LETTER ḌĀḌ.

Ḍaḥḥāk b. Ḥāritha b. Zayd al-Sulamī; Ḍaḥḥāk b. ʿAbd ʿAmr al-Najjārī; Ḍamra b. ʿAmr al-Juhanī: Mūsā b. ʿUqba gave his name as Ḍamra b. Kaʿb b. ʿAmr, ally of the Helpers, he being the brother of Ziyād b. ʿAmr.

THE LETTER ṬĀʾ.

Ṭalḥa b. ʿUbayd Allāh al-Taymī, one of the "ten": he came from Syria after their return from Badr and the Messenger of God (ṢAAS) gave him a share in the spoils; Ṭufayl b. al-Ḥārith b. al-Muṭṭalib b. ʿAbd Manāf, an Emigrant, and the brother of Ḥuṣayn and ʿUbayda; Ṭufayl b. Mālik b. Khansāʾ al-Sulamī; Ṭufayl b. al-Nuʿmān b. Khansāʾ al-Sulamī, the nephew of the preceding man; Ṭulayb b. ʿUmayr b. Wahb b. Abū Kabīr b. ʿAbd b. Quṣayy: al-Wāqidī mentioned him.

THE LETTER ẒĀʾ.

Ẓuhayr b. Rāfiʿ al-Awsī, mentioned by al-Bukhārī.

THE LETTER ʿAYN.

ʿĀṣim b. Thābit b. Abū al-Aqlaḥ al-Anṣārī, protected by bees after he was killed at al-Rajīʿ; ʿĀṣim b. ʿAdī b. al-Jidd b. ʿAjlān, sent back by the Messenger of God (ṢAAS) at al-Rawḥāʾ but awarded by him a share in the spoils; ʿĀṣim b. Qays b. Thābit al-Khazrajī; ʿĀqil b. al-Bukayr, brother of Iyās, Khālid and ʿĀmir; ʿĀmir b. Umayya b. Zayd b. al-Hashās al-Najjārī; ʿĀmir b. al-Ḥārith al-Fihrī, so referred to by Salama, quoting Ibn Isḥāq and Ibn ʿĀʾidh: Mūsā b. ʿUqba and Ziyād, quoting Ibn Isḥāq, gave his name as ʿAmr b. al-Ḥārith; ʿĀmir b. Rabīʿa b. Mālik al-ʿAnazī, ally of the Banū ʿAdī, one of the Emigrants; ʿĀmir b. Salama b. ʿĀmir b. ʿAbd Allāh al-Balawī al-Quḍāʿī, an ally of the Banū Sālim b. Mālik b. Sālim b. Ghanm: Ibn Hishām said he was known as ʿUmar b. Salama; ʿĀmir b. ʿAbd Allāh b. al-Jarrāḥ b. Hilāl b. Uhayb b. Ḍabba b. al-Ḥārith b. Fihr Abū ʿUbayda b. al-Jarrāḥ, one of the "ten", an initial Emigrant; ʿĀmir b. Fuhayra, a "client" of Abū Bakr; ʿĀmir b. Makhlid al-Najjārī; ʿĀʾidh b. Māʿid b. Qays al-Khazrajī; ʿAbbād b. Bishr b. Waqsh al-Awsī; ʿAbbād b. Qays b. ʿĀmir al-Khazrajī; ʿAbbād b. Qays b. ʿAysha al-Khazrajī, brother of Subayʿ referred to above; ʿAbbād b. al-Khashkhāsh al-Quḍāʿī; ʿUbāda b. al-Ṣāmit al-Khazrajī; ʿUbāda b. Qays b. Kaʿb b. Qays; ʿAbd Allāh b. Umayya b. ʿUrfuṭa; ʿAbd Allāh b. Thaʿlaba b. Khazama, brother of the Baḥḥāth mentioned above; ʿAbd Allāh b. Jaḥsh b. Riʾāb al-Asadī; ʿAbd Allāh b. Jubayr b. al-Nuʿmān al-Awsī.

ʿAbd Allāh b. al-Jidd b. Qays al-Sulamī; ʿAbd Allāh b. Ḥaqq b. Aws al-Sāʿidī: Mūsā b. ʿUqba, al-Wāqidī and Ibn ʿĀʾidh gave his name as ʿAbd Rabb b. Ḥaqq, while Ibn Hishām gave it as ʿAbd Rabbihī b. Ḥaqq.

ʿAbd Allāh b. al-Ḥumayr, ally of the Banū Harām, he being the brother of Khārija b. al-Ḥumayr of Ashjaʿ; ʿAbd Allāh b. al-Rabīʿ b. Qays al-Khazrajī; ʿAbd Allāh b. Rawāḥa al-Khazrajī; ʿAbd Allāh b. Zayd b. ʿAbd Rabbihī b. Thaʿlaba al-Khazrajī who was shown al-nidāʾ, the call to prayer.

ʿAbd Allāh b. Surāqa al-ʿAdawī, a name not mentioned by Mūsā b. ʿUqba, al-Wāqidī or Ibn ʿĀʾidh, though given by Ibn Isḥāq and others.

ʿAbd Allāh b. Salama b. Mālik al-ʿAjlān, an ally of the Anṣār; ʿAbd Allāh b. Sahl b. Rāfiʿ, brother of the Banū Zaʿūrā; ʿAbd Allāh b. Suhayl b. ʿAmr. He came out to battle with his father, on the side of the polytheists, but then he fled from them, joined the Muslims and fought with them. ʿAbd Allāh b. Ṭāriq b. Mālik al-Quḍāʿī, an ally of al-Aws; ʿAbd Allāh b. ʿĀmir of Baliyy, mentioned by Ibn Isḥāq.

ʿAbd Allāh b. ʿAbd Allāh b. Ubayy b. Salūl al-Khazrajī, whose father was the leader of the al-munāfiqūn, the "hypocrites". ʿAbd Allāh b. ʿAbd al-Asad b. Hilāl b. ʿAbd Allāh b. ʿAmr b. Makhzūm Abū Salama, husband of Umm Salama: ʿAbd Allāh was killed that day. ʿAbd Allāh b. ʿAbd Manāf b. al-Nuʿmān al-Sulamī; ʿAbd Allāh b. ʿAbs; ʿAbd Allāh b. ʿUthmān b. ʿĀmir b. ʿAmr b. Kaʿb b. Taym b. Murra b. Kaʿb Abū Bakr, "the Trusting", God bless him; ʿAbd Allāh b. ʿUrfaṭa b. ʿAdī al-Khazrajī.

ʿAbd Allāh b. ʿUmar b. Harām al-Sulamī Abū Jābir; ʿAbd Allāh b. ʿUmayr b. ʿAdī al-Khazrajī; ʿAbd Allāh b. Qays b. Khālid al-Najjārī; ʿAbd Allāh b. Qays b. Ṣakhr b. Harām al-Sulamī; ʿAbd Allāh b. Kaʿb b. ʿAmr b. ʿAwf b. Mabdhūl b. ʿAmr b. Ghanm b. Māzin b. al-Najjār, whom the Messenger of God (ṢAAS) put in charge of the spoils of Badr, along with ʿAdī b. Abū al-Zaghbāʾ.

ʿAbd Allāh b. Makhrama b. ʿAbd al-ʿUzzā, one of the initial Emigrants; ʿAbd Allāh b. Masʿūd al-Hudhalī, ally of Banū Zuhra, one of the initial Emigrants; ʿAbd Allāh b. Maẓʿūn al-Jumaḥī, one of the initial Emigrants; ʿAbd Allāh b. al-Nuʿmān b. Baldama al-Sulamī; ʿAbd Allāh b. Unaysa b. al-Nuʿmān al-Sulamī; ʿAbd al-Raḥmān b. Jabr b. ʿAmr Abū ʿUbays al-Khazrajī; ʿAbd al-Raḥmān b. ʿAbd Allāh b. Thaʿlaba, Abū ʿUqayl al-Quḍāʿī al-Balawī.

ʿAbd al-Raḥmān b. ʿAwf b. ʿAbd ʿAwf b. ʿAbd al-Ḥārith b. Zuhra b. Kilāb al-Zuhrī, one of the "ten", God be pleased with them all; ʿAbs b. ʿĀmir b. ʿAdī al-Sulamī; ʿUbayd b. al-Tayyihān, brother of Abū al-Haytham b. al-Tayyihān: his name is also given as ʿAtīk, instead of ʿUbayd.

ʿUbayd b. Thaʿlaba, of the Banū Ghanm b. Mālik; ʿUbayd b. Zayd b. ʿĀmir b. ʿAmr b. al-ʿAjlān b. ʿĀmir; ʿUbayd b. Abū ʿUbayd.

ʿUbayda b. al-Ḥārith b. al-Muṭṭalib b. ʿAbd Manāf, brother of al-Ḥuṣayn and al-Ṭufayl: he was one of the three champions who first went out to fight at Badr and whose arm (sic)[72] was cut off and who died following the battle. God bless him!

ʿUtbān b. Mālik b. ʿAmr al-Khazrajī; ʿUtba b. Rabīʿa b. Khālid b. Muʿāwiya al-Bahrānī, an ally of the Banū Umayya b. Lawdhān; ʿUtba b. ʿAbd Allāh b. Ṣakhr al-Sulamī; ʿUtba b. Ghazwān b. Jābir, one of the initial Emigrants.

---

72. Elsewhere in the text we learn that it was his leg that he lost.

ʿUthmān b. ʿAffān b. Abū al-ʿĀṣ b. Umayya b. ʿAbd Shams b. ʿAbd Manāf al-Umawī, (later) the "Commander of the Believers", one of the Four Caliphs, and one of the "ten". He remained behind with his wife Ruqayya, daughter of the Messenger of God (ṢAAS), nursing her until she died. He was given a full share of the spoils.

ʿUthmān b. Maẓʿūn al-Jumaḥī Abū al-Sāʾib, a brother of ʿAbd Allāh and Qudāma, one of the initial Emigrants.

ʿAdī b. Abū al-Zaghbāʾ al-Juhanī, who was sent ahead as a scout by the Messenger of God (ṢAAS), along with Basbas b. ʿAmr.

ʿIṣma b. al-Ḥuṣayn b. Wabra b. Khālid b. al-ʿAjlān; ʿUṣayma, an ally of the Banū al-Ḥārith b. Siwār of Ashjaʿ: he was also said to be of the Banū Asad b. Khuzayma; ʿAṭiyya b. Nuwayra b. ʿĀmir b. ʿAṭiyya al-Khazrajī; ʿUqba b. ʿĀmir b. Nābī al-Sulamī; ʿUqba b. ʿUthmān b. Khalda al-Khazrajī, brother of Saʿd b. ʿUthmān.

ʿUqba b. ʿAmr Abū Masʿūd al-Badrī: in the *ṣaḥīḥ* of al-Bukhārī it is stated that he was present at Badr. However, many of the scholars of the military expeditions of the Prophet (ṢAAS) express doubts over this and therefore do not include him.

ʿUqba b. Wahb b. Rabīʿa al-Asadī, the Asad of Khuzayma, an ally of the Banū ʿAbd Shams, he being a brother of Shujāʿ b. Wahb, one of the initial Emigrants; ʿUqba b. Wahb b. Kalda, an ally of the Banū Ghaṭfān.

ʿUkkāsha b. Miḥṣan al-Ghanmī, one of the initial Emigrants, one who will enter paradise without reckoning.

ʿAlī b. Abū Ṭālib al-Hāshimī, later "Commander of the Believers", one of the Four Caliphs, and one of the three champions who went forth at Badr. God be pleased with him!

ʿAmmār b. Yāsir al-ʿAnasī al-Madhḥijī, one of the initial Emigrants; ʿUmāra b. Ḥazm b. Zayd al-Najjārī. ʿUmar b. al-Khaṭṭāb, later "Commander of the Believers", one of the Four Caliphs, and one of the two sheikhs, learned elders, known as *al-muqtadā bihimā*, "those relied upon", who were viewed as exemplars. God be pleased with them both!

ʿUmar b. ʿAmr b. Iyās of Yemen, an ally of the Banū Lawdhān b. ʿAmr b. Sālim, said to be a brother of Rabīʿ and Waraqa; ʿAmr b. Thaʿlaba b. Wahb b. ʿAdī b. Mālik b. ʿAdī b. ʿĀmir Abū Ḥakīm.

ʿAmr b. al-Ḥārith b. Zuhayr b. Abū Shaddād b. Rabīʿa b. Hilāl b. Uhayb b. Ḍabsha b. al-Ḥārith b. Fihr al-Fihrī; ʿAmr b. Surāqa al-ʿAdawī, an Emigrant; ʿAmr b. Abū Sarḥ al-Fihrī, an Emigrant. Al-Wāqidī and Ibn ʿĀʾidh give his name as Maʿmar instead of ʿAmr.

ʿAmr b. Ṭalq b. Zayd b. Umayya b. Sinān b. Kaʿb b. Ghanm, of the Banū Ḥarām; ʿAmr b. al-Jumūḥ b. Ḥarām al-Anṣārī; ʿAmr b. Qays b. Zayd b. Sawwād b. Mālik b. Ghanm, mentioned by al-Wāqidī and al-Umawī.

ʿAmr b. Qays b. Mālik b. ʿAdī b. Khansāʾ b. ʿAmr b. Mālik b. ʿAdī b. ʿĀmir, the brother of Khārija: Mūsā b. ʿUqba did not mention him.

῾Amr b. ῾Āmir b. al-Ḥarith al-Fihrī, mentioned by Mūsā b. ῾Uqba; ῾Amr b. Ma῾bad b. al-Az῾ar al-Awsī; ῾Amr b. Mu῾ādh al-Awsī, brother of Sa῾d b. Mu῾ādh; ῾Umayr b. al-Ḥarith b. Tha῾laba, also known as ῾Amr b. al-Ḥārith b. Labda b. Tha῾laba al-Sulamī; ῾Umayr b. Ḥarām b. al-Jumūḥ al-Sulamī, mentioned by Ibn ῾Ā᾽idh and al-Wāqidī.

῾Umayr b. al-Ḥumām b. al-Jamūḥ, nephew of the next above, martyred at Badr; ῾Umayr b. ῾Āmir b. Mālik b. al-Khansā b. Mabdhūl b. ῾Amr b. Ghanm b. Māzin Abū Dā᾽ūd al-Māzinī.

῾Umayr b. ῾Awf, freed-man of Suhayl b. ῾Amr: his name is given by al-Umawī and others as ῾Amr b. ῾Awf. It is similarly given in both *ṣaḥīḥ* collections in the account of the dispatch of Abū ῾Ubayda to Baḥrayn.

῾Umayr b. Mālik b. Uhayb al-Zuhrī, brother of Sa῾d b. Abū Waqqāṣ, martyred that day; ῾Antara, freed-man of the Banū Sulaym and also said to be a member of that tribe, but God knows best.

῾Awf b. al-Ḥārith b. Rifā῾a b. al-Ḥārith al-Najjārī, he being the son of ῾Afrā᾽, daughter of ῾Ubayd b. Tha῾laba al-Najjāriyya: he was martyred that day; ῾Uwaym b. Sā᾽ida al-Anṣārī, of the Banū Umayya b. Zayd; ῾Iyāḍ b. Ghanm al-Fihrī, one of the initial Emigrants. May God be pleased with them all!

THE LETTER GHAYN.

Ghannām b. Aws al-Khazrajī: he was mentioned by al-Wāqidī, though there is no concensus about him.

THE LETTER FĀ᾽.

Al-Fākih b. Bishr b. al-Fākih al-Khazrajī; Farwa b. ῾Amr b. Wadfa al-Khazrajī.

THE LETTER QĀF.

Qatāda b. al-Nu῾mān al-Awsī: Qudāma b. Maẓ῾ūn al-Jumaḥī, an Emigrant, a brother of ῾Uthmān and ῾Abd Allāh. Quṭba b. ῾Āmir b. Hadīda al-Sulamī; Qays b. al-Sakn al-Najjārī; Qays b. Abū Ṣa῾ṣa῾a ῾Amr b. Zayd al-Māzinī, who was in command of the rearguard at Badr. Qays b. Muḥṣin b. Khālid al-Khazrajī; Qays b. Mukhallad b. Tha῾laba al-Najjārī.

THE LETTER KĀF.

Ka῾b b. Ḥammān, also known as Jammār and b. Jammāz. Ibn Hishām gave it as Ka῾b b. Ghubshān. He is also known as Ka῾b b. Mālik b. Tha῾laba b. Jammāz. Al-Umawī stated his identity to be Ka῾b b. Tha῾laba b. Ḥabāla b. Ghanm al-Ghassānī, one of the allies of the Banū al-Khazraj b. Sā῾ida.

Ka'b b. Zayd b. Qays al-Najjārī; Ka'b b. 'Amr Abū al-Yusr al-Sulamī; Kalāfa b. Tha'laba, one of the *bakkā'ūn*[73] mentioned by Mūsā b. 'Uqba; Kannāz b. Ḥuṣayn b. Yarbū' Abū Marthad al-Ghanawī, one of the initial Emigrants.

THE LETTER MĪM.

Mālik b. al-Dukhshum, known as Ibn al-Dukhshun (sic) al-Khazrajī; Mālik b. Abū Khawlā al-Ju'fī, an ally of the Banū 'Adī; Mālik b. Rabī'a Abū Usayd al-Sā'idī; Mālik b. Qudāma al-Awsī; Mālik b. 'Amr, brother of Thaqf b. 'Amr, both of whom were Emigrants and allies of the Banū Tamīm b. Dūdān b. Asad; Mālik b. Qudāma al-Awsī; Mālik b. Mas'ūd al-Khazrajī; Mālik b. Thābit b. Numayla al-Mazanī, an ally of the Banū 'Amr b. 'Awf; Mubashshir b. 'Abd al-Mundhir b. Zanbar al-Awsī, a brother of Abū Lubāba and Rifā'a: he was martyred at Badr; al-Mujadhdhar b. Dhiyād al-Balawī, an Emigrant; Muḥriz b. 'Āmir al-Najjārī; Muḥriz b. Naḍla al-Asadī, an ally of the Banū 'Abd Shams, an Emigrant; Muḥammad b. Maslama, an ally of the Banū 'Abd al-Ashhal; Mudlij, also known as Midlāj b. 'Amr, brother of Thaqf b. 'Amr, an Emigrant; Marthad b. Abū Marthad al-Ghanawī; Misṭaḥ b. Uthātha b. 'Abbād b. al-Muṭṭalib b. 'Abd Manāf, an initial Emigrant: his name is also given as 'Awf; Mas'ūd b. Aws al-Anṣārī al-Najjārī; Mas'ūd b. Khalda al-Khazrajī; Mas'ūd b. Rabī'a al-Qārī, an ally of the Banū Zahra, an Emigrant; Mas'ūd b. Sa'd, also known as Ibn 'Abd Sa'd b. 'Āmir b. 'Adī b. Jushm b. Majda'a b. Ḥāritha b. al-Ḥārith; Mas'ūd b. Sa'd b. Qays al-Khazrajī; Muṣ'ab b. 'Umayr al-'Abdarī, an Emigrant who bore the banner that day; Mu'ādh b. Jabal al-Khazrajī; Mu'ādh b. al-Ḥārith al-Najjārī: this man's mother was 'Afrā', and he was the brother of 'Awf and Mu'awwidh; Mu'ādh b. 'Amr b. al-Jumūḥ al-Khazrajī; Mu'ādh b. Mā'iḍ al-Khazrajī, brother of 'Ā'idh; Ma'bad b. 'Abbād b. Qushayr b. al-Qidhamm b. Sālim b. Ghanm: also known as Ma'bad b. 'Ubāda b. Qays. Al-Wāqidī gave his name as Qash'ar instead of Qushayr. Ibn Hishām gave his name as Qash'ar Abū Khumayṣa.

Ma'bad b. Qays b. Ṣakhr al-Sulamī, brother of 'Abd Allāh b. Qays; Mu'attib b. 'Ubayd b. Iyās al-Balawī al-Quḍā'ī; Mu'attib b. 'Awf al-Khuzā'ī, an ally of the Banū Makhzūm, an Emigrant; Mu'attib b. Qushayr al-Awsī; Ma'qil b. al-Mundhir al-Sulamī; Mu'ammar b. al-Ḥārith al-Jumaḥī, an Emigrant; Ma'an b. 'Adī al-Awsī; Mu'awwidh b. al-Ḥārith al-Jumaḥī, his mother being 'Afrā'. And he was a brother of Mu'ādh b. 'Awf. Mu'awwidh b. 'Amr b. al-Jumūḥ al-Sulamī, probably a brother of Mu'ādh b. 'Amr; al-Miqdād b. 'Amr al-Bahrānī, he being al-Miqdād b. al-Aswad, one of the initial Emigrants; it was he whose statement was praised by the Messenger of God (ṢAAS). He was the son of the man mentioned above and was one of the cavalry at Badr. Mulayl b. Wabra al-Khazrajī; al-Mundhir b. 'Amr b. Khunays al-Sā'idī; al-Mundhir b. Qudāma b. 'Arfaja al-Khazrajī; al-Mundhir b. Muḥammad b. 'Uqba al-Anṣārī of

---

73. The category of deeply pious Muslim converts who 'wept at', i.e. deeply repented, the tardiness of their conversion or participation in the struggles of the early Islamic community.

the Banū Jaḥjabī; Mihja', the freed-man of 'Umar b. al-Khaṭṭāb, whose origins were from Yemen: he was the first Muslim killed that day.

THE LETTER NŪN.

Naṣr b. al-Ḥārith b. 'Abd Razāḥ b. Ẓufr b. Ka'b; Nu'mān b. 'Abd 'Amr al-Najjārī, he being the brother of al-Ḍaḥḥāk; Nu'mān b. 'Amr b. Rifā'a al-Najjārī; Nu'mān b. 'Aṣr b. al-Ḥārith, an ally of the Banū 'Awf; Nu'mān b. Mālik b. Tha'laba al-Khazrajī, known as Qawqal; Nu'mān b. Yasār, freed-man of the Banū 'Ubayd, known as Nu'mān b. Sinān; Nawfal b. 'Ubayd Allāh b. Naḍla al-Khazrajī.

THE LETTER HĀ'.

Hāni' b. Niyār Abū Burda al-Balawī, uncle of al-Barā' b. 'Āzib.

Hilāl b. Umayya al-Wāqifī: he is included with those at Badr in both *ṣaḥīḥ* collections, in regard to the story of Ka'b b. Mālik. But none of the authors of the works on the military expeditions include him.

Hilāl b. al-Mu'allā al-Khazrajī, brother of Rāfi' b. al-Mu'allā.

THE LETTER WĀW.

Wāqid b. 'Abd Allāh al-Tamīmī, an ally of the Banū 'Adī, an Emigrant; Wadī'a b. 'Amr b. Jarād al-Juhanī, mentioned by al-Wāqidī and Ibn 'Ā'idh; Waraqa b. Iyās b. 'Amr al-Khazrajī, a brother of Rabī' b. Iyās; Wahb b. Sa'd b. Abū Sarḥ, mentioned by Mūsā b. 'Uqba, Ibn 'Ā'idh and al-Wāqidī among the Banū 'Āmir b. Lu'ayy. But Ibn Isḥāq did not mention him.

THE LETTER YĀ'.

Yazīd b. al-Akhnas b. Janāb b. Ḥabīb b. Jarra al-Sulamī. Al-Suhaylī stated that he was present along with his father and his son, something unique among the Companions. But Ibn Isḥāq and most of the other authorities do not mention them. They were, however, present with him at the *bay'at al-riḍwān*,[74] the "Pledge of Riḍwān".

Yazīd b. al-Ḥārith b. Qays al-Khazrajī. It was he who was called Ibn Fusḥum, the latter being his mother. He was martyred at Badr that day; Yazīd b. 'Āmir b. Ḥadīda Abū al-Mundhir al-Sulamī; Yazīd b. al-Mundhir b. Sarḥ al-Sulamī, he being the brother of Ma'qil b. al-Mundhir.

---

74. The Pledge of Riḍwān, or the Tree, also mentioned in the Qur'ān. It refers to the pledge given by the Companions to the Prophet (ṢAAS) during the treaty of al-Ḥudaybiyya. See *sūrat al-Fatḥ*; XLVIII, v.18.

THOSE MEN KNOWN BY 'KUNAN', AGNOMENA.

Abū Usayd Mālik b. Rabīʿa is listed above; Abū al-Aʿwar b. al-Ḥārith b. Ẓālim al-Najjārī: Ibn Hishām gave Abū al-Aʿwar's real name as al-Ḥārith b. Ẓālim, while al-Wāqidī gave it as Kaʿb b. al-Ḥārith b. Jundab b. Ẓālim; Abū Bakr, "the Trusting", ʿAbd Allāh b. ʿUthmān, listed above; Abū Ḥabba b. ʿAmr b. Thābit, one of the Banū Thaʿlaba b. ʿAmr b. ʿAwf al-Anṣārī; Abū Ḥudhayfa b. ʿUtba b. Rabīʿa was an Emigrant and his given name was said to be Mihsham; Abū al-Ḥamrāʾ, freed-man of al-Ḥārith b. Rifāʿa b. ʿAfrāʾ; Abū Khuzayma b. Aws b. Aṣram al-Najjārī; Abū Sabra, freed-man of Abū Ruhm b. ʿAbd al-ʿUzzā, an Emigrant; Abū Sinān b. Miḥṣan b. Hurthān, brother of ʿUkkāsha. With him he had his son Sinān. He was an Emigrant.

Abū al-Ṣiyāḥ b. al-Nuʿmān, said to be ʿUmayr b. Thābit b. al-Nuʿmān b. Umayya b. Imruʾ al-Qays b. Thaʿlaba. He returned while on the way there and was killed at the battle of Khaybar. He came back because of a wound he had from a rock and received a share of the spoils; Abū ʿArfaja, one of the allies of the Banū Jaḥjaba; Abū Kabsha, freed-man of the Messenger of God (ṢAAS); Abū Lubāba Bashīr b. ʿAbd al-Mundhir, listed above; Abū Marthad al-Ghanawī Kannāz b. Ḥuṣayn, listed above; Abū Masʿūd al-Badrī ʿUqba b. ʿAmr, listed above; Abū Mulayl b. al-Azʿar b. Zayd al-Awsī.

Division

The total number of Muslims who were present at Badr was 314, including the Messenger of God (ṢAAS).

As al-Bukhārī stated, "ʿAmr b. Khālid related to us, quoting Zuhayr, quoting Abū Isḥāq, 'I heard al-Barāʾ b. ʿĀzib say, "The Companions, God be pleased with them of Muḥammad, God's peace and blessings be upon him, who had been present at Badr, related to me that they were of the number of the Companions of Ṭalūt who crossed the river with him — that is 310 and a few more." Al-Barāʾ stated, "No, by God, no one crossed the river with him who was not a believer!"'"

Al-Bukhārī then related it through Isrāʾīl and Sufyān al-Thawrī, from Abū Isḥāq, from al-Barāʾ in similar terms.

Ibn Jarīr stated, "This is the concensus of the early authorities, that they were 310 men, and a few more."

He also stated, "Maḥmūd related to us, quoting Wahb, from Shuʿba, from Abū Isḥāq, from al-Barāʾ, who said, 'I and Ibn ʿUmar felt outnumbered at the battle of Badr. The Emigrants totalled only appoximately 60, whereas the Helpers were some 240.'"

This is what is given in this account.

Ibn Jarīr stated, "Muḥammad b. ʿUbayd al-Muḥāribī related to me, quoting Abū Mālik al-Jubanī, from al-Ḥajjāj, he being the son of Arṭāt, from al-Ḥakam, from Miqsam, from Ibn ʿAbbās, who said, 'The Emigrants at Badr totalled 70 men. The Helpers totalled 236 men. The bearer of the banner of the Prophet (ṢAAS) was ῾Alī b. Abū Ṭālib. The flag bearer for the Helpers was Sa῾d b. ῾Ubāda.'"

This determines their total to have been 306 men.

Ibn Jarīr stated, "It is said that they totalled 307 men."

I observe that this latter figure may have included the Messenger of God (ṢAAS); the former may have omitted him. But God knows best.

It was given earlier on the authority of Ibn Isḥāq that the Emigrants totalled 83 men, that of Aws there were 61, while Khazraj consisted of 170 men; and he enumerated them.

This is contrary to what al-Bukhārī reported and to what was related from Ibn ῾Abbās. But God knows best.

In the *ṣaḥīḥ* it is reported of Anas that he was asked whether he had been present at Badr. He replied, "And where else would I have been then?"

In the *Sunan* (*The Accepted Norms*) by Abū Dā᾽ūd, there is an account from Sa῾īd b. Manṣūr, from Abū Mu῾āwiya, from al-A῾mash, from Abū Sufyān Ṭalḥa b. Nāfi῾, from Jābir b. ῾Abd Allāh b. ῾Amr b. Ḥarām, who said, "I was drawing water from the well for my companions at the battle of Badr."

These two men are not mentioned by al-Bukhārī or by al-Ḍiyā᾽. But God knows best.

Among those included by Ibn Isḥāq in the total figure given of those who received a share of the spoils of Badr were some who were not actually there but who stayed behind for some good reason. These were the eight or nine men whose names follow: ῾Uthmān b. ῾Affān who stayed behind with Ruqayya, daughter of the Messenger of God (ṢAAS), nursing her until she died. He was given a full share of the spoils; Sa῾īd b. Zayd b. ῾Amr b. Nufayl who went to Syria but was given a full share; Ṭalḥa b. ῾Ubayd Allāh, who was also in Syria, was given a full share; Abū Lubāba Bashīr b. ῾Abd al-Mundhir, who was sent back by the Messenger of God (ṢAAS) from al-Rawḥā᾽ when news came of the departure of the enemy force from Mecca. The Messenger of God (ṢAAS) placed him in charge of Medina and awarded him a full share; al-Ḥārith b. Ḥāṭib b. ῾Ubayd b. Umayya, whom the Messenger of God (ṢAAS) also sent back while *en route*: he received a full share; al-Ḥārith b. al-Ṣimma, who broke his leg at al-Rawḥā᾽ and returned home, received a share. Al-Wāqidī added that he received compensation; Khawwāt b. Jubayr was also not present at the battle but was awarded a full share; Abū al-Ṣiyāḥ b. Thābit, who went forth with the Messenger of God (ṢAAS) but had a splinter of rock injure his foot, received a full share; al-Wāqidī stated, "And Sa῾d Abū Mālik who readied his equipment for battle but died at al-Rawḥā᾽: he was awarded a full share."

Those Muslims who were martyred that day totalled 14 men. Those who were Emigrants were 6 in number, as follows: ῾Ubayda b. al-Ḥārith b. al-Muṭṭalib, who had his leg cut off and died at al-Ṣafrā᾽, God bless him; ῾Umayr b. Abū Waqqāṣ, brother of Saʿd b. Abū Waqqāṣ al-Zuhrī, who was killed by al-ʿĀṣ b. Saʿīd, he being a youth of 16. It is said that the Messenger of God (ṢAAS) told him to return home because of his youth, but he wept, and was allowed to proceed and so was killed, God bless him: their ally Dhū al-Shimālayn b. ʿAbd ʿAmr al-Khuzāʿī; Ṣafwān b. Bayḍāʾ; ʿĀqil b. al-Bukayr al-Laythī, ally of the Banū ʿAdī; Mihjaʿ, freed-man of ʿUmar b. al-Khaṭṭāb who was the first of the Muslims killed that day.

Of the Helpers, there were eight men killed, as follows: Ḥāritha b. Surāqa who had an arrow shot at him by Ḥabbān b. al-ʿArqala that hit him in the neck and killed him; Muʿawwidh and ʿAwf, the two sons of ʿAfrāʾ; Yazīd b. al-Ḥārith, known as Ibn Fushum; ʿUmayr b. al-Ḥammām; Rāfiʿ b. al-Muʿallā b. Lawdhān; Saʿd b. Khaythama and Mubashshir b. ʿAbd al-Mundhir. May God be pleased with them all.

With the Muslims, as stated above, there were 70 baggage camels.

Ibn Isḥāq stated, "They had two men mounted on horses, one al-Miqdād b. al-Aswad, the name of the horse being Baʿzaja, also known as Sabḥa. The other was ridden by al-Zubayr b. al-ʿAwwām, its name being al-Yaʿsūb.

They had a banner that was carried by Muṣʿab b. ʿUmayr, and two flags, one carried for the Emigrants by ʿAlī b. Abū Ṭālib, the other for the Helpers by Saʿd b. ʿUbāda.

The leader of the council of the Emigrants was Abū Bakr, "the Trusting", while the leader of the council of the Helpers was Saʿd b. Muʿādh.

As for the polytheists' force, the best that can be said of them is that they totalled between 900 and 1,000. ʿUrwa and Qatāda stated that they numbered 930 men.

Al-Wāqidī stated, "They were 930 men."

This figure requires proof. In some of the accounts given above they are stated to have numbered more than 1,000; perhaps such figures include their attendants. But God knows best.

The authentic account given by al-Bukhārī from al-Barāʾ states that 70 of them were killed and 70 were wounded.

This is the majority view. It was because of this that Kaʿb b. Mālik stated in a poem:

> "He set up 70 of them that stank at the watering hole,
> ʿUtba and al-Aswad among them."

Al-Wāqidī stated that there was unanimity on that. Yet this statement is controversial. Mūsā b. ʿUqba and ʿUrwa b. al-Zubayr said the opposite, and they are prime authorities on this. No unanimity can be claimed without their agreement, even though their views are superceded by any authentic tradition. But God knows best.

Ibn Isḥāq and others list the names of those killed and taken captive and the *ḥāfiẓ* al-Ḍiyāʾ compiles these effectively in his work, *al-Aḥkām*.

In the course of the narration of the account it is stated which of them was killed first, he being al-Aswad b. ʿAbd al-Asad al-Makhzūmī. The first of them to take flight was Khālid b. al-Aʿlam al-Khuzāʿī – or al ʿUqaylī – an ally of the Banū Makhzūm. But that did not benefit him since he was captured. It was he who spoke the verse:

"It is not on our heels that our wounds bleed, but on
our feet the blood drips down."

He was not truthful in this!

The first prisoners taken were ʿUqba b. Abū Muʿayṭ and al-Naḍr b. al-Ḥārith. They were taken from the rest of the prisoners and killed stoically before the Messenger of God (ṢAAS). There are two different versions regarding which of them was killed first.

The Messenger of God (ṢAAS) released a group of prisoners without charge or ransom. These included Abū al-ʿĀṣ b. al-Rabīʿ al-Umawī, al-Muṭṭalib b. Ḥuntab b. al-Ḥārith al-Makhzūmī and Ṣayfī b. Abū Rifāʿa, as told above, Abū ʿAzza al-Shāʿir, Wahb b. ʿUmayr b. Wahb al-Jumaḥī, as told above. The rest he required to be ransomed, even including his uncle al-ʿAbbās, and he took more from him than from all the rest in order to give him no preferential treatment for being his uncle. He did this even though the Helpers who had captured him asked him to forgo the ransom for him, a request he refused. He insisted, "Don't let him off a single dirham!"

The ransom levied was variable. The least taken was 400 dirhams; for some 40 *awqiya* of gold was taken. Mūsā b. ʿUqba stated, "400 *awqiya* of gold was taken from al-Abbās."

Some were employed in labour to the value of their ransom; as the Imām Aḥmad stated, quoting ʿAlī b. ʿĀṣim, quoting ʿDāʾūd from ʿIkrima, who quoted Ibn ʿAbbās, as having said, "Some of the prisoners taken at Badr had no ransom money available, so the Messenger of God (ṢAAS) had some of them work off their ransom by teaching the children of the Helpers to write. One day a child came in tears to his mother who asked him what was the matter. He replied, 'My teacher hit me!' She commented, 'The lout! He's seeking blood-revenge for Badr! But, by God, he'll never get it!'"

Aḥmad is alone in giving this, but it accords with the criteria for traditions. This subject has been fully referenced above; and to God goes all praise and credit.

Chapter: On the excellence of those Muslims who were present at Badr.

Al-Bukhārī stated on this subject, "ʿAbd Allāh b. Muḥammad related to us, quoting Muʿāwiya b. ʿAmr, quoting Abū Isḥāq, from Ḥumayd, who said, 'I heard Anas say, "Ḥāritha was struck down at Badr and his mother went to the Messenger of God (ṢAAS) and said, 'O Messenger of God, you know how much Ḥāritha meant to me. If he be in heaven, I will be stoic and resigned; but if it be the other place, then tell me what I ought to do.' He replied, 'Woe unto you if you feel bereaved! Is heaven just one garden? It consists of many; he is in the garden of paradise.'"'"

Al-Bukhārī is alone in giving this *hadīth* through this path.

It is related on a different path from accounts of Thābit and Qatāda from Anas, to the effect that Ḥāritha was an observer and that the words used were, "Your son was awarded the highest paradise."

This provides a fine indication of the special status of those present at Badr, even if not engaged in the middle of the battle or the thick of the fray, but one observing it from a distance. Though merely struck by a stray arrow while drinking from the cistern, his position nevertheless won him that paradise that is the highest of all the gardens, in the very centre of heaven. It is from there that those rivers of heaven gush forth for which the law-giving Prophet (ṢAAS) recommended that his nation make their requests to God.

If this be the reward of such a man, what would such be for those who actually faced an enemy three times their own number?

Al-Bukhārī and Muslim both recounted, from Isḥāq b. Rāhawayh, from ʿAbd Allāh b. Idrīs, from Ḥuṣayn b. ʿAbd al-Raḥmān, from Saʿd b. ʿUbayda, from Abū ʿAbd al-Raḥmān al-Sulamī, from ʿAlī b. Abū Ṭālib, the story of Ḥātib b. Abū Baltaʿa and his despatch of the latter to the people of Mecca in the year of the conquest, and how ʿUmar sought the permission of the Messenger of God (ṢAAS) to strike off his head for having betrayed God, His Messenger and the believers. He responded, "He was present at Badr; do you realize that God looked down at those who took part at Badr and said, 'Do whatever you wish, for I have forgiven you!'"

Al-Bukhārī's text reads, "Is he not of those at Badr? Perhaps God looked down on those present there and said, 'Do whatever you wish, for I have guaranteed you heaven, and I have forgiven you.' Tears came to the eyes of ʿUmar, and he said, 'God and his Messenger know best.'"

Muslim related from Qutayba, from al-Layth, from Abū al-Zubayr, from Jābir, that a slave belonging to Ḥātib went to complain to the Messenger of God (ṢAAS) about his master, saying, "O Messenger of God, Ḥātib will certainly go to hell!" The Messenger of God (ṢAAS) replied, "You lie; he will not go there! He was present at Badr and at al-Ḥudaybiyya."

Imām Aḥmad stated, "Sulaymān b. Dāʾūd related to us, quoting Abū Bakr b. ʿAyyāsh; and al-Aʿmash related to me, from Abū Sufyān, from Jābir, who said, "The Messenger of God (ṢAAS) stated, 'No man who was present at Badr or al-Ḥudaybiyya will go to hell!'"

Aḥmad was alone in giving this, but it accords with the norms established by Muslim.

Imām Aḥmad stated that Yazīd related to him, quoting Ḥammād b. Salama, from ʿĀṣim b. Abū al-Nujūd, from Abū Ṣāliḥ, from Abū Hurayra who quoted the Prophet (ṢAAS) as saying, "God looked down at those present at Badr and said, 'Do what you wish, for I have forgiven you.'"

Abū Dāʾūd related it from Aḥmad b. Sinān and Mūsā b. Ismāʿīl, both of them quoting Yazīd b. Hārūn.

Al-Bazzār related in his *musnad*,[75] "Muḥammad b. Marzūq related to us, quoting Abū Ḥudhayfa, quoting ʿIkrima, from Yaḥyā b. Abū Kathīr, from Abū Salama, from Abū Hurayra, who said, 'The Messenger of God (ṢAAS) stated, "I certainly hope that no one who was present at Badr goes to hell, if God wills it so."'"

Al-Bazzār then commented, "We know of no other line of transmission of this *ḥadīth* from Abū Hurayra other than this."

I comment that al-Bazzār alone gives this *ḥadīth*, and the other authorities did not cite it. It does accord with the criteria for *ṣaḥīḥ* traditions. But God knows best.

Al-Bukhārī stated, in his chapter on the presence of the angels at Badr, "Isḥāq b. Ibrāhīm related to us, quoting Jarīr, from Yaḥyā b. Saʿīd, from Muʿādh b. Rifāʿa b. Rāfiʿ al-Zurqī, from his father who was present at Badr, who said, 'Gabriel came to the Prophet (ṢAAS) and asked him, "How do you view those of you who were present at Badr?" He replied, "As among the very finest Muslims" or he used some such phrase.

"He (Gabriel?) then stated, 'And likewise those of the angels who were present at Badr.'"

Al-Bukhārī alone gives this *ḥadīth*.

ON THE ARRIVAL OF ZAYNAB, DAUGHTER OF THE MESSENGER OF GOD (ṢAAS), AS AN EMIGRANT FROM MECCA TO MEDINA A MONTH AFTER THE BATTLE OF BADR IN FULFILLMENT OF THE CONDITION PLACED UPON HER HUSBAND BY THE PROPHET (ṢAAS).

Ibn Isḥāq stated, "When Abū al-ʿĀṣ returned to Mecca, he having been released, as related above, the Messenger of God (ṢAAS) sent for Zayd b. Ḥāritha and a Helper and told them, 'Go to the Yaʾjūj valley and stay there until Zaynab passes by, then bring her to me.'

"They left and took up their position, it being at that time approximately one month after the battle of Badr.

"When Abū al-ʿĀṣ reached Mecca he ordered Zaynab to join her father and she went off to equip herself for the journey."

Ibn Isḥāq continued, "ʿAbd Allāh b. Abū Bakr related to me as follows, 'I was told that Zaynab said, "While I was getting things ready Hind, daughter of ʿUtba, met me and said, 'O daughter of Muḥammad, haven't I heard that you are planning to join your father?' 'It wasn't my idea,' I told her, and she commented, 'Well then, cousin, don't do it; but if you need anything to take on the trip or money to reach your father, I can provide it. Don't be reluctant with me, for women don't let such matters come between them, as men do.' I really thought she would do as she had said, but I was afraid of her and denied I had any such plans."'"

---

75. A collection of traditions arranged by lines of their transmission.

Ibn Isḥāq went on, "So she continued making plans and when she was ready her husband's brother Kināna b. al-Rabīʿ brought a camel which she mounted and he, taking his bow and his quiver, led her away, she riding in a howdah and it being daytime. Some of the Quraysh men discussed this and followed after her, catching up with her at Dhū Ṭuwā. The first man to reach her was Habbār b. al-Aswad b. al-Muṭṭalib b. Asad b. ʿAbd al-ʿUzzā al-Fihrī. He scared her with his spear as she was there in the howdah and because, as they claim, she was pregnant at the time, she suffered a miscarriage. Her brother-in-law then knelt down and took the arrows from his quiver, saying, 'By God, if any man comes near me, I'll put an arrow into him!' The men drew away from him.

"Then Abū Sufyān arrived with some other Quraysh leaders and said, 'Put down your arrows so we can talk with you.' He did so and Abū Sufyān drew near him and said, 'You have not done well. You came forth with a woman openly, going over peoples' heads, even though you're aware of the injury and damage done us by Muhammad. When you took away his daughter, openly and regardless of anyone else, the people thought this was due to the humiliation we have undergone, and that this reflected our weakness and incapacity. I swear we don't want to keep her from her father and we're not after revenge, but you'd better return with the woman until the talk dies down and everyone says we have brought her back. Then you can secretly take her away to her father.' And so he did."

Ibn Isḥāq related that Hind spoke the following verse criticizing those men who brought Zaynab back to Mecca,

> "In peacetime, they're wild young asses, fearless and
> violent, but in war they're like women having periods!"

"She is also said to have spoken this line to those who returned from Badr after some of their force had been killed."

Ibn Isḥāq went on, "Zaynab stayed there for some days until the gossip had subsided and then Kināna conducted her away by night and delivered her over to Zayd b. Ḥāritha and his companion. They then took her by night to the Messenger of God (ṢAAS)."

Al-Bayhaqī related in the *Dalāʾil* (*The Signs*), giving a path of transmission through ʿUmar b. ʿAbd Allāh b. ʿUrwa b. al-Zubayr, from ʿUrwa, quoting ʿĀʾisha, the story of Zaynab's departure from Mecca and being brought back and having a miscarriage. His account relates that the Messenger of God (ṢAAS) then sent Zayd b. Ḥāritha off with a ring of his that she could use to arrive to him. Zayd then presented it to a shepherd from Mecca who gave the ring to Zaynab. When she saw it she recognized it and asked him who had given it to him, and he replied that it was someone on the outskirts of Mecca. Zaynab then left Mecca by night and rode behind Zayd who brought her to Medina.

(The account states), "The Messenger of God (ṢAAS) used to say, 'She was the best of my daughters who suffered on my account.'

"This comment reached ʿAlī b. al-Ḥusayn b. Zayn al-ʿĀbidīn, who then went to ʿUrwa and asked him, 'What is this *ḥadīth* I hear you have been relating?' ʿUrwa replied, 'By God, I really wouldn't diminish Fāṭima's reputation for all the world, and moreover, I'll never relate that again!'"

Ibn Isḥāq stated, "On that subject, it was either ʿAbd Allāh b. Rawāḥa or Abū Khaythama, brother of the Banū Sālim b. ʿAwf" -- Ibn Hishām said it was Abū Khaythama -- "who spoke the following verses,

> 'There has reached me unimaginable information about
> Zaynab's evil, terrible treatment by them.
> But by their expelling her over a battle, there being a
> fierce war between us, Muḥammad was not disgraced.
> By his alliance with Ḍamḍam and by making war on us,
> Abū Sufyān has earned only spite and regret,
> We bound his son ʿAmr and the man pledged to him in
> strong, well-wrought fetters,
> I swore we will never lack forces well-trained and
> numerous with which
> We will terrify the heathen Quraysh, attacking them
> again and again, placing muzzles over their noses and
> branding them,
> We will expel them up into Najd and Nakhla, and if they
> descend we will follow down on horse and foot,
> For ever, our forces never going astray; we will make
> them follow in the tracks of ʿĀd and Jurhum.
> Those who did not obey Muḥammad will regret their
> actions and how they will repent indeed!
> Tell Abū Sufyān, if you do meet him, "If you do not
> accept Islam and bow down sincerely,
> Then welcome that disgrace soon coming to you in this
> life, and that mantle of tar for ever upon you in hell!"'"

Ibn Isḥāq stated, "The 'man pledged' to Abū Sufyān referred to by the poet was ʿĀmir b. al-Ḥaḍramī." Ibn Hishām stated, "It was really ʿUqba b. ʿAbd al-Ḥārith b. al-Ḥaḍramī; ʿAmr b. al-Ḥaḍramī was killed at Badr."

Ibn Isḥāq stated, "Yazīd b. Abū Ḥabīb related to me, from Bukayr b. ʿAbd Allāh b. al-Ashajj, from Sulaymān b. Yasār, from Abū Isḥāq al-Dawsī, from Abū Hurayra, who said, 'The Messenger of God (ṢAAS) sent out a raiding party of which I was one, and told us, "If you capture Habbār b. al-Aswad and the other man who caught up with Zaynab, then burn them in fire!"

"'The next day he sent us a message saying, "I told you to burn those two men if you took them. But then I saw that no one should burn anyone by fire except God, Almighty and Glorious is He; so if you take them, then kill them both."'"

Ibn Isḥāq alone gave this *ḥadīth*, which conforms to criteria of the *ṣaḥīḥ* collections, though not cited therein.

Al-Bukhārī stated, "Qutayba related to us, quoting al-Layth, from Bukayr, from Sulaymān b. Yasār, from Abū Hurayra, who said, 'The Messenger of God (ṢAAS) sent us on a mission and told us, "If you should find so-and-so and so-and-so, then burn them in the fire." Later, as we were about to leave, he told us, "I ordered you to burn them in the fire; but only God punishes by the fire, so if you find them, execute them."'"

Ibn Isḥāq related that Abū al-ʿĀṣ remained an unbeliever in Mecca while Zaynab resided with her father in Medina. This was the situation until, shortly before the conquest (of Mecca) Abū al-ʿĀṣ left on a business trip on behalf of Quraysh. On his way back from Syria a raiding party met and overcame his caravan, and took all they had, though he escaped. He then went by night to his wife Zaynab and asked protection from her, which she gave him.

"When, next morning, the Messenger of God (ṢAAS) went forth for the prayer and spoke the words, *Allāhu Akbar*, God is most Great! and the people repeated this, someone cried out from the women's ranks, "O people, I have given protection to Abū al-ʿĀṣ b. al-Rabīʿ!"

"When the Messenger of God (ṢAAS) had finished the prayer, he turned to the worshippers and asked, 'Did you hear what I heard?' 'Yes, we did,' they answered. He then said, 'I swear by Him who holds the soul of Muḥammad in His hands, I heard nothing of this until I heard it when you did. And the lowest ranked Muslim may give protection on behalf of all.'

"He then went to his daughter Zaynab and said to her, 'Daughter, treat him with honour; but let him not come close to you, for you are not lawful to him.' The Messenger of God (ṢAAS) then sent word that what had been taken from him should be returned, and they did so, keeping nothing back.

"Abū al-ʿĀṣ then took it and returned with it to Mecca. There he paid off each person to whom he had a debt, making sure that he had omitted no one. He asked them, 'Quraysh, do I owe any of you money you have not yet received?' They responded, 'No, may God reward you well! We have found you to be fair and honourable.'

"He then said, 'I now bear witness that there is no god but God and that Muḥammad is His servant and His Messenger. I swear that the only thing that prevented my accepting Islam while I was with him was my concern that you would think that I was doing so only to appropriate your property. God having returned it to you and I being free of it, I now accept Islam.'

"He then returned to the Messenger of God (ṢAAS)."

Ibn Isḥāq stated, "Dāʾūd b. al-Ḥusayn related to me, from ʿIkrima, from Ibn ʿAbbās, who said, 'The Messenger of God (ṢAAS) returned Zaynab to her former marriage without further ceremony."

This *ḥadīth* was related by Imām Aḥmad, Abū Dāʾūd al-Tirmidhī and Ibn Mājah from an account given by Ibn Isḥāq. Al-Tirmidhī stated, "There is nothing wrong with its chain of authorities."

However, we do not know the provenance of this *hadīth*. It probably derived from the memory of Dā²ūd b. al-Ḥuṣayn. Al-Suhaylī stated, "As far as I know, none of the legal scholars vouched for it."

In one reading the words used are, "and the Messenger of God (ṢAAS) returned her to him after six years." And in another, "after two years, by the first marriage." Ibn Jarīr related it in this form. Yet another reading states, "he did not effect a marriage."

This *hadīth* has caused difficulties for many scholars. Their basic premise is that if a woman is a Muslim while her husband is an unbeliever, and this is the situation before the consummation, then the disunion should occur immediately. If, however, this occurs after the consummation of the marriage, then he ought to wait out the *ʿidda*[76] period. If he should accept Islam during that period then her marriage to him would continue. If he had not accepted Islam by the time that period had concluded, then her marriage would be dissolved.

Zaynab, God bless her, had become a Muslim when the Messenger of God (ṢAAS) received his mission, and emigrated one month after Badr. Muslim women were declared forbidden to polytheists in the year of Ḥudaybiyya, 6 AH, while Abū al-ʿĀṣ accepted Islam before the conquest (of Mecca) in 8 AH.

Therefore those who state that the Messenger of God (ṢAAS) returned her to him after six years, that is from the date of her emigration, are correct. And those who say it was after two years, that is two years after Muslim women were forbidden to polytheists, are also correct.

By any calculation it is obvious that the conclusion of her *ʿidda* period would have occurred during this period which was at least two years, or thereabouts, following the forbidding of Muslim women to unbelievers, and so the question remains how he could have returned her to him by the first marriage.

Some suggest that it is conceivable that her *ʿidda* period had not ended, and that this story relates to an oath that must be presumed. Some scholars oppose this *hadīth* with the previous one related by Aḥmad, al-Tirmidhī, and Ibn Mājah, from one of al-Ḥajjāj b. Arṭā², from ʿAmr b. Shuʿayb, from his father, from his grandfather, which has the Messenger of God (ṢAAS) returning his daughter to Abū al-ʿĀṣ b. al-Rabīʿ after a new dowry and a new wedding ceremony.

Imām Aḥmad stated, "This *hadīth* is weak and unfounded, and al-Ḥajjāj did not hear it from ʿAmr b. Shuʿayb, but rather from Muḥammad b. ʿUbayd Allāh al-ʿArzamī. And the *ahadīth* of al-ʿArzamī are worthless. The truth is that which related that the Prophet (ṢAAS) affirmed her in her first marriage."

Al-Dārquṭnī maintained the same, saying, "This *hadīth* lacks foundation; it is the *hadīth* of Ibn ʿAbbās that is correct, namely, that the Messenger of God (ṢAAS) returned her to him by the first marriage."

---

76. The period of waiting prescribed for a woman in Islamic law between the conclusion of one marriage and the commencement of another.

Al-Tirmidhī stated, "This *hadīth* has a controversial chain of authorities. Scholars therefore maintain that when a woman accepts Islam, and her husband does so later, then he is entitled to reconcile with her during the *ʿidda* period. This is the view of Mālik, al-Awzaʿī, al-Shāfiʿī, Aḥmad and Isḥāq. Others state that it is obvious that her *ʿidda* period was over. And that those who relate his having renewed her marriage are on weak grounds."

Regarding the case of Zaynab and the above circumstances, here is evidence that if a woman accepts Islam and her husband becomes a Muslim later, her *ʿidda* period having expired, then her marriage is not thereby nullified. It becomes a matter of choice whether she wishes to marry someone else or to bide her time and wait for her husband to accept Islam, whenever that might be. And she will still be his wife if she has not remarried.

There is force and good in this from the legal viewpoint. But God knows best.

Testimony in favour of this is given by al-Bukhārī when he states, "Regarding the marriage of non-believing women who become Muslims and the period of their *ʿidda*, Ibrāhīm b. Mūsā related to us, quoting Hishām, from Ibn Jarīḥ, from ʿAṭāʾ, from Ibn ʿAbbās, that the polytheists had two different kinds of relationship with the Messenger of God (ṢAAS) and the believers, depending upon whether they were enemies fighting and being fought or those with whom there was a mutual non-aggression pact. If a woman were to leave the declared enemy, she could not become engaged until she had had a period and become cleansed. Once cleansed, marriage to her would be permitted. If her husband were to leave (polytheism) before she remarried, then she could be returned to him. If slaves, whether male or female, should leave polytheism, then they would become free and would have the same rights as other Emigrants."

He then quoted from reliable authorities accounts similar to the *hadīth* of Mujāhid.

This is what he stated, to the letter.

His statement, "if a woman were to leave the declared enemy she could not become engaged until she had had a period and had become cleansed" necessitates that she be considered free after one period, not three menses; one group of authorities accepts this view.

And his statement, "if her husband were to leave polytheism before she remarried, then she could be returned to him," necessitates that even if he left after her being considered free, following the *ʿidda* period, that she would be returned to her first husband provided she had not married someone else. This is clearly the case for Zaynab, daughter of the Prophet (ṢAAS), and this is accepted by some scholars. But God knows best.

Section: Verses composed about the glorious battle of Badr.

These include the following given by Ibn Isḥāq quoting Ḥamza b. ʿAbd al-Muṭṭalib. Ibn Hishām declared these verses inauthentic:

"Did you not see one of time's great wonders? And to
destiny there are causes clear to see.
It was nothing but a people destroying themselves,
perishing by advising towards disrespect and disbelief,
One evening they went forth with their forces towards
Badr, being fate's pawns destined for its water hole.
We had sought for the caravan, desiring nothing else,
but they advanced towards us and destiny made us meet.
And when we clashed we did not wish to retreat but only
to strike with well-made blades,
And to strike off heads with their edges, weapons that
shone as they made their mark.
We left the evil ʿUtba lying there, and Shayba among
the dead who dropped into the pit.
And ʿAmr fell dead among those of their guard who
fell, and the clothes of mourning women were rent for ʿAmr,
The clothes of women of Luʾayy b. Ghālib, noble women,
shedding tears more abundantly than the Fihr.
Those were people killed in their error, and they
abandoned a banner not brought there for victory,
The banner of error, whose forces Satan was leading; he
betrayed them – the evil one engages in deception.
He told them, having seen the matter clearly, 'I am
quit of you. I have no endurance today.
And I see what you do not; I fear God's punishment,
and God has power.'
He led them to doom and they were embroiled, for he had
knowledge unknown to them.
On the morning of the battle at the well they were a
thousand strong, while we were 300, shining like fine young
horses
Among us were God's forces, helping us at that place
whose reputation will always be famous.
Gabriel attacked them beneath our banner in that battle
where their destiny would come."

Ibn Isḥāq also quoted their reply composed by al-Ḥārith b. Hishām, but we have
deliberately omitted this.

ʿAlī b. Abū Ṭālib spoke the following verses, though these are disputed by Ibn
Hishām:

"Did you not see that God put His Messenger to the
test, as one tests someone well-loved, respected and good,
By which He reduced the unbelievers to humiliation;
they encountered the shame of capture and death,
And so the Messenger of God's victory was glorious;
God's Messenger was sent with justice.

He brought a *furqān*, clear evidence, from God, its
verses clear to all of intelligence,
Some believed in that and were convinced, becoming –
praise be to God – fully united,
While others denied and were confused and God on His
throne compounded their agitation.
At the battle of Badr He delivered them over to His
Messenger, giving him a raging force, their actions superb,
Their hands bearing and wielding fine swords that they
had furbished, smoothed and polished.
Many young, brave warriors they have felled, as well as
others mature and courageous,
Wakeful the eyes of their women mourning them, their
tears flowing fast and slow.
In bereavement they weep for ʿUtba the misguided and
for his son, lamenting for Shayba and Abū Jahl.
And for him whose leg was severed,[77] and for Ibn
Judʿān, garbed in mourning clothes, dry-mouthed, grieving,
A group of the men dropped into the pit at Badr, men
who had been unselfish both in battle and in times of famine.
Falsehood had called to them and they had answered, for
falsehood has paths easily travelled.
And so they sacrificed before the house of hell, far
removed now from mischief-making and enmity, in its deepest
depths."

Ibn Isḥāq also gives their response to these verses, but we have deliberately
omitted them here.

Kaʿb b. Mālik stated,

"I was amazed at what God did, and God has power to do
what He wills, there being none able to overcome God.
He had decreed that at Badr we would confront a group
who had acted in evil; the path of evil leads men to doom.
They had so gathered and assembled their allies that
their force was huge,
And they came at us, none else, all of Kaʿb and ʿAmir
united,
While with us was the Messenger of God, with Aws about
him, they providing him a strong, victorious fortress,
With the Banū al-Najjār under his banner, advancing in
their flexible armour, while the dust flew.
When we clashed with them all our warriors were heroic,
stoic and protective of their comrades.

---

77. The reference is presumably to al-Aswad b. ʿAbd al-Asad, whose leg was cut off at the cistern.

We saw that there is no Lord but God, and that the
Messenger of God was making truth plain,
Our light, naked swords were like firebrands that
someone wielded before your eyes,
With them we destroyed their force and they scattered,
and those who were evil met their doom.
Abū Jahl was cast down dead upon his face and I left
ʿUtba staggering.
Shayba and al-ʿTaymī I left dead in the tumult, and all
of these had disbelieved in Him of the throne,
And so they became fuel for fire in its abode (hell),
and all who disbelieve are moving towards hell.
It will consume them, its fires stoked with molten
metal and rock.
The Messenger of God had told them to come forward, but
they had turned away, calling him a sorcerer.
All this for a purpose God had willed, that they perish
by it; and there is no diverting any command God decreed."

Kaʿb spoke the following verses about the battle of Badr:

"Has it reached Ghassān, in their far-off abode – and
the best to tell of matters are those who know them well –
That Maʿadd, cruel in their enmity, their young and
mature alike, have attacked us,
Because we worshipped God, hoping for none but Him and
for the gardens of paradise, when its leader came to us,
A Prophet, a man with a patrimony of honour and
inherited qualities of veracity fed by their roots.
They advanced and so did we, meeting like lions, their
roaring impossible to quiet.
We struck them until they fell in our attacks so that
the greatest of Luʾayy stank to the nose.
They fled, our sharp swords felling them, and we cared
not whether it be their ancilliaries or their core forces."

Kaʿb also spoke the following verses,

"By your father's life, O two sons of Luʾayy, regret
your pride and haughtiness,
Now that your horsemen circled at Badr but did not
persist when the forces met.
We came to it with God's light illuminating and
alleviating from us the obscurity of the shadows,
The Messenger of God leading us with orders from God,
the ultimate decision-maker.
Your horsemen did not gain mastery at Badr and did not
bring back to you any solution,

So do not rush to Abū Sufyān and watch the finest of
horses come up from Kudā',
By God's assistance – with that of the Holy Spirit
(Gabriel) and Michael included – Oh, the best of the
notables!"

Ḥassān b. Thābit spoke the following verses, though Ibn Hishām said they are
also attributed to 'Abd Allāh b. al-Ḥārith al-Sahmī:

"A man wearing a fine, light chain-mail as an
undergarment led them, a man steady of temperament,
effective, no coward he.
I mean the Messenger of the God of creation, who
favoured him above all men in his piety and goodness,
You claimed you would protect your valuables and
insisted that Badr's waters could not be reached.
Then we did reach it, not heeding your words, and we
drank our fill, not stinting ourselves,
Gripping that unbreakable rope of God stretched out and
well-made,
With us was the Messenger of God, with us was the truth
we will follow until death, and unlimited help,
Trustworthy, effective, a light-giving star, a full
moon illuminating all men of valour."

Ḥassān b. Thābit also said,

"Would that the people of Mecca knew how we destroyed
the unbelievers in their hour of reckoning,
We killed their leaders on our battlefield and when
they retired their backs were broken,
We killed Abū Jahl and 'Utba before him, along with
Shayba falling with hands outstretched for sacrifice.
We killed Suwayd, then 'Utba after him, and Ṭu'ma too
as the dust flew,
How many men we killed of nobility, leadership, respect
and good repute among their people,
We left them for yelping animals to attend, later to
cook in the hot depths of hell-fire.
I swear, Mālik's horsemen and their attendants were no
defence when we clashed at Badr."

'Ubayda b. al-Ḥārith b. 'Abd al-Muṭṭalib spoke the following verses about Badr,
concerning the loss of his leg in the competition that he, Ḥamza and 'Alī fought
with 'Utba, Shayba and al-Walīd b. 'Utba. Ibn Hishām considered these verses
inauthentic:

"A battle will tell the people of Mecca about us, one
in which even those far away embarked upon,

About ʿUtba as he fled, and Shayba after him, and
ʿUtba's first-born also had no joy in it.
      Though you cut off my leg, I am a Muslim still and by
it will earn a life close to God,
      With the houris like statues, set aside at the highest
heaven for those up high,
      For that I have exchanged a life the best of which I
have known, and I rushed to it even though losing those
close to me.
      The All-Merciful has honoured me by his generosity with
the gown of Islam that covers over my faults,
      And to fight them was not distasteful to me on that
morning when men called forth their peers to fight.
      When they asked the Prophet, he wanted none but us, we
three, so we answered the call,
      We confronted them like lions, flourishing our spears,
fighting for the All-Merciful those who disobeyed.
      Our feet did not leave our stand, we three, until they
met their fate."

Ibn Isḥāq stated, "Ḥassān b. Thābit also spoke the following verses criticizing
al-Ḥārith b. Hishām for fleeing at Badr and abandoning his people and not fighting for them:

      'A lovely woman disturbs your heart while you sleep,
      reviving you while lying there with cool, smiling lips,
      Like musk mixed with rain-water, or fine, vintage wine,
      like blood from sacrifice,
      Her buttocks high, their cheeks rising, carefree and
      not prone to oath-swearing.
      Her body is built at the waist as though boneless, when
      she sits it becomes like a mortar of marble,
      She is seductive as she moves to her bed, her body
      gorgeous, her figure superb.
      In daytime I never tire of thinking of her, while at
      night my dreams of her excite me.
      I swore I would forget her and think of her no more
      until my bones disappear in the grave.
      Could a generous woman reproach for foolishness? I
      reject being blamed for my passion.
      She came to me early, at dawn when I was newly awake,
      life's cares just intruding upon me.
      She claimed that a man suffers all his life from a lack
      of a plentitude of camels.
      If you were lying in what you told me, then may you
      avoid the lot of al-Ḥārith b. Hishām.

He left his beloved ones to fight for them, and fled by
giving his steed free rein.
It outstripped the fine horses in the desert, with the
speed of a rock on a rope descending a well,
Joyfully it sped away with him, while his friends lay
prostrate there in a terrible state.
His brothers and people locked in battle in which God
was giving his support to the Muslims.
God fulfils His purpose, and so the war, its flames
flaring on them, ground them to dust.
If not for God and the horses' racing, they would have
left him for the beasts, and for them to tread underfoot.
There were some who were captive and firmly bound, like
an eagle defending itself against the spears.
And others who lay prostrate, answering no call, until the
highest mountains might cease to exist.
In shame and clear humiliation when he saw the swords'
blades driving off all the chiefs,
Swords held by noblemen, great lords whose ancestry lines
can be traced and found blemish-free,
Swords that flash like lightning when striking iron in the
gloom beneath the rain clouds.'"

Ibn Hishām stated, "We have omitted three verses from the ending of the above
poem since I found them obscene."

He went on, "He was answered by al-Ḥārith b. Hishām, brother of Abū Jahl
ʿAmr b. Hishām, who spoke the following verses:

'The people well know that I did not abandon their battle
until they had covered my horse with red foam.
I knew that if I battled on alone I would be killed, yet my
martyrdom would not harm my enemy.
And so I left them, my friends among them, intending to
bring them punishment some other terrible day.'"

Ḥassān also said,

"O Ḥārith, you acted badly, not like someone to be relied
upon, at the battle, at the time for noble valour,
When you rode a swift-footed thoroughbred, fast and long-
flanked.
Your people left behind you, you having quit the battle,
hoping for escape when it was no time to leave.
Had you not compassion for your brother, lying there
pierced with spears and plundered?
The Almighty had hastened to him, destroying his force
in base dishonour and terrible punishment."

Ḥassān also spoke the following,

"Quraysh learned at Badr, that day of captive-taking
and terrible fighting,
That we were the war's champions at that battle of Abū
al-Walīd, when the long spears clashed,
We fought both sons of Rabī'a when they came at us
dressed in double suits of chain-mail,
With which Ḥakīm fled on that day when the Banū
al-Najjār wheeled in battle like lions,
Whereupon the Fihr forces ran away, little Ḥarith
giving them up from a distance,
You met humiliation and death that came quickly,
penetrating beneath the jugular.
All the force fled together, caring nothing for their
inherited honour."

Hind, daughter of Uthātha b. 'Ibād b. al-Muṭṭalib, spoke the following elegy for
'Ubayda b. al-Ḥārith b. al-Muṭṭalib:

"It was 'Ubayda who ensured glory, leadership and a
well-bred gentility full of intelligence and wisdom,
Weep for him, a towering mountain visible from afar, for
guests and for widows bent over dishevelled infants.
Mourn him for the masses every winter when the sky's
horizons turn red with the drought,
Mourn him for the orphans when the storms blow, for
whom he would heat a pot that would boil and foam,
 And if the light of its fires died down, he would
relight it with cut sticks,
Mourn him for those who would knock during the night,
or those seeking food, or the travellers he would comfort."

Al-Umawī stated in his work on the *maghāzī*, the early military expeditions,
"Sa'īd b. Quṭn related to me as follows: "Ātika, daughter of 'Abd al-Muṭṭalib
spoke the following verses about the visions she saw, and in commemoration of
the battle of Badr:

"Were my visions not true, now that a fugitive fleeing
from the force brings you its interpretation?
He saw and brought you the certainty he had seen with
his own eyes; swords striking do not lie.
You spoke; I did not lie to you, rather it was those
who lied who charged me with lying.
He came back in flight for fear of death, Ḥakīm,
knowing no other way out.
Indian swords were there in front of your heads, along
with spears glinting and victorious,
As though flames of fire on their edges when the raging
lions charged.

I swear by my father, the day of the rendezvous with
Muhammad, when with the help of wars the upper flanks were
bitten,
Your souls were drawn forth with whetted swords in
fighting as the South winds draw the clouds along.
Many were the covetous who were chilled by his swords,
while stable watering-holes were made to shake.
What does it mean for those slain to be in the pit and for
their like to be kept captive by my cousin and not to fight,
They being like women? Or did God bring some end to their
spirits that took effect, for an end does come.
How did Muhammad's cousins feel when they met in battle?
Warfare certainly brings its trials.
Did he not surprise you with blows that would shock even a
coward, making stars appear in full day?
I swear that if they repeat this we will overwhelm them
with oceans of death through which the horsemen will race,
As though the light of the sun is the reflection of the edges
of their swords, emitting light in conjunction and as a covering.""'"

ʿĀtika also spoke the following, according to al-Umawī's account,

"Why could you not persevere against the Prophet
Muhammad at Badr?
Who is able to overcome, with true perseverence, the tumult
(of war)?
You did not respond to the thin sword blades sharp in the
hands of the believers,
You failed to stand firm against the swords, until you
suffered but little at the hands of the Believers.
You fled in haste, yet heroes do not flee from the weapons'
impact when they do battle.
He brought you what the prophets before him also brought.
And my nephew, that good and truthful man, is certainly not a
poet.
Let it be enough what you have lost from your prophet;
instead, the two tribes of ʿAmr and ʿĀmir are helping him to
victory."

Tālib b. Abū Tālib spoke the following verses in praise of the Messenger of God
(ṢAAS), and in mourning for those of his tribe of Quraysh who were dropped
into the pit. He was still following his people's old religion at that time:

"My eyes send forth floods of tears, weeping for Kaʿb though
seeing them not.
In the battles Kaʿb betrayed one another and fate
overwhelmed them, for they had sinned,

And this day ʿĀmir lament their misfortunes; how I would
wish to see them at hand!

They are my brothers, their parentage above suspicion, and
one under their protection would never be harmed.

Our brothers ʿAbd Shams and Nawfal, may I be your
ransom! Do not excite war between us!

Do not become, following love and friendship, mere tales
you all fill with complaint.

Do you not know how it was with the war of Dāḥis, and that
of Abū Yaksūm when they filled the defile?

Were it not for the protection of God and Him alone, you
would have ended by not defending your people.

We in Quraysh have committed no great sin, but merely
protected the best man who ever trod the earth,

A man of trust and a support in troubles, a man noble in
repute, neither miserly not evil.

Supplicants resort to him, crowding his door, seeking a river
that never fails nor dries up.

By God, my soul will always be sad and ill at ease until you
smite Khazraj full well."

DIVISION

Ibn Isḥāq quoted much fine poetry of the polytheists in which they mourn their
dead at the battle of Badr.

One poem he gives is that of Ḍirār b. al-Khaṭṭāb b. Mirdās, a brother of the
Banū Muḥārib b. Fihr. He eventually accepted Islam; al-Suhaylī wrote in his
work al-*Rawaḍ* (*The Meadows*) about the verses of those poets who later became
Muslims:

"I am amazed at the pride of Aws, for tomorrow fate will
turn against them, and destiny can be foreseen,

And at that of the Banū al-Najjār, though a group were
struck down at Badr, all of whom there being fine men,

Even if some of our men were left there dead, we have
others after them yet to be so left.

Our swift horses will carry us in your midst, O Banū
al Aws, until vengeance quiets our spirits.

Amidst the Banū al-Najjār we will charge, panting
beneath the mail-clad spearsmen.

We will leave corpses with vultures circling above them
and with only their hopes to give them aid.

The women of Yathrib will mourn them who will have
passed sleepless nights there.

And that is because our swords will keep hacking at
them, dripping with the blood of those they struck.

Even though you are victorious at the battle of Badr,
it was only due to Aḥmad, and that is plain, that you won.
　　And due to those fine champions who were his supporters
who gave protection in the heat of battle, with death all
around.
　　Abū Bakr and Ḥamza are counted among them, and ʿAlī
could be named amidst those you remember.
　　It is those men, not those from whose abodes came the
Aws and the Najjār, whom you should vaunt,
　　Rather those whose ancestors were Luʾayy b. Ghālib,
Kaʿb and ʿĀmir, if lineage be considered.
　　It was they, the finest and the most important on the
morning of battle who repelled the cavalry at every fight."

Kaʿb b. Mālik replied to this with his ode given above, which begins:

　　"I was amazed at what God did, and God has power to do
what He wills, there being none able to overcome God."

Ibn Isḥāq stated, "Abū Bakr, his full name being Shaddād b. al-Aswad b. Shuʿūb (and here I comment that al-Bukhārī tells that he had a child by the ex-wife of Abū Bakr, 'the Trusting', after the latter had divorced her, that being when God had made non-believing women forbidden to Muslims. Her name was Umm Bakr) spoke the verses,

　　'Umm Bakr greeted me with peace, but now my people are
gone, can I ever have peace?
　　What of the pit, the pit of Badr, how can there be for
me singers and fine friends with whom to drink?
　　What of the pit, the pit of Badr, how can there be for
me plates piled high with fine meat?
　　What of the grave, the grave of Badr, how many grazing
camels and cattle will you enjoy henceforth?
　　What of the grave, the grave of Badr, and great
ambitions, fine gifts.
　　What of the friends, of that fine man Abū ʿAlī, my
brother of the generous glass and companionship!
　　Were you to see Abū ʿAqīl and the fighters at the Naʿam
pass,
　　Then you would be as distraught as the mother bereft of
a camel newborn,
　　The messenger informs us that we shall live, but what
life is there for corpses and heads?'"[78]

I would comment that al-Bukhārī quoted some of this in his *ṣaḥīḥ* collection to demonstrate the poet's state of mind.

78. Guillaume offers an interesting comment on the word *ṣadaʾ*, here translated as "heads" (plural), relating it to an ancient Arabian belief that an owl-like bird, the *ṣadaʾ* would emerge from the head of a slain man and demand revenge for his death. *Op. cit.* p.353, note 2.

Ibn Isḥāq stated, "Umayya b. Abū al-Ṣalt spoke the following verses expressing his lament for those of Quraysh killed at the battle of Badr:

'Have you not wept over those noble men, sons of
nobles, worthy of praise,
  Mourning like doves on swaying, pliant branches,
  Weeping as they coo softly as they return at night.
  The women who mourn are like them, the hired women
who wail.
  Whoever mourns for them does so in sorrow and whoever
praises them speaks true.
  What chieftains, what great leaders there were at Badr
and al-ʿAqanqal,
  And at Mudāfi al-Barqayn, and at al-Ḥannān by the side
of al-Awāshiḥ,
  Mature men and youthful were there, in nights of
raiding, and strong men too,
  Do you not see what I see, plain for all who look on?
  The Mecca valley has changed, its plains now deserted,
  By every prince and prince's son, pure in friendship,
confident,
  Frequent visitors at the gates of kings, eminent men
defeating the deserts.
  Men of broad necks, tall and well-built, influential
and successful,
  Men who say, do and order all things proper,
  Who serve rich meat piled high above the bread,
  Men who pass around dish after dish after dish big as
pools,
  Not mere nothings for those who are guests, plates not
merely flat,
  Serving guest after guest after guest from huge
platters,
  Men who give as gifts hundreds of the pregnant camels
they own to hundreds of friends,
  Driving the herds of camels over to the others coming
forth from Balādiḥ,
  Their men of nobility having qualities outweighing
other nobles on the scale.
  Like the weights on a scale being held down by the
measurer,
  One group deserted them while they were busy protecting
things open to shame,
  Men who struck blows against the vanguard with their
Indian-made broadswords,
  Their voices hurt me as they cried out, some for water,
others in pain.

> May God reward all the tribes of ʿAli, whether widowed
> or married,
> If they do not attack so fiercely that all the barking
> dogs slink home.
> On horses trained for journeys short or long, their
> heads held high and accompanying the unsubmissive ones.
> Brave men on fine horses as though attacking fierce,
> scowling lions.
> Each combatant meets his foe as though merely walking
> to shake his hand,
> About a thousand or a thousand more, some lancers, some
> in chain-mail.'"

Ibn Hishām stated, "We have omitted from this poetry two lines that impugn the Companions of the Messenger of God, may God be pleased with them."

I would comment that this is the poetry of a man who is feeble-minded and degenerate, a man whose ignorance and limited intelligence led him to praise the polytheists and to damn the believers.

He expressed affection in Mecca for Abū Jahl b. Hishām and other accursed unbelievers and ignorant and insignificant persons, but felt none for God's servant, Messenger and true friend, the pride of mankind, none for him whose face was more luminous than the moon, a man possessed of perfect knowledge, complete intelligence, none for God's trustworthy Companion who is ready to give trust, a man eager for good works and honourable deeds, a man willing to spend thousands and hundreds more in obedience to the Lord of the earth and of the heavens.

And similar praise can be given to the rest of his noble and eminent Companions who emigrated from the abode of disbelief and ignorance to that of knowledge and Islam. May God be pleased with them all as long as light and dark intermingle, and as long as the days and the nights follow one another in succession.

We have omitted many poems quoted by Ibn Isḥāq, God bless him, due to our fear of being long-winded and tiresome. There is enough in the poetry we have given. And to God is all praise and credit.

Al-Umawī has stated in his work on the military expeditions, as follows, "I heard my father say, and Sulaymān b. Arqam related to us, from Ibn Sīrīn, from Abū Hurayra, that the Messenger of God (ṢAAS) expressed forgiveness for the poetry before Islam. Sulaymān said, "Al-Zuhrī reported that, saying, 'He forgave it all except for two odes; one was the words of Umayya in which he recalled those fallen at Badr, and the poem of al-Aʿshā in which he made reference to a man with sunken eyes.'"

This is a strange *ḥadīth*. And this Sulaymān b. Arqam is to be disregarded. But God knows best.

Section: On the expedition against the Banū Sulaym in the second year after the emigration of the Prophet (ṢAAS).

Ibn Isḥāq stated, "The Messenger of God (ṢAAS) had finished with Badr by the end of Ramaḍān or in Shawwāl.

"He remained only seven nights in Medina before he himself conducted an expedition against the Banū Sulaym."

Ibn Hishām stated, "He placed Sibā' b. 'Urfuṭa al-Ghifārī, or Ibn Umm Maktūm, the blind, in charge of Medina."

Ibn Isḥāq stated, "He reached one of their wells at a place called al-Kadr, where he stayed for three days before returning to Medina without engaging in battle. He remained there for the rest of Shawwāl and Dhū al-Qaʿda and it was while he stayed there that he accepted ransom for the majority of the Quraysh captives."

Section: On the expedition against al-Sawīq in Dhū al-Ḥijja that year, it also being known as the expedition to Qarqarat al-Kadr.

Al-Suhaylī stated, "The word *al-qarqara* means 'smooth ground'. The word *al-kadr* refers to a bird whose colours are dingy."

Ibn Isḥāq stated, "According to what I was told by Muḥammad b. Jaʿfar b. al-Zubayr and Yazīd b. Rūmān, as well as by others whose word I do not doubt, from 'Abd Allāh b. Kaʿb b. Mālik, one of the most knowledgeable of the Helpers, that when Abū Sufyān and later the captives of Quraysh returned to Mecca, he swore that he would abstain from intercourse until he had carried out an attack against Muḥammad.

"He therefore went forth with 200 mounted warriors of Quraysh to fulfil his oath. He travelled along the Nejd road and stopped at the head of a water-course into the mountain called Nayb which is approximately one postal stage from Medina.

"From there he went on by night to the Banū al-Naḍīr and called at the home of Ḥuyayy b. Akhṭab. He knocked on the door, but he refused to open up, being afraid. So Abū Sufyān went on to Sallām b. Mishkam, who was at that time the chief of the Banū al-Naḍīr and the custodian of their treasure. He asked to go in and was invited to do so; he was treated as a guest and given wine and food.

"When the night was over he left and returned to his companions, sending some men of Quraysh ahead. They then went on to a place in that vicinity called al-'Urayḍ, where they burnt some young date-palms. They came across one of the Helpers and a man allied to him in a garden there, killed them both and then left again.

"People were warned about them, and the Messenger of God (ṢAAS) left in pursuit."

Ibn Hishām stated, "He left Abū Lubāba Bashīr b. 'Abd al-Mundhir in command of Medina."

Ibn Isḥāq went on, "The Messenger of God (ṢAAS) reached Qarqarat al-Kadr, but then headed back since Abū Sufyān and his companions had eluded him.

"The men with the Messenger of God (ṢAAS) found substantial supplies that the polytheists had discarded to lighten their load. Most of what they left behind was known as *al-sawīq*[79] and this name is therefore associated with this expedition.

"The Muslims asked him whether this would be credited to them as a military expedition, and he said that it would.

"Abū Sufyān composed the following verses about these actions of his and in praise of Sallām b. Mishkam, the Jew:

'I chose one man in Medina to ally with, and I did not
regret it, though I stayed only briefly.
Sallām b. Mishkam gave me refreshment with good wine,
though I was hurried.
When my force turned away I told him, to alleviate his
concern, "Take pleasure in glory and in booty.
Take thought, for these men are the best, pure-bred of
Luʾayy, not of some Jurhum mixed-breed.
What happened here was merely that a rider stayed a
while, one who was hungry but not needy or poor."'"

Section: On the marriage of ʿAlī b. Abū Ṭālib, God be pleased with him, to his wife Fāṭima, daughter of the Messenger of God (ṢAAS).

This took place in 2 AH, following the battle of Badr, according to the account given by al-Bukhārī and Muslim through al-Zuhrī, from ʿAlī b. al-Ḥusayn, from his father al-Ḥusayn b. ʿAlī, from ʿAlī b. Abū Ṭālib, who said, "I had a camel as my share of the spoils of the battle of Badr, the Prophet (ṢAAS) having given me one as my fifth share of what God had provided that day. When I wanted to marry Fāṭima, daughter of the Prophet (ṢAAS), I made an arrangement with a jeweller of the Banū Qaynuqāʿ to travel with me and to get some sweet-smelling rushes. I wanted to sell this to the jewellers and use the proceeds for a wedding feast for my bride. I gathered green fodder, sacks and ropes, having left my two camels tied down beside the house of one of the Helpers. When I had finished gathering things together, I found to my surprise that their humps had been sliced open, their flanks cut and their livers removed. I could scarcely believe my eyes at this sight. I asked who had done this and was told that it might well have been Ḥamza b. ʿAbd al-Muṭṭalib who was there in that house drinking with some of the Helpers, accompanied by his songstress and some friends. She was singing,

'O Ḥamza who cuts down the camels.'

79. This word refers to a mush-like dish made of wheat and barley.

"On hearing this, Ḥamza had jumped up for his sword, sliced open their humps, cut open their sides and removed their livers."

'Alī went on, "So I went off to see the Prophet (ṢAAS) who was with Zayd b. Ḥāritha. He knew something had happened to me and asked what was wrong. I replied by telling him what Ḥamza had done and where he was drinking.

"The Messenger of God (ṢAAS) then called for his cloak, put it on and walked away with myself and Zayd b. Ḥāritha following him. When he reached the house where Ḥamza was, he asked permission to enter and it was given. He set about upbraiding Ḥamza for what he had done, with Ḥamza before him drunk and red-eyed. Ḥamza stared towards the Prophet (ṢAAS) raising his eyes up to his knees, then to his face, whereupon he commented, 'What are you but slaves to my father!'

"The Prophet (ṢAAS) realized he was drunk and so turned on his heels and left, with us following him."

This is the wording of al-Bukhārī in the *Kitāb al-Maghāzī* (*The Book of Military Expeditions*). He also gives the account in several other places in his *ṣaḥīḥ* collection in various versions.

In this there is proof of the information we have given above that the spoils taken at Badr were divided into fives, contrary to what is claimed by Abū 'Ubayd al-Qāsim b. Salām in his book *al-Amwāl* (*Monies*). Therein he states that the revelation concerning division into fives only came thereafter. A number of authorities have disagreed with him in that, including al-Bukhārī and Ibn Jarīr. We have made clear his mistake regarding this in our *Tafsīr* (*Exegesis*) and in our previous comments. But God knows best.

This behaviour of Ḥamza and his companions, God be pleased with them, occurred before wine was prohibited. Indeed, Ḥamza was killed at Uḥud, as will be related, and that event preceded the prohibition of wine. But God knows best.

This *ḥadīth* may be cited as evidence by those who maintain that anything expressed by someone drunk is of no account and without effect in such cases as divorce or the giving of testimony, or such matters, as some scholars have maintained and as is established in the *Kitāb al-Aḥkām* (*The Book of Statutes*).

Imām Aḥmad stated, "Sufyān related to us, from Ibn Abū Najīḥ, from his father, from a man who heard 'Alī say, 'I wanted to seek from the Messenger of God (ṢAAS) my betrothal to his daughter but recognized that I owned nothing. But then I remembered his compassion and his relationship (to me) and so I did ask him to agree to my engagement to her.

"'He replied, "Do you own anything?" "No," I replied. "Where is your Ḥuṭamī chain-mail I gave you on such-and-such an occasion?" he asked. I replied, "At my place." "Well then," he said, "give me that for her." And so I did.'"

Aḥmad relates this similarly in his *ḥadīth* collection, though in his chain of transmission there is one link who is dubious.

Abū Dāʾūd stated, "Isḥāq b. Ismāʿīl al-Ṭāliqānī related to us, quoting ʿAbda, quoting Saʿīd, from Ayyūb, from ʿIkrima, from Ibn ʿAbbās, who said, 'When ʿAlī married Fāṭima, God bless them both, the Messenger of God (ṢAAS) told him, "Give her something." He replied, "I have nothing." "Where is your Huṭamī chain-mail?" he was asked.'"

Al-Nasāʾī related this from Hārūn b. Isḥāq, from ʿAbda b. Sulaymān, from Saʿīd b. Abū ʿUrūba, from an account of Ayyūb al-Sakhtiyānī.

Abū Dāʾūd stated, "Kathīr b. ʿUbayd al-Ḥimṣī related to us, quoting Abū Ḥaywa, from Shuʿayb b. Abū Ḥamza; Ghaylān b. Anas related to me, from the people of Ḥimṣ; and Muḥammad b. ʿAbd al-Raḥmān b. Thawbān related to me, from one of the Companions of the Prophet (ṢAAS) that when ʿAlī married Fāṭima and wanted to consummate the marriage, the Messenger of God (ṢAAS) prevented him from doing so until he gave her something. ʿAlī replied, 'O Messenger of God, I have nothing.' The Messenger of God (ṢAAS) told him, 'Give her your chain-mail.' He did so and then went in to her."

Al-Bayhaqī stated in *al-Dalāʾil* (*The Signs*), "The *ḥāfiz* Abū ʿAbd Allāh informed us, quoting Abū al-ʿAbbās Muḥammad b. Yaʿqūb al-Aṣamm, quoting Aḥmad b. ʿAbd al-Jabbār, quoting Yūnus b. Bukayr, from Ibn Isḥāq, that ʿAbd Allāh b. Abū Najīh related, from Mujāhid, from ʿAlī, who said, 'I did ask the Messenger of God (ṢAAS) to become engaged to Fāṭima. A freed-woman of mine asked, "Did you know that someone has asked the Messenger of God (ṢAAS) for permission to become engaged to Fāṭima?" "No," I replied. "Well," she went on, "she has been asked for; but what prevents you from going to the Messenger of God (ṢAAS) and having him marry you?" I asked her, "Do I own anything with which to get married?" She replied, "If you go to the Messenger of God (ṢAAS) he will marry you."

"'She kept on encouraging me until I did go in to him. When I sat down before him, I was struck dumb, I swear, and could not speak I was so much in awe.

"'The Messenger of God (ṢAAS) then asked me, "What brought you here? Is there something I can do for you?" I remained silent but he said, "Have you perhaps come to become engaged to Fāṭima?" "Yes, I have," I replied. "Do you have something to give her in marriage?" he asked. "No, O Messenger of God, I don't," I replied. He then enquired, "What did you do with the chain-mail I provided for you?"

"'Now I swear by Him who holds ʿAlī's soul in His hand, it was just a Huṭamī chain-mail, not worth four dirhams. I replied, "Yes, I have it." "Then I marry her to you for it; send it to her as her marriage payment," he said. This, then became the dowry paid for Fāṭima, daughter of the Messenger of God (ṢAAS).'"

Ibn Isḥāq stated, "Fāṭima bore to ʿAlī, Ḥasan, Ḥusayn and Muḥsin – the last of whom died young – Umm Kulthūm and Zaynab."

Al-Bayhaqī then related through ʿAṭāʾ b. al-Sāʾib, from his father, from ʿAlī, who said, "The Messenger of God (ṢAAS) gave to Fāṭima as her trousseau a soft gown, a water-skin, and a leather pillow stuffed with sweet-smelling rushes."

Al-Bayhaqī quoted from the *Kitāb al-Maʿrifa* (*The Book of Knowledge*) of Abū ʿAbd Allāh b. Munaddah, that ʿAlī became engaged to Fāṭima one year after the hegira and that he consummated the marriage with her one year thereafter.

I would comment that by that account the consummation took place early in the third year of the hegira. However, it is obvious that the anecdote relating to the two camels must involve the period shortly after the battle of Badr, that is, as we have related, at the end of the year 2 AH. But God knows best.

Section: Reference to a variety of events that occurred in the year 2 AH.

We have given details above about the marriage of the Messenger of God (ṢAAS) to ʿĀʾisha, mother of the believers, God bless her, and have already referred to the famous engagements that had occurred; these accounts include information on the deaths of famous men, both Muslim and polytheist.

Among those who died that year were the martyrs of the battle of Badr. These numbered 14 including both Emigrants and Helpers. Their names have been given above, as well as those of the chiefs of the Quraysh polytheists who numbered 70, as is widely known. Shortly after the battle, Abū Lahab ʿAbd al-ʿUzzā b. ʿAbd al-Muṭṭalib, God damn him, died. As is told above.

When the good news was brought to the Muslims of Medina by Zayd b. Ḥāritha and ʿAbd Allāh b. Rawāḥa concerning how God had afflicted the polytheists and given victory to the believers, they found Ruqayya, daughter of the Messenger of God (ṢAAS), had died and they were levelling the soil on her grave.

Her husband ʿUthmān b. ʿAffān had stayed behind to nurse her, on the orders of the Prophet (ṢAAS). This is why he was given a share of the spoils of Badr and also assured his reward from God at Judgement Day.

ʿUthmān thereafter married her sister Umm Kulthūm, daughter of the Messenger of God (ṢAAS); this is why he was known as *dhū al-nūrayn*, "he of the two lights". It is said that no man but him was married consecutively to two daughters of a prophet. May God be pleased with him and make him content.

That year the direction of prayer was changed, as we have related above. And there was an addition made to the prayer performed when in residence, as explained above.

That year fasting was prescribed, that of Ramaḍān, as related. The *zakāt dhāt al-nuṣab* and the *zakat al-fiṭr*[80] were imposed at that time.

That year the polytheists and Jews of Medina, among the Banū Qaynuqāʿ, the Banū al-Naḍīr and the Banū Qurayẓa who lived there, along with the Jews of the Banū Ḥāritha, pretended co-operation with the Muslims. A large number of the

---

80. The *zakāt dhāt al-nusab* (plural of a singular noun *nisab*) is a tax payable on certain categories of possessions, provided the tax-payer possessed a defined minimum (*nisāb*) value of these. The *zakat al-fiṭr* is an obligatory payment of provisions by all Muslims of means to the poor at the end of the fasting month of Ramaḍān.

polytheists and Jews professed Islam while secretly being hypocrites. Some did remain as they had been, while others were totally indecisive, tending first this way then the other, as God has depicted them in His Book.

Ibn Jarīr stated, "In that year the Messenger of God (ṢAAS) wrote his *al-maʿāqil*[81] which were kept attached to his sword."

Ibn Jarīr stated, "It is said that al-Ḥasan, ʿAlī's son was born that year."

He went on, "Al-Wāqidī, however, claimed that Ibn Abū Sabra related to him, from Isḥāq b. ʿAbd Allāh, from Abū Jaʿfar, that ʿAlī b. Abū Ṭālib consummated his marriage with Fāṭima in the month of Dhū al-Ḥijja that year.

"And if that account is true, then the former one is inaccurate."

81. The word refers to arrangements concerning the payment of the bloodwit in the case of murder or manslaughter.

GLOSSARY

ABBREVIATIONS AND NAME-RELATED TERMS

Abū means father. According to Arabic grammatical rules, this word changes to Abī when governed by a preceding word. While, therefore, Abū Ṭālib would mean Ṭālib's father, when the word Ibn, son, is prefixed to the name, the form changes to Abī, and so Ibn Abī Ṭālib, would mean 'the son of Ṭālib's father'. To avoid confusion in this text, however, the term is left here universally as Abū.

The letters 'al-' before a noun represent in Arabic the definite article, 'the'.

The letter b. when part of a name represents a shortened form of the word 'Ibn', 'son'. Thus, the name 'Yaʿqūb b. ʿUtba' means 'Yaʿqūb, son of ʿUtba'. In a composite name, as are often given in this text, such as 'Yaʿqūb b. ʿUtba b. al-Mughīra b. al-Akhnas' the names of Yaʿqūb's father, grandfather, and great grand-father are given.

The letters bt. a shortened form of the Arabic *bint*, indicates 'girl' or 'daughter'. Thus the name ʿĀʾisha bt. Abū Bakr refers to ʿĀʾisha, daughter of Abū Bakr.

The letters ṢAAS are inserted after mention of the Prophet Muḥammad. These letters stand for the Arabic words *ṣallā Allāhu ʿalayhi wa sallam*; this invocation, recited by Muslims after every reference to the Prophet, whether by name or inference, is normally translated as 'May God's peace and blessings be upon him'.

GLOSSARY ITEMS

Words defined in footnotes associated with the text are not generally included in this glossary.

afkhādh: plural of *fakhdh* (q.v.).

aḥādīth: plural of *ḥadīth* (q.v.).

agnatic: related through descent on the father's side.

ʿālim (pl. *ʿulamāʾ*): scholars or theologians of Islam.

anṣār: the plural of *nāṣir*, helper, or victor. Most commonly met, in this text, in the plural form, it refers to the early Medinan allies of the Prophet who officially fraternized with the *muhājirīn*, those Muslims who had initially gone into exile from Mecca to Medina in their support for Islam.

ʿarab al-ʿāriba: the original Arabs, who are assumed to have spoken the language of Yaʿrub b. Qaḥtān.

ʿarab al-mustaʿriba: 'the arabized Arabs', initially referring to those who spoke the Arabic of Ishmael, the dialects of the Ḥijāz, that is. The term is also applied to those not descended from the Arabs of Arabia, but who have been assimilated into Arab culture and who speak Arabic as their native tongue.

ʿArafāt (also ʿArafa): a plain some 13 miles east of Mecca. Essential parts of the *ḥajj* pilgrimage ceremonies occur there, centered on a small granite hill, also known by the same name.

ʿashīra (pl. *ʿashāʾir*): an agnatic group. The word is commonly translated as tribe. An *ʿashīra* is composed of several *afkhādh* (q.v.), while several *ʿashāʾir* form a single qabīla (q.v.).

badana: an animal, commonly a camel, to be offered for sacrifice by a pilgrim at the *ḥajj* (q.v.).

baraka: blessing, in particular that divine force that enables prosperity and happiness. Persons of great piety or holiness are believe suffused with *baraka*, which radiates from them to those around them.

Bakka: an ancient alternative or original name for Mecca. In legend, the name comes from the Arabic verb *bakā*, he wept, applied to Adam's sadness at descending to the barren environment of Arabia after his expulsion from paradise.

baṭn (pl. *buṭūn*): an agnatic group smaller than a *qabīla* (q.v.) but larger than a *fakhdh* (q.v.).

dafʿ: the word used to denote the act of departure from ʿArafāt during the pilgrimage rites.

fakhdh (pl. *afkhādh*): a group of several families claiming descent from the same ancestor.

al-fajr: the dawn; also the superogatory prayer, recommended but not required, performed immediately after dawn. It consists of two *rakʿāt* (q.v.) to be recited audibly.

faṣīla (pl. *faṣāʾil*): an agnatic group consisting of the nearest members of one's *ʿashīra* (q.v.).

ghazwa (pl. *ghazawāt*): armed engagements in which the Prophet Muḥammad participated personally. Those he initiated but without his own direct participation are known as *sarāyā* (pl. of *sariyya*).

ḥadīth (pl. *aḥādīth*): a saying, reported action or anecdote relating the words or deeds of the Prophet Muḥammad. An *isnād* (q.v.) precedes the *ḥadīth* and lists the persons by whom the reported material was transmitted.

ḥadīth marfūʿ: a *ḥadīth* related by one of the Companions of the Prophet (see *ṣāḥib*) and quoted directly from the latter.

ḥāfiẓ (pl. *ḥufāẓ*): a person who has memorized the entire *Qurʾān*. Also one of the sacred attributes – the Guardian, the Protector – by which God is known.

ḥajj: the pilgrimage to the holy places of Mecca set annually to take place in the first half of the month of *Dhū al-Ḥijja*.

ḥanīf: 1) a devout pre-Islamic monotheist. 2) a person sincerely searching for the ancient religion practised by Abraham, with whom the word is particularly associated.

ḥanīfiyya: the religion of Abraham and the *ḥanīfs*.

ḥaram (or *ḥarām*): a term denoting what is sacred, forbidden or inviolable.

ḥijāba: the office of the custodian of the *kaʿba*; he is known as the *ḥājib*.

ḥijra (or hegira): the emigration of the Prophet Muḥammad and his supporters from Mecca into exile in Medina. The date of this event was later adopted as the commencement of the Muslim era, calculated as 622 AD.

ijāza: 1) rendering something legal or permissible. 2) the act of transmitting a *ḥadīth* and attributing the same to an authority without actually having heard that person recite it.

ifāḍa: the movement or departure of pilgrims from ʿArafāt following their performance of the *wuqūf*, 'the standing'.

iḥrām: 1) the rendering sacred or inviolate. 2) the name given to the clothing donned by Muslims entering the *iḥrām* state prior to their participation in the pilgrimage.

isnād: the prefatory material to a *ḥadīth* (q.v.) that lists the sequence of scholars or witnesses who transmitted the account from the time of the Prophet Muḥammad up to the time when it was written down.

izār: the cloth that covers the pilgrim from waist to knees when he commits himself to the sacred state of *iḥrām*.

jāhiliyya: denoting childlike foolishness or ignorance, the word is commonly applied to the period prior to the advent of Islam.

jamra (pl. *jamrāt*): ancient stone pillars symbolizing Satan at Minā. These are pelted with pebbles during the pilgrimage rites, the stones being known as *jamrāt*.

kaᶜba: the ancient cube-like structure within the great mosque in Mecca positioned some feet from the sacred spring *zamzam* (q.v.). It is towards this site that Muslims direct their prayers (see *qibla*).

al-Khalīl: 1) a town, also known as Hebron, some 32 miles south of Jerusalem and the site of the Tomb of the Patriarchs, sacred both to Jews and to Muslims. 2) a name or attribute implying close friend or confidant; the word is particularly associated with Abraham.

liwāʾ: 1) a flag, banner or signpost. 2) the issuance of this to those making the pilgrimage to the *kaᶜba*.

maqām Ibrāhīm: the 'station' of Abraham. A sanctuary positioned a few feet from the *kaᶜba* where Abraham and his co-religionaries would stand for prayer during the summer months.

maghrib: the west or direction in which the sun sets. Also, the fourth canonical Islamic prayer performed at dusk. It consists of three *rakᶜāt*; at the first two of these the prayers are spoken audibly, the third in silence.

masjid: the place where the Muslim prostrates in prayer, usually a mosque.

Minā: a location some four miles east of Mecca on the road to ᶜArafāt.

ḥadīth mursal: a *ḥadīth* which is considered by scholars to have a fault or inconsistency in the chain of its transmission.

al-Muzdalifa: a location some half way between Minā and ᶜArafāt. It is there that pilgrims returning from ᶜArafāt spend the night.

nadwa: the act of presiding over assemblies of pilgrims at the *ka͑ba*.

parasang: a Persian term for a unit of length, also known as a *farsakh*. One *parasang* equals approximately one league, some three miles, that is.

qabīla (pl. *qabā͗il*): a large agnatic group whose members trace descent from a single ancestor. Often translated as tribe. A *qabīla* is larger than an *͑ashīra* (q.v.) but smaller than a *sha͑b* (q.v.).

qāḍī: a judge appointed by a Muslim community to administer and adjudicate issues of Islamic law.

qibla: the direction to which a Muslim faces when praying. Initially towards Jerusalem but later changed by the Prophet Muḥammad so that Muslims would face Mecca and the *ka͑ba* there.

rak͑a (pl. *rak͑āt*): a unit of prayer consisting of a variety of gestures and postures. These *rak͑āt* total 17 each day, divided between the five canonical prayer periods.

al-raḥīm: The All-Compassionate; one of the sublime epithets applied to God.

al-raḥmān: the All-Merciful; one of the sublime epithets applied to God.

Ramaḍān: the ninth month of the Muslim lunar calendar. The month of fasting, it was during *Ramaḍān* that divine revelation first came to the Prophet Muhammad, and it is therefore particularly venerated.

ridā͗: a length of unsewn cloth that is draped over the left shoulder and around the torso of the pilgrim. This garb is donned by the pilgrim when he enters the *iḥrām* state.

rifāda: the provision of pilgrims with wheat and raisins by certain members of Quraysh of Mecca.

al-sa͑y: the ritual rapid walk or jog performed during the pilgrimage between al-Ṣafā and al-Marwa.

saba͗: the community and kingdom ruling South-West Arabia for centuries prior to the mission of the Prophet Muḥammad.

ṣāḥib (pl. *aṣḥāb*, *ṣaḥāba*): companion; that community of men who knew and supported the Prophet Muḥammad during his mission.

ṣaḥīḥ: a *ḥadīth* (q.v.) the chain of transmission of which is considered by Muslim scholars to be reliable beyond any reasonable doubt; also, a collection comprised only of such *aḥādīth*.

samʿan: the receipt of a *ḥadīth* (q.v.) from a scholar by listening to him or her recite it and then repeating it back. This method of transmitting and receiving a *ḥadīth* was considered the most trustworthy of all.

shaʿb (pl. *shuʿūb*): a tribal group larger than a *qabīla* (q.v.); a nation, race or people.

shahāda: the profession of faith in Islam by reciting in Arabic the words: 'There is no God but God and Muḥammad is His Messenger'.

shaykh (pl. *shuyūkh*): an elderly man; a tribal or spiritual leader; a distinguished and devout scholar.

shīʿa: the doctrine and its adherent, a *shīʿī*, that considers ʿAlī, son of Abū Ṭālib and husband of the Prophet Muḥammad's daughter Fāṭima, was the legitimate spiritual and political heir to the Caliphate of Islam.

sunna: the body of recorded words, actions, gestures and practices of the Prophet Muḥammad. This material constitutes the second foundation of Islam and its legal system, the holy Qurʾān being the first and prime source. In the plural form, *sunan*, reference is made to the compilation, by various authorities of the reported words and actions of the Prophet.

tafsīr: exegesis and commentary, particularly applied to the Qurʾān.

tasmiyya: the enunciation by a Muslim of the formula: 'In the name of God, the All-Merciful, the All-Compassionate' prior to any act or activity in which he or she might engage.

ṭawāf: ritual circumambulation of a religious site, normally the *kaʿba*.

tubbaʿ (pl. *tabābiʿa*): the title applied to the kings of pre-Islamic Yemen.

wudūʾ: the ritual ablution necessarily practiced by Muslims prior to their performance of prayer.

zamzam: the sacred well positioned close to the *kaʿba* (q.v.) within the *ḥarām al-sharīf*, the sacred enclosure encompassing the great mosque in Mecca. Muslims believe the well to have been miraculously opened through the agency of Gabriel to provide water for Abraham's wife Hagar and their son Ishmael.

INDEX